# Romanticism

# ROMANTICISM

AN ANTHOLOGY

*Fifth Edition*

EDITED BY DUNCAN WU

WILEY Blackwell

This edition first published 2025


Edition history: Blackwell Publishers Ltd (1e, 1994 and 2e, 1998); Blackwell Publishing Ltd (3e, 2006); Wiley-Blackwell (4e, 2012)



*Registered Offices*
John Wiley & Sons, Inc., 111 River Street, Hoboken, NJ 07030, USA
John Wiley & Sons Ltd, The Atrium, Southern Gate, Chichester, West Sussex, PO19 8SQ, UK

For details of our global editorial offices, customer services, and more information about Wiley products visit us at www.wiley.com.

Wiley also publishes its books in a variety of electronic formats and by print-on-demand. Some content that appears in standard print versions of this book may not be available in other formats.



*Library of Congress Cataloging-in-Publication Data*

Names: Wu, Duncan, editor.
Title: Romanticism : an anthology / edited by Duncan Wu.
Description: Fifth edition. | Hoboken, NJ : Wiley-Blackwell, 2025. | Includes bibliographical references and index.
Identifiers: LCCN 2024026574 (print) | LCCN 2024026575 (ebook) | ISBN 9781394210855 (paperback) | ISBN 9781394210862 (adobe pdf) | ISBN 9781394210879 (epub)
Subjects: LCSH: English literature–19th century. | English literature–18th century. | Romanticism–Great Britain. | LCGFT: Literature.
Classification: LCC PR1139 .R66 2025 (print) | LCC PR1139 (ebook) | DDC 820.8/0145–dc23/eng/20240618
LC record available at https://lccn.loc.gov/2024026574
LC ebook record available at https://lccn.loc.gov/2024026575

Cover Design: Wiley
Cover Image: © Artefact/Alamy Stock Photo

Set in 10.5/12pt Dante by Straive, Pondicherry, India
Printed and bound by CPI Group (UK) Ltd, Croydon, CR0 4YY

C9781394210855_190924

## OTHER BOOKS BY DUNCAN WU

*Poetry of Witness: The Tradition in English, 1500–2001* (co-edited with Carolyn Forché)
*Wordsworth's Reading 1770–1799*
*Wordsworth's Reading 1800–1815*
*Making Plays: Interviews with Contemporary British Dramatists and Directors*
*Wordsworth: An Inner Life*
*Wordsworth's Poets*
*Six Contemporary Dramatists: Bennett, Potter, Gray, Brenton, Hare, Ayckbourn*
*William Hazlitt: The First Modern Man*

*William Wordsworth: Selected Poems* (co-edited with Stephen Gill)
*Romanticism: A Critical Reader* (editor)
*William Wordsworth: The Five-Book Prelude* (editor)
*Women Romantic Poets: An Anthology* (editor)
*A Companion to Romanticism* (editor)
*William Hazlitt, The Plain Speaker: Key Essays* (editor)
*The Selected Writings of William Hazlitt, nine volumes* (editor)
*British Romanticism and the Edinburgh Review* (co-edited with Massimiliano Demata)
*William Wordsworth: The Earliest Poems 1785–1790* (editor)
*Metaphysical Hazlitt* (co-edited with Uttara Natarajan and Tom Paulin)
*New Writings of William Hazlitt* (editor)
*Immortal Bird: Romantic Poems about Nightingales* (editor)
*The Happy Fireside: Romantic Poems about Cats and Dogs* (editor)
*Poetry of Witness: The Tradition in English, 1500–2001* (co-edited with Carolyn Forché)
*'All that is worth remembering': Selected Essays of William Hazlitt*
*30 Great Myths about the Romantics*
*Keats and Shelley: Essential Poems* with a Preface by Julian Sands
*Love is my religion: Keats on Love* with a Preface by Bob Geldof
*She walks in beauty: The Best of Byron* with a Preface by Julian Sands
*Dog-Eared: Poems About Humanity's Best Friend*

# Contents

# Introduction

*I perceive that in Germany as well as in Italy there is a great struggle about what they call* Classical *and* Romantic, *terms which were not subjects of Classification in England – at least when I left it four or five years ago.*

(Byron, in the rejected Dedication to *Marino Faliero*, 14 August 1820)

When *Lyrical Ballads* first appeared in 1798 the word 'Romantic' was no compliment. It meant 'fanciful', 'light', even 'inconsequential'. Wordsworth and Coleridge would have resisted its application; twenty years later, the new generation of writers would recognize it as the counter in a debate conducted by European intellectuals, barely relevant to what they were doing. Perhaps that is the nature of academic discourse: even when conducted by practitioners, it may not bear greatly on the creative process, which has its own customs and rules which vary between writers.

Originally a descriptive term, 'Romance' used to refer to the verse epics of Tasso and Ariosto. Eighteenth-century critics like Thomas Warton used it in relation to fiction, often European, and in that context Novalis applied it to German literature. The idea didn't take flight until August Wilhelm Schlegel used it in a lecture course at Berlin, 1801–4, when he made the distinction mentioned by Byron. Romantic literature, he argued, appeared in the Middle Ages with the work of Dante, Petrarchis and Boccaccio; in reaction to Classicism it was identified with progressive and Christian views. In another course of lectures in Vienna, 1808–9, he went further: Romanticism was 'organic' and 'plastic', as against the 'mechanical' tendencies of Classicism. By 1821, when Byron dedicated *Marino Faliero* to Goethe, the debate was in full flood: Schlegel's ideas had been picked up and extrapolated by Madame de Staël, and in 1818 Stendhal became the first Frenchman to claim himself *un romantique* – for Shakespeare and against Racine; for Byron and against Boileau. Within a year Spanish and Portuguese critics too were wading in.

Having originated in disagreement, and largely in the academe, the concept has remained fluid ever since, and though many definitions are suggested, none commands universal agreement. In that respect Romanticism is distinct from movements formed by artists, which tend to be more coherent in their ambitions, at least to begin with. When the Pre-Raphaelite Brotherhood turned themselves into a school, they wanted to challenge received notions about pictorial representation; the Imagists published a manifesto of sorts in *Blast* that presented an agreed line of attack. The British Romantic poets could not have done this. Blake, Wordsworth, Coleridge, Byron, Shelley and Keats never all met in the same room and, had they done so, would have quarrelled.

One factor was the generation gap. Byron, Shelley and Keats might have enjoyed the company of Wordsworth as he was in his later twenties and early thirties, but by the time they reached artistic maturity – *c.*1816 for Shelley and Byron, 1819 for Keats – he was well into middle age, had accepted the job of Distributor of Stamps for Westmorland, and appeared to have forsaken the religious and political views of his youth. His support for the Tory Lord Lonsdale in the 1818 general election confirmed his association with a brand of conservatism they loathed. So far as they were concerned, he had betrayed the promise of 'Tintern Abbey' for a sinecure. All this makes it doubly unfortunate they could not read 'The Prelude', unpublished until 1850, by which time they were dead. Had they done so, they would have seen him differently.

Byron caught up with the critical debate surrounding Romanticism in 1821, but Coleridge beat him to it by a year. In 1820 the sage of Highgate compiled a list of 'Romantic' writers in which the only English poets of the day were Southey, Scott and Byron. Byron would have disliked being placed in the same class as Southey, whom he hated. But this only goes to show how resistant the concept is to codification – or at least to a form of codification that makes any sense. Perhaps the best advice one can offer is to be suspicious of anyone who claims to have the answer.

## Romanticism: Culture and Society

The Romantic period has an immediacy earlier ones tend to lack. This is because so many of our values and preoccupations derive from it. It coincides with the moment at which Britain became an industrial economy. Factories sprang up in towns and cities across the country, and the agrarian lives people had known for centuries stopped being taken for granted. Instead, labourers moved from the country into large conurbations, working long hours in close proximity to each other. This had a number of consequences, not least that they began to fight for their 'rights'. Today we take our rights for granted, forgetting the intellectual journey working people had to make merely to understand they had such things. For many, something very similar to the feudal system of medieval times continued to dictate their place in society – though things were changing.

The process by which people were awakened to a sense of self-determination was global. It began with the American Revolution and continued with that in France. And the impact of those upheavals cannot be overstated. Whole populations began to question the legitimacy of hereditary monarchs whose right to rule had once been accepted without question. It was not surprising that struggles elsewhere to do away with monarchical government affected the British; in fact, the real surprise is their refusal to take the same step – a testament to the determination with which their government stifled unrest. By the summer of 1817, it had in place a sophisticated network of spies practised in thwarting popular uprisings in Yorkshire, Derbyshire and Nottinghamshire. A favoured technique was for *agents provocateurs* to incite revolutionary activity, and for the government to execute supporters.

Revolution in America and France generated conflict because of the effect on international trade. By the time Wordsworth was in his mid-twenties, Britain was embroiled in nothing less than world war which, unlike those in the twentieth century, would last not for years but decades. From 1793 to 1802, and then from 1803 until 1815, Britain grappled with France across the globe, often fighting single-handedly against a well-equipped and resourceful enemy who, for much of that time, had the advantage. On an island-bound people like the British, the constant threat of invasion over more than two decades had a powerful effect. Whatever one's sympathies with the ideals of the American and French Revolutions, it became difficult to express anything but support for the national cause. Patriotic feeling in its most jingoistic form ran high, something vividly indicated by the caricatures of James Gillray.

Then as now, the cost of war was exorbitant and, in order to pay its debts, the post-war government of Lord Liverpool had to levy higher taxes. On 14 June 1815, additional expenditure arising from Napoleon's escape from Elba and its consequences led Nicholas Vansittart, Chancellor of the Exchequer, to raise £79 million through tax revenues. On 18 March 1816, the government decided to repeal income tax altogether, causing the burden disproportionately to fall upon the poor, in the form of duties on tobacco, beer, sugar and tea. This generated intense hardship at a time when jobs were scarce and pay low.

International conflict, the threat of invasion by Napoleon, social and political discontent – the writers in this book lived with these things, and were shaped by them. To that extent, it is appropriate to consider them as war poets, surrounded by upheaval and conflict, and passionately engaged with it. That engagement was made possible by another important development: the rise of the media.

This period was the first in history in which the population could keep abreast of political developments through newsprint. Historians have long acknowledged that the French press played an important part in the Revolution, enjoying unprecedented freedom between the fall of the Bastille in July 1789 and that of the monarchy in August 1792. It was not for nothing that J. L. Carra and Antoine-Joseph Gorsas, both journalists, were among those guillotined by Robespierre. The inventions of the steam-press (by which *The Times* was produced from 1814 onwards) and the paper-making machine (in 1803) meant it was easier than ever to produce newspapers on an industrial scale. And from around 1810 the mail-coach, which travelled at the hitherto unimaginable speed of 12 miles an hour, enabled publishers to distribute on a nationwide scale. For the first time, it was possible for Coleridge in Keswick to receive the papers the day after publication before sending them on to Wordsworth in Grasmere; there is no sense in which those living in the provinces were cut off from world affairs.

Nor was it only poets in the Lake District who kept up with the news: bulletins were now available to the poor and illiterate. Cobbett sold his *Political Register* at a price that made it accessible to the labouring folk he addressed – twopence, which led Tory critics to christen it 'twopenny trash'. Groups of men would club together and buy a single copy, which would be read aloud.

The new-found influence of the press was hard to control, but the government did its utmost to suppress unfavourable comment: Peter Finnerty was imprisoned in October 1797 for his report of the trial and execution of William Orr, which criticized Lord Castlereagh; Cobbett was imprisoned in June 1810 for having condemned the flogging of five English militiamen by German mercenaries; in 1813 John and Leigh Hunt were imprisoned for ridiculing the debauched lifestyle of the Prince Regent in *The Examiner*. All received sentences of two years. There were calls for stiffer penalties such as transportation, not least from such erstwhile revolutionaries as Robert Southey, now a contributor to the Tory *Quarterly Review*. In an article published in February 1817, less than a month prior to the suspension of habeas corpus, he asked:

> Why is it that this convicted incendiary [Cobbett], and others of the same stamp, are permitted week after week to sow the seeds of rebellion, insulting the government, and defying the laws of the country? [...] Men of this description, like other criminals, derive no lessons from experience. But it behoves the Government to do so, and curb sedition in time; lest it should be called upon to crush rebellion and to punish treason.

Not content with pleading that liberal journalists be arrested while suspension of habeas corpus allowed it, Southey took it upon himself to write a private memorandum to the Prime Minister, Lord Liverpool, telling him that laws, however repressive, are 'altogether nugatory while such manifestoes as those of Cobbett, Hone, and the *Examiner*, &c., are daily and weekly issued, fresh and fresh, and read aloud in every alehouse where the men are quartered, or where they meet together'. This was supported by a typically convoluted letter by that other distinguished former revolutionary, Samuel Taylor Coleridge, who expressed his 'support of those principles [...] of the measures and means, which have at length secured the gratitude and reverence of the wise and good to your Lordship and your Lordship's fellow-combatants in the long-agonizing contest' – by which he meant the government's suppression of dissident opinion. This was not Coleridge at his best, in terms of either sentiment or eloquence, and Liverpool confessed that, despite the distinction of his correspondent, 'I cannot well understand him.' The Prime Minister felt less threatened by the liberal press than did his correspondents, for he declined to take the steps they urged. Cobbett, however, took no risks: believing suspension of habeas corpus in March 1817 would curtail his freedom, and not relishing the prospect of another prison term, he fled to America where he remained for the next two years.

Time and again, newspaper and journal reports were the means by which authors in this volume learnt of developments at home and abroad: it was how Wordsworth kept up with events in France when he returned from Paris in late 1792, and how Shelley heard of the Peterloo Massacre in 1819. Not only that; they published in newspapers – including Wordsworth and Coleridge in *The Morning Post*, Shelley and Keats in *The Examiner*. Coleridge was invited to write for the *Morning Chronicle* in early July 1796, and possibly to edit it. In June 1794, avowing his disapproval 'of monarchical and aristocratical governments', Wordsworth proposed to his friend William Mathews that they co-edit a journal addressed to 'the dispassionate advocates of liberty and discussion'. Not only were these writers shaped by their historical moment – they sought to shape it.

The most obvious evidence of the media's effect on the populace was the new-found appetite for scandal. As is the case today, the press was excited by stories in which sex and politics were intertwined. Mary Anne Clarke hit the headlines in early 1809 when it was revealed she had been paid by army officers to commend them for promotion to her lover – Frederick Augustus, Duke of York and Albany, second son of George III, and the army's commander-in-chief. The matter was raised in the Commons and referred to a Select Committee, which found the Duke culpable, precipitating his resignation (though he was reappointed in 1811). Eight years later Hazlitt could have referred in passing to 'the droll affair of Mrs Clarke', confident his readers would remember how much entertainment it had given them.

Another symptom was the cult of celebrity, the first and biggest beneficiary being one of the authors in this volume – Byron. He was colourful enough not to have required the assistance of gossip-columnists, but he had it anyway, and during his years in London, 1812–16, day-to-day reports of his affairs and adventures filled their pages. It is hard to imagine any poet generating such speculation today, or crowds of people following him (or her) through the streets – but that was the case with Byron. The world, as Samuel Rogers observed, went 'stark mad' about him. He found fame both intoxicating and tiresome. And not surprisingly: he was sufficiently indiscreet about his incestuous passion for his half-sister for London to have been ablaze with it in the weeks prior to his exile from Britain. When he died, helping Greece in its fight for independence, scenes of mass hysteria greeted his coffin as it journeyed from London to Nottinghamshire, the like of which had not previously been seen.

The new mass society even had its own entertainment industry – which, more than the media, gripped the imaginations of the writers in this book. Another century would pass before radio would enable performers to address the nation, but in the meantime, the two licensed theatres in London – Drury Lane and Covent Garden – were capable of accommodating audiences of over 3,000, more than three times the size of the Olivier Theatre in London's National Theatre today. Every night of the working week these venues drew capacity crowds from across the social spectrum, who quickly learnt how to exercise a collective influence: when the management attempted to increase admission prices in September 1809, they orchestrated sixty-seven nights of riots, making performance impossible – a state of affairs that ended only by negotiation with the management. It is hard to imagine such a thing happening today.

Should there be any doubt as to the importance of theatre to the Romantics, it is worth recalling that one of the distinctions of which Byron was most proud was his seat on the management committee of Drury Lane Theatre. Along with Wordsworth, Coleridge, Keats, Hazlitt and Lamb, he was an enthusiastic playgoer. Hazlitt collected his theatre reviews into the greatest theatre book of the time – *A View of the English Stage* (1818), while Coleridge, Shelley, Wordsworth, Keats and Byron all wrote plays of their own.

## Romantic Poets

There were reasons for being cynical about the affairs of the world during the Romantic period. The every-day squalor of the lives of working people made it impossible to believe they could revolt against the conservative interests that kept them in their place. To Burke, they were 'a swinish multitude', while for Shelley, who believed in change, the Dublin poor were 'one mass of animated filth'. Extreme poverty and lack of education meant that social and political justice were decades in the future, with no attempt at political reform until 1832 (after the deaths of Blake, Keats, Shelley and Byron). In the meantime there were obstacles aplenty, one being the instability of the monarchy. George III, to whom the British looked for leadership, was subject (1788 onwards) to periodic fits of insanity, and was declared totally mad in 1811. This was more serious than it would be today, when the monarch is little more than a figurehead; in those days he had the power to dissolve Parliament, appoint and dismiss governments and declare wars. Without his full involvement, laws could not be passed. When he suffered relapses, his administration was effectively suspended, arousing the power-hungry tendencies of his son, the Prince of Wales.

Perhaps we have seen too much in our lifetimes to feel much hope. If so, that is where we differ from the Romantics, whose capacity for belief defines them. They were 'optimists for human nature'. Some were activists, seeking to foment revolution where they could – Shelley during his stay in Ireland, or Byron, willing to die in the cause of Greek independence; others, though not activists, sided with revolution at times when to do so placed them at considerable risk – Wordsworth, who lived in France, 1791–2, adopted many of the ideas and convictions of Robespierre.

They were products of their time in believing in a more just world than that in which they lived, and even more so for believing that poetry had the potential to accomplish revolutionary aims. The most obvious example is Wordsworth's 'The Recluse', the poem designed to persuade readers that love of nature leads to love of mankind. Yet such views as this made Wordsworth and Coleridge prime targets of interest to the surveillance services. Spies monitored their movements and discussions from 1797 to 1798.

Even after the Napoleonic Wars, the government did not relax its grip: the Ely and Littleport bread-riots of 1816 resulted in the execution of five ringleaders, who were no threat to anyone; 600 starving weavers set out from Manchester in March 1817 to petition for help for the ailing cotton trade, but were rounded up by government forces as they crossed from Staffordshire into Derbyshire; and in August 1819, in the worst example (the Peterloo Massacre), armed militiamen cut down hundreds of men, women and children demonstrating peacefully at St Peter's Fields, Manchester – a measure that won the endorsement of the Prince Regent and his government.

In spite of this, the writers in this book refused to succumb to despair, preferring to believe in a better, fairer world. It is not just their capacity for optimism that distinguishes them, but the kind of belief to which they clung. Where earlier generations looked to an afterlife, the Romantics tended to reject formalized religion. This was partly because the Church of England then wielded a degree of political power it no longer possesses, and was complicit in the injustice the writers opposed. Typical of this is the reference by Blake's chimney sweeper to 'God and his Priest and King / Who make up a heaven of our misery'. Instead, they thought they could create, through their writing, a promised land in which property was of no consequence and people would live in harmony. It lay neither in the distant future nor in the abstract; it was attainable in the here and now. Wordsworth's 'Tintern Abbey' speaks of how his engagement with nature was the direct path to a transcendent, almost godlike, apprehension of the world, when he refers to

> A presence that disturbs me with the joy
> Of elevated thoughts, a sense sublime
> Of something far more deeply interfused,
> Whose dwelling is the light of setting suns,
> And the round ocean, and the living air,
> And the blue sky, and in the mind of man –
> A motion and a spirit that impels
> All thinking things, all objects of all thought,
> And rolls through all things.
> ('Tintern Abbey' 95–103)

The feeling he has while standing on the banks of the Wye is in itself divine, generated by a 'presence' that will redeem humanity from the post-lapsarian 'weariness' encountered earlier in the poem. Wordsworth is famous for having said he had no need of a redeemer; when he wrote 'Tintern Abbey', he had little need of God, at least in the generally accepted sense. For him, mankind is redeemed through self-realization – something that explains the appeal of 'Tintern Abbey' to Shelley and Keats. What excited them was its faith – not in formalized religion, but in the redemptive potential of the mind. It can be traced to 'The Eolian Harp' (1795), in which Coleridge had asked himself whether all living things might be

> organic harps diversely framed,
> That tremble into thought, as o'er them sweeps,
> Plastic and vast, one intellectual breeze,
> At once the soul of each, and God of all?
> (ll. 37–40)

The answer Coleridge receives from his wife-to-be is (in effect) 'no', reflecting his awareness of the radical nature of what he asks. As a Unitarian he could not accept many aspects of the Anglican faith, yet Coleridge was emphatically Christian in his poetry, more so than Wordsworth. The conceit that human beings were instruments waiting to be struck by the divine spirit within the universe is precisely such a notion, valuable for affirming our susceptibility *en masse* to God's will. This was what revolution meant to Coleridge: he reconceived it as a religious event on a universal scale, by which God's 'intellectual' (spiritual) influence would redeem fallen humanity.

Some critics have accused Wordsworth of suppressing his knowledge of the hardships of working people in his poetry, particularly 'Tintern Abbey'. This is not the occasion for a refutation but it is worth saying that Wordsworth thought his work engaged fully with life as it was lived; indeed, it was on those grounds he was attacked by reviewers. He considered his millenarian aspirations had to be grounded in an awareness of suffering – the 'still, sad music of humanity'. When Keats raved about Wordsworth in May 1818, it was to commend his ability to sharpen 'one's vision into the heart and nature of man, of convincing one's nerves that the world is full of misery and heartbreak, pain, sickness, and oppression'. And he was right. In that respect, Wordsworth was a crucial influence on how Keats conceived 'Hyperion: A Fragment' – a poem about the aspirations that spring out of dispossession.

Byron shared the radical aspirations expressed by Wordsworth and Coleridge in their youth, but rejected their philosophizing. For him, the word 'metaphysical' was an insult. He was more practical, something underlined by his readiness to die in the Greek War of Independence (for which he remains a national hero in Greece, with streets and squares named after him). Yet even he is capable of expressing, in 'Childe Harold's Pilgrimage' Canto III, something of Wordsworth's pantheist conviction in the redemptive power of nature:

> I live not in myself, but I become
> Portion of that around me; and to me
> High mountains are a feeling, but the hum
> Of human cities torture....
>
> (ll. 680–3)

Byron remained true to himself in that he knew the Wordsworthian response to nature affirmed something he took seriously – inner potential. Frustration with the restrictions of our earthly state permeates his poetry, compelling him to aspire to a level of existence beyond the merely human. Hence his ambiguous praise for that arch-overreacher Napoleon. As Wordsworth put it, 'We feel that we are greater than we know.'

In 'Don Juan', Byron's greatest achievement in verse, his setting is not the natural world favoured by Shelley and Wordsworth, nor the arena of philosophical disquisition to be found in Coleridge's 'Religious Musings'; it is the 'real' world of human affairs, masked balls, the perils of travel, and the passions of men and women. For Byron, the seclusion sought by Wordsworth was little more than a posture, one he was unwilling to assume for the few minutes it took him to write the relevant parts of 'Childe Harold' III. He is more at home when analyzing the random and the everyday in all their meaningless variety, or when studying human behaviour, marvelling at the follies and foibles of his characters, and addressing his reader in disarmingly familiar style, as if he were speaking to us from an armchair, a glass of claret in his lordly grasp. The life assumed by the poem seems to have surprised even him. 'Confess, you dog', he wrote to his friend Douglas Kinnaird, 'It may be profligate, but is it not *life*, is it not *the thing*? Could any man have written it who has not lived in the world? – and tooled in a post-chaise? In a hackney coach? In a gondola? Against a wall? In a court carriage? In a vis-à-vis? On a table – and under it?'

Blake is sometimes considered the exception to virtually anything one might want to say about these writers – and, in a sense, he is. He was born in 1757 – and is as much an eighteenth-century writer as a Romantic one. If, like his contemporaries, he read Wordsworth, it was late in life, and without much pleasure. However, it was he who, in 1789, on the brink of tumult in France, described the 'son of fire':

> Spurning the clouds written with curses, stamps the stony law to dust, loosing the eternal horses from the dens of night, crying, 'Empire is no more! And now the lion and wolf shall cease.'

Revolution as apocalypse: to Blake, events in France were harbingers not merely of political liberation, but of the spiritual millennium predicted in the Bible. And in this he was no less Romantic than the writers who were to follow. For him, as for them, the fallen world was a conundrum the resolution to which led back to paradise. He would spend much of his creative life explaining to the world, in his own distinctive manner, how paradise had been lost, and how it might be reclaimed. And never without grief at the 'Marks of weakness' and 'marks of woe' on the faces of those around him.

In that way he was, of course, as compelled by the privations of working people as other writers in this book – not least, perhaps, because he lived among them. He was as sensitive as they to the unfairnesses that dominated workers' lives. We know he was disturbed by scenes of anarchy and near revolution at the Gordon Riots in 1780, but there's no evidence he disagreed with the crowd's desire to even things up a little with the wealthy and privileged whose property they destroyed. In fact, his use of the image of fire to illustrate pictures of Revolution recalls the Riots.

Blake was too individualistic to simply 'subscribe' to others' thoughts or work – and from that perspective it's difficult to enlist him to a group of writers like the Romantics, diverse though they may be. But he certainly has much in common with them, sufficiently so as to warrant our regarding him as one of them rather than one of the eighteenth-century writers who preceded them.

# Editor's Note on the Fifth Edition

This is the fifth edition of *Romanticism: An Anthology* since its first publication in 1994, exactly three decades ago. The principle goal in revising has been to reduce the size of the book and the burden of carrying it round a university campus.

After running through the various possibilities, I have chosen to include only the six canonical authors: Blake, Wordsworth, Coleridge, Keats, Byron and Shelley. This decision was taken in the light of an assurance to make the fourth edition of the anthology available to readers online.

Texts are edited for this volume from both manuscript and early printed sources. Typically, readers are not restricted to highlights but have access to complete works, with all their fluctuations of tone, mood and rhythm. No attempt has been made to encompass the rich and extensive corpus of Romantic novel-writing. I have worked on the assumption that teachers will adopt separate volumes for novels they wish to include in their courses. Texts by European writers are not included either, on the grounds that Romanticism on the Continent is a world to itself, deserving more space than I have.

It is my hope that those using the fifth edition of *Romanticism: An Anthology* will find it helpful, and regard themselves as free to inform me of ways in which it may be further improved. The shaping of this book has been a gradual process that has continued at irregular intervals since 1994, and the advice of readers continues to be of paramount importance in determining how it should continue.

# Editorial Principles

This edition adopts the policy advocated by Coleridge on New Year's Day 1834, widely accepted as the basis for contemporary scholarly editions: 'After all you can say, I think the chronological order is the best for arranging a poet's works. All your divisions are in particular instances inadequate, and they destroy the interest which arises from watching the progress, maturity, and even the decay of genius.' Authors are introduced successively by their dates of birth; works are placed in order of composition where known and, when not known, by date of publication.

The edition is designed for the use of students and general readers, and textual procedures are geared accordingly. Except for works in dialect or in which archaic effects were deliberately sought, punctuation and orthography are normalized, pervasive initial capitals and italics removed, and contractions expanded except where they are of metrical significance (for instance, Keats's 'charact'ry' is demanded by the exigencies of metre, but 'thro'' is expanded to 'through'). Although the accidental features of late eighteenth- and early nineteenth-century printed texts have their own intrinsic interest and are of importance in considering the evolution of any given work, it should be noted that most poets were content to leave such matters to the printers or their collaborators. In many cases, therefore, accidental features of early printed texts cannot be assumed to be disposed according to the author's wishes. Conversely, I have taken the view that, on those occasions when capitalization is demonstrably authorial, and consistently applied, it should be allowed to stand – as in the case of Shelley's 'Adonais' and 'The Mask of Anarchy'. The punctuation applied by writers to their own works is another matter, as styles vary from one person to another, are sometimes eccentric and can mislead the modern reader. I have treated authorial punctuation as a good (though not infallible) guide as to emphasis, meaning and sentence structure, but have not followed it without question.

For this fifth edition I have checked and double-checked many editorial decisions I once took for granted. All texts have been edited for this anthology. I have followed procedures designed to produce a clear reading text. In editing from manuscript, I have aimed to present each draft as it stood on completion. Deletions are accepted only when alternative readings are provided; where they are not, the original is retained. Alternative readings are accepted only when the original has been deleted; where they are not, the original is retained. Where the original reading is deleted but legible, and the alternative fragmentary, illegible or inchoate, the original has been retained. Where, in the rush of composition, words are omitted, they have been supplied from adjacent drafts or manuscripts, or in some cases presented as hiatuses in the text, using square brackets. As a rule, I have silently corrected scribal errors. Ampersands are expanded to 'and' throughout.

Headnotes are provided for each author. Annotations gloss archaisms, difficult constructions, allusions, echoes, other verbal borrowings, provide points of information.

# Acknowledgements

## *First Edition (1994)*

Work on this volume began with consultation of numerous colleagues, who kindly offered advice on the anthology they wished to use. For that and help of various kinds it is a pleasure to thank Jonathan Bate, Shahin Bekhradnia, J. Drummond Bone, Geoffrey Brackett, Richard W. Clancey, David Fairer, Richard Gravil, Jack Haeger, Keith Hanley, Anthony Harding, Brooke Hopkins, M. C. Howatson, Kenneth Johnston, Grevel Lindop, Jerome J. McGann, Philip Martin, Michael O'Neill, Roy Park, Janice Patten, Tom Paulin, Cecilia Powell, Roger Robinson, Nicholas Roe, the late William Ruddick, Charles Rzepka, William S. Smith, Jane Stabler, David Stewart, Tim Trengove-Jones, J. R. Watson, Mary Wedd, Pamela Woof and Jonathan Wordsworth. I wish also to thank the advisers consulted by Blackwell for comments and advice.

This anthology is more dependent than most on original research for its texts, and in the course of editing I have incurred debts of many kinds to various librarians and archivists whom it is a pleasure to thank here: B. C. Barker-Benfield and the staff of the Upper Reading Room, Bodleian Library, Oxford; Elaine Scoble of the Wolfson Library, St Catherine's College, Oxford; the staff of the English Faculty Library, Oxford; Deborah Hedgecock of the Guildhall Library, London; and Jeff Cowton of the Wordsworth Library, Grasmere. It was my good fortune to have been a Fellow of St Catherine's College, Oxford, during work on this book, and among friends and colleagues there I acknowledge the generous help of Richard Parish, J. Ch. Simopoulos and J. B. McLaughlin. Nicola Trott was my collaborator at an early stage of work, and played a crucial part in formulating its aims and procedures, and in seeking advice from colleagues. My work has been expedited by the rapid and accurate typing of Pat Wallace; James Price of Woodstock Books kindly provided me with early printed texts of a number of works included; and Andrew McNeillie, my editor, offered enthusiastic help and advice through-out. This book was produced during tenure of a British Academy post-doctoral Fellowship; I am deeply grateful to the Academy for its kind support.

## *Second Edition (1998)*

Since this anthology was first published, I have received suggestions for revision from many people; I thank them all. I owe a particular debt to those students with whom I have used it as a course text, and who have helped determine the various ways in which revision might be implemented.

For expert advice and information I thank Douglas Gifford, Bonnie Woodbery, Nicholas Roe, Jane Stabler, Edwin Moïse, Nelson Hilton, Suzanne Gilbert, Bob Cummings, Richard W. Clancey, David Pirie, Roger Robinson, R. E. Cavaliero, Zachary Leader, David Fairer, David Birkett, Peter Cochran, Richard Cronin, Charles Branchini, Susan Castillo, E. A. Moignard, Michael O'Neill, Jonathan Wordsworth and Constance Parrish.

In researching new texts for this anthology, I am grateful once again to Jeff Cowton of the Wordsworth Library, Grasmere, and the staff of the Upper Reading Room, Bodleian Library, Oxford, and the British

Library, London. I am particularly indebted to my proof-reader, Henry Maas, and Alison Truefitt, my copy-editor, for the care they have taken over a challenging typescript. Once again, Andrew McNeillie has proved a patient and supportive editor.

## *Third Edition (2004)*

I thank all those who have suggested ways in which *Romanticism: An Anthology* might be revised. The NASSR-List continues to be an invaluable means of communicating with fellow Romanticists, and I am grateful to its subscribers for sending me information on their respective courses, in particular Kevin Binfield, Dan White, Brad Sullivan, Sara Guyer, SueAnn Schatz, Richard Matlak, Charles Snodgrass, Mary Waters, David Latane, Ann R. Hawkins and Patricia Matthew. I wish also to thank the many university professors who responded to the survey conducted by Blackwell Publishers into how this book might be revised. For specific help I thank Jane Stabler, Nicholas Roe, Susan J. Wolfson, Leslie Brisman, Nanora L. Sweet, Lucy Newlyn, Simon Kövesi, Jacqueline M. Labbe, Judith Pascoe, Ronald Tetreault, Hans Werner Breunig, Essaka Joshua, Grant Scott, Monika Class and Kim Wheatley. It has not been possible to adopt all suggestions, but the wealth of information and advice provided by all parties has been the most important single influence on the shape of this new edition.

At Blackwell Publishers I wish for the last time to thank Andrew McNeillie, who commissioned the first edition of this anthology over a decade ago, and who was responsible for commissioning this one. I am indebted to his successors, Al Bertrand and Emma Bennett, for the care they have taken in guiding this edition to the press, and to copy-editor Sandra Raphael and proof-reader Henry Maas, who have saved me from infelicities too numerous to mention.

## *Fourth Edition (2011)*

Preparation of this edition began with a survey of those who use, and do not use, this textbook. I wish to thank those who responded. Their comments have been at hand throughout work, and have been given careful consideration.

I have been greatly assisted by the advice of an editorial board. Their comments have guided me at every turn, and I am much in their debt. For assistance on particular points, I thank Michael O'Neill, Tony Reavell, Nicholas Roe, Jane Stabler, Susan Wolfson, and G. E. Bentley, Jr. Emma Bennett has been a receptive and sensitive editor throughout my labours. I am grateful to her, as well as to her colleagues at Wiley-Blackwell, in particular Brigitte Lee Messenger, who copy-edited this book.

## *Fifth Edition (2024)*

I wish to acknowledge, throughout the time this anthology has been available, the generous assistance of Leslie Brisman of Yale University, who has supplied me with detailed commentary designed to improve this volume.

*Georgetown University*

## Sources

The Bodleian Library, Oxford, for material from MS texts of Percy Bysshe Shelley.
The British Library for material from MS texts of the letters of William Blake.
The British Library, for material from MS texts of Samuel Taylor Coleridge.

The Corporation of the City of London for the Collections at Keats House, Hampstead, for John Keats's holograph texts, 'On Sitting Down to Read *King Lear* Once Again' and 'Bright Star, Would I Were Steadfast as Thou Art'.

The Morgan Library, New York, Victoria College Library, Toronto, the British Library and the Wordsworth Museum, Grasmere, for MS texts of the letters of Samuel Taylor Coleridge.

The Morgan Library, New York, the Bodleian Library, Oxford, the Houghton Library, Harvard, and the Library of Congress, Washington, DC, for material from the MS of the letters of Percy Bysshe Shelley.

The Houghton Library, Harvard University, for manuscript material by Mary Shelley, MS Eng 822, 2r–2v, and Percy Bysshe Shelley, MS Eng 258.3, 2r–3r.

The Houghton Library, Harvard University, and The Corporation of the City of London collections at Keats House, Hampstead, for material from MS texts of the letters of John Keats.

The Houghton Library, Harvard University, for material from the manuscripts of John Keats.

The John Murray Collection at the National Library of Scotland and the British Library for material from MS texts of the letters of Lord Byron.

The John Murray Collection at the National Library of Scotland for material from the MS of the works of Lord Byron.

Victoria College Library, Toronto, for material from *Table Talk* by Samuel Taylor Coleridge.

The Wordsworth Trust, Grasmere, for material from MS texts of Samuel Taylor Coleridge.

The Wordsworth Trust, Grasmere, for material from MS texts of William Wordsworth

# A Romantic Timeline 1770–1851

| Current affairs | Date | | Science and the Arts |
|---|---|---|---|
| Boston massacre | **1770** | 5 March | |
| | | 7 April | Wordsworth born, Cockermouth, Cumbria |
| | | 20 May | Hölderlin born |
| | | 24 August | Chatterton poisons himself in London, aged 17<br>Hegel born, Stuttgart |
| | | 16 December | Beethoven born, Bonn |
| | **1771** | 25 December | Dorothy Wordsworth born, Cockermouth, Cumbria |
| Emmanuel Swedenborg dies | **1772** | 29 March | |
| William Murray, Lord Mansfield, rules that there is no legal basis for slavery in England, giving a stimulus to the movement to abolish the slave trade in the colonies | | 14 May | |
| Lord Mansfield delivers judgement in the case of James Somersett, a runaway slave, ruling that no one has the right 'to take a slave by force to be sold abroad' – often regarded as the beginning of the end of slavery in England | | 22 June | |
| | | 4 August | Blake apprenticed to the antiquarian engraver James Basire |
| | | 9 October | Mary Tighe born, Dublin |
| | | 21 October | Coleridge born, Ottery St Mary, Devon |
| | | December | Anna Laetitia Aikin publishes her *Poems* (dated 1773 on title-page), including 'A Summer Evening's Meditation' |
| | **1773** | May | Hannah More publishes *The Search after Happiness* |

| Current affairs | Date | | Science and the Arts |
|---|---|---|---|
| | | September | Anna Laetitia Aikin and John Aikin publish *Miscellaneous Pieces in Prose* |
| Boston Tea Party | | 16 December | |
| | **1774** | 4 April | Goldsmith dies, London |
| | | 12 August | Southey born, Bristol |
| | **1775** | 10 February | Lamb born, London |
| | | 23 April | Turner born, London |
| | | 16 December | Jane Austen born, Steventon, Hampshire |
| | **1776** | 17 February | Gibbon publishes first volume of *Decline and Fall of the Roman Empire* |
| | | 10 June | Garrick's last appearance on stage as Don Felix in Centlivre's *The Wonder!* |
| | | 11 June | Constable born, Suffolk |
| American Declaration of Independence | | 4 July | |
| | | 25 August | David Hume dies |
| | | 10 December | Mary Robinson makes her debut as Juliet at Drury Lane Theatre |
| | **1777** | 8 May | Sheridan's *School for Scandal* opens at Drury Lane Theatre |
| | | 10 December | Hannah More's *Percy* opens at Covent Garden Theatre |
| | | 25 December | Sydney Owenson, Lady Morgan, born on the Dublin packet-boat in the Irish Sea |
| | **1778** | 29 January | Fanny Burney publishes *Evelina* |
| | | 8 March | Wordsworth's mother dies |
| | | 10 April | Hazlitt born, Maidstone, Kent |
| | | 30 May | Voltaire dies, Paris |
| | | 2 July | Rousseau dies, Paris |
| | **1779** | 20 January | Garrick dies, London |
| Captain Cook dies, Hawaii | | 14 February | |
| | | 29 April | Goethe's *The Sorrows of Werther* first published in London |
| | | 8 October | Blake admitted to study at the Royal Academy schools |
| | | 3 December | Mary Robinson's performance as Perdita is attended by the Prince of Wales, whose mistress she becomes shortly after |
| Gordon Riots in London | **1780** | 2–8 June | |
| | | 6 June | Blake involved in the attack on Newgate Prison |
| | | 29 August | Ingres born |
| Cornwallis surrenders to Washington at Yorktown, Virginia | **1781** | 19 October | Fuseli paints *The Nightmare* |

| Current affairs | Date | | Science and the Arts |
|---|---|---|---|
| | **1782** | January | Hannah More publishes *Sacred Dramas* (including 'Sensibility') |
| | | 18 August | Blake marries Catherine Boucher (b. 1762) |
| | | September | Coleridge goes to school at Christ's Hospital in London, where he meets Charles Lamb |
| | **1783** | 4 June | Montgolfier brothers give first publicdemonstration of their hot-air balloon |
| Treaty of Paris, confirming American Independence | | 3 September | |
| Pitt the Younger becomes Prime Minister at the age of 24 (until 1801) | | 19 December | |
| | | 30 December | Wordsworth's father dies |
| | **1784** | June | Charlotte Smith publishes first edition of *Elegiac Sonnets* |
| | | 19 October | Leigh Hunt born, Southgate |
| | | 13 December | Dr Johnson dies, London, aged 75 |
| | **1785** | June | Ann Yearsley publishes *Poems, on Several Occasions* |
| | | July | Cowper publishes *The Task* |
| | | 15 August | De Quincey born, Manchester |
| | | 18 October | Thomas Love Peacock born, Weymouth, Dorset |
| | **1786** | 25 January | Benjamin Robert Haydon born, Plymouth |
| | | 1 May | Mozart's *Marriage of Figaro* first performed in Prague |
| | | 7 June | Beckford's Vathek published, unauthorized |
| | | 25 June | Goya appointed painter to the King of Spain |
| | **1787** | 1 April | Wordsworth's first published poem, a sonnet addressed to Helen Maria Williams, appears in the *European Magazine* (for March) |
| Warren Hastings impeached by Burke in House of Commons for maladministration and corruption in Bengal | | May | |
| Committee for the Abolition of the Slave-Trade, composed mainly of Quakers, formed in London | | 22 May | |
| American Constitution drafted and signed | | 17 September | |
| | **1788** | 22 January | Byron born, London |
| | | 8 February | Hannah More publishes *Slavery: A Poem* |
| | | 22 February | Schopenhauer born, Danzig |
| Charles Wesley dies | | 28 March | |
| Sir William Dolben proposes a Bill to the House of Commons limiting the number of slaves who could be transported from Africa to British colonies in the West Indies (it is passed on 26 May, despite much opposition) | | 21 May | |

| Current affairs | Date | | Science and the Arts |
|---|---|---|---|
| | | 2 August | Gainsborough dies, London |
| George III suffers mental collapse | | November | Ann Yearsley publishes *Poem on the Inhumanity of the Slave-Trade* |
| Three Estates assemble at Versailles | **1789** | 4 May | |
| The Third estate names itself the National Assembly | | 17 June | |
| Storming of the Bastille | | 14 July | |
| March on Versaille; French royal family escorted to Paris | | 6 October | |
| Price addresses the London Revolution Society | | 4 November | Blake completes *Songs of Innocence* and begins 'The Book of Thel' (1789–90) |
| President Washington delivers the first 'State of the Union' address | **1790** | 8 January | |
| Fletcher Christian and fellow mutineers settle on the Pitcairn Islands | | 15 January | |
| | | 26 January | Mozart's *Cosi fan tutte* first performed in Vienna |
| Benjamin Franklin dies, Philadelphia, aged 84 | | 17 April | |
| | | June | Blake publishes the *Marriage of Heaven and Hell* |
| | | 13 July | Wordsworth arrives in France on his |
| Louis XVI swears oath of loyalty to the new constitution | | 14 July | first trip to the Continent |
| Suspension of habeas corpus in Britain | | October | |
| Slaves revolt in Haiti | | 23 October | |
| General election: Pitt returned with increased majority | | November | Helen Maria Williams publishes *Letters Written in France in Summer of 1790* |
| Congress moves from New York City to Philadelphia | | 1 November | Burke publishes *Reflections on the Revolution in France* |
| | | 29 November | Wollstonecraft publishes *A Vindication of the Rights of Men,* in response to Burke |
| | | 6 December | Kant publishes *The Critique of Pure Reason* |
| | **1791** | 1 January | Haydn arrives in England |
| | | 22 February | Paine publishes *The Rights of Man* Part I |
| The French royal family is prevented from leaving Paris by the National Guard | | 18 April | |
| French royal family flees, only to be captured at Varennes the following day | | 20 June | |
| Anti-Dissenter riots in Birmingham during which Joseph Priestley's house burned down by Church-and-King mob | | 14 July | |
| Louis XVI suspended from office until he agrees to ratify the constitution (which he does on 13 September) | | 16 July | |
| Slave riots in San Domingo | | August | |
| | | 22 September | Michael Faraday born, London (inventor of the dynamo and the electric motor) |

| Current affairs | Date | | Science and the Arts |
|---|---|---|---|
| | | 30 September | Mozart's *The Magic Flute* first performed in Vienna |
| French Legislative Assembly established | | 1 October | |
| United Irishmen founded by Wolfe Tone in Belfast to fight for Irish nationalism | | 14 October | |
| | | November | Wordsworth visits Charlotte Smith in Brighton |
| | | 5 December | Mozart dies, aged 35, in Vienna |
| | | 17 December | Ann Radcliffe publishes *The Romance of the Forest* |
| | | December | Wordsworth's second visit to France (for a year) |
| | | | Burns publishes 'Tam O'Shanter' |
| | **1792** | January | Mary Wollstonecraft publishes *A Vindication of the Rights of Woman* |
| | | 16 February | Paine publishes *The Rights of Man* Part II |
| | | 18 February | Thomas Holcroft's *The Road to Ruin* successfully performed at Covent Garden Theatre |
| | | 23 February | Joshua Reynolds dies, London |
| France declares war on Austria | | 20 April | |
| Paine charged with sedition | | 21 May | |
| | | 4 August | Shelley born, Field Place, Sussex |
| Tuileries stormed by Paris mob; French royal family placed in detention three days later | | 10 August | |
| September Massacres of royalist and other prisoners in Paris | | 3–7 September | |
| Robespierre elected to the National Assembly | | 5 September | |
| Paine flees to France | | 13 September | |
| France proclaims itself a Republic | | 22 September | |
| | | December | Mary Wollstonecraft in Paris |
| Louis XVI tried for treason by the National Assembly | | 11 December | |
| | | 15 December | Anne-Caroline Wordsworth, Wordsworth's natural daughter, born |
| Paine sentenced to death by British courts for seditious libel (*Rights of Man* Part II) | | 18 December | |
| | | 30 December | Hannah More publishes *Village Politics* (counter-revolutionary propaganda) |
| Louis XVI sentenced to death | **1793** | 19 January | |
| Louis XVI executed | | 21 January | |
| France declares war on Britain and Holland | | 1 February | |
| | | 14 February | Godwin publishes *Political Justice* |
| Suspension of habeas corpus in Britain | | March | Publication of William Frend's *Peace and Union Recommended* |

| Current affairs | Date | | Science and the Arts |
|---|---|---|---|
| Committee of Public Safety formed, led by Danton, Robespierre, Saint-Just and Couthon | | 6 April | |
| | | June | Smith publishes *The Emigrants* |
| Marat murdered in his bath by Charlotte Corday, heralding the Terror | | 13 July | John Clare born Helpstone, Northamptonshire |
| | | 25 September | Felicia Dorothea Browne born, Liverpool |
| France institutes a new calendar | | 7 April | |
| | | 10 October | Blake advertises *Songs of Experience* |
| Marie Antoinette executed | | 16 October | |
| | | 2 December | Coleridge enlists in the King's Regiment, 15th Light Dragoons, as Silas Tomkyn Comberbache |
| Paine imprisoned in the Luxembourg jail | | 28 December | Blake begins to produce copies of 'Visions of the Daughters of Albion' |
| | **1794** | April | Joseph Priestley emigrates to America |
| | | 10 May | Ann Radcliffe publishes *The Mysteries of Udolpho* |
| Arrest of Thomas Hardy and other radicals including John Thelwall | | 12 May | |
| Pitt's Bill to suspend habeas corpus receives royal assent | | 23 May | |
| | | 26 May | Godwin publishes *Caleb Williams* |
| | | 17 June | Coleridge's first meeting with Southey, Balliol College, Oxford |
| Robespierre executed; end of the Terror | | 28 July | |
| | | 20 October | Godwin publishes 'Cursory Strictures' in the *Morning Chronicle*, leading to acquittal of some defendants in the treason trials |
| Treason trials begin in London with the trial of Thomas Hardy | | 28 October | |
| Paine released from Luxembourg jail, having excaped execution by an oversight | | 4 November | |
| Thomas Hardy found not guilty | | 5 November | |
| Thelwall found not guilty at the treason trials | | 5 December | |
| France invades Holland | | 15 December (winter 1794–5) | |
| France abolishes slavery in its territories, conferring citizenship on former slaves | **1795** | 4 February | |
| | | 27 February | Wordsworth begins regular meetings with Godwin in London (until July) |
| | | March | Hannah More launches the Cheap Repository tracts (2 million distributed by the end of the year) |
| Prince of Wales marries his cousin, Caroline-Amelia of Brunswick-Wolfenbüttel, at St James's Palace | | 8 April | |

| Current affairs | Date | | Science and the Arts |
|---|---|---|---|
| | | 19 May | James Boswell dies, London |
| | | 4 October | Coleridge marries Sara Fricker at St Mary Redcliffe, Bristol, followed by a six-week honeymoon in Clevedon |
| King's coach stoned at opening of Parliament by crowd demanding bread and Pitt's resignation | | 29 October | |
| | | 31 October | Keats born, London |
| Pitt and Grenville introduce Bills outlawing treasonable practices and unlawful assemblies (they become law on 18 December) | | 6 November | |
| | | December | Southey publishes 'Joan of Arc' (which includes passages by Coleridge)<br>Helen Maria Williams publishes *Letters Containing a Sketch of the Politics of France* |
| | **1796** | 12 March | Matthew Lewis publishes *The Monk* |
| Napoleon commands Italian campaign, defeating Austrians in sequence of battles leading to the Peace of Leoben | | April | |
| | | 16 April | Coleridge publishes his first volume of *Poems* |
| | | May | Edward Jenner discovers vaccine against smallpox |
| | | 21 July | Burns dies |
| Washington's farewell address | | 18 September | |
| | | 19 September | Hartley Coleridge born |
| | | 22 September | Mary Lamb stabs her mother to death and badly injures her father |
| Catherine the Great, Empress of Russia, dies | | 17 November | |
| | | December | Coleridge moves to Nether Stowey, Somerset<br>Anna Seward publishes *Llangollen Vale with Other Poems*<br>Anna Yearsley publishes *The Rural Lyre* |
| | **1797** | 31 January | Schubert born, Vienna |
| John Adams elected second President in America; his Vice-President is Jefferson | | 4 March | |
| | | 15 April | Hölderlin begins to publish 'Hyperion' |
| Mutinies of the Royal Navy at Spithead and Nore | | 16 April until 15 May | |
| | | 7 July | Burke dies<br>Lamb arrives at Nether Stowey and goes walking with the Wordsworths, leaving Coleridge behind |
| | | 16 July | Wordsworth and his sister move into Alfoxden House near Coleridge at Nether Stowey |
| | | 17 July | Thelwall arrives at Nether Stowey (where he remains until the end of the month) |
| | | 29 August | Joseph Wright of Derby dies |

| Current affairs | Date | | Science and the Arts |
|---|---|---|---|
| | | 30 August | Mary Godwin born |
| | | 10 September | Mary Wollstonecraft dies; funeral on 15 September |
| | | October | Southey publishes 'Hannah, A Plaintive Tale' in the *Monthly Magazine* |
| | | 16 October | Coleridge sends a copy of the recently completed *Osorio* to Sheridan at Drury Lane Theatre, but it is rejected |
| | | 28 October | Coleridge publishes second edition of his *Poems* |
| | | 20 November | Wordsworth's play *The Borderers* sent to Covent Garden Theatre, but rejected as unperformable the following month |
| | | 10 December | Ann Radcliffe publishes *The Italian* |
| | **1798** | 14 January | Coleridge preaches at the Unitarian chapel in Shrewsbury and is heard by Hazlitt, aged 17 |
| | | 25 January | Wordsworth composes 'A Night-Piece', initiating a spate of composition including 'The Ruined Cottage', 'The Pedlar', and most of the 1798 *Lyrical Ballads* |
| | | February | Coleridge writes 'Frost at Midnight' and (until April) Christabel |
| | | 19 March | Wordsworth begins writing 'The Thorn' |
| | | 14 April | Coleridge, 'France: An Ode' published in *The Morning Post* |
| | | 20 May | Hazlitt visits Nether Stowey and is brought to Alfoxden where he reads the manuscript of *Lyrical Ballads* |
| Uprising of the United Irishmen, led by Lord Edward Fitzgerald and Wolfe Tone | | 23 May | |
| | | 7 June | Malthus publishes *Essay on Population* |
| | | 11 June | Hazlitt leaves Nether Stowey after a visit of three weeks |
| Napoleon invades Egypt | | July | |
| | | 10 July | Wordsworth and his sister depart from Bristol on a walking tour of the Wye Valley in the course of which he will compose 'Tintern Abbey' (returning to Bristol 13 July) |
| Battle of the Nile; Nelson victorious over the French | | 1 August | |
| | | 18 September | *Lyrical Ballads* published anonymously |
| | | 19 September<br>October | Coleridge and the Wordsworths arrive at Hamburg |
| | | 1 November | Wordsworth in Germany, begins 'The Two-Part Prelude' |
| | | | Southey's review of *Lyrical Ballads* appears in the *Critical Review* (October issue) |
| | | | Haydn composes *The Creation* |
| | | | Joanna Baillie publishes the first volume of her *Series of Plays* |

| Current affairs | Date | | Science and the Arts |
|---|---|---|---|
| Napoleon invades Syria | **1799** | 5 February | |
| | | 11 February | Berkeley Coleridge dies (b. 14 May 1798) |
| | | 12 February | Coleridge arrives at Göttingen |
| | | 19 February | Constable enrols at Royal Academy |
| | | 4 April | Coleridge hears of Berkeley Coleridge's death (in a letter from Poole, posted 15 March) |
| | | 21 April | The Wordsworths return to England |
| | | 23 May | Thomas Hood born, London |
| | | 6 June | Pushkin born, Moscow |
| Napoleon becomes First Consul | | 10 November | |
| | | 24 November | Coleridge's first meeting with Sara Hutchinson, Sockburn |
| | | 2 December | Godwin, *St Leon* published |
| Washington dies, Mount Vernon | | 14 December | |
| | | 20 December | Wordsworth and his sister move into Dove Cottage, Grasmere |
| | | | Wordsworth completes 'The Two-Part Prelude' |
| | | 24 December | Wordsworth begins writing 'The Brothers'<br>Goya begins etching his Caprichos, including 'The Sleep of Reason Begets Monsters' |
| First soup-kitchens in London to relieve the hungry and homeless | **1800** | January | Maria Edgeworth publishes *Castle Rackrent* anonymously |
| | | 28 February | Mary Robinson publishes 'The Haunted Beach' in *The Morning Post* |
| | | 2 April | Beethoven, *Symphony No. 1* first performed |
| | | 25 April | Cowper dies |
| | | 29 April | Joanna Baillie's *De Monfort* produced at Drury Lane Theatre by John Philip Kemble |
| | | 24 July | Coleridge and family take up residence at Greta Hall, Keswick |
| | | 14 September | Derwent Coleridge born, Keswick |
| | | 20 November | Mary Robinson publishes *Lyrical Tales* |
| | | 26 December | Mary Robinson dies, Englefield Green, Surrey<br>Volta invents galvanic cell (first electric battery) |
| Toussaint L'Ouverture takes command of Haiti, liberates black slaves | **1801** | 25 January | *Lyrical Ballads* (1800) published as by Wordsworth |
| Pitt resigns and is succeeded by Henry Addington in March | | February | |
| Jefferson delivers inaugral address as third US President | | 4 March | |
| First census in England and Wales compiled by John Rickman (published in December) | | 10 March | |
| Battle of Copenhagen | | 2 April | |

| Current affairs | Date | | Science and the Arts |
|---|---|---|---|
| General Enclosure Act, standardizing procedures for obtaining permission to enclose land | | June | |
| Truce between Britain and France | | 1 October | |
| Cobbett's *Weekly Political Register* begins publishing (until 1835) | **1802** | January | |
| | | 24 February | Scott publishes *Minstrelsy of the Scottish Border* |
| Peace of Amiens, bringing a temporary respite to the war between France and Britain (until May 1803) | | 27 March | |
| | | 4 April | Coleridge composes 'A Letter to Sara Hutchinson' |
| | | 18 April | Erasmus Darwin dies |
| Napoleon becomes Life Consul of France | | 2 August | |
| | | August | Wordsworth and his sister in Calais to meet Annette Vallon and her daughter, Anne-Caroline |
| | | 14 August | Letitia Landon born |
| | | October | Foundation of *Edinburgh Review* |
| | | 4 October | Wordsworth marries Mary Hutchinson at Brompton Church<br>Coleridge publishes 'Dejection: An Ode' in the *Morning Post* |
| | | 19 October | Coleridge, 'The Day-Dream' published in the *Morning Post* |
| | | 2 December | Harris Bigg-Wither proposes marriage to Jane Austen; she accepts, but changes her mind and formally retracts the following day |
| Toussaint L'Ouverture dies in prison | **1803** | 7 April | |
| Britain declares war on France, ending the Peace of Amiens | | 18 May | |
| | | 24 May | Beethoven, *Sonata in A for Violin* (Kreutzer) first performed |
| | | 25 May | Emerson born, Boston |
| Emmet leads an uprising in Ireland which fails due to lack of French support | | 30 June | Thomas Lovell Beddoes born, Clifton |
| | | July | Hazlitt visits Lake District to paint portraits of Coleridge and Wordsworth |
| | | August | Keats starts to attend the Revd John Clarke's school at Enfield |
| | | 12 August | Coleridge and the Wordsworths set out from Grasmere on their tour of Scotland<br>Warrant issued for arrest of Blake on charges of sedition |
| | | 5 September | Coleridge arrested in Fort Augustus as a spy; soon released |
| | | 10 September | Coleridge sends 'The Pains of Sleep' to Southey |
| Execution of Robert Emmet | | 20 September | Mary Tighe composes 'Psyche' (privately published, 1805) |

| Current affairs | Date | | Science and the Arts |
|---|---|---|---|
| | **1804** | 11–12 January | Blake tried and acquitted for sedition at Chichester Quarter Sessions |
| | | 6 February | Joseph Priestley dies, Pennsylvania |
| | | 12 February | Kant dies, Königsberg, Prussia |
| | | 21 February | Richard Trevithick's steam locomotive (the first to be built) makes its first run, Penydarren ironworks in Wales |
| | | 6 April | Coleridge sets sail on the *Speedwell* for the Mediterranean, in search of better health (returns August 1806) |
| | | 15 April | Keats's father dies after falling from his horse |
| Pitt's second ministry begins (until January 1806) | | 10 May | |
| Napoleon proclaimed Emperor (coronation 2 December) | | 18 May | |
| | | 4 July | Hawthorne born, Salem, MA |
| | **1805** | 12 January | Scott's 'Lay of the Last Minstrel' published (sells 44,000 copies) |
| | | 27 January | Samuel Palmer born, London |
| | | 5 February | John Wordsworth (the poet's brother) dies at sea |
| Jefferson inaugurated as US President for a second term | | 4 March | |
| | | 7 April | Beethoven, *Symphony No. 3 (Eroica)* first performed |
| | | 9 May | Schiller dies, Weimar |
| | | 19 May | Wordsworth completes 'The Prelude in Thirteen Books' |
| Napoleon declared King of Italy in Milan | | 26 May | |
| | | 19 July | Hazlitt publishes his first book, *An Essay on the Principles of Human Action* |
| Napoleon decides not to invade England | | September | |
| Battle of Trafalgar, Nelson mortally wounded | | 21 October | |
| Napoleon defeats Russian and Austrian armies at Austerlitz | | 2 December | |
| Pitt dies; Baron Grenville becomes head of the Coalition Ministry of All the Talents (until 26 March 1807) | **1806** | 23 January | |
| | | 6 March | Elizabeth Barrett (later Barrett Browning) born, Durham |
| | | 9 April | Brunel born, Portsmouth |
| | | May | Charlotte Dacre publishes Zofloya |
| | | 20 May | John Stuart Mill born, Pentonville |
| Francis II decrees an end to the Holy Roman Empire | | 6 August | |
| | | 17 August | Coleridge returns to England after Mediterranean sojourn |

| Current affairs | Date | | Science and the Arts |
|---|---|---|---|
| | | 13 September | James Fox dies, Devon |
| | | 9 October | Joseph Grimaldi, clown, makes his first appearance at Covent Garden Theatre |
| Napoleon defeats Prussians at Jena and occupies Berlin | | 14 October | |
| Napoleon declares blockade of Great Britain | | 21 November | |
| | **1807** | January | Charles and Mary Lamb, *Tales from Shakespeare* first published |
| | | 7 January | Coleridge writes 'To William Wordsworth', inspired by reading of 'The Prelude' |
| | | February | Charlotte Smith's *Beachy Head* published posthumously |
| Abolition Act receives royal assent, abolishing the slave trade | | 25 March | |
| Peninsular War begins | | 8 May | |
| | | December | Wordsworth publishes *Poem in Two Volumes* |
| America prohibits slave trade | **1808** | January | |
| | | 3 January | Leigh Hunt founds *The Examiner* |
| | | 15 January | Coleridge lectures on 'Poetry and Principles of Taste' at the Royal Institution, London (until June) |
| | | 22 February | Scott publishes 'Marmion' (2,000 copies sell in two months) |
| Spain invaded by France; Bonaparte made King | | March | |
| | | May | Felicia Dorothea Browne (later Hemans) publishes her first book of *Poems* |
| | | 1 May | Hazlitt marries Sarah Stoddart |
| | | 1 June | Coleridge begins to publish *The Friend* |
| | | September | Blake completes 'Milton' |
| | | 20 September | Covent Garden Theatre burns to the ground |
| | | December | Hannah More publishes *Coelebs in Search of a Wife* (which becomes a bestseller)<br>Goethe publishes *Faust* Part 1 |
| | **1809** | 19 January | Poe born, Boston |
| *Quarterly Review* founded | | February | |
| Lincoln born, Kentucky | | 12 February | Darwin born, Shrewsbury |
| Madison inaugurated as fourth US President | | 4 March | |
| Byron takes his seat in the House of Lords | | 13 March | |
| | | 16 March | Byron publishes *English Bards and Scotch Reviewers* |
| Napoleon takes Vienna | | 12 May | |
| | | 15 May | Blake exhibits his paintings in London (until September), visited by Crabb Robinson and Southey |

| Current affairs | Date | Science and the Arts |
|---|---|---|
| Papal States annexed to France | 17 May | |
| | 31 May | Haydn dies, Vienna |
| Pope Pius VII excommunicates Napoleon | 10 June | |
| Paine dies, New York State | 8 June | |
| Napoleon arrests and imprisons Pope Pius VII | July | |
| | 2 July | Byron sails for the Mediterranean with Hobhouse |
| | 18 September | Covent Garden Theatre reopens after being burnt down, with a new scale of ticket prices, precipitating the OP (or Old Price) riots which last sixty-seven nights |
| | 20 December | Joseph Johnson, bookseller and publisher, dies in London |
| | **1810** 1 March | Chopin born, Warsaw |
| | 24 March | Mary Tighe dies, Woodstock |
| Sir John Burdett imprisoned in the Tower of London for libellous article against the House of Commons in the *Weekly Political Register*; riots in London | April | |
| | 3 May | Byron swims the Hellespont |
| | 8 May | Scott's 'The Lady of the Lake' published (sells 20,300 copies) |
| Cobbett sentenced to two years' imprisonment for an article against the flogging of five English militiamen by German mercenaries in his *Political Register* | 9 July | |
| | 28 October | Basil Montagu tells Coleridge of remarks made by Wordsworth about Coleridge's opium addiction, suggesting that Wordsworth had commissioned him to do so, resulting in an irreparable breach<br>Goya etching *The Disasters of War* |
| Prince of Wales declared Regent, his father having been recognized as insane | **1811** 5 February | |
| First Luddite riots in Nottingham | 11 March | |
| | 25 March | Shelley expelled from Oxford for having co-written the *Necessity of Atheism* |
| | 14 July | Byron returns to England |
| | 18 July | Thackeray born, Calcutta |
| | 25 August | Shelley elopes with Harriet Westbrook |
| | 22 October | Liszt born, Raiding, Hungary |
| | 30 October | Austen's *Sense and Sensibility* published |
| | 18 November | Coleridge lectures on Shakespeare and Milton at Scot's Corporation Hall (until 17 January 1812) |
| | **1812** January | Anna Laetitia Barbauld publishes 'Eighteen Hundred and Eleven' |
| | 7 February | Dickens born, Portsmouth |

| Current affairs | Date | | Science and the Arts |
|---|---|---|---|
| | | 27 February | Byron delivers maiden speech in the Lords on behalf of the Luddites |
| | | 10 March | Byron publishes 'Childe Harold's Pilgrimage' Cantos I and II (500 copies sell in three days) |
| Leigh Hunt attacks the Prince Regent in *The Examiner* | | 22 March | |
| | | 21 April | Byron's second speech in the Lords |
| | | 7 May | Browning born, Camberwell |
| Assassination of the Prime Minister, Spencer Perceval, precipitating Liverpool's administration | | 11 May | |
| | | 4 June | Catherine Wordsworth dies in Grasmere (less than 4 years old) |
| America declares war on Britain | | 18 June | |
| Napoleon declares war on Russia | | 22 June | |
| Cobbett released from prison after two years, a ruined man | | 9 July | |
| Napoleon enters Moscow | | September | |
| | | 4 October | Shelley and Godwin meet in London |
| French begin retreat from Moscow | | 19 October | |
| | | 3 November | Coleridge lectures on Shakespeare, Surrey Institution (until 26 January 1813) |
| | | 11 November | Shelley meets Mary Godwin |
| | | 1 December | Thomas Wordsworth dies, Grasmere (6 years old) |
| | **1813** | 23 January | Coleridge's *Remorse* opens at Drury Lane Theatre in London, to widespread acclaim |
| | | 28 January | Austen's *Pride and Prejudice* published |
| Leigh Hunt sentenced to two years' imprisonment for libelling the Prince Regent | | 3 February | |
| | | 1 May | Wordsworth moves into Rydal Mount |
| | | 5 May | Søren Kierkegaard born |
| | | 18 May | Wordsworth assumes duties of his new office, Distributor of Stamps for Westmorland |
| | | 22 May | Wagner born, Leipzig |
| | | June | Shelley publishes 'Queen Mab' privately (250 copies only); it was pirated in 1821 |
| | | 11 August | Henry James Pye, Poet Laureate, dies |
| Napoleon's last major victory at Dresden | | 27 August | |
| Napoleon defeated at Leipzig | | 19 October | |
| | | October | Madame de Staël, *De l'Allemagne* published in French and English |
| | | 4 November | Southey takes oath as Poet Laureate |
| Metternich, with reluctant approval of Russia and Prussia, offers peace to Napoleon (proposal withdrawn by 2 December) | | 9 November | |

| Current affairs | Date | | Science and the Arts |
|---|---|---|---|
| Allies begin invasion of France | **1814** | 1 January | |
| | | 26 January | Edmund Kean makes his debut on the London stage as Shylock at Drury Lane Theatre (Hazlitt is in the audience) |
| | | 1 February | Byron publishes 'The Corsair' (10,000 copies sell in a day) |
| | | March | Burney, *The Wanderer* published |
| | | 24 March | Shelley marries Harriet Westbrook |
| Allies take Paris (news reaches London 5 April) | | 31 March | |
| Napoleon defeated at Toulouse; exiled to Elba | | 10 April | |
| | | 9 May | Austen's *Mansfield Park* published |
| | | 7 July | Scott's *Waverley* published anonymously |
| | | 28 July | Shelley elopes with Mary Godwin and her half-sister, Jane (later Claire) Clairmont, to the continent |
| | | 17 August | Wordsworth publishes 'The Excursion' |
| Washington, DC captured by the British | | September | |
| | | 14 September | Shelley, Mary Godwin and Jane Clairmont return from the continent |
| | | October | J. C. Spurzheim, phrenologist, visits Britain |
| | | November | John Walter, proprietor of *The Times*, introduces the steam-press |
| Peace of Ghent ends war between America and Britain | | 24 December | |
| | | 29 December | Jeffrey's hostile review of 'The Excursion' appears in the *Edinburgh Review* for November |
| | **1815** | 2 January | Byron marries Annabella Milbanke (separated 1816) |
| Battle of New Orleans, in which General Jackson defeats British troops | | 8 January | |
| Leigh Hunt released from prison | | 3 February | |
| | | 24 February | Scott publishes *Guy Mannering* (entire edition sells out the day after publication) |
| Napoleon escapes from Elba (news of which reaches London on 10 March) | | 26 February | |
| | | 7 April | Byron first meets Walter Scott at offices of John Murray, London |
| | | 27 April | Wordsworth publishes his first collected Poems |
| | | 12 May | Wordsworth publishes 'The White Doe of Rylstone', late May |
| | | | Byron appointed to the subcommittee of management at Drury Lane Theatre |
| | | 30 May | Coleridge writes to Wordsworth expressing disappointment with 'The Excursion' |
| | | 1 June | James Gillray dies, London (aged 58) |

| Current affairs | Date | | Science and the Arts |
|---|---|---|---|
| Napoleon defeated at Waterloo; exiled to St Helena in August | | 18 June | |
| | | 1 October | Keats enrols as medical student at Guy's Hospital, Southwark |
| | | December | Austen publishes *Emma* (dedicated to the Prince Regent)<br>Peacock publishes *Headlong Hall* |
| | | 17 December | Indian jugglers perform at Olympic New Theatre, Strand, London, precipitating Hazlitt's essay 'The Indian Jugglers' |
| | **1816** | 10 February | Shelley's 'Alastor' published in London |
| | | 15 February | Leigh Hunt publishes 'Rimini' |
| | | 10 April | Coleridge recites 'Kubla Khan' to Byron at his home in London |
| | | 15 April | Coleridge becomes house-guest and patient of Dr and Mrs Gillman, Highgate, London |
| | | 21 April | Charlotte Brontë born |
| | | 25 April | Byron sets out for the Continent from London |
| | | 2 May | Shelley, Mary Godwin and Claire Clairmont leave London for Geneva |
| | | 4 May | Byron visits the battlefield at Waterloo<br>Scott's *The Antiquary* published (sells 6,000 copies in six days) |
| | | 5 May | Keats' 'To Solitude' (his first published poem) appears in the *Examiner* |
| | | 9 May | Maturin's *Bertram* opens at Drury Lane Theatre, to wild acclaim |
| | | 25 May | Byron and Shelley meet at the Hotel Angleterre in Sécheron near Geneva |
| | | | Coleridge publishes 'Kubla Khan', 'Christabel' and 'The Pains of Sleep' to unfavourable reviews |
| | | 10 June | Byron moves into Villa Diodati, only a few hundred yards up the hill from the Shelleys at Montalègre |
| | | 17 June | Mary Godwin begins writing the story that will become *Frankenstein* |
| | | 7 July | Sheridan dies |
| | | 6 August | Austen completes *Persuasion* |
| | | 8 September | Shelley, Mary Godwin and Claire Clairmont return to England |
| | | 5 October | Byron leaves Geneva for Milan |
| Spa Fields riots in London | | 9 November | Harriet Shelley commits suicide, her body discovered 10 December |
| | | 18 November | Byron publishes 'Childe Harold's Pilgrimage' Canto III |
| | | 1 December | Hunt praises 'Young Poets' (including Shelley and Keats) in *The Examiner* |
| | | 2 December | |
| | | 30 December | Shelley marries Mary Godwin |

| Current affairs | Date | | Science and the Arts |
|---|---|---|---|
| | **1817** | 19 January | Shelley's 'Hymn to Intellectual Beauty' published in *The Examiner* |
| Southey publishes an article in the *Quarterly Review* for October 1816 saying that radical journalists should be prevented from 'insulting the government, and defying the laws of the country' | | 11 February | |
| | | 13 February | Southey's Wat Tyler published |
| | | 14 February | Hazlitt and Hunt publish *The Round Table* |
| | | 1 March | Keats's *Poems* published |
| Suspension of habeas corpus, which precipitates Cobbett's flight to America | | 4 March | |
| Monroe becomes fifth President of US | | | |
| Southey writes to Lord Liverpool asking for more repressive laws to control the press | | 19 March | |
| *Blackwood's Edinburgh Magazine* founded | | April | |
| Popular uprisings in the provinces | | June | |
| William Hone (radical publisher) tried for publishing 'blasphemous parodies' | | 18 June | |
| | | 23 June | John Philip Kemble's farewell performance as Coriolanus at Covent Garden Theatre |
| | | 3 July | Byron publishes *'Manfred'* |
| | | 9 July | Hazlitt publishes *Characters of Shakespeare's Plays* |
| | | 11 July | Coleridge publishes *Biographia Literaria* and *Sibylline Leaves* |
| | | 12 July | Thoreau born, Concord, MA |
| | | 14 July | Madame de Staël dies, Paris |
| | | 18 July | Austen dies, Winchester; buried Winchester Cathedral 24 July |
| | | October | Lockhart publishes the first of the Cockney School attacks in *Blackwood's* |
| Princess Charlotte dies in childbirth | | 6 November | |
| | | December | Austen's *Northanger Abbey* and *Persuasion* published posthumously |
| William Hone finally acquitted | | 20 December | |
| | | 26–8 December | Shelley writes 'Ozymandias' in a competition with Horace Smith at Marlow; it is published in *The Examiner*, 11 January 1818 |
| | | 28 December | Haydon hosts 'the immortal dinner' |
| | **1818** | 1 January | Mary Shelley publishes *Frankenstein* anonymously |
| | | 12 January | Shelley publishes 'The Revolt of Islam' |
| | | 13 January | Hazlitt begins to lecture on English Poetry at the Surrey Institution (until March) |
| | | 27 January | Coleridge begins lecturing on Poetry and Drama at Flower-de-Luce Court, Fetter Lane (until March) |

| Current affairs | Date | Science and the Arts |
|---|---|---|
| Habeas corpus restored | 28 January | |
| | 31 January | Scott publishes *Rob Roy* |
| | 6 February | Coleridge begins to lecture on Shakespeare in London |
| | 16 February | Fuseli as Professor of Painting begins a course of lectures at the Royal Academy, Somerset House |
| | 28 February | Byron publishes 'Beppo' |
| | 28 April | Byron publishes 'Childe Harold' Canto IV (4,000 copies sold) |
| | 29 April | Hazlitt publishes *A View of the English Stage* |
| | 30 April | Emily Brontë born, Thornton |
| | 5 May | Karl Marx born, Trier, Rhine Province, Prussia |
| | 18 May | Lamb publishes his Works (2 vols.) with C. and J. Ollier |
| | 19 May | Keats publishes 'Endymion' |
| | 22 June | Keats and Charles Brown depart for their walking tour of the Lake District and Scotland |
| | 18 August | Keats returns to London from Inverness (by boat) |
| | 1 September | Lockhart's attack on Keats, 'The Cockney School of Poetry' No. IV (signed 'Z'), published in *Blackwood's* (for August) |
| | 27 September | Croker publishes a hostile review of Keats's 'Endymion' in the April number of the *Quarterly Review* |
| | 15 November | Thomas Love Peacock publishes *Nightmare Abbey*<br>Shelley arrives in Rome (until 22 November) |
| | | Shelley arrives in Rome (until 22 November) |
| Queen Charlotte dies | 17 November | |
| University of Virginia founded by Jefferson | **1819** 25 January | |
| | 8 February | Ruskin born, London |
| | 1 April | Polidori publishes 'The Vampyre: A Tale by Lord Byron' in the *New Monthly Magazine* |
| | 15 April | John Hamilton Reynolds publishes *Peter Bell. A Lyrical Ballad* |
| | 22 April | Wordsworth's 'Peter Bell' published |
| Princess Victoria born | 24 May | |
| | 31 May | Whitman born |
| | 15 July | Byron's 'Don Juan' Cantos I and II published anonymously by Murray |
| | 1 August | Melville born, New York |
| | 14 August | Hazlitt publishes *Political Essays* |
| Peterloo Massacre takes place, | 16 August | |
| St Peter's Fields, Manchester | Early September | Shelley prints *The Cenci* in Livorno |
| | 5 September | Shelley composes 'The Mask of Anarchy' (until 23 September) |

| Current affairs | Date | | Science and the Arts |
|---|---|---|---|
| Trial of Richard Carlile, radical publisher, for criticizing the Government over the Peterloo Massacre and publishing Paine's *The Age of Reason*, critical of the Church of England (he is sentenced 21 November) | | 12 October | |
| | | 25 October | Shelley composes 'Ode to the West Wind' |
| Richard Carlile imprisoned for 3 years and fined £1,500 (£62,500/US$116,000 today) | | 21 November | |
| | | 26 November | William Hone and George Cruikshank publish *The Political House that Jack Built* |
| | | December | Shelley composes 'England in 1819' |
| Bolivar becomes President and military dictator of Colombia | | 17 December | |
| Military insurrection at Cadiz precipitates revolution in Spain, leading to restoration of 1812 constitution in March | **1820** | 1 January | *London Magazine* begins publishing |
| | | 16 January | Hunt publishes *The Indicator*<br>Clare, *Poems Descriptive of Rural Life and Scenery* published; it runs to four editions and sells over 3,500 copies |
| | | 28 January | Southey's *Poetical Works* (14 vols.) published |
| George III dies at Windsor Castle, to be succeeded by his son, Prince Regent since 1811, as George IV | | 29 January | |
| | | 3 February | Keats has his first haemorrhage indicating that he is suffering from tubercolosis |
| Cato Street Conspiracy (plan to blow up Cabinet) foiled; the principals are executed on 1 May | | 23 February | |
| | | 25 March | Haydon's *Christ's Entry into Jerusalem* exhibited in London |
| | | May | Hartley Coleridge deemed to have forfeited his Fellowship at Oriel College, Oxford |
| | | June | Shelley composes 'To a Skylark' |
| | | Late June | Peacock publishes 'The Four Ages of Poetry' in *Ollier's Literary Miscellany*, No. 1 |
| | | 1 July | Keats publishes *Lamia, Isabella, The Eve of St Agnes, and Other Poems* |
| | | 6 July | Wordsworth publishes *The River Duddon* |
| Start of the trial of Queen Caroline to prove her infidelities so that George IV can divorce her; she is eventually acquitted | | 17 August | |
| | | 14 August | Shelley's *Prometheus Unbound ... with Other Poems* published in London |
| | | September | Blake finishes work on the first illuminated copy of 'Jerusalem' |
| | | 1 September | Lamb publishes the first of his *Elia* essays, 'Recollections of the South Sea House', in the *London Magazine* (for August) |

| Current affairs | Date | | Science and the Arts |
|---|---|---|---|
| | | 17 September | Keats sails for Rome |
| | | 13 October | Wordsworth meets Helen Maria Williams for the first time in Paris (they meet again 20 October) |
| | | 15 November | Keats and Severn move into 26 Piazza di Spagna, Rome |
| | **1821** | February | Shelley writing 'A Defence of Poetry' (not published until 1840) |
| | | 23 February | Keats dies, Rome |
| | | 27 February | John Scott, editor of the *London Magazine,* killed in a duel |
| | | 6 April | Hazlitt, *Table Talk* Vol. 1 published |
| Napoleon dies, St Helena | | 5 May | |
| | | July | Shelley publishes 'Adonais' in Pisa |
| Coronation of George IV | | 19 July | |
| Queen Caroline (wife of George IV) dies | | 7 August | |
| | | September | Clare, 'The Village Minstrel' published (sells 800 copies in three months) |
| | | October | Cobbett sets out on the rural rides |
| | | 1 October | De Quincey's *Confessions of an English Opium-Eater* Part I appears in the *London Magazine*, followed by Part II in November |
| | | 1 November | Byron moves to Pisa |
| | | 11 November | Dostoyevsky born, Moscow |
| | | 11 December | Fight between Tom Hickman (the Gas-man) and Bill Neat at Hungerford, Berkshire, attended by Hazlitt |
| | | 12 December | Flaubert born, Rouen |
| | | 19 December | Byron publishes *Sardanapalus, The Two Foscari, and Cain* |
| | **1822** | February | Hazlitt's 'The Fight' published in *New Monthly Magazine* |
| | | 15 June | Hazlitt, *Table Talk* Vol. 2 published |
| | | 8 July | Shelley drowned off Livorno |
| Castlereagh commits suicide by slitting his own throat; succeeded as Foreign Secretary by Canning | | 12 August | |
| | | 16 August | Shelley cremated on beach not far from Viareggio, Italy |
| | | October | De Quincey publishes *Confessions of an English Opium-Eater* in book form |
| | | | Schubert composes Symphony No. 8 |
| | | 14 October | *The Liberal* No. 1 published |
| | | December | Lamb's *Elia* published - the first collected volume of *Elia* essays |
| | | 24 December | Matthew Arnold born |

| Current affairs | Date | | Science and the Arts |
|---|---|---|---|
| | **1823** | February | Mary Shelley publishes *Valperga* |
| | | 23 April | Hazlitt's 'My First Acquaintance with Poets' published in *The Liberal* |
| | | 9 May | Hazlitt publishes *Liber Amoris* |
| | | June | Hemans publishes *The Siege of Valencia* |
| | | 28 July | Richard Brinsley Peake's *Presumption, or the Fate of Frankenstein* opens at the Lyceum, London, for a run of thirty-seven performances – the first of many adaptations |
| | | 25 August | Mary Shelley returns to England |
| Monroe Doctrine enunciated in America | | 2 December | |
| | | 12 December | Hemans's *The Vespers of Palermo* performed at Covent Garden Theatre |
| | **1824** | 4 January | Byron lands at Missolonghi to great welcome |
| | | 22 January | Byron composes 'On this day I completed my thirty-sixth year' |
| | | March | Coleridge elected Fellow of the Royal Society |
| | | 19 April | Byron dies, Missolonghi, from marsh fever and excessive bleeding |
| | | 7 May | Beethoven, *Symphony No. 9 in D minor* first performed |
| | | June | Shelley's *Posthumous Poems* published, edited by Mary Shelley |
| | | 12 July | James Hogg's *Private Memoirs and Confessions of a Justified Sinner* published in London |
| | | September | Shelley's *Posthumous Poems* suppressed, at the insistence of Sir Timothy Shelley |
| | **1825** | 11 January | Hazlitt, *The Spirit of the Age* published anonymously |
| John Quincy Adams elected sixth US President | | 4 March | |
| | | 9 March | Anna Laetitia Barbauld dies, Stoke Newington |
| | | 16 April | Fuseli dies |
| | | May | Hemans publishes *The Forest Sanctuary and Other Poems* |
| | | June | Barbauld's *Works* posthumously published by her niece, Lucy Aikin |
| | | September | Stockton to Darlington railway becomes the first line open to the public |
| | | 7 November | Charlotte Dacre dies, London |
| | **1826** | 14 January | Constable (publisher) bankrupted, precipitating financial ruin for Sir Walter Scott and others |
| | | 23 January | Mary Shelley publishes *The Last Man* |
| | | March | Blake publishes *Job* |
| | | 28 April | Hazlitt publishes *The Plain Speaker* anonymously |
| Jefferson dies, Monticello, VA | | 4 July | |

| Current affairs | Date | | Science and the Arts |
|---|---|---|---|
| | **1827** | 26 March | Beethoven dies, Vienna |
| | | April | Clare, *The Shepherd's Calendar, with Village Stories and Other Poems* published (sells only 425 copies over two and a half years) |
| Lord Liverpool, Prime Minister since 1811, succeeded by Canning | | 30 April | |
| Canning dies | | 8 August | |
| | | 12 August | Blake dies, London |
| | | 15 December | Helen Maria Williams dies |
| Wellington becomes Prime Minister | **1828** | January | First two volumes of Hazlitt's *Life of Napoleon Buonaparte* published |
| | | 16 April | Goya dies in Spain, but is buried in France |
| Repeal of Test and Corporation Act that kept non-Anglicans from holding office | | 28 April | |
| | | May | Hemans publishes *Records of Woman*; goes into a second edition in October |
| | | 12 May | D.G. Rossetti born, London |
| | | 21 June | Coleridge, Wordsworth and Dora Wordsworth tour the Netherlands and the Rhine (until 7 August) |
| | | 19 November | Schubert dies, Vienna |
| Jackson elected seventh President of the US | **1829** | 4 March | |
| Catholic Emancipation Act | | 4 April | |
| Metropolitan Police Act puts 'Peelers' on the streets of London | | June | |
| | | December | Coleridge publishes *On the Constitution of Church and State* |
| | **1830** | May | Hazlitt's *Life of Napoleon Buonaparte* Vols. 3 and 4 published |
| George IV dies; accession of William IV, his brother | | 25 June | |
| 'Captain Swing' agrarian riots | | August | |
| | | 18 September | Hazlitt dies, Frith Street, Soho |
| The Whig, Earl Grey, succeeds Wellington (Tory) as Prime Minister, bringing an era of reform | | 16 November | |
| | | 5 December | Christina Rossetti born, London |
| | | 10 December | Emily Dickinson born, Amherst, MA |
| Bolivar dies, Colombia | | 17 December | |
| Lord John Russell introduces Reform Bill | **1831** | 1 March | |
| Government defeated on Reform Bill; Parliament dissolved | | 10 April | |
| | | 8 June | Sarah Siddons dies |
| New Parliament with Whig majority | | 14 June | |

| Current affairs | Date | | Science and the Arts |
|---|---|---|---|
| Reform Bill defeated in Lords | | 8 October | |
| | | 31 October | Mary Shelley publishes revised edition of *Frankenstein* |
| | | 14 November | Hegel dies, Berlin |
| | **1832** | 23 January | Manet born, Paris |
| | | 3 February | Crabbe dies |
| | | 22 March | Goethe dies in Weimar |
| Revised Reform Bill defeated in Lords; Grey resigns as Prime Minister 9 May; recalled 15 May | | 7 May | |
| | | 6 June | Bentham dies |
| Reform Bill receives royal assent | | 7 June | |
| | | 21 September | Scott dies, Abbotsford |
| | | October | Hunt publishes Shelley's 'The Mask of Anarchy' |
| | | December | Posthumous publication of Goethe's *Faust* Part 2 |
| | **1833** | 15 March | Edmund Kean dies |
| Emancipation Act receives its final reading, abolishing slavery in British colonies | | 26 July | |
| Wilberforce dies, London | | 29 July | |
| | | 5 August | Emerson visits Coleridge at Highgate |
| | | 7 September | Hannah More dies, leaving her sizeable fortune to a range of charities and religious institutions |
| | **1834** | 17 February | John Thelwall dies |
| Hunt begins publishing *Leigh Hunt's London Journal* (until December 1835) | | 2 April | |
| | | 19 July | Degas born, Paris |
| | | 25 July | Coleridge dies, Highgate |
| Poor Law Reform Act | | 14 August | |
| Slaves throughout the British Empire become legally free | | August | |
| Fire destroys Houses of Parliament | | 16 October | |
| | | 23 December | Malthus dies |
| | | 27 December | Lamb dies (buried 3 January, Edmonton) |
| | **1835** | March | Mary Shelley publishes *Lodore* |
| | | 16 May | Felicia Hemans dies, Dublin |
| | | July | Clare's *The Rural Muse* published |
| | | 15 October | Marx enrolled as a student at the University of Bonn |
| Siege of the Alamo; Davy Crockett killed | **1836** | March | |
| | | 7 April | William Godwin dies |
| Madison dies, Montpelier, VA | | 28 June | |

| Current affairs | Date | | Science and the Arts |
|---|---|---|---|
| | **1837** | 10 February | Pushkin dies, St Petersburg |
| Van Buren elected eighth US President | | 4 March | |
| William IV dies, succeeded by his 17-year-old niece as Queen Victoria | | June | |
| Charter presented to Parliament by National Convention of Chartists; rejection leads to riots in Birmingham and elsewhere in July | **1838** | 13 May | |
| | | 15 October | Letitia Landon dies, Gold Coast |
| Outbreak of Opium War with China | | November | |
| | **1839** | January | Shelley's collected *Poetical Works* (4 vols.) edited by Mary Shelley begins publishing (until May) |
| | | 1 February | De Quincey begins his 'Lake Reminiscences' in *Tait's Edinburgh Magazine* (for January) with the first part of his essay on Wordsworth |
| | **1840** | 6 January | Fanny Burney dies, London |
| Queen Victoria marries her first cousin, Albert of Saxe-Coburg-Gotha, St James's Palace London | | 10 February | |
| | | 2 June | Thomas Hardy born, Upper Bockhampton, Dorset |
| | | 14 November | Monet born, Paris |
| | **1841** | 25 February | Renoir born, Limoges |
| Harrison elected ninth President of the US | | 4 March | |
| | | 31 March | Schumann, *Symphony No. 1* first performed |
| | **1843** | 21 March | Southey dies |
| Harrison dies to be succeeded as tenth US President by Tyler | | 4 April | Wordsworth accepts the post of Poet Laureate in a letter to Sir Robert Peel |
| | **1844** | 2 May | William Beckford dies, after a severe attack of influenza |
| | | 28 July | Gerard Manley Hopkins born, Stratford, Essex |
| | | 15 October | Friedrich Nietzsche born |
| Polk elected eleventh President of US | **1845** | 4 March | |
| | | 1 April | De Quincey begins *Suspiria de Profundis in Blackwood's* (for March), which continues in issues for April, June and July |
| | **1846** | May | Brontë sisters publish *Poems by Currer, Ellis and Acton Bell* |
| | | 22 June | Benjamin Robert Haydon commits suicide |
| | | 12 September | Robert Browning marries Elizabeth Barrett |
| | **1847** | 20 May | Mary Lamb dies, aged 82 |
| | | 19 October | Charlotte Brontë publishes *Jane Eyre* |
| | | December | Emily Brontë publishes *Wuthering Heights* |

| Current affairs | Date | | Science and the Arts |
|---|---|---|---|
| Gold discovered in California; beginning of the gold rush | **1848** | 24 January | |
| Second Republic proclaimed in France | | February | Marx and Engels publish *Communist Manifesto* |
| June Days (until 26 June), bloody civil war in Paris | | 23 June | |
| Louis Napoleon Bonaparte elected President of France | | December | |
| | | 19 December | Emily Brontë dies |
| | **1849** | 6 January | Hartley Coleridge dies |
| Roman Republic is established | | 5 February | |
| Taylor elected twelfth President of US | | 4 March | |
| | | 22 May | Maria Edgeworth dies, Edgeworthstown |
| | | 7 October | Poe dies, Baltimore |
| | | 17 October | Chopin dies, Paris |
| | | 1 November | Wordsworth's *Poetical Works* (6 vols.), last edition in his lifetime, begins publishing |
| | | | De Quincey publishes 'The English Mail-Coach', anonymously, in *Blackwood's* (for October) |
| American Express founded | **1850** | 18 March | |
| | | 23 April | Wordsworth dies, aged 80 |
| | | July | 'The Prelude' first published, posthumously |
| Taylor dies, to be succeeded as thirteenth US President by Fillmore | | 9 July | |
| | | 18 August | Balzac dies, Paris |
| California admitted to the Union | | September | |
| | **1851** | 1 February | Mary Shelley dies, Chester Square, London, aged 53 |

# About the Companion Website

This book is accompanied by a companion website

**www.wiley.com/go/Wu/Romanticism5e** 

This website includes additional texts by authors not present in the print edition, including Thomas De Quincey, Charlotte Smith, Mary Robinson, John Clare, and many more.

# William Blake (1757–1827)

A native Londoner, William Blake was born on 28 November 1757 in Soho, London. His father, James Blake, was a hosier who with his wife Catherine Hermitage brought up their seven children as Dissenting Whigs. They were understandably dismayed when Blake's older brother claimed to have encountered Moses and Abraham, and young William insisted he had seen angels in the treetops on Peckham Rye. On another occasion William said he saw the prophet Ezekiel beneath a tree and got thrashed by his mother.

William's formal education began at the age of 10 when he was sent to Henry Pars's Drawing School in the Strand to become a draughtsman. At 14 he was apprenticed to James Basire, engraver to the Society of Antiquaries. During the next seven years he learnt the basic skills that would provide him with a living – etching onto prepared copper plates. Thanks to the authors who passed through Basire's workshop, Blake became acquainted with the natural sciences, philology and archaeology. At this period he also learnt about the English Gothic tradition, partly by drawing the monuments in Westminster Abbey. There he saw a vision of monks, priests, choristers and censer-bearers marching in procession. Blake began his career as a copy engraver in 1779, at the same time enrolling at the Royal Academy of Arts to train as an artist. His many sketches of classical sculpture indicate his ambitions to be a 'historical' painter.

At around this time, Blake befriended Catherine Boucher, the daughter of a market-gardener; he would marry her on 18 August 1782 at the Church of St Mary, Battersea. Soon after, they moved to 23 Green Street, near Leicester Square.

Blake's first volume of poems, *Poetical Sketches* (1783), was the first and last to use traditional letterpress; from then on his books were produced with his 'infernal' printing method developed during work on *All Religions Are One* and *There Is No Natural Religion*, etched around 1788. He would inscribe design and text, in reverse, directly onto a copper plate using a varnish resistant to the acid bath into which it would afterwards be immersed.[1] Once the plate was removed, the areas left in relief could be inked and printed with low pressure. Each page would then be water-coloured by him or his wife; consequently, no two books were identical. He did not care that they could not be mass produced; in fact the entire process was designed to make that impossible. The point was that every book would be, from start to finish, an artistic venture over which the artist retained complete control. Because each character of each word was the work of his own hand, it was susceptible to variation and emphasis as he saw fit. He was also in charge of page layout – integral to the meaning of the work, as it incorporated ornament and illustration that complemented or counterpointed the text. Indeed, the interweaving of word and image is essential to a full understanding of his poems and prophecies; readers may wish to use the Blake Trust/Tate Gallery editions of his work, which combine colour reproductions of each page of his books with detailed commentaries.

## Notes

[1] The process is explained by Joseph Viscomi, *Blake and the Idea of the Book* (Princeton,1993), part III.

*Romanticism: An Anthology*, Fifth Edition. Edited by Duncan Wu.

Companion website: www.wiley.com/go/Wu/Romanticism5e

It is worth bearing in mind that, though known today for his own works, Blake depended for an income on his commercial labours, which used traditional printing methods, commissioned by publishers such as Joseph Johnson. Johnson engaged Blake to illustrate works by Mary Wollstonecraft and Erasmus Darwin, and introduced Blake to Henry Fuseli, the volatile Swiss-German artist, as well as Thomas Paine and Joseph Priestley.

'Thel' (1789) is a sustained attempt to examine the 'fall' into the physical world and sexual experience. Only Blake would have approached such a subject through a narrative that concerns a girl's encounters with a curious series of characters – lily, cloud, clod of clay and worm – loaded with allegorical significance that is never precisely spelt out. Much hinges on the virgin's return to the Vales of Har, which signifies reluctance to submit to the descent into experience. Some readers take this to reflect badly on her, while others question the advice dispensed by those she encounters. 'Thel' is a good place to begin a study of Blake's unusual way of thinking: it takes us into a world in which, as in life, judgements as to meaning and morality are anything but straightforward. The parallel world, fall from grace and concern with sexual initiation were to be revisited.

*Songs of Innocence* (1789) and its companion volume, *Songs of Experience* (1794), contain Blake's most popular and influential poems. Their titles imply a binary opposition, but Blake was resistant to simplistic formulations, and it is typical that when producing joint copies of *Songs of Innocence and of Experience*, he moved some poems from one book to the other. Accordingly, 'Holy Thursday' (*Innocence*) can be read ironically, just as the corresponding poem in *Experience* can be read in a positive manner. Rather than thinking in terms of thematic opposition, it is more helpful to think of the two groups as engaged in dialogue.

'Every child may joy to hear', Blake wrote – except that the *Songs* contain some sophisticated ideas. Blakean innocence entails a complex mixture of qualities including unfettered energy, simplicity and love. He doesn't write about sin and divine punishment (usual elements of didactic poetry for children); instead such poems as 'The Lamb' and 'Spring' emphasize the intensity and purity of childhood vision. There is a political subtext too: publication of *Innocence* in 1789 coincided with the Revolution in France, that of *Experience* with the events that led to the execution of Louis XVI and the Reign of Terror. This is most obvious in 'London', 'Holy Thursday' (*Experience*) and 'The Chimney Sweeper' (*Experience*).

It may have been grief at the death of his brother Robert that prompted Blake to study the writings of Emanuel Swedenborg, the theologian and philosopher who theorized that the spirits of the dead rise from the body and assume physical form in another world. Though Swedish, Swedenborg died in London in 1772, when he was 84 and Blake 14, but his ideas were as widely discussed as ever. Such was their popularity that, in the 1780s, his followers formed the New Church, or Church of the New Jerusalem, which continues today. A visionary who conversed with angels and spirits, Swedenborg's brand of religion for a while had a powerful appeal for Blake, and he may have had a permanent influence on Blake's way of thinking, as when he wrote, 'God is a man, all angels and spirits are men in a perfect form'.

The Swedenborgian faith soon became institutionalized; it ordained ministers with robes and rituals, and was administered by conservatives who pledged loyalty to king and country, adhering to such doctrines as predestination (in favour of which Swedenborg had written). These developments were anathema to Blake who rejected the faith, and within a year of joining he wrote in his copy of Swedenborg's *Divine Providence*: 'Lies and Priestcraft', 'Predestination ... more abominable than Calvin's' and 'Cursed Folly!' Blake hated the systematizing tendencies of religious beliefs, and it was in part that disgust that inspired his satire on Swedenborgianism, *The Marriage of Heaven and Hell* (which echoes the title of Swedenborg's own *Heaven and Hell*).

The argument of Blake's *Marriage* is that Swedenborg, though pretending to the status of a radical, was a stooge for the forces of reaction. This is most explicitly articulated in Plate 11, where Blake explains how systems generated by institutionalized religions exiled the true poets of ancient times who were also, by implication, true priests; the result has been to make people forget that 'All deities reside in the human breast'. Despite appearances to the contrary, he argues, Swedenborg is a type of false prophet. Blake aims to prove this by imitating his literary devices, such as the 'correspondences' and 'memorable relations', to expose the underlying complacency of his thought. To that end, Blake condenses Swedenborgian ideas and literary techniques in a helter-skelter manner, producing a comically distorted version of them. For instance, the title of Blake's work echoes Swedenborg's opposition of heaven and hell, proposing a relationship that most theologians would have found either inappropriate or nonsensical.

Blake was for years regarded as operating outside the normal boundaries of literature, and ignored accordingly. As late as the 1950s, it was possible to teach a course on Romanticism without mentioning him. All that has changed, and if Blake has a claim to be regarded not just as a Romantic, but as a herald of the movement, it is never stronger than in the *Marriage*, when he declares his faith in a spiritual world: 'If the doors of perception were cleansed, everything would appear to man as it is: Infinite.'

'A Song of Liberty' is the great apocalyptic finale of the *Marriage*, which some scholars suggest originated as a separate work. Even if they are right, it resolves the *Marriage* in a way that could hardly be better by extending Blake's argument into the historical moment, where he finds the 'outing' of Swedenborg (and, more generally, institutionalized religions as a whole) to be the harbinger of revolution. Imagination is not just the agent of artistic creation, but the vehicle of revolutionary change in the 'real' world.

In autumn 1790 the Blakes moved to Lambeth in south London, where they produced a series of books now referred to as the Lambeth prophecies, which include *Visions of the Daughters of Albion* (1793). This work takes us straight into Blake's mythical universe. On her way to her beloved Theotormon, Oothoon is raped by Bromion. Having impregnated her, he casts her off; they are nonetheless bound back to back. Theotormon refuses to marry her, and sits weeping on the threshold of Bromion's cave. The rest of the poem consists of their lamentations. Thematically, it extends Blake's preoccupation with the journey from innocence to experience in 'Thel', but the obvious distinction is that where Thel retreated from the body, Oothoon accepts it.

The extent to which Oothoon is a feminist or a tool of male ideology is debated by critics. All the same, it is worth remembering that Blake knew Mary Wollstonecraft[2] and read her *Vindication of the Rights of Woman* (1792). He may even have been aware of her proposal to Henry Fuseli's wife that she move into their home and form a platonic *ménage à trois*, a scenario that may have inspired aspects of the *Visions*.

While working on *Visions of the Daughters*, Blake continued to pursue his career as engraver, supplying a number of illustrations to John Gabriel Stedman's *Narrative of a Five Years' Expedition against the Revolted Negroes of Surinam* (1796), one of the best known of which is an image of a captured black man hanging by the ribs from a gallows. Stedman's text left its mark on *Visions of the Daughters*: Bromion is a slave-owner – 'Stamped with my signet are the swarthy children of the sun' (l. 29) – and Theotormon hears the 'voice of slaves' (l. 39). For Blake the plight of women and slaves was the result of the failure to comprehend fully what the eye sees.

In these books, Blake worries at the nagging question: why did God permit the Fall? He attempts an answer in *The Book of Urizen* (1794), which contains the kernel of the mythology elaborated in subsequent works. *Urizen* was Blake's first attempt to rewrite the Scriptures, in this case the Book of Genesis. His central innovation is to postulate a primal unity before the act of creation when heaven and earth were one. The Fall occurs as part of the creation of the known universe, not the later stage claimed by the Bible. In Blake's retelling, the act of creation ('An activity unknown and horrible') cannot avoid destroying a perfect unity. Creation of the physical world is the first in a series of repressive acts responsible for enslaving the

## Notes

[2] Wollstonecraft probably met Blake when he engraved the illustrations for her *Original Stories from Real Life* in 1791.

human spirit. It culminates with the imposition of a tyranny Blake's readers well understood: 'One king, one God, one law.'

The myth is rehearsed three times. In the first, Urizen's story is told beginning at the moment he splits off from 'eternity' (chapter I). In the second, Urizen recalls the moment before creation as 'The heavens / Awoke' (chapter II). After the creation of Los (and Death), the 'changes of Urizen' are described as a series of 'Ages' in a parody of the Bible. During the course of what follows, time, institutionalized religion and the human body itself are seen as different kinds of tyranny imposed on humanity in the aftermath of the Fall.

If Blake's sceptical attitude towards the Bible seems extreme, it is as well to bear in mind he was one of a number of radicals (including Paine) who questioned the political and social control exercised by government and clergy through the Bible.

Blake would compose other visionary works, including *Vala, or the Four Zoas* (first version, 1797, revised 1802, 1807), 'Milton' (1804–?8) and 'Jerusalem' (1804–?20), none of which has the clarity or (comparative) simplicity of *Urizen*. They are all masterpieces and should be read complete – preferably in the Blake Trust editions, which reproduce the plates.

Blake encountered severe financial difficulties at the beginning of the new century, in part because Johnson stopped commissioning him. He became more dependent on patrons such as William Hayley, who housed the Blakes in a cottage in the Sussex village of Felpham, on the south coast. This was a happier situation than the confines of the city, and here Blake wrote much of 'Milton'. A strong-willed artist determined to follow his own path, he found it distasteful to work to Hayley's prescription, and tensions formed in their relationship.

Blake moved back to London and continued to work less on commissions than on watercolour illustrations, often at the behest of Thomas Butts, a clerk to the commissary general of musters, the office in charge of military pay. Butts thought highly of Blake and remained his patron for years. It took independence of thought because Blake's powers as writer and artist were unacknowledged. The Royal Academy rejected his paintings, and in response he mounted an exhibition at his home from May 1809 until around June 1810. Few people visited the exhibition and fewer still were tempted to buy his work. Among them was the journalist and friend of Wordsworth and Coleridge, Charles Lamb who thought Blake's paintings 'extraordinary': 'He paints in watercolours, marvelous strange pictures, visions of his brain which he asserts that he has seen. They have great merit.' The sole review of Blake's exhibition, in *The Examiner* newspaper, branded him 'an unfortunate lunatic'.

In his final years Blake was the hero of a number of young artists all of whom recognized his genius including John Linnell, Samuel Palmer, George Richmond, and John Varley. For Varley, Blake sketched a series of visionary faces, including those of Julius Caesar, William Wallace and 'the man who built the pyramids'. Blake said these people, though spiritual beings, were in the room as he worked. Linnell was an enthusiastic patron and commissioned Blake's *Illustrations of the Book of Job* and watercolours of 'Paradise Lost' and 'Paradise Regained'. He introduced Blake to Samuel Palmer in 1824; only nineteen, Palmer found him a powerful influence. 'Do you work with fear and trembling?' Blake asked. Having walked to Linnell's Hampstead retreat, Blake would sing old ballads or songs of his own invention.

He remained as creative as ever, engraving the Laocoön in 1826, and illustrating Dante's *Divine Comedy* and Bunyan's *Pilgrim's Progress*. He died on 12 August 1827 at Fountain Court in London, perhaps from cirrhosis contracted from inhalation of poisonous fumes while etching, and was buried at Bunhill Fields, now in the City of London.

The hermeticism of Blakean myth can tempt us to think of its creator as if he lived in a vacuum, detached from reality. But this is disproved if only by reference to the Gordon Riots, an anti-Catholic demonstration whipped up by sectarians in London. The marchers swept towards the 22-year-old Blake on the evening of 6 June 1780; he would have quickly realized the marchers were mostly of a similar age to himself, and he would have shared their hatred of the social and economic inequalities of Georgian London. He followed them to Newgate Prison, where some of their number were detained, and watched as they demolished the building, liberating some 300 prisoners including one under sentence of death. Then they torched what was left of it, some clambering onto precarious pieces of masonry, urinating into the flames and shouting obscenities across the rooftops. It was an intoxicating experience for the young poet, and he probably witnessed events the following night when the district around Holborn was 'like a volcano'; the King's Bench and Fleet prisons burned down; tollhouses on Blackfriars Bridge set on fire; a full-scale battle waged on the steps of the Bank of England; and scores of fires were set around the capital. From then on, fire had tremendous imaginative significance for Blake – for instance, when composing 'A Song of Liberty' for *The Marriage of Heaven and Hell*, he conceived of revolution as 'the new-born fire' with 'fiery limbs', bringing an end to the financial system, the Empire, and organized religion.

If Blake was that sensitive to current events, it becomes harder to think of him as mad. Contrary to the myth, he was never confined to a madhouse, nor did he and his wife sit naked in their summerhouse declaiming 'Paradise Lost'. Admittedly Robert Southey (who met him) described him as 'evidently insane', Wordsworth (who never met him) said 'this poor man was mad', while Blake's friend Henry Fuseli said he 'has something of madness about him'.

But to assume anyone mad without hard evidence is to tread a dangerous path. Another way of approaching Blake's achievements – which are remarkable – is to say that only a sane person could have managed them. This is all the more evident in the illustrations Blake provided for books as a commercial artist, where any suggestion of madness would have rendered him unemployable. And there were many acquaintances who saw no trace of madness in him. Looking back, years after Blake's death, Samuel Palmer described him 'as one of the sanest, if not the most thoroughly sane man I have ever known'.

Though many years would pass before Blake was understood to be one of the foremost writers and artists of his time, there were some who perceived his greatness early on. When he read the *Songs* in 1812, Wordsworth 'considered Blake as having the elements of poetry a thousand times more than either Byron or Scott' – high praise from someone not known for admiring other people's poetry. And when he caught up with *The Marriage of Heaven and Hell* in 1818, Coleridge bestowed on its author the ultimate compliment:

> He is a man of Genius – and I apprehend, a Swedenborgian – certainly, a mystic *emphatically*. You perhaps smile at *my* calling another Poet, a *Mystic*; but verily I am in the very mire of common-place common-sense compared with Mr Blake, apo- or rather anacalyptic Poet, and Painter!

In these texts I have retained Blake's capital letters; though punctuation is editorial, it preserves most of that used in his published texts, which sometimes allows for nuances and ambiguities that would otherwise be lost. There are occasions on which I have retained Blake's orthography, as in the cases of 'Tyger', 'appalls' and 'ecchoing'. I am indebted to the labours of those responsible for the Blake Trust/Tate Gallery editions, as all scholars of Blake must be; their datings and bibliographical observations are authoritative.

Admirers of Blake should visit 'The Blake Archive', an invaluable resource particularly in the cases of *Songs of Innocence and of Experience* and *The Book of Urizen*, where the relationship of text and illustration is important. The illustrations are also available in the Blake Trust/Tate Gallery editions.

## *All Religions Are One* (composed *c.*1788)

*The voice of one crying in the wilderness* [1]

*The Argument.* As the true method of knowledge is experiment, the true faculty of knowing must be the faculty which experiences. This faculty I treat of.

Notes

All Religions Are One

[1] Matthew 5:5; Mark 1:3; Luke 3:4; John 1:23. Blake's illustration shows John the Baptist, prophet of the coming of Christ; by implication, his situation – that of one crying in the wilderness – is one that Blake shares.

Principle 1st. That the Poetic Genius is the true Man, and that the body or outward form of Man is derived from the Poetic Genius. Likewise that the forms of all things are derived from their Genius which, by the Ancients, was called an Angel and Spirit and Demon.

Principle 2d. As all men are alike in outward form, so (and with the same infinite variety) all are alike in the Poetic Genius.

Principle 3d. No man can think, write or speak from his heart, but he must intend truth. Thus all sects of Philosophy are from the Poetic Genius adapted to the weaknesses of every individual.

Principle 4. As none by travelling over known lands can find out the unknown, so, from already acquired knowledge, man could not acquire more. Therefore an universal Poetic Genius exists.

Principle 5. The Religions of all Nations are derived from each Nation's different reception of the Poetic Genius, which is everywhere called the Spirit of Prophecy.

Principle 6. The Jewish and Christian Testaments are an original derivation from the Poetic Genius. This is necessary from the confined nature of bodily sensation.

Principle 7th. As all men are alike (though infinitely various); so all Religions: and as all similars have one source the true Man is the source, he being the Poetic Genius.

## *There Is No Natural Religion* (composed *c.*1788)[1]

*The Argument.* Man has no notion of moral fitness but from Education. Naturally he is only a natural organ subject to Sense.

I Man cannot naturally Perceive but through his natural or bodily organs.
II Man by his reasoning power can only compare and judge of what he has already perceived.
III From a perception of only 3 senses or 3 elements none could deduce a fourth or fifth.
IV None could have other than natural or organic thoughts if he had none but organic perceptions.
V Man's desires are limited by his perceptions; none can desire what he has not perceived.
VI The desires and perceptions of man, untaught by anything but organs of sense, must be limited to objects of sense.

I Man's perceptions are not bounded by organs of perception. He perceives more than sense (though ever so acute) can discover.
II Reason, or the ratio of all we have already known, is not the same that it shall be when we know more.
III [*missing*][2]
IV The bounded is loathed by its possessor. The same dull round, even of a universe, would soon become a mill with complicated wheels.
V If the many become the same as the few when possessed, 'More! More!' is the cry of a mistaken soul; less than all cannot satisfy Man.
VI If any could desire what he is incapable of possessing, despair must be his eternal lot.
VII The desire of man being Infinite, the possession is Infinite, and himself Infinite.

## Notes

There Is No Natural Religion

[1] This has traditionally been presented as two separate and distinct works, featuring the (a) and (b) series of plates; however, recent editorial discoveries have led to its being regarded as one work consisting of two parts, the second answering the first. The first six principles present apparently straightforward statements of Lockean thought which are refuted by the seven statements that follow.

[2] The plate etched for proposition III is lost.

*Conclusion.* If it were not for the Poetic or Prophetic character, the Philosophic and Experimental would soon be at the ratio of all things, and stand still, unable to do other than repeat the same dull round over again.

*Application.* He who sees the infinite in all things, sees God. He who sees the Ratio only, sees himself only.

Therefore God becomes as we are, that we may be as He is.

## *The Book of Thel* (1789)

[Plate 1]

### *Thel's Motto*

Does the Eagle know what is in the pit?
Or wilt thou go ask the Mole:
Can Wisdom be put in a silver rod?
Or Love in a golden bowl? [1]

[Plate 3]

### *Thel*[2]

I

The daughters of Mne Seraphim[3] led round their sunny flocks,
All but the youngest; she in paleness sought the secret air,
To fade away like morning beauty from her mortal day;
Down by the river of Adona[4] her soft voice is heard,
And thus her gentle lamentation falls like morning dew.
'Oh life of this our spring! Why fades the lotus of the water?
Why fade these children of the spring, born but to smile and fall?
 Ah! Thel is like a wat'ry bow, and like a parting cloud,
Like a reflection in a glass, like shadows in the water,
Like dreams of infants, like a smile upon an infant's face,
Like the dove's voice, like transient day, like music in the air:
Ah! gentle may I lay me down, and gentle rest my head;
And gentle sleep the sleep of death, and gentle hear the voice
Of him that walketh in the garden in the evening time.'[5]
 The Lily of the valley[6] breathing in the humble grass
Answered the lovely maid and said, 'I am a wat'ry weed,
And I am very small, and love to dwell in lowly vales;
So weak, the gilded butterfly scarce perches on my head.

## Notes

The Book of Thel

[1] The first two lines of the motto question the perspective from which knowledge can be gained; the second two question the containers of knowledge, either as verbal metaphor or the incarnation of spirit in body. *Silver rod...golden bowl* In Ecclesiastes 12:6 a 'silver cord' and 'golden bowl' are images of mortality.

[2] *Thel* Various meanings have been suggested, including 'will', 'wish' or 'desire'.

[3] *Mne Seraphim* No one is sure of Blake's meaning. Some suggest that it is an error for 'Bne Seraphim', the sons of the Seraphim. The Seraphim are the order of angels nearest to God, whose duty is to love him.

[4] *Adona* related to Adonis, a figure in Greek myth associated with the cycles of the vegetable world.

[5] *hear the voice...time* cf. Genesis 3:8: 'And they heard the voice of the Lord God walking in the garden in the cool of the day.'

[6] *Lily of the valley* flower of innocence, symbol of Thel's virginity; cf. Song of Solomon 2:1: 'the lily of the valleys'.

Yet I am visited from heaven, and he that smiles on all
Walks in the valley, and each morn over me spreads his hand
Saying, "Rejoice, thou humble grass, thou new-born lily flower,
Thou gentle maid of silent valleys, and of modest brooks;
For thou shalt be clothed in light and fed with morning manna,[7]
Till summer's heat melts thee beside the fountains and the springs
To flourish in eternal vales!" Then why should Thel complain?

[Plate 4]
Why should the mistress of the vales of Har[8] utter a sigh?'
She ceased and smiled in tears, then sat down in her silver shrine.
   Thel answered: 'Oh thou little virgin of the peaceful valley,
Giving to those that cannot crave – the voiceless, the o'ertired;
Thy breath doth nourish the innocent lamb, he smells thy milky garments,
He crops[9] thy flowers while thou sittest smiling in his face,
Wiping his mild and meekin[10] mouth from all contagious taints.
Thy wine doth purify the golden honey; thy perfume,
Which thou dost scatter on every little blade of grass that springs,
Revives the milked cow, and tames the fire-breathing steed.
But Thel is like a faint cloud kindled at the rising sun:
I vanish from my pearly throne, and who shall find my place?'[11]
   'Queen of the vales', the Lily answered, 'ask the tender cloud[12]
And it shall tell thee why it glitters in the morning sky,
And why it scatters its bright beauty through the humid air:
Descend, oh little cloud, and hover before the eyes of Thel.'
   The Cloud descended, and the Lily bowed her modest head
And went to mind her numerous charge among the verdant grass.

[Plate 5]

II

'Oh little Cloud', the virgin said, 'I charge thee tell to me
Why thou complainest not when in one hour thou fade away;
Then we shall seek thee but not find. Ah, Thel is like to thee:
I pass away – yet I complain, and no one hears my voice.'
   The Cloud then showed his golden head and his bright form emerged,
Hovering and glittering on the air before the face of Thel.
   'Oh virgin, know'st thou not our steeds drink of the golden springs[13]
Where Luvah[14] doth renew his horses? Look'st thou on my youth,
And fearest thou because I vanish and am seen no more.
Nothing remains; oh maid, I tell thee, when I pass away,
It is to tenfold life – to love, to peace, and raptures holy;
Unseen descending, weigh my light wings upon balmy flowers,

## Notes

[7] *morning manna* God provided the Israelites with manna (food) in the wilderness, Exodus 16:14–26.

[8] *Har* another character of Blake's, the father of Tiriel. His valley is a place of innocence.

[9] *crops* eats.

[10] *meekin* meek.

[11] *But Thel…place* cf. Job 7:9: 'As the cloud is consumed and vanisheth away: so he that goeth down to the grave shall come up no more.'

[12] *the tender cloud* the male principle, the fructifier.

[13] *Oh virgin…springs* cf. Shakespeare, *Cymbeline* II iii 21–2: 'and Phoebus gins arise, / His steeds to water at those springs.'

[14] *Luvah* god of desire, Prince of Love; one of Blake's Four Zoas (the four principles which rule human life).

And court the fair-eyed dew to take me to her shining tent:
The weeping virgin trembling kneels before the risen sun
Till we arise linked in a golden band, and never part,
But walk united, bearing food to all our tender flowers.'
'Dost thou, oh little Cloud? I fear that I am not like thee;
For I walk through the vales of Har and smell the sweetest flowers,
But I feed not the little flowers; I hear the warbling birds,
But I feed not the warbling birds – they fly and seek their food.
But Thel delights in these no more because I fade away,
And all shall say, "Without a use this shining woman lived –
Or did she only live to be at death the food of worms."'
The Cloud reclined upon his airy throne and answered thus:
'Then if thou art the food of worms, oh virgin of the skies,
How great thy use, how great thy blessing; everything that lives
Lives not alone, nor for itself: fear not and I will call
The weak worm from its lowly bed, and thou shalt hear its voice.
Come forth, worm of the silent valley, to thy pensive queen.'
The helpless worm arose and sat upon the Lily's leaf,
And the bright Cloud sailed on, to find his partner in the vale.

[Plate 6]

III

Then Thel, astonished, viewed the Worm upon its dewy bed.
'Art thou a Worm? Image of weakness, art thou but a Worm?
I see thee like an infant wrapped in the Lily's leaf;
Ah, weep not, little voice, thou canst not speak[15] but thou canst weep.
Is this a Worm? I see thee lay helpless and naked – weeping,
And none to answer, none to cherish thee with mother's smiles.'
The Clod of Clay[16] heard the Worm's voice and raised her pitying head;
She bowed over the weeping infant, and her life exhaled
In milky fondness, then on Thel she fixed her humble eyes.
'Oh beauty of the vales of Har, we live not for ourselves.
Thou seest me the meanest thing, and so I am indeed;
My bosom of itself is cold, and of itself is dark,

[Plate 7]

But he that loves the lowly pours his oil upon my head,
And kisses me, and binds his nuptial bands around my breast,
And says, "Thou mother of my children, I have loved thee,
And I have given thee a crown that none can take away."[17]
But how this is, sweet maid, I know not and I cannot know;
I ponder and I cannot ponder; yet I live and love.'

## Notes

[15] *thou canst not speak* a pun on the word 'infant', which means 'without speech' (*in-fans*).

[16] The worm and the clod are the baby and its mother.

[17] *a crown that none can take away* cf. 1 Peter 5:4: 'a crown of glory that fadeth not away'; see also Revelation 3.

The daughter of beauty wiped her pitying tears with her white veil
And said, 'Alas! I knew not this, and therefore did I weep.
That God would love a Worm I knew, and punish the evil foot
That, wilful, bruised its helpless form. But that he cherished it
With milk and oil I never knew; and therefore did I weep,
And I complained in the mild air because I fade away,
And lay me down in thy cold bed, and leave my shining lot.'
'Queen of the vales', the matron Clay answered, 'I heard thy sighs,
And all thy moans flew o'er my roof, but I have called them down.
Wilt thou, oh Queen, enter my house?[18] 'Tis given thee to enter
And to return; fear nothing, enter with thy virgin feet.'

[Plate 6]

IV

The eternal gate's terrific porter lifted the northern bar;[19]
Thel entered in and saw the secrets of the land unknown;
She saw the couches of the dead, and where the fibrous roots
Of every heart on earth infixes deep its restless twists:
A land of sorrows and of tears where never smile was seen.
She wandered in the land of clouds through valleys dark, list'ning
Dolours and lamentations; waiting oft beside a dewy grave
She stood in silence, list'ning to the voices of the ground,
Till to her own grave-plot she came, and there she sat down[20]
And heard this voice of sorrow breathed from the hollow pit:
'Why cannot the Ear be closed to its own destruction?
Or the glist'ning Eye, to the poison of a smile?
Why are Eyelids stored with arrows ready drawn,
Where a thousand fighting men in ambush lie?
Or an Eye of gifts and graces, show'ring fruits and coined gold?
Why a Tongue impressed with honey from every wind?[21]
Why an Ear, a whirlpool fierce to draw creations in?
Why a Nostril wide inhaling terror, trembling and affright?
Why a tender curb upon the youthful burning boy?
Why a little curtain of flesh[22] on the bed of our desire?'
The virgin started from her seat, and with a shriek
Fled back unhindered till she came into the vales of Har.

The End

## Notes

[18] *my house* cf. Job 17:13: 'the grave is mine house: I have made my bed in the darkness.'

[19] *The eternal gate's…bar* The exact meaning is unclear, although many interpretations have been offered. The porter is variously identified as Pluto, god of the underworld, or as Death, among others.

[20] *there she sat down* cf. Psalm 137:1: 'By the rivers of Babylon, there we sat down, yea, we wept.'

[21] *Why a Tongue…wind* probably a recollection of Spenser, 'Faerie Queene' I ix st. 31, 5: 'His subtill tongue, like dropping honny.'

[22] *a little curtain of flesh* the hymen.

## *Songs of Innocence* (1789)

### *Introduction*

Piping down the valleys wild,
Piping songs of pleasant glee,
On a cloud I saw a child
And he laughing said to me:

'Pipe a song about a Lamb!'
So I piped with a merry cheer;
'Piper, pipe that song again!'
So I piped, he wept to hear.

'Drop thy pipe, thy happy pipe,
Sing thy songs of happy cheer!'
So I sung the same again
While he wept with joy to hear.

'Piper, sit thee down and write
In a book, that all may read.'
So he vanished from my sight
And I plucked a hollow reed.

And I made a rural pen,
And I stained the water clear,
And I wrote my happy songs
Every child may joy to hear.

### *The Shepherd*

How sweet is the Shepherd's sweet lot,
From the morn to the evening he strays;
He shall follow his sheep all the day
And his tongue shall be filled with praise.

For he hears the lambs innocent call,[1]
And he hears the ewes tender reply;
He is watchful while they are in peace,
For they know when their Shepherd is nigh.

### *The Ecchoing Green*

The Sun does arise,
And make happy the skies;

## Notes

The Shepherd

[1] *the lambs innocent call* The stray sheep is a biblical symbol; see, for instance, Psalm 119:176; Isaiah 53:6; Matthew 18:12.

The merry bells ring
To welcome the Spring;
The skylark and thrush,
The birds of the bush,
Sing louder around
To the bells' cheerful sound,
While our sports shall be seen
On the Ecchoing Green.

Old John with white hair
Does laugh away care,
Sitting under the oak
Among the old folk.
They laugh at our play
And soon they all say,
'Such, such were the joys
When we all, girls and boys,
In our youth-time were seen
On the Ecchoing Green.'

Till the little ones weary
No more can be merry,
The sun does descend
And our sports have an end:
Round the laps of their mothers,
Many sisters and brothers
Like birds in their nest
Are ready for rest,
And sport no more seen
On the darkening Green.

### *The Lamb*

   Little Lamb who made thee?
   Dost thou know who made thee?
Gave thee life and bid thee feed
By the stream and o'er the mead;
Gave thee clothing of delight,
Softest clothing woolly bright;
Gave thee such a tender voice,
Making all the vales rejoice:
   Little Lamb who made thee?
   Dost thou know who made thee?

   Little Lamb I'll tell thee,
   Little Lamb I'll tell thee;
He is called by thy name,
For he calls himself a Lamb;
He is meek and he is mild,
He became a little child:
I a child and thou a lamb,

We are called by his name,[1]
Little Lamb God bless thee,
Little Lamb God bless thee.

## *The Little Black Boy*[1]

My mother bore me in the southern wild
And I am black, but O! my soul is white.
White as an angel is the English child,
But I am black as if bereaved of light.

My mother taught me underneath a tree,
And sitting down before the heat of day,
She took me on her lap and kissed me,
And pointing to the east began to say,

'Look on the rising sun: there God does live[2]
And gives his light, and gives his heat away;
And flowers and trees and beasts and men receive
Comfort in morning, joy in the noonday.

And we are put on earth a little space
That we may learn to bear the beams of love;
And these black bodies and this sunburnt face
Is but a cloud, and like a shady grove.

For when our souls have learned the heat to bear
The cloud will vanish; we shall hear his voice
Saying, "Come out from the grove, my love and care,
And round my golden tent like lambs rejoice."'

Thus did my mother say and kissed me;
And thus I say to little English boy,
When I from black and he from white cloud free,
And round the tent of God like lambs we joy,

I'll shade him from the heat till he can bear
To lean in joy upon our Father's knee;
And then I'll stand and stroke his silver hair,
And be like him, and he will then love me.

## Notes

The Lamb

[1] *I a child…his name* Critics note the child's identification with Christ and the lamb.

The Little Black Boy

[1] Blake was aware of the passing of a Bill proposed in the House of Commons on 21 May 1788 by Sir William Dolben MP, which restricted the number of slaves who could be transported from Africa to British colonies in the West Indies.

[2] *Look on the rising sun…live* The association of God with the rising sun echoes Isaiah 45:6; 59:19: 'So shall they fear the name of the Lord from the west, and his glory from the rising of the sun.'

## *The Blossom*

Merry Merry Sparrow
Under leaves so green,
A happy Blossom
Sees you swift as arrow;
Seek your cradle narrow
Near my Bosom.

Pretty Pretty Robin
Under leaves so green,
A happy Blossom
Hears you sobbing sobbing,
Pretty Pretty Robin
Near my bosom.

## *The Chimney Sweeper*[1]

When my mother died I was very young,
And my father sold me while yet my tongue
Could scarcely cry weep weep weep weep,[2]
So your chimneys I sweep, and in soot I sleep.

There's little Tom Dacre, who cried when his head
That curled like a lamb's back, was shaved; so I said,
'Hush Tom never mind it, for when your head's bare
You know that the soot cannot spoil your white hair.'

And so he was quiet, and that very night,
As Tom was a-sleeping he had such a sight,
That thousands of sweepers – Dick, Joe, Ned and Jack –
Were all of them locked up in coffins of black,

And by came an Angel who had a bright key,
And he opened the coffins and set them all free.
Then down a green plain leaping laughing they run
And wash in a river and shine in the Sun.

Then naked and white, all their bags left behind,
They rise upon clouds and sport in the wind;
And the Angel told Tom, if he'd be a good boy;
He'd have God for his father and never want joy.

And so Tom awoke and we rose in the dark
And got with our bags and our brushes to work.
Though the morning was cold, Tom was happy and warm
So if all do their duty, they need not fear harm.

## Notes

The Chimney Sweeper

[1] Blake knew that an attempt was made in 1788 to improve the conditions of child chimney sweeps: eight was the proposed minimum age; hours of work would be limited; regulations were proposed to ensure that sweeps were properly washed every week; and a ban was proposed on the use of children in chimneys on fire. In the event, the Porter's Act was not passed.

[2] *weep weep weep weep* suggestive of both the child's cry as he touts for work, as well as his grief.

## *The Little Boy Lost*

'Father, father, where are you going?
Oh do not walk so fast.
Speak, father, speak to your little boy
Or else I shall be lost.'

The night was dark, no father was there,
The child was wet with dew;
The mire was deep,[1] and the child did weep,
And away the vapour flew.[2]

## *The Little Boy Found*

The little boy lost in the lonely fen,
Led by the wand'ring light,[1]
Began to cry, but God ever nigh,
Appeared like his father in white.[2]

He kissed the child and by the hand led
And to his mother brought,
Who in sorrow pale through the lonely dale
Her little boy weeping sought.

## *Laughing Song*

When the green woods laugh with the voice of joy
And the dimpling stream runs laughing by,
When the air does laugh with our merry wit,
And the green hill laughs with the noise of it.

When the meadows laugh with lively green
And the grasshopper laughs in the merry scene;
When Mary and Susan and Emily
With their sweet round mouths sing, 'Ha, ha, he!'

When the painted birds laugh in the shade
Where our table with cherries and nuts is spread,
Come live and be merry and join with me
To sing the sweet chorus of 'Ha, ha, he!'

### Notes

The Little Boy Lost

[1] *The mire was deep* a biblical image; e.g. Psalm 69:2: 'I sink in deep mire.'

[2] *away the vapour flew* The boy is led astray by a will-o'-the-wisp.

The Little Boy Found

[1] *the wand'ring light* will-o'-the-wisp.

[2] *like his father in white* cf. the transfigured Christ; Matthew 17:2; Luke 9:29: 'And as he prayed, the fashion of his countenance was altered, and his raiment was white and glistering.'

## *A Cradle Song*

Sweet dreams form a shade
O'er my lovely infant's head;
Sweet dreams of pleasant streams
By happy silent moony beams.

Sweet sleep with soft down
Weave thy brows an infant crown;
Sweet sleep Angel mild,
Hover o'er my happy child.

Sweet smiles in the night
Hover over my delight;
Sweet smiles, Mother's smiles
All the livelong night beguiles.

Sweet moans, dovelike sighs,
Chase not slumber from thy eyes;
Sweet moans, sweeter smiles,
All the dovelike moans beguiles.

Sleep sleep happy child,
All creation slept and smiled;
Sleep sleep, happy sleep,
While o'er thee thy mother weep.

Sweet babe in thy face,
Holy image I can trace;
Sweet babe once like thee
Thy maker lay and wept for me,

Wept for me, for thee, for all,
When he was an infant small;
Thou his image ever see,
Heavenly face that smiles on thee –

Smiles on thee, on me, on all,
Who became an infant small:
Infant smiles are his own smiles;
Heaven and earth to peace beguiles.[1]

## *The Divine Image*

To Mercy, Pity, Peace and Love
All pray in their distress;
And to these virtues of delight
Return their thankfulness.

### Notes

A Cradle Song

[1] *Heaven and earth...beguiles* perhaps an echo of Milton's 'On the Morning of Christ's Nativity', where Christ's birth is accompanied by a divine harmony which 'alone / Could hold all heaven and earth in happier union' (ll. 107–8).

For Mercy, Pity, Peace and Love
Is God our Father dear;
And Mercy, Pity, Peace and Love
Is Man his child and care.

For Mercy has a human heart,
Pity a human face;
And Love, the human form divine,
And Peace, the human dress.

Then every man of every clime
That prays in his distress,
Prays to the human form divine
Love, Mercy, Pity, Peace.

And all must love the human form
In heathen, turk or jew;
Where Mercy, Love and Pity dwell
There God is dwelling too.[1]

## *Holy Thursday*[1]

'Twas on a Holy Thursday, their innocent faces clean,
The children walking two and two in red and blue and green,
Grey-headed beadles walked before with wands as white as snow
Till into the high dome of Paul's they like Thames' waters flow.

Oh what a multitude they seemed, these flowers of London town,
Seated in companies they sit with radiance all their own;
The hum of multitudes was there but multitudes of lambs –
Thousands of little boys and girls raising their innocent hands.

Now like a mighty wind they raise to heaven the voice of song,
Or like harmonious thunderings the seats of heaven among;
Beneath them sit the aged men, wise guardians of the poor –
Then cherish pity, lest you drive an angel from your door.

## *Night*

The sun descending in the west,
The evening star does shine;
The birds are silent in their nest

### Notes

The Divine Image

[1] *Where mercy…dwelling too* cf. 1 John 4:16: 'God is love; and he that dwelleth in love dwelleth in God, and God in him.'

Holy Thursday

[1] Blake describes the service for 6,000 or so of the poorest children in the charity schools of London, held in St Paul's Cathedral on the first Thursday in May from 1782 onwards. They would be marched there by their beadles (parish officers) for what Keynes called 'a compulsory exhibition of their piety and gratitude to their patrons'.

And I must seek for mine.
The moon like a flower
In heaven's high bower
With silent delight
Sits and smiles on the night.

Farewell green fields and happy groves,
Where flocks have took delight;
Where lambs have nibbled, silent moves
The feet of angels bright;
Unseen they pour blessing
And joy without ceasing
On each bud and blossom
And each sleeping bosom.

They look in every thoughtless nest
Where birds are covered warm,
They visit caves of every beast
To keep them all from harm;
If they see any weeping
That should have been sleeping
They pour sleep on their head
And sit down by their bed.

When wolves and tygers howl for prey
They pitying stand and weep,
Seeking to drive their thirst[1] away
And keep them from the sheep.
But if they rush dreadful,
The angels most heedful
Receive each mild spirit,
New worlds to inherit.

And there the lion's ruddy eyes
Shall flow with tears of gold,
And pitying the tender cries,
And walking round the fold,
Saying, 'Wrath by his[2] meekness,
And by his health sickness
Is driven away
From our immortal day.

And now beside thee bleating lamb,
I can lie down and sleep,
Or think on him who bore thy name,
Graze after thee and weep.
For, washed in life's river,[3]

## Notes

Night

[1] *thirst* i.e. for blood.

[2] *his* i.e. Christ's.

[3] *life's river* The River of Life is biblical; see Revelation 22:1–2.

My bright mane for ever
Shall shine like the gold
As I guard o'er the fold.'

## *Spring*

Sound the flute!
Now it's mute.
Birds delight
Day and Night;
Nightingale
In the dale,
Lark in Sky
Merrily
Merrily Merrily to welcome in the Year.

Little boy
Full of joy;
Little girl
Sweet and small;
Cock does crow,
So do you;
Merry voice,
Infant noise –
Merrily Merrily to welcome in the Year.

Little Lamb
Here I am,[1]
Come and lick
My white neck!
Let me pull
Your soft Wool,
Let me kiss
Your soft face;
Merrily Merrily we welcome in the Year.

## *Nurse's Song*

When the voices of children are heard on the green
And laughing is heard on the hill,
My heart is at rest within my breast
And everything else is still.

'Then come home my children, the sun is gone down
And the dews of night arise;
Come come, leave off play, and let us away
Till the morning appears in the skies.'

Notes

Spring

[1] *Here I am* frequently used in the Bible; see Genesis 22:1, 11; 31:11.

'No no let us play, for it is yet day
And we cannot go to sleep;
Besides in the sky, the little birds fly
And the hills are all covered with sheep.'

'Well well, go and play till the light fades away
And then go home to bed.'
The little ones leaped and shouted and laughed
And all the hills ecchoed.

## *Infant Joy*

'I have no name
I am but two days old.' –
What shall I call thee?
'I happy am,
Joy is my name.' –
Sweet joy befall thee!

Pretty joy!
Sweet joy but two days old,
Sweet joy I call thee;
Thou dost smile,
I sing the while,[1]
Sweet joy befall thee.

## *A Dream*

Once a dream did weave a shade
O'er my Angel-guarded bed,
That an Emmet[1] lost its way
Where on grass methought I lay.

Troubled wildered and forlorn
Dark benighted travel-worn,
Over many a tangled spray,
All heart-broke I heard her say,

'Oh my children! Do they cry,
Do they hear their father sigh?
Now they look abroad to see;
Now return and weep for me.'

### Notes

Infant Joy

[1] When he read this poem in February 1818, Coleridge marked it as one of his favourites, while proposing a new reading of lines 9–10: 'O smile, O smile! / I'll sing the while' – 'For a babe two days old does not, cannot *smile* – and innocence and the very truth of Nature must go together' (Griggs iv 837).

A Dream

[1] *Emmet* ant.

Pitying I dropped a tear;
But I saw a glow-worm near
Who replied, 'What wailing wight
Calls the watchman of the night?

I am set to light the ground
While the beetle goes his round;
Follow now the beetle's hum,
Little wanderer hie thee home.'[2]

### *On Another's Sorrow*

Can I see another's woe
And not be in sorrow too?
Can I see another's grief
And not seek for kind relief?

Can I see a falling tear
And not feel my sorrow's share?
Can a father see his child
Weep, nor be with sorrow filled?

Can a mother sit and hear
An infant groan, an infant fear?
No no never can it be,
Never never can it be.

And can he who smiles on all
Hear the wren with sorrows small,
Hear the small bird's grief and care,
Hear the woes that infants bear –

And not sit beside the nest
Pouring pity in their breast?
And not sit the cradle near
Weeping tear on infant's tear?

And not sit both night and day
Wiping all our tears away?
O! no never can it be,
Never never can it be.

He doth give his joy to all,
He becomes an infant small;
He becomes a man of woe,
He doth feel the sorrow too.

## Notes

[2] *Little wanderer, hie thee home* The dor-beetle, which flies after sunset with a humming sound, was known as 'the watchman'. The glow-worm was said, in a folk-song, to light people 'home to bed' on moonless nights.

Think not thou canst sigh a sigh
And thy maker is not by;
Think not thou canst weep a tear
And thy maker is not near.

O! he gives to us his joy,
That our grief he may destroy;
Till our grief is fled and gone
He doth sit by us and moan.

## *Songs of Experience* (1794)

### *Introduction*

Hear the voice of the Bard!
Who Present, Past and Future sees;
Whose ears have heard
The Holy Word
That walked among the ancient trees

Calling the lapsed Soul,[1]
And weeping in the evening dew;
That might control
The starry pole,
And fallen fallen light renew!

'Oh Earth oh Earth return!
Arise from out the dewy grass;
Night is worn,
And the morn
Rises from the slumberous mass.

Turn away no more:
Why wilt thou turn away?
The starry floor
The wat'ry shore
Is giv'n thee till the break of day.'

### *Earth's Answer*

Earth raised up her head
From the darkness dread and drear;
Her light fled,
Stony dread!
And her locks covered with grey despair.

## Notes

INTRODUCTION

[1] *Whose ears have heard...Soul* cf. Genesis 3:8, where Adam and Eve, now fallen, 'heard the voice of the Lord God walking in the garden in the cool of the day: and Adam and his wife hid themselves from the presence of the Lord God amongst the trees of the garden'.

'Prisoned on wat'ry shore
Starry Jealousy[1] does keep my den
Cold and hoar,
Weeping o'er,
I hear the father of the ancient men.

Selfish father of men
Cruel jealous selfish fear
Can delight
Chained in night
The virgins of youth and morning bear?

Does spring hide its joy
When buds and blossoms grow?
Does the sower
Sow by night,
Or the ploughman in darkness plough?

Break this heavy chain
That does freeze my bones around!
Selfish! vain!
Eternal bane!
That free Love with bondage bound.'

## *The Clod and the Pebble*

'Love seeketh not Itself to please,
Nor for itself hath any care;
But for another gives its ease
And builds a Heaven in Hell's despair.'

So sung a little Clod of Clay
Trodden with the cattle's feet,
But a Pebble of the brook
Warbled out these metres meet:

'Love seeketh only Self to please,
To bind another to Its delight;
Joys in another's loss of ease,
And builds a Hell in Heaven's despite.'

## *Holy Thursday*

Is this a holy thing to see
In a rich and fruitful land,
Babes reduced to misery,
Fed with cold and usurous hand?

Notes

Earth's Answer

[1] *Starry Jealousy* The idea of God as jealous is biblical; see Exodus 20:5; 34:14, and Deuteronomy 4:24: 'For the Lord thy God is a consuming fire, even a jealous God.'

Is that trembling cry a song?
Can it be a song of joy?
And so many children poor?
It is a land of poverty!

And their sun does never shine,
And their fields are bleak and bare,
And their ways are filled with thorns,
It is eternal winter there.

For where'er the sun does shine
And where'er the rain does fall,
Babe can never hunger there,
Nor poverty the mind appall.

## *The Little Girl Lost*[1]

In futurity
I prophetic see
That the earth from sleep
(Grave the sentence deep)

Shall arise and seek
For her maker meek,
And the desert wild
Become a garden mild.

In the southern clime,
Where the summer's prime
Never fades away,
Lovely Lyca lay.

Seven summers old
Lovely Lyca told;
She had wandered long
Hearing wild birds' song.

'Sweet sleep, come to me
Underneath this tree;
Do father, mother weep?
Where can Lyca sleep?

Lost in desert wild
Is your little child;
How can Lyca sleep
If her mother weep?

## Notes

THE LITTLE GIRL LOST

[1] This poem and 'The Little Girl Found' originally appeared in *Songs of Innocence*; in some respects they are counterparts to 'The Little Boy Lost' and 'The Little Boy Found'.

If her heart does ache
Then let Lyca wake;
If my mother sleep
Lyca shall not weep.

Frowning, frowning night,
O'er this desert bright,
Let thy moon arise
While I close my eyes.'

Sleeping Lyca lay
While the beasts of prey,
Come from caverns deep,
Viewed the maid asleep.

The kingly lion stood
And the virgin viewed,
Then he gambolled round
O'er the hallowed ground.

Leopards, tygers play
Round her as she lay,
While the lion old
Bowed his mane of gold,

And her bosom lick,
And upon her neck
From his eyes of flame
Ruby tears there came;

While the lioness
Loosed her slender dress,
And naked they conveyed
To caves the sleeping maid.[2]

### *The Little Girl Found*

All the night in woe
Lyca's parents go;
Over valleys deep,
While the deserts weep.

Tired and woe-begone,
Hoarse with making moan,
Arm in arm seven days
They traced the desert ways.

## Notes

[2] The obvious parallel is with Daniel in the lions' den; cf. Daniel 6:16–22, though compare also Isaiah 11:6: 'The wolf also shall dwell with the lamb, and the leopard shall lie down with the kid; and the calf and the young lion and the fatling together; and a little child shall lead them.'

Seven nights they sleep
Among shadows deep,
And dream they see their child
Starved in desert wild.

Pale through pathless ways
The fancied image strays –
Famished, weeping, weak,
With hollow piteous shriek.

Rising from unrest,
The trembling woman pressed
With feet of weary woe;
She could no further go.

In his arms he bore
Her, armed with sorrow sore;
Till before their way
A couching lion lay.

Turning back was vain;
Soon his heavy mane
Bore them to the ground:
Then he stalked around

Smelling to his prey.
But their fears allay
When he licks their hands,
And silent by them stands.

They look upon his eyes
Filled with deep surprise,
And wondering behold
A spirit armed in gold.

On his head a crown,
On his shoulders down
Flowed his golden hair;
Gone was all their care.

'Follow me', he said,
'Weep not for the maid;
In my palace deep
Lyca lies asleep.'

Then they followed
Where the vision led,
And saw their sleeping child
Among tygers wild.

To this day they dwell
In a lonely dell;
Nor fear the wolvish howl,
Nor the lion's growl.

### *The Chimney Sweeper*

A little black thing among the snow,
Crying weep, weep, in notes of woe!
'Where are thy father and mother, say?'
'They are both gone up to the church to pray.

Because I was happy upon the heath
And smiled among the winter's snow,
They clothed me in the clothes of death,
And taught me to sing the notes of woe.

And because I am happy and dance and sing,[1]
They think they have done me no injury,
And are gone to praise God and his Priest and King
Who make up a heaven of our misery.'

### *Nurse's Song*

When the voices of children are heard on the green
And whisp'rings are in the dale,
The days of my youth rise fresh in my mind,
My face turns green and pale.

Then come home, my children, the sun is gone down,
And the dews of night arise;
Your spring and your day are wasted in play,
And your winter and night in disguise.

### *The Sick Rose*

Oh Rose thou art sick;
The invisible worm
That flies in the night
In the howling storm

Has found out thy bed
Of crimson joy,
And his dark secret love
Does thy life destroy.

### *The Fly*

Little Fly
Thy summer's play
My thoughtless hand
Has brushed away.[1]

## Notes

THE CHIMNEY SWEEPER

[1] *And because...sing* Erdman suggests a reference to May Day, when sweeps and milkmaids danced in the streets of London in return for alms.

THE FLY

[1] In his notebook, Blake drafted another stanza at this point:

The cut worm
Forgives the plough
And dies in peace
And so do thou.

Am not I
A fly like thee?
Or art not thou
A man like me?

For I dance
And drink and sing,
Till some blind hand
Shall brush my wing.

If thought is life
And strength and breath,
And the want
Of thought is death,

Then am I
A happy fly,
If I live
Or if I die.

## *The Angel*

I dreamt a Dream! What can it mean?
And that I was a maiden Queen
Guarded by an Angel mild:
Witless woe was ne'er beguiled!

And I wept both night and day,
And he wiped my tears away,
And I wept both day and night,
And hid from him my heart's delight.

So he took his wings and fled,
Then the morn blushed rosy red;
I dried my tears, and armed my fears
With ten thousand shields and spears.

Soon my Angel came again;
I was armed, he came in vain:
For the time of youth was fled
And grey hairs were on my head.

## *The Tyger*[1]

Tyger Tyger burning bright
In the forests of the night;

## Notes

The Tyger

[1] This is regarded as the contrary poem to 'The Lamb' in *Songs of Innocence*. Charles Lamb read it in 1824, and memorized its opening two lines, describing them as 'glorious, but alas! I have not the book; for the man is flown, whither I know not – to Hades or a madhouse. But I must look on him as one of the most extraordinary persons of the age.'

What immortal hand or eye
Could frame thy fearful symmetry?

In what distant deeps or skies
Burnt the fire of thine eyes?
On what wings dare he aspire?
What the hand dare seize the fire?

And what shoulder and what art
Could twist the sinews of thy heart?
And when thy heart began to beat,
What dread hand and what dread feet?

What the hammer? What the chain?
In what furnace was thy brain?
What the anvil? What dread grasp
Dare its deadly terrors clasp?

When the stars threw down their spears
And watered heaven with their tears
Did he smile his work to see?
Did he who made the Lamb make thee?

Tyger Tyger burning bright
In the forests of the night:
What immortal hand or eye
Dare frame thy fearful symmetry?

## *My Pretty Rose-Tree*

A flower was offered to me,
Such a flower as May never bore;
But I said, 'I've a Pretty Rose-tree',
And I passed the sweet flower o'er.

Then I went to my Pretty Rose-tree
To tend her by day and by night;
But my Rose turned away with jealousy:
And her thorns were my only delight.

## *Ah, Sunflower!*

Ah, sunflower! weary of time,
Who countest the steps of the Sun,
Seeking after that sweet golden clime
Where the traveller's journey is done;

Where the Youth pined away with desire,
And the pale Virgin shrouded in snow,
Arise from their graves and aspire
Where my Sunflower wishes to go.

## *The Lily*

The modest Rose puts forth a thorn,
The humble Sheep a threat'ning horn;
While the Lily white shall in Love delight,
Nor a thorn nor a threat stain her beauty bright.

## *The Garden of Love*

I went to the Garden of Love
And saw what I never had seen:
A Chapel was built in the midst
Where I used to play on the green.[1]

And the gates of this Chapel were shut,
And 'Thou shalt not' writ over the door;
So I turned to the Garden of Love
That so many sweet flowers bore,

And I saw it was filled with graves
And tombstones where flowers should be;
And Priests in black gowns[2] were walking their rounds,
And binding with briars my joys and desires.

## *The Little Vagabond*

Dear Mother, dear Mother, the Church is cold
But the Alehouse is healthy and pleasant and warm;
Besides I can tell where I am used well –
Such usage in heaven will never do well.

But if at the Church they would give us some Ale,
And a pleasant fire our souls to regale,
We'd sing and we'd pray all the livelong day,
Nor ever once wish from the Church to stray.

Then the Parson might preach and drink and sing,
And we'd be as happy as birds in the spring;
And modest dame Lurch, who is always at Church,
Would not have bandy[1] children nor fasting nor birch.

And God like a father rejoicing to see
His children as pleasant and happy as he,
Would have no more quarrel with the Devil or the Barrel,
But kiss him and give him both drink and apparel.

### Notes

THE GARDEN OF LOVE

[1] *A chapel…green* Possibly a reference to the building of a chapel on South Lambeth green in 1793. Members of the congregation were required to pay for their places.

[2] *black gowns* In his notebook Blake originally wrote 'black gounds', a Cockney pronunciation, thus giving the line an internal rhyme.

THE LITTLE VAGABOND

[1] *bandy* Bandy legs are a symptom of rickets, caused by vitamin deficiency.

## *London*

I wander through each chartered[1] street
Near where the chartered Thames does flow,
And mark in every face I meet
Marks of weakness, marks of woe.

In every cry of every Man,
In every Infant's cry of fear,
In every voice, in every ban,
The mind-forged manacles[2] I hear.

How the Chimney-sweeper's cry
Every black'ning church appalls,
And the hapless Soldier's sigh
Runs in blood down Palace walls.

But most through midnight streets I hear
How the youthful Harlot's curse
Blasts the new born Infant's tear,
And blights with plagues the Marriage hearse.[3]

## *The Human Abstract*[1]

Pity would be no more
If we did not make somebody Poor;
And Mercy no more could be,
If all were as happy as we.

And mutual fear brings peace
Till the selfish loves increase;
Then Cruelty knits a snare
And spreads his baits with care.

He sits down with holy fears
And waters the ground with tears;
Then Humility takes its root
Underneath his foot.

Soon spreads the dismal shade
Of Mystery over his head,
And the Caterpillar and Fly
Feed on the Mystery.

### Notes

London

[1] *chartered* mapped, but also owned by corporations (by the terms of a charter). In Blake's notebook, this originally read, 'dirty'.

[2] *mind-forged manacles* The original MS reading is 'German-forged links' – a reference to the House of Hanover, which provided Britain with its monarchs.

[3] *blights with plagues the Marriage hearse* apparently a reference to the passing on of sexually transmitted diseases by mothers to their children.

The Human Abstract

[1] This song is a counterpart of 'The Divine Image'. Above it in Blake's notebook appear some lines related to it:

How came pride in Man
From Mary it began
How contempt and scorn

And it bears the fruit of Deceit,
Ruddy and sweet to eat;
And the Raven his nest has made
In its thickest shade.

The Gods of the earth and sea
Sought through Nature to find this Tree,
But their search was all in vain:
There grows one in the Human Brain.

## *Infant Sorrow*

My mother groaned! my father wept,
Into the dangerous world I leapt:
Helpless, naked, piping loud:
Like a fiend hid in a cloud.

Struggling in my father's hands,
Striving against my swaddling bands,
Bound and weary I thought best
To sulk upon my mother's breast.

## *A Poison Tree*[1]

I was angry with my friend;
I told my wrath, my wrath did end.
I was angry with my foe;
I told it not, my wrath did grow.

And I watered it in fears,
Night and morning with my tears;
And I sunned it with smiles,
And with soft deceitful wiles.

And it grew both day and night
Till it bore an apple bright;
And my foe beheld it shine,
And he knew that it was mine.

And into my garden stole
When the night had veiled the pole –
In the morning glad I see
My foe outstretched beneath the tree.

## Notes

A Poison Tree

[1] In Blake's notebook this poem was originally entitled 'Christian Forbearance'.

## *A Little Boy Lost*

'Nought loves another as itself
Nor venerates another so,
Nor is it possible to Thought
A greater than itself to know.

And Father, how can I love you
Or any of my brothers more?
I love you like the little bird
That picks up crumbs around the door.'

The Priest sat by and heard the child,
In trembling zeal he seized his hair;
He led him by his little coat
And all admired the Priestly care.

And standing on the altar high,
'Lo, what a fiend is here!' said he,
'One who sets reason up for judge
Of our most holy Mystery.'

The weeping child could not be heard,
The weeping parents wept in vain;
They stripped him to his little shirt
And bound him in an iron chain,

And burned him in a holy place[1]
Where many had been burned before.
The weeping parents wept in vain –
Are such things done on Albion's shore?

## *A Little Girl Lost*

*Children of the future Age*
*Reading this indignant page,*
*Know that in a former time*
*Love! sweet Love! was thought a crime.*

In the Age of Gold,
Free from winters cold,
Youth and maiden bright
To the holy light,
Naked in the sunny beams delight.

### Notes

A Little Boy Lost

[1] *a holy place* biblical name for the sanctuary in the Temple.

Once a youthful pair
Filled with softest care
Met in garden bright
Where the holy light
Had just removed the curtains of the night.

There in rising day
On the grass they play;
Parents were afar,
Strangers came not near,
And the maiden soon forgot her fear.

Tired with kisses sweet,
They agree to meet
When the silent sleep
Waves o'er heavens deep,
And the weary tired wanderers weep.

To her father white
Came the maiden bright,
But his loving look,
Like the holy book
All her tender limbs with terror shook.

'Ona! pale and weak!
To thy father speak:
Oh the trembling fear!
Oh the dismal care!
That shakes the blossoms of my hoary hair!'

## *To Tirzah*[1]

Whate'er is Born of Mortal Birth
Must be consumed with the Earth
To rise from Generation free;
Then what have I to do with thee?

The Sexes sprung from Shame and Pride –
Blowed in the morn, in evening died;
But Mercy changed Death into Sleep –
The Sexes rose to work and weep.

Thou Mother of my Mortal part,
With cruelty didst mould my Heart
And with false self-deceiving tears
Didst bind my Nostrils Eyes and Ears;

## Notes

To Tirzah

[1] This poem does not appear in early copies of the *Songs*. Tirzah was the first capital of the northern kingdom of Israel, a counterpart of Jerusalem in the south; cf. Song of Solomon 6:4: 'Thou art beautiful, O my love, as Tirzah, comely as Jerusalem, terrible as an army with banners.' See also Numbers 27:1–11; Blake associated Tirzah with the fallen realm of the senses, a power that confines humanity within a vision of the human body as finite and corrupt.

Didst close my Tongue in senseless clay
And me to Mortal Life betray:
The Death of Jesus set me free –
Then what have I to do with thee?[2]

It is Raised

a Spiritual Body[3]

## *The Schoolboy*[1]

I love to rise in a summer morn
When the birds sing on every tree;
The distant huntsman winds his horn,
And the skylark sings with me –
Oh what sweet company!

But to go to school in a summer morn,
Oh! it drives all joy away;
Under a cruel eye outworn,
The little ones spend the day
In sighing and dismay.

Ah! then at times I drooping sit
And spend many an anxious hour;
Nor in my book can I take delight,
Nor sit in learning's bower,
Worn through with the dreary shower.

How can the bird that is born for joy
Sit in a cage and sing?
How can a child, when fears annoy,
But droop his tender wing
And forget his youthful spring?

Oh! father and mother, if buds are nipped
And blossoms blown away,
And if the tender plants are stripped
Of their joy in the springing day
By sorrow and care's dismay,

How shall the summer arise in joy
Or the summer fruits appear?
Or how shall we gather what griefs destroy,
Or bless the mellowing year
When the blasts of winter appear?

## Notes

[2] *Then what …thee* cf. Jesus to his mother, John 2:4: 'what have I to do with thee? Mine hour is not yet come.'

[3] *It is…Body* On Blake's plate, these words appear on the garment of an old man ministering to a dead body; they come from 1 Corinthians 15:44: 'It is sown a natural body; it is raised a spiritual body.'

The Schoolboy

[1] This song was originally included in *Songs of Innocence*.

### *The Voice of the Ancient Bard*[1]

Youth of delight come hither
And see the opening morn –
Image of truth new-born;
Doubt is fled and clouds of reason,
Dark disputes and artful teasing.
Folly is an endless maze,
Tangled roots perplex her ways –
How many have fallen there!
They stumble all night over bones of the dead,
And feel they know not what but care,
And wish to lead others, when they should be led.

### *A Divine Image*[1]

Cruelty has a Human Heart
And Jealousy a Human Face;
Terror the Human Form Divine,
And Secrecy the Human Dress.

The Human Dress is forged Iron,
The Human Form a fiery Forge,
The Human Face a Furnace sealed,
The Human Heart its hungry Gorge.

## *The Marriage of Heaven and Hell*[1] (1790)[2]

[Plate 2]

### *The Argument*

Rintrah[3] roars and shakes his fires in the burdened air;[4]
Hungry clouds swag[5] on the deep.

Once meek, and in a perilous path,
The just man kept his course along
The vale of death;
Roses are planted where thorns grow,
And on the barren heath
Sing the honey bees.

## Notes

The Voice of the Ancient Bard

[1] This song was originally included in *Songs of Innocence*.

A Divine Image

[1] This poem is known to us only through a print made after Blake's death; it appears in one copy of the *Songs*, and was not usually included in the volume. It was apparently composed as a counterpart to 'The Divine Image' in *Songs of Innocence*. Blake's design shows a blacksmith hammering at a wall round the sun.

The Marriage of Heaven and Hell

[1] Blake's title alludes to two of Swedenborg's: *De coelo ...et de inferno* and *De amore conjugali* (*A Treatise Concerning Heaven and Hell* and *Marital Love*). For more on Blake's attitude to Swedenborg, see headnote above.

[2] Various dates have been suggested over the years, but the editors of the Blake Trust/Tate Gallery edition settle on 1790.

[3] *Rintrah* the just wrath of the prophet, presaging revolution.

[4] *Rintrah...air* cf. Amos 1:2: 'The Lord will roar from Zion, and utter his voice from Jerusalem.'

[5] *swag* sway, sag.

Then the perilous path was planted;
And a river, and a spring
On every cliff and tomb;
And on the bleached bones[6]
Red clay[7] brought forth.

Till the villain left the paths of ease
To walk in perilous paths, and drive
The just man into barren climes.

Now the sneaking serpent walks
In mild humility
And the just man rages in the wilds
Where lions roam.

Rintrah roars and shakes his fires in the burdened air;
Hungry clouds swag on the deep.

[Plate 3]

As a new heaven is begun, and it is now thirty-three years since its advent: the Eternal Hell revives.[8] And lo! Swedenborg is the Angel sitting at the tomb; his writings are the linen clothes folded up.[9] Now is the dominion of Edom,[10] and the return of Adam into Paradise; see Isaiah 34 and 35.[11]

Without Contraries is no progression. Attraction and Repulsion, Reason and Energy, Love and Hate, are necessary to Human existence.[12]

From these contraries spring what the religious call Good and Evil. Good is the passive that obeys Reason. Evil is the active springing from Energy.[13]

Good is Heaven. Evil is Hell.

### *The Voice of the Devil*

All Bibles or sacred codes have been the causes of the following errors.

1. That man has two real existing principles, viz. a Body and a Soul.
2. That Energy,[14] called Evil, is alone from the Body, and that Reason, called Good, is alone from the Soul.
3. That God will torment man in eternity for following his Energies.

## Notes

[6] *bleached bones* a valley of dry bones symbolizes the exiled 'house of Israel', Ezekiel 37:3–4.

[7] *Red clay* sometimes taken to mean Adam, the first man, formed from the dust of the ground.

[8] *As a new heaven…revives* In 1790 it was 33 years since 1757, the year of the Swedenborgian Last Judgement and (coincidentally) Blake's birth. Christ was 33 at the time of his crucifixion and resurrection. Thus, Blake identifies his lifetime with Christ's and the eternal hell resurrected.

[9] *his writings…folded up* Jesus's body was wrapped in a linen shroud, laid in a sepulchre, and closed with a rock (Mark 15:46). When three women came to anoint the body, they found the stone rolled aside and the body gone.

[10] *Edom* Esau, cheated of his birthright by his brother Jacob (Genesis 25:29–34); his dominion is foreseen by his father, Isaac (Genesis 27:40). The dominion of Edom is a time when the just man has restored to him what is his due – effectively, a time of revolution.

[11] *Isaiah 34 and 35* Isaiah 34 prophesies the 'day of the Lord's vengeance' against the enemies of Israel; Isaiah 35 concerns the restoration of power to Israel. Blake may have interpreted them as being about the French Revolution.

[12] *Without contraries…existence* a swipe at Swedenborg's theory of correspondence and equilibrium.

[13] *Good is…Energy* cf. Blake's marginalia in Lavater's *Aphorisms*: 'Active evil is better than passive good.'

[14] *Energy* a term associated with revolutionary action, particularly in discussions of current events in Revolutionary France; Burke commented on 'this dreadful and portentous energy' in 1790.

But the following Contraries to these are True

1. Man has no Body distinct from his Soul, for that called Body is a portion of Soul discerned by the five Senses (the chief inlets of Soul in this age).
2. Energy is the only life and is from the Body, and Reason is the bound or outward circumference of Energy.
3. Energy is Eternal Delight.

[Plate 5]

Those who restrain desire do so because theirs is weak enough to be restrained; and the restrainer (or Reason) usurps its place and governs the unwilling.

And, being restrained, it by degrees becomes passive, till it is only the shadow of desire.

The history of this is written in *Paradise Lost*, and the Governor (or Reason) is called Messiah.

And the original Archangel, or possessor of the command of the heavenly host, is called the Devil or Satan, and his children are called Sin and Death.[15]

But in the Book of Job, Milton's Messiah is called Satan.[16] For this history has been adopted by both parties. It indeed appeared to Reason as if Desire was cast out, but the Devil's account is that the Messi- [Plate 6] -ah fell, and formed a heaven of what he stole from the Abyss.

This is shown in the Gospel, where he prays to the Father to send the comforter, or Desire,[17] that Reason may have Ideas to build on, the Jehovah of the Bible being no other than he[18] who dwells in flaming fire.

Know that after Christ's death he became Jehovah.

But in Milton the Father is Destiny, the Son a Ratio of the five senses, and the Holy Ghost, Vacuum!

Note: The reason Milton wrote in fetters when he wrote of Angels and God, and at liberty when of Devils and Hell, is because he was a true Poet and of the Devil's party without knowing it.

### *A Memorable Fancy*[19] [The Five Senses]

As I was walking among the fires of hell,[20] delighted with the enjoyments of Genius (which to Angels look like torment and insanity), I collected some of their Proverbs, thinking that as the sayings used in a nation mark its character, so the Proverbs of Hell show the nature of infernal wisdom better than any description of buildings or garments.

When I came home,[21] on the abyss of the five senses, where a flat-sided steep frowns over the present world,[22] I saw a mighty Devil[23] folded in black clouds hovering on the sides of the rock; with cor- [Plate 7] -roding fires[24] he wrote the following sentence, now perceived by the minds of men, and read by them on earth.

How do you know but ev'ry Bird that cuts the airy way,
Is an immense world of delight, closed by your senses five?[25]

## Notes

[15] *The history...Death* a deliberate inversion of the plan of Milton's poem, by which it becomes the story of how desire and energy are usurped by restraint and reason. Blake casts Jesus as Reason and Satan as the hero. In 'Paradise Lost' Satan's daughter, Sin, is born from his head, and Death is the product of their incestuous union.

[16] *But in the Book...Satan* In Job, Satan accuses and torments Job (as God's agent); likewise, 'Milton's Messiah' accuses and torments Adam and Eve.

[17] *This is shown...Desire* a reference to John 14:16–17, 26, where Jesus tells his disciples that he will pray to the 'Father' to 'give you another Comforter', which is 'the Spirit of truth' and 'the Holy Ghost'.

[18] *he* Blake originally etched 'the Devil'.

[19] The 'Memorable Fancy' parodies Swedenborg's 'Memorable Relations' – short tales used to underline particular ideas.

[20] *As I was walking...Hell* parodic of Swedenborg's excursions in the spiritual world.

[21] *home* various interpretations have been suggested: the world of daily business; Blake's workshop; or England.

[22] *on the abyss...world* In Blake's metaphor the abyss is the head, where all five senses are located, and the cliff is the face.

[23] *a mighty Devil* Blake himself, who has hell inside his head. He sees himself reflected in the copper plate.

[24] *With corroding fires* acids; Blake etched sentences into copper plates with acids.

[25] *How do you know...five* an echo of Chatterton, 'Bristowe Tragedie, or the Dethe of Syr Charles Bawdin' (1768): 'How dydd I knowe thatt ev'ry darte / That cutte the airie waie / Myghte nott fynde passage toe my harte / And close myne eyes for aie?'

### *Proverbs of Hell*[26]

In seed-time learn, in harvest teach, in winter enjoy.
Drive your cart and your plough over the bones of the dead.
The road of excess leads to the palace of wisdom.
Prudence is a rich ugly old maid courted by Incapacity.
He who desires but acts not breeds pestilence.
The cut worm forgives the plough.
Dip him in the river who loves water.
A fool sees not the same tree that a wise man sees.
He whose face gives no light shall never become a star.
Eternity is in love with the productions of time.
The busy bee has no time for sorrow.
The hours of folly are measured by the clock, but of wisdom: no clock can measure.
All wholesome food is caught without a net or a trap.
Bring out number, weight and measure in a year of dearth.
No bird soars too high, if he soars with his own wings.
A dead body revenges not injuries.
The most sublime act is to set another before you.
If the fool would persist in his folly he would become wise.
Folly is the cloak of knavery.
Shame is Pride's cloak.
[Plate 8]
Prisons are built with stones of Law, Brothels with bricks of Religion.
The pride of the peacock is the glory of God.
The lust of the goat is the bounty of God.
The wrath of the lion is the wisdom of God.
The nakedness of woman is the work of God.
Excess of sorrow laughs. Excess of joy weeps.
The roaring of lions, the howling of wolves, the raging of the stormy sea, and the destructive sword, are portions of eternity too great for the eye of man.
The fox condemns the trap, not himself.
Joys impregnate, Sorrows bring forth.
Let man wear the fell[27] of the lion, woman the fleece of the sheep.
The bird a nest, the spider a web, man friendship.
The selfish smiling fool and the sullen frowning fool shall be both thought wise, that they may be a rod.
What is now proved, was once only imagined.
The rat, the mouse, the fox, the rabbit, watch the roots; the lion, the tiger, the horse, the elephant, watch the fruits.
The cistern contains; the fountain overflows.
One thought fills immensity.
Always be ready to speak your mind, and a base man will avoid you.
Every thing possible to be believed is an image of truth.
The eagle never lost so much time as when he submitted to learn of the crow.
[Plate 9]
The fox provides for himself, but God provides for the lion.
Think in the morning, Act in the noon, Eat in the evening, Sleep in the night.

## Notes

[26] The proverb or aphorism was a widely employed literary form; Blake knew the biblical Book of Proverbs and Lavater's *Aphorisms on Man* (1788), among others.

[27] *fell* skin.

He who has suffered you to impose on him knows you.
As the plough follows words, so God rewards prayers.
The tygers of wrath are wiser than the horses of instruction.
Expect poison from the standing water.
You never know what is enough unless you know what is more than enough.
Listen to the fool's reproach! It is a kingly title!
The eyes of fire, the nostrils of air, the mouth of water, the beard of earth.
The weak in courage is strong in cunning.
The apple tree never asks the beech how he shall grow; nor the lion, the horse how he shall take his prey.
The thankful receiver bears a plentiful harvest.
If others had not been foolish, we should be so.
The soul of sweet delight can never be defiled.
When thou seest an Eagle, thou seest a portion of Genius, lift up thy head!
As the caterpillar chooses the fairest leaves to lay her eggs on, so the priest lays his curse on the fairest joys.[28]
To create a little flower is the labour of ages.
'Damn!' braces; 'Bless!' relaxes.
The best wine is the oldest, the best water the newest.
Prayers plough not! Praises reap not!
Joys laugh not! Sorrows weep not!
[Plate 10]
The head Sublime, the heart Pathos, the genitals Beauty, the hands and feet Proportion.
As the air to a bird or the sea to a fish, so is contempt to the contemptible.
The crow wished everything was black; the owl that everything was white.
Exuberance is Beauty.
If the lion was advised by the fox, he would be cunning.
Improvement makes straight roads, but the crooked roads without improvement are roads of Genius.
Sooner murder an infant in its cradle than nurse unacted desires.
Where man is not nature is barren.
Truth can never be told so as to be understood, and not be believed.

Enough! or Too much.

[Plate 11]

The ancient Poets animated all sensible objects with Gods or Geniuses, calling them by the names and adorning them with the properties of woods, rivers, mountains, lakes, cities, nations, and whatever their enlarged and numerous senses could perceive.

And particularly they studied the genius of each city and country, placing it under its mental deity.

Till a system was formed, which some took advantage of, and enslaved the vulgar by attempting to realize or abstract the mental deities from their objects: thus began Priesthood.

Choosing forms of worship from poetic tales.

And at length they pronounced that the Gods had ordered such things.

Thus men forgot that All deities reside in the human breast.

Notes

[28] Cf. 'The Garden of Love' 11–12.

[Plate 12]

## *A Memorable Fancy* [Isaiah and Ezekiel]

The Prophets Isaiah and Ezekiel dined with me, and I asked them how they dared so roundly to assert that God spake to them, and whether they did not think at the time that they would be misunderstood, and so be the cause of imposition?

Isaiah answered, 'I saw no God, nor heard any, in a finite organical perception.[29] But my senses discovered the infinite in everything, and, as I was then persuaded, and remain confirmed, that the voice of honest indignation[30] is the voice of God, I cared not for consequences, but wrote.'

Then I asked, 'Does a firm persuasion that a thing is so, make it so?'

He replied, 'All poets believe that it does, and in ages of imagination this firm persuasion removed mountains;[31] but many are not capable of a firm persuasion of anything.'

Then Ezekiel said, 'The philosophy of the east taught the first principles of human perception. Some nations held one principle for the origin and some another. We of Israel taught that the Poetic Genius (as you now call it) was the first principle and all the others merely derivative, which was the cause of our despising the Priests and Philosophers of other countries, and prophesying that all Gods would [Plate 13] at last be proved to originate in ours and to be the tributaries of the Poetic Genius. It was this that our great poet King David[32] desired so fervently, and invokes so pathetic'ly,[33] saying by this he conquers enemies and governs kingdoms. And we so loved our God that we cursed in his name all the deities of surrounding nations,[34] and asserted that they had rebelled. From these opinions the vulgar came to think that all nations would at last be subject to the jews.

'This', said he, 'like all firm persuasions, is come to pass, for all nations believe the jews' code and worship the jews' god, and what greater subjection can be?'

I heard this with some wonder, and must confess my own conviction. After dinner I asked Isaiah to favour the world with his lost works; he said none of equal value was lost. Ezekiel said the same of his.

I also asked Isaiah what made him go naked and barefoot three years? He answered, 'The same that made our friend Diogenes the Grecian.'[35]

I then asked Ezekiel why he ate dung, and lay so long on his right and left side?[36] He answered, 'The desire of raising other men into a perception of the infinite: this the North American tribes practise, and is he honest who resists his genius or conscience, only for the sake of present ease or gratification?'

[Plate 14]

The ancient tradition that the world will be consumed in fire at the end of six thousand years is true,[37] as I have heard from Hell.

For the cherub with his flaming sword is hereby commanded to leave his guard at the tree of life;[38] and when he does, the whole creation will be consumed and appear infinite and holy, whereas it now appears finite and corrupt.

## Notes

[29] *I saw no God...perception* Though appropriated for the priesthood by the religious, Isaiah is here reclaimed for the just man. The statement is highly subversive of the Bible, where Isaiah is inclined to say such things as 'Moreover the Lord said unto me' (Isaiah 8:1).

[30] *honest indignation* at, for instance, social or political injustice. In the Bible indignation is attributed, by contrast, to God: 'his lips are full of indignation' (Isaiah 30:27).

[31] *removed mountains* an allusion to Jesus, who withers a fig tree with his words, and tells his disciples, 'if ye have faith, and doubt not ... if ye shall say unto this mountain, Be thou removed, and be thou cast into the sea; it shall be done' (Matthew 21:21).

[32] *our great poet King David* second king of Judah and Israel, author of the Psalms.

[33] *pathetic'ly* movingly.

[34] *And we so loved...nations* ironic; Isaiah and Ezekiel curse the deities of other nations, and predict their destruction (Isaiah 19; Ezekiel 29–32).

[35] *Diogenes the Grecian* Greek philosopher of the Cynic school (d. 320 BC), said to have wandered through Athens with a lantern searching for one honest person; also said to have lived in a barrel.

[36] *I then asked Ezekiel...side* Ezekiel lay 390 days on his left side, 40 on his right. He did not eat dung but cooked with it (Ezekiel 4).

[37] *The ancient tradition...true* In the fashion of Swedenborg, Blake predicts the end of the world. It was widely believed, at the end of the eighteenth century, that the 6,000 year lifespan of the world was about to end.

[38] *For the cherub...life* At Genesis 3:22, 24, cherubim are commanded to guard the way of the tree of life with a flaming sword.

This will come to pass by an improvement of sensual enjoyment. But first the notion that man has a body distinct from his soul is to be expunged.

This I shall do by printing in the infernal method, by corrosives,[39] which in Hell are salutary and medicinal, melting apparent surfaces away, and displaying the infinite which was hid.

If the doors of perception were cleansed, everything would appear to man as it is: Infinite.

For man has closed himself up till he sees all things through narrow chinks of his cavern.

[Plate 15]

## *A Memorable Fancy* [A Printing-House in Hell][40]

I was in a printing-house in Hell and saw the method in which knowledge is transmitted from generation to generation.

In the first chamber was a Dragon-Man, clearing away the rubbish from a cave's mouth; within, a number of Dragons were hollowing the cave.

In the second chamber was a Viper[41] folding round the rock and the cave, and others adorning it with gold, silver, and precious stones.

In the third chamber was an Eagle with wings and feathers of air[42] – he caused the inside of the cave to be infinite; around were numbers of Eagle-like men, who built palaces in the immense cliffs.

In the fourth chamber were Lions of flaming fire, raging around and melting the metals into living fluids.

In the fifth chamber were unnamed forms, which cast the metals into the expanse.[43] There they were received by Men who occupied the sixth chamber, and took the forms of books and were arranged in libraries.

[Plate 16]

The Giants who formed this world into its sensual existence and now seem to live in it in chains are, in truth, the causes of its life and the sources of all activity;[44] but the chains are the cunning of weak and tame minds, which have power to resist energy. According to the proverb, the weak in courage is strong in cunning.

Thus one portion of being is the Prolific; the other, the Devouring. To the devourer it seems as if the producer was in his chains, but it is not so: he only takes portions of existence and fancies that the whole.

But the Prolific would cease to be Prolific unless the Devourer as a sea received the excess of his delights.

Some will say, 'Is not God alone the Prolific?' I answer, 'God only acts and is in existing beings or men.'

These two classes of men are always upon earth, and they should be enemies; whoever tries [Plate 17] to reconcile them seeks to destroy existence.

Religion is an endeavour to reconcile the two.

Note: Jesus Christ did not wish to unite, but to separate them (as in the parable of sheep and goats),[45] and he says, 'I came not to send Peace but a Sword.'[46]

Messiah or Satan or Tempter was formerly thought to be one of the Antediluvians who are our Energies.

## Notes

[39] *corrosives* Blake's printing technique involved the use of acid.

[40] This memorable fancy picks up the metaphor of body as cave, in order to show how the 'doors of perception' can be cleansed by 'a printing-house in hell' with five chambers (one for each sense) and a sixth where men receive the products of the first five. The printing-house produces imaginative ('infernal') thoughts.

[41] *Viper* perhaps a brush or pen, or the lines made by such implements.

[42] *feathers of air* Blake used feathers in his printing process, perhaps to stir the acid over his plates.

[43] *cast the metals...expanse* probably copper plates 'cast ... into the expanse' of paper, during the printing process.

[44] *The Giants...activity* By contrast, Swedenborg condemned the antediluvian giants at Genesis 6:4 for self-love and sensuality.

[45] Matthew 25:32–3.

[46] Matthew 10:34. See also Luke 12:51, where Jesus asks: 'Suppose ye that I am come to give peace on earth? I tell you, nay; but rather division.'

### *A Memorable Fancy* [The Vanity of Angels][47]

An Angel came to me and said, 'Oh pitiable foolish young man! Oh horrible! Oh dreadful state! Consider the hot burning dungeon thou art preparing for thyself to all eternity, to which thou art going in such career.'

I said, 'Perhaps you will be willing to show me my eternal lot, and we will contemplate together upon it and see whether your lot or mine is most desirable.'

So he took me through a stable, and through a church, and down into the churchvault, at the end of which was a mill.[48] Through the mill we went, and came to a cave. Down the winding cavern we groped our tedious way, till a void, boundless as a nether sky, appeared beneath us, and we held by the roots of trees and hung over this immensity. But I said, 'If you please, we will commit ourselves to this void, and see whether providence is here also; if you will not, I will'. But he answered, 'Do not presume, oh young man; but as we here remain, behold thy lot which will soon appear when the darkness passes away.'

So I remained with him, sitting in the twisted [Plate 18] root of an oak. He was suspended in a fungus which hung with the head downward into the deep.

By degrees we beheld the infinite Abyss,[49] fiery as the smoke of a burning city; beneath us, at an immense distance, was the sun, black but shining; round it were fiery tracks on which revolved vast spiders, crawling after their prey, which flew, or rather swum, in the infinite deep, in the most terrific shapes of animals sprung from corruption. And the air was full of them, and seemed composed of them. These are Devils, and are called Powers of the air. I now asked my companion which was my eternal lot? He said, 'Between the black and white spiders.'[50]

But now, from between the black and white spiders, a cloud and fire burst and rolled through the deep, black'ning all beneath so that the nether deep grew black as a sea, and rolled with a terrible noise: beneath us was nothing now to be seen but a black tempest, till, looking east[51] between the clouds and the waves, we saw a cataract of blood mixed with fire; and, not many stones' throw from us, appeared and sunk again the scaly fold of a monstrous serpent. At last, to the east, distant about three degrees,[52] appeared a fiery crest above the waves. Slowly it reared, like a ridge of golden rocks, till we discovered two globes of crimson fire from which the sea fled away in clouds of smoke. And now we saw it was the head of Leviathan.[53] His forehead was divided into streaks of green and purple, like those on a tiger's forehead; soon we saw his mouth and red gills hang just above the raging foam, tinging the black deep with beams of blood, advancing toward us [Plate 19] with all the fury of a spiritual existence.

My friend the Angel climbed up from his station into the mill; I remained alone, and then this appearance was no more, but I found myself sitting on a pleasant bank beside a river by moonlight, hearing a harper who sung to the harp.[54] And his theme was, 'The man who never alters his opinion is like standing water, and breeds reptiles of the mind.'

But I arose and sought for the mill, and there I found my Angel who, surprised, asked me how I escaped.

## Notes

[47] This memorable fancy is based on an episode in Swedenborg's *Conjugal Love* in which an angel shows a young man various contrary visions by alternately opening his internal, and closing his external sight. Blake satirizes Swedenborg by giving his narrator the energy and wisdom to challenge his angelic guide.

[48] *So he took me…mill* The church is entered through a stable of rationalism and leads to the mill of mechanistic philosophy that Blake so thoroughly despised.

[49] *the infinite Abyss* presumably hell.

[50] *Between the black and white spiders* In Swedenborgian terms, an existence between false reasoners, perhaps between false contraries such as good and evil.

[51] *east* In Swedenborg the Lord is always 'to the east'.

[52] *distant…degrees* Paris, centre of the French Revolution, is three degrees in longitude from London.

[53] *Leviathan* huge sea-dragon associated with eclipses of sun and moon, who threatens the natural order; see Isaiah 27:1 and Revelation 13:2, for instance. Blake probably has in mind the prophecy in Revelation that the Leviathan will be cast in a pit for a thousand years before being loosed – effectively turning him into a version of the just man whose time has come (Revelation 11:7; 20:1–3).

[54] *and then this…harp* The abrupt transition mimics, and to some extent parodies, that at Revelation 13–14, where the vision of the beast suddenly gives way to a vision of the Lamb where John hears 'the voice of harpers harping with their harps' (Revelation 14:2–3).

I answered, 'All that we saw was owing to your metaphysics. For when you ran away, I found myself on a bank by moonlight hearing a harper. But now we have seen my eternal lot, shall I show you yours?' He laughed at my proposal, but I by force suddenly caught him in my arms, and flew westerly through the night, till we were elevated above the earth's shadow.[55] Then I flung myself with him directly into the body of the sun; here I clothed myself in white, and, taking in my hand Swedenborg's volumes, sunk from the glorious clime, and passed all the planets till we came to Saturn. Here I stayed to rest, and then leaped into the void between saturn and the fixed stars.[56]

'Here', said I, 'is your lot – in this space (if space it may be called).'[57] Soon we saw the stable and the church, and I took him to the altar, and opened the Bible, and lo! it was a deep pit, into which I descended, driving the angel before me. Soon we saw seven houses of brick.[58] One we entered; in it were a [Plate 20] number of monkeys, baboons, and all of that species, chained by the middle, grinning and snatching at one another, but withheld by the shortness of their chains. However, I saw that they sometimes grew numerous, and then the weak were caught by the strong, and, with a grinning aspect, first coupled with, and then devoured, by plucking off first one limb and then another, till the body was left a helpless trunk. This, after grinning and kissing it with seeming fondness, they devoured too. And here and there I saw one savourily picking the flesh off of his own tail. As the stench terribly annoyed us both, we went into the mill, and I in my hand brought the skeleton of a body, which in the mill was Aristotle's Analytics.[59]

So the Angel said, 'Thy fantasy has imposed upon me and thou oughtest to be ashamed.'

I answered, 'We impose on one another, and it is but lost time to converse with you whose works are only Analytics.'

Opposition is true friendship.

[Plate 21]

I have always found that Angels have the vanity to speak of themselves as the only wise; this they do with a confident insolence sprouting from systematic reasoning.

Thus Swedenborg boasts that what he writes is new, though it is only the contents or index of already published books.

A man carried a monkey about for a show, and, because he was a little wiser than the monkey, grew vain, and conceived himself as much wiser than seven men. It is so with Swedenborg: he shows the folly of churches and exposes hypocrites, till he imagines that all are religious, and himself the single [Plate 22] one on earth that ever broke a net.

Now hear a plain fact: Swedenborg has not written one new truth. Now hear another: he has written all the old falsehoods.

And now hear the reason: he conversed with Angels, who are all religious, and conversed not with Devils who all hate religion, for he was incapable through his conceited notions.

Thus Swedenborg's writings are a recapitulation of all superficial opinions, and an analysis of the more sublime – but no further.

Have now another plain fact: any man of mechanical talents may, from the writings of Paracelsus or Jacob Behmen,[60] produce ten thousand volumes of equal value with Swedenborg's – and, from those of Dante or Shakespeare, an infinite number.

But when he has done this, let him not say that he knows better than his master, for he only holds a candle in sunshine.

## Notes

[55] *I by force...shadow* a parody of Swedenborgian space travel.

[56] *into the void...stars* i.e. into an intellectual vacuum.

[57] *if space it may be called* The phrasing echoes Milton's description of Death.

[58] *seven houses of brick* houses in Swedenborg signify states of mind; possibly also a reference to the seven churches of Asia castigated by John, Revelation 1:4.

[59] *Analytics* Aristotle wrote two volumes of *Analytics*, which serve to symbolize an inhuman rationality. Its transformation from the monkey skeleton parodies similar transformations in Swedenborg.

[60] *Paracelsus or Jacob Behmen* Philippus Aureolus Theophrastus Bombastus von Hohenheim, known as Paracelsus (1493–1541), a Swiss-German physician and alchemist; Jakob Boehme (1575–1624), German cobbler and mystic. Blake placed Paracelsus and Boehme alongside Shakespeare among his closest spiritual friends.

## *A Memorable Fancy* [A Devil, My Friend]

Once I saw a Devil in a flame of fire, who arose before an Angel that sat on a cloud, and the Devil uttered these words:

'The worship of God is honouring his gifts in other men, each according to his genius, and loving the [Plate 23] greatest men best. Those who envy or calumniate great men hate God, for there is no other God.'

The Angel hearing this became almost blue; but, mastering himself, he grew yellow, and, at last, white, pink and smiling. And then replied:

'Thou idolater! Is not God One? And is not he visible in Jesus Christ? And has not Jesus Christ given his sanction to the law of ten commandments, and are not all other men fools, sinners and nothings?'

The Devil answered, 'Bray a fool in a mortar with wheat, yet shall not his folly be beaten out of him.[61] If Jesus Christ is the greatest man, you ought to love him in the greatest degree; now hear how he has given his sanction to the law of ten commandments. Did he not mock at the Sabbath, and so mock the Sabbath's God? Murder those who were murdered because of him? Turn away the law from the woman taken in adultery? Steal the labour of others to support him? Bear false witness when he omitted making a defence before Pilate? Covet when he prayed for his disciples, and when he bid them shake off the dust of their feet against such as refused to lodge them? I tell you, no virtue can exist without breaking these ten commandments: Jesus was all virtue and acted from impulse, [Plate 24] not from rules.'

When he had so spoken, I beheld the Angel who stretched out his arms embracing the flame of fire, and he was consumed and arose as Elijah.[62]

Note: This Angel, who is now become a Devil, is my particular friend: we often read the Bible together in its infernal or diabolical sense, which the world shall have if they behave well.

I have also the Bible of Hell:[63] which the world shall have whether they will or no.

One law for the lion and ox is oppression.[64]

[Plate 25]

## *A Song of Liberty*[65]

1. The Eternal Female groaned![66] It was heard over all the Earth:
2. Albion's[67] coast is sick, silent; the American meadows faint!
3. Shadows of Prophecy shiver along by the lakes and the rivers, and mutter across the ocean! France, rend down thy dungeon;[68]
4. Golden Spain, burst the barriers of old Rome;[69]
5. Cast thy keys,[70] oh Rome, into the deep down falling, even to eternity down falling,

### Notes

[61] *Bray a fool…him* cf. Proverbs 27:22: 'Though thou shouldest bray [crush] a fool in a mortar among wheat with a pestle, yet will not his foolishness depart from him.'

[62] *I beheld…Elijah* Elijah is taken up to heaven in a chariot of fire, 2 Kings 2:11.

[63] *the Bible of Hell* possibly a work projected by Blake, which might have included the Proverbs of Hell and *Urizen*.

[64] Above this motto in Blake's plate, a bearded man, looking at the reader with an expression of anguish, crawls along the ground on all fours, naked.

[65] Some have argued that this originated as a separate work from the *Marriage*.

[66] *The Eternal Female groaned* This momentous birth (of Revolution) heralds an apocalypse.

[67] *Albion* England.

[68] *France, rend down thy dungeon* The Bastille prison was stormed by the mob, and demolished, in July 1789. It was a powerful symbol of liberation.

[69] *Rome* the Roman Catholic Church.

[70] *keys* keys of St Peter, symbolic of papal power.

6. And weep![71]
7. In her trembling hands, she took the new-born terror howling;
8. On those infinite mountains of light now barred out by the Atlantic sea,[72] the new-born fire stood before the starry king![73]
9. Flagged[74] with grey-browed snows and thunderous visages, the jealous wings[75] waved over the deep.
10. The speary hand burned aloft, unbuckled was the shield, forth went the hand of jealousy among the flaming hair, and [Plate 26] hurled the new-born wonder[76] through the starry night.
11. The fire, the fire, is falling!
12. Look up! Look up! Oh citizen of London, enlarge thy countenance! Oh Jew, leave counting gold, return to thy oil and wine! Oh African! Black African! (Go, winged thought, widen his forehead.)[77]
13. The fiery limbs, the flaming hair, shot like the sinking sun into the western sea.
14. Waked from his eternal sleep, the hoary element[78] roaring fled away;
15. Down rushed, beating his wings in vain the jealous king;[79] his grey-browed counsellors, thunderous warriors, curled veterans, among helms and shields and chariots, horses, elephants: banners, castles, slings and rocks,
16. Falling, rushing, ruining! buried in the ruins, on Urthona's[80] dens.
17. All night beneath the ruins; then their sullen flames faded emerge round the gloomy king.
18. With thunder and fire: leading his starry hosts through the waste wilderness [Plate 27] he promulgates his ten commands,[81] glancing his beamy eyelids over the deep in dark dismay,
19. Where the son of fire[82] in his eastern cloud, while the morning plumes her golden breast,
20. Spurning the clouds written with curses, stamps the stony law[83] to dust, loosing the eternal horses from the dens of night, crying, 'Empire is no more! And now the lion and wolf shall cease.'[84]

### *Chorus*

Let the priests of the Raven of dawn no longer, in deadly black, with hoarse note, curse the sons of joy; nor his accepted brethren (whom, tyrant, he calls free) lay the bound or build the roof; nor pale religious lechery call that virginity that wishes but acts not!

For everything that lives is Holy.[85]

## Notes

[71] This line originally read: 'And weep and bow thy reverend locks.'

[72] *On those…sea* the mythical ancient kingdom of Atlantis.

[73] *the starry king* Urizen, the primeval priest, in this case a type of the oppressive ruler.

[74] *Flagged* covered.

[75] *the jealous wings* of Urizen; cf. 'Earth's Answer' 7 and note.

[76] *the new-born wonder* Orc, spirit of revolution.

[77] *Oh, citizen…forehead* Blake foresees revolution across the world, from England to the Middle East and Africa.

[78] *the hoary element* The sea retreats, in preparation for the re-emergence of Atlantis. The disappearance of the sea is prophesied Revelation 21:1.

[79] *the jealous king* Urizen, who is falling.

[80] Urthona is the creative, imaginative principle.

[81] *ten commands* cf. God's handing down to Moses of the Ten Commandments, Exodus 20.

[82] *the son of fire* a Christ-like anti-Moses, anti-Jehovah figure, who is to liberate mankind.

[83] *the stony law* The Ten Commandments were inscribed on tablets of stone.

[84] *And now…cease* cf. Isaiah's prophecy of a new heaven and new earth where 'the wolf and the lamb shall feed together (Isaiah 65:25).

[85] *For everything…Holy* a parodic reversal of Revelation 15:4: 'For thou [God] only art holy: for all nations shall come and worship before thee.'

## Visions of the Daughters of Albion (1793)

[Plate 1]

The Eye sees more than the Heart knows.[1]

[Plate 3]

### *The Argument*

I loved Theotormon[2]
And I was not ashamed;
I trembled in my virgin fears
And I hid in Leutha's vale!

I plucked Leutha's flower,[3]
And I rose up from the vale;
But the terrible thunders tore
My virgin mantle[4] in twain.

### *Visions*

Enslaved,[5] the Daughters of Albion[6] weep: a trembling lamentation
Upon their mountains, in their valleys, sighs toward America.
For the soft soul of America,[7] Oothoon wandered in woe
Along the vales of Leutha seeking flowers to comfort her;
And thus she spoke to the bright Marigold of Leutha's vale:
'Art thou a flower? Art thou a nymph? I see thee now a flower,
Now a nymph! I dare not pluck thee from thy dewy bed!'
The golden nymph replied, 'Pluck thou my flower, Oothoon the mild;
Another flower shall spring, because the soul of sweet delight
Can never pass away.' She ceased and closed her golden shrine.
Then Oothoon plucked the flower, saying, 'I pluck thee from thy bed,
Sweet flower, and put thee here to glow between my breasts;[8]
And thus I turn my face to where my whole soul seeks.'
Over the waves she went in winged exulting swift delight,
And over Theotormon's reign[9] took her impetuous course.
Bromion rent her with his thunders.[10] On his stormy bed
Lay the faint maid, and soon her woes appalled his thunders hoarse.
Bromion spoke: 'Behold this harlot here on Bromion's bed,

## Notes

[1] The motto appears on the poem's title-page.

[2] *Theotormon* Blake's coinage; the speaker in the argument is Oothoon, who represents thwarted love. The name Theotormon probably means 'tormented of god' or 'tormented of law'.

[3] *I plucked Leutha's flower* symbolic of an attempt to acquire sexual experience.

[4] *My virgin mantle* the hymen.

[5] *Enslaved* Wollstonecraft had described women as 'the slaves of injustice'.

[6] *Albion* England.

[7] America has been 'raped' by European exploitation.

[8] *between my breasts* In Homer's *Iliad*, Juno places the 'bridle' (girdle) of Venus between her breasts as a sign of sexual awakening.

[9] *Theotormon's reign* the sea.

[10] *Bromion...thunders* On her way to her beloved Theotormon, Oothoon is raped by Bromion. Bromion also embodies the cruelty of slave-owners (lines 29–30). His name means 'roarer' in Greek.

And let the jealous dolphins[11] sport around the lovely maid.
Thy soft American plains are mine, and mine thy north and south.
Stamped with my signet are the swarthy children of the sun[12] –
They are obedient, they resist not, they obey the scourge;
Their daughters worship terrors and obey the violent.
[Plate 5]
Now thou may'st marry Bromion's harlot, and protect the child
Of Bromion's rage that Oothoon shall put forth in nine moons' time.'
  Then storms rent Theotormon's limbs; he rolled his waves around
And folded his black jealous waters round the adulterate pair.
Bound back to back in Bromion's caves,[13] terror and meekness dwell.
At entrance Theotormon sits wearing the threshold hard
With secret tears; beneath him sound like waves on a desert shore
The voice of slaves beneath the sun, and children bought with money
That shiver in religious caves beneath the burning fires
Of lust, that belch incessant from the summits of the earth.
Oothoon weeps not – she cannot weep! Her tears are locked up
But she can howl incessant writhing her soft snowy limbs,
And calling Theotormon's Eagles to prey upon her flesh.[14]
  'I call with holy voice, kings of the sounding air!
Rend away this defiled bosom that I may reflect
The image of Theotormon on my pure transparent breast.'
The Eagles at her call descend and rend their bleeding prey:
Theotormon severely smiles – her soul reflects the smile
As the clear spring mudded with feet of beasts grows pure and smiles.
The Daughters of Albion hear her woes, and echo back her sighs.
  'Why does my Theotormon sit weeping upon the threshold,
And Oothoon hovers by his side, persuading him in vain?[15]
I cry, "Arise, oh Theotormon, for the village dog
Barks at the breaking day; the nightingale has done lamenting;
The lark does rustle in the ripe corn, and the Eagle returns
From nightly prey, and lifts his golden beak to the pure east,
Shaking the dust from his immortal pinions to awake
The sun that sleeps too long. Arise, my Theotormon, I am pure
Because the night is gone that closed me in its deadly black."
They told me that the night and day were all that I could see;
They told me that I had five senses to enclose me up,
And they enclosed my infinite brain into a narrow circle,
And sunk my heart into the Abyss, a red round globe hot burning,
Till all from life I was obliterated and erased.

## Notes

[11] *jealous dolphins* representative of the feelings of Theotormon, whom Bromion is addressing.

[12] *Stamped...sun* Newly bought slaves were branded with their owner's name.

[13] *Bound back to back...caves* Oothoon and Bromion are bound back to back in Theotormon's cave, while he guards its entrance. This is depicted in one of the most famous, and impressive, of Blake's illustrations (see Blake, *Early Illuminated Books* 268–9).

[14] *And calling...flesh* When Zeus chained Prometheus on the mountain-top (when he refused to reveal the prophecy of Zeus's fall), an eagle preyed on Prometheus's liver.

[15] Theotormon's ineffectual response to the rape of Oothoon by Bromion is probably suggested by the behaviour of J.G. Stedman, who wrote of how he fell in love with Joanna, a slave. After a brief affair, he failed to buy her freedom and returned to England without her. He remembered how 'I fancied I saw her tortured, insulted, and bowing under the weight of her chains, calling aloud, but in vain, for my assistance'. Although he disapproved of the treatment of female slaves, Stedman did nothing to prevent the cruelty he witnessed.

Instead of morn arises a bright shadow like an eye
In the eastern cloud; instead of night, a sickly charnel house,
That Theotormon hears me not! To him the night and morn
Are both alike: a night of sighs, a morning of fresh tears –
[Plate 6]
And none but Bromion can hear my lamentations.
With what sense is it that the chicken shuns the ravenous hawk?
With what sense does the tame pigeon measure out the expanse?
With what sense does the bee form cells? Have not the mouse and frog
Eyes and ears and sense of touch? Yet are their habitations
And their pursuits as different as their forms and as their joys.
Ask the wild ass why he refuses burdens; and the meek camel
Why he loves man – is it because of eye, ear, mouth or skin
Or breathing nostrils? No, for these the wolf and tiger have.
Ask the blind worm the secrets of the grave, and why her spires
Love to curl round the bones of death; and ask the rav'nous snake
Where she gets poison; and the winged eagle why he loves the sun –
And then tell me the thoughts of man that have been hid of old.
Silent I hover all the night, and all day could be silent
If Theotormon once would turn his loved eyes upon me.
How can I be defiled when I reflect thy image pure?
Sweetest the fruit that the worm feeds on, and the soul preyed on by woe,
The new-washed lamb tinged with the village smoke, and the bright swan
By the red earth of our immortal river! I bathe my wings
And I am white and pure to hover round Theotormon's breast.'
Then Theotormon broke his silence, and he answered.
'Tell me what is the night or day to one o'erflowed with woe?
Tell me what is a thought, and of what substance is it made?
Tell me what is a joy, and in what gardens do joys grow?
And in what rivers swim the sorrows, and upon what mountains
[Plate 7]
Wave shadows of discontent? And in what houses dwell the wretched
Drunken with woe forgotten, and shut up from cold despair?
Tell me where dwell the thoughts forgotten till thou call them forth?
Tell me where dwell the joys of old, and where the ancient loves?
And when will they renew again, and the night of oblivion past?[16]
That I might traverse times and spaces far remote, and bring
Comforts into a present sorrow and a night of pain.
Where goest thou, oh thought? To what remote land is thy flight?
If thou returnest to the present moment of affliction
Wilt thou bring comforts on thy wings, and dews and honey and balm?
Or poison from the desert wilds, from the eyes of the envier?'
Then Bromion said (and shook the cavern with his lamentation),
'Thou knowest that the ancient trees seen by thine eyes have fruit,
But knowest thou that trees and fruits flourish upon the earth
To gratify senses unknown? Trees, beasts and birds unknown?
Unknown, not unperceived, spread in the infinite microscope,

Notes

[16] *And when…past?* i.e. when will the thoughts, joys, and loves renew; when will the night of oblivion be past?

In places yet unvisited by the voyager, and in worlds
Over another kind of seas, and in atmospheres unknown.
Ah, are there other wars, beside the wars of sword and fire?
And are there other sorrows, beside the sorrows of poverty?
And are there other joys, beside the joys of riches and ease?
And is there not one law for both the lion and the ox?
And is there not eternal fire, and eternal chains
To bind the phantoms of existence from eternal life?'
  Then Oothoon waited silent all the day and all the night,
[Plate 8]
But when the morn arose, her lamentation renewed –
The Daughters of Albion hear her woes, and echo back her sighs.
'Oh Urizen![17] Creator of men! Mistaken Demon of heaven!
Thy joys are tears, thy labour vain – to form men to thine image.
How can one joy absorb another? Are not different joys
Holy, eternal, infinite? And each joy is a Love!
Does not the great mouth laugh at a gift, and the narrow eyelids mock
At the labour that is above payment? And wilt thou take the ape
For thy counsellor? Or the dog, for a schoolmaster to thy children?
Does he who contemns poverty, and he who turns with abhorrence
From usury, feel the same passion? Or are they moved alike?
How can the giver of gifts experience the delights of the merchant?
How the industrious citizen the pains of the husbandman?
How different far the fat-fed hireling with hollow drum
Who buys whole cornfields into wastes,[18] and sings upon the heath –
How different their eye and ear! How different the world to them!
With what sense does the parson claim the labour of the farmer[19]
What are his nets and gins and traps, and how does he surround him
With cold floods of abstraction, and with forests of solitude,
To build him castles and high spires where kings and priests may dwell?
Till she who burns with youth, and knows no fixed lot, is bound
In spells of law to one she loathes. And must she drag the chain
Of life in weary lust?[20] Must chilling murderous thoughts obscure
The clear heaven of her eternal spring? – to bear the wintry rage
Of a harsh terror, driv'n to madness, bound to hold a rod[21]
Over her shrinking shoulders all the day, and all the night
To turn the wheel of false desire? – and longings that wake her womb
To the abhorred birth of cherubs in the human form
That live a pestilence and die a meteor, and are no more?
Till the child dwell with one he hates, and do the deed he loathes,
And the impure scourge force his seed into its unripe birth
Ere yet his eyelids can behold the arrows of the day.

## Notes

[17] *Urizen* ('your reason') the creator of the fallen, fragmented world.

[18] *cornfields into wastes* Expenditure of harvests and men on war is associated with enclosure and agricultural decline. The enlistment of young men in the army left a dearth of farmers to till the land, which in turn led to food shortages.

[19] *With what sense...farmer* a reference to tithes, taxes paid by peasants to the church.

[20] *And must...lust* Wollstonecraft probably inspired the notion of marriage as slavery.

[21] *rod* yoke for bearing burdens over the shoulders; though perhaps also the rod or whip of her slave-driving husband.

Does the whale worship at thy footsteps as the hungry dog?
Or does he scent the mountain prey because his nostrils wide
Draw in the ocean? Does his eye discern the flying cloud
As the raven's eye? Or does he measure the expanse like the vulture?
Does the still spider view the cliffs where eagles hide their young?
Or does the fly rejoice because the harvest is brought in?
Does not the eagle scorn the earth and despise the treasures beneath?
But the mole knoweth what is there, and the worm shall tell it thee.
Does not the worm erect a pillar in the mouldering churchyard,
[Plate 9]
And a palace of eternity in the jaws of the hungry grave?
Over his porch these words are written: "Take thy bliss O Man!
And sweet shall be thy taste, and sweet thy infant joys renew!"
Infancy, fearless, lustful, happy! – nestling for delight
In laps of pleasure; Innocence! Honest, open, seeking
The vigorous joys of morning light, open to virgin bliss –
Who taught thee modesty, subtle modesty, child of night and sleep?
When thou awakest, wilt thou dissemble all thy secret joys
Or wert thou not awake when all this mystery was disclosed?
Then com'st thou forth a modest virgin knowing to dissemble[22]
With nets found under thy night pillow, to catch virgin joy,
And brand it with the name of whore, and sell it in the night[23]
In silence, ev'n without a whisper, and in seeming sleep.
Religious dreams and holy vespers light thy smoky fires;
Once were thy fires lighted by the eyes of honest morn.
And does my Theotormon seek this hypocrite modesty,
This knowing, artful, secret, fearful, cautious, trembling hypocrite?
Then is Oothoon a whore indeed! And all the virgin joys
Of life are harlots, and Theotormon is a sick man's dream,
And Oothoon is the crafty slave of selfish holiness.
But Oothoon is not so: a virgin filled with virgin fancies,
Open to joy and to delight wherever beauty appears.
If in the morning sun I find it, there my eyes are fixed
[Plate 10]
In happy copulation; if in evening mild, wearied with work,
Sit on a bank and draw the pleasures of this free-born joy.
The moment of desire! The moment of desire! The virgin
That pines for man shall awaken her womb to enormous joys
In the secret shadows of her chamber;[24] the youth shut up from
The lustful joy shall forget to generate, and create an amorous image
In the shadows of his curtains and in the folds of his silent pillow.[25]
Are not these the places of religion? The rewards of continence?

## Notes

[22] *a modest virgin...dissemble* Wollstonecraft lamented the tendency of women to spend so much time in front of mirrors, 'for this exercise of cunning is only an instinct of nature to enable them to obtain indirectly a little of that power of which they are unjustly denied a share'.

[23] *sell it in the night* prostitution.

[24] *The virgin...chamber* female masturbation.

[25] *the youth...pillow* male masturbation.

The self-enjoyings of self-denial? Why dost thou seek religion?
Is it because acts are not lovely that thou seekest solitude
Where the horrible darkness is impressed with reflections of desire?
Father of Jealousy,[26] be thou accursed from the earth!
Why hast thou taught my Theotormon this accursed thing?
Till beauty fades from off my shoulders, darkened and cast out,
A solitary shadow wailing on the margin of nonentity.
I cry, "Love! Love! Love! Happy, happy Love! Free as the mountain wind!"
Can that be Love, that drinks another as a sponge drinks water?
That clouds with jealousy his nights, with weepings all the day?
To spin a web of age around him, grey and hoary, dark,
Till his eyes sicken at the fruit that hangs before his sight?[27]
Such is self-love that envies all! – a creeping skeleton
With lamp-like eyes, watching around the frozen marriage bed.
But silken nets and traps of adamant will Oothoon spread,
And catch for thee girls of mild silver, or of furious gold;
I'll lie beside thee on a bank and view their wanton play
In lovely copulation, bliss on bliss, with Theotormon;
Red as the rosy morning, lustful as the first-born beam,
Oothoon shall view his dear delight, nor e'er with jealous cloud
Come in the heaven of generous love, nor selfish blightings bring.
Does the sun walk in glorious raiment on the secret floor
[Plate 11]
Where the cold miser spreads his gold? Or does the bright cloud drop
On his stone threshold? Does his eye behold the beam that brings
Expansion to the eye of pity? Or will he bind himself
Beside the ox to thy hard furrow? Does not that mild beam blot
The bat, the owl, the glowing tiger, and the king of night?
The sea-fowl takes the wintry blast for a cov'ring to her limbs
And the wild snake the pestilence to adorn him with gems and gold;
And trees and birds and beasts and men behold their eternal joy.
Arise, you little glancing wings, and sing your infant joy!
Arise and drink your bliss, for every thing that lives is holy!'
Thus every morning wails Oothoon, but Theotormon sits
Upon the margined ocean, conversing with shadows dire.
The Daughters of Albion hear her woes, and echo back her sighs.

The End

Notes

[26] *Father of jealousy* Urizen.

[27] *Till his eyes…sight* cf. Tantalus who, in Hades, has delicious fruit growing just beyond reach in Greek myth.

## The First Book of Urizen[1] (1794)

[Plate 2]

*Preludium to the First Book of Urizen*

Of the primeval Priest's assumed power,[2]
When Eternals spurned back his[3] religion
And gave him a place in the north –
Obscure, shadowy, void, solitary.

Eternals, I hear your call gladly[4] –
Dictate swift-winged words, and fear not
To unfold your dark visions of torment.

[Plate 3]

### *Chapter I*

1. Lo, a shadow of horror is risen
In Eternity! Unknown, unprolific!
Self-closed, all-repelling; what Demon
Hath formed this abominable void,[5]
This soul-shudd'ring vacuum? Some said,
'It is Urizen'.[6] But unknown, abstracted,
Brooding secret,[7] the dark power hid.

2. Times on times he divided,[8] and measured
Space by space in his ninefold darkness,[9]
Unseen, unknown; changes appeared
In his desolate mountains,[10] rifted furious
By the black winds of perturbation.

3. For he strove in battles dire,
In unseen conflictions, with shapes
Bred from his forsaken wilderness,
Of beast, bird, fish, serpent and element,
Combustion, blast, vapour and cloud.[11]

## Notes

[1] The title is designed to contrast Blake's poem with the title of Genesis in the Authorized Version of the Bible – 'The First Book of Moses'. Perhaps *Urizen* was intended to be the first part of Blake's 'Bible of Hell' mentioned in *The Marriage of Heaven and Hell.* Urizen himself has been aligned in the past with Reason – 'your reason'. Blake was no admirer of reason in its purest state; it is, in the present context, the force of division and separation, responsible for the making of unjust laws.

[2] *Of the...power* Blake imitates the usual opening to an epic poem (e.g. 'Of arms and the man I sing ...', 'Of man's first disobedience ...'). It echoes the anti-clericalism of *The Marriage of Heaven and Hell.*

[3] *his* Urizen's.

[4] *I hear your call gladly* Blake, the poet, receives the dictation of the Eternals.

[5] *What demon...void* cf. Genesis 1:2: 'And the earth was without form, and void.'

[6] *Some said...Urizen* the first act of naming in the poem.

[7] *Brooding secret* an allusion to the moment of creation in *Paradise Lost* i 21–2, where the Holy Spirit 'Dove-like sat'st brooding on the vast abyss / And madest it pregnant'.

[8] *divided* The Creation begins with Urizen's splitting away from the Eternals into self hood.

[9] *ninefold darkness* Milton's Satan lay for nine days in the abyss of hell.

[10] *mountains* Urizen becomes a landscape: Creation and the Fall are one and the same.

[11] *Of beast ... cloud* The elements (l. 24) are accompanied by emblematic beasts (l. 23).

4. Dark, revolving in silent activity,
Unseen in tormenting passions,
An activity unknown and horrible;
A self-contemplating shadow
In enormous labours occupied.

5. But Eternals beheld his vast forests.
Age on ages he lay, closed, unknown,
Brooding, shut in the deep; all avoid
The petrific[12] abominable chaos.

6. His cold horrors silent, dark Urizen
Prepared: his ten thousands of thunders
Ranged in gloomed array stretch out across
The dread world, and the rolling of wheels,
As of swelling seas, sound in his clouds,
In his hills of stored snows, in his mountains
Of hail and ice; voices of terror
Are heard, like thunders of autumn,
When the cloud blazes over the harvests.

## *Chapter II*[13]

1. Earth was not, nor globes of attraction.[14]
The will of the Immortal[15] expanded
Or contracted his all-flexible senses.
Death was not, but eternal life sprung.

2. The sound of a trumpet! The heavens
Awoke, and vast clouds of blood rolled
Round the dim rocks of Urizen (so named
That solitary one in Immensity).

3. Shrill the trumpet, and myriads of Eternity
[Plate 4]
Muster around the bleak deserts
Now filled with clouds darkness and waters
That rolled perplexed, lab'ring, and uttered
Words articulate, bursting in thunders
That rolled on the tops of his mountains.

4. 'From the depths of dark solitude,[16] From
The eternal abode in my holiness,
Hidden, set apart in my stern counsels,

## Notes

[12] *petrific* a Miltonic coinage meaning stony, static (see *Paradise Lost* x 294). The point is that chaos is static when compared to all-flexible eternity.

[13] In this chapter Blake tells the story of the Creation a second time.

[14] *globes of attraction* solar systems; planets held together by gravity. In Blake's plate, 'attraction' is split into two parts, 'attrac-/-tion', with the second part hovering above the first, mimicking a gravity-less state.

[15] *the Immortal* Urizen.

[16] Lines 57–91 comprise Urizen's account of the Creation.

Reserved for the days of futurity,
I have sought for a joy without pain,
For a solid without fluctuation.
Why will you die oh Eternals?[17]
Why live in unquenchable burnings?

5. First I fought with the fire, consumed
Inwards, into a deep world within:
A void immense, wild dark and deep
Where nothing was; Nature's wide womb.
And self-balanced, stretched o'er the void
I alone, even I! the winds merciless
Bound; but condensing in torrents
They fall and fall; strong, I repelled
The vast waves, and arose on the waters –
A wide world of solid obstruction.

6. Here alone I, in books formed of metals,
Have written the secrets of wisdom,[18]
The secrets of dark contemplation,
By fightings and conflicts dire
With terrible monsters sin-bred,
Which the bosoms of all inhabit,
Seven deadly sins of the soul.

7. Lo! I unfold my darkness: and on
This rock place with strong hand the Book
Of eternal brass, written in my solitude.

8. Laws of peace, of love, of unity,
Of pity,[19] compassion, forgiveness.
Let each choose one habitation,
His ancient infinite mansion.
One command, one joy, one desire,
One curse, one weight, one measure,
One King, one God, one Law.'[20]

## *Chapter III*

1. The voice ended. They saw his pale visage
Emerge from the darkness, his hand
On the rock of eternity unclasping
The Book of brass. Rage seized the strong,

## Notes

[17] *Why will you die, oh Eternals?* an echo of Ezekiel 18:31: 'why will ye die, oh house of Israel?'

[18] *Here alone…wisdom* parodic of God's handing down to Moses of the Ten Commandments, Exodus 20.

[19] *pity* not, for Blake, a desirable quality, as it consolidates division.

[20] *One King, one God, one Law* Blake regarded the imposition of these things as tyranny.

2. Rage, fury, intense indignation,
In cataracts of fire blood and gall,
In whirlwinds of sulphurous smoke
And enormous forms of energy;
All the seven deadly sins of the soul
[Plate 5]
In living creations appeared
In the flames of eternal fury.

3. Sund'ring, dark'ning, thund'ring!
Rent away with a terrible crash,
Eternity rolled wide apart,
Wide asunder rolling
Mountainous all around
Departing; departing; departing:
Leaving ruinous fragments of life,
Hanging frowning cliffs, and all between
An ocean of voidness unfathomable.

4. The roaring fires ran o'er the heav'ns
In whirlwinds and cataracts of blood,
And o'er the dark deserts of Urizen
Fires pour through the void on all sides
On Urizen's self-begotten armies.

5. But no light from the fires: all was darkness
In the flames of Eternal fury.

6. In fierce anguish and quenchless flames
To the deserts and rocks he ran raging
To hide, but he could not: combining,
He dug mountains and hills in vast strength,
He piled them in incessant labour,
In howlings and pangs and fierce madness
Long periods in burning fires labouring
Till hoary and age-broke and aged,
In despair and the shadows of death.

7. And a roof vast, petrific, around,
On all sides he framed, like a womb
Where thousands of rivers in veins
Of blood pour down the mountains to cool
The eternal fires beating without
From Eternals; and, like a black globe
Viewed by sons of Eternity, standing
On the shore of the infinite ocean,
Like a human heart struggling and beating,
The vast world of Urizen appeared.

8. And Los[21] round the dark globe of Urizen
Kept watch for Eternals to confine
The obscure separation alone;
For Eternity stood wide apart
[Plate 7]
As the stars are apart from the earth.

9. Los wept, howling around the dark Demon
And cursing his lot; for in anguish
Urizen was rent from his side:[22]
And a fathomless void for his feet,
And intense fires for his dwelling.

10. But Urizen laid in a stony sleep
Unorganized, rent from Eternity.

11. The Eternals said: 'What is this? Death.[23]
Urizen is a clod of clay.'

[Plate 9]
12. Los howled in a dismal stupor,
Groaning! Gnashing! Groaning!
Till the wrenching apart was healed.

13. But the wrenching of Urizen healed not;
Cold, featureless, flesh or clay,
Rifted with direful changes
He lay in a dreamless night.

14. Till Los roused his fires, affrighted
At the formless unmeasurable death.

[Plate 10]

### *Chapter IVa*

1. Los, smitten with astonishment,
Frightened at the hurtling bones,

2. And at the surging sulphureous
Perturbed Immortal mad-raging

3. In whirlwinds and pitch and nitre
Round the furious limbs of Los;

## Notes

[21] *Los* the imagination, now separated from Urizen.

[22] *Urizen was rent from his side* cf. the creation of Eve from Adam's rib, Genesis 2:21.

[23] *What is…Death* the second act of naming in the poem.

4. And Los formed nets and gins[24]
And threw the nets round about.

5. He watched in shudd'ring fear
The dark changes, and bound every change
With rivets of iron and brass;
And these were the changes of Urizen.

[Plate 12]

## *Chapter IVb*

1. Ages on ages rolled over him!
In stony sleep ages rolled over him!
Like a dark waste stretching changeable
By earthquakes riv'n, belching sullen fires,
On ages rolled ages in ghastly
Sick torment; around him in whirlwinds
Of darkness, the Eternal Prophet[25] howled,
Beating still on his rivets of iron,
Pouring sodor[26] of iron, dividing
The horrible night into watches.

2. And Urizen (so his eternal name)
His prolific delight obscured more and more
In dark secrecy, hiding in surging
Sulphureous fluid his fantasies.
The Eternal Prophet heaved the dark bellows
And turned restless the tongs, and the hammer
Incessant beat, forging chains new and new,
Numb'ring with links, hours, days, and years.[27]

3. The Eternal Mind bounded began to roll
Eddies of wrath ceaseless round and round,
And the sulphureous foam surging thick
Settled – a lake, bright and shining clear,
White as the snow on the mountains cold.

4. Forgetfulness, dumbness, necessity!
In chains of the mind locked up
Like fetters of ice shrinking together
Disorganized, rent from Eternity.
Los beat on his fetters of iron,
And heated his furnaces, and poured
Iron sodor and sodor of brass.

Notes

[24] *gins* snares, traps.
[25] *the Eternal Prophet* Los.
[26] *sodor* solder – which, like rivets, is used to join metal components.
[27] *Numb'ring…years* Los constructs a calendar.

5. Restless turned the Immortal enchained,
Heaving dolorous! Anguished! Unbearable
Till a roof shaggy wild enclosed
In an orb[28] his fountain of thought.

6. In a horrible dreamful slumber
Like the linked infernal chain
A vast spine writhed in torment
Upon the winds, shooting pained
Ribs, like a bending cavern,
And bones of solidness froze
Over all his nerves of joy.
And a first Age passed over
And a state of dismal woe.

[Plate 13]
7. From the caverns of his jointed Spine
Down sunk with fright a red
Round globe[29] hot burning, deep
Deep down into the abyss:
Panting, conglobing, trembling,
Shooting out ten thousand branches
Around his solid bones.
And a second Age passed over
And a state of dismal woe.

8. In harrowing fear rolling round;
His nervous brain shot branches
Round the branches of his heart
On high into two little orbs;[30]
And fixed in two little caves
Hiding carefully from the wind,
His eyes beheld the deep,
And a third Age passed over:
And a state of dismal woe.

9. The pangs of hope began,
In heavy pain striving, struggling;
Two Ears in close volutions[31]
From beneath his orbs of vision
Shot spiring out and petrified
As they grew. And a fourth Age passed
And a state of dismal woe.

## Notes

[28] *an orb* the skull.
[29] *a red / Round globe* the heart.
[30] *two little orbs* the eyes.
[31] *close volutions* inner ear.

10. In ghastly torment sick;
Hanging upon the wind;
[Plate 15]
Two Nostrils bent down to the deep.
And a fifth Age passed over,
And a state of dismal woe.

11. In ghastly torment sick;
Within his ribs bloated round,
A craving hungry cavern;
Thence arose his channelled Throat,
And like a red flame a Tongue
Of thirst and of hunger appeared.
And a sixth Age passed over:
And a state of dismal woe.

12. Enraged and stifled with torment,
He threw his right Arm to the north,
His left Arm to the south,
Shooting out in anguish deep;
And his Feet stamped the nether Abyss
In trembling and howling and dismay.
And a seventh Age passed over
And a state of dismal woe.

## *Chapter V*

1. In terrors Los shrunk from his task –
His great hammer fell from his hand;
His fires beheld and, sickening,
Hid their strong limbs in smoke.
For with noises ruinous loud
With hurtlings and clashings and groans
The Immortal endured his chains
Though bound in a deadly sleep.

2. All the myriads of Eternity
All the wisdom and joy of life
Roll like a sea around him,
Except what his little orbs
Of sight by degrees unfold.

3. And now his eternal life,
Like a dream, was obliterated.

4. Shudd'ring, the Eternal Prophet smote
With a stroke, from his north to south region.
The bellows and hammer are silent now,
A nerveless silence; his prophetic voice
Seized; a cold solitude and dark void
The Eternal Prophet and Urizen closed.

5. Ages on ages rolled over them,
Cut off from life and light, frozen
Into horrible forms of deformity.
Los suffered his fires to decay,
Then he looked back with anxious desire,
But the space undivided by existence
Struck horror into his soul.

6. Los wept obscured with mourning;
His bosom earthquaked with sighs;
He saw Urizen, deadly black,
In his chains bound, and Pity began,

7. In anguish dividing and dividing
(For pity divides the soul),[32]
In pangs, eternity on eternity,
Life in cataracts poured down his cliffs.
The void shrunk the lymph into Nerves
Wand'ring wide on the bosom of night,
And left a round globe of blood
Trembling upon the void.
[Plate 16]
Thus the Eternal Prophet was divided
Before the death-image of Urizen;
For in changeable clouds and darkness
In a winterly night beneath,
The Abyss of Los stretched immense.
And now seen, now obscured, to the eyes
Of Eternals the visions remote
Of the dark separation appeared.
As glasses discover Worlds
In the endless Abyss of space,
So the expanding eyes of Immortals
Beheld the dark visions of Los,
And the globe of life-blood trembling.

[Plate 18]
8. The globe of life-blood trembled
Branching out into roots:
Fibrous, writhing upon the winds:
Fibres of blood, milk, and tears:[33]
In pangs, eternity on eternity.
At length, in tears and cries embodied,
A female form trembling and pale
Waves before his deathy face.

## Notes

[32] *For pity divides the soul* Pity is a divisive – and therefore unfavourable – quality for Blake, since it is allied to fear and selfishness. It leads Los to split into two parts, a fallen Los (or Adam) and Enitharmon (or Eve).

[33] *Fibrous…tears* Blake's description of blood seems strange to us, but was up-to-date at the time of writing. Blood was thought to contain fibres and red globules. Other vessels were believed to carry blood, milk, chyle and tears.

9. All Eternity shuddered at sight
Of the first female now separate,[34]
Pale as a cloud of snow
Waving before the face of Los.

10. Wonder, awe, fear, astonishment,
Petrify the eternal myriads
At the first female form now separate.
[Plate 19]
They called her Pity, and fled.

11. 'Spread a tent,[35] with strong curtains around them;
Let cords and stakes bind in the Void,[36]
That Eternals may no more behold them!'

12. They began to weave curtains of darkness;
They erected large pillars round the Void
With golden hooks fastened in the pillars.
With infinite labour the Eternals
A woof wove, and called it 'Science'.

## *Chapter VI*

1. But Los saw the female and pitied;
He embraced her, she wept, she refused.
In perverse and cruel delight
She fled from his arms, yet he followed.

2. Eternity shuddered when they saw
Man begetting his likeness
On his own divided image.

3. A time passed over, the Eternals
Began to erect the tent;
When Enitharmon sick,
Felt a Worm[37] within her womb.

4. Yet helpless it lay like a Worm
In the trembling womb
To be moulded into existence.

### Notes

[34] *All Eternity...separate* The Eternals are horrified at the creation of the first female because it implies infinite human division.
[35] *a tent* the sky, the firmament.
[36] *Spread a tent...Void* Blake recalls Isaiah 54:2: 'Enlarge the place of thy tent, and let them stretch forth the curtains of thine habitations: spare not, lengthen thy cords, and strengthen thy stakes.'
[37] *a Worm* 'seminal worms' were believed to be the seed of the human nervous system.

5. All day the worm lay on her bosom;
All night within her womb
The worm lay till it grew to a serpent,
With dolorous hissings and poisons
Round Enitharmon's loins folding.

6. Coiled within Enitharmon's womb,
The serpent grew, casting its scales;
With sharp pangs the hissings began
To change to a grating cry;
Many sorrows and dismal throes,
Many forms of fish, bird and beast,
Brought forth an Infant form[38]
Where was a worm before.

7. The Eternals their tent finished
Alarmed with these gloomy visions,
When Enitharmon groaning
Produced a man Child to the light.

8. A shriek ran through Eternity:
And a paralytic stroke
At the birth of the Human shadow.

9. Delving earth in his resistless way,
Howling, the Child with fierce flames
Issued from Enitharmon.

10. The Eternals closed the tent.
They beat down the stakes, the cords
[Plate 20]
Stretched for a work of eternity;
No more Los beheld Eternity.

11. In his hands he seized the infant,[39]
He bathed him in springs of sorrow,
He gave him to Enitharmon.

## *Chapter VII*

1. They named the child Orc, he grew
Fed with milk of Enitharmon.

2. Los awoke her; oh sorrow and pain!
A tight'ning girdle grew
Around his bosom. In sobbings

## Notes

[38] *Brought forth an Infant form* The apocalyptic tone is heightened by the echo of Revelation 12:5, where the 'woman clothed with the sun' 'brought forth a man child'.

[39] *he seized the infant* cf. the child of the 'woman clothed with the sun' in Revelation, which 'was caught up unto God, and to his throne' (Revelation 12:5).

He burst the girdle in twain,
But still another girdle
Oppressed his bosom. In sobbings
Again he burst it. Again
Another girdle succeeds;
The girdle was formed by day,
By night was burst in twain.

3. These falling down on the rock
Into an iron chain
In each other link by link locked.

4. They took Orc to the top of a mountain –
Oh how Enitharmon wept!
They chained his young limbs to the rock[40]
With the Chain of Jealousy
Beneath Urizen's deathful shadow.

5. The dead heard the voice of the child
And began to awake from sleep;
All things heard the voice of the child
And began to awake to life.

6. And Urizen craving with hunger
Stung with the odours of Nature
Explored his dens around.

7. He formed a line and a plummet
To divide the Abyss beneath.
He formed a dividing rule;

8. He formed scales to weigh;
He formed massy weights;
He formed a brazen quadrant;
He formed golden compasses
And began to explore the Abyss,
And he planted a garden of fruits.

9. But Los encircled Enitharmon
With fires of Prophecy
From the sight of Urizen and Orc.

10. And she bore an enormous race.

## Notes

[40] *They chained...rock* cf. Abraham's binding of Isaac to the altar (Genesis 22:9); Laius's piercing of Oedipus's ankles when abandoning him to the wolves; and Jupiter's nailing of Prometheus to the rock of the Caucasus.

## Chapter VIII

1. Urizen explored his dens –
Mountain, moor and wilderness,
With a globe of fire lighting his journey,
A fearful journey, annoyed
By cruel enormities, forms
[Plate 22]
Of life on his forsaken mountains.

2. And his world teemed vast enormities
Fright'ning, faithless, fawning
Portions of life; similitudes
Of a foot, or a hand, or a head,
Or a heart, or an eye, they swam, mischievous
Dread terrors! delighting in blood.

3. Most Urizen sickened to see
His eternal creations appear –
Sons and daughters of sorrow on mountains
Weeping! wailing! First Thiriel appeared,
Astonished at his own existence
Like a man from a cloud born; and Utha
From the waters emerging, laments;
Grodna rent the deep earth howling
Amazed! his heavens immense cracks
Like the ground parched with heat; then Fuzon
Flamed out! – first begotten, last born.[41]
All his eternal sons in like manner,
His daughters from green herbs and cattle,
From monsters and worms of the pit;

4. He, in darkness closed, viewed all his race
And his soul sickened![42] He cursed
Both sons and daughters, for he saw
That no flesh nor spirit could keep
His iron laws one moment.

5. For he saw that life lived upon death;
[Plate 25]
The ox in the slaughterhouse moans,
The dog at the wintry door.
And he wept, and he called it 'Pity',
And his tears flowed down on the winds.

## Notes

[41] Thiriel (air), Utha (water), Grodna (earth) and Fuzon (fire) correspond to the four elements.

[42] *He…sickened* There is no way the fall from a state of original innocence can be reversed, as Urizen realizes.

6. Cold he wandered on high, over their cities
In weeping and pain and woe;
And wherever he wandered in sorrows
Upon the aged heavens
A cold shadow followed behind him
Like a spider's web – moist, cold and dim,
Drawing out from his sorrowing soul
The dungeon-like heaven dividing,
Wherever the footsteps of Urizen
Walked over the cities in sorrow.

7. Till a Web dark and cold throughout all
The tormented element stretched
From the sorrows of Urizen's soul;
And the Web is a Female in embryo.
None could break the Web, no wings of fire,

8. So twisted the cords and so knotted
The meshes: twisted like to the human brain.

9. And all called it The Net of Religion.

## *Chapter IX*

1. Then the inhabitants of those Cities[43]
Felt their Nerves change into Marrow,
And hardening bones began
In swift diseases and torments,
In throbbings and shootings and grindings
Through all the coasts; till weakened
The Senses inward rushed, shrinking,
Beneath the dark net of infection;

2. Till the shrunken eyes, clouded over,
Discerned not the woven hypocrisy.
But the streaky slime in their heavens
Brought together by narrowing perceptions
Appeared transparent air; for their eyes
Grew small like the eyes of a man
And in reptile forms shrinking together
Of seven feet stature they remained.

3. Six days they shrunk up from existence
And on the seventh day they rested;

### Notes

[43] *the inhabitants of those Cities* an allusion to the inhabitants of Sodom and Gomorrah, Genesis 19:25: 'And he overthrew those cities, and all the plain, and all the inhabitants of those cities, and that which grew upon the ground.'

And they blessed the seventh day, in sick hope,
And forgot their eternal life.

4. And their thirty cities divided
In form of a human heart;
No more could they rise at will
In the infinite void, but bound down
To earth by their narrowing perceptions
[Plate 27]
They lived a period of years
Then left a noisome[44] body
To the jaws of devouring darkness.

5. And their children wept, and built
Tombs in the desolate places,
And formed laws of prudence, and called them
The eternal laws of God.

6. And the thirty cities remained
Surrounded by salt floods, now called
Africa; its name was then Egypt.

7. The remaining sons of Urizen
Beheld their brethren shrink together
Beneath the net of Urizen:
Persuasion was in vain
For the ears of the inhabitants
Were withered and deafened and cold!
And their eyes could not discern
Their brethren of other cities.

8. So Fuzon called all together
The remaining children of Urizen:
And they left the pendulous earth:[45]
They called it Egypt, and left it.[46]

9. And the salt ocean rolled englobed.

The End of the first book of Urizen

## Notes

[44] *noisome* noxious, foul, rotten.

[45] *the pendulous earth* cf. 'Paradise Lost' iv 1000: 'The pendulous round earth with balanced air.'

[46] *They called it Egypt, and left it* a reworking of the story of how the Israelites were conducted out of Egypt by God, commemo rated in the Passover: 'Remember this day, in which ye came out from Egypt, out of the house of bondage; for by strength of hand the Lord brought you out from this place' (Exodus 18:3).

## *Letter from William Blake to the Revd Dr Trusler,*[1] *23 August 1799* (extract)

Reverend Sir,

I really am sorry that you are fall'n out with the spiritual world, especially if I should have to answer for it. I feel very sorry that your ideas and mine on moral painting differ so much as to have made you angry with my method of study. If I am wrong, I am wrong in good company. I had hoped your plan comprehended all species of this art, and especially that you would not regret that species which gives existence to every other – namely, visions of eternity. You say that I want somebody to elucidate my ideas, but you ought to know that what is grand is necessarily obscure to weak men. That which can be made explicit to the idiot is not worth my care. The wisest of the ancients considered what is not too explicit as the fittest for instruction because it rouses the faculties to act – I name Moses, Solomon, Aesop, Homer, Plato...

I have therefore proved your reasonings ill-proportioned, which you can never prove my figures to be. They are those of Michelangelo, Raphael, and the antique, and of the best living models. I perceive that your eye is perverted by caricature prints, which ought not to abound so much as they do. Fun I love, but too much fun is, of all things, the most loathsome. Mirth is better than fun, and happiness is better than mirth. I feel that a man may be happy in this world. And I know that this world is a world of imagination and vision. I see everything I paint in this world, but everybody does not see alike. To the eyes of a miser, a guinea[2] is more beautiful than the sun, and a bag worn with the use of money has more beautiful proportions than a vine filled with grapes. The tree which moves some to tears of joy is, in the eyes of others, only a green thing that stands in the way. Some see nature all ridicule and deformity (and by these I shall not regulate my proportions), and some scarce see nature at all. But to the eyes of the man of imagination, nature is imagination itself. As a man is, so he sees; as the eye is formed, such are its powers.

You certainly mistake when you say that the visions of fancy are not be found in this world. To me, this world is all one continued vision of fancy or imagination, and I feel flattered when I am told so. What is it sets Homer, Virgil, and Milton in so high a rank of art? Why is the Bible more entertaining and instructive than any other book? Is it not because they are addressed to the imagination (which is spiritual sensation), and but mediately to the understanding or reason? Such is true painting, and such was alone valued by the Greeks and the best modern artists. Consider what Lord Bacon says: 'Sense sends over to imagination before reason have judged, and reason sends over to imagination before the decree can be acted' (see *Advancement of Learning* Part 2, p. 47 of first edition).[3]

But I am happy to find a great majority of fellow mortals who can elucidate my visions – and particularly they have been elucidated by children, who have taken a greater delight in contemplating my pictures than I even hoped. Neither youth nor childhood is folly or incapacity; some children are fools and so are some old men. But there is a vast majority on the side of imagination or spiritual sensation...

## Notes

LETTER FROM WILLIAM BLAKE

[1] Blake had been introduced to John Trusler with a view to his illustrating some of his works, but they fell out when Trusler told him that 'Your fancy seems to be in the other world, or the world of spirits, which accords not with my intentions.' Trusler wrote on this letter the comment: 'Blake, dimmed with superstition'.

[2] *guinea* gold coin worth 21 shillings, not minted since 1813.

[3] Francis Bacon, Baron Verulam, Viscount St Albans (1561–1626) published his *Of the Advancement of Learning* in 1605.

## FROM 'THE PICKERING MANUSCRIPT' (composed 1800–4)

### *The Mental Traveller*

I travelled through a land of men,
A land of men and women too,
And heard and saw such dreadful things
As cold earth-wanderers never knew.

For there the babe is born in joy
That was begotten in dire woe;
Just as we reap in joy the fruit
Which we in bitter tears did sow.

And, if the babe is born a boy,
He's given to a woman old
Who nails him down upon a rock,
Catches his shrieks in cups of gold.

She binds iron thorns around his head,
She pierces both his hands and feet,
She cuts his heart out at his side
To make it feel both cold and heat.

Her fingers number every nerve
Just as a miser counts his gold,
She lives upon his shrieks and cries,
And she grows young as he grows old.

Till he becomes a bleeding youth
And she becomes a virgin bright;
Then he rends up his manacles
And binds her down for his delight.

He plants himself in all her nerves
Just as a husbandman[1] his mould,[2]
And she becomes his dwelling-place,
And garden fruitful seventy-fold.

An aged shadow soon he fades,
Wand'ring round an earthly cot,[3]
Full filled all with gems and gold
Which he by industry had got.

And these are the gems of the human soul,
The rubies and pearls of a lovesick eye,

Notes

[1] *husbandman* farmer.
[2] *mould* soil, earth.
[3] *cot* cottage.

The countless gold of the aching heart,
The martyr's groan and the lover's sigh.

They are his meat, they are his drink;
He feeds the beggar and the poor,
And the wayfaring traveller –
Forever open is his door.

His grief is their eternal joy;
They make the roofs and walls to ring,
Till from the fire on the hearth
A little female babe does spring.

And she is all of solid fire,
And gems and gold, that none his hand
Dares stretch to touch her baby form
Or wrap her in his swaddling-band.

But she comes to the man she loves,
If young or old, or rich or poor.
They soon drive out the aged host –
A beggar at another's door.

He wanders weeping far away
Until some other take him in;
Oft blind and age-bent, sore distressed,
Until he can a maiden win.

And to allay his freezing age
The poor man takes her in his arms;
The cottage fades before his sight,
The garden and its lovely charms;

The guests are scattered through the land.
For the eye altering, alters all;
The senses roll themselves in fear
And the flat earth becomes a ball;

The stars, sun, moon – all shrink away,
A desert vast without a bound;
And nothing left to eat or drink,
And a dark desert all around.

The honey of her infant lips,
The bread and wine of her sweet smile,
The wild game[4] of her roving eye
Does him to infancy beguile.

Notes

[4] *game* sport.

For as he eats and drinks he grows
Younger and younger every day,
And on the desert wild they both
Wander in terror and dismay.

Like the wild stag she flees away,
Her fear plants many a thicket wild;
While he pursues her night and day,
By various arts of love beguiled,

By various arts of love and hate;
Till the wide desert planted o'er
With labyrinths of wayward love,
Where roams the lion, wolf, and boar;

Till he becomes a wayward babe
And she a weeping woman old.
Then many a lover wanders here;
The sun and stars are nearer rolled;

The trees bring forth sweet ecstasy
To all who in the desert roam –
Till many a city there is built,
And many a pleasant shepherd's home.

But when they find the frowning babe,
Terror strikes through the region wide;
They cry, 'The babe, the babe is born!'
And flee away on every side.

For who dare touch the frowning form –
His arm is withered to its root;
Lions, boars, wolves, all howling flee
And every tree does shed its fruit.

And none can touch that frowning form
Except it be a woman old;
She nails him down upon the rock
And all is done as I have told.

### *The Crystal Cabinet*

The maiden caught me in the wild
Where I was dancing merrily,
She put me into her cabinet
And locked me up with a golden key.

This cabinet is formed of gold
And pearl and crystal, shining bright,
And within it opens into a world
And a little lovely moony night.

Another England there I saw,
Another London with its Tower,
Another Thames and other hills
And another pleasant Surrey bower,

Another maiden like herself,
Translucent, lovely, shining clear –
Threefold each in the other closed:
Oh, what a pleasant trembling fear!

Oh, what a smile, a threefold smile
Filled me that like a flame I burned;
I bent to kiss the lovely maid
And found a threefold kiss returned.

I strove to seize the inmost form
With ardour fierce and hands of flame,
But burst the crystal cabinet
And like a weeping babe became –

A weeping babe upon the wild
And weeping woman, pale, reclined.
And in the outward air again
I filled with woes the passing wind.

## FROM 'MILTON' (composed 1803–8)

### *And did those feet in ancient time*[1]

And did those feet in ancient time
Walk upon England's mountains green?
And was the holy lamb of God
On England's pleasant pastures seen?

And did the countenance divine
Shine forth upon our clouded hills?
And was Jerusalem builded here,
Among these dark Satanic mills?

Bring me my bow of burning gold!
Bring me my arrows of desire!
Bring me my spear – oh clouds unfold!
Bring me my chariot of fire![2]

I will not cease from mental fight
Nor shall my sword sleep in my hand,
Till we have built Jerusalem
In England's green and pleasant land.[3]

## Notes

[1] This poem is best known today as a hymn, 'Jerusalem', having been set to music by Hubert Parry in 1916 and arranged by Edward Elgar in 1922.

[2] *Bring me my chariot of fire* a reference to the chariot of fire that carried Elijah to heaven, 2 Kings 2:11.

[3] Would to God that all the Lord's people were Prophets. Numbers XI. Ch 29.v.

# William Wordsworth and Samuel Taylor Coleridge, *Lyrical Ballads* (1798)

*Lyrical Ballads* (1798) is arguably the most important single volume of the period. It signalled a revolution in literary history, and is presented here in its entirety, separately from the author selections, so that readers can experience it in something approaching the shape in which it was first published.

It sprang directly out of the *annus mirabilis* of 1797–8. Its authors spent days in each other's company, from the moment the Wordsworths moved into Alfoxden House in June 1797, four miles' walk from Coleridge's cottage at Nether Stowey, until the following summer when they moved out. That year would change the lives and careers of both men forever. Wordsworth was 27, Coleridge 25 and Dorothy 26. In some ways Coleridge was the more innovatory: he would compose his three greatest poems – 'The Ancient Mariner', 'Kubla Khan' and 'Christabel' (Part I) – and concoct the plan for the poem that would help precipitate the millennium (Christ's thousand-year rule on earth), 'The Recluse', persuading Wordsworth he was the poet who could write it. Together they would plan, write and publish the *Lyrical Ballads*. Dorothy played an indispensable part in all this; her account of these months in her Alfoxden journal is essential reading for anyone wishing to understand the work of this time, not least because its descriptions of the natural world and human psychology constitute a literary achievement in their own right.

The proposal for a joint volume was in the air when, on 20 November 1797, Dorothy noted 'The Ancient Mariner' was to be published 'with some pieces of William's'. In those days poetry tended to be written in ornate rhyming couplets, a style in fashion since the days of Alexander Pope. With the exception of such writers as Cowper and Burns, there were few who wrote in an informal or even a colloquial style. Wordsworth and Coleridge say nothing about 'The Recluse' directly in this volume, but *Lyrical Ballads* is inspired by the vision of a world in which a life-force could enter into the lives of ordinary people through nature, improving them morally, and leading ultimately to a form of non-violent revolution. This underpins 'Tintern Abbey', one of the finest poems in the collection, as well as 'Goody Blake and Harry Gill', 'The Thorn' and 'The Idiot Boy'.

In 'Goody Blake and Harry Gill' Wordsworth explores a medical history that demonstrates how words are capable of altering the physical constitution of an individual. In this case they are delivered in the form of a curse, but the argument of the poem is that blessings have an equal potency. In 'Essays upon Epitaphs' (1810), Wordsworth argued that '[w]ords are too awful an instrument for good and evil to be trifled with: they hold above all other external powers a dominion over thoughts.' The spell Goody Blake casts over Harry Gill is proof of that. Wordsworth does not explain why Gill is stricken – presumably it is due to an unconscious awareness he has behaved unjustly – but that is not what concerns him. The point is to acknowledge the power of words and thus legitimize the idea that a poem could materially alter the political sphere.

'The Thorn' is daring because Wordsworth provides so little commentary on the retired sea-captain who narrates it – for its true subject, disclosed only in passing, is not Martha Ray but the 'adhesive' sensibility of the man obsessed with her. Did she smother her child? Did she bury its corpse? The answers are irrelevant because Martha Ray, who appears to be the subject of the poem, is really a vector for the captain's prurient inquisitiveness. Rather than offer her shelter, he prefers to watch her through his telescope. Nor is he the only one. Despite being aware of her suffering, the village allows her to remain on the hillside, using her as the focus for lurid speculation. And that, rather than the conjectured history of Martha Ray, is Wordsworth's true subject. 'The Thorn' is about a village (and, by implication, a world) that no longer knows how to be human. As with 'Goody Blake and Harry Gill', Wordsworth believed it was only by confronting the fallen world, with all its injustices and cruelties, that paradise could be regained.

In this context, 'The Idiot Boy' is one of the most daring poems in the volume. One of its earliest readers was Scottish man of letters John Wilson, then a student at the University of Glasgow, who told Wordsworth that Johnny Foy generated feelings of 'disgust and contempt': 'It appears almost unnatural that a person in a state of complete idiotism, should excite the warmest feelings of attachment in the breast even of his mother.' Wordsworth answered, 'I have often applied to Idiots, in my own mind, that sublime expression of scripture that, "their life is hidden with God." They are worshipped, probably from a feeling of this sort, in several parts of the East.'

This was an extraordinary thing to say. Far from attempting to compromise, Wordsworth insists Johnny Foy is closer to God, and to visionary enlightenment, than those around him. The poem is designed to bear that out. His mother's fears, though indicative of her love, are shown to be unfounded; the natural forces to which he is surrendered guarantee his well-being, returning him to Betty at the end of the poem. And his uncanny ability to transcend the physical limitations of the world is heightened by transfiguration first into a fairy-tale wanderer riding the night skies, then into a 'silent horseman-ghost' and finally into a 'fierce and dreadful' sheep-hunter. He is at once all of those things and none of them – as if these possibilities, fantastic though they sound, are incapable of containing him for more than the instant it takes us to think of them. 'Mighty prophet! Seer blessed!' Wordsworth would write of Hartley Coleridge in 1804; Johnny Foy's disability, insofar as he has one, manifests itself not in the kind of behaviour John Wilson expected, but in precisely the kind of exalted status attributed to Hartley. Of all the characters in the volume, Johnny Foy is closest to the protagonist of 'The Recluse'.

Although Coleridge was an inspirational force at the time of this collaboration, he had difficulty writing poems to order for *Lyrical Ballads*. Originally it was hoped the finished 'Christabel' would appear in the volume, but Coleridge got no further than Part I. 'The Nightingale' was not written specifically for it, while 'The Dungeon' and 'The Foster Mother's Tale' were quarried from *Osorio*, a play completed in 1797. All the same, 'The Ancient Mariner' remains enduringly popular, and makes an important statement by being the first poem in the book. Wordsworth would come to regret that, and in later editions moved it. For the 1800 edition he wrote a 'note' apologizing for the poem's 'great defects'.

Coleridge may not have composed as many poems as he hoped, but his influence is found throughout, permeating Wordsworth's writing more than at any other time in their careers. His pantheist beliefs strongly colour 'Lines written at a small distance from my house' and the core statement of 'Tintern Abbey':

> And I have felt
> A presence that disturbs me with the joy
> Of elevated thoughts, a sense sublime
> Of something far more deeply interfused,
> Whose dwelling is the light of setting suns,
> And the round ocean, and the living air,
> And the blue sky, and in the mind of man –
> A motion and a spirit that impels
> All thinking things, all objects of all thought,
> And rolls through all things.
>
> (ll. 94–103)

No one recognized the significance of *Lyrical Ballads* when it first appeared in early October 1798. Sales were respectable (such that by 1807 Francis Jeffrey could remark that 'The Lyrical Ballads were unquestionably popular') but few copies sold at first, and along with one or two good reviews it attracted some bad ones. But in due course, *Lyrical Ballads* changed the way in which people read and interpreted poetry. Sales were sufficiently good for the book to be enlarged by a second volume (consisting of poems by Wordsworth only), and for revised editions in 1802 and 1805.

Constituent poems are presented in the order in which they first appeared in *Lyrical Ballads* (1798) – not chronologically as is the case elsewhere in this anthology. Dates of composition and attribution are provided. This information was not available to readers of the first edition, which appeared anonymously (although the authors' identities were widely known in literary circles).

## *Advertisement* (by Wordsworth, working from Coleridge's notes, composed June 1798)

It is the honourable characteristic of poetry that its materials are to be found in every subject which can interest the human mind. The evidence of this fact is to be sought not in the writings of critics, but in those of poets themselves.

The majority of the following poems are to be considered as experiments. They were written chiefly with a view to ascertain how far the language of conversation in the middle and lower classes of society is adapted to the purposes of poetic pleasure.

Readers accustomed to the gaudiness and inane phraseology of many modern writers, if they persist in reading this book to its conclusion, will perhaps frequently have to struggle with feelings of strangeness and awkwardness: they will look round for poetry, and will be induced to enquire by what species of courtesy these attempts can be permitted to assume that title. It is desirable that such readers, for their own sakes, should not suffer the solitary word 'poetry' (a word of very disputed meaning) to stand in the way of their gratification, but that while they are perusing this book, they should ask themselves if it contains a natural delineation of human passions, human characters and human incidents; and, if the answer be favourable to the author's wishes, that they should consent to be pleased in spite of that most dreadful enemy to our pleasures: our own pre-established codes of decision.[1]

Readers of superior judgement may disapprove of the style in which many of these pieces are executed. It must be expected that many lines and phrases will not exactly suit their taste. It will perhaps appear to them that, wishing to avoid the prevalent fault of the day,[2] the author has sometimes descended too low, and that many of his expressions are too familiar, and not of sufficient dignity. It is apprehended that the more conversant the reader is with our elder writers, and with those in modern times who have been the most successful in painting manners[3] and passions,[4] the fewer complaints of this kind will he have to make.

An accurate taste in poetry and in all the other arts, Sir Joshua Reynolds[5] has observed, is an acquired talent which can only be produced by severe thought, and a long continued intercourse with the best models of composition. This is mentioned not with so ridiculous a purpose as to prevent the most inexperienced reader from judging for himself, but merely to temper the rashness of decision, and to suggest that if poetry be a subject on which much time has not been bestowed, the judgement may be erroneous, and that in many cases it necessarily will be so.

### Notes

ADVERTISEMENT

1 *pre-established codes of decision* prejudices.

2 *the prevalent fault of the day* gaudy and inane phraseology.

3 *manners* In a letter of 1799, Wordsworth commends the appearance, in Burns's poetry, of 'manners connected with the permanent objects of nature, and partaking of the simplicity of those objects'.

4 *elder writers...passions* Wordsworth probably has in mind Milton and Shakespeare ('elder writers'), and Burns, Cowper and Joanna Baillie ('those in modern times').

5 Sir Joshua Reynolds (1723–92) was the most renowned portrait-painter of the age. His first discourse was delivered in 1769, and subsequent lectures became yearly fixtures at the Royal Academy.

The tale of 'Goody Blake and Harry Gill' is founded on a well-authenticated fact which happened in Warwickshire.[6] Of the other poems in the collection, it may be proper to say that they are either absolute inventions of the author, or facts which took place within his personal observation or that of his friends.

The poem of 'The Thorn', as the reader will soon discover, is not supposed to be spoken in the author's own person: the character of the loquacious narrator will sufficiently show itself in the course of the story. 'The Rime of the Ancyent Marinere' was professedly written in imitation of the style, as well as of the spirit, of the elder poets. But with a few exceptions, the author believes that the language adopted in it has been equally intelligible for these three last centuries. The lines entitled 'Expostulation and Reply', and those which follow, arose out of conversation with a friend[7] who was somewhat unreasonably attached to modern books of moral philosophy.

## *The Rime of the Ancyent Marinere, in Seven Parts* (by Coleridge, composed November 1797–March 1798)

### *Argument*

How a ship, having passed the line,[1] was driven by storms to the cold country towards the South Pole, and how from thence she made her course to the tropical latitude of the great Pacific Ocean; and of the strange things that befell, and in what manner the ancyent marinere came back to his own country.

I

It is an ancyent marinere,
  And he stoppeth one of three:
'By thy long grey beard and thy glittering eye
  Now wherefore stoppest me?

The bridegroom's doors are opened wide,
  And I am next of kin;
The guests are met, the feast is set –
  Mayst hear the merry din.'

But still he holds the wedding-guest:
  'There was a ship', quoth he –
'Nay, if thou'st got a laughsome tale,
  Marinere, come with me!'

He holds him with his skinny hand,
  Quoth he, 'There was a ship –'
'Now get thee hence, thou grey-beard loon,
  Or my staff shall make thee skip!'

Notes

[6] It was a case history in a medical text, Erasmus Darwin's *Zoönomia* (1794–6).

[7] *a friend* William Hazlitt.

THE RIME OF THE ANCYENT MARINERE, IN SEVEN PARTS

[1] *line* equator.

He holds him with his glittering eye –
  The wedding-guest stood still,
And listens like a three years' child:
  The marinere hath his will.[2]

The wedding-guest sat on a stone,
  He cannot choose but hear;
And thus spake on that ancyent man,
  The bright-eyed marinere:

'The ship was cheered, the harbour cleared,
  Merrily did we drop
Below the kirk, below the hill,
  Below the lighthouse top.

The sun came up upon the left,
  Out of the sea came he;
And he shone bright, and on the right
  Went down into the sea.

Higher and higher every day,
  Till over the mast at noon –'
The wedding-guest here beat his breast,
  For he heard the loud bassoon.

The bride hath paced into the hall,
  Red as a rose is she;
Nodding their heads before her goes
  The merry minstrelsy.

The wedding-guest he beat his breast,
  Yet he cannot choose but hear;
And thus spake on that ancyent man,
  The bright-eyed marinere.

'Listen, stranger! Storm and wind,
  A wind and tempest strong!
For days and weeks it played us freaks –
  Like chaff we drove along.

Listen, stranger! Mist and snow,
  And it grew wondrous cauld:
And ice mast-high came floating by
  As green as emerauld.

Notes

[2] Lines 19–20 are by Wordsworth.

And through the drifts[3] the snowy clifts[4]
Did send a dismal sheen;
Ne shapes of men ne beasts we ken –
The ice was all between.

The ice was here, the ice was there,
The ice was all around;
It cracked and growled, and roared and howled
Like noises of a swound.[5]

At length did cross an albatross,
Thorough the fog it came;
And an[6] it were a Christian soul,[7]
We hailed it in God's name.

The marineres gave it biscuit-worms,
And round and round it flew:
The ice did split with a thunder-fit;
The helmsman steered us through.

And a good south wind sprung up behind,
The albatross did follow;
And every day, for food or play,
Came to the marineres' hollo!

In mist or cloud, on mast or shroud,
It perched for vespers[8] nine,
Whiles all the night, through fogsmoke white,
Glimmered the white moonshine.'

'God save thee, ancyent marinere,
From the fiends that plague thee thus!
Why look'st thou so?' 'With my crossbow
I shot the albatross.[9]

## Notes

[3] *drifts* floating ice.

[4] *clifts* clefts.

[5] *swound* swoon.

[6] *an* as if.

[7] *a Christian soul* i.e. a human being.

[8] *vespers* evenings.

[9] No explanation for the action is given; it was suggested by Wordsworth after reading Shelvocke's *Voyage Round the World* (1726): '[W]e had continual squalls of sleet, snow and rain, and the heavens were perpetually hid from us by gloomy dismal clouds. In short, one would think it impossible that any thing living could subsist in so rigid a climate; and, indeed, we all observed, that we had not had the sight of one fish of any kind, since we were come to the southward of the straits of le Mair, nor one seabird, except a disconsolate black albatross, who accompanied us for several days, hovering about us as if he had lost himself, till Hatley (my second Captain), observing, in one of his melancholy fits, that this bird was always hovering near us, imagined, from his colour, that it might be some ill omen. That which, I suppose, induced him the more to encourage his superstition, was the continued series of contrary tempestuous winds, which had oppressed us ever since we had got into this sea. But be that as it would, he, after some fruitless attempts, at length, shot the albatross, not doubting (perhaps) that we should have a fair wind after it. I must own that this navigation is truly melancholy, and was the more so to us, who were by ourselves without a companion, which would have somewhat diverted our thoughts from the reflection of being in such a remote part of the world.'

II

The sun came up upon the right,
Out of the sea came he;
And broad as a weft[10] upon the left
Went down into the sea.

And the good south wind still blew behind,
But no sweet bird did follow,
Ne any day for food or play
Came to the marineres' hollo!

And I had done an hellish thing
And it would work 'em woe:
For all averred[11] I had killed the bird
That made the breeze to blow.

Ne dim ne red, like God's own head
The glorious sun uprist:
Then all averred I had killed the bird
That brought the fog and mist.
"'Twas right", said they, "such birds to slay,
That bring the fog and mist."

The breezes[12] blew, the white foam flew,
The furrow followed free:
We were the first that ever burst
Into that silent sea.

Down dropt the breeze, the sails dropt down,
'Twas sad as sad could be,
And we did speak only to break
The silence of the sea.

All in a hot and copper sky
The bloody sun at noon
Right up above the mast did stand,
No bigger than the moon.

Day after day, day after day,
We stuck, ne breath ne motion,
As idle as a painted ship
Upon a painted ocean.

Water, water, everywhere,
And all the boards did shrink;
Water, water, everywhere,
Ne any drop to drink.

Notes

[10] *weft* signal-flag.

[11] *averred* maintained that.

[12] *breezes* trade winds.

The very deeps did rot: oh Christ,
  That ever this should be!
Yea, slimy things did crawl with legs
  Upon the slimy sea.

About, about, in reel and rout
  The death-fires danced at night;
The water, like a witch's oils,
  Burnt green and blue and white.

And some in dreams assured were
  Of the spirit that plagued us so;
Nine fathom deep he had followed us
  From the land of mist and snow.

And every tongue, through utter drouth,[13]
  Was withered at the root;
We could not speak, no more than if
  We had been choked with soot.

Ah wel-a-day! what evil looks
  Had I from old and young!
Instead of the cross the albatross
  About my neck was hung.

III

I saw a something in the sky
  No bigger than my fist;
At first it seemed a little speck
  And then it seemed a mist;
It moved and moved, and took at last
  A certain shape, I wist.[14]

A speck, a mist, a shape, I wist!
  And still it nered and nered:
And an it dodged a water-sprite,
  It plunged and tacked and veered.

With throat unslaked, with black lips baked,
  Ne could we laugh, ne wail;
Then while through drouth all dumb they stood,
I bit my arm, and sucked the blood,
  And cried, "A sail! A sail!"

Notes

[13] *drouth* dryness.

[14] *wist* was aware of.

With throat unslaked, with black lips baked,
   Agape they heard me call:
Gramercy![15] they for joy did grin
And all at once their breath drew in
   As they were drinking all.

She doth not tack from side to side
   Hither to work us weal;[16]
Withouten wind, withouten tide
   She steddies with upright keel.

The western wave was all aflame,
   The day was well nigh done!
Almost upon the western wave
   Rested the broad bright sun;
When that strange shape[17] drove suddenly
   Betwixt us and the sun.

And strait the sun was flecked with bars
   (Heaven's Mother send us grace!),
As if through a dungeon-grate he peered
   With broad and burning face.

Alas! thought I, and my heart beat loud,
   How fast she neres and neres!
Are those *her* sails that glance in the sun
   Like restless gossameres?

Are these *her* naked ribs, which flecked
   The sun that did behind them peer?
And are these two all, all the crew,
   That woman and her fleshless pheere?[18]

*His* bones were black with many a crack,
   All black and bare, I ween;
Jet black and bare, save where with rust
Of mouldy damps and charnel crust
   They're patched with purple and green.

*Her* lips are red, *her* looks are free,
   *Her* locks are yellow as gold;
Her skin is as white as leprosy,
And she is far liker death than he,
   Her flesh makes the still air cold.

## Notes

[15] *Gramercy!* mercy on us!
[16] *weal* harm.
[17] *strange shape* According to Wordsworth, the ghost-ship was suggested by a dream of Coleridge's friend and neighbour John Cruikshank, who is said to have seen 'a skeleton ship with figures in it'.
[18] *pheere* companion.

The naked hulk alongside came,
  And the twain were playing dice;
"The game is done! I've won! I've won!"
  Quoth she, and whistled thrice.

A gust of wind sterte up behind
  And whistled through his bones;
Through the holes of his eyes and the hole of his mouth
  Half-whistles and half-groans.

With never a whisper in the sea
  Off darts the spectre-ship;
While clombe[19] above the eastern bar
The horned moon, with one bright star
  Almost atween the tips.[20]

One after one by the horned moon
  (Listen, oh stranger, to me!)
Each turned his face with a ghastly pang
  And cursed me with his ee.

Four times fifty living men,
  With never a sigh or groan,
With heavy thump, a lifeless lump,
  They dropped down one by one.

Their souls did from their bodies fly,
  They fled to bliss or woe;
And every soul, it passed me by
  Like the whiz of my crossbow.'

IV

'I fear thee, ancyent marinere,
  I fear thy skinny hand;
And thou art long and lank and brown
  As is the ribbed sea-sand.[21]

I fear thee and thy glittering eye,
  And thy skinny hand so brown –'
'Fear not, fear not, thou wedding-guest,
  This body dropt not down.

Alone, alone, all all alone,
  Alone on the wide wide sea;
And Christ would take no pity on
  My soul in agony.

## Notes

[19] *clombe* climbed; still used in everyday speech at the time of writing.

[20] *The horned moon…tips* In a copy of *Lyrical Ballads* (1798) now at Trinity College, Cambridge, Coleridge explained: 'It is a common superstition among sailors that something evil is about to happen whenever a star dogs the moon.'

[21] *And thou art long…sea-sand* These two lines are by Wordsworth.

The many men so beautiful,
   And they all dead did lie!
And a million million slimy things
   Lived on – and so did I.

I looked upon the rotting sea
   And drew my eyes away;
I looked upon the eldritch[22] deck,
   And there the dead men lay.

I looked to heaven and tried to pray
   But or ever a prayer had gusht,
A wicked whisper came and made
   My heart as dry as dust.

I closed my lids and kept them close
   Till the balls like pulses beat;
For the sky and the sea, and the sea and the sky
Lay like a load on my weary eye,
   And the dead were at my feet.

The cold sweat melted from their limbs,
   Ne rot, ne reek did they;
The look with which they looked on me
   Had never passed away.

An orphan's curse would drag to hell
   A spirit from on high;
But oh! more horrible than that
   Is the curse in a dead man's eye!
Seven days, seven nights, I saw that curse
   And yet I could not die.

The moving moon went up the sky
   And nowhere did abide;
Softly she was going up
   And a star or two beside;

Her beams bemocked the sultry main
   Like morning frosts yspread;
But where the ship's huge shadow lay
The charmed[23] water burnt alway
   A still and awful red.

Beyond the shadow of the ship
   I watched the water-snakes;
They moved in tracks of shining white,
And when they reared, the elfish light
   Fell off in hoary flakes.

Notes

[22] *eldritch* ghostly.

[23] *charmed* dead calm.

Within the shadow of the ship
   I watched their rich attire:
Blue, glossy green, and velvet black,
They coiled and swam, and every track
   Was a flash of golden fire.

Oh happy living things! no tongue
   Their beauty might declare:
A spring of love gusht from my heart
   And I blessed them unaware!
Sure my kind saint took pity on me,
   And I blessed them unaware.

The self-same moment I could pray,
   And from my neck so free
The albatross fell off and sank
   Like lead into the sea.

V

Oh sleep, it is a gentle thing
   Beloved from pole to pole!
To Mary Queen[24] the praise be yeven;[25]
She sent the gentle sleep from heaven
   That slid into my soul.

The silly[26] buckets on the deck
   That had so long remained,
I dreamt that they were filled with dew
   And when I awoke it rained.

My lips were wet, my throat was cold,
   My garments all were dank;
Sure I had drunken in my dreams
   And still my body drank.

I moved and could not feel my limbs,
   I was so light, almost
I thought that I had died in sleep
   And was a blessed ghost.

The roaring wind – it roared far off,
   It did not come anear;
But with its sound it shook the sails
   That were so thin and sere.[27]

Notes

[24] *Mary Queen* the Virgin Mary.

[25] *yeven* given.

[26] *silly* plain, rustic, homely.

[27] *sere* worn.

The upper air bursts into life
   And a hundred fire-flags sheen,[28]
To and fro they are hurried about;
And to and fro, and in and out
   The stars dance on between.[29]

The coming wind doth roar more loud,
   The sails do sigh like sedge;
The rain pours down from one black cloud,
   And the moon is at its edge.

Hark, hark! The thick black cloud is cleft
   And the moon is at its side;
Like waters shot from some high crag,
The lightning falls with never a jag,
   A river steep and wide.

The strong wind reached the ship, it roared
   And dropped down like a stone!
Beneath the lightning and the moon
   The dead men gave a groan.

They groaned, they stirred, they all uprose,
   Ne spake, ne moved their eyes;
It had been strange, even in a dream,
   To have seen those dead men rise.

The helmsman steered, the ship moved on,
   Yet never a breeze up-blew;
The marineres all gan work the ropes
   Where they were wont to do;
They raised their limbs like lifeless tools –
   We were a ghastly crew.

The body of my brother's son
   Stood by me, knee to knee;
The body and I pulled at one rope
   But he said nought to me –
And I quaked to think of my own voice,
   How frightful it would be!

The daylight dawned, they dropped their arms
   And clustered round the mast;
Sweet sounds rose slowly through their mouths
   And from their bodies passed.

Notes

[28] *sheen* shining.

[29] *The upper air…between* the aurora borealis, which also features in Wordsworth's 'The Complaint of a Forsaken Indian Woman'.

Around, around, flew each sweet sound
   Then darted to the sun;
Slowly the sounds came back again,
   Now mixed, now one by one.

Sometimes a-dropping from the sky
   I heard the lavrock[30] sing;
Sometimes all little birds that are,
How they seemed to fill the sea and air
   With their sweet jargoning![31]

And now 'twas like all instruments,
   Now like a lonely flute,
And now it is an angel's song
   That makes the heavens be mute.

It ceased, yet still the sails made on
   A pleasant noise till noon,
A noise like of a hidden brook
   In the leafy month of June,
That to the sleeping woods all night
   Singeth a quiet tune –

Listen, oh listen, thou wedding-guest!'
   'Marinere, thou hast thy will!
For that which comes out of thine eye doth make
   My body and soul to be still.'

'Never sadder tale was told
   To a man of woman born;
Sadder and wiser thou wedding-guest
   Thou'lt rise tomorrow morn!

Never sadder tale was heard
   By a man of woman born;
The marineres all returned to work
   As silent as beforne.

The marineres all gan pull the ropes,
   But look at me they n'old;[32]
Thought I, I am as thin as air –
   They cannot me behold.

Till noon we silently sailed on,
   Yet never a breeze did breathe;
Slowly and smoothly went the ship,
   Moved onward from beneath.

## Notes

[30] *lavrock* lark.

[31] *jargoning* birdsong.

[32] *n'old* would not.

Under the keel nine fathom deep,
   From the land of mist and snow,
The spirit slid, and it was he
   That made the ship to go.
The sails at noon left off their tune
   And the ship stood still also.

The sun right up above the mast
   Had fixed her to the ocean;
But in a minute she gan stir
   With a short uneasy motion –
Backwards and forwards half her length,
   With a short uneasy motion.

Then like a pawing horse let go,
   She made a sudden bound;
It flung the blood into my head,
   And I fell into a swound.

How long in that same fit I lay,
   I have not to declare;
But ere my living life returned,
I heard and in my soul discerned
   Two voices in the air.

"Is it he?" quoth one, "Is this the man?
   By him who died on cross,
With his cruel bow he laid full low
   The harmless albatross.

The spirit who bideth by himself
   In the land of mist and snow,
He loved the bird that loved the man
   Who shot him with his bow."

The other was a softer voice,
   As soft as honey-dew;
Quoth he, "The man hath penance done
   And penance more will do."'

VI

First Voice
But tell me, tell me! speak again,
   Thy soft response renewing –
What makes that ship drive on so fast?
   What is the ocean doing?

Second Voice
Still as a slave before his lord,
   The ocean hath no blast;
His great bright eye most silently
   Up to the moon is cast –

If he may know which way to go,
For she guides him smooth or grim.
See, brother, see – how graciously
She looketh down on him!

First Voice
But why drives on that ship so fast
Withouten wave or wind?

Second Voice
The air is cut away before
And closes from behind.

Fly, brother, fly! more high, more high,
Or we shall be belated;
For slow and slow that ship will go
When the marinere's trance is abated.

'I woke, and we were sailing on
As in a gentle weather;
'Twas night, calm night, the moon was high –
The dead men stood together.

All stood together on the deck,
For a charnel-dungeon[33] fitter;
All fixed on me their stony eyes
That in the moon did glitter.

The pang, the curse, with which they died
Had never passed away;
I could not draw my een from theirs
Ne turn them up to pray.

And in its time the spell was snapt
And I could move my een;
I looked far forth but little saw
Of what might else be seen –

Like one that on a lonely road
Doth walk in fear and dread,
And having once turned round walks on
And turns no more his head,
Because he knows a frightful fiend
Doth close behind him tread.

But soon there breathed a wind on me,
Ne sound ne motion made;
Its path was not upon the sea,
In ripple or in shade.

Notes

[33] *charnel-dungeon* dungeon containing dead bodies.

It raised my hair, it fanned my cheek,
  Like a meadow-gale of spring –
It mingled strangely with my fears,
  Yet it felt like a welcoming.

Swiftly, swiftly flew the ship,
  Yet she sailed softly too;
Sweetly, sweetly blew the breeze –
  On me alone it blew.

Oh dream of joy! Is this indeed
  The lighthouse top I see?
Is this the hill? Is this the kirk?
  Is this mine own countrée?

We drifted o'er the harbour-bar,[34]
  And I with sobs did pray,
"Oh let me be awake, my God!
  Or let me sleep alway!"

The harbour-bay was clear as glass,
  So smoothly it was strewn![35]
And on the bay the moonlight lay
  And the shadow of the moon.

The moonlight bay was white all o'er
  Till rising from the same,
Full many shapes that shadows were
  Like as of torches came.

A little distance from the prow
  Those dark red shadows were;
But soon I saw that my own flesh
  Was red as in a glare.

I turned my head in fear and dread
  And by the holy rood,[36]
The bodies had advanced, and now
  Before the mast they stood.

They lifted up their stiff right arms,
  They held them strait and tight;
And each right arm burnt like a torch,
  A torch that's borne upright.
Their stony eyeballs glittered on
  In the red and smoky light.

Notes

[34] *harbour-bar* bank of silt across the mouth of the harbour.

[35] *strewn* levelled.

[36] *rood* cross.

I prayed and turned my head away
  Forth looking as before;
There was no breeze upon the bay,
  No wave against the shore.

The rock shone bright, the kirk no less
  That stands above the rock;
The moonlight steeped in silentness
  The steady weathercock.

And the bay was white with silent light,
  Till rising from the same
Full many shapes that shadows were
  In crimson colours came.

A little distance from the prow
  Those crimson shadows were;
I turned my eyes upon the deck –
  Oh Christ! what saw I there?

Each corse lay flat, lifeless and flat,
  And by the holy rood
A man all light, a seraph-man[37]
  On every corse there stood.

This seraph-band, each waved his hand –
  It was a heavenly sight!
They stood as signals to the land,
  Each one a lovely light;

This seraph-band, each waved his hand,
  No voice did they impart –
No voice, but oh! the silence sank
  Like music on my heart.

Eftsones I heard the dash of oars,
  I heard the pilot's cheer;
My head was turned perforce away
  And I saw a boat appear.

Then vanished all the lovely lights,
  The bodies rose anew;
With silent pace each to his place
  Came back the ghastly crew.
The wind that shade nor motion made,
  On me alone it blew.

## Notes

[37] *seraph-man* The seraphim were the highest order of angels, whose purpose was to glow with the love of God.

The pilot and the pilot's boy,
I heard them coming fast –
Dear Lord in heaven! it was a joy
The dead men could not blast.

I saw a third, I heard his voice –
It is the hermit good!
He singeth loud his godly hymns
That he makes in the wood.
He'll shrieve my soul, he'll wash away
The albatross's blood.

VII

This hermit good lives in that wood
Which slopes down to the sea;
How loudly his sweet voice he rears!
He loves to talk with marineres
That come from a far countrée.

He kneels at morn, and noon and eve,
He hath a cushion plump;
It is the moss that wholly hides
The rotted old oak-stump.

The skiff-boat nered, I heard them talk:
"Why, this is strange, I trow!
Where are those lights so many and fair,
That signal made but now?"

"Strange, by my faith!" the hermit said,
"And they answered not our cheer!
The planks look warped, and see those sails,
How thin they are and sere!
I never saw aught like to them
Unless perchance it were

The skeletons of leaves that lag
My forest brook along,
When the ivy-tod[38] is heavy with snow
And the owlet whoops to the wolf below
That eats the she-wolf's young."

"Dear Lord! it has a fiendish look,"
The pilot made reply,
"I am a-feared." "Push on, push on!"
Said the hermit cheerily.

Notes

[38] *ivy-tod* ivy-bush.

The boat came closer to the ship
   But I ne spake ne stirred;
The boat came close beneath the ship
   And strait a sound was heard!

Under the water it rumbled on,
   Still louder and more dread;
It reached the ship, it split the bay –
   The ship went down like lead.

Stunned by that loud and dreadful sound
   Which sky and ocean smote,
Like one that hath been seven days drowned,
   My body lay afloat;
But swift as dreams, myself I found
   Within the pilot's boat.

Upon the whirl where sank the ship
   The boat spun round and round,
And all was still, save that the hill
   Was telling of the sound.

I moved my lips – the pilot shrieked
   And fell down in a fit;
The holy hermit raised his eyes
   And prayed where he did sit.

I took the oars; the pilot's boy,
   Who now doth crazy go,
Laughed loud and long, and all the while
   His eyes went to and fro:
"Ha! ha!" quoth he, "full plain I see
   The Devil knows how to row."

And now all in my own countrée
   I stood on the firm land!
The hermit stepped forth from the boat,
   And scarcely he could stand.

"Oh shrieve me, shrieve me, holy man!"
   The hermit crossed his brow.
"Say quick," quoth he, "I bid thee say
   What manner man art thou?"

Forthwith this frame of mine was wrenched
   With a woeful agony,
Which forced me to begin my tale –
   And then it left me free.

Since then, at an uncertain hour,
   Now oft-times and now fewer,
That anguish comes and makes me tell
   My ghastly aventure.

I pass, like night, from land to land,
  I have strange power of speech;
  The moment that his face I see
I know the man that must hear me –
  To him my tale I teach.

What loud uproar bursts from that door!
  The wedding-guests are there;
But in the garden bower the bride
  And bridemaids singing are;
And hark, the little vesper bell[39]
  Which biddeth me to prayer.

Oh wedding-guest! this soul hath been
  Alone on a wide wide sea;
So lonely 'twas, that God himself
  Scarce seemed there to be.

Oh sweeter than the marriage-feast,
  'Tis sweeter far to me
To walk together to the kirk
  With a goodly company!

To walk together to the kirk
  And all together pray,
While each to his great Father bends,
Old men, and babes, and loving friends,
  And youths and maidens gay.

Farewell, farewell! but this I tell
  To thee, thou wedding-guest!
He prayeth well who loveth well
  Both man and bird and beast.

He prayeth best who loveth best
  All things both great and small,
For the dear God who loveth us,
  He made and loveth all.'

The Marinere, whose eye is bright,
  Whose beard with age is hoar,
Is gone; and now the wedding-guest
  Turned from the bridegroom's door.

He went, like one that hath been stunned
  And is of sense forlorn:
A sadder and a wiser man
  He rose the morrow morn.

Notes

[39] *vesper bell* bell used to summon the congregation for vespers, evensong.

## *The Foster-Mother's Tale: A Dramatic Fragment* (by Coleridge, extracted from *Osorio,* composed April–September 1797)

FOSTER-MOTHER. I never saw the man whom you describe.
MARIA. 'Tis strange! He spake of you familiarly
As mine and Albert's common foster-mother.
FOSTER-MOTHER. Now blessings on the man, whoe'er he be,
That joined your names with mine! Oh my sweet lady,
As often as I think of those dear times
When you two little ones would stand at eve
On each side of my chair, and make me learn
All you had learnt in the day; and how to talk
In gentle phrase, then bid me sing to you
'Tis more like heaven to come than what *has* been!
MARIA. Oh my dear mother! This strange man has left me
Troubled with wilder fancies than the moon
Breeds in the lovesick maid who gazes at it,
Till, lost in inward vision, with wet eye
She gazes idly! But that entrance,[1] Mother!
FOSTER-MOTHER. Can no one hear? It is a perilous tale.
MARIA. No one.
FOSTER-MOTHER. My husband's father told it me,
Poor old Leoni! (Angels rest his soul!)
He was a woodman, and could fell and saw
With lusty[2] arm. You know that huge round beam
Which props the hanging wall of the old chapel?
Beneath that tree, while yet it was a tree,
He found a baby wrapped in mosses lined
With thistle-beards[3] and such small locks of wool
As hang on brambles. Well, he brought him home
And reared him at the then Lord Velez's cost.
And so the babe grew up a pretty boy –
A pretty boy, but most unteachable,
And never learnt a prayer, nor told a bead,[4]
But knew the names of birds, and mocked[5] their notes,
And whistled as he were a bird himself.
And all the autumn 'twas his only play
To get the seeds of wild-flowers, and to plant them
With earth and water on the stumps of trees.
A friar who gathered simples[6] in the wood,
A grey-haired man, he loved this little boy,
The boy loved him. And when the friar taught him,

### Notes

THE FOSTER-MOTHER'S TALE: A DRAMATIC FRAGMENT

[1] *entrance* the entrance to a dungeon.

[2] *lusty* strong.

[3] *thistle-beards* the down or pappus which crowns the 'seeds' of the thistle, by which they are carried along by the wind.

[4] *told a bead* i.e. counted a bead on a rosary.

[5] *mocked* imitated.

[6] *simples* medicinal herbs.

He soon could write with the pen, and from that time
Lived chiefly at the convent or the castle.
So he became a very learned youth.
  But oh, poor wretch – he read, and read, and read,
Till his brain turned! And ere his twentieth year
He had unlawful thoughts of many things,
And though he prayed, he never loved to pray
With holy men, nor in a holy place.
But yet his speech – it was so soft and sweet,
The late Lord Velez ne'er was wearied with him.
And once, as by the north side of the chapel
They stood together, chained in deep discourse,
The earth heaved under them with such a groan
That the wall tottered, and had well-nigh fallen
Right on their heads. My Lord was sorely frightened;
A fever seized him, and he made confession
Of all the heretical and lawless talk
Which brought this judgement: so the youth was seized
And cast into that hole. My husband's father
Sobbed like a child – it almost broke his heart.
And once as he was working in the cellar,
He heard a voice distinctly: 'twas the youth's,
Who sung a doleful song about green fields,
How sweet it were on lake or wild savannah[7]
To hunt for food and be a naked man,[8]
And wander up and down at liberty.
He always doted on the youth and now
His love grew desperate; and, defying death,
He made that cunning entrance I described –
And the young man escaped.
MARIA. 'Tis a sweet tale,
Such as would lull a listening child to sleep,
His rosy face besoiled with unwiped tears.
And what became of him?
FOSTER-MOTHER. He went on shipboard
With those bold voyagers who made discovery
Of golden lands.[9] Leoni's younger brother
Went likewise, and when he returned to Spain,
He told Leoni that the poor mad youth,
Soon after they arrived in that new world,
In spite of his dissuasion, seized a boat,
And all alone set sail by silent moonlight
Up a great river, great as any sea,
And ne'er was heard of more. But 'tis supposed
He lived and died among the savage men.

## Notes

[7] *savannah* treeless plain in tropical America.

[8] *naked man* i.e. savage.

[9] *golden lands* South and Central America.

## *Lines Left upon a Seat in a Yew-Tree which Stands near the Lake of Esthwaite, on a Desolate Part of the Shore, yet Commanding a Beautiful Prospect*[1] (by Wordsworth, composed April–May 1797)

Nay, traveller, rest! This lonely yew-tree stands
Far from all human dwelling. What if here
No sparkling rivulet spread the verdant herb?[2]
What if these barren boughs the bee not loves?
Yet, if the wind breathe soft, the curling waves
That break against the shore shall lull thy mind,
By one soft impulse saved from vacancy.

————————————Who he was
That piled these stones, and with the mossy sod
First covered o'er, and taught this aged tree,
Now wild, to bend its arms in circling shade,[3]
I well remember. He was one who owned
No common soul. In youth by genius nursed,
And big with[4] lofty views, he to the world
Went forth, pure in his heart, against the taint
Of dissolute tongues, 'gainst jealousy and hate
And scorn, against all enemies prepared –
All but neglect. And so his spirit damped
At once, with rash disdain he turned away,
And with the food of pride sustained his soul
In solitude. Stranger, these gloomy boughs
Had charms for him[5] – and here he loved to sit,
His only visitants a straggling sheep,
The stonechat or the glancing sandpiper;
And on these barren rocks, with juniper
And heath and thistle thinly sprinkled o'er,
Fixing his downward eye, he many an hour
A morbid pleasure nourished, tracing here
An emblem of his own unfruitful life.
And lifting up his head, he then would gaze
On the more distant scene – how lovely 'tis
Thou seest – and he would gaze till it became
Far lovelier, and his heart could not sustain
The beauty still more beauteous. Nor, that time,
Would he forget those beings to whose minds,
Warm from the labours of benevolence,
The world, and man himself, appeared a scene
Of kindred loveliness: then he would sigh

### Notes

LINES LEFT UPON A SEAT IN A YEW-TREE

1 Wordsworth had in mind a particular place near Esthwaite Water; the solitary man he describes is partly based on the Revd William Braithwaite, who built a yew-tree seat there.

2 *spread the verdant herb* help the grass to grow.

3 *to bend...shade* In his *Unpublished Tour* Wordsworth recalled how 'the boughs had been trained to bend round the seat and almost embrace the person who might occupy the seat within, allowing only an opening for the beautiful landscape'.

4 *big with* full of.

5 *Had charms for him* an echo of Charlotte Smith's 'Sonnet XII. Written on the Sea Shore' 7: 'But the wild gloomy scene has charms for me.'

With mournful joy, to think that others felt
What he must never feel. And so, lost man,
On visionary views would fancy feed,
Till his eye streamed with tears. In this deep vale
He died, this seat his only monument.
   If thou be one whose heart the holy forms
Of young imagination have kept pure,
Stranger, henceforth be warned – and know that pride,
Howe'er disguised in its own majesty,
Is littleness; that he who feels contempt
For any living thing hath faculties
Which he has never used; that thought with him
Is in its infancy. The man whose eye
Is ever on himself doth look on one
The least of nature's works – one who might move
The wise man to that scorn which wisdom holds
Unlawful ever. Oh be wiser thou!
Instructed that true knowledge leads to love,
True dignity abides with him alone
Who, in the silent hour of inward thought,
Can still suspect, and still revere himself,
In lowliness of heart.

## *The Nightingale; A Conversational Poem, Written in April 1798* (by Coleridge, composed April–May 1798)

No cloud, no relic of the sunken day
Distinguishes the west,[1] no long thin slip
Of sullen[2] light, no obscure trembling hues.
Come, we will rest on this old mossy bridge.
You see the glimmer of the stream beneath
But hear no murmuring: it flows silently
O'er its soft bed of verdure. All is still,
A balmy night, and though the stars be dim
Yet let us think upon the vernal showers
That gladden the green earth, and we shall find
A pleasure in the dimness of the stars.
And hark, the nightingale begins its song –
'Most musical, most melancholy' bird![3]
A melancholy bird? Oh idle thought!
In nature there is nothing melancholy.
   But some night-wandering man whose heart was pierced

## Notes

The Nightingale

[1] *the west* The sun sets in the west.

[2] *sullen* dim.

[3] *'Most musical, most melancholy' bird* Milton, 'Il Penseroso' 62. 'This passage in Milton possesses an excellence far superior to that of mere description: it is spoken in the character of the melancholy man, and has therefore a *dramatic* propriety. The author makes this remark to rescue himself from the charge of having alluded with levity to a line in Milton – a charge than which none could be more painful to him, except perhaps that of having ridiculed his Bible' (Coleridge's note).

With the remembrance of a grievous wrong
Or slow distemper[4] or neglected love
(And so, poor wretch, filled all things with himself
And made all gentle sounds tell back the tale
Of his own sorrows) – he, and such as he,
First named these notes a melancholy strain,
And many a poet echoes the conceit[5] –
Poet who hath been building up the rhyme
When he had better far have stretched his limbs
Beside a brook in mossy forest-dell[6]
By sun or moonlight, to the influxes[7]
Of shapes and sounds and shifting elements
Surrendering his whole spirit, of his song
And of his fame forgetful! So his fame
Should share in nature's immortality
(A venerable thing!), and so his song
Should make all nature lovelier, and itself
Be loved, like nature! But 'twill not be so;
And youths and maidens most poetical[8]
Who lose the deep'ning twilights of the spring
In ballrooms and hot theatres, they still,
Full of meek sympathy, must heave their sighs
O'er Philomela's[9] pity-pleading strains.
   My friend, and my friend's sister,[10] we have learnt
A different lore; we may not thus profane
Nature's sweet voices always full of love
And joyance! 'Tis the merry nightingale
That crowds and hurries and precipitates
With fast thick warble his[11] delicious notes,
As he were fearful that an April night
Would be too short for him to utter forth
His love-chant, and disburden his full soul
Of all its music! And I know a grove
Of large extent, hard by a castle huge[12]
Which the great lord inhabits not – and so
This grove is wild with tangling underwood,
And the trim walks are broken up, and grass,
Thin grass and king-cups grow within the paths.
But never elsewhere in one place I knew
So many nightingales. And far and near
In wood and thicket over the wide grove,

## Notes

[4] *distemper* depression.

[5] *conceit* thought, fancy.

[6] *stretched his limbs…forest-dell* cf. Gray, 'Elegy' 103: 'His listless length at noontide would he stretch, / And pore upon the brook that babbles by.'

[7] *influxes* perceptions entering the mind.

[8] *poetical* immersed in poetical conventions.

[9] *Philomela* Most poets of the time identified the nightingale with Philomela, raped by her brother-in-law, Tereus, King of Thrace. When she revealed what had happened to her sister, she was saved from his rage by being turned into a nightingale.

[10] *My friend, and my friend's sister* William and Dorothy Wordsworth.

[11] *his* Despite the traditional identification of the nightingale with Philomela, Coleridge is technically correct; male nightingales sing as part of the courtship ritual.

[12] *a castle huge* Coleridge probably has in mind Enmore Castle, home of Lord Egmont. It was demolished in 1834.

They answer and provoke each other's songs
With skirmish and capricious passagings,[13]
And murmurs musical and swift jug jug
And one low piping sound more sweet than all,
Stirring the air with such an harmony,
That should you close your eyes, you might almost
Forget it was not day. On moonlight bushes
Whose dewy leafits are but half-disclosed,
You may perchance behold them on the twigs,
Their bright, bright eyes, their eyes both bright and full,
Glist'ning, while many a glow-worm in the shade
Lights up her love-torch.[14]
A most gentle maid[15]
Who dwelleth in her hospitable home
Hard by the castle, and at latest eve
(Even like a lady vowed and dedicate
To something more than nature in the grove)
Glides through the pathways. She knows all their notes,
That gentle maid, and oft, a moment's space,
What time the moon was lost behind a cloud,
Hath heard a pause of silence; till the moon
Emerging hath awakened earth and sky
With one sensation, and those wakeful birds
Have all burst forth in choral minstrelsy,
As if one quick and sudden gale had swept
An hundred airy harps![16] And she hath watched
Many a nightingale perch giddily
On blos'my twig still swinging from the breeze,
And to that motion tune his wanton song,
Like tipsy joy that reels with tossing head.
Farewell, oh warbler, till tomorrow eve!
And you, my friends – farewell, a short farewell!
We have been loitering long and pleasantly,
And now for our dear homes. That strain again!
Full fain it would delay me! My dear babe[17]
Who, capable of no articulate sound,
Mars all things with his imitative lisp –
How he would place his hand beside his ear,
His little hand, the small forefinger up,
And bid us listen! And I deem it wise
To make him nature's playmate. He knows well
The evening star; and once, when he awoke
In most distressful mood (some inward pain
Had made up that strange thing, an infant's dream)

## Notes

[13] *passagings* of music.

[14] *Lights up her love-torch* technically correct; the female glow-worm emits a green light to attract males.

[15] *A most gentle maid* Various real-life counterparts have been suggested, including Dorothy Wordsworth and Ellen Cruikshank, whose father was agent to the Earl of Egmont.

[16] *airy harps* i.e. Aeolian harps.

[17] *My dear babe* Hartley Coleridge. In a notebook entry for 1797, Coleridge describes how Hartley 'fell down and hurt himself. I caught him up crying and screaming, and ran out of doors with him. The moon caught his eye, he ceased crying immediately, and his eyes and the tears in them – how they glittered in the moonlight!'

I hurried with him to our orchard-plot
And he beholds the moon, and hushed at once
Suspends his sobs and laughs most silently,
While his fair eyes that swam with undropped tears
Did glitter in the yellow moonbeam! Well,
It is a father's tale. But if that Heaven
Should give me life, his childhood shall grow up
Familiar with these songs, that with the night
He may associate joy. Once more farewell,
Sweet nightingale! Once more, my friends, farewell!

## *The Female Vagrant* (by Wordsworth, derived from 'Salisbury Plain', initially composed late summer 1793 and revised for inclusion in *Lyrical Ballads*, 1798)

'By Derwent's side[1] my father's cottage stood',
The woman thus her artless story told,
'One field, a flock, and what the neighbouring flood
Supplied, to him were more than mines of gold.
Light was my sleep, my days in transport[2] rolled;
With thoughtless joy I stretched along the shore
My father's nets, or watched (when from the fold
High o'er the cliffs I led my fleecy store),[3]
A dizzy depth below, his boat and twinkling oar.

My father was a good and pious man,
An honest man by honest parents bred,
And I believe that, soon as I began
To lisp, he made me kneel beside my bed,
And in his hearing there my prayers I said;
And afterwards, by my good father taught,
I read, and loved the books in which I read –
For books in every neighbouring house I sought,
And nothing to my mind a sweeter pleasure brought.

Can I forget what charms did once adorn
My garden, stored with peas and mint and thyme,
And rose and lily for the Sabbath morn?
The Sabbath bells, and their delightful chime;
The gambols and wild freaks at shearing time;
My hen's rich nest through long grass scarce espied;
The cowslip-gathering at May's dewy prime;
The swans that, when I sought the waterside,
From far to meet me came, spreading their snowy pride.

## Notes

THE FEMALE VAGRANT

[1] *By Derwent's side* Her father was a fisherman on Derwentwater.

[2] *transport* happiness.

[3] *fleecy store* sheep.

The staff I yet remember, which upbore
The bending body of my active sire;
His seat beneath the honeyed sycamore
When the bees hummed, and chair by winter fire;
When market-morning came, the neat attire
With which, though bent on haste, myself I decked;
My watchful dog, whose starts of furious ire
When stranger passed, so often I have checked;
The redbreast known for years, which at my casement[4] pecked.

The suns of twenty summers danced along –
Ah, little marked, how fast they rolled away!
Then rose a mansion proud our woods among,
And cottage after cottage owned its sway;[5]
No joy to see a neighbouring house, or stray
Through pastures not his own, the master took.
My father dared his greedy wish gainsay:
He loved his old hereditary nook,
And ill could I the thought of such sad parting brook.

But when he had refused the proffered gold,
To cruel injuries he became a prey –
Sore traversed[6] in whate'er he bought and sold.
His troubles grew upon him day by day
Till all his substance fell into decay:
His little range of water was denied,[7]
All but the bed where his old body lay,
All, all was seized, and weeping side by side
We sought a home where we uninjured might abide.

Can I forget that miserable hour
When from the last hilltop my sire surveyed,
Peering above the trees, the steeple tower
That on his marriage-day sweet music made?
Till then he hoped his bones might there be laid
Close by my mother in their native bowers.
Bidding me trust in God, he stood and prayed;
I could not pray – through tears that fell in showers
Glimmered our dear loved home: alas, no longer ours!

There was a youth whom I had loved so long
That when I loved him not I cannot say.
Mid the green mountains many and many a song
We two had sung like little birds in May.
When we began to tire of childish play

## Notes

[4] *casement* window.

[5] *owned its sway* yielded to its power, i.e. was abandoned by its inhabitants.

[6] *traversed* thwarted.

[7] 'Several of the lakes in the north of England are let out to different fishermen, in parcels marked out by imaginary lines drawn from rock to rock' (Wordsworth's note).

We seemed still more and more to prize each other:
We talked of marriage and our marriage-day,
And I in truth did love him like a brother,
For never could I hope to meet with such another.

His father said that to a distant town
He must repair to ply the artist's[8] trade:
What tears of bitter grief till then unknown!
What tender vows our last sad kiss delayed!
To him we turned – we had no other aid.
Like one revived, upon his neck I wept,
And her whom he had loved in joy, he said
He well could love in grief: his faith he kept,
And in a quiet home once more my father slept.

Four years each day with daily bread was blessed,
By constant toil and constant prayer supplied.
Three lovely infants lay upon my breast,
And often, viewing their sweet smiles, I sighed
And knew not why. My happy father died
When sad distress reduced the children's meal –
Thrice happy, that from him the grave did hide
The empty loom,[9] cold hearth and silent wheel,[10]
And tears that flowed for ills which patience could not heal.

'Twas a hard change, an evil time was come:
We had no hope, and no relief could gain.
But soon with proud parade, the noisy drum
Beat round to sweep the streets of want and pain.[11]
My husband's arms now only served to strain
Me and his children hungering in his view.
In such dismay my prayers and tears were vain;
To join those miserable men he flew,
And now to the sea-coast, with numbers more we drew.

There foul neglect for months and months we bore,
Nor yet the crowded fleet its anchor stirred.
Green fields before us and our native shore,
By fever, from polluted air incurred,[12]
Ravage was made for which no knell was heard.[13]
Fondly we wished and wished away, nor knew
Mid that long sickness, and those hopes deferred,
That happier days we never more must view.
The parting signal streamed,[14] at last the land withdrew,

## Notes

[8] *artist* craftsman, artisan.

[9] *empty loom* Her husband was a weaver, and can no longer find work.

[10] *wheel* spinning-wheel, which, in former times, she would have used when work was to be found.

[11] *the noisy drum...pain* Soldiers were enlisted for the American War of Independence in exactly this manner: drummer-boys would parade round provincial towns, followed by conscription officers promising relief from poverty and hunger if men signed up for war. In 1793, when this poem was written, Wordsworth would have seen this process taking place in aid of the war with Revolutionary France (declared February 1793).

[12] *incurred* caught.

[13] *Ravage...heard* Those who died from fever were not given a church funeral.

[14] *streamed* the signal flag streamed in the wind.

But from delay the summer calms were passed.
On as we drove, the equinoctial[15] deep
Ran mountains high before the howling blast.
We gazed with terror on the gloomy sleep
Of them that perished in the whirlwind's sweep,
Untaught that soon such anguish must ensue,
Our hopes such harvest of affliction reap,
That we the mercy of the waves should rue.
We reached the western world,[16] a poor devoted[17] crew.

Oh dreadful price of being to resign
All that is dear *in* being: better far
In Want's most lonely cave till death to pine,
Unseen, unheard, unwatched by any star;
Or, in the streets and walks where proud men are,
Better our dying bodies to obtrude,[18]
Than dog-like, wading at the heels of war,
Protract a cursed existence with the brood
That lap (their very nourishment) their brother's blood.

The pains and plagues that on our heads came down –
Disease and famine, agony and fear,
In wood or wilderness, in camp or town –
It would thy brain unsettle even to hear.
All perished; all, in one remorseless year,
Husband and children! One by one, by sword
And ravenous plague, all perished. Every tear
Dried up, despairing, desolate, on board
A British ship I waked, as from a trance restored.

Peaceful as some immeasurable plain
By the first beams of dawning light impressed,[19]
In the calm sunshine slept the glittering main.
The very ocean has its hour of rest
That comes not to the human mourner's breast.
Remote from man and storms of mortal care,
A heavenly silence did the waves invest;[20]
I looked and looked along the silent air,
Until it seemed to bring a joy to my despair.

Ah, how unlike those late terrific[21] sleeps!
And groans, that rage of racking[22] famine spoke,
Where looks inhuman dwelt on festering heaps![23]

## Notes

[15] *equinoctial* equatorial.
[16] *the western world* America, where the female vagrant's husband was to fight in the War of Independence on the British side.
[17] *devoted* doomed.
[18] *Better...obtrude* Very poor people did starve to death in the streets of London at this time.
[19] *impressed* imprinted, as when, in 'Paradise Lost', the sun 'impressed his beams' on Eden (iv 150).
[20] *the waves invest* cf. Milton's invocation to 'holy light', which 'as with a mantle didst invest / The rising world of waters' ('Paradise Lost' iii 10–11).
[21] *terrific* terrifying.
[22] *racking* Hunger racks the body with pain.
[23] *Where looks...heaps* The image is of heaps of decomposing, unburied corpses, dead from hunger.

The breathing pestilence that rose like smoke![24]
The shriek that from the distant battle broke!
The mine's[25] dire earthquake, and the pallid host[26]
Driven by the bomb's incessant thunderstroke
To loathsome vaults[27] where heartsick anguish tossed,
Hope died, and fear itself in agony was lost!

Yet does that burst of woe congeal my frame
When the dark streets appeared to heave and gape,
While like a sea the storming army[28] came,
And Fire from hell reared his gigantic shape,
And Murder, by the ghastly gleam, and Rape
Seized their joint prey – the mother and the child!
But from these crazing thoughts, my brain, escape!
For weeks the balmy air breathed soft and mild,
And on the gliding vessel heaven and ocean smiled.

Some mighty gulf of separation passed,
I seemed transported to another world:
A thought resigned with pain, when from the mast
The impatient mariner the sail unfurled,
And, whistling, called the wind that hardly curled
The silent sea. From the sweet thoughts of home
And from all hope I was forever hurled.
For me, farthest from earthly port to roam
Was best, could I but shun the spot where man might come.

And oft, robbed of my perfect mind,[29] I thought
At last my feet a resting-place had found.
Here will I weep in peace (so fancy wrought),
Roaming the illimitable waters[30] round;
Here watch, of every human friend disowned,
All day, my ready tomb the ocean flood.
To break my dream the vessel reached its bound,
And homeless near a thousand homes I stood,
And near a thousand tables pined, and wanted[31] food.

By grief enfeebled was I turned adrift,
Helpless as sailor cast on desert rock;
Nor morsel to my mouth that day did lift,
Nor dared my hand at any door to knock.

## Notes

[24] *The breathing…smoke* Disease was thought to be airborne; there is a hint that the 'festering heaps' of corpses mentioned in the preceding line were the source of disease.

[25] *mine* tunnel in which explosives, once detonated, would cause the ground to give way.

[26] *the pallid host* The host (of soldiers) are 'pallid' (wan, pale) because they are starving.

[27] *loathsome vaults* Soldiers blown up by mines would be buried alive by the 'dire earthquake'.

[28] *the storming army* American troops storm the town occupied by the British.

[29] *robbed of…mind* cf. *King Lear* IV vii 62: 'I fear I am not in my perfect mind.'

[30] *the illimitable waters* The sea is like Chaos, 'a dark / Illimitable ocean without bound' ('Paradise Lost' ii 891–2).

[31] *wanted* needed.

I lay where, with his drowsy mates, the cock
From the cross timber of an outhouse[32] hung.
How dismal tolled that night the city clock!
At morn my sick heart-hunger scarcely stung,
Nor to the beggar's language could I frame my tongue.

So passed another day, and so the third.
Then did I try (in vain) the crowd's resort;
In deep despair by frightful wishes stirred,
Near the seaside I reached a ruined fort.
There pains which nature could no more support,
With blindness linked, did on my vitals fall;
Dizzy my brain, with interruption short
Of hideous sense.[33] I sunk, nor step could crawl,
And thence was borne away to neighbouring hospital.

Recovery came with food. But still my brain
Was weak, nor of the past had memory.
I heard my neighbours in their beds complain
Of many things which never troubled me:
Of feet still bustling round with busy glee,
Of looks where common kindness had no part,
Of service done with careless cruelty,
Fretting the fever round the languid heart,
And groans which, as they said, would make a dead man start.

These things just served to stir the torpid sense,
Nor pain nor pity in my bosom raised;
Memory, though slow, returned with strength; and thence
Dismissed, again on open day I gazed
At houses, men and common light, amazed.
The lanes I sought and, as the sun retired,
Came where beneath the trees a faggot blazed.
The wild brood saw me weep, my fate enquired,
And gave me food and rest – more welcome, more desired.

My heart is touched to think that men like these,
The rude earth's tenants, were my first relief.
How kindly did they paint their vagrant ease!
And their long holiday[34] that feared not grief –
For all belonged to all, and each was chief.
No plough their sinews strained; on grating road
No wain they drove; and yet the yellow sheaf
In every vale for their delight was stowed:
For them in nature's meads the milky udder flowed.[35]

## Notes

[32] *outhouse* barn.

[33] *hideous sense* When conscious she was in severe pain.

[34] *their long holiday* Life, to them, was a holiday from care.

[35] *and yet the yellow sheaf... flowed* They took milk and corn wherever they found it.

Semblance, with straw and panniered ass, they made
Of potters wandering on from door to door.
But life of happier sort to me portrayed,
And other joys my fancy to allure:
The bagpipe dinning on the midnight moor
In barn uplighted, and companions boon
Well-met from far with revelry secure
In depth of forest glade, when jocund June
Rolled fast along the sky his warm and genial moon.

But ill it suited me, in journey dark
O'er moor and mountain, midnight theft to hatch;
To charm the surly housedog's faithful bark,
Or hang on tiptoe at the lifted latch.
The gloomy lantern and the dim blue match,
The black disguise, the warning whistle shrill,
And ear still busy on its nightly watch,
Were not for me, brought up in nothing ill.
Besides, on griefs so fresh my thoughts were brooding still.

What could I do, unaided and unblessed?
Poor father, gone was every friend of thine!
And kindred of dead husband are at best
Small help, and after marriage such as mine,
With little kindness would to me incline.
Ill was I then for toil or service fit:
With tears whose course no effort could confine,
By highway-side forgetful would I sit
Whole hours, my idle arms in moping sorrow knit.[36]

I lived upon the mercy of the fields,
And oft of cruelty the sky accused;
On hazard, or what general bounty yields[37] –
Now coldly given, now utterly refused.
The fields I for my bed have often used.
But what afflicts my peace with keenest ruth[38]
Is that I have my inner self abused,
Foregone the home[39] delight of constant truth
And clear and open soul, so prized in fearless youth.

Three years a wanderer, often have I viewed,
In tears, the sun towards that country tend[40]
Where my poor heart lost all its fortitude.
And now across this moor my steps I bend –
Oh tell me whither, for no earthly friend
Have I!' She ceased and, weeping, turned away,
As if because her tale was at an end.
She wept because she had no more to say
Of that perpetual weight which on her spirit lay.

## Notes

[36] *knit* folded.

[37] *On hazard…yields* She lived on charity or what she chanced to find.

[38] *ruth* remorse.

[39] *home* inner.

[40] *the sun…tend* The sun sets in the west.

## *Goody Blake and Harry Gill: A True Story* (by Wordsworth, composed 7–13 March 1798)[1]

Oh what's the matter? What's the matter?
What is't that ails young Harry Gill,
That evermore his teeth they chatter,
Chatter, chatter, chatter still?
Of waistcoats Harry has no lack,
Good duffle grey, and flannel fine;
He has a blanket on his back,
And coats enough to smother nine.

In March, December, and in July,[2]
'Tis all the same with Harry Gill;
The neighbours tell, and tell you truly,
His teeth they chatter, chatter still.
At night, at morning, and at noon,
'Tis all the same with Harry Gill;
Beneath the sun, beneath the moon,
His teeth they chatter, chatter still.

Young Harry was a lusty drover,[3]
And who so stout of limb as he?
His cheeks were red as ruddy clover,
His voice was like the voice of three.
Auld Goody[4] Blake was old and poor,
Ill fed she was, and thinly clad;
And any man who passed her door
Might see how poor a hut she had.

All day she spun in her poor dwelling,
And then her three hours' work at night –
Alas, 'twas hardly worth the telling,
It would not pay for candlelight.
This woman dwelt in Dorsetshire,[5]
Her hut was on a cold hillside,
And in that country[6] coals are dear,[7]
For they come far by wind and tide.

## Notes

Goody Blake and Harry Gill

[1] This poem has a source in a medical treatise, Erasmus Darwin's *Zoönomia* (1794–6), which Wordsworth read in early March 1798: 'A young farmer in Warwickshire, finding his hedges broke, and the sticks carried away during a frosty season, determined to watch for the thief. He lay many cold hours under a haystack, and at length an old woman, like a witch in a play, approached and began to pull up the hedge. He waited till she had tied up her bottle of sticks and was carrying them off, that he might convict her of the theft; and then, springing from his concealment, he seized his prey with violent threats. After some altercation, in which her load was left upon the ground, she kneeled upon her bottle of sticks, and raising her arms to heaven, beneath the bright moon, then at the full, spoke to the farmer (already shivering with cold): "Heaven grant that thou never mayest know again the blessing to be warm!" He complained of cold all the next day, and wore an upper coat – and in a few days another – and in a fortnight took to his bed, always saying nothing made him warm. He covered himself with very many blankets, and had a sieve over his face as he lay; and from this one insane idea he kept his bed above twenty years for fear of the cold air, till at length he died.'

[2] *July* stressed on the first syllable.

[3] *drover* cattle farmer.

[4] *Goody* 'goodwife'; traditional address for a countrywoman, often implying age.

[5] *Dorsetshire* Although Erasmus Darwin (Wordsworth's source) located the story in Warwickshire, Wordsworth places it in Dorset, where he and Dorothy lived, 1795–7.

[6] *country* region.

[7] *coals are dear* Coal was shipped from Wales; it was of poor quality and expensive.

By the same fire to boil their pottage,[8]
Two poor old dames (as I have known)
Will often live in one small cottage,
But she, poor woman, dwelt alone.
'Twas well enough when summer came,
The long, warm, lightsome summer day;
Then at her door the canty[9] dame
Would sit, as any linnet gay.

But when the ice our streams did fetter,[10]
Oh, then how her old bones would shake!
You would have said, if you had met her,
'Twas a hard time for Goody Blake.
Her evenings then were dull and dead –
Sad case it was, as you may think,
For very cold to go to bed,
And then for cold not sleep a wink.

Oh joy for her, whene'er in winter
The winds at night had made a rout,[11]
And scattered many a lusty splinter,
And many a rotten bough about.
Yet never had she, well or sick
(As every man who knew her says),
A pile beforehand, wood or stick,
Enough to warm her for three days.

Now when the frost was past enduring
And made her poor old bones to ache,
Could anything be more alluring
Than an old hedge to Goody Blake?
And now and then, it must be said,
When her old bones were cold and chill,
She left her fire or left her bed
To seek the hedge of Harry Gill.

Now Harry he had long suspected
This trespass of old Goody Blake,
And vowed that she should be detected,
And he on her would vengeance take.
And oft from his warm fire he'd go,
And to the fields his road would take,
And there at night, in frost and snow,
He watched to seize old Goody Blake.

## Notes

[8] *pottage* soup.

[9] *canty* cheerful.

[10] *fetter* chain, bind. The 1790s were a decade notorious for the coldness of its winters; it was a mini ice age.

[11] *rout* party.

And once, behind a rick[12] of barley,
Thus looking out did Harry stand;
The moon was full and shining clearly,
And crisp with frost the stubble-land.
He hears a noise, he's all awake –
Again? On tiptoe down the hill
He softly creeps: 'tis Goody Blake,
She's at the hedge of Harry Gill.

Right glad was he when he beheld her:
Stick after stick did Goody pull.
He stood behind a bush of elder
Till she had filled her apron full.
When with her load she turned about,
The by-road back again to take,
He started forward with a shout
And sprang upon poor Goody Blake.

And fiercely by the arm he took her,
And by the arm he held her fast,
And fiercely by the arm he shook her,
And cried, 'I've caught you then at last!'
Then Goody, who had nothing said,
Her bundle from her lap let fall,
And kneeling on the sticks she prayed
To God that is the judge of all.

She prayed, her withered hand uprearing,
While Harry held her by the arm:
'God, who art never out of hearing –
Oh may he never more be warm!'
The cold, cold moon above her head,
Thus on her knees did Goody pray,
Young Harry heard what she had said,
And icy cold he turned away.

He went complaining all the morrow
That he was cold and very chill;
His face was gloom, his heart was sorrow –
Alas that day for Harry Gill!
That day he wore a riding-coat
But not a whit the warmer he;
Another was on Thursday brought,
And ere the Sabbath he had three.

## Notes

[12] *rick* corn-stack; barley and other grain was cut with a scythe and bound into sheaves, which were stacked and thatched to await threshing.

'Twas all in vain, a useless matter,
And blankets were about him pinned;
Yet still his jaws and teeth they clatter
Like a loose casement[13] in the wind.
And Harry's flesh it fell away,
And all who see him say 'tis plain
That, live as long as live he may,
He never will be warm again.

No word to any man he utters,
Abed or up, to young or old,
But ever to himself he mutters,
'Poor Harry Gill is very cold.'[14]
Abed or up, by night or day,
His teeth they chatter, chatter still:
Now think, ye farmers all, I pray,
Of Goody Blake and Harry Gill.

## *Lines Written at a Small Distance from My House,[1] and Sent by My Little Boy[2] to the Person to Whom They are Addressed* (by Wordsworth, composed 1–9 March 1798)[3]

It is the first mild day of March,
Each minute sweeter than before,
The redbreast sings from the tall larch
That stands beside our door.

There is a blessing in the air
Which seems a sense of joy to yield
To the bare trees and mountains bare,[4]
And grass in the green field.

My sister, 'tis a wish of mine
Now that our morning meal is done –
Make haste, your morning task resign,
Come forth and feel the sun!

Edward[5] will come with you – and pray
Put on with speed your woodland dress,
And bring no book, for this one day
We'll give to idleness.

## Notes

[13] *casement* window.

[14] *Poor…cold* cf. *King Lear* III iv 147: 'Poor Tom's a-cold.'

Lines Written at a Small Distance

[1] *my house* Alfoxden House, where the Wordsworths resided, June 1797–July 1798.

[2] *my little boy* Basil Montagu Jr, whose mother had died, and whose father, a friend of Wordsworth's, was unable to look after him.

[3] Wordsworth later exchanged the cumbersome original title for 'To my Sister'.

[4] *mountains bare* an exaggeration; the Quantock Hills in which Alfoxden House is located do not compare with the mountains of the Lake District.

[5] *Edward* Basil Montagu Jr.

No joyless forms[6] shall regulate
Our living calendar;
We from today, my friend, will date
The opening of the year.[7]

Love, now an universal birth,
From heart to heart is stealing,
From earth to man, from man to earth –
It is the hour of feeling.

One moment now may give us more
Than fifty years of reason;
Our minds shall drink at every pore
The spirit of the season.

Some silent laws[8] our hearts may make
Which they shall long obey;
We for the year to come may take
Our temper[9] from today.

And from the blessed power that rolls
About, below, above,
We'll frame the measure[10] of our souls –
They shall be tuned to love.[11]

Then come, my sister, come, I pray,
With speed put on your woodland dress;
And bring no book, for this one day
We'll give to idleness.

## *Simon Lee, the Old Huntsman, with an Incident in which He Was Concerned* (by Wordsworth, composed between March and 16 May 1798)

In the sweet shire of Cardigan[1]
Not far from pleasant Ivor Hall,
An old man dwells, a little man,
I've heard he once was tall.
Of years he has upon his back,
No doubt, a burden weighty;
He says he is three score and ten,
But others say he's eighty.

## Notes

[6] *forms* rules, conventions.

[7] *We from…year* In 1793 the French completely reorganized their calendar to begin from the birth of the republic (22 September 1792) rather than that of Christ.

[8] *silent laws* effectively, New Year's resolutions.

[9] *temper* constitution.

[10] *measure* rhythm, harmony.

[11] *And from…love* a memorable expression of the pantheistic credo that was imparted to Wordsworth by Coleridge, also to be found in 'Tintern Abbey' 94–103.

Simon Lee

[1] *Cardigan* Cardiganshire is on the west coast of Wales; however, Simon Lee's real-life counterpart was Christopher Tricky, the huntsman who lived in a cottage on the common near Alfoxden Park.

A long blue livery-coat[2] has he
That's fair behind and fair before;
Yet meet him where you will, you see
At once that he is poor.
Full five and twenty years he lived
A running huntsman[3] merry,
And though he has but one eye left,
His cheek is like a cherry.

No man like him the horn could sound,
And no man was so full of glee;
To say the least, four counties round
Had heard of Simon Lee.
His master's dead, and no one now
Dwells in the Hall of Ivor,
Men, dogs, and horses – all are dead;
He is the sole survivor.

His hunting feats have him bereft
Of his right eye, as you may see;
And then, what limbs those feats have left
To poor old Simon Lee!
He has no son, he has no child;
His wife, an aged woman,
Lives with him near the waterfall,
Upon the village[4] common.

And he is lean and he is sick,
His little body's half awry,[5]
His ankles they are swoln and thick,
His legs are thin and dry.
When he was young he little knew
Of husbandry or tillage,[6]
And now he's forced to work, though weak –
The weakest in the village.

He all the country[7] could outrun,
Could leave both man and horse behind;
And often, ere the race was done,
He reeled and was stone-blind.[8]
And still there's something in the world
At which his heart rejoices,
For when the chiming[9] hounds are out
He dearly loves their voices!

## Notes

[2] *livery-coat* as worn by the retainer of an aristocratic family.

[3] *running huntsman* Simon would have hunted on foot, running alongside the gentry who rode on horseback.

[4] *village* Holford.

[5] *awry* twisted, bent.

[6] *tillage* cultivation of the land.

[7] *country* region.

[8] *stone-blind* totally blind.

[9] *chiming* barking together.

Old Ruth works out of doors with him
And does what Simon cannot do;
For she, not over-stout of limb,
Is stouter of the two.
And though you with your utmost skill
From labour could not wean them,
Alas, 'tis very little, all
Which they can do between them!

Beside their moss-grown hut of clay
Not twenty paces from the door,
A scrap of land they have, but they
Are poorest of the poor.
This scrap of land he from the heath
Enclosed when he was stronger,
But what avails the land to them
Which they can till no longer?

Few months of life has he in store
As he to you will tell,
For still, the more he works, the more
His poor old ankles swell.
My gentle reader, I perceive
How patiently you've waited,
And I'm afraid that you expect
Some tale will be related.

Oh reader, had you in your mind
Such stores as silent thought can bring –
Oh gentle reader, you would find
A tale in every thing.
What more I have to say is short,
I hope you'll kindly take it;
It is no tale, but, should you think,
Perhaps a tale you'll make it.

One summer day I chanced to see
This old man doing all he could
About the root of an old tree,
A stump of rotten wood.
The mattock[10] tottered in his hand;
So vain was his endeavour,
That at the root of the old tree
He might have worked forever.

'You're overtasked, good Simon Lee,
Give me your tool,' to him I said;
And at the word, right gladly he
Received my proffered aid.

Notes

[10] *mattock* tool for tilling the ground.

I struck, and with a single blow
The tangled root I severed,
At which the poor old man so long
And vainly had endeavoured.

The tears into his eyes were brought,
And thanks and praises seemed to run
So fast out of his heart, I thought
They never would have done.
I've heard of hearts unkind, kind deeds
With coldness still returning;
Alas, the gratitude of men
Has oft'ner left me mourning.

## *Anecdote for Fathers, Showing How the Art of Lying May Be Taught* (by Wordsworth, composed between April and 16 May 1798)

I have a boy of five years old,[1]
His face is fair and fresh to see,
His limbs are cast in beauty's mould,
And dearly he loves me.

One morn we strolled on our dry walk,
Our quiet house all full in view,
And held such intermitted talk
As we are wont[2] to do.

My thoughts on former pleasures ran;
I thought of Kilve's[3] delightful shore –
My pleasant home when spring began
A long long year before.

A day it was when I could bear
To think, and think, and think again;
With so much happiness to spare
I could not feel a pain.

My boy was by my side, so slim
And graceful in his rustic dress!
And oftentimes I talked to him
In very idleness.

## Notes

Anecdote for Fathers

[1] *a boy of five years old* Basil Montagu Jr, the son of Wordsworth's friend Basil Montagu.

[2] *wont* used.

[3] *Kilve* small village on the Somersetshire coast, not far from Alfoxden. It is pronounced as a single syllable.

The young lambs ran a pretty race,
The morning sun shone bright and warm;
'Kilve', said I, 'was a pleasant place,
And so is Liswyn farm.[4]

My little boy, which like you more?'
I said and took him by the arm,
'Our home by Kilve's delightful shore,
Or here at Liswyn farm?

And tell me, had you rather be
(I said and held him by the arm)
At Kilve's smooth shore by the green sea
Or here at Liswyn farm?'

In careless mood he looked at me
While still I held him by the arm
And said, 'At Kilve I'd rather be
Than here at Liswyn farm.'

'Now, little Edward, say why so,
My little Edward, tell me why.'
'I cannot tell, I do not know.'
'Why this is strange!' said I.

'For here are woods and green hills warm;
There surely must some reason be
Why you would change sweet Liswyn farm
For Kilve by the green sea.'

At this, my boy, so fair and slim,
Hung down his head, nor made reply,
And five times did I say to him,
'Why? Edward, tell me why?'

His head he raised; there was in sight –
It caught his eye, he saw it plain –
Upon the house-top, glittering bright,
A broad and gilded vane.[5]

Then did the boy his tongue unlock
And thus to me he made reply;
'At Kilve there was no weathercock,
And that's the reason why.'

## Notes

[4] *Liswyn farm* John Thelwall, who visited Wordsworth and Coleridge in Somerset in July 1797, had retreated to Llys Wen farm in Wales. Dorothy and William went there for the first time in early August 1798.

[5] *vane* weather-cock.

Oh dearest, dearest boy! my heart
For better lore would seldom yearn,
Could I but teach the hundredth part
Of what from thee I learn.

## *We Are Seven* (by Wordsworth, composed between April and 16 May 1798)

A simple child, dear brother Jim,[1]
That lightly draws its breath,
And feels its life in every limb –
What should it know of death?

I met a little cottage girl,[2]
She was eight years old, she said;
Her hair was thick with many a curl
That clustered round her head.

She had a rustic woodland air
And she was wildly clad;
Her eyes were fair, and very fair –
Her beauty made me glad.

'Sisters and brothers, little maid,
How many may you be?'
'How many? Seven in all', she said,
And wondering looked at me.

'And where are they, I pray you tell?'
She answered, 'Seven are we,
And two of us at Conway[3] dwell,
And two are gone to sea.

Two of us in the churchyard lie
(My sister and my brother),
And in the churchyard cottage I
Dwell near them with my mother.'

'You say that two at Conway dwell
And two are gone to sea,
Yet you are seven – I pray you tell,
Sweet maid, how this may be?'

## Notes

We Are Seven

[1] *Jim* James Tobin, a friend of Wordsworth and Coleridge's. The first line of the poem was written impromptu by Coleridge.

[2] *I met…girl* The poem is based on Wordsworth's meeting with a child near Goodrich Castle on the River Wye in summer 1793.

[3] *Conway* a seaport in north Wales, about 120 miles north of Goodrich Castle.

Then did the little maid reply,
'Seven boys and girls are we;
Two of us in the churchyard lie
Beneath the churchyard tree.'

'You run about, my little maid,
Your limbs they are alive;
If two are in the churchyard laid,
Then ye are only five.'

'Their graves are green, they may be seen',[4]
The little maid replied,
'Twelve steps or more from my mother's door,
And they are side by side.

My stockings there I often knit,
My kerchief[5] there I hem,
And there upon the ground I sit,
I sit and sing to them.

And often after sunset, sir,
When it is light and fair,
I take my little porringer[6]
And eat my supper there.

The first that died was little Jane,
In bed she moaning lay,
Till God released her of her pain
And then she went away.

So in the churchyard she was laid
And all the summer dry,
Together round her grave we played,
My brother John and I.

And when the ground was white with snow,
And I could run and slide,
My brother John was forced to go,
And he lies by her side.'

'How many are you then', said I,
'If they two are in heaven?'
The little maiden did reply,
'Oh master, we are seven!'

## Notes

[4] *Their graves…seen* The child regards the graves as proof her siblings are alive.

[5] *kerchief* headscarf.

[6] *porringer* wooden soup-bowl.

'But they are dead – those two are dead!
Their spirits are in heaven!'
'Twas throwing words away, for still
The little maid would have her will
And said, 'Nay, we are seven!'

## *Lines Written in Early Spring* (by Wordsworth, composed *c.*12 April 1798)[1]

I heard a thousand blended notes[2]
While in a grove I sat reclined
In that sweet mood when pleasant thoughts
Bring sad thoughts to the mind.

To her fair works did nature link
The human soul that through me ran,
And much it grieved my heart to think
What man has made of man.

Through primrose-tufts, in that sweet bower,
The periwinkle[3] trailed its wreaths;
And 'tis my faith that every flower
Enjoys the air it breathes.[4]

The birds around me hopped and played,
Their thoughts I cannot measure,
But the least motion which they made –
It seemed a thrill of pleasure.

The budding twigs spread out their fan
To catch the breezy air;
And I must think, do all I can,
That there was pleasure there.

If I these thoughts may not prevent,
If such be of my creed[5] the plan,
Have I not reason to lament
What man has made of man?

## Notes

Lines Written in Early Spring

[1] According to Wordsworth this poem was 'composed while I was sitting by the side of the brook that runs down the coomb (in which stands the village of Holford), through the grounds of Alfoxden. It was a chosen resort of mine. The brook fell down a sloping rock so as to make a waterfall considerable for that country, and, across the pool below, had fallen a tree, an ash if I rightly remember, from which rose perpendicularly boughs in search of the light intercepted by the deep shade above'.

[2] *notes* pronounced so as to rhyme with 'thoughts', as Wordsworth, with his Cumbrian accent, would have done.

[3] *periwinkle* evergreen trailing plant with light blue flowers (US myrtle).

[4] *And 'tis…breathes* Wordsworth was up-to-date in his botanical knowledge; in 1791 Erasmus Darwin had written, in *The Economy of Vegetation*, that leaves function as lungs.

[5] *creed* credo, belief.

# *The Thorn* (by Wordsworth, composed between 19 March and 20 April 1798)[1]

I

'There is a thorn, it looks so old,
In truth you'd find it hard to say
How it could ever have been young,
It looks so old and grey.
Not higher than a two years' child,
It stands erect, this aged thorn;
No leaves it has, no thorny points –
It is a mass of knotted joints,
A wretched thing forlorn.
It stands erect and, like a stone,
With lichens[2] it is overgrown.

II

Like rock or stone, it is o'ergrown
With lichens to the very top,
And hung with heavy tufts of moss,
A melancholy crop;
Up from the earth these mosses creep,
And this poor thorn they clasp it round
So close, you'd say that they were bent
With plain and manifest intent
To drag it to the ground –
And all had joined in one endeavour
To bury this poor thorn for ever.

III

High on a mountain's highest ridge
Where oft the stormy winter gale
Cuts like a scythe, while through the clouds
It sweeps from vale to vale;
Not five yards from the mountain path
This thorn you on your left espy,
And to the left, three yards beyond,
You see a little muddy pond
Of water, never dry.
I've measured it from side to side;
'Tis three feet long and two feet wide.

## Notes

The Thorn

[1] Wordsworth recalled this poem 'arose out of my observing, on the ridge of Quantock Hill, on a stormy day, a thorn which I had often passed in calm and bright weather without noticing it. I said to myself, "Cannot I by some invention do as much to make this thorn permanently an impressive object as the storm has made it to my eyes at this moment?" I began the poem accordingly, and composed it with great rapidity.'

[2] *lichens* slow-growing grey-green plants encrusting the surface of old walls, trees and thorn bushes.

IV

And close beside this aged thorn
There is a fresh and lovely sight,
A beauteous heap, a hill of moss,
Just half a foot in height.
All lovely colours there you see,
All colours that were ever seen,
And mossy net-work[3] too is there,
As if by hand of lady fair
The work had woven been,
And cups,[4] the darlings of the eye,
So deep is their vermilion dye.

V

Ah me, what lovely tints are there
Of olive-green and scarlet bright!
In spikes, in branches, and in stars,
Green, red, and pearly white.
This heap of earth o'ergrown with moss,
Which close beside the thorn you see,
So fresh in all its beauteous dyes,
Is like an infant's grave in size,
As like as like can be;
But never, never, anywhere
An infant's grave was half so fair.

VI

Now would you see this aged thorn,
This pond and beauteous hill of moss,
You must take care and choose your time
The mountain when to cross.
For oft there sits, between the heap
That's like an infant's grave in size
And that same pond of which I spoke,
A woman in a scarlet cloak,[5]
And to herself she cries,
"Oh misery! Oh misery!
Oh woe is me! Oh misery!"

VII

At all times of the day and night
This wretched woman thither goes,
And she is known to every star
And every wind that blows;
And there beside the thorn she sits

Notes

[3] *net-work* embroidery.

[4] *cups* blooms.

[5] *a scarlet cloak* traditionally associated with guilt and sin; cf. the whore of Babylon 'arrayed in purple, and scarlet colour' (Revelation 17:4).

When the blue daylight's in the skies,
And when the whirlwind's on the hill,
Or frosty air is keen and still,
And to herself she cries,
"Oh misery! Oh misery!
Oh woe is me! Oh misery!"'

VIII

'Now wherefore thus, by day and night,
In rain, in tempest, and in snow,
Thus to the dreary mountain-top
Does this poor woman go?
And why sits she beside the thorn
When the blue daylight's in the sky,
Or when the whirlwind's on the hill,
Or frosty air is keen and still,
And wherefore does she cry?
Oh wherefore, wherefore, tell me why
Does she repeat that doleful cry?'

IX

'I cannot tell, I wish I could;
For the true reason no one knows.
But if you'd gladly view the spot,
The spot to which she goes –
The heap that's like an infant's grave,
The pond, and thorn so old and grey –
Pass by her door ('tis seldom shut),
And if you see her in her hut,[6]
Then to the spot away!
I never heard of such as dare
Approach the spot when she is there.'

X

'But wherefore to the mountain-top
Can this unhappy woman go,
Whatever star is in the skies,
Whatever wind may blow?'
'Nay rack your brain, 'tis all in vain –
I'll tell you everything I know;
But to the thorn, and to the pond
Which is a little step beyond,
I wish that you would go.
Perhaps when you are at the place
You something of her tale may trace.

Notes

[6] *hut* cottage.

XI

I'll give you the best help I can:
Before you up the mountain go,
Up to the dreary mountain-top,
I'll tell you all I know.
'Tis now some two and twenty years
Since she (her name is Martha Ray)[7]
Gave with a maiden's true goodwill
Her company to Stephen Hill,
And she was blithe and gay,
And she was happy, happy still
Whene'er she thought of Stephen Hill.

XII

And they had fixed the wedding-day,
The morning that must wed them both,
But Stephen to another maid
Had sworn another oath,
And with this other maid to church
Unthinking Stephen went –
Poor Martha! On that woeful day
A cruel, cruel fire, they say,
Into her bones was sent:
It dried her body like a cinder
And almost turned her brain to tinder.

XIII

They say full six months after this,
While yet the summer leaves were green,
She to the mountain-top would go,
And there was often seen;
'Tis said a child was in her womb,
As now to any eye was plain –
She was with child and she was mad,
Yet often she was sober-sad
From her exceeding pain.
Oh me! Ten thousand times I'd rather
That he had died, that cruel father!

XIV

Sad case for such a brain to hold
Communion with a stirring child!
Sad case (as you may think) for one
Who had a brain so wild!
Last Christmas when we talked of this,

## Notes

[7] *Martha Ray* the mother of Wordsworth's friend Basil Montagu, and grandmother of Basil Montagu Jr, whom he and Dorothy were looking after at Alfoxden. Ray had been the mistress of the 4th Earl of Sandwich, and on 7 April 1779 was shot dead on the steps of Covent Garden Theatre by a jealous lover, the Revd James Hackman.

Old Farmer Simpson did maintain
That in her womb the infant wrought
About its mother's heart, and brought
Her senses back again;
And when at last her time drew near,
Her looks were calm, her senses clear.

XV

No more I know – I wish I did,
And I would tell it all to you.
For what became of this poor child
There's none that ever knew;
And if a child was born or no,
There's no one that could ever tell;
And if 'twas born alive or dead,
There's no one knows, as I have said.
But some remember well
That Martha Ray about this time
Would up the mountain often climb.

XVI

And all that winter, when at night
The wind blew from the mountain-peak,
'Twas worth your while, though in the dark,
The churchyard path to seek:
For many a time and oft were heard
Cries coming from the mountain-head.
Some plainly living voices were,
And others, I've heard many swear,
Were voices of the dead.
I cannot think, whate'er they say,
They had to do with Martha Ray.

XVII

But that she goes to this old thorn,
The thorn which I've described to you,
And there sits in a scarlet cloak,
I will be sworn is true.
For one day with my telescope,
To view the ocean wide and bright,
When to this country[8] first I came,
Ere I had heard of Martha's name,
I climbed the mountain's height;
A storm came on, and I could see
No object higher than my knee.

Notes

[8] *country* area, district.

XVIII

'Twas mist and rain, and storm and rain,
No screen, no fence could I discover;[9]
And then the wind – in faith, it was
A wind full ten times over!
I looked around, I thought I saw
A jutting crag, and off I ran
Head-foremost through the driving rain,
The shelter of the crag to gain;
And, as I am a man,
Instead of jutting crag, I found
A woman seated on the ground.

XIX

I did not speak – I saw her face,
Her face it was enough for me;
I turned about and heard her cry,
"Oh misery! Oh misery!"
And there she sits, until the moon
Through half the clear blue sky will go,
And when the little breezes make
The waters of the pond to shake,
As all the country know,
She shudders and you hear her cry,
"Oh misery! Oh misery!"'

XX

'But what's the thorn? And what's the pond?
And what's the hill of moss to her?
And what's the creeping breeze that comes
The little pond to stir?'
'I cannot tell, but some will say
She hanged her baby on the tree;
Some say she drowned it in the pond
Which is a little step beyond;
But all and each agree
The little babe was buried there,
Beneath that hill of moss so fair.

XXI

I've heard the scarlet moss is red
With drops of that poor infant's blood –
But kill a new-born infant thus?
I do not think she could.
Some say, if to the pond you go,
And fix on it a steady view,

Notes

[9] *discover* see.

The shadow of a babe you trace,
A baby and a baby's face,
And that it looks at you;
Whene'er you look on it, 'tis plain
The baby looks at you again.

XXII

And some had sworn an oath that she
Should be to public justice brought,
And for the little infant's bones
With spades they would have sought.
But then the beauteous hill of moss
Before their eyes began to stir,
And for full fifty yards around,
The grass it shook upon the ground.
But all do still aver[10]
The little babe is buried there,
Beneath that hill of moss so fair.

XXIII

I cannot tell how this may be,
But plain it is, the thorn is bound
With heavy tufts of moss that strive
To drag it to the ground.
And this I know, full many a time
When she was on the mountain high,
By day, and in the silent night,
When all the stars shone clear and bright,
That I have heard her cry,
"Oh misery! Oh misery!
Oh woe is me! Oh misery!"'

## *The Last of the Flock* (by Wordsworth, composed between March and 16 May 1798)[1]

In distant countries I have been,
And yet I have not often seen
A healthy man, a man full grown,
Weep in the public roads alone.
But such a one on English ground
And in the broad highway, I met;

Notes

[10] *aver* maintain.

The Last of the Flock

[1] In later years Wordsworth recalled the encounter described here 'occurred in the village of Holford, close by Alfoxden'. It was apparently relayed to him by one of those who had taken part: 'I never in my whole life saw a man weep alone in the roads; but a friend of mine did see this poor man weeping alone, with the lamb, the last of the flock, in his arms.'

Along the broad highway he came,
His cheeks with tears were wet.
Sturdy he seemed, though he was sad,
And in his arms a lamb he had.

He saw me and he turned aside
As if he wished himself to hide;
Then with his coat he made essay[2]
To wipe those briny tears away.
I followed him, and said, 'My friend,
What ails you? Wherefore weep you so?'
'Shame on me, sir! This lusty lamb,
He makes my tears to flow;
Today I fetched him from the rock –
He is the last of all my flock.

When I was young, a single man,
And after youthful follies ran,
Though little given to care and thought,
Yet so it was a ewe I bought;
And other sheep from her I raised,
As healthy sheep as you might see.
And then I married, and was rich
As I could wish to be;
Of sheep I numbered a full score,[3]
And every year increased my store.

Year after year my stock it grew,
And from this one, this single ewe,
Full fifty comely sheep I raised –
As sweet a flock as ever grazed!
Upon the mountain did they feed,
They throve, and we at home did thrive.
This lusty lamb of all my store
Is all that is alive;
And now I care not if we die
And perish all of poverty.

Ten children, sir, had I to feed –
Hard labour in a time of need!
My pride was tamed, and in our grief
I of the parish asked relief.
They said I was a wealthy man;
My sheep upon the mountain fed
And it was fit that thence I took
Whereof to buy us bread.
"Do this. How can we give to you"
They cried, "what to the poor is due?"

Notes

[2] *made essay* tried.

[3] *a full score* twenty.

I sold a sheep as they had said,
And bought my little children bread,
And they were healthy with their food;
For me it never did me good.
A woeful time it was for me
To see the end of all my gains,
The pretty flock which I had reared
With all my care and pains,
To see it melt like snow away!
For me it was a woeful day.

Another still, and still another!
A little lamb and then its mother!
It was a vein that never stopped,
Like blood-drops from my heart they dropped
Till thirty were not left alive;
They dwindled, dwindled, one by one,
And I may say that many a time
I wished they all were gone:
They dwindled one by one away –
For me it was a woeful day.

To wicked deeds I was inclined,
And wicked fancies crossed my mind,
And every man I chanced to see,
I thought he knew some ill of me.
No peace, no comfort could I find,
No ease, within doors or without,
And crazily, and wearily,
I went my work about.
Oft-times I thought to run away;
For me it was a woeful day.

Sir, 'twas a precious flock to me,
As dear as my own children be;
For daily with my growing store
I loved my children more and more.
Alas, it was an evil time,
God cursed me in my sore distress;
I prayed, yet every day I thought
I loved my children less;
And every week, and every day
My flock, it seemed to melt away.

They dwindled, sir, sad sight to see,
From ten to five, from five to three –
A lamb, a wether,[4] and a ewe;
And then at last, from three to two.

## Notes

[4] *wether* castrated male sheep.

And of my fifty, yesterday
I had but only one,
And here it lies upon my arm –
Alas, and I have none!
Today I fetched it from the rock;
It is the last of all my flock.'

## *The Dungeon* (by Coleridge, extracted from *Osorio,* composed April–September 1797)[1]

And this place our forefathers made for man!
This is the process of our love and wisdom
To each poor brother who offends against us;
Most innocent, perhaps – and what if guilty?
Is this the only cure, merciful God?
Each pore and natural outlet shrivelled up
By ignorance and parching poverty,
His energies roll back upon his heart
And stagnate and corrupt; till, changed to poison,
They break out on him like a loathsome plague-spot.
Then we call in our pampered mountebanks
And this is their best cure: uncomforted
And friendless solitude, groaning and tears
And savage faces at the clanking hour,
Seen through the steams and vapour of his dungeon,
By the lamp's dismal twilight. So he lies
Circled with evil, till his very soul
Unmoulds its essence, hopelessly deformed
By sights of ever more deformity!
With other ministrations, thou, oh nature,
Healest thy wandering and distempered child:
Thou pourest on him thy soft influences,
Thy sunny hues, fair forms, and breathing sweets,
Thy melodies of woods, and winds, and waters,
Till he relent, and can no more endure
To be a jarring and a dissonant thing
Amid this general dance and minstrelsy;
But, bursting into tears, wins back his way,
His angry spirit healed and harmonized
By the benignant touch of love and beauty.

### Notes

The Dungeon

[1] In Coleridge's play, this was part of a soliloquy by the protagonist, Albert, when jailed by the Inquisition. Like Wordsworth's 'The Convict', this poem is a plea for penal reform.

## *The Mad Mother* (by Wordsworth, composed between March and 16 May 1798)[1]

Her eyes are wild, her head is bare,
The sun has burnt her coal-black hair,
Her eyebrows have a rusty stain,
And she came far from over the main.[2]
She has a baby on her arm,
Or else she were alone;
And underneath the haystack warm,
And on the greenwood stone,
She talked and sung the woods among –
And it was in the English tongue.

'Sweet babe, they say that I am mad,
But nay, my heart is far too glad;
And I am happy when I sing
Full many a sad and doleful thing.
Then, lovely baby, do not fear!
I pray thee, have no fear of me,
But safe as in a cradle, here
My lovely baby, thou shalt be;
To thee I know too much I owe,
I cannot work thee any woe.

A fire was once within my brain,
And in my head a dull, dull pain;
And fiendish faces – one, two, three,
Hung at my breasts, and pulled at me.
But then there came a sight of joy,
It came at once to do me good;
I waked and saw my little boy,
My little boy of flesh and blood –
Oh joy for me that sight to see!
For he was here, and only he.

Suck, little babe, oh suck again!
It cools my blood, it cools my brain;
Thy lips I feel them, baby, they
Draw from my heart the pain away.
Oh, press me with thy little hand,
It loosens something at my chest;
About that tight and deadly band
I feel thy little fingers pressed.
The breeze I see is in the tree,
It comes to cool my babe and me.

### Notes

THE MAD MOTHER

[1] In later years, Wordsworth recalled: 'The subject was reported to me by a lady of Bristol who had seen the poor creature.'

[2] *main* sea.

Oh love me, love me, little boy!
Thou art thy mother's only joy;
And do not dread the waves below,
When o'er the sea-rock's edge[3] we go.
The high crag cannot work me harm,
Nor leaping torrents when they howl;
The babe I carry on my arm,
He saves for me my precious soul.
Then happy lie, for blessed am I –
Without me my sweet babe would die.

Then do not fear, my boy, for thee
Bold as a lion I will be;
And I will always be thy guide
Through hollow snows and rivers wide.
I'll build an Indian bower;[4] I know
The leaves that make the softest bed;
And if from me thou wilt not go,
But still be true till I am dead –
My pretty thing, then thou shalt sing,
As merry as the birds in spring.

Thy father cares not for my breast;
'Tis thine, sweet baby, there to rest,
'Tis all thine own! And if its hue
Be changed, that was so fair to view,
'Tis fair enough for thee, my dove!
My beauty, little child, is flown;
But thou wilt live with me in love –
And what if my poor cheek be brown?
'Tis well for me; thou canst not see
How pale and wan it else would be.

Dread not their taunts, my little life!
I am thy father's wedded wife,
And underneath the spreading tree
We two will live in honesty.
If his sweet boy he could forsake,
With me he never would have stayed;
From him no harm my babe can take,
But he, poor man, is wretched made;
And every day we two will pray
For him that's gone and far away.

I'll teach my boy the sweetest things,
I'll teach him how the owlet sings.
My little babe, thy lips are still,
And thou hast almost sucked thy fill.

## Notes

[3] *o'er the sea-rock's edge* along the cliff-top.

[4] *I'll build…bower* The mad mother was either an American Indian, or lived among them.

Where art thou gone, my own dear child?
What wicked looks are those I see?
Alas, alas! that look so wild,
It never, never came from me;
If thou art mad, my pretty lad,
Then I must be forever sad.

Oh smile on me, my little lamb,
For I thy own dear mother am.
My love for thee has well been tried;
I've sought thy father far and wide.
I know the poisons of the shade,
I know the earth-nuts fit for food;
Then, pretty dear, be not afraid –
We'll find thy father in the wood.
Now laugh and be gay, to the woods away,
And there, my babe, we'll live for aye.'

## *The Idiot Boy* (by Wordsworth, composed between March and 16 May 1798)

'Tis eight o'clock, a clear March night,
The moon is up, the sky is blue,
The owlet[1] in the moonlight air –
He shouts from nobody knows where,
He lengthens out his lonely shout:
Halloo, halloo! A long halloo!

Why bustle thus about your door?
What means this bustle, Betty Foy?
Why are you in this mighty fret?
And why on horseback have you set
Him whom you love, your idiot boy?

Beneath the moon that shines so bright,
Till she is tired, let Betty Foy
With girt[2] and stirrup fiddle-faddle;
But wherefore set upon a saddle
Him whom she loves, her idiot boy?

There's scarce a soul that's out of bed –
Good Betty, put him down again!
His lips with joy they burr at you,
But, Betty, what has he to do
With stirrup, saddle, or with rein?

Notes

The Idiot Boy

[1] *owlet* full-grown owl.

[2] *girt* saddle-girth.

The world will say 'tis very idle –
Bethink you of the time of night?
There's not a mother – no not one,
But when she hears what you have done,
Oh Betty, she'll be in a fright!

But Betty's bent on her intent,
For her good neighbour, Susan Gale
(Old Susan, she who dwells alone)
Is sick and makes a piteous moan
As if her very life would fail.

There's not a house within a mile,
No hand to help them in distress,
Old Susan lies abed in pain,
And sorely puzzled are the twain,
For what she ails[3] they cannot guess.

And Betty's husband's at the wood
Where by the week he doth abide,
A woodman in the distant vale;
There's none to help poor Susan Gale –
What must be done? What will betide?

And Betty from the lane has fetched
Her pony that is mild and good
Whether he be in joy or pain,
Feeding at will along the lane,
Or bringing faggots[4] from the wood.

And he is all in travelling trim,[5]
And by the moonlight, Betty Foy
Has up upon the saddle set
(The like was never heard of yet)
Him whom she loves, her idiot boy.

And he must post[6] without delay
Across the bridge that's in the dale,
And by the church and o'er the down
To bring a Doctor from the town,
Or she will die, old Susan Gale.

There is no need of boot or spur,
There is no need of whip or wand,[7]
For Johnny has his holly-bough,
And with a hurly-burly now
He shakes the green bough in his hand.

## Notes

[3] *what she ails* what ails her.

[4] *faggots* bundles of sticks for fuel.

[5] *in travelling trim* i.e. saddled.

[6] *post* travel quickly.

[7] *wand* stick, cane.

And Betty o'er and o'er has told
The boy who is her best delight
Both what to follow, what to shun,
What do, and what to leave undone,
How turn to left, and how to right,

And Betty's most especial charge[8]
Was, 'Johnny, Johnny! Mind that you
Come home again, nor stop at all,
Come home again whate'er befall –
My Johnny do, I pray you do.'

To this did Johnny answer make
Both with his head and with his hand,
And proudly shook the bridle too,
And then! his words were not a few,
Which Betty well could understand.

And now that Johnny is just going,
Though Betty's in a mighty flurry,
She gently pats the pony's side
On which her idiot boy must ride,
And seems no longer in a hurry.

But when the pony moved his legs –
Oh then for the poor idiot boy!
For joy he cannot hold the bridle,
For joy his head and heels are idle,
He's idle all for very joy.

And while the pony moves his legs,
In Johnny's left hand you may see
The green bough's motionless and dead;
The moon that shines above his head
Is not more still and mute than he.

His heart it was so full of glee
That till full fifty yards were gone
He quite forgot his holly whip
And all his skill in horsemanship –
Oh happy, happy, happy John!

And Betty's standing at the door,
And Betty's face with joy o'erflows,
Proud of herself and proud of him,
She sees him in his travelling trim;
How quietly her Johnny goes!

Notes

[8] *charge* instruction.

The silence of her idiot boy –
What hopes it sends to Betty's heart!
He's at the guide-post,[9] he turns right,
She watches till he's out of sight,
And Betty will not then depart.

Burr, burr, now Johnny's lips they burr
As loud as any mill or near it;
Meek as a lamb the pony moves,
And Johnny makes the noise he loves,
And Betty listens, glad to hear it.

Away she hies to Susan Gale,
And Johnny's in a merry tune;[10]
The owlets hoot, the owlets curr,
And Johnny's lips they burr, burr, burr,
And on he goes beneath the moon.

His steed and he right well agree,
For of this pony there's a rumour
That should he lose his eyes and ears,
And should he live a thousand years,
He never will be out of humour.

But then he is a horse that thinks!
And when he thinks his pace is slack;
Now, though he knows poor Johnny well,
Yet for his life he cannot tell
What he has got upon his back.

So through the moonlight lanes they go
And far into the moonlight dale,
And by the church and o'er the down
To bring a Doctor from the town
To comfort poor old Susan Gale.

And Betty, now at Susan's side,
Is in the middle of her story,
What comfort Johnny soon will bring,
With many a most diverting thing
Of Johnny's wit and Johnny's glory.

And Betty's still at Susan's side –
By this time she's not quite so flurried;
Demure with porringer[11] and plate
She sits, as if in Susan's fate
Her life and soul were buried.

## Notes

[9] *guide-post* signpost.
[10] *tune* mood.
[11] *porringer* wooden soup-bowl.

But Betty (poor good woman!), she –
You plainly in her face may read it –
Could lend out of that moment's store
Five years of happiness or more
To any that might need it.

But yet I guess that now and then
With Betty all was not so well,
And to the road she turns her ears,
And thence full many a sound she hears,
Which she to Susan will not tell.

Poor Susan moans, poor Susan groans;
'As sure as there's a moon in heaven',
Cries Betty, 'he'll be back again –
They'll both be here, 'tis almost ten;
They'll both be here before eleven.'

Poor Susan moans, poor Susan groans,
The clock gives warning for eleven –
'Tis on the stroke. 'If Johnny's near',
Quoth Betty, 'he will soon be here,
As sure as there's a moon in heaven.'

The clock is on the stroke of twelve
And Johnny is not yet in sight;
The moon's in heaven, as Betty sees,
But Betty is not quite at ease –
And Susan has a dreadful night.

And Betty, half an hour ago,
On Johnny vile reflections cast;
'A little idle sauntering thing!'
With other names, an endless string,
But now that time is gone and past.

And Betty's drooping at the heart,
That happy time all past and gone;
'How can it be he is so late?
The Doctor, he has made him wait –
Susan, they'll both be here anon!'

And Susan's growing worse and worse,
And Betty's in a sad quandary,[12]
And then there's nobody to say
If she must go or she must stay –
She's in a sad quandary.

Notes

[12] *quandary* stressed on the second syllable.

The clock is on the stroke of one,
But neither Doctor nor his guide
Appear along the moonlight road;
There's neither horse nor man abroad,
And Betty's still at Susan's side.

And Susan, she begins to fear
Of sad mischances not a few;
That Johnny may perhaps be drowned,
Or lost perhaps, and never found –
Which they must both forever rue.

She prefaced half a hint of this
With, 'God forbid it should be true!'
At the first word that Susan said,
Cried Betty, rising from the bed,
'Susan, I'd gladly stay with you;

I must be gone, I must away.
Consider, Johnny's but half-wise;
Susan, we must take care of him,
If he is hurt in life or limb –'
'Oh God forbid!' poor Susan cries.

'What can I do?' says Betty, going,
'What can I do to ease your pain?
Good Susan tell me, and I'll stay;
I fear you're in a dreadful way,
But I shall soon be back again.'

'Good Betty go, good Betty go,
There's nothing that can ease my pain.'
Then off she hies, but with a prayer
That God poor Susan's life would spare
Till she comes back again.

So through the moonlight lane she goes
And far into the moonlight dale;
And how she ran and how she walked
And all that to herself she talked
Would surely be a tedious tale.

In high and low, above, below,
In great and small, in round and square,
In tree and tower was Johnny seen,
In bush and brake, in black and green,
'Twas Johnny, Johnny, everywhere.

She's past the bridge that's in the dale,
And now the thought torments her sore –
Johnny perhaps his horse forsook
To hunt the moon that's in the brook,
And never will be heard of more.

And now she's high upon the down,
Alone amid a prospect wide;
There's neither Johnny nor his horse
Among the fern or in the gorse;
There's neither Doctor nor his guide.

'Oh saints! What is become of him?
Perhaps he's climbed into an oak
Where he will stay till he is dead;
Or sadly he has been misled
And joined the wandering gipsy-folk;

Or him that wicked pony's carried
To the dark cave, the goblin's hall;
Or in the castle he's pursuing,
Among the ghosts, his own undoing,
Or playing with the waterfall.'

At poor old Susan then she railed,
While to the town she posts away;
'If Susan had not been so ill,
Alas! I should have had him still,
My Johnny, till my dying day.'

Poor Betty, in this sad distemper,
The Doctor's self would hardly spare;
Unworthy things she talked, and wild –
Even he, of cattle[13] the most mild,
The pony had his share.

And now she's got into the town
And to the Doctor's door she hies;
'Tis silence all on every side –
The town so long, the town so wide
Is silent as the skies.

And now she's at the Doctor's door,
She lifts the knocker – rap, rap, rap!
The Doctor at the casement[14] shows
His glimmering eyes that peep and doze,
And one hand rubs his old nightcap.

'Oh Doctor, Doctor! Where's my Johnny?'
'I'm here, what is't you want with me?'
'Oh sir, you know I'm Betty Foy
And I have lost my poor dear boy –
You know him, him you often see;

He's not so wise as some folks be.'
'The devil take his wisdom!' said

Notes

[13] *cattle* animals.

[14] *casement* window.

The Doctor, looking somewhat grim,
'What, woman, should I know of him?'
And grumbling, he went back to bed.

'Oh woe is me! Oh woe is me!
Here will I die, here will I die;
I thought to find my Johnny here,
But he is neither far nor near –
Oh what a wretched mother I!'

She stops, she stands, she looks about,
Which way to turn she cannot tell.
Poor Betty, it would ease her pain
If she had heart to knock again;
The clock strikes three – a dismal knell!

Then up along the town she hies,
No wonder if her senses fail,
This piteous news so much it shocked her
She quite forgot to send the Doctor
To comfort poor old Susan Gale.

And now she's high upon the down
And she can see a mile of road;
'Oh cruel! I'm almost threescore;
Such night as this was ne'er before,
There's not a single soul abroad.'

She listens, but she cannot hear
The foot of horse, the voice of man;
The streams with softest sound are flowing,
The grass you almost hear it growing,
You hear it now if e'er you can.

The owlets through the long blue night
Are shouting to each other still,
Fond lovers, yet not quite hob-nob,
They lengthen out the tremulous sob
That echoes far from hill to hill.

Poor Betty now has lost all hope,
Her thoughts are bent on deadly sin;
A green-grown pond she just has passed
And from the brink she hurries fast
Lest she should drown herself therein.

And now she sits her down and weeps,
Such tears she never shed before;
'Oh dear, dear pony! My sweet joy!
Oh carry back my idiot boy
And we will ne'er o'erload thee more.'

A thought is come into her head;
'The pony he is mild and good
And we have always used him well;
Perhaps he's gone along the dell
And carried Johnny to the wood.'

Then up she springs as if on wings –
She thinks no more of deadly sin;
If Betty fifty ponds should see,
The last of all her thoughts would be
To drown herself therein.

Oh reader, now that I might tell
What Johnny and his horse are doing,
What they've been doing all this time –
Oh could I put it into rhyme,
A most delightful tale pursuing!

Perhaps (and no unlikely thought)
He with his pony now doth roam
The cliffs and peaks so high that are,
To lay his hands upon a star
And in his pocket bring it home.

Perhaps he's turned himself about,
His face unto his horse's tail,
And still and mute, in wonder lost,
All like a silent horseman-ghost
He travels on along the vale.

And now, perhaps, he's hunting sheep,
A fierce and dreadful hunter he!
Yon valley that's so trim and green,
In five months' time, should he be seen,
A desert wilderness will be.

Perhaps, with head and heels on fire,
And like the very soul of evil,
He's galloping away, away,
And so he'll gallop on for aye,
The bane of all that dread the devil.

I to the muses have been bound
These fourteen years by strong indentures;[15]
Oh gentle muses, let me tell
But half of what to him befell,
For sure he met with strange adventures.

## Notes

[15] *indentures* contract by which apprentice is bound to a master who will teach him a trade. Wordsworth's apprenticeship to the muses of poetry, by his reckoning, began in 1784, when he was 14.

Oh gentle muses, is this kind?
Why will ye thus my suit repel?
Why of your further aid bereave[16] me?
And can ye thus unfriended leave me,
Ye muses, whom I love so well?

Who's yon, that, near the waterfall
Which thunders down with headlong force,
Beneath the moon, yet shining fair,
As careless as if nothing were,
Sits upright on a feeding horse?

Unto his horse that's feeding free
He seems, I think, the rein to give;
Of moon or stars he takes no heed,
Of such we in romances read –
'Tis Johnny, Johnny, as I live!

And that's the very pony too!
Where is she, where is Betty Foy?
She hardly can sustain her fears;
The roaring waterfall she hears,
And cannot find her idiot boy.

Your pony's worth his weight in gold,
Then calm your terrors, Betty Foy!
She's coming from among the trees,
And now, all full in view, she sees
Him whom she loves, her idiot boy,

And Betty sees the pony too.
Why stand you thus, good Betty Foy?
It is no goblin, 'tis no ghost –
'Tis he whom you so long have lost,
He whom you love, your idiot boy.

She looks again, her arms are up,
She screams, she cannot move for joy;
She darts as with a torrent's force,
She almost has o'erturned the horse,
And fast she holds her idiot boy.

And Johnny burrs and laughs aloud –
Whether in cunning or in joy
I cannot tell; but while he laughs,
Betty a drunken pleasure quaffs
To hear again her idiot boy.

Notes

[16] *bereave* deprive.

And now she's at the pony's tail,
And now she's at the pony's head,
On that side now, and now on this,
And almost stifled with her bliss,
A few sad tears does Betty shed.

She kisses o'er and o'er again
Him whom she loves, her idiot boy;
She's happy here, she's happy there,
She is uneasy everywhere;
Her limbs are all alive with joy.

She pats the pony, where or when
She knows not, happy Betty Foy!
The little pony glad may be,
But he is milder far than she,
You hardly can perceive his joy.

'Oh Johnny, never mind the Doctor;
You've done your best, and that is all.'
She took the reins when this was said,
And gently turned the pony's head
From the loud waterfall.

By this the stars were almost gone,
The moon was setting on the hill
So pale you scarcely looked at her;
The little birds began to stir,
Though yet their tongues were still.

The pony, Betty, and her boy,
Wind slowly through the woody dale;
And who is she, betimes abroad,
That hobbles up the steep rough road?
Who is it but old Susan Gale?

Long Susan lay deep lost in thought
And many dreadful fears beset her,
Both for her messenger and nurse;
And as her mind grew worse and worse,
Her body it grew better.

She turned, she tossed herself in bed,
On all sides doubts and terrors met her,
Point after point did she discuss,
And while her mind was fighting thus,
Her body still grew better.

'Alas, what is become of them?
These fears can never be endured –
I'll to the wood.' The word scarce said,
Did Susan rise up from her bed,
As if by magic cured.

Away she posts up hill and down,
And to the wood at length is come,
She spies her friends, she shouts a greeting –
Oh me, it is a merry meeting
As ever was in Christendom!

The owls have hardly sung their last
While our four travellers homeward wend;
The owls have hooted all night long,
And with the owls began my song,
And with the owls must end.

For while they all were travelling home,
Cried Betty, 'Tell us Johnny, do,
Where all this long night you have been,
What you have heard, what you have seen –
And Johnny, mind you tell us true.'

Now Johnny all night long had heard
The owls in tuneful concert strive;
No doubt too he the moon had seen,
For in the moonlight he had been
From eight o'clock till five.

And thus to Betty's question he
Made answer like a traveller bold
(His very words I give to you):
'The cocks did crow to-whoo, to-whoo,
And the sun did shine so cold.'
Thus answered Johnny in his glory,
And that was all his travel's story.

## *Lines Written near Richmond, upon the Thames, at Evening*<br>(by Wordsworth, derived from a sonnet written 1789, complete in this form by 29 March 1797)[1]

How rich the wave in front, impressed
With evening twilight's summer hues,
While, facing thus the crimson west,
The boat her silent path pursues!
And see how dark the backward stream,
A little moment past, so smiling!
And still, perhaps, with faithless gleam,
Some other loiterer beguiling.

## Notes

LINES WRITTEN NEAR RICHMOND, UPON THE THAMES, AT EVENING

[1] The title was concocted for the poem's appearance in *Lyrical Ballads*: 'The title is scarcely correct. It was during a solitary walk on the banks of the Cam that I was first struck with this appearance, and applied it to my own feelings in the manner here expressed, changing the scene to the Thames, near Windsor.'

Such views the youthful bard allure,
But heedless of the following gloom,
He deems their colours shall endure
Till peace go with him to the tomb.
And let him nurse his fond deceit;
And what if he must die in sorrow?
Who would not cherish dreams so sweet,
Though grief and pain may come tomorrow?

Glide gently, thus forever glide,
Oh Thames! that other bards may see
As lovely visions by thy side
As now, fair river; come to me!
Oh glide, fair stream, forever so;
Thy quiet soul on all bestowing,
Till all our minds forever flow,
As thy deep waters now are flowing.

Vain thought! Yet be as now thou art,
That in thy waters may be seen
The image of a poet's heart,
How bright, how solemn, how serene!
Such heart did once the poet bless
Who, pouring here a *later* ditty,
Could find no refuge from distress
But in the milder grief of pity.

Remembrance! as we glide along,
For him suspend the dashing oar,
And pray that never child of song
May know his freezing sorrows more.
How calm, how still! the only sound
The dripping of the oar suspended!
The evening darkness gathers round
By virtue's holiest powers attended.

## *Expostulation and Reply* (by Wordsworth, composed probably 23 May 1798)

'Why, William, on that old grey stone,
Thus for the length of half a day,
Why, William, sit you thus alone
And dream your time away?

Where are your books that light bequeathed
To beings else forlorn and blind?
Up, up, and drink the spirit breathed
From dead men to their kind!

You look round on your mother earth
As if she for no purpose bore you;
As if you were her first-born birth,
And none had lived before you!'

One morning thus, by Esthwaite Lake,[1]
When life was sweet I knew not why,
To me my good friend Matthew spake,
And thus I made reply.

'The eye it cannot choose but see,
We cannot bid the ear be still;
Our bodies feel where'er they be,
Against or with our will.

Nor less I deem that there are powers[2]
Which of themselves our minds impress,
That we can feed this mind of ours
In a wise passiveness.

Think you, mid all this mighty sum
Of things forever speaking,
That nothing of itself will come,
But we must still[3] be seeking?

Then ask not wherefore, here, alone,
Conversing as I may,[4]
I sit upon this old grey stone
And dream my time away.'

## *The Tables Turned: An Evening Scene, on the Same Subject* (by Wordsworth, composed probably 23 May 1798)

Up, up, my friend, and clear your looks!
Why all this toil and trouble?
Up, up, my friend, and quit your books,
Or surely you'll grow double!

The sun above the mountain's head
A freshening lustre mellow
Through all the long green fields has spread,
His first sweet evening yellow.

Books! 'tis a dull and endless strife;
Come hear the woodland linnet –
How sweet his music! On my life,
There's more of wisdom in it.

## Notes

Expostulation and Reply

[1] *Esthwaite Lake* Wordsworth attended school at Hawkshead, on Esthwaite Water in the Lake District.

[2] *powers* i.e. external to us; natural forces.

[3] *still* always.

[4] *Conversing...may* i.e. with the natural world.

And hark, how blithe the throstle[1] sings!
And he is no mean preacher;
Come forth into the light of things,
Let nature be your teacher.

She has a world of ready wealth,
Our minds and hearts to bless –
Spontaneous wisdom breathed by health,
Truth breathed by cheerfulness.

One impulse from a vernal wood
May teach you more of man,
Of moral evil and of good
Than all the sages can.

Sweet is the lore which nature brings,
Our meddling intellect
Misshapes the beauteous forms of things –
We murder to dissect.

Enough of science[2] and of art,[3]
Close up these barren leaves;[4]
Come forth, and bring with you a heart
That watches and receives.

## *Old Man Travelling; Animal Tranquillity and Decay, A Sketch* (by Wordsworth, composed by June 1797)

The little hedgerow birds
That peck along the road, regard him not.
He travels on, and in his face, his step,
His gait, is one expression; every limb,
His look and bending figure, all bespeak
A man who does not move with pain, but moves
With thought. He is insensibly subdued
To settled quiet; he is one by whom
All effort seems forgotten, one to whom
Long patience has such mild composure given,
That patience now doth seem a thing of which
He hath no need. He is by nature led
To peace so perfect that the young behold
With envy what the old man hardly feels.
I asked him whither he was bound, and what
The object of his journey; he replied:
'Sir, I am going many miles to take
A last leave of my son, a mariner,
Who from a sea-fight has been brought to Falmouth,
And there is dying in an hospital.'

### Notes

The Tables Turned, An Evening Scene

[1] *throstle* thrush.

[2] *science* knowledge.

[3] *art* skill, artfulness.

[4] *barren leaves* pages of books.

## *The Complaint of a Forsaken Indian Woman* (by Wordsworth, composed between early March and 16 May 1798)

When a Northern Indian, from sickness, is unable to continue his journey with his companions, he is left behind, covered over with deer-skins, and is supplied with water, food, and fuel, if the situation of the place will afford it. He is informed of the track which his companions intend to pursue, and, if he is unable to follow or overtake them, he perishes alone in the desert (unless he should have the good fortune to fall in with some other tribes of Indians). It is unnecessary to add that the females are equally, or still more, exposed to the same fate; see that very interesting work, Hearne's *Journey from Hudson's Bay to the Northern Ocean*.[1] When the Northern Lights[2] (as the same writer informs us) vary their position in the air, they make a rustling and a crackling noise. This circumstance is alluded to in the first stanza of the following poem.

Before I see another day
Oh let my body die away!
In sleep I heard the northern gleams,[3]
The stars they were among my dreams;
In sleep did I behold the skies,
I saw the crackling flashes drive,
And yet[4] they are upon my eyes,
And yet I am alive.
Before I see another day
Oh let my body die away!

My fire is dead[5] – it knew no pain,
Yet is it dead, and I remain.
All stiff with ice the ashes lie,
And they are dead, and I will die.
When I was well, I wished to live,
For[6] clothes, for warmth, for food and fire;
But they to me no joy can give,
No pleasure now, and no desire.
Then here contented will I lie,
Alone I cannot fear to die.

Alas, you might have dragged me on
Another day, a single one!
Too soon despair o'er me prevailed,
Too soon my heartless[7] spirit failed;

## Notes

THE COMPLAINT OF A FORSAKEN INDIAN WOMAN

[1] A reference to Samuel Hearne's *Journey from Prince of Wales' Fort in Hudson Bay, to the Northern Ocean* (1795), which describes the plight of a sick Indian woman left behind by her tribe: 'The poor woman … came up with us three several times, after having been left in the manner described. At length, poor creature, she dropped behind, and no one attempted to go back in search of her.'

[2] *Northern Lights* the aurora borealis.

[3] *northern gleams* Hearne writes: 'I do not remember to have met with any travellers into high northern latitudes, who remarked their having heard the Northern Lights make any noise in the air as they vary their colours or position – which may probably be owing to the want of perfect silence at the time they made their observations on those meteors. I can positively affirm that in still nights I have frequently heard them make a rustling and crackling noise, like the waving of a large flag in a fresh gale of wind.'

[4] *yet* still.

[5] *My fire is dead* According to Hearne, members of the tribe abandoned to die were left with some provisions: '[T]he friends or relations of the sick generally leave them some victuals and water, and, if the situation of the place will afford it, a little firing. When those articles are provided, the person to be left is acquainted with the road which the others intend to go, and then, after covering them well up with deer-skins, etc., they take their leave, and walk away crying.'

[6] *For* i.e. I wished for …

[7] *heartless* disheartened.

When you were gone my limbs were stronger –
And oh, how grievously I rue
That afterwards, a little longer,
My friends, I did not follow you!
For strong and without pain I lay,
My friends, when you were gone away.

My child, they gave thee to another,
A woman who was not thy mother;
When from my arms my babe they took,
On me how strangely did he look!
Through his whole body something ran,
A most strange something did I see –
As if he strove to be a man,
That he might pull the sledge for me.
And then he stretched his arms, how wild!
Oh mercy, like a little child!

My little joy! My little pride!
In two days more I must have died.
Then do not weep and grieve for me;
I feel I must have died with thee.
Oh wind, that o'er my head art flying
The way my friends their course did bend,
I should not feel the pain of dying
Could I with thee a message send.
Too soon, my friends, you went away,
For I had many things to say.

I'll follow you across the snow,
You travel heavily and slow;
In spite of all my weary pain,
I'll look upon your tents again.
My fire is dead, and snowy white
The water which beside it stood;
The wolf has come to me tonight
And he has stolen away my food.
Forever left alone am I,
Then wherefore should I fear to die?

My journey will be shortly run,
I shall not see another sun,
I cannot lift my limbs to know
If they have any life or no.
My poor forsaken child, if I
For once could have thee close to me,
With happy heart I then would die
And my last thoughts would happy be.
I feel my body die away,
I shall not see another day.

## *The Convict* (by Wordsworth, composed between 21 March and October 1796)

The glory of evening was spread through the west –
On the slope of a mountain I stood;
While the joy that precedes the calm season of rest[1]
Rang loud through the meadow and wood.

'And must we then part from a dwelling so fair?'
In the pain of my spirit I said,
And with a deep sadness I turned to repair
To the cell where the convict is laid.

The thick-ribbed walls that o'ershadow the gate
Resound, and the dungeons unfold;
I pause,[2] and at length through the glimmering grate[3]
That outcast of pity behold.

His black matted head on his shoulder is bent,
And deep is the sigh of his breath,
And with steadfast dejection his eyes are intent
On the fetters that link him to death.

'Tis sorrow enough on that visage to gaze,
That body dismissed from his care;
Yet my fancy has pierced to his heart, and portrays[4]
More terrible images there.

His bones are consumed and his life-blood is dried,
With wishes the past to undo;
And his crime, through the pains that o'erwhelm him, descried,
Still[5] blackens and grows on his view.

When from the dark synod[6] or blood-reeking field,[7]
To his chamber the monarch is led,
All soothers of sense their soft virtue shall yield,
And quietness pillow his head.

But if grief, self-consumed, in oblivion would doze,
And conscience her tortures appease,
Mid tumult and uproar this man must repose
In the comfortless vault of disease.

When his fetters at night have so pressed on his limbs
That the weight can no longer be borne,
If, while a half-slumber his memory bedims,
The wretch on his pallet should turn;

## Notes

The Convict

[1] *the calm season of rest* i.e. night-time.

[2] *I pause* to allow his eyes to adjust to the darkness.

[3] *grate* barred window to the prison cell.

[4] *portrays* visualizes.

[5] *Still* continually.

[6] *dark synod* secret council.

[7] *blood-reeking field* battlefield that stinks of blood. The monarch is, by implication, far more culpable than the convict. Britain had been at war with France since 1793.

While the jail-mastiff howls at the dull-clanking chain,
From the roots of his hair there shall start
A thousand sharp punctures of cold-sweating pain,
And terror shall leap at his heart.

But now he half-raises his deep-sunken eye,
And the motion unsettles a tear;
The silence of sorrow it seems to supply,
And asks of me why I am here.

'Poor victim! No idle intruder has stood
With o'erweening complacence our state to compare –
But one whose first wish is the wish to be good
Is come as a brother thy sorrows to share.

At thy name, though Compassion her nature resign,
Though in Virtue's proud mouth thy report be a stain,
My care, if the arm of the mighty were mine,
Would plant thee where yet thou might'st blossom again.'

## *Lines Written a Few Miles above Tintern Abbey, on Revisiting the Banks of the Wye during a Tour, 13 July 1798* (by Wordsworth, composed 10–13 July 1798)

Five years have passed; five summers, with the length
Of five long winters![1] And again I hear
These waters, rolling from their mountain springs
With a sweet inland murmur.[2] Once again
Do I behold these steep and lofty cliffs,
Which on a wild secluded scene impress
Thoughts of more deep seclusion, and connect
The landscape with the quiet of the sky.
The day is come when I again repose
Here, under this dark sycamore, and view
These plots of cottage-ground, these orchard-tufts,
Which, at this season, with their unripe fruits,
Among the woods and copses lose themselves,
Nor, with their green and simple hue, disturb
The wild green landscape. Once again I see
These hedgerows – hardly hedgerows, little lines
Of sportive wood run wild; these pastoral farms[3]
Green to the very door; and wreaths of smoke
Sent up in silence from among the trees,
With some uncertain notice,[4] as might seem,
Of vagrant dwellers in the houseless woods,
Or of some hermit's cave, where by his fire

### Notes

LINES WRITTEN A FEW MILES ABOVE TINTERN ABBEY

[1] *Five years...winters* Wordsworth's first visit to the Wye was in August 1793.

[2] 'The river is not affected by the tides a few miles above Tintern' (Wordsworth's note).

[3] *pastoral farms* sheep farms.

[4] *With some uncertain notice* faintly discernible.

The hermit sits alone.[5]
Though absent long,
These forms of beauty[6] have not been to me
As is a landscape to a blind man's eye;
But oft, in lonely rooms, and mid the din
Of towns and cities, I have owed to them,
In hours of weariness, sensations sweet,
Felt in the blood, and felt along the heart,
And passing even into my purer mind[7]
With tranquil restoration;[8] feelings too
Of unremembered pleasure – such, perhaps,
As may have had no trivial influence
On that best portion of a good man's life,
His little, nameless, unremembered acts
Of kindness and of love. Nor less, I trust,
To them I may have owed another gift,
Of aspect more sublime; that blessed mood
In which the burden of the mystery,
In which the heavy and the weary weight
Of all this unintelligible world
Is lightened – that serene and blessed mood
In which the affections gently lead us on
Until the breath of this corporeal frame[9]
And even the motion of our human blood
Almost suspended, we are laid asleep
In body, and become a living soul,
While with an eye made quiet by the power
Of harmony, and the deep power of joy,
We see into the life of things.
If this
Be but a vain belief – yet oh, how oft
In darkness, and amid the many shapes
Of joyless daylight, when the fretful stir
Unprofitable, and the fever of the world,
Have hung upon the beatings of my heart,
How oft, in spirit, have I turned to thee,
Oh sylvan[10] Wye! Thou wanderer through the woods,
How often has my spirit turned to thee!
And now, with gleams of half-extinguished thought,
With many recognitions dim and faint
And somewhat of a sad perplexity,
The picture of the mind revives again;
While here I stand, not only with the sense
Of present pleasure, but with pleasing thoughts
That in this moment there is life and food
For future years. And so I dare to hope,

## Notes

[5] *as might seem…alone* The 'vagrant dwellers' (gypsies) and hermit are figments of the imagination; the smoke comes from the charcoal-furnaces.

[6] *forms of beauty* natural objects, impressed on the mind.

[7] *my purer mind* i.e. the spiritual element of his being.

[8] *restoration* The memory of the 'forms of beauty' is spiritually restorative..

[9] *corporeal frame* the physical body.

[10] *sylvan* wooded.

Though changed, no doubt, from what I was when first
I came among these hills, when like a roe[11]
I bounded o'er the mountains by the sides
Of the deep rivers and the lonely streams
Wherever nature led, more like a man
Flying from something that he dreads than one
Who sought the thing he loved. For nature then
(The coarser pleasures of my boyish days
And their glad animal movements all gone by)
To me was all in all.
I cannot paint
What then I was. The sounding cataract
Haunted me like a passion; the tall rock,
The mountain, and the deep and gloomy wood,
Their colours and their forms, were then to me
An appetite, a feeling and a love
That had no need of a remoter charm
By thought supplied, or any interest
Unborrowed from the eye. That time is past,
And all its aching joys are now no more,
And all its dizzy raptures. Not for this
Faint I, nor mourn, nor murmur; other gifts
Have followed – for such loss, I would believe,
Abundant recompense. For I have learned
To look on nature not as in the hour
Of thoughtless youth, but hearing oftentimes
The still, sad music of humanity,
Not harsh nor grating, though of ample power
To chasten and subdue. And I have felt
A presence that disturbs me with the joy
Of elevated thoughts, a sense sublime
Of something far more deeply interfused,
Whose dwelling is the light of setting suns,
And the round ocean, and the living air,
And the blue sky, and in the mind of man –
A motion and a spirit that impels
All thinking things, all objects of all thought,
And rolls through all things. Therefore am I still
A lover of the meadows and the woods
And mountains, and of all that we behold
From this green earth, of all the mighty world
Of eye and ear (both what they half-create[12]
And what perceive) – well-pleased to recognize
In nature and the language of the sense,[13]
The anchor of my purest[14] thoughts, the nurse,
The guide, the guardian of my heart, and soul
Of all my moral being.

## Notes

[11] *roe* small deer.

[12] *half-create* Wordsworth notes a borrowing from Young, *Night Thoughts* vi 427: 'And half-create the wondrous world they [the senses] see.'

[13] *the language of the sense* what the senses perceive.

[14] *purest* most spiritual.

Nor, perchance,
If I were not thus taught, should I the more
Suffer my genial spirits[15] to decay;
For thou[16] art with me, here, upon the banks
Of this fair river – thou, my dearest friend,
My dear, dear friend, and in thy voice I catch
The language of my former heart, and read
My former pleasures in the shooting lights
Of thy wild eyes. Oh, yet a little while
May I behold in thee what I was once,
My dear, dear sister! And this prayer I make,
Knowing that Nature never did betray
The heart that loved her; 'tis her privilege,
Through all the years of this our life, to lead
From joy to joy, for she can so inform[17]
The mind that is within us, so impress
With quietness and beauty, and so feed
With lofty thoughts, that neither evil tongues,
Rash judgements, nor the sneers of selfish men,
Nor greetings where no kindness is, nor all
The dreary intercourse of daily life,
Shall e'er prevail against us, or disturb
Our cheerful faith that all which we behold
Is full of blessings. Therefore let the moon
Shine on thee in thy solitary walk,
And let the misty mountain-winds be free
To blow against thee. And in after-years,
When these wild ecstasies shall be matured
Into a sober pleasure, when thy mind
Shall be a mansion[18] for all lovely forms,
Thy memory be as a dwelling-place
For all sweet sounds and harmonies – oh then
If solitude, or fear, or pain, or grief
Should be thy portion,[19] with what healing thoughts
Of tender joy wilt thou remember me,
And these my exhortations! Nor perchance,
If I should be where I no more can hear
Thy voice, nor catch from thy wild eyes these gleams
Of past existence, wilt thou then forget
That on the banks of this delightful stream
We stood together; and that I, so long
A worshipper of nature, hither came
Unwearied in that service – rather say
With warmer love, oh with far deeper zeal
Of holier love! Nor wilt thou then forget
That, after many wanderings, many years
Of absence, these steep woods and lofty cliffs
And this green pastoral landscape, were to me
More dear, both for themselves, and for thy sake.

## Notes

[15] *genial spirits* creative energies, vitality; cf. *Samson Agonistes* 594: 'So much I feel my genial spirits droop.'

[16] *thou* Dorothy Wordsworth.

[17] *inform* imbue.

[18] *mansion* home, resting-place.

[19] *portion* lot, fate.

# William Wordsworth (1770–1850)

William Wordsworth was born on 7 April 1770, the second son of John Wordsworth Sr (1741–83), legal agent for Sir James Lowther, later Earl of Lonsdale, the most powerful landowner in the Lake District. The family was relatively well off and lived in the grandest house in the main street of the market town of Cockermouth. In March 1778 Wordsworth's mother Ann died of pneumonia; he was sent to Hawkshead Grammar School in May 1779, on the other side of the Lake District. Here he received a good education in the English grammar-school tradition, acquiring expertise in Latin, Greek and mathematics. He lodged with Ann Tyson in Colthouse, and prospered under two teachers, William Taylor and Thomas Bowman, recent graduates from Cambridge University. They loved contemporary poetry, and with their encouragement Wordsworth became an enthusiastic reader of Cowper, Charlotte Smith, Helen Maria Williams, Robert Burns and Anna Laetitia Barbauld.

When he was 13 his father died, leaving him and his siblings (Richard, Christopher, John and Dorothy) orphans. It was a devastating event and its most immediate effect was to render the Wordsworth children homeless and at the mercy of relatives, not all of whom were happy to support their upbringing and education. This would be a problem throughout the next decade, as the sums necessary for Wordsworth's university years were stinted, and pressure exerted on him to become a clergyman.

His good relationships with friends and teachers at school seem partly to have insulated him from the full impact of his parents' deaths. It was at Hawkshead, when he was 15, that he began to compose poetry; his teachers saw he was producing something better than much of what was published at the time and when he was 16 one of his sonnets appeared in a major periodical, the *European Magazine*. By the time he left Hawkshead he had composed a long poem, 'The Vale of Esthwaite', which included an early version of the spot of time in which he waited for the horses to take him home to see his dying father.

'Beside the pleasant mills of Trompington / I laughed with Chaucer', he would write in 'The Prelude'– and Wordsworth's Cambridge years seem to have been happy ones. He continued to write poetry but after his first year failed to distinguish himself in academic studies. The University syllabus was concerned chiefly with Euclid, whose work he had mastered at Hawkshead; in later years he suggested the level of proficiency he had reached at school left him unchallenged by the Cambridge course. Nonetheless, he did well in College examinations on Latin and Greek literature. His relatives were impatient for him to enter the church and become financially independent but Wordsworth had other ideas. There was certainly no clerical reason for his visit to France, with his friend Robert Jones, in summer 1790. Instead, it was a sort of political excursion.

France was in the grip of Revolution, and they were swept up in it. Wordsworth liked it so much he went back there in 1791–2, and stayed for a time at Blois, near Orléans. There he met Michel Beaupuy, the soldier who served as mentor, and had an affair with a French girl, Annette Vallon. She gave birth to Caroline Wordsworth in December 1792. But by then he was back in London, publishing his poems, 'An Evening Walk' and 'Descriptive Sketches', as a means of raising money before returning to France. Though he succeeded in getting the poems into print (they appeared in late January 1793), the execution of Louis XVI in January 1793, which precipitated war between Britain and France, made return impossible.

His inability to return to Annette and their child caused Wordsworth intense distress – a response that strengthened his devotion to the French cause. One result was the composition in early 1793 of a pamphlet defending regicide, 'A Letter to the Bishop of Llandaff'. It argued from a republican position that popular violence was the inevitable (and excusable) by-product of revolution. Had it been published at the time, Wordsworth would have been tried for treason; it would not appear in print until 1876.

At this period the philosophy of William Godwin's *Political Justice* had an appeal for him in its non-violent affirmation of revolutionary ideals, and when he returned to London in 1795 the two men became friends, often breakfasting together. What he liked about Godwinism was its imposition of justice on a society that was (in his view) corrupt; Godwin envisaged that reason would assume a compulsory power over human conduct. It was, in political terms, necessitarian, though we might see in it hints of totalitarian thought. Wordsworth tired of it not for that reason but because Godwin outlawed emotion. And as he matured in his early twenties, Wordsworth began to confront the grief stemming from his parents' deaths.

By 1796 he had rejected Godwinian rationalism and was living with his sister Dorothy at Racedown Lodge in Dorset. There he followed politics while continuing to write poetry, though at this stage he published comparatively little. They lived together as early as 1794, at Windy Brow near Keswick and it seemed natural to set up house together now. Dorothy had no one else with whom she could live, and in those days it was not respectable for single women to live on their own. Her healing influence helped Wordsworth compose the earliest version of 'The Ruined Cottage', which Coleridge probably heard when he visited Racedown in June 1797.

'The Ruined Cottage' is Wordsworth's first indisputably great poem. It was described by Jonathan Wordsworth as a tragedy; what distinguishes the version presented here (completed in the spring of 1798) is the optimism of its conclusion in which, confronted by Margaret's pain and suffering, we are directed to the sight of the speargrass in her garden:

> I well remember that those very plumes,
> Those weeds, and the high speargrass on
> that wall,
> By mist and silent raindrops silvered o'er,
> As once I passed did to my mind convey
> So still an image of tranquillity,
> So calm and still, and looked so beautiful
> Amid the uneasy thoughts which filled my
> mind,
> That what we feel of sorrow and despair
> From ruin and from change, and all the grief
> The passing shows of being leave behind,
> Appeared an idle dream that could not live
> Where meditation was.
>
> (ll. 513–24)

This is a central statement in Romantic poetry: through Margaret's incorporation into the wildness of the speargrass and weeds that have taken over her garden, grief at her passing is reduced to an 'idle dream'. Her earthly fate is part of a process of becoming. In another poem, written in late 1798, Wordsworth would describe a woman whose corpse is 'Rolled round in earth's diurnal course / With rocks and stones and trees!' – as if part of a larger harmony. Grief is a powerful force throughout Wordsworth's poetry, and in the great work of 1797–8 it finds consolation through apprehension of a cosmic unity.

But it was part of a larger view of the power of nature to communicate 'that pure principle of love' to anyone who perceived it. You could call that mysticism, as indeed it was, but it was typical of a conviction in the redemptive power of the nature, something he would continue to believe in to his dying day.

Wordsworth's philosophical views were influenced by Coleridge, who proposed that Wordsworth compose a poem called 'The Recluse', of which 'The Ruined Cottage' was to have been part. Seeing around them the continued hardship and suffering which the French Revolution was intended to relieve, Wordsworth and Coleridge asked themselves how poetry could play its part. The answer would embody elements of both men's thought. Its central tenet (later to be the subject of 'The Prelude' Book VIII) was that love of Nature led to love of mankind; that is to say, the intensely perceived, and imaginatively enhanced, engagement with the life-force running through the natural world could lead, in turn, to sympathy and compassion for all things, including other members of the human race. Essentially, 'The Recluse' would argue that if everyone were 'converted' by imaginative process, the world would be improved, and a sort of Utopia created in which humanity could live in harmony with Nature. (This is a rough and ready paraphrase of what remains, to some extent, a conjectural work.) Once again there was a compulsory element that prefigures elements of twentieth-century political thought.

The emphasis on the redemptive function of Nature was distinctively Wordsworthian, and is attributed to him when it appears for the first time in Coleridge's 'This Lime-Tree Bower my Prison', in July 1797; the pantheism came from Coleridge, who had espoused his views in a unifying, all-embracing divinity since 1794, when he wrote the first version of 'Religious Musings'. A poem that explained how love of Nature could lead to universal brotherhood would, Wordsworth and Coleridge believed, begin the process. They foresaw a world in which, filled with the divine life-force that flowed through nature, people would be compelled to feel love for one other. It was something they had experienced for themselves:

> And from the blessed power that rolls
> About, below, above,
> We'll frame the measure of our souls –
> They shall be tuned to love.
>
> ('Lines written at a small distance from My House' 33–6)

This would lead irresistibly to the millennium – Christ's thousand-year rule on earth. Such beliefs were not as mad as they sound. It was widely believed, as the eighteenth century came to an end, that the American and French Revolutions were harbingers of universal betterment, and that the scriptural prophecies of St John the Divine were soon to reach fulfilment. 'The ancient tradition that the world will be consumed in fire at the end of six thousand years is true, as I have heard from Hell', Blake had written in *The Marriage of Heaven and Hell.* Neither Wordsworth nor Coleridge would have declared their views so nakedly, but both wanted to write poetry that spoke of what would happen after the end of the money system and the power system. What more noble aim than to write the poem that would, in effect, precipitate the end of the world? It would dominate Wordsworth's poetic ambitions for the next forty years.

Despite Wordsworth's initial enthusiasm for the concept of pantheism – the view that God is all, and all is God – it played little part in his poetry *after* 1798. Perhaps that was because he found Coleridge's optimistic philosophy increasingly hard to credit. And that, in turn, was why he would never complete 'The Recluse'. Not that he didn't try. 'Home at Grasmere', Part I, Book I of 'The Recluse', was probably composed in 1800; 'A Tuft of Primroses' in 1806; 'The Excursion', a lengthy preliminary to 'The Recluse', was published in 1814; and he continued to write fragmentary drafts towards it until the 1830s. But Wordsworth was aware that none of these writings, all of which contain poetry worthy of our attention, fulfilled the ambitions of the work originally conceived in 1797–8. Nor did they amount to a complete poem. Claims that his entire published output constituted 'The Recluse' were symptomatic of growing desperation at the knowledge that the great epic that would justify his career was slipping from his grasp. When Coleridge expressed disappointment with 'The Excursion' in a letter of 1815, Wordsworth seems to have lost conviction he could continue with 'The Recluse', though he would make spasmodic attempts to revive it. In truth, the original scheme was so unrealistic, so grandiose, and so intellectually complex, that no one could have composed it. However, for a short while in 1798, it helped Wordsworth write a number of works he would otherwise not have written, now regarded as among his finest, all of which are included here: 'The Ruined Cottage', 'The Pedlar', 'There is an Active Principle', 'Not Useless do I Deem' and 'The Discharged Soldier' among them.

Besides 'The Recluse', Wordsworth and Coleridge spent their remarkable year of creative work together planning and writing the first volume of *Lyrical Ballads*, designed to help them raise money to visit Germany – then the intellectual hub of Europe. They travelled there in early autumn 1798. Confined to Goslar, a small market-town in the Hartz mountains, by what he believed the severest winter of the eighteenth century, Wordsworth began a six-week period of intense work which included composition of most of the first part of 'The Two-Part Prelude'. He could not proceed with 'The Recluse', but 'The Prelude' was the epic poem he was destined to write, and it was his masterpiece. It demanded no academic study, as would 'The Recluse', for its subject matter was his own life. Autobiography was in those days virtually unknown. The only precedent of recent vintage was Rousseau's *Confessions* (1782–9) – a prose work; poetic autobiography was unheard of, even offensive, to late eighteenth-century taste, and in pursuing it, Wordsworth created a new kind of poem, the latter-day descendants of which include Ginsberg's 'Howl' (1956) and Bunting's 'Briggflatts' (1965).

'The Two-Part Prelude' begins with a despairing question – 'Was it for this ...?' – because he had lost hope of continuing with 'The Recluse'. And yet the poetry of 'The Prelude' poured out of him. It was not essentially philosophical, as 'The Recluse' was to be, but surveyed his teenage years in Hawkshead, before and after the death of his father. Throughout the intervening years those powerful memories had acquired layers of reflection and meditation, and the changes wrought by time on what seems to be an unshakeable hold on the past are the subject of 'The Prelude'. At first we may not notice how our first glance of the woman with the pitcher on her head in the second of the concluding spots of time in Part I has altered, however subtly, when we see her the second time, so that it is not the pitcher, but 'her garments vexed and tossed' that strike us. Wordsworth wants to be faithful to the way in which the mind works on our memories – reconstituting them in the light of the powerful emotions attached to them. We may not be fully conscious of those emotions (in this case fear and apprehension), but they are present nonetheless.

Part II of the poem was finished in late 1799, just as the Wordsworths, back in England, moved into Dove Cottage in Grasmere. Wordsworth always thought of 'The Prelude' as an autobiographical work addressed to Coleridge – out of guilt, because it wasn't 'The Recluse'. He intended to write a third part, and attempted it in 1801. In early 1804 he reconceived it as a longer poem, and drafted many hundreds of lines that resulted in 'The Thirteen-Book Prelude' in early 1806. It still had no formal title, and would not be given one until after his death. He thought of it as 'the poem on my life', which would explain his qualifications to write 'The Recluse'. For that reason, he knew he could not to publish it until 'The Recluse' was finished, and over the rest of his life revised it compulsively. Modern editors have uncovered no less than sixteen distinct versions in his manuscripts, the most important of which are in print. After his demise it was further altered by his executors prior to publication in 1850. So it was that one of the masterpieces of the Romantic period was known at first hand only to a small coterie – Coleridge, Dorothy, Hazlitt, De Quincey and the poet's family. Byron, Shelley and Keats knew of it only by repute.

'The Prelude' had little appeal to Victorian readers, but its importance grew in the twentieth century. We should not be surprised. The story it tells – of promise under constant threat; of a man scarred by loss; of a poetic sensibility and its long, arduous journey to maturity (it is, in essence, a Bildungsroman) – is one for the modern era, that speaks to our own preoccupation with the individual psyche and the perilous course we trace from youth to adulthood.

Today Wordsworth is regarded as one of the foremost of the Romantics; during the early 1800s, however, his poetry was neither admired nor understood – in particular, 'The Thorn', 'We Are Seven' and 'The Excursion' came in for attack. Yet by the 1820s Wordsworth had acquired the status of father-figure to second-generation writers such as Keats, Byron and Shelley, who accused him of having forsaken the radical leanings of his youth (see, for instance, 'To Wordsworth', and the Dedication to *Don Juan*). It is true that he became more conservative, as the apostrophe to Burke in 'The Fourteen-Book Prelude' reveals. In 1821, in his defence, he told a correspondent:

> If I were addressing those who have dealt so liberally with the words 'renegado', 'apostate', etc., I should retort the charge upon them, and say, you have been deluded by places and persons, while I have stuck to principles – I abandoned France and her rulers when they abandoned the struggle for Liberty, gave themselves up to Tyranny, and endeavoured to enslave the world. I disapproved of the war against France at its commencement, thinking (which was perhaps an error) that it might have been avoided. But after Buonaparte had violated the independence of Switzerland, my heart turned against him and the nation that could submit to be the instrument of such an outrage.

Politics aside, Wordsworth is sometimes said to have become a worse poet as he got older. That remains a matter of vigorous debate. He was certainly a different kind of poet in his fifties, sixties and seventies but not by any means less competent or less inspired. The conclusion to 'The River Duddon' (1820) is one of the finest sonnets he ever composed – a meditation on the past and the damage wrought by time on human potential. 'Airey-Force Valley' is as good as anything in 'The Prelude', while the 'Extempore Effusion Upon the Death of James Hogg' stands as one of the most impressive elegies of the Romantic period, if only for the remarkable stanza at its heart:

Like clouds that rake the mountain-summits,
Or waves that own no curbing hand,
How fast has brother followed brother,
From sunshine to the sunless land!

(ll. 21–4)

In 1843, when he was appointed Poet Laureate, Wordsworth's reputation was at its height. At the age of 73, he had outlived other Romantic writers and was still composing and revising. In his final years he was awarded honorary degrees from Durham and Oxford and supervised the final lifetime edition of his poetry. He remains among the most highly regarded, and enduringly popular, of the Romantics.

## *A Night-Piece* (composed by 25 January 1798)[1]

The sky is overspread
With a close veil of one continuous cloud
All whitened by the moon, that just appears
A dim-seen orb, yet chequers not the ground
With any shadow – plant, or tower, or tree.
At last, a pleasant gleam breaks forth at once,
An instantaneous light; the musing man
Who walks along with his eyes bent to earth
Is startled. He looks about, the clouds are split
Asunder, and above his head he views
The clear moon, and the glory of the heavens.
There in a black-blue vault she sails along,
Followed by multitudes of stars, that small,
And bright, and sharp, along the gloomy vault
Drive as she drives. How fast they wheel away,
Yet vanish not! The wind is in the trees,
But they are silent; still they roll along
Immeasurably distant, and the vault
Built round by those white clouds, enormous clouds,
Still deepens its interminable depth.

## Notes

A Night-Piece

[1] This poem was, Wordsworth recalled many years after its composition, 'Composed upon the road between Nether Stowey and Alfoxden, extempore. I distinctly recollect the very moment I was struck, as described, "He looks up at the clouds, etc."' Critics note that it reworks a number of images and expressions from a journal entry by Dorothy of 25 January 1798: 'The sky spread over with one continuous cloud, whitened by the light of the moon, which, though her dim shape was seen, did not throw forth so strong a light as to chequer the earth with shadows. At once the clouds seemed to cleave asunder, and left her in the centre of a black-blue vault. She sailed along, followed by multitudes of stars, small, and bright, and sharp. Their brightness seemed concentrated (half-moon).'

At length the vision closes, and the mind,
Not undisturbed by the deep joy it feels,
Which slowly settles into peaceful calm,
Is left to muse upon the solemn scene.

## *The Discharged Soldier* (composed late January 1798)[1]

I love to walk
Along the public way, when, for the night
Deserted in its silence, it assumes
A character of deeper quietness
Than pathless solitudes. At such a time
I slowly mounted up a steep ascent[2]
Where the road's watery surface, to the ridge
Of that sharp rising, glittered in the moon,
And seemed before my eyes another stream[3]
Stealing with silent lapse[4] to join the brook[5]
That murmured in the valley.
On I passed
Tranquil, receiving in my own despite
Amusement as I slowly passed along,
From such near objects as from time to time
Perforce disturbed the slumber of the sense
Quiescent[6] and disposed to sympathy,
With an exhausted mind worn out by toil
And all unworthy of the deeper joy
Which waits on distant prospect – cliff or sea,
The dark blue vault, and universe of stars.
Thus did I steal along that silent road,
My body from the stillness drinking in
A restoration like the calm of sleep,
But sweeter far. Above, before, behind,
Around me, all was peace and solitude:
I looked not round, nor did the solitude
Speak to my eye, but it was heard and felt.
Oh happy state, what beauteous pictures now
Rose in harmonious imagery! They rose
As from some distant region of my soul
And came along like dreams; yet such as left
Obscurely mingled with their passing forms
A consciousness of animal delight,
A self-possession felt in every pause
And every gentle movement of my frame.[7]

## Notes

THE DISCHARGED SOLDIER

[1] This poem was revised in 1804 to form part of 'The Thirteen-Book Prelude'.

[2] *a steep ascent* Briers Brow, above the ferry on the western shore of Windermere.

[3] *And seemed…stream* Days before this line was composed, 31 January 1798, Dorothy had written: 'The road to the village of Holford glittered like another stream.'

[4] *lapse* flow; cf. 'Paradise Lost' viii 263: 'And liquid lapse of murmuring streams.'

[5] *brook* Sawrey Brook.

[6] *Quiescent* at repose, inert.

[7] *self-possession…frame* awareness of physical well-being diffused through the body and its activity.

While thus I wandered, step by step led on,
It chanced a sudden turning of the road
Presented to my view an uncouth shape,[8]
So near that, stepping back into the shade
Of a thick hawthorn, I could mark him well,
Myself unseen. He was in stature tall,
A foot above man's common measure tall,
And lank, and upright. There was in his form
A meagre stiffness. You might almost think
That his bones wounded him. His legs were long,
So long and shapeless that I looked at them
Forgetful of the body they sustained.
His arms were long and lean, his hands were bare;
His visage, wasted though it seemed, was large
In feature, his cheeks sunken, and his mouth
Showed ghastly[9] in the moonlight; from behind
A milestone propped him,[10] and his figure seemed
Half-sitting and half-standing. I could mark
That he was clad in military garb,
Though faded yet entire. His face was turned
Towards the road, yet not as if he sought
For any living object. He appeared
Forlorn and desolate, a man cut off
From all his kind, and more than half detached
From his own nature.
He was alone,
Had no attendant, neither dog, nor staff,
Nor knapsack; in his very dress appeared
A desolation, a simplicity
That appertained[11] to solitude. I think
If but a glove had dangled in his hand,
It would have made him more akin to man.
Long time I scanned him with a mingled sense
Of fear and sorrow. From his lips meanwhile
There issued murmuring sounds, as if of pain
Or of uneasy thought, yet still his form
Kept the same fearful steadiness. His shadow
Lay at his feet and moved not.
In a glen
Hard by, a village stood, whose silent doors
Were visible among the scattered trees,
Scarce distant from the spot an arrow's flight.[12]
I wished to see him move, but he remained
Fixed to his place, and still from time to time
Sent forth a murmuring voice of dead[13] complaint,

## Notes

[8] *an uncouth shape* perhaps a reminiscence of 'Paradise Lost' ii 666, which describes Death: 'The other shape, / If shape it might be called that shape had none.'

[9] *ghastly* ghost-like, pale

[10] *A milestone propped him* the third milestone from Hawkshead, just beyond Far Sawrey; the milestone has since disappeared from that spot.

[11] *appertained* belonged.

[12] *an arrow's flight* approximately 300 yards.

[13] *dead* muffled, deadened.

A groan scarce audible. Yet all the while
The chained mastiff in his wooden house
Was vexed, and from among the village trees
Howled, never ceasing. Not without reproach
Had I prolonged my watch, and now, confirmed,
And my heart's specious cowardice[14] subdued,
I left the shady nook where I had stood
And hailed the stranger. From his resting-place
He rose, and with his lean and wasted arm
In measured gesture lifted to his head
Returned my salutation. A short while
I held discourse on things indifferent
And casual matter. He meanwhile had ceased
From all complaint, his station he resumed,
Propped by the milestone as before. And when, erelong,
I asked his history, he in reply
Was neither slow nor eager; but, unmoved,[15]
And with a quiet uncomplaining voice,
A stately air of mild indifference,
He told a simple fact – that he had been
A soldier, to the tropic isles[16] had gone,
Whence he had landed now some ten days past;
That on his landing he had been dismissed,
And with the little strength he yet had left
Was travelling to regain his native home.
At this I turned and through the trees looked down
Into the village. All were gone to rest,
Nor smoke nor any taper[17] light appeared,
But every silent window to the moon
Shone with a yellow glitter. 'No one there',
Said I, 'is waking; we must measure back
The way which we have come. Behind yon wood
A labourer dwells, an honest man and kind;
He will not murmur should we break his rest,
And he will give you food (if food you need)
And lodging for the night.' At this he stooped
And from the ground took up an oaken staff
By me yet unobserved – a traveller's staff
Which I suppose from his slack hand had dropped,
And, such the languor of the weary man,
Had lain till now neglected in the grass,
But not forgotten.
Back we turned and shaped
Our course toward the cottage. He appeared
To travel without pain, and I beheld

## Notes

[14] *my heart's specious cowardice* he was motivated by fear rather than kindness.

[15] *unmoved* without emotion.

[16] *tropic isles* West Indies. An anachronism: Wordsworth has in mind the campaigns against the French that occurred in the mid-1790s, although the encounter took place during the long vacation of 1788. Conditions were bad – 40,000 British troops had died of yellow fever by 1796. Survivors were often diseased, and had no alternative but to beg in the streets.

[17] *taper* candle.

With ill-suppressed astonishment his tall
And ghostly figure moving at my side.
As we advanced I asked him for what cause
He tarried there, nor had demanded rest
At any inn or cottage. He replied,
'My weakness made me loath to move; in truth
I felt myself at ease, and much relieved,
But that the village mastiff fretted me,
And every second moment rang a peal
Felt at my very heart. I do not know
What ailed him, but it seemed as if the dog
Were howling to the murmur of the stream.'
While thus we travelled on I did not fail
To question him of what he had endured
From war, and battle, and the pestilence.[18]
He all the while was in demeanour calm,
Concise in answer. Solemn and sublime
He might have seemed, but that in all he said
There was a strange half-absence, and a tone
Of weakness and indifference, as of one
Remembering the importance of his theme
But feeling it no longer. We advanced
Slowly, and ere we to the wood were come,
Discourse had ceased. Together on we passed
In silence through the shades gloomy and dark;
Then, turning up along an open field,
We gained the cottage. At the door I knocked,
And called aloud, 'My friend, here is a man
By sickness overcome. Beneath your roof
This night let him find rest, and give him food –
The service if need be I will requite.'
Assured that now my comrade would repose
In comfort, I entreated that henceforth
He would not linger in the public ways
But at the door of cottage or of inn
Demand the succour which his state required,
And told him, feeble as he was, 'twere fit
He asked relief or alms. At this reproof,
With the same ghastly mildness in his look,
He said, 'My trust is in the God of Heaven,
And in the eye of him that passes me.'
By this the labourer had unlocked the door,
And now my comrade touched his hat again
With his lean hand, and in a voice that seemed
To speak with a reviving interest
Till then unfelt, he thanked me; I returned
The blessing of the poor unhappy man,
And so we parted.

Notes

[18] *the pestilence* yellow fever.

## *The Ruined Cottage* (composed 1797–8)

### *First Part*

'Twas summer and the sun was mounted high;
Along the south the uplands feebly glared
Through a pale steam, and all the northern downs,
In clearer air ascending, showed far off
Their surfaces with shadows dappled o'er
Of deep embattled clouds.[1] Far as the sight
Could reach those many shadows lay in spots
Determined and unmoved, with steady beams
Of clear and pleasant sunshine interposed –
Pleasant to him who on the soft cool moss
Extends his careless limbs beside the root
Of some huge oak whose aged branches make
A twilight[2] of their own, a dewy shade
Where the wren warbles while the dreaming man,
Half-conscious of that soothing melody,
With sidelong eye looks out upon the scene,
By those impending branches made more soft,
More soft and distant.
                    Other lot was mine.
Across a bare wide common I had toiled
With languid feet which by the slippery ground
Were baffled still; and when I stretched myself
On the brown earth my limbs from very heat
Could find no rest, nor my weak arm disperse
The insect host which gathered round my face
And joined their murmurs to the tedious noise
Of seeds of bursting gorse that crackled round.
I rose and turned towards a group of trees
Which midway in that level stood alone;
And thither come at length, beneath a shade
Of clustering elms[3] that sprang from the same root
I found a ruined house, four naked walls
That stared upon each other. I looked round,
And near the door I saw an aged man
Alone and stretched upon the cottage bench;
An iron-pointed staff lay at his side.
With instantaneous joy I recognized
That pride of nature and of lowly life,
The venerable Armytage, a friend

## Notes

THE RUINED COTTAGE

[1] *deep embattled clouds* an allusion to Charlotte Smith, 'Sonnet LIX' 3–4: 'Sudden, from many a deep embattled cloud / Terrific thunders burst.'

[2] *twilight* The 'twilight' in the midst of sunshine is highly reminiscent of Milton's 'darkness visible', and looks back to Virgil's 'ingenti ramorum protegat umbra' (*Georgics* ii 489).

[3] *clustering elms* Elms tend to grow in clusters as groups of them spring from a single root; they are now a rare sight in England thanks to the ravages of Dutch elm disease in the 1970s.

As dear to me as is the setting sun.
Two days before
We had been fellow-travellers. I knew
That he was in this neighbourhood, and now
Delighted found him here in the cool shade.
He lay, his pack of rustic merchandise
Pillowing his head. I guess he had no thought
Of his way-wandering life. His eyes were shut,
The shadows of the breezy elms above
Dappled his face. With thirsty heat oppressed
At length I hailed him, glad to see his hat
Bedewed with water-drops, as if the brim
Had newly scooped a running stream. He rose
And pointing to a sunflower, bade me climb
The [ ][4] wall where that same gaudy flower
Looked out upon the road.
It was a plot
Of garden-ground now wild, its matted weeds
Marked with the steps of those whom as they passed,
The gooseberry-trees that shot in long lank slips,
Or currants hanging from their leafless stems
In scanty strings, had tempted to o'erleap
The broken wall. Within that cheerless spot,
Where two tall hedgerows of thick willow boughs
Joined in a damp cold nook, I found a well
Half covered up with willow-flowers and weeds.
I slaked my thirst and to the shady bench
Returned, and while I stood unbonneted[5]
To catch the motion of the cooler air
The old man said, 'I see around me here
Things which you cannot see. We die, my friend,
Nor we alone, but that which each man loved
And prized in his peculiar nook of earth
Dies with him, or is changed, and very soon
Even of the good is no memorial left.
The poets, in their elegies and songs
Lamenting the departed, call the groves,
They call upon the hills and streams to mourn,
And senseless rocks – nor idly, for they speak
In these their invocations with a voice
Obedient to the strong creative power
Of human passion. Sympathies there are
More tranquil, yet perhaps of kindred birth,
That steal upon the meditative mind
And grow with thought. Beside yon spring I stood,
And eyed its waters till we seemed to feel
One sadness, they and I. For them a bond

## Notes

[4] There is a gap in the manuscript at this point. The missing word would presumably have been of one syllable.

[5] *unbonneted* without his hat.

Of brotherhood is broken: time has been
When every day the touch of human hand
Disturbed their stillness, and they ministered
To human comfort. When I stooped to drink
A spider's web hung to the water's edge,
And on the wet and slimy footstone lay
The useless fragment of a wooden bowl;[6]
It moved my very heart.
The day has been
When I could never pass this road but she
Who lived within these walls, when I appeared,
A daughter's welcome gave me, and I loved her
As my own child. Oh sir! The good die first,
And they whose hearts are dry as summer dust
Burn to the socket.[7] Many a passenger[8]
Has blessed poor Margaret for her gentle looks
When she upheld the cool refreshment drawn
From that forsaken spring, and no one came
But he was welcome, no one went away
But that it seemed she loved him. She is dead,
The worm is on her cheek,[9] and this poor hut,
Stripped of its outward garb of household flowers,
Of rose and sweetbriar, offers to the wind
A cold bare wall whose earthy top is tricked[10]
With weeds and the rank speargrass. She is dead,
And nettles rot and adders sun themselves
Where we have sat together while she nursed
Her infant at her breast. The unshod colt,
The wandering heifer and the potter's ass,
Find shelter now within the chimney-wall
Where I have seen her evening hearthstone blaze
And through the window spread upon the road
Its cheerful light. You will forgive me, sir,
But often on this cottage do I muse
As on a picture, till my wiser mind
Sinks, yielding to the foolishness of grief.
She had a husband, an industrious man,
Sober and steady. I have heard her say
That he was up and busy at his loom
In summer ere the mower's scythe had swept
The dewy grass, and in the early spring
Ere the last star had vanished. They who passed

## Notes

[6] *The useless…bowl* cf. the final chapter of Ecclesiastes, 'Remember now thy Creator in the days of thy youth Or ever the silver cord be loosed, or the golden bowl be broken, or the pitcher be broken at the fountain, or the wheel broken at the cistern. Then shall the dust return to the earth as it was: and the spirit shall return unto God who gave it.'

[7] *Burn to the socket* The image is of a candle burning down to its socket in a candlestick.

[8] *passenger* passer-by.

[9] *The worm is on her cheek* cf. Viola, in *Twelfth Night* II iv 110–12: 'she never told her love, / But let concealment, like a worm in the bud, / Feed on her damask cheek.'

[10] *tricked* decked.

At evening, from behind the garden-fence
Might hear his busy spade, which he would ply
After his daily work till the daylight
Was gone, and every leaf and flower were lost
In the dark hedges. So they passed their days
In peace and comfort, and two pretty babes
Were their best hope next to the God in heaven.
You may remember, now some ten years gone,
Two blighting seasons when the fields were left
With half a harvest. It pleased heaven to add
A worse affliction in the plague of war;[11]
A happy land was stricken to the heart –
'Twas a sad time of sorrow and distress.
A wanderer among the cottages,
I with my pack of winter raiment[12] saw
The hardships of that season. Many rich
Sunk down as in a dream among the poor,
And of the poor did many cease to be,
And their place knew them not. Meanwhile, abridged
Of daily comforts, gladly reconciled
To numerous self-denials, Margaret
Went struggling on through those calamitous years
With cheerful hope. But ere the second autumn,
A fever seized her husband. In disease
He lingered long, and when his strength returned
He found the little he had stored to meet
The hour of accident, or crippling age,
Was all consumed. As I have said, 'twas now
A time of trouble: shoals of artisans[13]
Were from their daily labour turned away
To hang for bread on parish charity,[14]
They and their wives and children – happier far
Could they have lived as do the little birds
That peck along the hedges, or the kite[15]
That makes her dwelling in the mountain rocks.
Ill fared it now with Robert, he who dwelt
In this poor cottage. At his door he stood
And whistled many a snatch of merry tunes
That had no mirth in them, or with his knife
Carved uncouth[16] figures on the heads of sticks;
Then idly sought about through every nook
Of house or garden any casual task

## Notes

[11] *war* England had been at war with France for five years as Wordsworth was writing in 1798; it should be borne in mind, however, that the poem is set during the aftermath of the American War, which had ended in 1783.

[12] *winter raiment* warm clothes to sell to cottagers.

[13] *shoals of artisans* crowds of workmen.

[14] *parish charity* Until the early part of the century, the poor were the responsibility of their local parish, which received no government funding to help them.

[15] *kite* large hawk.

[16] *uncouth* grotesque, ugly.

Of use or ornament, and with a strange,
Amusing but uneasy novelty
He blended where he might the various tasks
Of summer, autumn, winter, and of spring.
But this endured not; his good humour soon
Became a weight in which no pleasure was,
And poverty brought on a petted[17] mood
And a sore temper. Day by day he drooped,[18]
And he would leave his home, and to the town
Without an errand would he turn his steps,
Or wander here and there among the fields.
One while he would speak lightly of his babes
And with a cruel tongue; at other times
He played with them wild freaks of merriment,
And 'twas a piteous thing to see the looks
Of the poor innocent children. "Every smile",
Said Margaret to me here beneath these trees,
"Made my heart bleed."'
At this the old man paused,
And looking up to those enormous elms
He said, ''Tis now the hour of deepest noon.
At this still season of repose and peace,
This hour when all things which are not at rest
Are cheerful, while this multitude of flies
Fills all the air with happy melody,
Why should a tear be in an old man's eye?
Why should we thus with an untoward[19] mind,
And in the weakness of humanity,
From natural wisdom turn our hearts away,
To natural comfort shut our eyes and ears,
And feeding on disquiet, thus disturb
The calm of Nature with our restless thoughts?'

## *Second Part*

He spake with somewhat of a solemn tone,
But when he ended there was in his face
Such easy cheerfulness, a look so mild,
That for a little time it stole away
All recollection, and that simple tale
Passed from my mind like a forgotten sound.
A while on trivial things we held discourse,
To me soon tasteless.[20] In my own despite
I thought of that poor woman as of one
Whom I had known and loved. He had rehearsed

## Notes

[17] *petted* peevish.

[18] *he drooped* an echo of Milton, *Samson Agonistes* 594: 'So much I feel my genial spirits droop.'

[19] *untoward* stubborn, perverse.

[20] *tasteless* without taste, insipid.

Her homely tale with such familiar power,
With such an active countenance, an eye
So busy, that the things of which he spake
Seemed present, and, attention now relaxed,
There was a heartfelt chillness in my veins.
I rose, and turning from that breezy shade
Went out into the open air, and stood
To drink the comfort of the warmer sun.
Long time I had not stayed ere, looking round
Upon that tranquil ruin, I returned
And begged of the old man that for my sake
He would resume his story.
He replied,
'It were a wantonness,[21] and would demand
Severe reproof, if we were men whose hearts
Could hold vain dalliance with[22] the misery
Even of the dead, contented thence to draw
A momentary pleasure, never marked
By reason, barren of all future good.
But we have known that there is often found
In mournful thoughts, and always might be found,
A power to virtue friendly; were't not so
I am a dreamer among men, indeed
An idle dreamer. 'Tis a common tale
By moving accidents uncharactered,
A tale of silent suffering, hardly clothed
In bodily form, and to the grosser sense
But ill adapted – scarcely palpable
To him who does not think. But at your bidding
I will proceed.
While thus it fared with them
To whom this cottage till that hapless year
Had been a blessed home, it was my chance
To travel in a country far remote;
And glad I was when, halting by yon gate
That leads from the green lane, again I saw
These lofty elm-trees. Long I did not rest –
With many pleasant thoughts I cheered my way
O'er the flat common. At the door arrived,
I knocked, and when I entered, with the hope
Of usual greeting, Margaret looked at me
A little while, then turned her head away
Speechless, and sitting down upon a chair
Wept bitterly. I wist[23] not what to do,

Notes

[21] *wantonness* self-indulgence.

[22] *hold vain dalliance with* draw entertainment from.

[23] *wist* knew.

Or how to speak to her. Poor wretch! At last
She rose from off her seat – and then, oh sir!
I cannot tell how she pronounced my name:
With fervent love, and with a face of grief
Unutterably helpless, and a look
That seemed to cling upon me, she enquired
If I had seen her husband. As she spake
A strange surprise and fear came to my heart,
Nor had I power to answer ere she told
That he had disappeared – just two months gone.
He left his house: two wretched days had passed,
And on the third by the first break of light,
Within her casement[24] full in view she saw
A purse of gold.[25] "I trembled at the sight",
Said Margaret, "for I knew it was his hand
That placed it there. And on that very day
By one, a stranger, from my husband sent,
The tidings came that he had joined a troop
Of soldiers going to a distant land.[26]
He left me thus. Poor man, he had not heart
To take a farewell of me, and he feared
That I should follow with my babes, and sink
Beneath the misery of a soldier's life."
   This tale did Margaret tell with many tears,
And when she ended I had little power
To give her comfort, and was glad to take
Such words of hope from her own mouth as served
To cheer us both. But long we had not talked
Ere we built up a pile of better thoughts,
And with a brighter eye she looked around
As if she had been shedding tears of joy.
We parted. It was then the early spring;
I left her busy with her garden tools,
And well remember, o'er that fence she looked,
And, while I paced along the footway path,
Called out and sent a blessing after me,
With tender cheerfulness, and with a voice
That seemed the very sound of happy thoughts.
   I roved o'er many a hill and many a dale
With this my weary load, in heat and cold,
Through many a wood and many an open ground,
In sunshine or in shade, in wet or fair,
Now blithe, now drooping, as it might befall;
My best companions now the driving winds
And now the "trotting brooks"[27] and whispering trees,

## Notes

[24] *casement* window.

[25] *A purse of gold* A 'bounty' of three guineas was paid to men when they enlisted – a strong incentive for poor men with starving families.

[26] *a distant land* America.

[27] *trotting brooks* an allusion to Burns's 'To William Simpson', about the poet and his relationship to nature:

The Muse, nae poet ever fand her,
Till by himsel he learned to wander
Adown some trottin burn's meander …
(ll. 85–7)

And now the music of my own sad steps,
With many a short-lived thought that passed between
And disappeared. I came this way again
Towards the wane of summer, when the wheat
Was yellow, and the soft and bladed grass
Sprang up afresh and o'er the hayfield spread
Its tender green. When I had reached the door
I found that she was absent. In the shade
Where we now sit, I waited her return.
Her cottage in its outward look appeared
As cheerful as before, in any show
Of neatness little changed – but that I thought
The honeysuckle crowded round the door
And from the wall hung down in heavier wreaths,
And knots of worthless stonecrop started out
Along the window's edge, and grew like weeds
Against the lower panes. I turned aside
And strolled into her garden. It was changed.
The unprofitable bindweed spread his bells
From side to side, and with unwieldy wreaths
Had dragged the rose from its sustaining wall
And bent it down to earth.[28] The border tufts,
Daisy, and thrift, and lowly camomile,
And thyme, had straggled out into the paths
Which they were used to deck.
Ere this an hour
Was wasted. Back I turned my restless steps,
And as I walked before the door it chanced
A stranger passed, and guessing whom I sought,
He said that she was used to ramble far.
The sun was sinking in the west, and now
I sat with sad impatience. From within
Her solitary infant cried aloud.
The spot though fair seemed very desolate,
The longer I remained more desolate;
And looking round I saw the corner-stones,
Till then unmarked, on either side the door
With dull red stains discoloured, and stuck o'er
With tufts and hairs of wool, as if the sheep
That feed upon the commons thither came
Familiarly, and found a couching-place
Even at her threshold.
The house-clock struck eight:
I turned and saw her distant a few steps.
Her face was pale and thin, her figure too
Was changed. As she unlocked the door she said,
"It grieves me you have waited here so long,

Notes

[28] *the rose...earth* a symbol of Margaret herself, without the support of her husband.

But in good truth I've wandered much of late,
And sometimes – to my shame I speak – have need
Of my best prayers to bring me back again."
While on the board[29] she spread our evening meal
She told me she had lost her elder child,
That he for months had been a serving-boy,
Apprenticed by the parish. "I perceive
You look at me, and you have cause. Today
I have been travelling far, and many days
About the fields I wander, knowing this
Only, that what I seek I cannot find.
And so I waste my time: for I am changed,
And to myself ", said she, "have done much wrong,
And to this helpless infant. I have slept
Weeping, and weeping I have waked. My tears
Have flowed as if my body were not such
As others are, and I could never die.
But I am now in mind and in my heart
More easy, and I hope", said she, "that Heaven
Will give me patience to endure the things
Which I behold at home."
It would have grieved
Your very soul to see her. Sir, I feel
The story linger in my heart. I fear
'Tis long and tedious, but my spirit clings
To that poor woman. So familiarly
Do I perceive her manner and her look
And presence, and so deeply do I feel
Her goodness, that not seldom in my walks
A momentary trance comes over me
And to myself I seem to muse on one
By sorrow laid asleep or borne away,
A human being destined to awake
To human life, or something very near
To human life, when he shall come again
For whom she suffered. Sir, it would have grieved
Your very soul to see her: evermore
Her eyelids drooped, her eyes were downward cast,
And when she at her table gave me food
She did not look at me. Her voice was low,
Her body was subdued. In every act
Pertaining to her house-affairs appeared
The careless stillness which a thinking mind
Gives to an idle matter. Still she sighed,
But yet no motion of the breast was seen,
No heaving of the heart. While by the fire
We sat together, sighs came on my ear –
I knew not how, and hardly whence, they came.

Notes

[29] *board* table.

I took my staff, and when I kissed her babe
The tears stood in her eyes. I left her then
With the best hope and comfort I could give:
She thanked me for my will, but for my hope
It seemed she did not thank me.
                                                I returned
And took my rounds along this road again
Ere on its sunny bank the primrose flower
Had chronicled the earliest day of spring.
I found her sad and drooping. She had learned
No tidings of her husband. If he lived,
She knew not that he lived: if he were dead,
She knew not he was dead. She seemed the same
In person or appearance, but her house
Bespoke a sleepy hand of negligence.
The floor was neither dry nor neat, the hearth
Was comfortless,[30]
The windows too were dim, and her few books,[31]
Which one upon the other heretofore
Had been piled up against the corner-panes
In seemly order, now with straggling leaves
Lay scattered here and there, open or shut,
As they had chanced to fall. Her infant babe
Had from its mother caught the trick[32] of grief,
And sighed among its playthings. Once again
I turned towards the garden-gate, and saw
More plainly still that poverty and grief
Were now come nearer to her. The earth was hard,
With weeds defaced and knots of withered grass;
No ridges there appeared of clear black mould,[33]
No winter greenness. Of her herbs and flowers
It seemed the better part were gnawed away
Or trampled on the earth. A chain of straw,
Which had been twisted round the tender stem
Of a young apple-tree, lay at its root;
The bark was nibbled round by truant sheep.
Margaret stood near, her infant in her arms,
And, seeing that my eye was on the tree,
She said, "I fear it will be dead and gone
Ere Robert come again."
                                    Towards the house
Together we returned, and she enquired
If I had any hope. But for her babe,
And for her little friendless boy, she said,
She had no wish to live – that she must die

## Notes

[30] Line incomplete in the manuscript.

[31] *her few books* Margaret is literate; this was unusual. In 1795 60 per cent of the female population was unable to read or write. Most received little, if any, formal education.

[32] *trick* habit.

[33] *mould* earth.

Of sorrow. Yet I saw the idle loom
Still in its place. His Sunday garments hung
Upon the self-same nail, his very staff
Stood undisturbed behind the door. And when
I passed this way beaten by autumn winds,
She told me that her little babe was dead
And she was left alone. That very time,
I yet remember, through the miry lane
She walked with me a mile, when the bare trees
Trickled with foggy damps, and in such sort
That any heart had ached to hear her, begged
That wheresoe'er I went I still would ask
For him whom she had lost. We parted then,
Our final parting; for from that time forth
Did many seasons pass ere I returned
Into this tract[34] again.
Five tedious years
She lingered in unquiet widowhood,
A wife and widow. Needs must it have been
A sore heart-wasting. I have heard, my friend,
That in that broken arbour she would sit
The idle length of half a sabbath day –
There, where you see the toadstool's lazy head –
And when a dog passed by she still would quit
The shade and look abroad. On this old bench
For hours she sat, and evermore her eye
Was busy in the distance, shaping things
Which made her heart beat quick. Seest thou that path? –
The greensward now has broken its grey line –
There to and fro she paced through many a day
Of the warm summer, from a belt of flax
That girt her waist, spinning the long-drawn thread
With backward steps.[35] Yet ever as there passed
A man whose garments showed the soldier's red,[36]
Or crippled mendicant[37] in sailor's garb,
The little child who sat to turn the wheel
Ceased from his toil, and she, with faltering voice,
Expecting still[38] to learn her husband's fate,
Made many a fond enquiry; and when they
Whose presence gave no comfort were gone by,
Her heart was still more sad. And by yon gate
Which bars the traveller's road, she often stood,
And when a stranger horseman came, the latch
Would lift, and in his face look wistfully,

## Notes

[34] *tract* district.

[35] *from a belt...steps* Robert had been a weaver, and Margaret supports herself in her last years by spinning flax.

[36] *the soldier's red* The British army wore red uniforms, making them easy targets on the battlefield.

[37] *mendicant* beggar.

[38] *still* always.

Most happy if from aught discovered there
Of tender feeling she might dare repeat
The same sad question.
                                        Meanwhile her poor hut
Sunk to decay; for he was gone, whose hand
At the first nippings of October frost
Closed up each chink, and with fresh bands of straw
Chequered the green-grown thatch. And so she lived
Through the long winter, reckless[39] and alone,
Till this reft[40] house, by frost, and thaw, and rain,
Was sapped; and when she slept, the nightly damps
Did chill her breast, and in the stormy day
Her tattered clothes were ruffled by the wind
Even at the side of her own fire. Yet still
She loved this wretched spot, nor would for worlds
Have parted hence; and still that length of road,
And this rude bench, one torturing hope endeared,
Fast rooted at her heart. And here, my friend,
In sickness she remained; and here she died,
Last human tenant of these ruined walls.'
    The old man ceased; he saw that I was moved.
From that low bench, rising instinctively,
I turned aside in weakness, nor had power
To thank him for the tale which he had told.
I stood, and leaning o'er the garden gate
Reviewed that woman's sufferings; and it seemed
To comfort me while with a brother's love
I blessed her in the impotence of grief.
At length towards the cottage I returned
Fondly, and traced with milder interest
That secret spirit of humanity
Which, mid the calm oblivious[41] tendencies
Of Nature, mid her plants, her weeds and flowers,
And silent overgrowings, still survived.
The old man, seeing this, resumed, and said,
'My friend, enough to sorrow have you given,
The purposes of wisdom ask no more:
Be wise and cheerful, and no longer read
The forms of things with an unworthy eye:
She sleeps in the calm earth, and peace is here.
I well remember that those very plumes,
Those weeds, and the high speargrass on that wall,
By mist and silent raindrops silvered o'er,
As once I passed did to my mind convey
So still an image of tranquillity,
So calm and still, and looked so beautiful
Amid the uneasy thoughts which filled my mind,

## Notes

[39] *reckless* not caring (i.e. for herself ).

[40] *reft* bereft (i.e. without Robert).

[41] *oblivious* Nature carries on oblivious to human affairs.

That what we feel of sorrow and despair
From ruin and from change, and all the grief
The passing shows of being leave behind,
Appeared an idle dream that could not live
Where meditation was. I turned away,
And walked along my road in happiness.'
   He ceased. By this the sun declining shot
A slant and mellow radiance, which began
To fall upon us where beneath the trees
We sat on that low bench. And now we felt,
Admonished thus, the sweet hour coming on:
A linnet warbled from those lofty elms,
A thrush sang loud, and other melodies
At distance heard peopled the milder air.
The old man rose and hoisted up his load;
Together casting then a farewell look
Upon those silent walls, we left the shade,
And ere the stars were visible attained
A rustic inn, our evening resting-place.

## *The Pedlar* (composed February–March 1798, edited from MS)[1]

Him had I seen the day before, alone
And in the middle of the public way,
Standing to rest himself. His eyes were turned
Towards the setting sun, while, with that staff
Behind him fixed, he propped a long white pack
Which crossed his shoulders, wares for maids who live
In lonely villages or straggling huts.[2]
I knew him – he was born of lowly race
On Cumbrian hills, and I have seen the tear
Stand in his luminous[3] eye when he described
The house in which his early youth was passed,
And found I was no stranger to the spot.
I loved to hear him talk of former days
And tell how when a child, ere[4] yet of age
To be a shepherd, he had learned to read
His bible in a school that stood alone,
Sole building on a mountain's dreary edge,
Far from the sight of city spire, or sound
Of minster clock. From that bleak tenement[5]

## Notes

THE PEDLAR

[1] 'The Pedlar' begins abruptly because it was composed originally as part of 'The Ruined Cottage'. It is Wordsworth's earliest piece of autobiographical and philosophical poetry, and was to be a dry run for both 'The Recluse' and 'The Prelude'.

[2] *huts* cottages.

[3] *luminous* shining.

[4] *ere* before.

[5] *tenement* building.

He many an evening to his distant home
In solitude returning saw the hills
Grow larger in the darkness, all alone
Beheld the stars come out above his head,
And travelled through the wood, no comrade near
To whom he might confess the things he saw.
  So the foundations of his mind were laid.
In such communion, not from terror free,[6]
While yet a child, and long before his time,
He had perceived the presence and the power
Of greatness, and deep feelings had impressed
Great objects on his mind with portraiture
And colour so distinct that on his mind
They lay like substances, and almost seemed
To haunt the bodily sense.[7] He had received
A precious gift, for as he grew in years
With these impressions would he still compare
All his ideal stores, his shapes and forms,
And, being still unsatisfied with aught
Of dimmer character, he thence attained
An *active* power to fasten images
Upon his brain, and on their pictured lines
Intensely brooded, even[8] till they acquired
The liveliness of dreams. Nor did he fail,
While yet a child, with a child's eagerness
Incessantly to turn his ear and eye
On all things which the rolling seasons brought
To feed such appetite. Nor this alone
Appeased his yearning – in the after-day[9]
Of boyhood, many an hour in caves forlorn
And in the hollow depths of naked crags
He sate, and even in their fixed lineaments,
Or[10] from the power of a peculiar eye,[11]
Or by creative feeling[12] overborne,
Or by predominance of thought[13] oppressed,
Even in their fixed and steady lineaments
He traced an ebbing and a flowing mind,
Expression ever varying.
                                        Thus informed,
He had small need of books; for many a tale
Traditionary round the mountains hung,
And many a legend peopling the dark woods
Nourished imagination in her growth,

## Notes

[6] *not from terror free* Burke had celebrated the importance of fear in aesthetic terms in his *Sublime and Beautiful* (1757). For Wordsworth, fear is important as it stimulates and intensifies imaginative thought.

[7] *deep feelings...sense* Sublime natural forms are literally stamped ('impressed') on the child's mind as mental 'images', thanks partly to strong feelings (of fear, pain, pleasure) that he experienced in their presence.

[8] *even* to be scanned as a single syllable, 'e'en'.

[9] *after-day* later time.

[10] *Or* either.

[11] *the power of a peculiar eye* especially sharp observation.

[12] *creative feeling* imaginative sympathy.

[13] *predominance of thought* dominance of thought over other kinds of response.

And gave the mind that apprehensive power
By which she is made quick to recognize
The moral properties and scope of things.
But greedily he read and read again
Whate'er the rustic vicar's shelf supplied:
The life and death of martyrs who sustained
Intolerable pangs,[14] and here and there
A straggling volume, torn and incomplete,
Which left half-told the preternatural tale,
Romance of giants, chronicle of fiends,
Profuse in garniture of wooden cuts[15]
Strange and uncouth, dire faces, figures dire,
Sharp-kneed, sharp-elbowed, and lean-ankled too,
With long and ghostly shanks, forms which once seen
Could never be forgotten – things though low,
Though low and humble, not to be despised
By such as have observed the curious links
With which the perishable hours of life
Are bound together, and the world of thought
Exists and is sustained.[16] Within his heart
Love was not yet, nor the pure joy of love,
By sound diffused, or by the breathing air,
Or by the silent looks of happy things,
Or flowing from the universal face –
Of earth and sky. But he had felt the power
Of Nature, and already was prepared
By his intense conceptions to receive
Deeply the lesson deep of love, which he
Whom Nature, by whatever means, has taught
To feel intensely, cannot but receive.
  Ere his ninth year he had been sent abroad[17]
To tend his father's sheep; such was his task
Henceforward till the later day of youth.
Oh then, what soul was his, when on the tops
Of the high mountains he beheld the sun
Rise up and bathe the world in light! He looked,
The ocean and the earth beneath him lay
In gladness and deep joy. The clouds were touched,
And in their silent faces he did read
Unutterable love. Sound needed none,
Nor any voice of joy: his spirit drank
The spectacle. Sensation, soul, and form,
All melted into him; they swallowed up

## Notes

[14] *The life and death…pangs* Wordsworth read Foxe's *Book of Martyrs* as a schoolboy at Hawkshead.

[15] *Profuse in garniture of wooden cuts* with many woodcut illustrations.

[16] *the curious links…sustained* a reference to the associationist philosophy of David Hartley, which informs much of Wordsworth's thinking at this moment. The 'links' that connect the 'perishable hours of life' are emotions (arising, in this case, out of the romances of giants and chronicles of fiends) that confirm the underlying unity and order of the imaginative mind.

[17] *abroad* out.

His animal being. In them did he live,
And by them did he live – they were his life.
In such access of mind, in such high hour
Of visitation from the living God,
He did not feel the God, he felt his works.
Thought was not; in enjoyment it expired.
Such hour by prayer or praise was unprofaned;
He neither prayed, nor offered thanks or praise;
His mind was a thanksgiving to the power
That made him. It was blessedness and love.
   A shepherd on the lonely mountain-tops,
Such intercourse[18] was his, and in this sort
Was his existence oftentimes possessed.
Oh *then* how beautiful, how bright, appeared
The written promise. He had early learned
To reverence the volume which displays
The mystery, the life which cannot die,
But in the mountains did he FEEL his faith,
There did he see the writing. All things there
Breathed immortality, revolving life,
And greatness still revolving, infinite.
There littleness was not, the least of things
Seemed infinite, and there his spirit shaped
Her prospects – nor did he *believe;* he saw.
What wonder if his being thus became
Sublime and comprehensive? Low desires,
Low thoughts, had there no place; yet was his heart
Lowly, for he was meek in gratitude
Oft as he called to mind those ecstacies,
And whence they flowed; and from them he acquired
Wisdom which works through patience – thence he learned
In many a calmer hour of sober thought
To look on Nature with an humble heart,
Self-questioned where it did not understand,
And with a superstitious[19] eye of love.
   Thus passed the time, yet to the neighbouring town
He often went with what small overplus
His earnings might supply, and brought away
The book which most had tempted his desires
While at the stall he read. Among the hills
He gazed upon that mighty orb[20] of song,
The divine Milton.[21] Lore of different kind,
The annual savings of a toilsome life,
The schoolmaster supplied – books that explain
The purer elements of truth involved
In lines and numbers, and by charm severe,

## Notes

[18] *intercourse* communion.

[19] *superstitious* conscientious.

[20] *orb* world.

[21] *Milton* a favourite poet with young Wordsworth.

Especially perceived where Nature droops
And feeling is suppressed, preserve the mind
Busy in solitude and poverty.
And thus employed he many a time o'erlooked[22]
The listless hours when in the hollow vale,
Hollow and green, he lay on the green turf
In lonesome idleness. What could he do?
Nature was at his heart, and he perceived,
Though yet he knew not how, a wasting[23] power
In all things which from her sweet influence
Might tend to wean[24] him. Therefore with her hues,
Her forms, and with the spirit of her forms,
He clothed the nakedness of austere truth.[25]
While yet he lingered in the elements
Of science, and among her simplest laws,
His triangles they were the stars of heaven,
The silent stars; his altitudes[26] the crag
Which is the eagle's birthplace, or some peak
Familiar with forgotten years which shows
Inscribed, as with the silence of the thought,
Upon its bleak and visionary[27] sides
The history of many a winter storm,
Or obscure records of the path of fire.[28]
Yet with these lonesome sciences he still
Continued to amuse the heavier hours
Of solitude. Yet not the less he found
In cold elation, and the lifelessness
Of truth by oversubtlety dislodged
From grandeur and from love, an idle toy,[29]
The dullest of all toys. He saw in truth
A holy spirit and a breathing soul;
He reverenced her and trembled at her look,
When with a moral beauty in her face
She led him through the worlds.
    But now, before his twentieth year was passed,
Accumulated feelings pressed his heart
With an increasing weight; he was o'erpowered
By Nature, and his spirit was on fire
With restless thoughts. His eye became disturbed,[30]
And many a time he wished the winds might rage
When they were silent. Far more fondly now
Than in his earlier season did he love

## Notes

[22] *o'erlooked* didn't notice, whiled away.
[23] *wasting* destructive, consuming.
[24] *wean* A child is 'weaned' from its mother when she ceases to breastfeed it. Nature will wean the boy away from the destructive tendency of geometrical analysis.
[25] *Therefore...truth* The boy clothes the 'austere truth' of geometry with the colours and shapes of the landscape he loves.
[26] *altitudes* in geometrical terms, the height of a triangle measured by a perpendicular from the peak to the base.
[27] *visionary* embodying truth.
[28] *the path of fire* an apocalyptic and tumultuous event in the past, to which the mountains bear witness by their markings.
[29] *toy* hobby.
[30] *disturbed* i.e. with intense passion and creative thought.

Tempestuous nights, the uproar and the sounds
That live in darkness. From his intellect,
And from the stillness of abstracted thought,
He sought repose in vain. I have heard him say
That at this time he scanned the laws of light
Amid the roar of torrents, where they send
From hollow clefts up to the clearer air
A cloud of mist, which in the shining sun
Varies its rainbow hues.[31] But vainly thus,
And vainly by all other means he strove
To mitigate[32] the fever of his heart.
    From Nature and her overflowing soul
He had received so much that all his thoughts
Were steeped in feeling.[33] He was only then
Contented when with bliss ineffable[34]
He felt the sentiment of being spread
O'er all that moves, and all that seemeth still,[35]
O'er all which, lost beyond the reach of thought
And human knowledge, to the human eye
Invisible, yet liveth to the heart;
O'er all that leaps, and runs, and shouts, and sings,
Or beats the gladsome air; o'er all that glides
Beneath the wave, yea, in the wave itself,
And mighty depth of waters. Wonder not
If such his transports[36] were; for in all things
He saw one life, and felt that it was joy.
One song they sang, and it was audible –
Most audible then when the fleshly ear,
O'ercome by grosser prelude of that strain,[37]
Forgot its functions, and slept undisturbed.
    These things he had sustained[38] in solitude
Even till his bodily strength began to yield
Beneath their weight.[39] The mind within him burnt,
And he resolved to quit his native hills.
The father strove to make his son perceive
As clearly as the old man did himself
With what advantage he might teach a school
In the adjoining village. But the youth,
Who of this service made a short essay,[40]
Found that the wanderings of his thought were then
A misery to him, that he must resign
A task he was unable to perform.

## Notes

[31] *I have heard…hues* The Pedlar attempts to reconcile Newtonian optics with his perceptions of Nature.

[32] *mitigate* reduce.

[33] *steeped in feeling* filled with emotion.

[34] *ineffable* indescribable.

[35] *He felt…still* The Pedlar is aware of some divine presence, not unlike the Platonic world soul, infused throughout the natural world.

[36] *transports* raptures.

[37] *grosser prelude of that strain* The 'music' of ordinary sense experience – so intense that it leads to loss of bodily awareness and a perception of the mystic 'song' of the one life.

[38] *sustained* suffered.

[39] *These things…weight* The transcendent experiences are so intense they sap his strength.

[40] *essay* trial.

He asked his father's blessing, and assumed
This lowly occupation. The old man
Blessed him and prayed for him, yet with a heart
Foreboding[41] evil.
From his native hills
He wandered far. Much did he see of men,
Their manners,[42] their enjoyments and pursuits,
Their passions and their feelings, chiefly those
Essential and eternal in the heart,
Which mid the simpler forms of rural life
Exist more simple in their elements,
And speak a plainer language. Many a year
Of lonesome meditation and impelled
By curious thought he was content to toil
In this poor calling, which he now pursued
From habit and necessity. He walked
Among the impure haunts of vulgar men
Unstained; the talisman[43] of constant thought
And kind sensations in a gentle heart
Preserved him. Every show of vice to him
Was a remembrancer[44] of what he knew,
Or a fresh seed of wisdom, or produced
That tender interest[45] which the virtuous feel
Among the wicked, which when truly felt
May bring the bad man nearer to the good,
But, innocent of evil, cannot sink
The good man to the bad.
Among the woods
A lone enthusiast, and among the hills,
Itinerant[46] in this labour he had passed
The better portion of his time, and there
From day to day had his affections[47] breathed
The wholesome air of Nature; there he kept
In solitude and solitary thought,
So pleasant were those comprehensive views,
His mind in a just equipoise[48] of love.
Serene it was, unclouded by the cares
Of ordinary life – unvexed, unwarped
By partial bondage.[49] In his steady course
No piteous revolutions[50] had he felt,
No wild varieties of joy or grief.
Unoccupied by sorrow of its own,
His heart lay open; and, by Nature tuned
And constant disposition of his thoughts

## Notes

[41] *Foreboding* anticipating.
[42] *manners* way of life.
[43] *talisman* The Pedlar's thoughts act as a charm that protects him.
[44] *remembrancer* reminder.
[45] *tender interest* compassion.
[46] *Itinerant* travelling.
[47] *affections* feelings.
[48] *equipoise* balance.
[49] *partial bondage* i.e. to the cares of daily life.
[50] *revolutions* reversals, changes.

To sympathy with man, he was alive
To all that was enjoyed where'er he went,
And all that was endured; and, in himself
Happy, and quiet in his cheerfulness,
He had no painful pressure from within
Which made him turn aside from wretchedness
With coward fears. He could afford to suffer
With those whom he saw suffer. Hence it was
That in our best experience he was rich,
And in the wisdom of our daily life.
For hence, minutely, in his various rounds
He had observed the progress and decay
Of many minds, of minds and bodies too –
The history of many families,
And how they prospered, how they were o'erthrown
By passion or mischance, or such misrule
Among the unthinking masters of the earth
As makes the nations groan. He was a man,
One whom you could not pass without remark[51] –
If you had met him on a rainy day
You would have stopped to look at him. Robust,
Active, and nervous,[52] was his gait; his limbs
And his whole figure breathed intelligence.
His body, tall and shapely, showed in front
A faint line of the hollowness of age,
Or rather what appeared the curvature
Of toil; his head looked up steady and fixed.
Age had compressed the rose upon his cheek
Into a narrower circle of deep red,
But had not tamed his eye, which, under brows
Of hoary grey, had meanings which it brought
From years of youth, which, like a being made
Of many beings, he had wondrous skill
To blend with meanings of the years to come,
Human, or such as lie beyond the grave.
Long had I loved him. Oh, it was most sweet
To hear him teach in unambitious style
Reasoning and thought, by painting as he did
The manners[53] and the passions. Many a time
He made a holiday and left his pack
Behind, and we two wandered through the hills
A pair of random travellers. His eye
Flashing poetic fire he would repeat
The songs of Burns, or many a ditty wild
Which he had fitted to the moorland harp –
His own sweet verse – and, as we trudged along,
Together did we make the hollow grove

Notes

[51] *without remark* without noticing.

[52] *nervous* vigorous.

[53] *manners* way of life.

Ring with our transports.
Though he was untaught,
In the dead lore of schools[54] undisciplined,
Why should he grieve? He was a chosen son.
He yet retained an ear which deeply felt
The voice of Nature in the obscure wind,
The sounding mountain, and the running stream.
From deep analogies by thought supplied,
Or consciousnesses not to be subdued,
To every natural form, rock, fruit, and flower,
Even the loose stones that cover the highway,
He gave a moral life;[55] he saw them feel,
Or linked them to some feeling. In all shapes
He found a secret and mysterious soul,
A fragrance and a spirit of strange meaning.
Though poor in outward show, he was most rich:
He had a world about him – 'twas his own,
He made it – for it only lived to him,
And to the God who looked into his mind.
Such sympathies would often bear him far
In outward gesture, and in visible look,
Beyond the common seeming[56] of mankind.
Some called it madness; such it might have been,
But that he had an eye which evermore
Looked deep into the shades of difference[57]
As they lie hid in all exterior forms,
Near or remote, minute or vast – an eye
Which from a stone, a tree, a withered leaf,
To the broad ocean and the azure heavens
Spangled with kindred multitudes of stars,
Could find no surface where its power might sleep –
Which spake perpetual logic to his soul,
And by an unrelenting agency
Did bind his feelings even as in a chain.

## Notes

[54] *the dead lore of schools* philosophy.

[55] *To every…life* He attributed to natural things the ability to act as independent moral agents; effectively, he endowed them with human emotions.

[56] *seeming* conduct, behaviour.

[57] *shades of difference* small and subtle differences perceptible only to the trained mind.

## *The Two-Part Prelude* (Part I composed October 1798–February 1799; Part II, autumn 1799)[1]

### First Part

Was it for this
That one, the fairest of all rivers, loved
To blend his murmurs with my nurse's song,
And from his alder shades and rocky falls,
And from his fords and shallows, sent a voice
That flowed along my dreams? For this didst thou,
Oh Derwent, travelling over the green plains
Near my 'sweet birthplace', didst thou, beauteous stream,
Make ceaseless music through the night and day,
Which with its steady cadence tempering
Our human waywardness, composed my thoughts
To more than infant softness, giving me,
Among the fretful dwellings of mankind,
A knowledge, a dim earnest[2] of the calm
Which nature breathes among the fields and groves?
Beloved Derwent, fairest of all streams,
Was it for this that I, a four years' child,
A naked boy, among thy silent pools,
Made one long bathing of a summer's day,
Basked in the sun, or plunged into thy streams
Alternate all a summer's day, or coursed[3]
Over the sandy fields, and dashed the flowers
Of yellow grunsel;[4] or, when crag and hill,
The woods, and distant Skiddaw's lofty height[5]
Were bronzed with a deep radiance, stood alone,
A naked savage in the thunder shower?
And afterwards, 'twas in a later day,
Though early,[6] when upon the mountain-slope
The frost and breath of frosty wind had snapped
The last autumnal crocus, 'twas my joy
To wander half the night among the cliffs
And the smooth hollows where the woodcocks ran
Along the moonlight turf. In thought and wish
That time, my shoulder all with springes[7] hung,
I was a fell destroyer. Gentle powers
Who give us happiness and call it peace,
When scudding on from snare to snare I plied
My anxious visitation – hurrying on,
Still hurrying, hurrying onward – how my heart

## Notes

The Two-Part Prelude: First Part

[1] This is the earliest complete version of Wordsworth's masterpiece, 'The Two-Part Prelude'. It would go through numerous revisions but was not published in his lifetime.

[2] *earnest* foretaste, pledge.

[3] *coursed* run.

[4] *grunsel* ragwort.

[5] *distant Skiddaw's lofty height* Skiddaw is the fourth highest peak in the Lake District at 3,053 feet.

[6] *And…early* Wordsworth jumps forward to his time at Hawkshead Grammar School, which he joined in May 1779; he left Hawkshead for Cambridge in the autumn of 1787.

[7] *springes* traps.

Panted among the scattered yew-trees and the crags
That looked upon me, how my bosom beat
With expectation! Sometimes strong desire,
Resistless, overpowered me, and the bird
Which was the captive of another's toils[8]
Became my prey; and when the deed was done
I heard among the solitary hills
Low breathings coming after me, and sounds
Of undistinguishable motion, steps
Almost as silent as the turf they trod.[9]
   Nor less in springtime, when on southern banks
The shining sun had from his knot of leaves
Decoyed the primrose flower, and when the vales
And woods were warm, was I a rover then
In the high places, on the lonesome peaks
Among the mountains and the winds. Though mean
And though inglorious were my views, the end
Was not ignoble.[10] Oh, when I have hung
Above the raven's nest, by knots of grass
Or half-inch fissures in the slipp'ry rock
But ill sustained, and almost (as it seemed)
Suspended by the blast which blew amain,[11]
Shouldering the naked crag[12] – oh, at that time,
While on the perilous ridge I hung alone,
With what strange utterance did the loud dry wind
Blow through my ears! The sky seemed not a sky
Of earth, and with what motion moved the clouds!
   The mind of man is fashioned and built up
Even as a strain of music; I believe
That there are spirits which, when they would form
A favoured being, from his very dawn
Of infancy do open out the clouds
As at the touch of lightning, seeking him
With gentle visitation – quiet powers,
Retired and seldom recognized, yet kind
And to the very meanest not unknown.
With me, though rarely, in my early days,
They communed; others too there are who use,
Yet haply aiming at the self-same end,
Severer interventions, ministry[13]
More palpable – and of their school was I.
   They guided me. One evening, led by them,
I went alone into a shepherd's boat,
A skiff that to a willow-tree was tied
Within a rocky cave, its usual home.
The moon was up, the lake was shining clear

## Notes

[8] *toils* a pun, meaning both 'trap' and 'labours'.

[9] *and when…trod* woodcock were a delicacy and fetched sixteen or twenty pence a couple on the spot before being sent to London on the Kendal stagecoach. They were trapped by snares set at the end of narrowing avenues of stones which the birds would not jump over.

[10] *the end…ignoble* ravens preyed on lambs and anyone who destroyed their eggs was rewarded by the parish.

[11] *amain* strongly.

[12] *Shouldering the naked crag* Wordsworth recalls Atlas, Titan of myth, who bore the world on his shoulders.

[13] *ministry* guidance.

Among the hoary mountains; from the shore
I pushed, and struck the oars, and struck again
In cadence, and my little boat moved on
Just like a man who walks with stately step
Though bent on speed. It was an act of stealth
And troubled pleasure; not without the voice
Of mountain-echoes did my boat move on,
Leaving behind her still on either side
Small circles glittering idly in the moon
Until they melted all into one track
Of sparkling light. A rocky steep uprose
Above the cavern of the willow-tree,
And now, as suited one who proudly rowed
With his best skill, I fixed a steady view
Upon the top of that same craggy ridge,
The bound of the horizon, for behind
Was nothing but the stars and the grey sky.
She was an elfin pinnace;[14] twenty times
I dipped my oars into the silent lake,
And, as I rose upon the stroke, my boat
Went heaving through the water like a swan –
When, from behind that rocky steep (till then
The bound of the horizon), a huge cliff,[15]
As if with voluntary power instinct,[16]
Upreared its head. I struck and struck again,
And, growing still in stature, the huge cliff
Rose up between me and the stars, and still,
With measured motion, like a living thing
Strode after me. With trembling hands I turned,
And through the silent water stole my way
Back to the cavern of the willow-tree.
There in her mooring-place I left my bark,
And through the meadows homeward went with grave
And serious thoughts; and after I had seen
That spectacle, for many days my brain
Worked with a dim and undetermined sense
Of unknown modes of being. In my thoughts
There was a darkness – call it solitude
Or blank desertion; no familiar shapes
Of hourly objects, images of trees,
Of sea or sky, no colours of green fields,
But huge and mighty forms that do not live
Like living men moved slowly through my mind
By day, and were the trouble of my dreams.
  Ah, not in vain, ye beings of the hills,
And ye that walk the woods and open heaths
By moon or starlight, thus from my first dawn

## Notes

[14] *elfin pinnace* The language embodies the child's imaginative absorption; the boat seems to be enchanted.

[15] *a huge cliff* Glenridding Dodd, the stepped-back summit of which causes its peak to make a sudden delayed appearance above the 'craggy steep' of Stybarrow Crag.

[16] *instinct* imbued, filled.

Of childhood did ye love to intertwine
The passions that build up our human soul,
Not with the mean and vulgar works of man,
But with high objects, with eternal things,
With life and nature, purifying thus
The elements of feeling and of thought,
And sanctifying by such discipline
Both pain and fear, until we recognize
A grandeur in the beatings of the heart.
   Nor was this fellowship vouchsafed to me
With stinted kindness. In November days,
When vapours rolling down the valleys made
A lonely scene more lonesome, among woods
At noon, and mid the calm of summer nights
When by the margin of the trembling lake
Beneath the gloomy hills I homeward went
In solitude, such intercourse[17] was mine.
   And in the frosty season, when the sun
Was set, and visible for many a mile,
The cottage windows through the twilight blazed,
I heeded not the summons;[18] clear and loud
The village clock tolled six; I wheeled about,
Proud and exulting like an untired horse
That cares not for its home. All shod with steel
We hissed along the polished ice in games
Confederate,[19] imitative of the chase
And woodland pleasures – the resounding horn,
The pack loud bellowing, and the hunted hare.
So through the darkness and the cold we flew,
And not a voice was idle. With the din,
Meanwhile, the precipices rang aloud,
The leafless trees and every icy crag
Tinkled like iron, while the distant hills
Into the tumult sent an alien sound
Of melancholy not unnoticed – while the stars
Eastward were sparkling clear, and in the west
The orange sky of evening died away.
   Not seldom from the uproar I retired
Into a silent bay, or sportively
Glanced sideway, leaving the tumultuous throng,
To cut across the shadow[20] of a star
That gleamed upon the ice. And oftentimes,
When we had given our bodies to the wind,
And all the shadowy banks on either side
Came sweeping through the darkness, spinning still
The rapid line of motion – then at once
Have I, reclining back upon my heels,

## Notes

[17] *intercourse* companionship (with Nature).

[18] *The cottage...summons* Candle- and fire-light through the cottage windows tell the boy it is time to go home.

[19] *Confederate* collective; games played in groups.

[20] *shadow* reflection.

Stopped short: yet still the solitary cliffs
Wheeled by me, even as if the earth had rolled
With visible motion her diurnal[21] round;
Behind me did they stretch in solemn train[22]
Feebler and feebler, and I stood and watched
Till all was tranquil as a summer sea.
 Ye powers of earth, ye genii of the springs!
And ye that have your voices in the clouds
And ye that are familiars of the lakes
And of the standing pools, I may not think
A vulgar hope was yours when ye employed
Such ministry[23] – when ye through many a year
Thus by the agency of boyish sports
On caves and trees, upon the woods and hills,
Impressed[24] upon all forms the characters[25]
Of danger or desire, and thus did make
The surface of the universal earth
With meanings of delight, of hope and fear,
Work like a sea.
 Not uselessly employed,
I might pursue this theme through every change
Of exercise and sport to which the year
Did summon us in its delightful round.
We were a noisy crew; the sun in heaven
Beheld not vales more beautiful than ours,
Nor saw a race in happiness and joy
More worthy of the fields where they were sown.
I would record with no reluctant voice
Our home amusements by the warm peat-fire
At evening, when with pencil and with slate,
In square divisions parcelled out, and all
With crosses and with cyphers scribbled o'er,[26]
We schemed and puzzled, head opposed to head,
In strife too humble to be named in verse;
Or round the naked table, snow-white deal,
Cherry or maple, sat in close array,
And to the combat, loo or whist, led on
A thick-ribbed army[27] – not (as in the world)
Discarded and ungratefully thrown by
Even for the very service they had wrought,
But husbanded[28] through many a long campaign.
Oh with what echoes on the board they fell!
Ironic diamonds, hearts of sable hue,
Queens gleaming through their splendour's last decay,
Knaves wrapped in one assimilating gloom,
And kings indignant at the shame incurred
By royal visages. Meanwhile abroad

## Notes

[21] *diurnal* daily.
[22] *train* sequence, succession.
[23] *ministry* guidance.
[24] *Impressed* stamped, printed.
[25] *characters* signs, marks.
[26] *With crosses…o'er* noughts and crosses (tick-tack-toe).
[27] *A thick-ribbed army* The cards' edges have thickened through use.
[28] *husbanded* saved up; they were survivors.

The heavy rain was falling, or the frost
Raged bitterly with keen and silent tooth,
Or, interrupting the impassioned game,
Oft from the neighbouring lake the splitting ice,
While it sank down towards the water, sent
Among the meadows and the hills its long
And frequent yellings,[29] imitative some
Of wolves that howl along the Bothnic main.[30]
  Nor with less willing heart would I rehearse
The woods of autumn and their hidden bowers
With milk-white clusters[31] hung, the rod and line
(True symbol of the foolishness of hope)
Which with its strong enchantment led me on
By rocks and pools where never summer star
Impressed its shadow,[32] to forlorn cascades
Among the windings of the mountain-brooks;
The kite, in sultry calms from some high hill
Sent up, ascending thence till it was lost
Among the fleecy clouds, in gusty days
Launched from the lower grounds, and suddenly
Dashed headlong – and rejected by the storm.
All these and more with rival claims demand
Grateful acknowledgement. It were a song
Venial, and such as if I rightly judge
I might protract unblamed, but I perceive
That much is overlooked, and we should ill
Attain our object if from delicate fears
Of breaking in upon the unity
Of this my argument[33] I should omit
To speak of such effects as cannot here
Be regularly classed, yet tend no less
To the same point, the growth of mental power
And love of nature's works.
                                        Ere I had seen
Eight summers[34] – and 'twas in the very week
When I was first entrusted to thy vale,
Beloved Hawkshead! – when thy paths, thy shores
And brooks, were like a dream of novelty
To my half-infant mind, I chanced to cross
One of those open fields which, shaped like ears,[35]
Make green peninsulas on Esthwaite's Lake.
Twilight was coming on, yet through the gloom
I saw distinctly on the opposite shore,
Beneath a tree and close by the lakeside,
A heap of garments, as if left by one
Who there was bathing. Half an hour I watched

## Notes

[29] *its long…yellings* The ice makes a yelling noise as it breaks up.

[30] *Bothnic main* the northern Baltic.

[31] *milk-white clusters* hazel nuts.

[32] *shadow* reflection.

[33] *argument* theme.

[34] *Ere I had…summers* Despite Wordsworth's claims, he went to Hawkshead Grammar School in May 1779 at the age of nine.

[35] *shaped like ears* There are three such peninsulas; Wordsworth has in mind Strickland Ees.

And no one owned them; meanwhile the calm lake
Grew dark with all the shadows on its breast,
And now and then a leaping fish disturbed
The breathless stillness. The succeeding day
There came a company, and in their boat
Sounded with iron hooks and with long poles.
At length the dead man,[36] mid that beauteous scene
Of trees and hills and water, bolt upright
Rose with his ghastly face. I might advert[37]
To numerous accidents in flood or field,
Quarry or moor, or mid the winter snows,
Distresses and disasters, tragic facts
Of rural history that impressed my mind
With images to which, in following years,
Far other feelings were attached, with forms
That yet exist with independent life,
And, like their archetypes, know no decay.
There are in our existence spots of time
Which with distinct pre-eminence retain
A fructifying[38] virtue, whence, depressed
By trivial occupations and the round
Of ordinary intercourse, our minds
(Especially the imaginative power)
Are nourished, and invisibly repaired.
Such moments chiefly seem to have their date
In our first childhood.
I remember well
('Tis of an early season that I speak,
The twilight of rememberable life)
While I was yet an urchin,[39] one who scarce
Could hold a bridle, with ambitious hopes
I mounted, and we rode towards the hills.
We were a pair of horsemen: honest James[40]
Was with me, my encourager and guide.
We had not travelled long ere some mischance
Disjoined me from my comrade and, through fear
Dismounting, down the rough and stony moor
I led my horse, and, stumbling on, at length
Came to a bottom where in former times
A man, the murderer of his wife, was hung
In irons; mouldered was the gibbet-mast,
The bones were gone, the iron and the wood,
Only a long green ridge of turf remained
Whose shape was like a grave.[41] I left the spot

## Notes

[36] *the dead man* John Jackson, village schoolmaster from Sawrey, was drowned while bathing in Esthwaite Water, 18 June 1779.

[37] *advert* refer.

[38] *fructifying* the power to make fruitful.

[39] *an urchin* Wordsworth was five at the time this incident took place. He was staying with his grandparents at Penrith.

[40] *honest James* identified in 'The Fourteen-Book Prelude' as 'An ancient Servant of my Father's house'.

[41] *Mouldered was the gibbet-mast...like a grave* The valley bottom was Cowdrake Quarry, east of Penrith, where Thomas Nicholson was hanged in 1767 for murdering a butcher. However, 'The Prelude' is not a record of fact, and it is worth noting that Nicholson's gibbet had not 'mouldered down' in 1775, and a 5-year-old would not have ridden that far. Wordsworth may also have in mind a rotted gibbet in the water-meadows near Ann Tyson's cottage, the last remains of Thomas Lancaster, hanged in 1672 for poisoning his wife.

And, reascending the bare slope, I saw
A naked pool that lay beneath the hills,
The beacon on the summit,[42] and, more near,
A girl who bore a pitcher on her head
And seemed with difficult steps to force her way
Against the blowing wind. It was in truth
An ordinary sight, but I should need
Colours and words that are unknown to man
To paint the visionary dreariness[43]
Which, while I looked all round for my lost guide,
Did at that time invest the naked pool,
The beacon on the lonely eminence,
The woman and her garments vexed and tossed
By the strong wind.
                                        Nor less I recollect,
Long after, though my childhood had not ceased,
Another scene which left a kindred power
Implanted in my mind. One Christmas-time,
The day before the holidays began,[44]
Feverish and tired and restless, I went forth
Into the fields, impatient for the sight
Of those three horses which should bear us home,
My brothers and myself.[45] There was a crag,[46]
An eminence which from the meeting-point
Of two highways ascending, overlooked
At least a long half-mile of those two roads,
By each of which the expected steeds might come,
The choice uncertain. Thither I repaired
Up to the highest summit. 'Twas a day
Stormy, and rough, and wild, and on the grass
I sat, half-sheltered by a naked wall;
Upon my right hand was a single sheep,
A whistling hawthorn on my left, and there,
Those two companions at my side, I watched,
With eyes intensely straining, as the mist
Gave intermitting prospects of the wood
And plain beneath. Ere I to school returned
That dreary time, ere I had been ten days
A dweller in my father's house, he died,[47]
And I and my two brothers, orphans then,

## Notes

[42] *The beacon on the summit* built in 1719 to warn of invasion from Scotland; it is still to be seen, even from the nearby M6, a short building with a pointed roof on the hill above Penrith.

[43] *visionary dreariness* Wordsworth's point is that in spite of the ordinariness and bleakness of the scene, it was impressed on his mind with all the intensity and power of a vision.

[44] *One Christmas-time...began* probably 19 December 1783, when Wordsworth was 13.

[45] *My brothers and myself* Wordsworth's brothers Richard (1768–1816) and John (1772–1805) also attended Hawkshead Grammar School. The horses were to take them home to Cockermouth; it was a lengthy journey as Hawkshead and Cockermouth were at opposite ends of the Lake District. Whether they chose to go round the coastal route or towards the east, to Keswick, through Ambleside and then to Hawkshead, it was necessary to travel around the central mountains. The horses were in fact delayed.

[46] *a crag* probably the ridge north of Borwick Lodge, a mile and a half from Hawkshead Grammar School.

[47] *he died* John Wordsworth Sr died on 30 December 1783. His wife, Ann, had died five years previously, before Wordsworth's eighth birthday.

Followed his body to the grave. The event,
With all the sorrow which it brought, appeared
A chastisement,[48] and when I called to mind
That day so lately past, when from the crag
I looked in such anxiety of hope,
With trite reflections of morality,
Yet with the deepest passion, I bowed low
To God, who thus corrected my desires.[49]
And afterwards the wind and sleety rain
And all the business of the elements,
The single sheep, and the one blasted tree,
And the bleak music of that old stone wall,
The noise of wood and water, and the mist
Which on the line of each of those two roads
Advanced in such indisputable shapes –
All these were spectacles and sounds to which
I often would repair, and thence would drink
As at a fountain.[50] And I do not doubt
That in this later time, when storm and rain
Beat on my roof at midnight, or by day
When I am in the woods, unknown to me
The workings of my spirit thence are brought.[51]
   Nor, sedulous[52] as I have been to trace
How nature by collateral[53] interest
And by extrinsic passion[54] peopled first
My mind with forms or beautiful or grand[55]
And made me love them, may I well forget
How other pleasures have been mine, and joys
Of subtler origin – how I have felt,
Not seldom, even in that tempestuous time,
Those hallowed and pure motions of the sense
Which seem in their simplicity to own
An intellectual[56] charm, that calm delight
Which, if I err not, surely must belong
To those first-born affinities[57] that fit
   Our new existence to existing things,
And in our dawn of being constitute
The bond of union betwixt life and joy.
   Yes, I remember when the changeful earth
And twice five seasons on my mind had stamped
The faces of the moving year; even then,
A child, I held unconscious intercourse

## Notes

[48] *chastisement* (stressed on the first syllable) punishment.

[49] *I bowed low to God…desires* The child believes he has been punished for looking forward too eagerly to the Christmas holidays – in effect, he has killed his father.

[50] *fountain* stream or well.

[51] *unknown to me…brought* Spots of time mould the adult mind by power of association.

[52] *sedulous* careful, anxious.

[53] *collateral* indirect, sideways.

[54] *extrinsic passion* emotions not directly related to the natural scenes that were to 'educate' the poet. Nature operated on the boy without his being aware of it.

[55] *or…or* either…or.

[56] *intellectual* spiritual – the sense in which Wordsworth often uses the word.

[57] *first-born affinities* affinities with which the child is born.

With the eternal beauty, drinking in
A pure organic[58] pleasure from the lines
Of curling mist, or from the level plain
Of waters coloured by the steady clouds.
   The sands of Westmorland, the creeks and bays
Of Cumbria's rocky limits, they can tell
How when the sea threw off his evening shade
And to the shepherd's hut beneath the crags
Did send sweet notice of the rising moon,
How I have stood, to images like these
A stranger, linking with the spectacle
No body of associated forms[59]
And bringing with me no peculiar sense
Of quietness or peace – yet I have stood,
Even while my eye has moved o'er three long leagues[60]
Of shining water, gathering, as it seemed,
Through the wide surface of that field of light
New pleasure like a bee among the flowers.
   Thus often in those fits of vulgar[61] joy
Which through all seasons on a child's pursuits
Are prompt attendants, mid that giddy bliss
Which like a tempest works along the blood
And is forgotten – even then I felt
Gleams like the flashing of a shield. The earth
And common face of nature spake to me
Rememberable things – sometimes, 'tis true,
By quaint associations, yet not vain
Nor profitless if haply they impressed
Collateral objects and appearances,[62]
Albeit lifeless then, and doomed to sleep
Until maturer seasons called them forth
To impregnate and to elevate the mind.
And if the vulgar joy by its own weight
Wearied itself out of the memory,
The scenes which were a witness of that joy
Remained in their substantial lineaments
Depicted on the brain, and to the eye
Were visible, a daily sight. And thus,
By the impressive agency of fear,[63]
By pleasure, and repeated happiness,
So frequently repeated, and by force
Of obscure feelings representative

## Notes

[58] *organic* sensuous, bodily.

[59] *linking...forms* Wordsworth emphasizes that he has enjoyed these things in and for themselves, rather than for any association they may have with other things. He has been a 'stranger' to them in so far as he has not seen them before and sees them freshly.

[60] *three long leagues* at least nine miles (a league is a varying measure of about three miles).

[61] *vulgar* ordinary, unremarkable.

[62] *sometimes...appearances* The 'associations' (or juxtapositions) are quaint, but not vain or without benefit if indirectly ('collaterally') they impress natural objects and appearances on the mind.

[63] *the impressive agency of fear* fear's ability to stamp 'impressions' on the memory.

Of joys that were forgotten, these same scenes
So beauteous and majestic in themselves,
Though yet the day was distant, did at length
Become habitually dear, and all
Their hues and forms were by invisible links[64]
Allied to the affections.[65]
                                        I began
My story early, feeling, as I fear,
The weakness of a human love for days
Disowned by memory, ere the birth of spring
Planting my snowdrops among winter snows.
Nor will it seem to thee, my friend,[66] so prompt
In sympathy, that I have lengthened out
With fond and feeble tongue a tedious tale.
Meanwhile my hope has been that I might fetch
Reproaches from my former years, whose power
May spur me on, in manhood now mature,
To honourable toil.[67] Yet should it be
That this is but an impotent desire,
That I by such enquiry am not taught
To understand myself, nor thou to know
With better knowledge how the heart was framed
Of him thou lovest, need I dread from thee
Harsh judgements if I am so loath to quit
Those recollected hours that have the charm
Of visionary things,[68] and lovely forms
And sweet sensations that throw back our life
And make our infancy a visible scene
On which the sun is shining?

## SECOND PART

Thus far, my friend, have we retraced the way
Through which I travelled when I first began
To love the woods and fields. The passion yet
Was in its birth, sustained (as might befall)
By nourishment that came unsought;[1] for still
From week to week, from month to month, we lived
A round of tumult. Duly were our games
Prolonged in summer till the daylight failed;
No chair remained before the doors; the bench
And threshold steps were empty; fast asleep
The labourer, and the old man who had sat

### Notes

[64] *invisible links* associative links in the mind.

[65] *And thus…affections* Fear, pleasure and repeated happiness all work to make the natural world constantly precious ('habitually dear'), and to connect its colours and shapes to the poet's emotions ('affections').

[66] *my friend* Coleridge, to whom the poem is addressed.

[67] *honourable toil* When he composed these lines in February 1799, Wordsworth expected to go on with 'The Recluse'.

[68] *Missionary things* things seen imaginatively.

[1] *nourishment that came unsought* Where in Part I Wordsworth discussed his unconscious reponse to the influence of nature, he aims to show in Part II how nature in adolescence was 'sought / For her own sake'.

A later lingerer – yet the revelry
Continued, and the loud uproar! At last,
When all the ground was dark, and the huge clouds
Were edged with twinkling stars, to bed we went,
With weary joints and with a beating mind.
   Ah, is there one who ever has been young
And needs a monitory voice to tame
The pride of virtue and of intellect?[2]
And is there one, the wisest and the best
Of all mankind, who does not sometimes wish
For things which cannot be, who would not give,
If so he might, to duty and to truth
The eagerness of infantine desire?
A tranquillizing spirit presses now
On my corporeal frame, so wide appears
The vacancy between me and those days
Which yet have such self-presence in my heart
That sometimes, when I think of them, I seem
Two consciousnesses – conscious of myself
And of some other being. A grey stone
Of native rock, left midway in the square
Of our small market-village, was the home
And centre of these joys; and when, returned
After long absence, thither I repaired,
I found that it was split, and gone to build
A smart assembly-room[3] that perked and flared
With wash and rough-cast, elbowing the ground
Which had been ours. But let the fiddle scream
And be ye happy! Yet I know, my friends,[4]
That more than one of you will think with me
Of those soft starry nights, and that old dame
From whom the stone was named, who there had sat
And watched her table with its huckster's wares,
Assiduous for the length of sixty years.[5]
We ran a boisterous race, the year span round
With giddy motion. But the time approached
That brought with it a regular desire
For calmer pleasures, when the beauteous scenes
Of nature were collaterally attached
To every scheme of holiday delight
And every boyish sport – less grateful[6] else,
And languidly pursued.[7]
                    When summer came

## Notes

[2] *Ah, is…intellect* 'How can anyone who remembers what it was like to be young need a warning ("monitory voice") not to overrate the achievements of maturity?'

[3] *A smart assembly-room* Hawkshead Town Hall, built 1790, covered with gravel stucco ('rough-cast') and whitewash.

[4] *my friends* An address to Coleridge and John Wordsworth (the poet's brother), with whom the poet visited Hawkshead on 2 November 1799.

[5] *that old dame…years* Ann Holme, who set out her wares – cakes, pies and sweets – on the large stone at the end of the market square in Hawkshead.

[6] *grateful* pleasing.

[7] *languidly pursued* Natural beauty is still only an additional ('collateral') pleasure, though it is beginning to be valued.

It was the pastime of our afternoons
To beat along the plain[8] of Windermere
With rival oars, and the selected bourn[9]
Was now an island musical with birds
That sang for ever; now a sister isle
Beneath the oak's umbrageous[10] covert, sown
With lilies-of-the-valley like a field;
And now a third small island[11] where remained
An old stone table and one mouldered cave –
A hermit's history. In such a race,
So ended, disappointment could be none,
Uneasiness, or pain, or jealousy;
We rested in the shade, all pleased alike,
Conquered and conqueror. Thus our selfishness
Was mellowed down, and thus the pride of strength
And the vainglory of superior skill
Were interfused[12] with objects which subdued
And tempered them, and gradually produced
A quiet independence of the heart.
And to my friend who knows me, I may add,
Unapprehensive of reproof, that hence
Ensued a diffidence and modesty,
And I was taught to feel, perhaps too much,
The self-sufficing power of solitude.
  No delicate viands[13] sapped our bodily strength;
More than we wished we knew the blessing then
Of vigorous hunger, for our daily meals
Were frugal, Sabine fare;[14] and then, exclude
A little weekly stipend,[15] and we lived
Through three divisions of the quartered year
In penniless poverty. But now, to school
Returned from the half-yearly holidays,
We came with purses more profusely filled,[16]
Allowance which abundantly sufficed
To gratify the palate with repasts
More costly than the dame of whom I spake,
That ancient woman,[17] and her board, supplied.
Hence inroads into distant vales, and long
Excursions far away among the hills;
Hence rustic dinners on the cool green ground,
Or in the woods, or by a riverside

## Notes

[8] *plain* flat surface of the lake.

[9] *bourn* aim, destination.

[10] *umbrageous* shady.

[11] *a third small island* Lady Holm, where there was once a chapel to the Virgin Mary.

[12] *interfused* mingled.

[13] *delicate viands* decorative foods of scant nutritional value.

[14] *Sabine fare* The Sabine region of Italy has for centuries been famous for olives, but Wordsworth is likely to be referring to fish, which are as plentiful in its rivers and lakes as in those of the English Lake District. A good classicist, Wordsworth knew the Roman poet Horace owned a farm in Sabina.

[15] *A little weekly stipend* In 1787, the year he left Hawkshead, Wordsworth received sixpence a week.

[16] *But now…filled* When Wordsworth returned to school in January 1787, after the half-yearly holiday, he had an extra guinea (worth 42 'weekly stipends').

[17] *That ancient woman* Ann Tyson was 73 in January 1787.

Or fountain[18] – festive banquets that provoked
The languid action of a natural scene
By pleasure of corporeal appetite.
   Nor is my aim neglected if I tell
How twice in the long length of those half-years
We from our funds perhaps with bolder hand
Drew largely – anxious for one day, at least,
To feel the motion of the galloping steed.
And with the good old innkeeeper,[19] in truth,
I needs must say that sometimes we have used
Sly subterfuge, for the intended bound
Of the day's journey was too distant far
For any cautious man – a structure famed
Beyond its neighbourhood, the antique walls
Of that large abbey with its fractured arch,[20]
Belfry, and images, and living trees,
A holy scene! Along the smooth green turf
Our horses grazed. In more than inland peace
Left by the winds that overpass the vale
In that sequestered ruin trees and towers,
Both silent and both motionless alike,
Hear all day long the murmuring sea that beats
Incessantly upon a craggy shore.
   Our steeds remounted, and the summons given,
With whip and spur we by the chantry[21] flew
In uncouth[22] race, and left the cross-legged knight,
And the stone abbot,[23] and that single wren
Which one day sang so sweetly in the nave
Of the old church that, though from recent showers
The earth was comfortless, and, touched by faint
Internal breezes from the roofless walls,
The shuddering ivy dripped large drops, yet still
So sweetly mid the gloom the invisible bird
Sang to itself that there I could have made
My dwelling-place, and lived for ever there
To hear such music.[24] Through the walls we flew
And down the valley, and, a circuit made
In wantonness of heart, through rough and smooth
We scampered homeward. Oh, ye rocks and streams,
And that still spirit of the evening air,
Even in this joyous time I sometimes felt
Your presence, when with slackened step we breathed[25]
Along the sides of the steep hills, or when,

## Notes

[18] *fountain* spring or stream.

[19] *innkeeper* who hired out the horses.

[20] *that large abbey with its fractured arch* Furness Abbey is about 20 miles south of Hawkshead, near Barrow-in-Furness. It was founded by Cistercian monks in 1127 and dissolved by Henry VIII in 1539. The fractured arch is still to be seen. Its roof-timbers, stripped of their valuable lead, had long since fallen by Wordsworth's day.

[21] *chantry* chapel where masses were once said for the dead.

[22] *uncouth* unseemly, indecorous (because of their surroundings).

[23] *the cross-legged knight…abbot* The stone figures of several cross-legged knights and an abbot may be seen in the Furness Abbey visitor centre.

[24] *So sweetly…music* cf. Shakespeare, 'Sonnet 73': 'Bare ruined choirs, where late the sweet birds sang.'

[25] *breathed* i.e. let the horses get their breath back.

Lightened by gleams of moonlight from the sea,
We beat with thundering hoofs the level sand.
  There was a row of ancient trees, since fallen,
That on the margin of a jutting land
Stood near the lake of Coniston, and made
With its long boughs above the water stretched
A gloom through which a boat might sail along
As in a cloister. An old hall[26] was near,
Grotesque and beautiful, its gavel-end[27]
And huge round chimneys to the top o'ergrown
With fields of ivy. Thither we repaired,
'Twas even a custom with us, to the shore
And to that cool piazza.[28] They who dwelt
In the neglected mansion-house supplied
Fresh butter, tea-kettle, and earthenware,
And chafing-dish with smoking coals,[29] and so
Beneath the trees we sat in our small boat
And in the covert[30] ate our delicate meal
Upon the calm smooth lake. It was a joy
Worthy the heart of one who is full-grown
To rest beneath those horizontal boughs
And mark the radiance of the setting sun,
Himself unseen, reposing on the top
Of the high eastern hills. And there I said,
That beauteous sight before me, there I said
(Then first beginning in my thoughts to mark
That sense of dim similitude which links
Our moral feelings with external forms)
That in whatever region I should close
My mortal life I would remember you,
Fair scenes, that dying I would think on you,
My soul would send a longing look to you,
Even as that setting sun while all the vale
Could nowhere catch one faint memorial gleam
Yet with the last remains of his last light
Still lingered, and a farewell lustre threw
On the dear mountain-tops where first he rose.[31]
'Twas then my fourteenth summer, and these words
Were uttered in a casual access
Of sentiment, a momentary trance
That far outran the habit of my mind.
  Upon the eastern shore of Windermere

## Notes

[26] *An old hall* Coniston Hall, dating from 1580, was the seat of the wealthy Le Fleming family.
[27] *gavel-end* gable.
[28] *cool piazza* the shady colonnade formed by the branches of the sycamore trees.
[29] *chafing-dish with smoking coals* portable charcoal stove used to cook trout, or char, from the lake.
[30] *covert* shade.
[31] *Even as…rose* In later years Wordsworth recalled that this image 'suggested itself to me while I was resting in a boat along with my companions under the shade of a magnificent row of sycamores, which then extended their branches from the shore of the promontory upon which stands the ancient, and at that time the more picturesque, Hall of Coniston, the seat of the Le Flemings, from very early times'.

Above the crescent of a pleasant bay,
There was an inn[32] – no homely-featured shed,
Brother of the surrounding cottages,
But 'twas a splendid place, the door beset
With chaises,[33] grooms, and liveries,[34] and within
Decanters, glasses, and the blood-red wine.[35]
In ancient times, or ere the hall was built
On the large island,[36] had this dwelling been
More worthy of a poet's love, a hut[37]
Proud of its one bright fire and sycamore shade.
But though the rhymes were gone which once inscribed
The threshold, and large golden characters[38]
On the blue-frosted signboard had usurped
The place of the old lion, in contempt
And mockery of the rustic painter's hand,
Yet to this hour the spot to me is dear
With all its foolish pomp. The garden lay
Upon a slope surmounted by the plain
Of a small bowling-green; beneath us stood
A grove, with gleams of water through the trees
And over the tree-tops – nor did we want
Refreshment, strawberries and mellow cream.
And there, through half an afternoon, we played
On the smooth platform, and the shouts we sent
Made all the mountains ring. But ere the fall
Of night, when in our pinnace we returned
Over the dusky lake, and to the beach
Of some small island steered our course, with one,[39]
The minstrel of our troop, and left him there,
And rowed off gently while he blew his flute
Alone upon the rock – oh then the calm
And dead still water lay upon my mind
Even with a weight of pleasure, and the sky,
Never before so beautiful, sank down
Into my heart, and held me like a dream.
   Thus day by day my sympathies increased,
And thus the common range of visible things
Grew dear to me. Already I began
To love the sun – a boy I loved the sun
Not as I since have loved him (as a pledge
And surety[40] of our earthly life, a light

## Notes

[32] *an inn* the White Lion at Bowness, now the Royal Hotel.

[33] *chaises* light carriages.

[34] *liveries* uniforms.

[35] *the blood-red wine* an echo of the anonymous ballad, *Sir Patrick Spens*: 'The king sits in Dunfermling toune, / Drinking the blude-reid wine' (ll. 1–2).

[36] *the hall…island* The first and finest of the neoclassical villas in the Lakes was the circular mansion on Belle Isle in Windermere, designed by John Plaw in 1774 for Thomas English, but not completed until the early 1780s when John Christian Curwen had become its owner. Dorothy had harsh words for the circular mansion in June 1802: '…& that great house! Mercy upon us! If it *could* be concealed it would be well for all who are not pained to see the pleasantest of earthly spots deformed by man' (her italics).

[37] *hut* cottage.

[38] *characters* letters.

[39] *one* Robert Greenwood, another of Ann Tyson's boarders, who was elected Fellow of Trinity College, Cambridge in 1792. Wordsworth remained in touch with him for many years.

[40] *surety* guarantee.

Which while I view I feel I am alive),
But for this cause: that I had seen him lay
His beauty on the morning hills, had seen
The western mountain touch his setting orb
In many a thoughtless hour, when from excess
Of happiness my blood appeared to flow
With its own pleasure, and I breathed with joy.
And from like feelings, humble though intense
(To patriotic and domestic love
Analogous[41]), the moon to me was dear,
For I would dream away my purposes,
Standing to look upon her while she hung
Midway between the hills, as if she knew
No other region, but belonged to thee –
Yea, appertained by a peculiar right
To thee and thy grey huts,[42] my native vale.
   Those incidental charms which first attached
My heart to rural objects day by day
Grew weaker, and I hasten on to tell
How Nature – intervenient till this time,
And secondary[43] – now at length was sought
For her own sake. But who shall parcel out[44]
His intellect by geometric rules,
Split like a province into round and square?
Who knows the individual hour in which
His habits were first sown, even as a seed?
Who that shall point as with a wand, and say,
'This portion of the river of my mind
Came from yon fountain'? Thou, my friend,[45] art one
More deeply read in thy own thoughts, no slave
Of that false secondary power[46] by which
In weakness we create distinctions, then
Believe our puny boundaries are things
Which we perceive, and not which we have made.
To thee, unblinded by these outward shows,
The unity of all has been revealed;[47]
And thou wilt doubt with me, less aptly skilled
Than many are to class the cabinet
Of their sensations,[48] and in voluble[49] phrase
Run through the history and birth of each
As of a single independent thing.

## Notes

[41] *To patriotic…analogous* His love for the moon was like love of country and family ('domestic love') because it gave him pleasure in the region where he lived.

[42] *grey huts* cottages built of grey stone, which are everywhere in the Lake District.

[43] *intervenient…secondary* Nature had been experienced in the midst of other distractions.

[44] *parcel out* divide up, categorize, analyse.

[45] *my friend* Wordsworth turns once more to Coleridge, to whom this poem is dedicated.

[46] *that false secondary power* the power of rational analysis, as opposed to the imaginative perception of unity.

[47] *To thee…revealed* Coleridge was a Unitarian.

[48] *to class…sensations* classify sensations as if they were exhibits in a cabinet.

[49] *voluble* glib, fluent.

Hard task[50] to analyse a soul, in which
Not only general habits and desires,
But each most obvious and particular thought –
Not in a mystical[51] and idle sense,
But in the words of reason deeply weighed
Hath no beginning.
Blessed the infant babe[52]
(For with my best conjectures I would trace
The progress of our being) – blessed the babe
Nursed in his mother's arms, the babe who sleeps
Upon his mother's breast, who when his soul
Claims manifest kindred with an earthly soul,
Doth gather passion from his mother's eye![53]
Such feelings pass into his torpid[54] life
Like an awakening breeze, and hence his mind,
Even in the first trial of its powers,
Is prompt and watchful, eager to combine
In one appearance all the elements
And parts of the same object, else detached
And loath to coalesce.[55] Thus day by day
Subjected to the discipline of love,
His organs and recipient faculties[56]
Are quickened,[57] are more vigorous; his mind spreads,
Tenacious of the forms which it receives.[58]
In one beloved presence – nay and more,
In that most apprehensive habitude[59]
And those sensations which have been derived
From this beloved presence, there exists
A virtue which irradiates and exalts
All objects through all intercourse of sense.[60]
No outcast he, bewildered and depressed:
Along his infant veins are interfused
The gravitation and the filial bond
Of nature that connect him with the world.[61]
Emphatically such a being lives
An inmate of this *active* universe.
From nature largely he receives, nor so

## Notes

[50] *Hard task* a deliberate echo of Milton, who speaks of having to describe the war in heaven as 'Sad task and hard' ('Paradise Lost' v 564); describing the growth of the mind is just as worthy of epic treatment for Wordsworth.

[51] *mystical* mysterious, occult.

[52] *Blessed the infant babe* The Infant Babe passage was inspired partly by the death of Coleridge's baby son Berkeley, news of which reached Coleridge in Germany in April 1799, several months after it had taken place.

[53] *who when...eye* When his soul first forms a relationship with another, the baby learns to love by seeing its mother's love in her eyes.

[54] *torpid* dormant.

[55] *loath to coalesce* reluctant to come together, making wholes. Inspired by its mother's love, the baby becomes able to form parts into wholes, ordering what he perceives; in other words, his mind is working imaginatively.

[56] *recipient faculties* senses.

[57] *quickened* enlivened.

[58] *Tenacious...receives* The mind retains visual images.

[59] *most apprehensive habitude* A relationship ('habitude') best suited to learning ('most apprehensive').

[60] *this beloved presence...sense* The mother's love is a power ('virtue') that infuses all objects which the child perceives, exalting them.

[61] *Along his infant veins...world* The child's loving relationship with his mother is what connects him to natural objects.

Is satisfied, but largely[62] gives again –
For feeling has to him imparted strength;
And, powerful in all sentiments of grief,
Of exultation, fear and joy, his mind,
Even as an agent of the one great mind
Creates, creator and receiver both,[63]
Working but in alliance with the works
Which it beholds. Such, verily, is the first
Poetic spirit of our human life,
By uniform control of after-years
In most abated and suppressed, in some
Through every change of growth or of decay
Pre-eminent till death.
From early days,
Beginning not long after that first time
In which, a babe, by intercourse of touch,
I held mute dialogues with my mother's heart,
I have endeavoured to display the means
Whereby the infant sensibility,
Great birthright of our being, was in me
Augmented and sustained. Yet is a path
More difficult before me, and I fear
That in its broken windings we shall need
The chamois'[64] sinews and the eagle's wing.
For now a trouble came into my mind
From unknown causes: I was left alone,
Seeking this visible world, nor knowing why.
The props of my affections were removed,
And yet the building stood, as if sustained
By its own spirit.[65] All that I beheld
Was dear to me, and from this cause it came:
That now to nature's finer influxes[66]
My mind lay open to that more exact
And intimate communion which our hearts
Maintain with the minuter properties[67]
Of objects which already are beloved,
And of those only.
Many are the joys
Of youth, but oh what happiness to live
When every hour brings palpable access[68]
Of knowledge, when all knowledge is delight,
And sorrow is not there! The seasons came,
And every season brought a countless store

## Notes

[62] *largely* abundantly.

[63] *Creates…both* The child's mind becomes creative as well as receptive; it is imaginative – working in harmony with Nature.

[64] *chamois* mountain antelope.

[65] *The props…spirit* The 'props' of the boy's feelings are the 'incidental charms which first attached / My heart to rural objects day by day' (ll. 237–8); they are no longer required for his love of nature to exist in its own right.

[66] *influxes* influences.

[67] *minuter properties* qualities known to those who possess a well-established love of nature.

[68] *palpable access* perceptible increase.

Of modes and temporary qualities[69]
Which, but for this most watchful power of love,
Had been neglected – left a register
Of permanent relations,[70] else unknown.
Hence life, and change, and beauty, solitude
More active even than 'best society',[71]
Society made sweet as solitude
By silent inobtrusive sympathies
And gentle agitations of the mind
From manifold distinctions (difference
Perceived in things where to the common eye
No difference is) – and hence, from the same source,
Sublimer joy.[72] For I would walk alone
In storm and tempest, or in starlight nights
Beneath the quiet heavens, and at that time
Would feel whate'er there is of power in sound
To breathe[73] an elevated mood, by form
Or image unprofaned. And I would stand
Beneath some rock, listening to sounds that are
The ghostly language of the ancient earth
Or make their dim abode in distant winds:
Thence did I drink the visionary power.
I deem not profitless these fleeting moods
Of shadowy exultation – not for this,
That they are kindred to our purer mind[74]
And intellectual life, but that the soul,
Remembering how she felt, but what she felt
Remembering not, retains an obscure sense
Of possible sublimity, to which
With growing faculties she doth aspire,
With faculties still growing, feeling still
That whatsoever point they gain they still
Have something to pursue.
                                          And not alone
In grandeur and in tumult, but no less
In tranquil scenes, that universal power
And fitness[75] in the latent qualities
And essences of things, by which the mind
Is moved with feelings of delight, to me
Came strengthened with a superadded soul,[76]

## Notes

[69] *modes and temporary qualities* short-lived weather or seasonal conditions.

[70] *register…relations* permanent recollection in the mind of changing scenes in nature.

[71] *best society* Wordsworth alludes to 'Paradise Lost', where Adam in Eden says: 'For solitude sometimes is best society' (ix 249).

[72] *sublimer joy* A series of things follows from the permanently impressed features of Nature on the poet's mind: change, beauty, solitude more active than society, society as sweet as solitude and the 'gentle agitations' produced by noticing many distinctions not observable to the untrained eye. From this last feature is produced 'sublimer joy'.

[73] *breathe* inspire.

[74] *kindred to our purer mind* of a spiritual nature.

[75] *fitness* harmony.

[76] *superadded soul* The 'superadded soul' is presumably an element of the 'visionary power' of l. 360. It is additional to natural objects, and is not conferred on them by the perceiving mind: it comes from beyond.

A virtue not its own. My morning walks
Were early; oft before the hours of school[77]
I travelled round our little lake, five miles
Of pleasant wandering – happy time more dear
For this, that one was by my side, a friend
Then passionately loved. With heart how full
Will he peruse these lines, this page (perhaps
A blank to other men), for many years
Have since flowed in between us, and, our minds
Both silent to each other, at this time
We live as if those hours had never been.
Nor seldom did I lift our cottage latch
Far earlier, and before the vernal[78] thrush
Was audible, among the hills I sat
Alone upon some jutting eminence
At the first hour of morning, when the vale
Lay quiet in an utter solitude.
How shall I trace the history, where seek
The origin of what I then have felt?
Oft in those moments such a holy calm
Did overspread my soul, that I forgot
The agency of sight, and what I saw
Appeared like something in myself – a dream,
A prospect[79] in my mind.
                    'Twere long to tell
What spring and autumn, what the winter snows,
And what the summer shade, what day and night,
The evening and the morning, what my dreams
And what my waking thoughts supplied, to nurse
That spirit of religious love in which
I walked with nature. But let this at least
Be not forgotten – that I still retained
My first creative sensibility,
That by the regular action of the world
My soul was unsubdued. A plastic[80] power
Abode with me, a forming hand, at times
Rebellious, acting in a devious mood,
A local spirit of its own, at war
With general tendency, but for the most
Subservient strictly to the external things
With which it communed.[81] An auxiliar[82] light
Came from my mind, which on the setting sun
Bestowed new splendour; the melodious birds,

## Notes

[77] *oft before the hours of school* School began at 6 or 6.30 a.m. during the summer; the five-mile walk would have taken Wordsworth round Esthwaite Water – though that seems a generous estimate for a lake which is little more than a mile long. The friend was John Fleming, who went up to Cambridge in 1785.

[78] *vernal* spring-time.

[79] *prospect* landscape, view.

[80] *plastic* shaping, forming.

[81] *at times…communed* The imagination sometimes behaves with a will of its own, but is usually subordinate to the natural world (i.e. prepared to enhance it).

[82] *auxiliar* enhancing; the 'auxiliar light' is the imagination.

The gentle breezes, fountains that ran on
Murmuring so sweetly in themselves, obeyed
A like dominion, and the midnight storm
Grew darker in the presence of my eye.
Hence my obeisance, my devotion hence,
And *hence* my transport.[83]
                    Nor should this perchance
Pass unrecorded, that I still had loved
The exercise and produce of a toil
Than analytic industry to me
More pleasing, and whose character I deem
Is more poetic, as resembling more
Creative agency – I mean to speak
Of that interminable building[84] reared
By observation of affinities
In objects where no brotherhood exists
To common minds. My seventeenth year was come,
And, whether from this habit[85] rooted now
So deeply in my mind, or from excess
Of the great social principle of life[86]
Coercing all things into sympathy,
To unorganic natures I transferred
My own enjoyments, or, the power of truth
Coming in revelation, I conversed
With things that really are; I at this time
Saw blessings spread around me like a sea.
Thus did my days pass on, and now at length
From Nature and her overflowing soul
I had received so much that all my thoughts
Were steeped in feeling.
                    I was only then
Contented when with bliss ineffable[87]
I felt the sentiment of being spread
O'er all that moves, and all that seemeth still,
O'er all that, lost beyond the reach of thought
And human knowledge, to the human eye
Invisible, yet liveth to the heart;
O'er all that leaps and runs, and shouts and sings,
Or beats the gladsome air; o'er all that glides
Beneath the wave, yea in the wave itself
And mighty depth of waters. Wonder not
If such my transports[88] were, for in all things
I saw one life, and felt that it was joy.
One song they sang, and it was audible –

## Notes

[83] *transport* ecstasy. It is because the mind is believed to be 'lord and master' over what it perceives that the poet devotes himself to Nature.

[84] *interminable building* mental structure.

[85] *this habit* the 'observation of affinities' (l. 433).

[86] *the great social principle of life* love, which might have led Wordsworth to see his feelings reflected in inanimate objects ('unorganic natures').

[87] *ineffable* indescribable.

[88] *transports* raptures.

Most audible then when the fleshly ear,
O'ercome by grosser prelude of that strain,[89]
Forgot its functions and slept undisturbed.
  If this be error, and another faith
Find easier access to the pious mind,
Yet were I grossly destitute of all
Those human sentiments which make this earth
So dear, if I should fail with grateful voice
To speak of you, ye mountains and ye lakes
And sounding cataracts, ye mists and winds
That dwell among the hills where I was born.
If in my youth I have been pure in heart,
If, mingling with the world, I am content
With my own modest pleasures, and have lived
With God and nature communing, removed
From little enmities and low desires,
The gift is yours; if in these times of fear,
This melancholy waste[90] of hopes o'erthrown,
If, mid indifference and apathy
And wicked exultation, when good men
On every side fall off we know not how,
To selfishness, disguised in gentle names
Of peace and quiet and domestic love,
Yet mingled not unwillingly with sneers
On visionary minds[91] – if in this time
Of dereliction and dismay I yet
Despair not of our nature, but retain
A more than Roman confidence, a faith
That fails not, in all sorrow my support,
The blessing of my life, the gift is yours,
Ye mountains! – thine, oh nature! Thou hast fed
My lofty speculations, and in thee,
For this uneasy heart of ours, I find
A never-failing principle[92] of joy
And purest passion.
                    Thou, my friend, wast reared
In the great city, mid far other scenes,[93]
But we by different roads at length have gained
The self-same bourn. And from this cause to thee
I speak unapprehensive of contempt,
The insinuated scoff of coward tongues,
And all that silent language which so oft

## Notes

[89] *grosser prelude of that strain* sensual joy preceding the more refined pleasures of response to the pantheist one life.

[90] *waste* desert.

[91] *when good men…minds* Wordsworth is reacting to Coleridge's exhortation to incorporate into 'The Recluse' an address to 'those, who, in consequence of the complete failure of the French Revolution, have thrown up all hopes of the amelioration of mankind, and are sinking into an almost epicurean selfishness, disguising the same under the soft titles of domestic attachment and contempt for visionary *philosophes*'.

[92] *principle* source.

[93] *Thou, my friend…other scenes* In 'Frost at Midnight', Coleridge had written: 'For I was reared / In the great city, pent mid cloisters dim' (ll. 56–7).

In conversation betwixt man and man
Blots from the human countenance all trace
Of beauty and of love. For thou hast sought
The truth in solitude, and thou art one,
The most intense of nature's worshippers,
In many things my brother, chiefly here
In this my deep devotion.
Fare thee well![94]
Health and the quiet of a healthful mind
Attend thee, seeking oft the haunts of men,
And yet more often living with thyself,
And for thyself. So haply shall thy days
Be many, and a blessing to mankind.

End of the Second Part[95]

## *There Was a Boy* (composed between 6 October and early December 1798)

There was a boy – ye knew him well, ye cliffs
And islands of Winander![1] Many a time
At evening, when the stars had just begun
To move along the edges of the hills,
Rising or setting, would he stand alone
Beneath the trees or by the glimmering lake,
And there, with fingers interwoven, both hands
Pressed closely palm to palm and to his mouth
Uplifted, he, as through an instrument,
Blew mimic hootings to the silent owls
That they might answer him. And they would shout
Across the watery vale, and shout again
Responsive to his call, with quivering peals
And long halloos, and screams, and echoes loud
Redoubled and redoubled – a wild scene
Of mirth and jocund din! And when it chanced
That pauses of deep silence mocked his skill,
Then sometimes in that silence while he hung
Listening, a gentle shock of mild surprise
Has carried far[2] into his heart the voice
Of mountain torrents; or the visible scene
Would enter unawares[3] into his mind

## Notes

[94] *Fare thee well!* Coleridge in November 1799 was about to go south to become a journalist in London; the Wordsworths were about to move into Dove Cottage.

[95] *End of the Second Part* entered by Dorothy when she copied the poem. She thought it would be continued, and Wordsworth indeed attempted to write a third Part at the end of 1801.

There Was a Boy

[1] *Winander* Windermere.

[2] 'The very expression, "far", by which space and its infinities are attributed to the human heart, and to its capacities of re-echoing the sublimities of nature, has always struck me as with a flash of sublime revelation', wrote De Quincey of this passage in 1839.

[3] *unawares* unconsciously; it is important to Wordsworth and Coleridge that moments of vision occur spontaneously.

With all its solemn imagery, its rocks,
Its woods, and that uncertain heaven, received
Into the bosom of the steady lake.[4]
Fair are the woods, and beauteous is the spot,
The vale where he was born. The churchyard hangs
Upon a slope above the village school,
And there, along that bank, when I have passed
At evening, I believe that near his grave
A full half-hour together I have stood
Mute – for he died when he was ten years old.[5]

## *Nutting* (composed between 6 October and 28 December 1798)[1]

It seems a day,
One of those heavenly days which cannot die,
When forth I sallied from our cottage-door,
And with a wallet o'er my shoulder slung,
A nutting-crook in hand, I turned my steps
Towards the distant woods, a figure quaint,
Tricked out in proud disguise of beggar's weeds[2]
Put on for the occasion, by advice
And exhortation of my frugal dame.[3]
Motley accoutrement! of power to smile
At thorns, and brakes, and brambles, and, in truth,
More ragged than need was. Among the woods,
And o'er the pathless rocks, I forced my way
Until, at length, I came to one dear nook
Unvisited, where not a broken bough
Drooped with its withered leaves (ungracious sign
Of devastation), but the hazels rose
Tall and erect, with milk-white clusters hung,
A virgin scene! A little while I stood,
Breathing with such suppression of the heart
As joy delights in; and, with wise restraint
Voluptuous, fearless of a rival, eyed

## Notes

[4] After reading 'There was a boy' in December 1798, Coleridge wrote of ll. 24–5: 'I should have recognised [them] any where; and had I met these lines running wild in the deserts of Arabia, I should have instantly screamed out "Wordsworth!"' Wordsworth offered a gloss on ll. 21–5 in his 1815 Preface: 'The Boy, there introduced, is listening, with something of a feverish and restless anxiety, for the recurrence of the riotous sounds which he had previously excited; and, at the moment when the intenseness of his mind is beginning to remit, he is surprised into a perception of the solemn and tranquillizing images which the Poem describes'.

[5] Although, as Wordsworth later recalled, the boy who hooted at the owls was a conflation of himself and a schoolfriend called William Raincock, the grave he has in mind is that of his schoolfriend John Tyson, who died in 1782 at the age of 12.

Nutting

[1] Written in Germany, intended as part of a poem on my own life ['The Two-Part Prelude'], but struck out as not being wanted there. Like most of my schoolfellows I was an impassioned nutter… These verses arose out of the remembrance of feelings I had often had when a boy, and particularly in the extensive woods that still stretch from the side of Esthwaite Lake towards Graythwaite, the seat of the ancient family of Sandys.'

[2] *weeds* clothes.

[3] *my frugal dame* Ann Tyson, Wordsworth's landlady at Hawkshead. Cf. 'The Two-Part Prelude' ii 88–90.

The banquet, or beneath the trees I sate
Among the flowers, and with the flowers I played;
A temper known to those who, after long
And weary expectation, have been blessed
With sudden happiness beyond all hope.
   Perhaps it was a bower beneath whose leaves
The violets of five seasons reappear
And fade, unseen by any human eye,
Where fairy water-breaks[4] do murmur on
For ever; and I saw the sparkling foam,
And, with my cheek on one of those green stones
That, fleeced with moss, beneath the shady trees,
Lay round me scattered like a flock of sheep,
I heard the murmur and the murmuring sound,
In that sweet mood when pleasure loves to pay
Tribute to ease; and, of its joy secure,
The heart luxuriates with indifferent[5] things,
Wasting its kindliness on stocks[6] and stones,
And on the vacant air. Then up I rose,
And dragged to earth both branch and bough, with crash
And merciless ravage, and the shady nook
Of hazels, and the green and mossy bower,
Deformed and sullied, patiently gave up
Their quiet being; and, unless I now
Confound my present feelings with the past,
Even then, when from the bower I turned away,
Exulting, rich beyond the wealth of kings,
I felt a sense of pain when I beheld
The silent trees, and the intruding sky.
   Then, dearest maiden,[7] move along these shades
In gentleness of heart; with gentle hand
Touch – for there is a spirit in the woods.

## *Strange Fits of Passion I Have Known* (composed between 6 October and 28 December 1798)[1]

Strange fits of passion I have known,
And I will dare to tell,
But in the lover's ear alone,
What once to me befell.

## Notes

[4] *water-breaks* stretches of rapid water.

[5] *indifferent* not insensible but neutral, impartial, disinterested.

[6] *stocks* tree-stumps, dead wood.

[7] *dearest maiden* The anonymous 'maiden' (perhaps associated with Wordsworth's sister Dorothy) is bidden to establish contact with a wood-spirit.

STRANGE FITS OF PASSION I HAVE KNOWN

[1] This poem, the three that follow it and 'I travelled among unknown men', comprise what have come to be known as the Lucy poems. 'She was a phantom of delight' is often classed among them. Much ink has been expended on the question of Lucy's identity. But Wordsworth has no interest in that question; the poems have other concerns.

When she I loved was strong and gay
And like a rose in June,
I to her cottage bent my way
Beneath the evening moon.

Upon the moon I fixed my eye,
All over the wide lea;[2]
My horse trudged on, and we drew nigh
Those paths so dear to me.

And now we reached the orchard-plot,
And as we climbed the hill,
Towards the roof of Lucy's cot
The moon descended still.

In one of those sweet dreams I slept,
Kind nature's gentlest boon!
And all the while my eyes I kept
On the descending moon.

My horse moved on; hoof after hoof
He raised and never stopped:
When down behind the cottage roof
At once the planet dropped.

What fond[3] and wayward thoughts will slide
Into a lover's head;
'Oh mercy!' to myself I cried,
'If Lucy should be dead!'

## *Song* (composed between 6 October and 28 December 1798)

She dwelt among th' untrodden ways
  Beside the springs of Dove,
A maid whom there were none to praise
  And very few to love.

A violet by a mossy stone
  Half-hidden from the eye,
Fair as a star when only one
  Is shining in the sky!

She lived unknown, and few could know
  When Lucy ceased to be;
But she is in her grave, and oh!
  The difference to me.

Notes

[2] *lea* meadow.

[3] *fond* meaning either 'foolish' or 'loving, affectionate'.

## *A Slumber Did My Spirit Seal* (composed between 6 October and 28 December 1798)[1]

A slumber did my spirit seal,[2]
I had no human fears;
She seemed a thing that could not feel
The touch of earthly years.

No motion has she now, no force;
She neither hears nor sees;
Rolled round in earth's diurnal[3] course
With rocks and stones and trees!

## *Three Years She Grew in Sun and Shower* (composed between 6 October and 28 December 1798)

Three years she grew in sun and shower,
Then Nature said, 'A lovelier flower
On earth was never sown;
This child I to myself will take,
She shall be mine, and I will make
A lady of my own.

Myself will to my darling be
Both law and impulse, and with me
The girl in rock and plain,
In earth and heaven, in glade and bower,
Shall feel an overseeing power
To kindle or restrain.

She shall be sportive as the fawn
That wild with glee across the lawn
Or up the mountain springs,
And hers shall be the breathing balm
And hers the silence and the calm
Of mute insensate things.

The floating clouds their state shall lend
To her, for her the willow bend,
Nor shall she fail to see
Even in the motions of the storm

## Notes

A Slumber Did My Spirit Seal

[1] When first composed, this poem was sent to Coleridge. In a letter to his friend Thomas Poole of 6 April 1799, Coleridge remarked: 'Oh, this strange, strange, strange scene-shifter, Death! that giddies one with insecurity, and so unsubstantiunsubstanti ates the living things that one has grasped and handled! Some months ago Wordsworth transmitted to me a most sublime Epitaph. Whether it had any reality, I cannot say. Most probably, in some gloomier moments he had fancied the moment in which his sister might die.'

[2] *seal* contain, lock up.

[3] *diurnal* daily.

A beauty that shall mould her form
By silent sympathy.

The stars of midnight shall be dear
To her, and she shall lean her ear
In many a secret place
Where rivulets dance their wayward round
And beauty born of murmuring sound
Shall pass into her face.

And vital feelings of delight
Shall rear her form to stately height,
Her virgin bosom swell,
Such thoughts to Lucy I will give
While she and I together live
Here in this happy dell.'

Thus Nature spake – the work was done –
How soon my Lucy's race was run!
She died and left to me
This heath, this calm and quiet scene,
The memory of what has been,
And never more will be.

## *The Brothers: A Pastoral Poem* (composed December 1799–early March 1800)[1]

'These tourists,[2] Heaven preserve us, needs must live
A profitable life! Some glance along,
Rapid and gay, as if the earth were air,
And they were butterflies to wheel about
Long as their summer lasted; some, as wise,
Upon the forehead of a jutting crag
Sit perched with book and pencil on their knee,
And look and scribble, scribble on and look,
Until a man might travel twelve stout miles[3]
Or reap an acre of his neighbour's corn.
   But, for that moping[4] son of idleness –
Why can he tarry yonder? In our churchyard
Is neither epitaph nor monument,

## Notes

THE BROTHERS: A PASTORAL POEM

[1] 'The Brothers' is based on a story told to Wordsworth and Coleridge while on a walking tour of the Lakes in 1799. They heard about Jerome Bowman (who broke his leg near Scale Force, crawled three miles at night on hands and knees, and then died from his injuries) and his son who 'broke his neck before this, by falling off a crag', as Coleridge put it. The son was believed 'to have laid down and slept, but walked in his sleep, and so came to this crag and fell off. This was at Proud Knot on the mountain called Pillar up Ennerdale. His pikestaff stuck midway and stayed there till it rotted away' (*Notebooks* i 540). In 1800 Wordsworth appended the following note to the title: 'This poem was intended to be the concluding poem of a series of pastorals the scene of which was laid among the mountains of Cumberland and Westmorland. I mention this to apologise for the abruptness with which the poem begins.'

[2] *tourists* Even in 1800, the Lake District was a popular tourist resort.

[3] *stout miles* the English 'long mile' of 2,428 yards.

[4] *moping* aimless, purposeless.

Tombstone nor name,[5] only the turf we tread
And a few natural graves.' To Jane, his wife,
Thus spake the homely priest of Ennerdale.
It was a July evening, and he sat
Upon the long stone-seat beneath the eaves
Of his old cottage – as it chanced that day,
Employed in winter's work. Upon the stone
His wife sat near him, teasing matted wool,
While from the twin cards[6] toothed with glittering wire,
He fed the spindle of his youngest child,
Who turned her large round wheel in the open air
With back and forward steps.[7] Towards the field
In which the parish chapel stood alone
Girt round with a bare ring of mossy wall,
While half an hour went by, the priest had sent
Many a long look of wonder; and at last,
Risen from his seat, beside the snowy ridge
Of carded wool which the old man had piled
He laid his implements with gentle care,
Each in the other locked, and down the path
Which from his cottage to the churchyard led
He took his way, impatient to accost
The stranger whom he saw still lingering there.
'Twas one well known to him in former days:
A shepherd-lad, who ere his thirteenth year[8]
Had changed his calling – with the mariners
A fellow-mariner – and so had fared
Through twenty seasons; but he had been reared
Among the mountains, and he in his heart
Was half a shepherd on the stormy seas.
Oft in the piping shrouds[9] had Leonard heard
The tones of waterfalls, and inland sounds
Of caves and trees. And when the regular wind
Between the tropics[10] filled the steady sail
And blew with the same breath through days and weeks,
Lengthening invisibly its weary line
Along the cloudless main, he, in those hours
Of tiresome indolence, would often hang
Over the vessel's side, and gaze and gaze;

## Notes

[5] *neither epitaph...name* Several Lake District churchyards had no tombstones.

[6] *twin cards* a pair of combs used for teasing out the hairs of wool before they are spun into thread.

[7] *Upon the stone...steps* In the Fenwick Notes of 1843, Wordsworth recalled: 'I could write a treatise of lamentation upon the changes brought about among the cottages of Westmorland by the silence of the spinning wheel. During long winter nights and wet days, the wheel upon which wool was spun gave employment to a great part of a family. The old man, however infirm, was able to card the wool, as he sat in the corner by the fireside; and often, when a boy, have I admired the cylinders of carded wool which were softly laid upon each other by his side. Two wheels were often at work on the same floor, and others of the family, chiefly the little children, were occupied in teasing and cleaning the wool to fit it for the hand of the carder. So that all except the smallest infants were contributing to mutual support.'

[8] *ere his thirteenth year* John Wordsworth, the poet's younger brother, also decided early on that he would be a sailor.

[9] *shrouds* ropes supporting the mast of a ship, climbed when changing sails. The wind plays ('pipes') through them.

[10] *the regular wind...tropics* trade winds blowing towards the equator from the tropics of Cancer and Capricorn.

And while the broad green wave and sparkling foam
Flashed round him images and hues that wrought
In union with the employment of his heart,
He – thus by feverish passion overcome –
Even with the organs of his bodily eye,
Below him in the bosom of the deep
Saw mountains, saw the forms of sheep that grazed
On verdant hills, with dwellings among trees,
And shepherds clad in the same country grey
Which he himself had worn.[11]
And now at length,
From perils manifold, with some small wealth
Acquired by traffic in the Indian Isles,[12]
To his paternal home he is returned
With a determined purpose to resume
The life which he lived there – both for the sake
Of many darling[13] pleasures, and the love
Which to an only brother he has borne
In all his hardships, since that happy time
When, whether it blew foul or fair, they two
Were brother shepherds on their native hills.
They were the last of all their race;[14] and now,
When Leonard had approached his home, his heart
Failed in him, and not venturing to enquire
Tidings of one whom he so dearly loved,
Towards the churchyard he had turned aside[15]
That (as he knew in what particular spot
His family were laid) he thence might learn
If still his brother lived, or to the file[16]
Another grave was added. He had found
Another grave, near which a full half-hour
He had remained; but as he gazed there grew
Such a confusion in his memory
That he began to doubt, and he had hopes
That he had seen this heap of turf before –
That it was not another grave, but one
He had forgotten. He had lost his path
As up the vale he came that afternoon
Through fields which once had been well known to him,
And oh, what joy the recollection now

## Notes

[11] The calenture was defined by Johnson as 'a distemper peculiar to sailors in hot climates, wherein they imagine the sea to be green fields, and will throw themselves into it'.

[12] *traffic in the Indian Isles* trade in the East Indies.

[13] *darling* dearly loved.

[14] *They were the last of all their race* As in 'Michael', Wordsworth is concerned in this poem with the dying out of small landowners – 'statesmen', whose small plots of land had descended through the same families for generations.

[15] *When Leonard…aside* probably based on John Wordsworth's arrival in Grasmere at the end of January 1800; according to Dorothy, 'twice did he approach the door and lay his hand upon the latch, and stop, and turn away without the courage to enter (we had not met for several years). He then went to the inn and sent us word that he was come'.

[16] *file* row, line.

Sent to his heart! He lifted up his eyes,
And looking round he thought that he perceived
Strange alteration wrought on every side
Among the woods and fields, and that the rocks,
And the eternal hills themselves, were changed.
  By this the priest, who down the field had come
Unseen by Leonard, at the churchyard gate
Stopped short; and thence, at leisure, limb by limb
He scanned him with a gay complacency.[17]
'Aye', thought the vicar, smiling to himself,
''Tis one of those who needs must leave the path
Of the world's business, to go wild alone –
His arms have a perpetual holiday.
The happy man will creep about the fields
Following his fancies by the hour, to bring
Tears down his cheek, or solitary smiles
Into his face, until the setting sun
Write Fool upon his forehead.' Planted thus
Beneath a shed[18] that overarched the gate
Of this rude churchyard, till the stars appeared
The good man might have communed with himself,
But that the stranger, who had left the grave,
Approached. He recognized the priest at once,
And after greetings interchanged (and given
By Leonard to the vicar as to one
Unknown to him), this dialogue ensued.

LEONARD

You live, sir, in these dales, a quiet life.
Your years make up one peaceful family,
And who would grieve and fret, if – welcome come
And welcome gone – they are so like each other
They cannot be remembered? Scarce a funeral
Comes to this churchyard once in eighteen months;
And yet, some changes must take place among you.
And you who dwell here, even among these rocks
Can trace the finger of mortality,[19]
And see that with our threescore years and ten[20]
We are not all that perish. I remember
(For many years ago I passed this road)
There was a footway all along the fields
By the brook-side; 'tis gone. And that dark cleft –
To me it does not seem to wear the face
Which then it had.

## Notes

[17] *complacency* self-satisfaction.
[18] *shed* porchway, roof.
[19] *the finger of mortality* signs of death or change.
[20] *threescore years and ten* seventy years, man's allotted lifespan: 'the days of our years are threescore years and ten' (Psalm 90:10).

PRIEST

Why, sir, for aught I know,
That chasm is much the same.

LEONARD

But surely, yonder –

PRIEST

Aye, there indeed your memory is a friend
That does not play you false. On that tall pike
(It is the loneliest place of all these hills)
There were two springs which bubbled side by side
As if they had been made that they might be
Companions for each other! Ten years back,
Close to those brother fountains, the huge crag
Was rent with lightning – one is dead and gone,
The other, left behind, is flowing still.[21]
For accidents and changes such as these,
Why, we have store[22] of them! A water-spout
Will bring down half a mountain – what a feast
For folks that wander up and down like you,
To see an acre's breadth of that wide cliff
One roaring cataract! A sharp May storm
Will come with loads of January snow
And in one night send twenty score of sheep
To feed the ravens; or a shepherd dies
By some untoward death among the rocks;
The ice breaks up, and sweeps away a bridge;
A wood is felled. And then, for our own homes –
A child is born or christened, a field ploughed,
A daughter sent to service,[23] a web spun,[24]
The old house-clock is decked with a new face[25] –
And hence, so far from wanting facts or dates
To chronicle the time, we all have here
A pair of diaries: one serving, sir,
For the whole dale, and one for each fireside.[26]
Yours was a stranger's judgment[27] – for historians
Commend me to these valleys!

LEONARD

Yet your churchyard
Seems (if such freedom may be used with you)
To say that you are heedless of the past:

## Notes

[21] 'The impressive circumstance here described actually took place some years ago in this country, upon an eminence called Kidstow Pike, one of the highest of the mountains that surround Hawes Water. The summit of the Pike was stricken by lightning, and every trace of one of the fountains disappeared, while the other continued to flow as before' (Wordsworth's note).

[22] *store* a good store, plenty.

[23] *sent to service* put to work as a servant.

[24] *a web spun* a piece of cloth woven.

[25] *decked with a new face* repainted.

[26] *we all…fireside* Time is measured by the public events, shared by the community, and private ones, known to each family.

[27] *Yours was a stranger's judgment* painfully ironic; the priest is still unaware of Leonard's identity.

An orphan could not find his mother's grave.
Here's neither head nor foot-stone, plate of brass,
Cross-bones or skull, type of our earthly state
Or emblem of our hopes. The dead man's home
Is but a fellow to that pasture field.[28]

PRIEST
Why there, sir, is a thought that's new to me.
The stonecutters, 'tis true, might beg their bread
If every English churchyard were like ours;
Yet your conclusion wanders from the truth.
We have no need of names and epitaphs,
We talk about the dead by our firesides.
And then for our immortal part[29] – we want
No symbols, sir, to tell us that plain tale.
The thought of death sits easy on the man
Who has been born and dies among the mountains.[30]

LEONARD
Your dalesmen, then, do in each other's thoughts
Possess a kind of second life. No doubt
You, sir, could help me to the history
Of half these graves?

PRIEST
For eight-score winters past[31] –
With what I've witnessed, and with what I've heard –
Perhaps I might; and on a winter's evening,
If you were seated at my chimney's nook,
By turning o'er these hillocks one by one
We two could travel, sir, through a strange round,
Yet all in the broad highway of the world.[32]
Now there's a grave – your foot is half upon it –
It looks just like the rest, and yet that man
Died broken-hearted.

LEONARD
'Tis a common case –
We'll take another. Who is he that lies
Beneath yon ridge, the last of those three graves? –
It touches on that piece of native[33] rock
Left in the churchyard wall.

## Notes

28 *The dead…field* The graveyard looks the same as the meadow.

29 *our immortal part* i.e. the soul.

30 'There is not anything more worthy of remark in the manners of the inhabitants of these mountains, than the tranquillity – I might say indifference – with which they think and talk upon the subject of death. Some of the country churchyards, as here described, do not contain a single tombstone, and most of them have a very small number' (Wordsworth's note).

31 *eight-score winters past* i.e. the last 160 years (a score is twenty).

32 *By turning…world* The life stories of those buried before them comprise a wide range ('strange round') of experience, which, taken as a whole, would be revealed as entirely normal ('in the broad highway of the world').

33 *native* a piece of rock embedded in the ground even before the graveyard was put there.

PRIEST

That's Walter Ewbank.
He had as white a head and fresh a cheek
As ever were produced by youth and age
Engendering in the blood of hale fourscore.[34]
For five long generations had the heart
Of Walter's forefathers o'erflowed the bounds
Of their inheritance[35] – that single cottage
(You see it yonder), and those few green fields.
They toiled and wrought, and still, from sire[36] to son,
Each struggled, and each yielded as before
A little – yet a little. And old Walter –
They left to him the family heart, and land
With other burdens than the crop it bore.
Year after year the old man still preserved
A cheerful mind, and buffeted with bond,
Interest and mortgages, at last he sank,
And went into his grave before his time.[37]
Poor Walter – whether it was care that spurred him
God only knows, but to the very last
He had the lightest foot in Ennerdale.
His pace was never that of an old man –
I almost see him tripping down the path
With his two grandsons after him. But you,
Unless our landlord be your host tonight,[38]
Have far to travel, and in these rough paths
Even in the longest day of midsummer –

LEONARD

But these two orphans...

PRIEST

Orphans – such they were,
Yet not while Walter lived. For though their parents
Lay buried side by side as now they lie,
The old man was a father to the boys –
Two fathers in one father – and if tears
Shed when he talked of them where they were not,
And hauntings from the infirmity of love,
Are aught of what makes up a mother's heart,
This old man in the day of his old age
Was half a mother to them. If you weep, sir,
To hear a stranger talking about strangers,[39]

## Notes

[34] *He had...fourscore* Walter was 80, but he was healthy and vigorous ('hale') thanks to his combination of youth and age.

[35] *the heart...inheritance* The Ewbanks were more generous than they could afford.

[36] *sire* father.

[37] *buffeted...time* The cost of Walter's independence was that the land he inherited was burdened by mortgages and debt.

[38] *Unless our landlord be your host tonight* unless you plan to stay at the inn.

[39] *If you weep...strangers* again, painfully ironic. The priest is still unaware that the story he has been telling is that of Leonard's family.

Heaven bless you when you are among your kindred!
Aye, you may turn that way – it is a grave
Which will bear looking at.

LEONARD

These boys, I hope
They loved this good old man?

PRIEST

They did, and truly –
But that was what we almost overlooked,
They were such darlings of each other. For
Though from their cradles they had lived with Walter,
The only kinsman near them in the house,
Yet he being old they had much love to spare,
And it all went into each other's hearts.
Leonard, the elder by just eighteen months,
Was two years taller – 'twas a joy to see,
To hear, to meet them! From their house the school
Was distant three short miles; and in the time
Of storm, and thaw, when every water-course
And unbridged stream (such as you may have noticed,
Crossing our roads at every hundred steps)
Was swoln into a noisy rivulet,
Would Leonard then, when elder boys perhaps
Remained at home, go staggering through the fords[40]
Bearing his brother on his back. I've seen him
On windy days, in one of those stray brooks –
Aye, more than once I've seen him mid-leg deep,
Their two books lying both on a dry stone
Upon the hither side. And once I said,
As I remember, looking round these rocks
And hills on which we all of us were born,
That God who made the great book of the world[41]
Would bless such piety.[42]

LEONARD

It may be then –

PRIEST

Never did worthier lads break English bread:
The finest Sunday that the autumn saw,
With all its mealy[43] clusters of ripe nuts,
Could never keep these boys away from church
Or tempt them to an hour of sabbath breach.[44]

## Notes

[40] *fords* A ford is a shallow place in a river where people and animals can wade across.

[41] *the great book of the world* i.e. the natural world.

[42] *piety* virtue.

[43] *mealy* meal-coloured.

[44] *sabbath breach* violating the command not to work on the Sabbath (Sunday).

Leonard and James! I warrant, every corner
Among these rocks, and every hollow place
Where foot could come, to one or both of them
Was known as well as to the flowers that grow there.
Like roebucks they went bounding o'er the hills;[45]
They played like two young ravens on the crags.
Then they could write, aye, and speak too, as well
As many of their betters.[46] And for Leonard –
The very night before he went away,
In my own house I put into his hand
A bible, and I'd wager twenty pounds
That if he is alive he has it yet.

LEONARD
It seems these brothers have not lived to be
A comfort to each other?

PRIEST
That they might
Live to that end, is what both old and young
In this our valley all of us have wished –
And what for my part I have often prayed.
But Leonard –

LEONARD
Then James still is left among you?

PRIEST
'Tis of the elder brother I am speaking –
They had an uncle (he was at that time
A thriving man and trafficked[47] on the seas[48]),
And but for this same uncle, to this hour
Leonard had never handled rope or shroud.
For the boy loved the life which we lead here;
And, though a very stripling, twelve years old,
His soul was knit[49] to this his native soil.
But, as I said, old Walter was too weak
To strive with such a torrent. When he died,
The estate and house were sold, and all their sheep –
A pretty flock, and which, for aught I know,
Had clothed the Ewbanks for a thousand years.
Well – all was gone, and they were destitute;
And Leonard, chiefly for his brother's sake,
Resolved to try his fortune on the seas.

## Notes

[45] *Like roebucks…hills* cf. 'Tintern Abbey' 68–9.

[46] *betters* social superiors.

[47] *trafficked* traded.

[48] *he was…seas* The poet's cousin, another John Wordsworth, was a successful captain working for the East India Company. Wordsworth's brother John succeeded him as captain of the *Earl of Abergavenny*.

[49] *knit* joined, attached.

'Tis now twelve years since we had tidings from him.
If there was one among us who had heard
That Leonard Ewbank was come home again,
From the Great Gavel, down by Leeza's Banks,
And down the Enna, far as Egremont,[50]
The day would be a very festival,
And those two bells of ours, which there you see
Hanging in the open air – but oh, good sir,
This is sad talk; they'll never sound for him,
Living or dead. When last we heard of him
He was in slavery among the Moors
Upon the Barbary Coast.[51] 'Twas not a little
That would bring down his spirit, and no doubt
Before it ended in his death, the lad
Was sadly crossed.[52] Poor Leonard, when we parted
He took me by the hand and said to me
If ever the day came when he was rich
He would return, and on his father's land
He would grow old among us.

LEONARD

If that day
Should come, 'twould needs be a glad day for him;
He would himself, no doubt, be then as happy
As any that should meet him.

PRIEST

Happy, sir –

LEONARD

You said his kindred were all in their graves,
And that he had one brother...

PRIEST

That is but
A fellow[53] tale of sorrow. From his youth
James, though not sickly, yet was delicate;
And Leonard being always by his side
Had done so many offices about him[54]
That, though he was not of a timid nature,
Yet still the spirit of a mountain boy
In him was somewhat checked. And when his brother
Was gone to sea and he was left alone,

## Notes

[50] 'The Great Gavel, so called, I imagine, from its resemblance to the gable end of a house, is one of the highest of the Cumberland mountains. It stands at the head of the several vales of Ennerdale, Wastdale, and Borrowdale. The Leeza is a river which flows into the Lake of Ennerdale; on issuing from the Lake, it changes its name and is called the End, or Eyne, or Enna. It falls into the sea a little below Egremont' (Wordsworth's note).

[51] *Barbary Coast* north coast of Africa.

[52] *crossed* grieved.

[53] *fellow* similar.

[54] *Had done so many offices about him* had looked after him so much.

The little colour that he had was soon
Stolen from his cheek; he drooped, and pined and pined...

LEONARD
But these are all the graves of full grown men...

PRIEST
Aye, sir, that passed away. We took him to us –
He was the child of all the dale. He lived
Three months with one, and six months with another,
And wanted neither food, nor clothes, nor love;
And many, many happy days were his.
But, whether blithe or sad, 'tis my belief
His absent brother still was at his heart.
And when he lived beneath our roof, we found
(A practice till this time unknown to him)
That often, rising from his bed at night,
He in his sleep would walk about, and sleeping
He sought his brother Leonard. You are moved;
Forgive me, sir – before I spoke to you
I judged you most unkindly.

LEONARD
But this youth,
How did he die at last?

PRIEST
One sweet May morning
(It will be twelve years since, when spring returns)
He had gone forth among the new-dropped lambs
With two or three companions, whom it chanced
Some further business summoned to a house
Which stands at the dale-head.[55] James, tired perhaps,
Or from some other cause, remained behind.
You see yon precipice? It almost looks
Like some vast building made of many crags,
And in the midst is one particular rock
That rises like a column from the vale,
Whence by our shepherds it is called the Pillar.[56]
James pointed to its summit, over which
They all had purposed to return together,
Informed them that he there would wait for them.
They parted, and his comrades passed that way
Some two hours after, but they did not find him
At the appointed place – a circumstance
Of which they took no heed. But one of them,
Going by chance, at night, into the house

Notes

[55] *dale-head* head of the valley.

[56] *the Pillar* a mountain in Ennerdale.

Which at this time was James' home, there learned
That nobody had seen him all that day.
The morning came, and still he was unheard of;
The neighbours were alarmed, and to the brook
Some went, and some towards the lake. Ere noon
They found him at the foot of that same rock,
Dead, and with mangled limbs. The third day after,
I buried him, poor lad, and there he lies.

LEONARD
And that then *is* his grave. Before his death
You said that he saw many happy years?

PRIEST
Aye, that he did.

LEONARD
And all went well with him?

PRIEST
If he had one, the lad had twenty homes.

LEONARD
And you believe then, that his mind was easy?

PRIEST
Yes, long before he died he found that time
Is a true friend to sorrow; and unless
His thoughts were turned on Leonard's luckless fortune,
He talked about him with a cheerful love.

LEONARD
He could not come to an unhallowed end![57]

PRIEST
Nay, God forbid! You recollect I mentioned
A habit which disquietude and grief
Had brought upon him; and we all conjectured
That as the day was warm he had lain down
Upon the grass, and waiting for his comrades
He there had fallen asleep – that in his sleep
He to the margin of the precipice
Had walked, and from the summit had fallen headlong.
And so no doubt he perished. At the time
We guess that in his hands he must have had
His shepherd's staff; for midway in the cliff

## Notes

[57] *an unhallowed end* In 1800 suicide was still regarded as a sin.

It had been caught, and there for many years
It hung – and mouldered there.

The priest here ended.
The stranger would have thanked him, but he felt
Tears rushing in. Both left the spot in silence,
And Leonard, when they reached the churchyard gate,
As the priest lifted up the latch, turned round,
And looking at the grave he said, 'My brother'.
The vicar did not hear the words; and now,
Pointing towards the cottage, he entreated
That Leonard would partake his homely fare.
The other thanked him with a fervent voice,
But added that, the evening being calm,
He would pursue his journey. So they parted.
It was not long ere Leonard reached a grove
That overhung the road. He there stopped short,
And sitting down beneath the trees, reviewed
All that the priest had said.
His early years
Were with him in his heart – his cherished hopes,
And thoughts which had been his an hour before,
All pressed on him with such a weight that now
This vale where he had been so happy seemed
A place in which he could not bear to live.
So he relinquished all his purposes.
He travelled on to Egremont; and thence
That night addressed a letter to the priest
Reminding him of what had passed between them,
And adding – with a hope to be forgiven –
That it was from the weakness of his heart
He had not dared to tell him who he was.
This done, he went on shipboard, and is now
A seaman, a grey-headed mariner.

## *Preface to Lyrical Ballads* (extracts; composed September 1800)[1]

The first volume of these Poems[2] has already been submitted to general perusal. It was published as an experiment which, I hoped, might be of some use to ascertain how far, by fitting to metrical arrangement a selection of the real language of men[3] in a state of vivid sensation, that sort of pleasure and that quantity of pleasure may be imparted, which a Poet may rationally endeavour to impart.

### Notes

PREFACE TO LYRICAL BALLADS

[1] This Preface, Wordsworth's most important critical work, was first published in this form in 1800, and revised for the 1802 edition of *Lyrical Ballads*. The Preface was written at Coleridge's insistence, and drew on ideas conceived or gathered by him; as he told Southey, 29 July 1802, 'Wordsworth's Preface is half a child of my own brain'. Throughout this essay, Wordsworth tends to capitalize such words as 'Poem' and 'Reader', and I have preserved those typographical features.

[2] *The first volume of these Poems* Wordsworth refers to *Lyrical Ballads* (1798).

[3] *the real language of men* Wordsworth's use of this phrase brought much criticism, because many people responded that no one spoke as people did in his poems.

I had formed no very inaccurate estimate of the probable effect of those Poems: I flattered myself that they who should be pleased with them would read them with more than common pleasure: and on the other hand I was well aware that by those who should dislike them they would be read with more than common dislike. The result has differed from my expectation in this only, that I have pleased a greater number than I ventured to hope I should please.

For the sake of variety and from a consciousness of my own weakness, I was induced to request the assistance of a Friend, who furnished me with the Poems of the 'Ancient Mariner', 'The Foster-Mother's Tale', 'The Nightingale', and the Poem entitled 'Love'.[4] I should not, however, have requested this assistance, had I not believed that the Poems of my Friend would in a great measure have the same tendency as my own, and that, though there would be found a difference, there would be found no discordance in the colours of our style as our opinions on the subject of poetry do almost entirely coincide.

Several of my Friends are anxious for the success of these Poems from a belief that, if the views with which they were composed were indeed realized, a class of Poetry would be produced well adapted to interest mankind permanently, and not unimportant in the multiplicity, and in the quality of its moral relations: and on this account they have advised me to prefix a systematic defence of the theory upon which the poems were written.[5] But I was unwilling to undertake the task because I knew that on this occasion the Reader would look coldly upon my arguments, since I might be suspected of having been principally influenced by the selfish and foolish hope of *reasoning* him into an approbation of these particular Poems: and I was still more unwilling to undertake the task because adequately to display my opinions and fully to enforce my arguments would require a space wholly disproportionate to the nature of a preface. For to treat the subject with the clearness and coherence of which I believe it susceptible, it would be necessary to give a full account of the present state of the public taste in this country, and to determine how far this taste is healthy or depraved: which again could not be determined without pointing out in what manner language and the human mind act and react on each other, and without retracing the revolutions not of literature alone but likewise of society itself. I have therefore altogether declined to enter regularly upon this defence; yet I am sensible that there would be some impropriety in abruptly obtruding upon the Public, without a few words of introduction, Poems so materially different from those upon which general approbation is at present bestowed.

It is supposed, that by the act of writing in verse an Author makes a formal engagement that he will gratify certain known habits of association, that he not only thus apprizes the Reader that certain classes of ideas and expressions will be found in his book, but that others will be carefully excluded. This exponent or symbol held forth by metrical language must in different eras of literature have excited very different expectations: for example, in the age of Catullus, Terence, and Lucretius, and that of Statius or Claudian;[6] and in our own country, in the age of Shakespeare and Beaumont and Fletcher, and that of Donne and Cowley, or Dryden, or Pope. I will not take upon me to determine the exact import of the promise which by the act of writing in verse an Author

## Notes

[4] *a Friend…'Love'* 'Love' did not appear in *Lyrical Ballads* (1798), but was added in 1800. The 'Friend' is Coleridge.

[5] *they have advised…written* The 'Friends' consist of Coleridge. 'I never cared a straw about the theory', Wordsworth told Barron Field, 'and the Preface was written at the request of Coleridge out of sheer good nature. I recollect the very spot, a deserted quarry in the vale of Grasmere, where he pressed the thing upon me, and but for that it would never have been thought of.'

[6] Catullus (?84–?54 BCE) was a Roman poet, remembered for a range of work including elegies, epigrams and love poems to his beloved 'Lesbia'; Terence (195–159 BCE) wrote comedies, a polished and urbane writer; Lucretius (99–55 BCE), Roman philosophic poet, author of *De rerum natura* ('On the nature of things'); Statius (*c.*45–*c.*96) was the author of the *Thebaid*, an epic in the manner of Virgil. Claudian (fourth–fifth century) was the last notable Latin classical poet. He is regarded as a vigorous, skilful, imaginative writer, the author of several epics including *The Rape of Proserpine*. The latter two authors use a more inflated manner than the earlier ones, and date from a period of general decline. Similarly, Wordsworth contrasts the writing of Dryden and Pope unfavourably with that of earlier times because he thinks of the Augustans as having been guilty of using a form of 'poetic diction' that took them away from life as experienced by ordinary people.

in the present day makes to his Reader; but I am certain it will appear to many persons that I have not fulfilled the terms of an engagement thus voluntarily contracted. I hope therefore the Reader will not censure me if I attempt to state what I have proposed to myself to perform, and also (as far as the limits of a preface will permit) to explain some of the chief reasons which have determined me in the choice of my purpose: that at least he may be spared any unpleasant feeling of disappointment, and that I myself may be protected from the most dishonourable accusation which can be brought against an Author – namely, that of an indolence which prevents him from endeavouring to ascertain what is his duty, or, when his duty is ascertained, prevents him from performing it.

The principal object, then, which I proposed to myself in these Poems, was to make the incidents of common life interesting by tracing in them (truly,[7] though not ostentatiously) the primary laws of our nature,[8] chiefly as far as regards the manner in which we associate ideas[9] in a state of excitement.[10] Low and rustic life was generally chosen because in that condition the essential passions of the heart find a better soil in which they can attain their maturity, are less under restraint, and speak a plainer and more emphatic language;[11] because in that situation our elementary feelings coexist in a state of greater simplicity, and consequently may be more accurately contemplated and more forcibly communicated; because the manners of rural life germinate from those elementary feelings,[12] and (from the necessary character of rural occupations) are more easily comprehended and are more durable; and lastly, because in that condition the passions of men are incorporated[13] with the beautiful and permanent forms of nature.[14]

The language too of these men is adopted (purified indeed from what appear to be its real defects – from all lasting and rational causes of dislike or disgust) because such men hourly communicate with the best objects[15] from which the best part of language is originally derived, and because, from their rank in society and the sameness and narrow circle of their intercourse being less under the influence of social vanity, they convey their feelings and notions in simple and unelaborated expressions. Accordingly, such a language, arising out of repeated experience and regular feelings, is a more permanent and a far more philosophical language[16] than that which is frequently substituted for it by poets who think that they are conferring honour upon themselves and their art, in proportion as they separate themselves from the sympathies of men and indulge in arbitrary and capricious habits of expression, in order to furnish food for fickle tastes and fickle appetites[17] of their own creation.[18]

I cannot, however, be insensible to the present outcry against the triviality and meanness both of thought and language which some of my contemporaries have occasionally introduced into their metrical compositions. And I acknowledge that this defect, where it exists, is more dishonourable to the writer's own character than false refinement or arbitrary innovation (though I should contend at the same time that it is far less pernicious in the sum of its consequences).

## Notes

[7] *truly* truthfully.

[8] *the primary laws of our nature* i.e. (in this context) the workings of the mind.

[9] *we associate ideas* The association of ideas – that is to say, the way in which emotions are connected with, for instance, memories, is an important element in Wordsworth's thinking.

[10] *a state of excitement* i.e. emotional excitement, when we feel intensely.

[11] *Low and rustic...language* a belief first expressed in February 1798.

[12] *the manners of rural life...feelings* There is an implied comparison with the social life ('manners') of the city, which has become detached from 'elementary' human emotion.

[13] *incorporated* interfused, united, blended.

[14] *the passions...nature* as, for instance, in the way that Michael's unfinished sheepfold becomes a symbol of his tragedy, or that Margaret's ruined cottage embodies hers. The search for permanence – of language and symbol – is fundamental to Wordsworth's aesthetic.

[15] *the best objects* for example, natural objects.

[16] *philosophical language* i.e. fit for philosophical discourse.

[17] *fickle tastes and fickle appetites* tastes and appetites governed by literary fashion.

[18] 'It is worthwhile here to observe that the affecting parts of Chaucer are almost always expressed in language pure and universally intelligible even to this day' (Wordsworth's note). Wordsworth believed that 'every great and original writer, in proportion as he is great or original, must himself create the taste by which he is to be relished'.

From such verses the poems in these volumes will be found distinguished at least by one mark of difference – that each of them has a worthy *purpose*. Not that I mean to say that I always began to write with a distinct purpose formally conceived, but I believe that my habits of meditation have so formed my feelings, as that my descriptions of such objects as strongly excite those feelings will be found to carry along with them a *purpose*. If in this opinion I am mistaken, I can have little right to the name of a poet; for all good poetry is the spontaneous overflow of powerful feelings.[19] But though this be true, poems to which any value can be attached were never produced on any variety of subjects but by a man who, being possessed of more than usual organic[20] sensibility, had also thought long and deeply.[21] For our continued influxes of feeling[22] are modified and directed by our thoughts, which are indeed the representatives of all our past feelings.[23] And, as by contemplating the relation of these general representatives[24] to each other, we discover what is really important to men, so by the repetition and continuance of this act, feelings connected with important subjects will be nourished, till at length (if we be originally possessed of much organic sensibility) such habits of mind will be produced that, by obeying blindly and mechanically[25] the impulses of those habits, we shall describe objects and utter sentiments of such a nature, and in such connection with each other, that the understanding of the being to whom we address ourselves – if he be in a healthful state of association[26] – must necessarily be in some degree enlightened, his taste exalted, and his affections ameliorated.[27]

I have said that each of these poems has a purpose. I have also informed my Reader what this purpose will be found principally to be: namely, to illustrate the manner in which our feelings and ideas are associated in a state of excitement.[28] But (speaking in less general language) it is to follow the fluxes and refluxes[29] of the mind when agitated by the great and simple affections of our nature. This object I have endeavoured in these short essays[30] to attain by various means: by tracing the maternal passion through many of its more subtle windings (as in the poems of 'The Idiot Boy' and 'The Mad Mother'); by accompanying the last struggles of a human being at the approach of death, cleaving in solitude to life and society (as in the poem of the forsaken Indian);[31] by showing, as in the stanzas entitled 'We Are Seven', the perplexity and obscurity which in childhood attend our notion of death – or rather our utter inability to admit that notion; or by displaying the strength of fraternal or (to speak more philosophically) of moral attachment when early associated with the great and beautiful objects of nature (as in 'The Brothers'); or, as in the incident of 'Simon Lee', by placing my Reader in the way of receiving from ordinary moral sensations another and more salutary impression than we are accustomed to receive from them.[32]

It has also been part of my general purpose to attempt to sketch characters under the influence of less impassioned feelings, as in the 'Old Man Travelling', 'The Two Thieves', etc. – characters of which the elements are simple, belonging rather to nature than to manners,[33] such as exist now and

## Notes

[19] *all good poetry...feelings* one of Wordsworth's best-known pronouncements; note, however, the sentence that follows, frequently omitted or forgotten.

[20] *organic* innate, inherent.

[21] *If in this opinion...deeply* Wordsworth's championing of 'powerful feelings' is strongly modified by the insistence on long and profound thought.

[22] *influxes of feeling* i.e. 'flowing-in' of emotion; cf. the Pedlar's 'access of mind' ('The Pedlar' 107).

[23] *For our ... feelings* Emotions in the past work in the present, as thoughts, to alter continuing influxes of emotion in the present.

[24] *these general representatives* thoughts deriving from feelings in the past.

[25] *by obeying blindly and mechanically* It is crucial to the creative act that the poet completely surrender to associations, and habits of thought and feeling.

[26] *a healthful state of association* i.e. a state of mind in which the reader is receptive, and does not impose on the poetry irrelevant prejudices or assumptions.

[27] *ameliorated* improved. Poetry should be emotionally uplifting.

[28] *the manner...excitement* the way in which emotions and ideas interact associatively when the mind is stimulated.

[29] *fluxes and refluxes* ebb and flow.

[30] *essays* attempts.

[31] *the poem of the forsaken Indian* i.e. 'The Complaint of a Forsaken Indian Woman'.

[32] *by placing...them* The initial pity, which leads the narrator to offer to help Simon Lee, gives way to the more complex sentiment expressed in the final lines of the poem.

[33] *manners* customs.

will probably always exist, and which from their constitution may be distinctly and profitably contemplated. I will not abuse the indulgence of my Reader by dwelling longer upon this subject, but it is proper that I should mention one other circumstance which distinguishes these Poems from the popular poetry of the day. It is this – that the feeling therein developed gives importance to the action and situation, and not the action and situation to the feeling.[34] My meaning will be rendered perfectly intelligible by referring my reader to the poems entitled 'Poor Susan' and 'The Childless Father'[35] (particularly to the last stanza of the latter Poem).

I will not suffer a sense of false modesty to prevent me from asserting that I point my Reader's attention to this mark of distinction far less for the sake of these particular Poems than from the general importance of the subject. The subject is indeed important![36] For the human mind is capable of excitement without the application of gross and violent stimulants,[37] and he must have a very faint perception of its beauty and dignity who does not know this, and who does not further know that one being is elevated above another in proportion as he possesses this capability.[38]

It has therefore appeared to me that to endeavour to produce or enlarge this capability is one of the best services in which (at any period) a Writer can be engaged – but this service, excellent at all times, is especially so at the present day. For a multitude of causes, unknown to former times, are now acting with a combined force to blunt the discriminating powers of the mind and, unfitting it for all voluntary exertion, to reduce it to a state of almost savage torpor.[39] The most effective of these causes are the great national events[40] which are daily taking place, and the increasing accumulation of men in cities, where the uniformity of their occupations produces a craving for extraordinary incident which the rapid communication[41] of intelligence hourly gratifies. To this tendency of life and manners the literature and theatrical exhibitions[42] of the country have conformed themselves. The invaluable works of our elder writers (I had almost said the works of Shakespeare and Milton) are driven into neglect by frantic novels, sickly and stupid German tragedies, and deluges of idle and extravagant stories in verse.[43]

When I think upon this degrading thirst after outrageous[44] stimulation, I am almost ashamed to have spoken of the feeble effort with which I have endeavoured to counteract it. And, reflecting upon the magnitude of the general evil, I should be oppressed with no dishonourable melancholy had I not a deep impression of certain inherent and indestructible qualities of the human mind (and likewise of certain powers in the great and permanent objects[45] that act upon it which are equally inherent and indestructible), and did I not further add to this impression a belief that the time is approaching when the evil will be systematically opposed by men of greater powers and with far more distinguished success.

Having dwelt thus long on the subjects and aim of these poems, I shall request the Reader's permission to apprise him of a few circumstances relating to their *style*, in order (among other reasons) that I may not be censured for not having performed what I never attempted. The Reader will find no personifications of abstract ideas in these volumes, not that I mean to censure such

## Notes

[34] *the feeling…feeling* a crucial distinction between Wordsworth's poetry and that of many of his more fashionable contemporaries: his poetry is inspired primarily by the emotion behind it rather than by the incidents or the social class of those it describes.

[35] *'Poor Susan' and 'The Childless Father'* These poems, first published in *Lyrical Ballads* (1800), are not included in this anthology, but Wordsworth's point is borne out by 'Simon Lee', 'The Last of the Flock', 'Complaint of a Forsaken Indian Woman', 'The Thorn' and 'The Idiot Boy'.

[36] In view of his stylistic conservatism when it came to prose, it is worth noting that the exclamation mark at this point is Wordsworth's.

[37] *gross and violent stimulants* a reference to the sort of violent or salacious detail often found in Gothic chillers of the day.

[38] *this capability* imaginative sympathy.

[39] *savage torpor* barbaric laziness.

[40] *national events* Britain had been at war with France since 1793.

[41] *rapid communication* the semaphore telegraph (invented 1792) and the stagecoach.

[42] *exhibitions* performances.

[43] *frantic novels…verse* Gothic novels, and plays by sentimental writers like Kotzebue, were popular.

[44] *outrageous* excessive.

[45] *the great and permanent objects* i.e. primarily the internalized images of objects in the natural world, such as mountains, lakes, trees.

personifications: they may be well fitted for certain sorts of composition, but in these Poems I propose to myself to imitate – and, as far as is possible, to adopt – the very language of men, and I do not find that such personifications make any regular or natural part of that language. I wish to keep my Reader in the company of flesh and blood, persuaded that by so doing I shall interest him. Not but that I believe that others who pursue a different track may interest him likewise. I do not interfere with their claim; I only wish to prefer a different claim of my own.

There will also be found in these volumes little of what is usually called 'poetic diction': I have taken as much pains to avoid it as others ordinarily take to produce it. This I have done for the reason already alleged – to bring my language near to the language of men, and, further, because the pleasure which I have proposed to myself to impart is of a kind very different from that which is supposed by many persons to be the proper object of poetry. I do not know how, without being culpably particular,[46] I can give my Reader a more exact notion of the style in which I wished these poems to be written than by informing him that I have at all times endeavoured to look steadily at my subject. Consequently, I hope that there is in these Poems little falsehood of description, and that my ideas are expressed in language fitted to their respective importance.[47] Something I must have gained by this practice, as it is friendly to one property of all good poetry – namely, good sense. But it has necessarily cut me off from a large portion of phrases and figures of speech which, from father to son, have long been regarded as the common inheritance of Poets. I have also thought it expedient to restrict myself still further, having abstained from the use of many expressions in themselves proper and beautiful, but which have been foolishly repeated by bad Poets till such feelings of disgust are connected with them as it is scarcely possible by any art of association to overpower.

If in a Poem there should be found a series of lines, or even a single line, in which the language, though naturally arranged and according to the strict laws of metre, does not differ from that of prose, there is a numerous class of critics who, when they stumble upon these prosaisms as they call them, imagine that they have made a notable discovery, and exult over the Poet as over a man ignorant of his own profession. Now these men would establish a canon of criticism which the Reader will conclude he must utterly reject if he wishes to be pleased with these volumes. And it would be a most easy task to prove to him that not only the language of a large portion of every good poem, even of the most elevated character, must necessarily, except with reference to the metre, in no respect differ from that of good prose, but likewise that some of the most interesting parts of the best poems will be found to be strictly the language of prose when prose is well written. The truth of this assertion might be demonstrated by innumerable passages from almost all the poetical writings, even of Milton himself. I have not space for much quotation; but, to illustrate the subject in a general manner, I will here adduce a short composition of Gray, who was at the head of those who by their reasonings[48] have attempted to widen the space of separation betwixt prose and metrical composition, and was more than any other man curiously elaborate in the structure of his own poetic diction.

In vain to me the smiling mornings shine,
And reddening Phoebus lifts his golden fire:
The birds in vain their amorous descant join,
Or cheerful fields resume their green attire:
These ears alas! for other notes repine;
*A different object do these eyes require;*

## Notes

[46] *culpably particular* too meticulously detailed.

[47] *fitted to their respective importance* i.e. by the weight of emotion behind them.

[48] *reasonings* Wordsworth was probably aware of Gray's dictum in his correspondence that 'the language of the age is never the language of poetry'. The poem is Gray's 'Sonnet on the Death of Richard West'.

*My lonely anguish melts no heart but mine;*
*And in my breast the imperfect joys expire;*
Yet Morning smiles the busy race to cheer,
And new-born pleasure brings to happier men;
The fields to all their wonted tribute bear;
To warm their little loves the birds complain.
*I fruitless mourn to him that cannot hear*
*And weep the more because I weep in vain.*

It will easily be perceived that the only part of this sonnet which is of any value is the lines printed in italics: it is equally obvious that, except in the rhyme, and in the use of the single word 'fruitless' for 'fruitlessly', which is so far a defect, the language of these lines does in no respect differ from that of prose.

Is there, then, it will be asked, no essential difference between the language of prose and metrical composition? I answer that there neither is nor can be any essential difference. We are fond of tracing the resemblance between poetry and painting, and, accordingly, we call them sisters.[49] But where shall we find bonds of connection sufficiently strict to typify the affinity betwixt metrical and prose composition? They both speak by and to the same organs; the bodies in which both of them are clothed may be said to be of the same substance, their affections are kindred and almost identical, not necessarily differing even in degree;[50] poetry sheds no tears 'such as angels weep',[51] but natural and human tears; she can boast of no celestial ichor[52] that distinguishes her vital juices from those of prose; the same human blood circulates through the veins of them both.

If it be affirmed that rhyme and metrical arrangement of themselves constitute a distinction which overturns what I have been saying on the strict affinity of metrical language with that of prose, and paves the way for other distinctions which the mind voluntarily admits, I answer that the distinction of rhyme and metre is regular and uniform, and not like that which is produced by what is usually called 'poetic diction' – arbitrary, and subject to infinite caprices upon which no calculation whatever can be made. In the one case, the Reader is utterly at the mercy of the Poet respecting what imagery or diction he may choose to connect with the passion, whereas in the other the metre obeys certain[53] laws, to which the Poet and Reader both willingly submit because they are certain, and because no interference is made by them with the passion but such as the concurring testimony of ages has shown to heighten and improve the pleasure which co-exists with it.

It will now be proper to answer an obvious question, namely, why, professing these opinions, have I written in verse? To this in the first place I reply, because, however I may have restricted myself, there is still left open to me what confessedly constitutes the most valuable object of all writing whether in prose or verse, the great and universal passions of men,[54] the most general and interesting of their occupations, and the entire world of nature, from which I am at liberty to supply myself with endless combinations of forms and imagery.[55] Now, granting for a moment that

## Notes

[49] *we call them sisters* This was a commonplace of eighteenth-century aesthetic theory.

[50] 'I here use the word "poetry" (though against my own judgement) as opposed to the word "prose", and synonymous with metrical composition. But much confusion has been introduced into criticism by this contradistinction of poetry and prose, instead of the more philosophical one of poetry and science. The only strict antithesis to prose is metre' (Wordsworth's note).

[51] *such as angels weep* from 'Paradise Lost' i 620, where Satan is lachrymose.

[52] *celestial ichor* the blood of the gods in Greek myth.

[53] *certain* fixed.

[54] *the great and universal passions of men* For 'passions' think of emotions, or psychological twists and turns. The task of understanding how the human mind worked prior to the existence of a 'science' of psychology, in the sense in which it now exists, is Wordsworth's main project. See also the 'Note to "The Thorn"'.

[55] *imagery* Wordsworth defined imagery as 'sensible objects really existing, and felt to exist'.

whatever is interesting in these objects may be as vividly described in prose, why am I to be condemned, if to such description I have endeavoured to superadd the charm which, by the consent of all nations, is acknowledged to exist in metrical language? To this, it will be answered, that a very small part of the pleasure given by Poetry depends upon the metre, and that it is injudicious to write in metre, unless it be accompanied with the other artificial distinctions of style with which metre is usually accompanied, and that by such deviation more will be lost from the shock which will be thereby given to the Reader's associations, than will be counterbalanced by any pleasure which he can derive from the general power of numbers. In answer to those who thus contend for the necessity of accompanying metre with certain appropriate colours of style in order to the accomplishment of its appropriate end, and who also, in my opinion, greatly underrate the power of metre in itself, it might perhaps be almost sufficient to observe, that poems are extant, written upon more humble subjects, and in a more naked and simple style than what I have aimed at, which poems have continued to give pleasure from generation to generation. Now, if nakedness and simplicity be a defect, the fact here mentioned affords a strong presumption that poems somewhat less naked and simple are capable of affording pleasure at the present day; and all that I am now attempting is to justify myself for having written under the impression of this belief.

But I might point out various causes why, when the style is manly, and the subject of some importance, words metrically arranged[56] will long continue to impart such a pleasure to mankind as he who is sensible of the extent of that pleasure will be desirous to impart. The end of Poetry is to produce excitement in coexistence with an overbalance of pleasure. Now, by the supposition, excitement is an unusual and irregular state of the mind; ideas and feelings do not in that state succeed each other in accustomed order. But, if the words by which this excitement is produced are in themselves powerful, or the images and feelings have an undue proportion of pain connected with them, there is some danger that the excitement may be carried beyond its proper bounds. Now the co-presence of something regular, something to which the mind has been accustomed when in an unexcited or a less excited state, cannot but have great efficacy in tempering and restraining the passion by an intertexture of ordinary feeling. This may be illustrated by appealing to the Reader's own experience of the reluctance with which he comes to the re-perusal of the distressful parts of *Clarissa Harlowe*, or *The Gamester*.[57] While Shakespeare's writings, in the most pathetic scenes, never act upon us as pathetic beyond the bounds of pleasure – an effect which is in a great degree to be ascribed to small but continual and regular impulses of pleasurable surprise from the metrical arrangement. On the other hand (what it must be allowed will much more frequently happen) if the Poet's words should be incommensurate with the passion, and inadequate to raise the Reader to a height of desirable excitement, then (unless the Poet's choice of his metre has been grossly injudicious) in the feelings of pleasure which the Reader has been accustomed to connect with metre in general, and in the feeling, whether cheerful or melancholy, which he has been accustomed to connect with that particular movement of metre, there will be found something which will greatly contribute to impart passion to the words, and to effect the complex end which the Poet proposes to himself.

If I had undertaken a systematic defence of the theory upon which these poems are written, it would have been my duty to develop the various causes upon which the pleasure received from metrical language depends. Among the chief of these causes is to be reckoned a principle which must be well known to those who have made any of the Arts the object of accurate reflection; I mean the pleasure which the mind derives from the perception of similitude in dissimilitude.[58] This principle is the great spring of the activity of our minds and their chief feeder. From this

## Notes

[56] *words metrically arranged* Wordsworth would probably have been aware of Johnson's claim that metre 'shackles attention and governs passions'.

[57] Wordsworth refers to Samuel Richardson's *Clarissa* (1747–8), about the noble but doomed heroine Clarissa Harlowe and the aristocratic rake Robert Lovelace; and Edward Moore's prose drama of family life, *The Gamester* (1753).

[58] *the perception of similitude in dissimilitude* The pleasure derived from the combination of uniformity and variety in a work of art was another commonplace of eighteenth-century aesthetics.

principle the direction of the sexual appetite, and all the passions connected with it take their origin: It is the life of our ordinary conversation; and upon the accuracy with which similitude in dissimilitude, and dissimilitude in similitude are perceived, depend our taste and our moral feelings. It would not have been a useless employment to have applied this principle to the consideration of metre, and to have shown that metre is hence enabled to afford much pleasure, and to have pointed out in what manner that pleasure is produced. But my limits will not permit me to enter upon this subject, and I must content myself with a general summary.

I have said that Poetry is the spontaneous overflow of powerful feelings: it takes its origin from emotion recollected in tranquillity: the emotion is contemplated till by a species of reaction the tranquillity gradually disappears, and an emotion similar to that which was before the subject of contemplation is gradually produced, and does itself actually exist in the mind.[59] In this mood successful composition generally begins, and in a mood similar to this it is carried on; but the emotion, of whatever kind and in whatever degree, from various causes is qualified by various pleasures, so that in describing any passions whatsoever (which are voluntarily described) the mind will upon the whole be in a state of enjoyment.[60]

Now, if Nature be thus cautious in preserving in a state of enjoyment a being thus employed, the Poet ought to profit by the lesson thus held forth to him, and ought especially to take care, that whatever passions he communicates to his Reader, those passions, if his Reader's mind be sound and vigorous, should always be accompanied with an overbalance of pleasure. Now the music of harmonious metrical language,[61] the sense of difficulty[62] overcome, and the blind association of pleasure which has been previously received from works of rhyme or metre of the same or similar construction – all these imperceptibly make up a complex feeling of delight, which is of the most important use in tempering[63] the painful feeling, which will always be found intermingled with powerful descriptions of the deeper passions.[64] This effect is always produced in pathetic[65] and impassioned poetry while, in lighter compositions, the ease and gracefulness with which the Poet manages his numbers[66] are themselves confessedly a principal source of the gratification of the Reader.

I might perhaps include all which it is *necessary* to say upon this subject by affirming what few persons will deny, that of two descriptions, either of passions, manners, or characters, each of them equally well-executed, the one in prose and the other in verse, the verse will be read a hundred times where the prose is read once. We see that Pope, by the power of verse alone, has contrived to render the plainest common sense interesting, and even frequently to invest it with the appearance of passion. In consequence of these convictions I related in metre the tale of 'Goody Blake and Harry Gill', which is one of the rudest[67] of this collection. I wished to draw attention to the truth that the power of the human imagination is sufficient to produce such changes even in our physical nature as might almost appear miraculous. The truth is an important one; the fact (for it is a *fact*)[68] is a valuable illustration of it. And I have the satisfaction of knowing that it has been communicated to many hundreds of people[69] who would never have heard of it, had it not been narrated as a Ballad, and in a more impressive metre than is usual in Ballads.

## Notes

[59] *The emotion…in the mind* What the poet experiences is related to the original emotion, rather than the original emotion itself.

[60] *so that…enjoyment* Wordsworth emphasizes that we gain aesthetic pleasure even from reading poetry that is tragic in theme.

[61] *harmonious metrical language* poetry.

[62] *the sense of difficulty* i.e. that of disciplining the 'language of prose' into metrical form.

[63] *tempering* modifying.

[64] *deeper passions* serious, darker emotions, such as grief.

[65] *pathetic* passionate, deeply felt.

[66] *numbers* i.e. verse, metre.

[67] *rudest* less sophisticated.

[68] It was important to Wordsworth to make clear that 'Goody Blake and Harry Gill' was not invented, but a true story.

[69] *it has been…people* 'Goody Blake and Harry Gill' was in 1800 the most reprinted of the 1798 *Lyrical Ballads*, having appeared in the *Edinburgh Magazine* 14 (1799) 387–9, the *Ipswich Magazine* (1799) 118–19, *New Annual Register* 19 (1799) 200–3 and the *Universal Magazine* 105 (1799) 270–1.

Having thus adverted to a few of the reasons why I have written in verse, and why I have chosen subjects from common life, and endeavoured to bring my language near to the real language of men, if I have been too minute[70] in pleading my own cause, I have at the same time been treating a subject of general interest; and it is for this reason that I request the Reader's permission to add a few words with reference solely to these particular poems, and to some defects which will probably be found in them. I am sensible that my associations must have sometimes been particular instead of general, and that, consequently, giving to things a false importance, sometimes from diseased impulses I may have written upon unworthy subjects; but I am less apprehensive on this account, than that my language may frequently have suffered from those arbitrary connections of feelings and ideas with particular words, from which no man can altogether protect himself. Hence I have no doubt that, in some instances, feelings even of the ludicrous may be given to my Readers by expressions which appeared to me tender and pathetic. Such faulty expressions, were I convinced they were faulty at present, and that they must necessarily continue to be so, I would willingly take all reasonable pains to correct. But it is dangerous to make these alterations on the simple authority of a few individuals, or even of certain classes of men; for where the understanding of an Author is not convinced, or his feelings altered, this cannot be done without great injury to himself: for his own feelings are his stay and support, and if he sets them aside in one instance, he may be induced to repeat this act till his mind loses all confidence in itself and becomes utterly debilitated. To this it may be added, that the Reader ought never to forget that he is himself exposed to the same errors as the Poet, and perhaps in a much greater degree: for there can be no presumption in saying, that it is not probable he will be so well acquainted with the various stages of meaning through which words have passed, or with the fickleness or stability of the relations of particular ideas to each other; and above all, since he is so much less interested in the subject, he may decide lightly and carelessly.

## *Note to 'The Thorn'* (composed late September 1800)[1]

This poem ought to have been preceded by an introductory poem which I have been prevented from writing by never having felt myself in a mood when it was probable that I should write it well.

The character which I have here introduced speaking is sufficiently common. The reader will perhaps have a general notion of it if he has ever known a man (a captain of a small trading vessel, for example)[2] who, being past the middle age of life, had retired upon an annuity or small independent income to some village or country town of which he was not a native, or in which he had not been accustomed to live. Such men, having little to do, become credulous and talkative from indolence. And from the same cause (and other predisposing causes by which it is probable that such men may have been affected) they are prone to superstition. On which account it appeared to me proper to select a character like this to exhibit some of the general laws by which superstition acts upon the mind. Superstitious men are almost always men of slow faculties and deep feelings. Their minds are not loose but adhesive.[3] They have a reasonable share of imagination, by which

### Notes

[70] *minute* detailed.

Note to 'The Thorn'

[1] 'The Thorn' was originally published in *Lyrical Ballads* (1798) without explanation. This essay, significant both for what it says about its subject as well as what it says about tautology, was published in the second edition of *Lyrical Ballads* (1800), in anticipation of the widespread misunderstanding of the poem that inevitably followed.

[2] *a captain…example* The telescope at line 181 of the poem is the only piece of evidence that supports this suggestion.

[3] *adhesive* persevering, tending to worry at certain ideas. Wordsworth is talking about the psychology of obsession.

word I mean the faculty which produces impressive effects out of simple elements. But they are utterly destitute of fancy – the power by which pleasure and surprise are excited by sudden varieties of situation and by accumulated imagery.

It was my wish in this poem to show the manner in which such men cleave[4] to the same ideas, and to follow the turns of passion (always different, yet not palpably different) by which their conversation is swayed. I had two objects to attain: first, to represent a picture which should not be unimpressive, yet consistent with the character that should describe it; secondly (while I adhered to the style in which such persons describe), to take care that words – which in their minds are impregnated with passion[5] – should likewise convey passion to readers who are not accustomed to sympathize with men feeling in that manner, or using such language. It seemed to me that this might be done by calling in the assistance of lyrical and rapid metre. It was necessary that the poem, to be natural, should in reality move slowly. Yet I hoped that by the aid of the metre, to those who should at all enter into the spirit of the poem, it would appear to move quickly. (The reader will have the kindness to excuse this note, as I am sensible that an introductory poem is necessary to give this poem its full effect.)

Upon this occasion I will request permission to add a few words closely connected with 'The Thorn', and many other poems in these volumes. There is a numerous class of readers who imagine that the same words cannot be repeated without tautology. This is a great error. Virtual tautology is much oftener produced by using different words when the meaning is exactly the same. Words – a poet's words more particularly – ought to be weighed in the balance of feeling, and not measured by the space which they occupy upon paper. For the reader cannot be too often reminded that poetry is passion: it is the history or science of feelings. Now every man must know that an attempt is rarely made to communicate impassioned feelings without something of an accompanying consciousness of the inadequateness of our own powers, or the deficiencies of language. During such efforts there will be a craving[6] in the mind, and as long as it is unsatisfied the speaker will cling to the same words, or words of the same character.

There are also various other reasons why repetition and apparent tautology are frequently beauties of the highest kind. Among the chief of these reasons is the interest which the mind attaches to words not only as symbols of the passion, but as *things*, active and efficient, which are of themselves part of the passion. And further, from a spirit of fondness, exultation, and gratitude, the mind luxuriates in the repetition of words which appear successfully to communicate its feelings.

The truth of these remarks might be shown by innumerable passages from the Bible, and from the impassioned poetry of every nation.

Awake, awake, Deborah! Awake, awake, utter a song!
Arise, Barak, and lead thy captivity captive, thou son of Abinoam!
At her feet he bowed, he fell, he lay down. At her feet he bowed, there he fell
down dead.
Why is his chariot so long in coming? Why tarry the wheels of his chariot?
(Judges 12: 27, and part of 28; see also the whole
of that tumultuous and wonderful poem)

## Notes

[4] *cleave* cling, stick.

[5] *passion* emotion.

[6] *craving* i.e. an emotional craving, or frustration.

## *Note to Coleridge's 'The Rime of the Ancient Mariner'*[1]

I cannot refuse myself the gratification of informing such readers as may have been pleased with this poem, or with any part of it, that they owe their pleasure in some sort to me, as the author[2] was himself very desirous that it should be suppressed. This wish had arisen from a consciousness of the defects of the poem, and from a knowledge that many persons had been much displeased with it.[3] The poem of my friend has indeed great defects: first, that the principal person has no distinct character, either in his profession of mariner, or as a human being who having been long under the control of supernatural impressions might be supposed himself to partake of something supernatural; secondly, that he does not act, but is continually acted upon; thirdly, that the events having no necessary connection do not produce each other; and lastly, that the imagery is somewhat too laboriously accumulated. Yet the poem contains many delicate touches of passion, and indeed the passion is everywhere true to nature; a great number of the stanzas present beautiful images and are expressed with unusual felicity of language; and the versification, though the metre is itself unfit for long poems, is harmonious and artfully varied, exhibiting the utmost powers of that metre, and every variety of which it is capable. It therefore appeared to me that these several merits (the first of which, namely that of the passion, is of the highest kind)[4] gave to the poem a value which is not often possessed by better poems. On this account I requested of my friend to permit me to republish it.

## *Michael: A Pastoral Poem* (composed October–December 1800)

If from the public way you turn your steps
Up the tumultuous brook of Greenhead Gill[1]
You will suppose that with an upright path
Your feet must struggle, in such bold ascent
The pastoral mountains front you, face to face.
But courage! for beside that boisterous brook
The mountains have all opened out themselves,
And made a hidden valley of their own.
No habitation there is seen; but such
As journey thither find themselves alone
With a few sheep, with rocks and stones, and kite[2]
That overhead are sailing in the sky.[3]
   It is in truth an utter solitude,
Nor should I have made mention of this dell

### Notes

NOTE TO COLERIDGE'S 'THE RIME OF THE ANCIENT MARINER'

[1] Wordsworth appended this note to Coleridge's poem when it appeared in the second edition of *Lyrical Ballads* (1800), sending it to the printer a few days before the decision not to include 'Christabel'. The note must have contributed to the 'change' in the relationship between the two men, lamented in Wordsworth's 'A Complaint'.

[2] *the author* Coleridge.

[3] *many persons...with it* probably a reference to Southey's damning comment that it was a 'poem of little merit'.

[4] *the first of which...kind* a comment consistent with Wordsworth's *Note to 'The Thorn'*, which states that 'poetry is passion; it is the history or science of feelings'.

MICHAEL: A PASTORAL POEM

[1] *Greenhead Gill* Greenhead Gill (a gill is a Lake District term for a mountain stream) is in the Vale of Grasmere, Cumbria. Wordsworth later recalled this poem is based on memories of a family who once owned Dove Cottage.

[2] *kite* small bird of prey.

[3] *but such...sky* lines indebted to Dorothy's account of her walk with her brother to the sheepfold on 11 October 1800: 'Kites sailing in the sky above our heads – sheep bleating and in lines and chains and patterns scattered over the mountains'.

But for one object which you might pass by –
Might see and notice not. Beside the brook
There is a straggling heap of unhewn stones;
And to that place a story appertains,
Which, though it be ungarnished with events,
Is not unfit, I deem, for the fireside
Or for the summer shade. It was the first,
The earliest of those tales that spake to me
Of shepherds, dwellers in the valleys, men
Whom I already loved – not verily
For their own sakes, but for the fields and hills
Where was their occupation and abode.
And hence this tale, while I was yet a boy –
Careless of books, yet having felt the power
Of nature – by the gentle agency
Of natural objects, led me on to feel
For passions that were not my own, and think
(At random and imperfectly indeed)
On man, the heart of man, and human life.[4]
Therefore, although it be a history[5]
Homely and rude,[6] I will relate the same
For the delight of a few natural hearts[7] –
And with yet fonder feeling, for the sake
Of youthful poets who among these hills
Will be my second self when I am gone.
Upon the forest-side in Grasmere vale
There dwelt a shepherd, Michael was his name,
An old man, stout of heart and strong of limb.
His bodily frame had been from youth to age
Of an unusual strength; his mind was keen,
Intense, and frugal, apt for all affairs;[8]
And in his shepherd's calling he was prompt
And watchful more than ordinary men.
Hence he had learned the meaning of all winds,
Of blasts of every tone; and oftentimes
When others heeded not, he heard the south
Make subterraneous music, like the noise
Of bagpipers on distant Highland hills.
The shepherd, at such warning, of his flock
Bethought him, and he to himself would say,
'The winds are now devising work for me!'
And truly at all times the storm that drives
The traveller to a shelter, summoned him

## Notes

[4] *man, the heart of man, and human life* subject of Wordsworth's never-completed epic, 'The Recluse'.

[5] *history* story.

[6] *rude* unsophisticated, simple.

[7] *a few natural hearts* Wordsworth is aware that in relating a story about poor country folk he is working against public taste. The 'few' for whom he saw himself writing would have included, primarily, Dorothy and Coleridge.

[8] *apt for all affairs* suitable for all kinds of work.

Up to the mountains: he had been alone
Amid the heart of many thousand mists
That came to him and left him on the heights.
So lived he till his eightieth year was passed;
And grossly that man errs who should suppose
That the green valleys, and the streams and rocks,
Were things indifferent to the shepherd's thoughts.[9]
Fields, where with cheerful spirits he had breathed
The common air, the hills which he so oft
Had climbed with vigorous steps – which had impressed
So many incidents upon his mind
Of hardship, skill or courage, joy or fear;
Which like a book preserved the memory
Of the dumb animals whom he had saved,
Had fed or sheltered, linking to such acts,
So grateful in themselves, the certainty
Of honourable gains – these fields, these hills,
Which were his living being even more
Than his own blood (what could they less?), had laid
Strong hold on his affections, were to him
A pleasurable feeling of blind love,
The pleasure which there is in life itself.
   He had not passed his days in singleness:
He had a wife, a comely matron – old,
Though younger than himself full twenty years.
She was a woman of a stirring life,
Whose heart was in her house. Two wheels she had
Of antique form – this, large for spinning wool,
That, small for flax – and if one wheel had rest
It was because the other was at work.
The pair had but one inmate[10] in their house,
An only child, who had been born to them
When Michael telling[11] o'er his years began
To deem that he was old – in shepherd's phrase,
With one foot in the grave. This only son,
With two brave sheep dogs tried in many a storm
(The one of an inestimable worth),
Made all their household. I may truly say
That they were as a proverb in the vale
For endless industry. When day was gone,
And from their occupations out of doors
The son and father were come home, even then
Their labour did not cease, unless when all
Turned to their cleanly supper-board, and there
Each with a mess of pottage[12] and skimmed milk,

## Notes

[9] *And grossly...thoughts* Wordsworth told the Whig leader, Charles James Fox, that this poem and 'The Brothers' 'were written with a view to show that men who do not wear fine clothes can feel deeply'.

[10] *inmate* dependent.

[11] *telling* counting.

[12] *pottage* porridge.

Sat round their basket piled with oaten cake,[13]
And their plain home-made cheese. Yet when their meal
Was ended, Luke (for so the son was named)
And his old father both betook themselves
To such convenient work as might employ
Their hands by the fireside – perhaps to card[14]
Wool for the housewife's spindle, or repair
Some injury done to sickle, flail, or scythe,[15]
Or other implement of house or field.
  Down from the ceiling by the chimney's edge
(Which in our ancient uncouth country style
Did with a huge projection overbrow[16]
Large space beneath) as duly as the light
Of day grew dim, the housewife hung a lamp,
An aged utensil which had performed
Service beyond all others of its kind.
Early at evening did it burn, and late,
Surviving comrade of uncounted[17] hours
Which going by from year to year had found
And left the couple neither gay perhaps
Nor cheerful, yet with objects[18] and with hopes
Living a life of eager industry.
And now, when Luke was in his eighteenth year,
There by the light of this old lamp they sat,
Father and son, while late into the night
The housewife plied her own peculiar[19] work,
Making the cottage through the silent hours
Murmur as with the sound of summer flies.
Not with a waste of words, but for the sake
Of pleasure which I know that I shall give
To many living now, I of this lamp
Speak thus minutely; for there are no few
Whose memories will bear witness to my tale.
The light was famous in its neighbourhood,
And was a public symbol of the life
The thrifty pair had lived. For as it chanced
Their cottage on a plot of rising ground
Stood single, with large prospect north and south,
High into Easedale, up to Dunmail Raise,
And westward to the village near the lake.
And from this constant light so regular
And so far-seen, the house itself by all
Who dwelt within the limits of the vale,
Both old and young, was named The Evening Star.

## Notes

[13] *oaten cake* a kind of bread eaten by local statesmen.

[14] *card* comb out.

[15] *sickle, flail, or scythe* implements that reveal Michael's other labours: growing hay (cut with the scythe) and corn (cut with the scythe or sickle and threshed with the flail).

[16] *overbrow* overhang.

[17] *uncounted* countless.

[18] *objects* objectives, aims.

[19] *peculiar* particular.

Thus living on through such a length of years
The shepherd, if he loved himself, must needs
Have loved his helpmate;[20] but to Michael's heart
This son of his old age was yet more dear –
Effect which might perhaps have been produced
By that instinctive tenderness, the same
Blind[21] spirit which is in the blood of all,
Or that a child more than all other gifts,
Brings hope with it, and forward-looking thoughts,
And stirrings of inquietude,[22] when they
By tendency of nature[23] needs must fail.
From such, and other causes, to the thoughts
Of the old man his only son was now
The dearest object that he knew on earth.
Exceeding was the love he bare to him,
His heart and his heart's joy! For oftentimes
Old Michael, while he was a babe in arms,
Had done him female service,[24] not alone
For dalliance[25] and delight, as is the use
Of fathers, but with patient mind enforced
To acts of tenderness; and he had rocked
His cradle with a woman's gentle hand.
And in a later time, ere yet the boy
Had put on boy's attire,[26] did Michael love
(Albeit of a stern unbending mind)
To have the young one in his sight when he
Had work by his own door, or when he sat
With sheep before him on his shepherd's stool
Beneath that large old oak, which near their door
Stood, and from its enormous breadth of shade
Chosen for the shearer's covert[27] from the sun,
Thence in our rustic dialect was called
The Clipping[28] Tree – a name which yet it bears.
There, while they two were sitting in the shade
With others round them, earnest all and blithe,
Would Michael exercise his heart with looks
Of fond correction and reproof, bestowed
Upon the child if he disturbed the sheep
By catching at their legs, or with his shouts
Scared them while they lay still beneath the shears.
And when by Heaven's good grace the boy grew up
A healthy lad, and carried in his cheek

## Notes

[20] *helpmate* wife.

[21] *Blind* unquestioning.

[22] *inquietude* anxiety about Luke.

[23] *tendency of nature* age.

[24] *Old Michael…female service* Michael tended his baby son as if he had been his mother.

[25] *For dalliance* for playfulness.

[26] *ere yet…attire* Until well into the nineteenth century, boys and girls were dressed in frocks until, between the ages of 3 and 7, boys were 'breeched'.

[27] *covert* shade.

[28] 'Clipping is the word used in the north of England for shearing' (Wordsworth's note).

Two steady roses that were five years old,
Then Michael from a winter coppice[29] cut
With his own hand a sapling, which he hooped
With iron, making it throughout in all
Due requisites a perfect shepherd's staff,
And gave it to the boy; wherewith equipped,
He as a watchman oftentimes was placed
At gate or gap, to stem[30] or turn the flock;
And, to his office[31] prematurely called,
There stood the urchin, as you will divine,
Something between a hindrance and a help –
And for this cause not always, I believe,
Receiving from his father hire[32] of praise,
Though nought was left undone which staff, or voice,
Or looks, or threatening gestures, could perform.
But soon as Luke, now ten years old, could stand
Against the mountain blasts, and to the heights,
Not fearing toil, nor length of weary ways,
He with his father daily went, and they
Were as companions – why should I relate
That objects which the shepherd loved before
Were dearer now? – that from the boy there came
Feelings and emanations, things which were
Light to the sun and music to the wind,
And that the old man's heart seemed born again?
Thus in his father's sight the boy grew up
And now when he had reached his eighteenth year,
He was his comfort and his daily hope.
    While this good household thus were living on
From day to day, to Michael's ear there came
Distressful tidings. Long before the time
Of which I speak, the shepherd had been bound
In surety for his brother's son,[33] a man
Of an industrious life and ample means,
But unforeseen misfortunes suddenly
Had pressed upon him, and old Michael now
Was summoned to discharge the forfeiture –
A grievous penalty, but little less
Than half his substance.[34] This unlooked-for claim,
At the first hearing, for a moment took
More hope out of his life than he supposed
That any old man ever could have lost.
As soon as he had gathered so much strength

## Notes

[29] *coppice* a small wood.

[30] *stem* stop.

[31] *office* job, work.

[32] *hire* reward.

[33] *In surety for his brother's son* Michael made himself liable for his nephew's debt.

[34] *Long before...substance* The failure of his nephew to pay off the loan Michael had guaranteed, using his land as security, means that he is now forced to pay the penalty – a sum amounting to only slightly less than half his entire capital.

That he could look his trouble in the face,
It seemed that his sole refuge was to sell
A portion of his patrimonial fields.[35]
Such was his first resolve; he thought again,
And his heart failed him. 'Isabel', said he,
Two evenings after he had heard the news,
'I have been toiling more than seventy years,
And in the open sunshine of God's love
Have we all lived, yet if these fields of ours
Should pass into a stranger's hand, I think
That I could not lie quiet in my grave.
Our lot is a hard lot;[36] the sun itself
Has scarcely been more diligent than I,
And I have lived to be a fool at last
To my own family. An evil man
That was, and made an evil choice, if he
Were false to us; and if he were not false,
There are ten thousand to whom loss like this
Had been no sorrow. I forgive him – but
'Twere better to be dumb than to talk thus.
When I began, my purpose was to speak
Of remedies and of a cheerful hope.
Our Luke shall leave us, Isabel; the land
Shall not go from us, and it shall be free –
He shall possess it, free as is the wind
That passes over it. We have, thou knowest,
Another kinsman; he will be our friend
In this distress. He is a prosperous man,
Thriving in trade, and Luke to him shall go
And with his kinsman's help and his own thrift
He quickly will repair this loss, and then
May come again to us. If here he stay
What can be done? Where everyone is poor
What can be gained?'[37]
At this the old man paused
And Isabel sat silent, for her mind
Was busy looking back into past times.
'There's Richard Bateman', thought she to herself,
'He was a parish-boy[38] – at the church door
They made a gathering for him, shillings, pence,[39]
And halfpennies, wherewith the neighbours bought
A basket which they filled with pedlar's wares,
And with this basket on his arm the lad
Went up to London, found a master[40] there,

## Notes

[35] *patrimonial fields* the land he had inherited from his forefathers. This poem is preoccupied with the plight of small landowners – families who passed the same small plot of land from one generation to the next over many centuries.

[36] *lot* way of life.

[37] *Where everyone…gained* No one in the village has enough money to employ Luke.

[38] *parish-boy* supported by the parish.

[39] *shillings, pence* before decimalization in 1970, there were 12 pence to the shilling, and 20 shillings to the pound.

[40] *master* employer.

Who out of many chose the trusty boy
To go and overlook his merchandise
Beyond the seas, where he grew wondrous rich
And left estates and monies to the poor,
And at his birthplace built a chapel, floored
With marble which he sent from foreign lands.'[41]
These thoughts, and many others of like sort,
Passed quickly through the mind of Isabel,
And her face brightened. The old man was glad,
And thus resumed: 'Well, Isabel, this scheme
These two days has been meat and drink to me:
Far more than we have lost is left us yet.
We have enough – I wish indeed that I
Were younger, but this hope is a good hope.
Make ready Luke's best garments; of the best
Buy for him more, and let us send him forth
Tomorrow, or the next day, or tonight –
If he could go, the boy should go tonight.'
    Here Michael ceased, and to the fields went forth
With a light heart. The housewife for five days
Was restless morn and night, and all day long
Wrought on with her best fingers[42] to prepare
Things needful for the journey of her son.
But Isabel was glad when Sunday came
To stop her in her work; for when she lay
By Michael's side, she for the last two nights
Heard him, how he was troubled in his sleep;
And when they rose at morning she could see
That all his hopes were gone. That day at noon
She said to Luke, while they two by themselves
Were sitting at the door: 'Thou must not go,
We have no other child but thee to lose,
None to remember – do not go away,
For if thou leave thy father he will die.'
The lad made answer with a jocund[43] voice,
And Isabel, when she had told her fears,
Recovered heart. That evening her best fare
Did she bring forth, and all together sat
Like happy people round a Christmas fire.
    Next morning Isabel resumed her work,
And all the ensuing week the house appeared
As cheerful as a grove in spring. At length
The expected letter from their kinsman came,
With kind assurances that he would do
His utmost for the welfare of the boy –

## Notes

[41] 'The story alluded to here is well known in the country. The chapel is called Ings Chapel, and is on the right hand side of the road leading from Kendal to Ambleside' (Wordsworth's note). Bateman's marble floor is still to be seen.

[42] *Wrought on with her best fingers* idiomatic; she worked as hard as she possibly could.

[43] *jocund* happy.

To which requests were added that forthwith
He might be sent to him. Ten times or more
The letter was read over; Isabel
Went forth to show it to the neighbours round;
Nor was there at that time on English land
A prouder heart than Luke's. When Isabel
Had to her house returned the old man said,
'He shall depart tomorrow.' To this word
The housewife answered, talking much of things
Which, if at such short notice he should go,
Would surely be forgotten – but at length
She gave consent, and Michael was at ease.
  Near the tumultuous brook of Greenhead Gill
In that deep valley, Michael had designed
To build a sheepfold,[44] and before he heard
The tidings of his melancholy loss
For this same purpose he had gathered up
A heap of stones, which close to the brook-side
Lay thrown together, ready for the work.
With Luke that evening thitherward[45] he walked,
And soon as they had reached the place he stopped,
And thus the old man spake to him: 'My son,
Tomorrow thou wilt leave me. With full heart
I look upon thee, for thou art the same
That wert a promise to me ere thy birth,
And all thy life hast been my daily joy.
I will relate to thee some little part
Of our two histories; 'twill do thee good
When thou art from me, even if I should speak
Of things thou canst not know of. After thou
First cam'st into the world, as it befalls
To new-born infants, thou didst sleep away
Two days, and blessings from thy father's tongue
Then fell upon thee. Day by day passed on,
And still I loved thee with increasing love.
Never to living ear came sweeter sounds
Than when I heard thee by our own fireside
First uttering without words a natural tune –
When thou, a feeding babe, didst in thy joy
Sing at thy mother's breast. Month followed month,
And in the open fields my life was passed,
And in the mountains, else I think that thou
Hadst been brought up upon thy father's knees.
But we were playmates, Luke; among these hills,
As well thou know'st, in us the old and young

## Notes

[44] 'It may be proper to inform some readers that a sheepfold in these mountains is an unroofed building of stone walls, with different divisions. It is generally placed by the side of a brook for the convenience of washing the sheep; but it is also useful as a shelter for them, and as a place to drive them into, to enable the shepherds conveniently to single out one or more for any particular purpose' (Wordsworth's note).

[45] *thitherward* in that direction, to that place.

Have played together – nor with me didst thou
Lack any pleasure which a boy can know.'
   Luke had a manly heart, but at these words
He sobbed aloud. The old man grasped his hand,
And said, 'Nay do not take it so – I see
That these are things of which I need not speak.
Even to the utmost I have been to thee
A kind and a good father; and herein
I but repay a gift which I myself
Received at others' hands, for, though now old
Beyond the common life of man,[46] I still
Remember them who loved me in my youth.
Both of them sleep together – here they lived
As all their forefathers had done; and when
At length their time was come, they were not loath
To give their bodies to the family mould.[47]
I wished that thou should'st live the life they lived;
But 'tis a long time to look back, my son,
And see so little gain from sixty years.
These fields were burdened when they came to me;[48]
Till I was forty years of age, not more
Than half of my inheritance was mine.
I toiled and toiled; God blessed me in my work,
And till these three weeks past the land was free –
It looks as if it never could endure
Another master. Heaven forgive me, Luke,
If I judge ill for thee, but it seems good
That thou should'st go.'
                              At this the old man paused,
Then pointing to the stones near which they stood,
Thus after a short silence he resumed:
'This was a work for us, and now, my son,
It is a work for me. But lay one stone –
Here, lay it for me, Luke, with thine own hands –
I for the purpose brought thee to this place.
Nay, boy, be of good hope: we both may live
To see a better day. At eighty-four
I still am strong and stout; do thou thy part,
I will do mine. I will begin again
With many tasks that were resigned to thee;
Up to the heights, and in among the storms,
Will I without thee go again, and do
All works which I was wont to do alone
Before I knew thy face. Heaven bless thee, boy;
Thy heart these two weeks has been beating fast

## Notes

[46] *the common life of man* the usual lifespan of a man (threescore years and ten); he is 84.

[47] *mould* the earth from which man was formed, and to which he returns in the grave.

[48] *These fields were burdened when they came to me* Michael inherited his land with the burden of a mortgage.

With many hopes. It should be so – yes, yes,
I knew that thou could'st never have a wish
To leave me, Luke – thou hast been bound to me
Only by links of love. When thou art gone
What will be left to us? But I forget
My purposes. Lay now the corner-stone
As I requested, and hereafter, Luke,
When thou art gone away, should evil men
Be thy companions, let this sheepfold be
Thy anchor and thy shield. Amid all fear
And all temptation, let it be to thee
An emblem of the life thy fathers lived,
Who, being innocent,[49] did for that cause
Bestir them in good deeds. Now fare thee well.
When thou return'st, thou in this place wilt see
A work which is not here. A covenant[50]
'Twill be between us – but whatever fate
Befall thee, I shall love thee to the last,
And bear thy memory with me to the grave.'
    The shepherd ended here, and Luke stooped down
And as his father had requested, laid
The first stone of the sheepfold. At the sight
The old man's grief broke from him; to his heart
He pressed his son, he kissed him and wept –
And to the house together they returned.
Next morning, as had been resolved, the boy
Began his journey; and when he had reached
The public way he put on a bold face,
And all the neighbours as he passed their doors
Came forth with wishes and with farewell prayers
That followed him till he was out of sight.
    A good report did from their kinsman come
Of Luke and his well-doing; and the boy
Wrote loving letters, full of wondrous news,
Which, as the housewife phrased it, were throughout
The prettiest letters that were ever seen.
Both parents read them with rejoicing hearts.
So many months passed on, and once again
The shepherd went about his daily work
With confident and cheerful thoughts; and now
Sometimes when he could find a leisure hour
He to that valley took his way, and there

## Notes

[49] *innocent* uncorrupted.

[50] *covenant* an echo of the biblical covenant made by God with Abraham, Genesis 17:19.

Wrought at the sheepfold. Meantime Luke began
To slacken in his duty, and at length
He in the dissolute city gave himself
To evil courses; ignominy and shame
Fell on him, so that he was driven at last
To seek a hiding-place beyond the seas.
   There is a comfort in the strength of love,
'Twill make a thing endurable which else
Would break the heart – old Michael found it so.
I have conversed with more than one who well
Remember the old man, and what he was
Years after he had heard this heavy news.
His bodily frame had been from youth to age
Of an unusual strength. Among the rocks
He went, and still looked up upon the sun,
And listened to the wind, and, as before,
Performed all kinds of labour for his sheep
And for the land, his small inheritance.
And to that hollow dell from time to time
Did he repair, to build the fold of which
His flock had need. 'Tis not forgotten yet
The pity which was then in every heart
For the old man; and 'tis believed by all
That many and many a day he thither went,
And never lifted up a single stone.
   There by the sheepfold sometimes was he seen
Sitting alone, with that his faithful dog –
Then old – beside him, lying at his feet.
The length of full seven years from time to time
He at the building of this sheepfold wrought,
And left the work unfinished when he died.[51]
   Three years, or little more, did Isabel
Survive her husband; at her death the estate
Was sold, and went into a stranger's hand.
The cottage which was named The Evening Star
Is gone; the ploughshare has been through the ground
On which it stood. Great changes have been wrought
In all the neighbourhood; yet the oak is left
That grew beside their door, and the remains
Of the unfinished sheepfold may be seen
Beside the boisterous brook of Greenhead Gill.

Notes

[51] *when he died* Michael would have been 91 or 92.

## *I Travelled among Unknown Men* (composed *c.*29 April 1801)

I travelled among unknown men
In lands beyond the sea;[1]
Nor, England, did I know till then
What love I bore to thee.

'Tis passed, that melancholy dream!
Nor will I quit thy shore
A second time, for still I seem
To love thee more and more.

Among thy mountains did I feel
The joy of my desire;
And she I cherished turned her wheel
Beside an English fire.

Thy mornings showed, thy nights concealed
The bowers where Lucy played;
And thine is, too, the last green field
Which Lucy's eyes surveyed!

## *Preface to Lyrical Ballads* (extracts; revised text composed January to April 1802)[1]

Taking up the subject, then, upon general grounds, I ask what is meant by the word poet? What is a poet? To whom does he address himself ? And what language is to be expected from him? He is a man speaking to men – a man (it is true) endued[2] with more lively sensibility, more enthusiasm and tenderness, who has a greater knowledge of human nature, and a more comprehensive[3] soul, than are supposed to be common among mankind; a man pleased with his own passions and volitions,[4] and who rejoices more than other men in the spirit of life that is in him, delighting to contemplate similar volitions and passions as manifested in the goings-on of the universe,[5] and habitually impelled to create them where he does not find them.

To these qualities he has added a disposition to be affected more than other men by absent things as if they were present,[6] an ability of conjuring up in himself passions which are indeed far from being the same as those produced by real events, yet (especially in those parts of the general sympathy which are pleasing and delightful) do more nearly resemble the passions produced by real events than anything

### Notes

I Travelled among Unknown Men

[1] *I travelled...sea* Wordsworth is probably recalling his visit to Germany, 1798–9.

Preface to Lyrical Ballads

[1] When revising the Preface in 1802 for a new edition of *Lyrical Ballads*, Wordsworth added this passage on the topic, 'What is a poet?' It is one of his most important comments on his craft and vocation.

[2] *endued* endowed.

[3] *more comprehensive* more intense, profound and all-embracing.

[4] *volitions* impulses, good deeds.

[5] *the universe* the created world.

[6] *To these qualities...present* So vividly does the poet recall natural objects, which have 'impressed' themselves on his mind, that they seem to be present.

which, from the motions of their own minds merely, other men are accustomed to feel in themselves – whence, and from practice, he has acquired a greater readiness and power in expressing what he thinks and feels, and especially those thoughts and feelings which, by his own choice, or from the structure of his own mind, arise in him without immediate external excitement.

But whatever portion of this faculty we may suppose even the greatest poet to possess, there cannot be a doubt but that the language which it will suggest to him must in liveliness and truth fall far short of that which is uttered by men in real life under the actual pressure of those passions – certain shadows of which the poet thus produces, or feels to be produced, in himself.

However exalted a notion we would wish to cherish of the character of a poet, it is obvious that, while he describes and imitates passions, his situation is altogether slavish and mechanical compared with the freedom and power of real and substantial action and suffering. So that it will be the wish of the poet to bring his feelings near to those of the persons whose feelings he describes – nay, for short spaces of time, perhaps, to let himself slip into an entire delusion, and even confound[7] and identify his own feelings with theirs, modifying only the language which is thus suggested to him by a consideration that he describes for a particular purpose: that of giving pleasure. Here, then, he will apply the principle on which I have so much insisted – namely, that of selection. On this he will depend for removing what would otherwise be painful or disgusting in the passion; he will feel that there is no necessity to trick out[8] or elevate nature.[9] And the more industriously he applies this principle, the deeper will be his faith that no words which his fancy or imagination can suggest will be compared with those which are the emanations of reality and truth….

Aristotle, I have been told,[10] hath said that poetry is the most philosophic of all writing.[11] It is so. Its object is truth,[12] not individual and local, but general and operative;[13] not standing upon external testimony, but carried alive into the heart by passion – truth which is its own testimony, which gives strength and divinity to the tribunal to which it appeals, and receives them from the same tribunal.

Poetry is the image of man and nature. The obstacles which stand in the way of the fidelity of the biographer and historian (and of their consequent utility) are incalculably greater than those which are to be encountered by the poet who has an adequate notion of the dignity[14] of his art. The poet writes under one restriction only – namely, that of the necessity of giving immediate pleasure to a human being possessed of that information which may be expected from him, not as a lawyer, a physician, a mariner, an astronomer, or a natural philosopher, but as a man.[15] Except this one restriction, there is no object standing between the poet and the image of things; between this, and the biographer and historian, there are a thousand.

Nor let this necessity of producing immediate pleasure be considered as a degradation of the poet's art; it is far otherwise. It is an acknowledgement of the beauty of the universe, an acknowledgement the more sincere because it is not formal, but indirect; it is a task light and easy to him who looks at the world in the spirit of love. Further, it is a homage paid to the native and naked dignity of man, to the grand elementary principle of pleasure[16] by which he knows, and feels, and lives, and moves….

## Notes

[7] *confound* confuse; effectively, the poet cannot tell the difference between his own feelings and those of his subject.

[8] *trick out* dress up.

[9] *nature* natural utterance.

[10] *I have been told* probably by Coleridge, who had been a Grecian (a boy in the highest class) at Christ's Hospital.

[11] *Aristotle…writing* Wordsworth aimed to compose the great philosophical epic of his day – 'The Recluse'. Aristotle thought poetry the most philosophical genre because it shows men not as they are but as they should be.

[12] *truth* effectively, the real world – real people and real things, as opposed to abstract personifications.

[13] *operative* practical.

[14] *dignity* high status.

[15] *not as…man* i.e. the poet is concerned with fidelity to psychological truth, rather than with facts.

[16] *pleasure* positive sensations (spiritual and physical) deriving from our involvement with the external world.

## *To H.C., Six Years Old* (composed probably between 4 March and 4 April 1802)[1]

Oh thou, whose fancies from afar are brought,
Who of thy words dost make a mock apparel,
And fittest to unutterable thought
The breeze-like motion and the self-born carol;
Thou fairy voyager, that dost float
In such clear water, that thy boat
May rather seem
To brood on air than on an earthly stream,[2]
Suspended in a stream as clear as sky,
Where earth and heaven do make one imagery;
Oh blessed vision, happy child,
That art so exquisitely wild,
I think of thee with many fears
For what may be thy lot in future years.

I thought of times when Pain might be thy guest,
Lord of thy house and hospitality;
And Grief, uneasy lover, never rest
But when she sate within the touch of thee.
Oh too industrious folly!
Oh vain and causeless melancholy!
Nature will either end thee quite,
Or, lengthening out thy season of delight,
Preserve for thee, by individual right,
A young lamb's heart among the full-grown flocks.
What hast thou to do with sorrow
Or the injuries of tomorrow?
Thou art a dew-drop, which the morn brings forth,
Not doomed to jostle with unkindly shocks,
Or to be trailed along the soiling earth;
A gem that glitters while it lives,
And no forewarning gives;
But, at the touch of wrong, without a strife,
Slips in a moment out of life.

## Notes

To H.C., Six Years Old

[1] Hartley Coleridge (b. 1796) had already featured in Coleridge's 'Frost at Midnight', 'Christabel' and 'The Nightingale', and would appear again in Wordsworth's 'Ode'.

[2] 'See Carver's description of his situation upon one of the lakes of America' (Wordsworth's note). Wordsworth has in mind Carver's account of Lake Superior: 'The water in general appeared to lie on a bed of rocks. When it was calm, and the sun shone bright, I could sit in my canoe, where the depth was upwards of six fathoms, and plainly see huge piles of stones at the bottom, of different shapes, some of which appeared as if they were hewn. The water at this time was as pure and transparent as air; and my canoe seemed as if it hung suspended in that element. It was impossible to look attentively through this limpid medium at the rocks below, without finding, before many minutes were elapsed, your head swim, and your eyes no longer able to behold the dazzling scene' (Jonathan Carver, *Travels Through the Interior Parts of North America* (1778), pp. 132–3).

## *The Rainbow* (composed probably 26 March 1802)

My heart leaps up when I behold
  A rainbow in the sky;
So was it when my life began,
So is it now I am a man,
So be it when I shall grow old
  Or let me die!
The child is father of the man,
And I could wish my days to be
Bound each to each by natural piety.

## *These Chairs They Have No Words to Utter* (composed *c.*22 April 1802)

These chairs they have no words to utter,
No fire is in the grate to stir or flutter,
The ceiling and floor are mute as a stone,
My chamber is hushed and still,
    And I am alone,
    Happy and alone.
Oh, who would be afraid of life,
The passion, the sorrow, and the strife,
    When he may lie
    Sheltered so easily –
May lie in peace on his bed,
Happy as they who are dead?

### *Half an hour afterwards*

I have thoughts that are fed by the sun;
  The things which I see
  Are welcome to me,
  Welcome every one;
  I do not wish to lie
    Dead, dead,
Dead, without any company.[1]
  Here alone on my bed,
With thoughts that are fed by the sun
And hopes that are welcome every one,
  Happy am I.

## Notes

These Chairs They Have No Words to Utter

[1] *without any company* Wordsworth echoes Arcite's dying speech in Chaucer's *Knight's Tale*:

What is this world? What askest men to have?
Now with his love, now in his colde grave
Allone, withouten any compaignye? (ll. 2777–9)

Oh life, there is about thee
A deep delicious peace;
I would not be without thee –
  Stay, oh stay!
Yet be thou ever as now,
Sweetness and breath with the quiet of death,
  Peace, peace, peace.

## *Resolution and Independence* (composed probably 3 May–4 July 1802)

There was a roaring in the wind all night,
The rain came heavily and fell in floods;
But now the sun is rising calm and bright,
The birds are singing in the distant woods;
Over his own sweet voice the stockdove broods,
The jay makes answer as the magpie chatters,
And all the air is filled with pleasant noise of waters.

All things that love the sun are out of doors,
The sky rejoices in the morning's birth,
The grass is bright with raindrops, on the moors
The hare is running races in her mirth
And with her feet she from the plashy earth
Raises a mist which, glittering in the sun,
Runs with her all the way, wherever she doth run.

I was a traveller then upon the moor;[1]
I saw the hare that raced about with joy;
I heard the woods and distant waters roar,
Or heard them not, as happy as a boy –
The pleasant season did my heart employ.
My old remembrances went from me wholly,
And all the ways of men, so vain and melancholy.

But as it sometimes chanceth, from the might
Of joy in minds that can no farther go,
As high as we have mounted in delight
In our dejection do we sink as low –
To me that morning did it happen so,
And fears and fancies thick upon me came,
Dim sadness, and blind thoughts I knew not nor could name.

## Notes

RESOLUTION AND INDEPENDENCE

[1] *I was then…moor* In the Fenwick Notes, Wordsworth recalls: 'This old man I met a few hundred yards from my cottage at Town End, Grasmere, and the account of him is taken from his own mouth.'

I heard the skylark singing in the sky,[2]
And I bethought me of the playful hare;
Even such a happy child of earth am I,
Even as these blissful creatures do I fare;
Far from the world I walk, and from all care.
But there may come another day to me –
Solitude, pain of heart, distress, and poverty.

My whole life I have lived in pleasant thought
As if life's business were a summer mood,
As if all needful things would come unsought
To genial faith, still rich in genial good;
But how can he expect that others should
Build for him, sow for him, and at his call
Love him, who for himself will take no heed at all?

I thought of Chatterton,[3] the marvellous boy,
The sleepless soul that perished in its pride;
Of him[4] who walked in glory and in joy
Behind his plough[5] upon the mountainside.
By our own spirits are we deified;[6]
We poets in our youth begin in gladness,
But thereof comes in the end despondency and madness.

Now whether it were by peculiar grace,[7]
A leading from above, a something given,
Yet it befell that, in this lonely place,
When up and down my fancy thus was driven,
And I with these untoward thoughts had striven,
I saw a man before me unawares –
The oldest man he seemed that ever wore grey hairs.

My course I stopped as soon as I espied
The old man in that naked wilderness;
Close by a pond, upon the further side,
He stood alone. A minute's space I guess
I watched him, he continuing motionless.
To the pool's further margin then I drew,
He being all the while before me full in view.

As a huge stone is sometimes seen to lie
Couched on the bald top of an eminence,
Wonder to all who do the same espy

## Notes

[2] *I heard...sky* cf. 'The Ancient Mariner' (1798) 347–8: 'Sometimes a-dropping from the sky / I heard the lavrock sing.'

[3] During his short life, Thomas Chatterton (1752–70) composed a number of forged medieval poems supposedly by the fifteenth-century poet, Thomas Rowley. Wordsworth and Coleridge both admired these works as schoolboys.

[4] Robert Burns.

[5] *Behind his plough* Burns was a farmer, and in some of his poems, such as 'To a Mouse', described himself at the plough.

[6] *deified* made god-like, divine.

[7] *grace* divine influence.

By what means it could thither come, and whence;
So that it seems a thing endued with sense,
Like a sea-beast crawled forth, which on a shelf
Of rock or sand reposeth, there to sun itself –

Such seemed this man, not all alive nor dead,
Nor all asleep, in his extreme old age.
His body was bent double, feet and head
Coming together in their pilgrimage,
As if some dire constraint of pain, or rage
Of sickness felt by him in times long past,
A more than human weight upon his frame had cast.

Himself he propped, his body, limbs, and face,
Upon a long grey staff of shaven wood;
And still as I drew near with gentle pace,
Beside the little pond or moorish flood,
Motionless as a cloud the old man stood
That heareth not the loud winds when they call,
And moveth altogether, if it move at all.

At length, himself unsettling, he the pond
Stirred with his staff, and fixedly did look
Upon the muddy water, which he conned[8]
As if he had been reading in a book.
And now such freedom as I could I took,
And drawing to his side, to him did say,
'This morning gives us promise of a glorious day.'

A gentle answer did the old man make
In courteous speech which forth he slowly drew,
And him with further words I thus bespake,
'What kind of work is that which you pursue?
This is a lonesome place for one like you.'
He answered me with pleasure and surprise,
And there was, while he spake, a fire about his eyes.

His words came feebly, from a feeble chest,
Yet each in solemn order followed each,
With something of a lofty utterance dressed,
Choice word and measured phrase, above the reach
Of ordinary men – a stately speech
Such as grave livers[9] do in Scotland use,
Religious men, who give to God and man their dues.

He told me that he to this pond had come
To gather leeches, being old and poor –

Notes

[8] *conned* studied.

[9] *livers* folk.

Employment hazardous and wearisome![10]
And he had many hardships to endure;
From pond to pond he roamed, from moor to moor,
Housing, with God's good help, by choice or chance;
And in this way he gained an honest maintenance.[11]

The old man still stood talking by my side,
But now his voice to me was like a stream
Scarce heard, nor word from word could I divide;
And the whole body of the man did seem
Like one whom I had met with in a dream,
Or like a man from some far region sent
To give me human strength, and strong admonishment.

My former thoughts returned: the fear that kills,
The hope that is unwilling to be fed,
Cold, pain, and labour, and all fleshly ills,
And mighty poets in their misery dead.
And now, not knowing what the old man had said,
My question eagerly did I renew,
'How is it that you live, and what is it you do?'

He with a smile did then his words repeat,
And said that gathering leeches far and wide
He travelled, stirring thus about his feet
The waters of the ponds where they abide.
'Once I could meet with them on every side
But they have dwindled long by slow decay;
Yet still I persevere, and find them where I may.'

While he was talking thus, the lonely place,
The old man's shape and speech, all troubled me;
In my mind's eye I seemed to see him pace
About the weary moors continually,
Wandering about alone and silently.
While I these thoughts within myself pursued,
He, having made a pause, the same discourse renewed.

And soon with this he other matter blended,
Cheerfully uttered, with demeanour kind,
But stately in the main; and when he ended,
I could have laughed myself to scorn to find
In that decrepit man so firm a mind.
'God', said I, 'be my help and stay[12] secure;
I'll think of the leech-gatherer on the lonely moor.'

## Notes

[10] *He told me…wearisome* Leeches were widely used in medical treatment. Many illnesses, including fevers, were thought to be caused by an excess of blood; leeches were applied to bleed the patient.

[11] *maintenance* living.

[12] *stay* support.

## *I Grieved for Buonaparte* (composed 21 May 1802)

I grieved for Buonaparte, with a vain
And an unthinking grief! The vital blood
Of that man's mind, what can it be? What food
Fed his first hopes? What knowledge could *he* gain?
'Tis not in battles[1] that from youth we train
The Governor who must be wise and good,
And temper with the sternness of the brain
Thoughts motherly, and meek as womanhood.
Wisdom doth live with children round her knees:
Books, leisure, perfect freedom, and the talk
Man holds with weekday man in the hourly walk
Of the mind's business: these are the degrees
By which true Sway doth mount; this is the stalk
True Power doth grow on; and her rights are these.

## *The World Is too Much with Us* (composed late May 1802)

The world is too much with us; late and soon,
Getting and spending, we lay waste our powers:
Little we see in nature that is ours;
We have given our hearts away, a sordid boon!
This sea that bares her bosom to the moon;
The winds that will be howling at all hours
And are up-gathered now like sleeping flowers;
For this, for every thing, we are out of tune;
It moves us not. Great God! I'd rather be
A Pagan suckled in a creed outworn;
So might I, standing on this pleasant lea,[1]
Have glimpses that would make me less forlorn;
Have sight of Proteus coming from the sea;[2]
Or hear old Triton blow his wreathed horn.[3]

### Notes

I Grieved for Buonaparte

[1] *'Tis not in battles* Wordsworth was aware that Napoleon's education had been almost exclusively in the army: five years at the military college of Brienne, and a year at the military academy of Paris, before (at the age of 16) becoming second lieutenant of artillery in the regiment of La Fère, training school for young artillery officers.

The World Is too Much with Us

[1] *lea* meadow.

[2] *Have sight…sea* cf. 'Paradise Lost' iii 603–4: 'call up unbound / In various shapes old Proteus from the sea.'

[3] *Have sight…horn* cf. Spenser, 'Colin Clouts Come Home Againe' 245–8: 'Triton blowing loud his wreathed horne … And Proteus eke with him does drive his heard.'

## *Composed upon Westminster Bridge, 3 September 1802* (composed probably 31 July 1802, possibly revised early September 1802)[1]

Earth has not any thing to show more fair:
Dull would he be of soul who could pass by
A sight so touching in its majesty:
This city now doth like a garment wear
The beauty of the morning; silent, bare,
Ships, towers, domes, theatres, and temples lie
Open unto the fields, and to the sky;
All bright and glittering in the smokeless air.
Never did sun more beautifully steep[2]
In his first splendour valley, rock, or hill;
Ne'er saw I, never felt, a calm so deep!
The river glideth at his own sweet will:[3]
Dear God! the very houses seem asleep;
And all that mighty heart is lying still!

## *To Toussaint L'Ouverture*[1] (composed August 1802)

Toussaint, the most unhappy man of men!
Whether the rural milkmaid by her cow
Sing in thy hearing, or thou liest now
Alone in some deep dungeon's earless den –
Oh miserable chieftain, where and when
Wilt thou find patience? Yet die not! Do thou
Wear rather in thy bonds a cheerful brow;
Though fallen thyself, never to rise again,
Live, and take comfort. Thou hast left behind
Powers that will work for thee – air, earth, and skies;

### Notes

Composed upon Westminster Bridge

[1] This famous sonnet was inspired by the view from Westminster Bridge, at about 5.30 or 6.30 on the morning of 31 July 1802, as Dorothy and William were heading out of London to France (where Wordsworth would be reunited with Annette Vallon and meet, for the first time, their daughter Caroline). Dorothy described the view in her journal: 'It was a beautiful morning. The City, St Paul's, with the river and a multitude of little boats, made a most beautiful sight as we crossed Westminster Bridge. The houses were not overhung by their cloud of smoke and they were spread out endlessly, yet the sun shone so brightly, with such a pure light, that there was even something like the purity of one of Nature's own grand spectacles. We rode on cheerfully.'

[2] *steep* bathe, envelop.

[3] *own sweet will* Shakespeare, 'Sonnet 16', l. 14: 'And you must live, drawn by your own sweet will.'

To Toussaint L'Ouverture

[1] François Dominique Toussaint L'Ouverture (1746–1803), son of a Negro slave, became governor of San Domingo (Haiti), then a French colony, in 1801. He resisted Napoleon's attempts to reintroduce slavery, leading a popular uprising. All slaves were freed, and non-blacks were amazed by his magnanimity. Toussaint made himself governor-general for life, and dictated a constitution that gave him absolute power. He attempted to convince Napoleon of his loyalty while remaining aware that Napoleon did not trust him and would attempt to reassert French rule as soon as he could. Napoleon invaded Haiti in January 1802 with a larger force than expected. After fierce fighting, Toussaint surrendered in May, and was taken to France, where he was tortured at the Fort-de-Joux in the French Alps. He died there, April 1803. His heroic life and death aroused sympathy in England, where the movement for the Abolition of the Slave Trade was gathering pace.

There's not a breathing of the common wind
That will forget thee; thou hast great allies;
Thy friends are exultations, agonies,
And love, and man's unconquerable mind.

## *It Is a Beauteous Evening, Calm and Free* (composed 1–29 August 1802)[1]

It is a beauteous evening, calm and free;
The holy time is quiet as a nun
Breathless with adoration; the broad sun
Is sinking down in its tranquillity;
The gentleness of heaven is on the sea:
Listen! The mighty Being is awake
And doth with his eternal motion make
A sound like thunder – everlastingly.
Dear Child![2] Dear Girl! that walkest with me here,
If thou appear'st untouched by solemn thought,
Thy nature is not therefore less divine:
Thou liest in Abraham's bosom[3] all the year;
And worshipp'st at the Temple's inner shrine,
God being with thee when we know it not.

## *1 September 1802* (composed 29 August–1 September 1802)[1]

We had a fellow-passenger who came
From Calais with us, gaudy in array –
A Negro woman, like a lady gay,
Yet silent as a woman fearing blame;
Dejected, meek – yea, pitiably tame
She sat, from notice turning not away,
But on our proffered kindness still did lay
A weight of languid speech, or at the same

## Notes

It Is a Beauteous Evening, Calm and Free

[1] This poem was composed on the beach at Calais. William and Dorothy took advantage of the Peace of Amiens in the summer of 1802 to visit France to meet Annette Vallon and their daughter, Caroline Wordsworth, whom he had not previously seen. Dorothy recorded in her journal for August: 'The weather was very hot. We walked by the sea-shore almost every evening with Annette and Caroline, or William and I alone.... The reflections in the water were more beautiful than the sky itself, purple waves brighter than precious stones for ever melting away upon the sands. The fort, a wooden building at the entrance of the harbour at Calais, when the evening twilight was coming on, and we could not see anything of the building but its shape which was far more distinct than in perfect daylight, seemed to be reared upon pillars of ebony, between which pillars the sea was seen in the most beautiful colours that can be conceived. Nothing in Romance was ever half so beautiful.'

[2] *Dear child* Wordsworth's daughter, Caroline.

[3] *Abraham's bosom* see Luke 16:22: 'And it came to pass that the beggar died, and was carried by the angels into Abraham's bosom.'

1 September 1802

[1] Composed during Wordsworth's brief visit to France during the Treaty of Amiens, 1802. In 1827, he added a headnote: 'Among the capricious acts of tyranny that disgraced these times was the chasing of all Negroes from France by decree of the government. We had a fellow-passenger who was one of the expelled.' In the wake of the disastrous San Domingo campaign, Napoleon deported colonial blacks from the French mainland.

Was silent, motionless in eyes and face.
She was a Negro woman driv'n from France,
Rejected like all others of that race,
Not one of whom may now find footing there;
This the poor outcast did to us declare,
Nor murmured at the unfeeling ordinance.

## *London 1802* (composed September 1802)

Milton, thou shouldst be living at this hour,
England hath need of thee! She is a fen
Of stagnant waters. Altar, sword, and pen,
Fireside, the heroic wealth of hall and bower,
Have forfeited their ancient English dower
Of inward happiness. We are selfish men;
Oh raise us up, return to us again,
And give us manners, virtue, freedom, power!
Thy soul was like a star and dwelt apart;
Thou hadst a voice whose sound was like the sea,
Pure as the naked heavens, majestic, free –
So didst thou travel on life's common way,
In cheerful godliness, and yet thy heart
The lowliest duties on itself did lay.

## *Great Men Have Been among Us* (composed summer 1802)

Great men have been among us; hands that penned
And tongues that uttered wisdom, better none:
The later Sidney, Marvell, Harrington,
Young Vane,[1] and others who called Milton friend.
These moralists could act and comprehend:
They knew how genuine glory was put on;
Taught us how rightfully a nation shone
In splendour; what strength was, that would not bend
But in magnanimous meekness. France, 'tis strange,
Hath brought forth no such souls as we had then.
Perpetual emptiness! Unceasing change!
No single volume paramount, no code,
No master spirit, no determined road;
But equally a want of books and men!

## Notes

Great Men Have Been among Us

[1] *Great men…Vane* English republicans of the civil war period. Algernon Sidney was a distinguished republican executed for complicity in the Rye House plot, 1683; he was the author of a republican tract, *Discourse concerning Civil Government* (1698), which Wordsworth probably read while an undergraduate. Wordsworth had also read the work of Andrew Marvell (1621–78), poet, friend and secretary to Milton, by 1795. James Harrington (1611–77) was the author of the republican classic, *Commonwealth of Oceana* (1656); Wordsworth is likely to have read it during his time in France, 1791–2. Wordsworth admired Milton's sonnet 'To Henry Vane the Younger', beginning: 'Vane, young in years, but in sage counsel old'. Vane was executed on 14 January 1662.

## *Ode* (composed between 27 March 1802 and 6 March 1804)[1]

*Paulò majora canamus.*[2]

There was a time when meadow, grove, and stream,
The earth, and every common sight,
To me did seem
Apparelled in celestial light,
The glory and the freshness of a dream.
It is not now as it has been of yore;
Turn wheresoe'er I may
By night or day
The things which I have seen I now can see no more.
The rainbow comes and goes
And lovely is the rose,
The moon doth with delight
Look round her when the heavens are bare;
Waters on a starry night
Are beautiful and fair;
The sunshine is a glorious birth;
But yet I know, where'er I go,
That there hath passed away a glory from the earth.

Now while the birds thus sing a joyous song,
And while the young lambs bound
As to the tabor's[3] sound,
To me alone there came a thought of grief;
A timely utterance gave that thought relief
And I again am strong.
The cataracts blow their trumpets from the steep –
No more shall grief of mine the season wrong;
I hear the echoes through the mountains throng,
The winds come to me from the fields of sleep
And all the earth is gay;
Land and sea
Give themselves up to jollity,
And with the heart of May
Doth every beast keep holiday.
Thou child of joy
Shout round me, let me hear thy shouts, thou happy shepherd-boy!

Ye blessed creatures, I have heard the call
Ye to each other make; I see

## Notes

ODE

[1] From 1815 entitled 'Ode. Intimations of Immortality from Recollections of Early Childhood'.

[2] 'Let us sing of somewhat more exalted things' (Virgil, *Eclogue* iv 1). From 1815 onwards, Wordsworth eliminated this epigraph and replaced it with:

The Child is Father of the Man;
And I could wish my days to be
Bound each to each by natural piety.

[3] *tabor* a small drum.

The heavens laugh with you in your jubilee;
My heart is at your festival,
My head hath its coronal[4] –
The fullness of your bliss, I feel, I feel it all.
Oh evil day! if I were sullen
While the earth herself is adorning
This sweet May morning,
And the children are pulling
On every side
In a thousand valleys far and wide
Fresh flowers, while the sun shines warm
And the babe leaps up on his mother's arm –
I hear, I hear, with joy I hear!
But there's a tree, of many one,
A single field which I have looked upon,
Both of them speak of something that is gone;
The pansy at my feet
Doth the same tale repeat:
Whither is fled the visionary gleam?
Where is it now, the glory and the dream?

Our birth is but a sleep and a forgetting.
The soul that rises with us, our life's star,
Hath had elsewhere its setting
And cometh from afar.[5]
Not in entire forgetfulness,
And not in utter nakedness,
But trailing clouds of glory do we come
From God, who is our home.
Heaven lies about us in our infancy!
Shades of the prison-house begin to close
Upon the growing boy,
But he beholds the light and whence it flows,
He sees it in his joy;
The youth who daily farther from the east
Must travel, still is nature's priest,
And by the vision splendid
Is on his way attended:
At length the man perceives it die away
And fade into the light of common day.

Earth fills her lap with pleasures of her own;
Yearnings she hath in her own natural kind,
And even with something of a mother's mind
And no unworthy aim,
The homely nurse doth all she can

## Notes

[4] *coronal* small garland of flowers worn on the head.

[5] *The soul...afar* Wordsworth suggests that we exist, before birth, in spiritual form.

To make her foster-child, her inmate man,
Forget the glories he hath known
And that imperial palace whence he came.

Behold the child among his new-born blisses,
A four years' darling of a pygmy size!
See where mid work of his own hand he lies,
Fretted by sallies of his mother's kisses
With light upon him from his father's eyes!
See at his feet some little plan or chart,
Some fragment from his dream of human life
Shaped by himself with newly-learned art –
A wedding or a festival,
A mourning or a funeral;
And this hath now his heart,
And unto this he frames his song.
Then will he fit his tongue
To dialogues of business, love, or strife;
But it will not be long
Ere this be thrown aside,
And with new joy and pride
The little actor cons[6] another part,
Filling from time to time his 'humorous stage'[7]
With all the persons down to palsied Age
That Life brings with her in her equipage[8] –
As if his whole vocation
Were endless imitation.

Thou[9] whose exterior semblance doth belie
Thy soul's immensity;
Thou best philosopher who yet dost keep
Thy heritage; thou eye among the blind
That, deaf and silent, read'st the eternal deep,
Haunted for ever by the eternal mind;
Mighty prophet! Seer blessed!
On whom those truths do rest
Which we are toiling all our lives to find;
Thou, over whom thy immortality
Broods like the day, a master o'er a slave,
A presence which is not to be put by,
To whom the grave
Is but a lonely bed without the sense or sight
Of day or the warm light,
A place of thought where we in waiting lie;
Thou little child, yet glorious in the might

## Notes

[6] *cons* learns.

[7] *humorous stage* The theatre is peopled by characters with different moods ('humours'). The quotation is from Samuel Daniel's dedicatory sonnet to 'Musophilus, To the Right Worthy and Judicious Favourer of Virtue, Mr Fulke Grevill' 1–2: 'I do not here upon this hum'rous stage / Bring my transformed verse.' Wordsworth is also recalling the seven ages of man speech, *As You Like It* II vii 139–66.

[8] *equipage* retinue, attendant following.

[9] *Thou* Hartley Coleridge.

Of untamed pleasures, on thy being's height –
Why with such earnest pains dost thou provoke
The years to bring the inevitable yoke,
Thus blindly with thy blessedness at strife?
Full soon thy soul shall have her earthly freight,
And custom lie upon thee with a weight
Heavy as frost, and deep almost as life.

Oh joy! that in our embers
Is something that doth live,
That nature yet remembers
What was so fugitive!
The thought of our past years in me doth breed
Perpetual benedictions, not indeed
For that which is most worthy to be blessed –
Delight and liberty, the simple creed
Of childhood, whether fluttering or at rest,
With new-born hope forever in his breast –
Not for these I raise
The song of thanks and praise;
But for those obstinate questionings
Of sense and outward things,[10]
Fallings from us, vanishings,[11]
Blank misgivings of a creature
Moving about in worlds not realized,
High instincts before which our mortal nature
Did tremble like a guilty thing surprised;[12]
But for those first affections,
Those shadowy recollections
Which, be they what they may,
Are yet the fountain-light of all our day,
Are yet a master-light of all our seeing;
Uphold us, cherish us, and make
Our noisy years seem moments in the being
Of the eternal silence – truths that wake
To perish never,
Which neither listlessness nor mad endeavour,
Nor man nor boy,
Nor all that is at enmity with joy
Can utterly abolish or destroy!
Hence, in a season of calm weather,
Though inland far we be,
Our souls have sight of that immortal sea
Which brought us hither,
Can in a moment travel thither

## Notes

[10] *obstinate...things* The soul constantly challenges the notion that the outward, material reality of the physical world might be all there is.

[11] *vanishings* Years later, Wordsworth is reported to have said, 'There was a time in my life when I had to push against something that resisted, to be sure that there was anything outside me. I was sure of my own mind; everything else fell away and vanished into thought.'

[12] *like a guilty thing surprised* cf. Horatio talking about the ghost: *Hamlet* I i 148–9: 'And then it started like a guilty thing / Upon a fearful summons.'

And see the children sport upon the shore,
And hear the mighty waters rolling evermore.

Then sing, ye birds; sing, sing a joyous song!
And let the young lambs bound
As to the tabor's sound!
We in thought will join your throng,
Ye that pipe and ye that play,
Ye that through your hearts today
Feel the gladness of the May!
What though the radiance which was once so bright
Be now for ever taken from my sight?
Though nothing can bring back the hour
Of splendour in the grass, of glory in the flower,
We will grieve not, rather find
Strength in what remains behind,
In the primal sympathy
Which having been must ever be,
In the soothing thoughts that spring
Out of human suffering,
In the faith that looks through death,
In years that bring the philosophic mind.

And oh, ye fountains, meadows, hills and groves,
Think not of any severing of our loves!
Yet in my heart of hearts I feel your might;
I only have relinquished one delight
To live beneath your more habitual sway.
I love the brooks which down their channels fret[13]
Even more than when I tripped lightly as they;
The innocent brightness of a new-born day
Is lovely yet;
The clouds that gather round the setting sun
Do take a sober colouring from an eye
That hath kept watch o'er man's mortality;
Another race hath been, and other palms are won.
Thanks to the human heart by which we live,
Thanks to its tenderness, its joys and fears,
To me the meanest flower[14] that blows can give
Thoughts that do often lie too deep for tears.

## Daffodils (composed March 1804–April 1807)

I wandered lonely as a cloud
That floats on high o'er vales and hills,
When all at once I saw a crowd,

### Notes

[13] *fret* Move in an agitated manner.

[14] *the meanest flower* Borrowed from Gray, 'Ode on the Pleasure Arising from Vicissitude' 49: 'The meanest flowret of the vale.'

A host of golden daffodils;[1]
Beside the lake, beneath the trees,
Fluttering and dancing in the breeze.

Continuous as the stars that shine
And twinkle on the milky way,
They stretched in never-ending line
Along the margin of a bay:
Ten thousand saw I at a glance,
Tossing their heads in sprightly dance.

The waves beside them danced, but they
Outdid the sparkling waves in glee: –
A Poet could not but be gay
In such a jocund company:
I gazed – and gazed – but little thought
What wealth the show to me had brought:

For oft when on my couch I lie
In vacant or in pensive mood,
They flash upon that inward eye
Which is the bliss of solitude,[2]
And then my heart with pleasure fills,
And dances with the daffodils.

## *Stepping Westward* (composed 3 June 1805)

*While my fellow-traveller and I were walking by the side of Loch Ketterine one fine evening after sunset,*[1] *in our road to a hut*[2] *where, in the course of our tour, we had been hospitably entertained some weeks before, we met in one of the loneliest parts of that solitary region two well-dressed women, one of whom said to us by way of greeting, 'What you are stepping westward?'*

'What you are stepping westward?' 'Yea.'
'Twould be a wildish destiny
If we, who thus together roam
In a strange land, and far from home,
Were in this place the guests of Chance –
Yet who would stop, or fear to advance,
Though home or shelter he had none,
With such a sky to lead him on?

The dewy ground was dark and cold;
Behind, all gloomy to behold;

## Notes

DAFFODILS

[1] *daffodils* Not the garden daffodils of today but the small, pale and wild *Narcissus pseudonarcissus*.

[2] *They flash…solitude* These two lines were written by Wordsworth's wife, Mary.

STEPPING WESTWARD

[1] *While…sunset* Wordsworth and Dorothy toured Scotland in 1803.

[2] *hut* cottage.

And stepping westward seemed to be
A kind of *heavenly* destiny.
I liked the greeting – 'twas a sound
Of something without place or bound,
And seemed to give me spiritual right
To travel through that region bright.

The voice was soft, and she who spake
Was walking by her native lake;
The salutation had to me
The very sound of courtesy:
Its power was felt, and while my eye
Was fixed upon the glowing sky,
The echo of the voice enwrought[3]
A human sweetness with the thought
Of travelling through the world that lay
Before me in my endless way.

## *The Solitary Reaper* (composed 5 November 1805)[1]

Behold her, single in the field,
Yon solitary highland lass!
Reaping and singing by herself –
Stop here, or gently pass!
Alone she cuts, and binds the grain,
And sings a melancholy strain;
Oh listen! for the vale profound
Is overflowing with the sound.

No nightingale did ever chaunt
So sweetly to reposing bands
Of travellers in some shady haunt
Among Arabian sands;
No sweeter voice was ever heard
In springtime from the cuckoo-bird,
Breaking the silence of the seas
Among the farthest Hebrides.

Will no one tell me what she sings?
Perhaps the plaintive numbers flow
For old, unhappy, far-off things

## Notes

[3] *enwrought* interwove, combined.

THE SOLITARY REAPER

[1] 'This poem was suggested by a beautiful sentence in a MS tour in Scotland written by a friend, the last line being taken from it verbatim' (Wordsworth's note). Thomas Wilkinson, the Lake District poet, was a friend of Wordsworth, and his *Tours to the British Mountains* was published in 1824. The sentence that inspired Wordsworth runs as follows: 'Passed a female who was reaping alone: she sung in Erse as she bended over her sickle; the sweetest human voice I ever heard: her strains were tenderly melancholy, and felt delicious, long after they were heard no more' (p. 12).

And battles long ago;
Or is it some more humble lay,
Familiar matter of today?
Some natural sorrow, loss, or pain
That has been, and may be again?

Whate'er the theme, the maiden sang
As if her song could have no ending;
I saw her singing at her work
And o'er the sickle bending;
I listened till I had my fill,
And as I mounted up the hill,
The music in my heart I bore
Long after it was heard no more.

## *Elegiac Stanzas, Suggested by a Picture of Peele Castle*[1] *in a Storm, Painted by Sir George Beaumont*[2] (composed between 20 May and 27 June 1806)

I was thy neighbour once, thou rugged pile![3]
Four summer weeks I dwelt in sight of thee;
I saw thee every day, and all the while
Thy form was sleeping on a glassy sea.

So pure the sky, so quiet was the air!
So like, so very like, was day to day!
Whene'er I looked, thy image still was there –
It trembled, but it never passed away.

How perfect was the calm; it seemed no sleep,
No mood which season takes away, or brings;
I could have fancied that the mighty deep
Was even the gentlest of all gentle things.

Ah *then*, if mine had been the painter's hand
To express what then I saw, and add the gleam,
The light that never was, on sea or land,
The consecration, and the poet's dream,

I would have planted thee, thou hoary pile,
Amid a world how different from this! –

### Notes

ELEGIAC STANZAS

[1] Piel Castle is in northern Lancashire, on a promontory opposite Rampside, where Wordsworth spent the summer of 1794. Beaumont's painting is now at the Wordsworth Museum, Grasmere.

[2] Sir George Howland Beaumont, 7th Baronet (1753–1827) of Coleorton Hall, near Ashby-de-la-Zouch, Leicestershire. He had sketched in the Lakes in 1798, and given Wordsworth a farmstead at Applethwaite, less than two miles north of Greta Hall at the foot of Skiddaw, in 1803.

[3] *thou rugged pile* Piel Castle.

Beside a sea that could not cease to smile,
On tranquil land, beneath a sky of bliss;

Thou shouldst have seemed a treasure-house, a mine
Of peaceful years, a chronicle of heaven –
Of all the sunbeams that did ever shine
The very sweetest had to thee been given.

A picture had it been of lasting ease,
Elysian quiet, without toil or strife;
No motion but the moving tide, a breeze,
Or merely silent nature's breathing life.

Such, in the fond delusion of my heart,
Such picture would I at that time have made;
And seen the soul of truth in every part –
A faith, a trust that could not be betrayed.

So once it would have been – 'tis so no more;
I have submitted to a new control:
A power is gone, which nothing can restore –
A deep distress hath humanized my soul.[4]

Not for a moment could I now behold
A smiling sea and be what I have been;
The feeling of my loss will ne'er be old –
This, which I know, I speak with mind serene.

Then, Beaumont, friend! who would have been the friend,
If he had lived, of him[5] whom I deplore,[6]
This work of thine[7] I blame not, but commend;
This sea in anger, and that dismal shore.

Oh 'tis a passionate work! – yet wise and well,
Well-chosen is the spirit that is here;
That hulk which labours in the deadly swell,
This rueful sky, this pageantry of fear!

And this huge castle, standing here sublime,
I love to see the look with which it braves,
Cased in the unfeeling armour of old time,
The lightning, the fierce wind, and trampling waves.

Farewell, farewell the heart that lives alone,
Housed in a dream, at distance from the kind![8]
Such happiness, wherever it be known,
Is to be pitied, for 'tis surely blind.

## Notes

[4] *A deep distress…soul* The drowning of Wordsworth's brother John (b. 1773) in the wreck of the *Earl of Abergavenny*, of which he was captain, 25 February 1805.

[5] *him* John Wordsworth.

[6] *deplore* lament.

[7] *This work of thine* Sir George Beaumont's *A Storm: Peele Castle* was exhibited at the Royal Academy, 2 May 1806, where Wordsworth probably saw it.

[8] *kind* humankind.

But welcome fortitude, and patient cheer,
And frequent sights of what is to be borne!
Such sights, or worse, as are before me here –
Not without hope we suffer and we mourn.

## *Star Gazers* (composed November 1806)[1]

What crowd is this? What have we here? We must not pass it by;
A telescope upon its frame and pointed to the sky,
Long is it as a barber's pole, or mast of little boat,
Some little pleasure-skiff that doth on Thames's waters float.

The showman chooses well his place – 'tis Leicester's busy Square;
And he's as happy in his night, for the heavens are blue and fair;
Calm, though impatient, are the crowd, each is ready with the fee,
And envies him that's looking – what an insight it must be!

Now, showman, where can lie the cause? Shall thy implement have blame –
A boaster that, when he is tried, fails and is put to shame?
Or is it good as others are, and be their eyes at fault?
Their eyes or minds? Or finally, is this resplendent vault?[2]

Is nothing of that radiant pomp so good as we have here?
Or gives a thing but small delight that never can be dear?
The silver moon with all her vales, and hills of mightiest fame,
Do they betray us when they're seen? And are they but a name?

Or is it rather that conceit[3] rapacious[4] is and strong?
And bounty[5] never yields so much but it seems to do her wrong?
Or is it that when human souls a journey long have had
And are returned into themselves they cannot but be sad?

Or does some deep and earnest thought the blissful mind employ[6]
Of him who gazes, or has gazed – a grave and steady joy
That doth reject all show of pride, admits no outward sign,
Because not of this noisy world, but silent and divine?

Or is it (last unwelcome thought!) that these spectators rude,
Poor in estate, of manners base, men of the multitude,
Have souls which never yet have risen, and therefore prostrate[7] lie,
Not to be lifted up at once to power and majesty?

Whate'er the cause, 'tis sure that they who pry and pore
Seem to meet with little gain, seem less happy than before;
One after one they take their turns, nor have I one espied
That does not slackly go away as if dissatisfied.

## Notes

Star Gazers

[1] Wordsworth probably saw the showman charging customers to look through his telescope when walking through Leicester Square during a visit to London, April–May 1806.

[2] *resplendent vault* the sky.

[3] *conceit* conception, expectation of what we will see down the telescope.

[4] *rapacious* greedy; i.e. people expect too much.

[5] *bounty* i.e. the reward of seeing the moon down the telescope.

[6] *employ* preoccupy.

[7] *prostrate* overcome, defeated.

## *St Paul's* (composed 1808)[1]

Pressed[2] with conflicting thoughts of love and fear,
I parted from thee, friend,[3] and took my way
Through the great city, pacing with an eye
Downcast, ear sleeping, and feet masterless,
That were sufficient guide unto themselves,
And step by step went pensively. Now, mark
Not how my trouble was entirely hushed
(That might not be), but how by sudden gift,
Gift of imagination's holy power,
My soul in her uneasiness received
An anchor of stability. It chanced
That, while I thus was pacing, I raised up
My heavy eyes and instantly beheld,
Saw at a glance in that familiar spot
A visionary scene: a length of street
Laid open in its morning quietness,
Deep, hollow, unobstructed, vacant, smooth,
And white with winter's purest white, as fair,
As fresh and spotless as he ever sheds
On field or mountain. Moving form was none,
Save here and there a shadowy passenger,
Slow, shadowy, silent, dusky, and beyond
And high above this winding length of street,
This noiseless and unpeopled avenue,
Pure, silent, solemn, beautiful, was seen
The huge majestic temple of St Paul
In awful sequestration,[4] through a veil,
Through its own sacred veil of falling snow.

## *Surprised by Joy – Impatient as the Wind* (composed between 1812 and 1814)

Surprised by joy – impatient as the wind
I wished to share the transport[1] – oh, with whom
But thee,[2] long buried in the silent tomb,
That spot which no vicissitude[3] can find?
Love, faithful love recalled thee to my mind –

### Notes

St Paul's

[1] This poem was inspired by Wordsworth's departure early on the morning of 3 April 1808 from Coleridge's lodgings to start his journey back to Grasmere. On 8 April he described it to Sir George Beaumont: 'I left Coleridge at 7 o'clock on Sunday morning; and walked towards the city in a very thoughtful and melancholy state of mind. I had passed through Temple Bar and by St Dunstan's, noticing nothing, and entirely occupied by my own thoughts, when, looking up, I saw before me the avenue of Fleet Street, silent, empty, and pure white, with a sprinkling of newfallen snow, not a cart or carriage to obstruct the view, no noise, only a few soundless and dusky foot-passengers here and there; you remember the elegant curve of Ludgate Hill in which this avenue would terminate, and beyond and towering above it was the huge and majestic form of St Paul's, solemnized by a thin veil of falling snow. I cannot say how much I was affected at this unthought-of sight in such a place, and what a blessing I felt there is in habits of exalted imagination. My sorrow was controlled, and my uneasiness of mind, not quieted and relieved altogether, seemed at once to receive the gift of an anchor of security.'

[2] *Pressed* oppressed.

[3] *friend* Coleridge.

[4] *awful sequestration* awe-inspiring seclusion.

Surprised by Joy – Impatient as the Wind

[1] *transport* ecstasy.

[2] *thee* his dead daughter Catherine who died 4 June 1812.

[3] *vicissitude* change, development in human affairs.

But how could I forget thee? Through what power,
Even for the least division of an hour,
Have I been so beguiled[4] as to be blind
To my most grievous loss? That thought's return
Was the worst pang that sorrow ever bore,
Save one, one only, when I stood forlorn,
Knowing my heart's best treasure was no more;
That neither present time, nor years unborn
Could to my sight that heavenly face restore.

## *Conclusion to The River Duddon* (composed 1818–20)[1]

I thought of thee,[2] my partner and my guide,
As being past away. Vain sympathies!
For *backward*, Duddon, as I cast my eyes,
I see what was, and is, and will abide;
Still glides the stream, and shall for ever glide;
The form remains, the function never dies,
While *we*, the brave, the mighty, and the wise,[3]
We men who, in our morn of youth, defied
The elements, must vanish; be it so!
Enough, if something from our hands have power
To live, and act, and serve the future hour;
And if, as tow'rd the silent tomb we go,
Through love, through hope, and faith's transcendent dower,[4]
We feel that we are greater than we know.

## *Airey-Force Valley* (composed September 1835)[1]

Not a breath of air
Ruffles the bosom of this leafy glen.
From the brook's margin, wide around, the trees
Are steadfast as the rocks; the brook itself,
Old as the hills that feed it from afar,
Doth rather deepen than disturb the calm
Where all things else are still and motionless.
And yet, even now, a little breeze, perchance
Escaped from boisterous winds that rage without,
Has entered, by the sturdy oaks unfelt,
But to its gentle touch how sensitive
Is the light ash that, pendent from the brow
Of yon dim cave, in seeming silence makes

## Notes

[4] *beguiled* deceived.

CONCLUSION TO THE RIVER DUDDON

[1] Wordsworth composed a sequence of sonnets describing the Duddon Valley, which he published in 1820. This concluding sonnet is probably the most famous. The River Duddon descends through one of the most picturesque valleys in the Lake District.

[2] *thee* the River Duddon.

[3] *While we…wise* Borrowed from Wordsworth's early translation of Moschus, 'Lament for Bion' (1789) 5: 'But we, the great, the mighty and the wise.'

[4] *dower* gift.

AIREY-FORCE VALLEY

[1] Aira Force is a waterfall on the north shore of Ullswater. This poem celebrates the gorge that rises above it.

A soft eye-music of slow-waving boughs,
Powerful almost as vocal harmony
To stay the wanderer's steps and soothe his thoughts.

## *Extempore Effusion upon the Death of James Hogg*[1] (composed between 21 November and 3 December 1835)

When first,[2] descending from the moorlands,
I saw the Stream of Yarrow glide
Along a bare and open valley,
The Ettrick Shepherd[3] was my guide.

When last[4] along its banks I wandered,
Through groves that had begun to shed
Their golden leaves upon the pathways,
My steps the Border Minstrel[5] led.

The mighty Minstrel breathes no longer,
Mid mouldering ruins[6] low he lies;
And death upon the braes of Yarrow
Has closed the Shepherd-poet's eyes:

Nor has the rolling year twice measured,
From sign to sign, its steadfast course,
Since every mortal power of Coleridge[7]
Was frozen at its marvellous source;

The rapt One of the godlike forehead,
The heaven-eyed creature sleeps in earth:
And Lamb,[8] the frolic and the gentle,
Has vanished from his lonely hearth.

Like clouds that rake the mountain-summits,
Or waves that own no curbing hand,
How fast has brother followed brother,
From sunshine to the sunless land!

Yet I, whose lids from infant slumbers
Were earlier raised, remain to hear
A timid voice that asks in whispers,
'Who next will drop and disappear?'

Our haughty life is crowned with darkness,
Like London with its own black wreath,[9]

## Notes

EXTEMPORE EFFUSION UPON THE DEATH OF JAMES HOGG

[1] James Hogg, poet, novelist and man of letters, died 21 November 1835.

[2] *When first* Wordsworth first walked along the banks of the River Yarrow in September 1814.

[3] *The Ettrick Shepherd* The name under which Hogg often published. After his father went bankrupt when he was 6, he was removed from school and spent most of his life as a shepherd.

[4] *When last* Wordsworth returned to the Yarrow in September–October 1831, when his guide was Sir Walter Scott, a friend since the early 1800s.

[5] *the Border Minstrel* Sir Walter Scott, died 21 September 1832. His earliest literary success had come with *The Minstrelsy of the Scottish Border* (1802–3).

[6] *Mid mouldering ruins* Scott was buried at Dryburgh Abbey, 26 September 1832.

[7] Samuel Taylor Coleridge died 25 July 1834.

[8] Charles Lamb died 27 December 1834. Lamb remained a friend of Wordsworth from the time of their first meeting at Nether Stowey in June 1797.

[9] *Like London…wreath* A reference to the pall of black smoke hanging over London, produced by the burning of household fires.

On which with thee, oh Crabbe![10] forth-looking,
I gazed from Hampstead's breezy heath.

As if but yesterday departed,
Thou too art gone before; but why
O'er ripe fruit, seasonably gathered,
Should frail survivors[11] heave a sigh?

Mourn rather for that holy Spirit,[12]
Sweet as the spring, as ocean deep;
For Her who, ere her summer faded,
Has sunk into a breathless sleep.

No more of old romantic[13] sorrows,
For slaughtered youth and love-lorn maid!
With sharper grief is Yarrow smitten,
And Ettrick[14] mourns with her their Poet dead.

## *From* The Fenwick Notes (dictated 1843)

### ***On the 'Ode'* (extract)**

Nothing was more difficult for me in childhood than to admit the notion of death as a state applicable to my own being. I have said elsewhere: 'A simple child ... that lightly draws its breath, / And feels its life in every limb – / What should it know of death?'[1] But it was not so much from [excess][2] of animal vivacity that *my* difficulty came, as from a sense of the indomitableness[3] of the spirit within me. I used to brood over the stories of Enoch and Elijah, and almost to persuade myself that, whatever might become of others, I should be translated in something of the same way to heaven.

With a feeling congenial to this, I was often unable to think of external things as having external existence, and I communed with all that I saw as something not apart from, but inherent in, my own immaterial nature.[4] Many times while going to school have I grasped at a wall or tree to recall myself from this abyss of idealism to the reality. At that time I was afraid of such processes. In later periods of life I have deplored (as we have all reason to do) a subjugation of an opposite character, and have rejoiced over the remembrances, as is expressed in the lines, 'obstinate questionings',[5] etc. To that dreamlike vividness and splendour which invest objects of sight in childhood, everyone (I believe, if he would look back) could bear testimony, and I need not dwell upon it here.

But having in the poem regarded it as presumptive evidence of a prior state of existence, I think it right to protest against a conclusion which has given pain to some good and pious persons that I meant to inculcate such a belief. It is far too shadowy a notion to be recommended to faith as more than an element in our instincts of immortality. But let us bear in mind that, though the idea is not advanced in revelation, there is nothing there to contradict it, and the fall of man presents an analogy in its favour.

## Notes

[10] George Crabbe died 3 February 1832.

[11] *frail survivors* Wordsworth was 65 at the time of composition.

[12] *that holy Spirit* Felicia Dorothea Hemans, who became a friend of Wordsworth during her visit to the Lake District in 1830, and corresponded with him until the end of her life. She was the most recently deceased of those celebrated here, having died on 16 May 1835.

[13] *romantic* i.e. from old medieval romances, which provided much of Scott's subject matter.

[14] *Ettrick* the village of Ettrick, where Hogg lived, worked and is buried, is in the Scottish lowlands.

The Fenwick Notes: On the 'Ode'

[1] 'We Are Seven' 1–4.

[2] *excess* editorial conjecture, to fill a gap in the MS.

[3] *indomitableness* effectively, strength, power.

[4] *my own immaterial nature* spirit.

[5] *obstinate questionings* See 'Ode' l. 144.

Accordingly, a pre-existent state has entered into the popular creeds of many nations, and among all persons acquainted with classic literature is known as an ingredient in Platonic philosophy.

Archimedes said that he could move the world if he had a point whereon to rest his machine. Who has not felt the same aspirations as regards the world of his own mind? Having to wield some of its elements when I was impelled to write this poem on the immortality of the soul, I took hold of the notion of pre-existence as having sufficient foundation in humanity for authorizing me to make for my purpose the best use of it I could as a poet.

### *On 'We Are Seven'* (extract)

In reference to this poem, I will here mention one of the most remarkable facts in my own poetic history and that of Mr Coleridge.

In the spring of the year 1798,[1] he, my sister and myself started from Alfoxden, pretty late in the afternoon, with a view to visit Lynton and the Valley of Stones near it. And as our united funds were very small, we agreed to defray the expense of the tour by writing a poem to be sent to the new *Monthly Magazine* set up by Phillips the bookseller, and edited by Dr Aikin.[2] Accordingly we set off and proceeded along the Quantock Hills towards Watchet, and in the course of this walk was planned the poem of 'The Ancient Mariner', founded on a dream (as Mr Coleridge said) of his friend Mr Cruikshank.[3] Much the greatest part of the story was Mr Coleridge's invention, but certain parts I myself suggested; for example, some crime was to be committed which should bring upon the Old Navigator (as Coleridge afterwards delighted to call him) the spectral persecution, as a consequence of that crime and his own wanderings.

I had been reading in Shelvocke's *Voyages*[4] a day or two before, that while doubling Cape Horn they frequently saw albatrosses – in that latitude the largest sort of seafowl, some extending their wings 12 or 13 feet. 'Suppose', I said, 'you represent him as having killed one of these birds on entering the South Sea, and that the tutelary spirits of these regions take upon them to avenge the crime?' The incident was thought fit for the purpose, and adopted accordingly. I also suggested the navigation of the ship by the dead men, but do not recollect that I had anything more to do with the scheme of the poem.

The gloss with which it was subsequently accompanied was not thought of by either of us at the time – at least, not a hint of it was given to me – and I have no doubt it was a gratuitous afterthought.[5] We began the composition together on that (to me) memorable evening; I furnished two or three lines at the beginning of the poem, in particular:

And listened like a three years' child:
The mariner had his will.[6]

These trifling contributions all but one (which Mr Coleridge has with unnecessary scrupulosity recorded) slipped out of his mind – as they well might. As we endeavoured to proceed conjointly[7] (I speak of the same evening), our respective manners[8] proved so widely different that it would have been quite presumptuous in me to do anything but separate from an undertaking upon which I could only have been a clog.

## Notes

THE FENWICK NOTES: ON 'WE ARE SEVEN'

[1] *In the year…1798* The walking tour took place not in spring 1798 but in mid-November 1797.

[2] *The Monthly Magazine*, An influential radical periodical founded in 1796 by Richard Phillips and edited by Dr John Aikin (1747–1822), brother of Mrs Barbauld.

[3] John Cruikshank, land agent to Lord Egmont at Nether Stowey, and Coleridge's neighbour there. He was the brother of Ellen Cruikshank, the 'most gentle maid' of Coleridge's 'The Nightingale' 69.

[4] George Shelvocke, *Voyage round the World, by the Way of the Great South Sea* (1726).

[5] *The gloss…afterthought* The 1817 text of 'The Ancient Mariner' carries a series of marginal glosses.

[6] 'The Ancient Mariner' (1798) 19–20.

[7] *conjointly* together.

[8] *manners* literary styles.

# Samuel Taylor Coleridge (1772–1834)

Samuel Taylor Coleridge was the tenth and last child of the Reverend John Coleridge, vicar of the village of Ottery St Mary and headmaster of the local grammar school. Though he died when his youngest son was only eight, John Coleridge had by then filled him with an unquenchable love of ideas and books. Shortly after his father's death, Coleridge was sent to Christ's Hospital School in the City of London, where he was to meet his lifelong friend, Charles Lamb. As a Grecian (a member of the highest class), he benefited from an excellent education in the classics, though the techniques used to impart such skills were by modern standards less than humane.

Coleridge had a turbulent time at Jesus College, Cambridge, where he matriculated in 1791 at the age of 19. It was here that he began to espouse republicanism and became interested in the brand of Unitarianism promoted by the Reverend Joseph Priestley, more famous today for his scientific experiments with electricity and gases than for his theological writings. (His experiments with 'phlogiston' led to the discovery of oxygen.) While at Cambridge Coleridge became a supporter of William Frend, whose *Peace and Union* (1793), a pamphlet advocating parliamentary reform and increased suffrage, led to its author's expulsion from the university. In the midst of this, Coleridge joined the King's Light Dragoons under the name Silas Tomkyn Comberbache. It took six weeks and the strenuous efforts of his brother George to gain his release – by no means a straightforward procedure. After an unofficial payment of 25 guineas, the Regimental Muster Roll recorded: 'discharged S.T. Comberbache, Insane; 10 April 1794'.

In June Coleridge met Robert Southey, at that time an undergraduate at Balliol College, Oxford. Southey's achievements included having edited *The Flagellant*, an anti-flogging journal, at Westminster School, which led swiftly to expulsion. Southey was then engaged on *Joan of Arc*, an epic poem of which 10,000 lines had already been consigned to the fire for being so bad. Together they devised a radical political scheme called 'pantisocracy' – a word deriving from the Greek *pantisocratia*, an all-equal society. Together with Southey's college friend Robert Lovell, they planned to establish a commune on the banks of the Susquehanna River in Pennsylvania, where Priestley had settled in April 1794. Coleridge and Southey hoped that twelve married couples could be converted to pantisocratic ideals, and would embark from Bristol for America in April 1795. In this society which rejected property ownership, the men would each contribute £125 to a common fund, and labour on a landholding for two or three hours a day. As a first step it was decided they would get married in England. Lovell had already married Mary Fricker, whose widowed mother kept a dress shop in Bristol. Mary had two sisters; Southey would marry the third sister, Edith, while Coleridge would marry the eldest, Sara.

Pantisocracy would not survive the pressure of the adult world and the much-hoped-for emigration to America never took place. All the same, Coleridge married Sara on 4 October 1795, something he would later regret. They were temperamentally ill-suited; she took no part in his intellectual life, and resented the increasing time he devoted to his work, much of which was conducted away from home. All the same, they were happy at the outset, Coleridge recording in a letter to his friend Thomas Poole that he was 'united to the woman whom I love best of all created beings ... Mrs Coleridge – MRS COLERIDGE!! – I like to *write* the name'. She is a key figure in Coleridge's poems of this period, notably 'The Eolian Harp', 'Reflections on Having Left a Place of Retirement' and 'This Lime-Tree Bower My Prison'.

The mid-1790s were a period of frenetic activity. Coleridge delivered lectures expounding his philosophical and religious beliefs in Bristol in 1795, and founded and largely wrote his own periodical, *The Watchman*, in 1796. He was convinced the millennium – Christ's thousand-year rule on earth – was nigh, and that the French Revolution was its harbinger: 'Speed it, oh Father! Let thy Kingdom come!' he wrote in 'Reflections on Having Left a Place of Retirement'. Humanity would not be able to resist these redemptive forces, and all would be united in a common apprehension of good, or so he hoped. In times as cynical as our own, it is hard to understand how anyone could subscribe to views so idealistic, but Coleridge was not alone in doing so. They had watched the French Revolution, which had promised so much, go sour; now they wanted to see whether there were other, non-violent means by which its ideals of *liberté, egalité* and *fraternité* might be achieved.

His year of intense association with William and Dorothy began in July 1797 when he brought them from Dorset to live at Alfoxden House near Holford, a few miles down the road from his cottage in Nether Stowey in Somerset. Wordsworth's influence registered immediately in 'This Lime-Tree Bower My Prison', which contains an element new to Coleridge's writing: love of nature. At its conclusion he is solaced by awareness of natural beauty even in that unloveable fowl, 'the last rook', on which he bestows a blessing.

But the principal achievement of his time with the Wordsworths would be his three great poems – 'The Ancient Mariner', 'Kubla Khan' and 'Christabel'. The first of them, 'The Ancient Mariner', is presented in this book in both the 1798 version (published in *Lyrical Ballads*) and that of 1817 (see later in this chapter) – the first to introduce the glosses that serve both as commentary and counterpoint to the narrative.

Its protagonist continues to fascinate. What is the cause of his woes? A thoughtless, random act of a kind little different from those committed by people every day of the week: 'With my crossbow / I shot the albatross.' The poem might have ended there, but its genius is that this is the beginning. The first thing that happens is that the boat in which he is sailing gets trapped in a dead calm – 'For all averred I had killed the bird / That made the breeze to blow.' Having run out of drinking water, the Mariner and his shipmates see 'deathfires', have nightmares and dehydrate for lack of moisture. Rightly identifying the Mariner as the cause, the sailors hang the albatross's corpse round his neck (a full-grown albatross can weigh as much as 26 pounds with a wingspan of 3.5 metres). And who should come visiting but both Death and Life-in-Death, 'who thicks man's blood with cold'? They play dice: Death wins the sailors and Life-in-Death the Mariner, who is condemned to watch mutely while his shipmates drop dead. 'The many men so beautiful, / And they all dead did lie!' By random turns the innocent are punished for the sins of others, or for no reason at all. To which there's not much to be said, other than it's a fact of life. No one else was writing in this way in 1797.

Perhaps Coleridge felt uncomfortable with it. At the time he composed the poem he was a Unitarian priest and would not have professed belief in a world in which random acts led to punishment of the innocent. Like any Christian, he believed in a universe governed by a benevolent, loving God, as described in the poem's concluding lines.

> He prayeth best who loveth best
> All things both great and small,
> For the dear God who loveth us,
> He made and loveth all.

This sentiment is desirable, but inadequate to account for what we have witnessed – the unexplained killing of the bird; the punishment of the crew, none of whom are implicated in what the mariner did; the dejection of the wedding-guest, who cannot attend the wedding; and the mariner's own fate. This is a story of damnation set in a godless, arbitrary world.

'Kubla Khan' is a poem like no other. After what we might imagine to be decades of exertion on the battlefield, the Khan Kubla yearns for repose and peace, to build an earthly paradise to which he can retire, walled round for his protection. And yet, for all his wealth and power, he cannot cleanse his Eden of such unsettling elements as 'Ancestral voices prophesying war!' Those voices come from the depths of humanity; they speak of violent, hostile urges which are genetically programmed. And, despite whatever urge we may feel to make our lives afresh, to find peace, calm and happiness, those ancestral voices will have their say. They are part of our genetic inheritance. A poem that went no further would be remarkable enough, but this one proceeds to describe a poet-figure attempting to build the Khan's pleasure-dome 'in air', inspired by the vision of 'an Abyssinian maid'. The poet is also a slave to his inspiration, which distinguishes him from those around him.

When he published 'Kubla Khan', Coleridge apologized for not having finished it, presenting it 'rather as a psychological curiosity than on the ground of any supposed *poetic* merits'; in truth, it could not have been more complete. Whatever his ambitions for it, 'Kubla Khan' stands as one of the most powerful poems of the period.

From Coleridge's perspective (and that of his contemporaries) 'Christabel' was also defective in being fragmentary. Only Part I was written in 1798; the remainder of what survives was completed by 1801. Its author had plans to conclude his strange adult fairy-tale, and on that basis the poem was at one stage to have been included in *Lyrical Ballads* (1800). But he could not bring it to a resolution, and in any case, finished or not, it was too weird for Wordsworth's taste, so was dropped. It remained in manuscript for years, to be read by Coleridge to horrified social gatherings, until Byron, having attended one such reading, instructed his publisher John Murray to put it into print. Anxious to please the most lucrative bestseller in his stable, Murray obliged. It was almost universally panned, perhaps not surprisingly. No one knew what to make of it.

Even in its unfinished state, 'Christabel' is a masterpiece. Its plot does not need resolving because it depends not on the intricacies of narrative, but on the forces that drive its characters. It is no accident the poem's protagonist has a name bringing together two suffering innocents from the Bible (Christ/Abel), nor that the 'hissing sound' she emits in Part II indicates possession by evil. Its key event is the stripping of Geraldine before she gets into bed with Christabel:

> Behold! her bosom and half her side –
> A sight to dream of, not to tell!
> And she is to sleep by Christabel.
> (ll. 246–8)

The nature of what Coleridge is trying to discuss is clearer in the manuscript, where we are told that Geraldine's side is 'lean and old and foul of hue', a detail excised from the published text. It was Hazlitt who pointed out this line 'is necessary to make common sense of the first and second part'. What he meant was that it reveals Geraldine as not human, that the poem is not concerned principally with a sexual act. For Geraldine is predatory by nature, like a snake or scorpion; she is doomed to 'infect', 'contaminate' or even 'deflower' the 'innocent' Christabel. From the moment of their meeting, she is compelled to convey to Christabel the pain and suffering we will witness in Part II. When Christabel falls to the ground with a hissing sound, we recognize that some essential part of Geraldine has contaminated her, and that the two women now share the same dark secret.

However carefully we explicate Coleridge's three great poems, their true meaning seems always to elude us – or perhaps, more accurately, it might be said they speak to a part of us that finds it impossible to articulate the fullest extent of what it perceives. That may be because they speak to the same part of the psyche that responds to fairy-tales, which need no explication. And therein lies their greatness.

In some ways the most important product of 1797–8 was another fragmentary work: Wordsworth's 'The Recluse'. For some time he had planned an epic poem about man, nature and society entitled 'The Brook', an amplification and development of 'Religious Musings' (1794–6). But his love and regard for Wordsworth was such that he 'gave' it to him, believing him the only person capable of writing it. Many of its central theories – such as its reworking of the idealist philosophy of Berkeley and the associationist thought of Hartley[1] – went straight into Wordsworth's poems of that moment. But the tragedy of Wordsworth's career was that he would never be able to complete it. Wordsworth framed 'The Excursion' (1814) as 'the second part of a long and laborious work, which is to consist of three parts' (that is, 'The Recluse'), but Coleridge was disappointed with what Wordsworth made of his ideas, and his letter to Wordsworth of 1815 elucidates the mind-boggling ambitions of the poem Coleridge had conceived.

Though an exhilarating period, 1797–8, the year of close association with the Wordsworths was precarious. Coleridge lived on very little, with a growing family to support. In December 1797 the Wedgwood brothers sent him a gift of £100, but Coleridge returned it, saying he needed a secure income. Instead, he took the post of Unitarian minister and travelled to Shrewsbury, where he delivered a sermon on 14 January 1798. A career as clergyman might have brought the close working relationship with Wordsworth to a premature conclusion had it not been for the Wedgwoods. After spending the night at Hazlitt's home in Wem, Coleridge received a letter from them offering him an annuity of £150 a year for life, were he to devote himself to poetry and philosophy. Two days later he wrote to accept, and returned to Nether Stowey, via the Wedgwoods, in early February.

With Wordsworth, Coleridge devised the *Lyrical Ballads* principally as a means of raising money to visit Germany, which they believed to be the centre of the intellectual world and the most appropriate place for the poet of 'The Recluse' to gather his materials. At first Coleridge expected to write as many poems as Wordsworth, but he experienced writer's block, probably the result of opium addiction. Instead he quarried two extracts from his play, *Osorio*, and sent them to Wordsworth with 'The Ancient Mariner' and 'The Nightingale', neither of which were written specifically for *Lyrical Ballads*.

When he composed 'A Letter to Sara Hutchinson' in April 1802, Coleridge was at odds with his wife and hopelessly in love with Sara Hutchinson (who would become Wordsworth's sister-in-law); within hours of its composition, he would sit up all night encouraging Wordsworth to propose marriage to Mary Hutchinson. That would always pain him because he could not help but feel jealous at his inability to take the same step with regard to Sara. The misery of his 'coarse domestic life' would make him increasingly bitter. That, combined with frequent bouts of illness and dependence on opium, led him to resent Wordsworth's satisfying home life. He solaced himself with the thought of how, in happier times, he, Sara and Mary sat together in front of the fire – an occasion recalled in 'The Day-Dream', 'A Letter to Sara Hutchinson' and 'A Day-Dream'. But as the years passed even that failed to ease the suspicion that Wordsworth had cheated him, and in December 1806 he claim to have seen him and Sara Hutchinson in bed: 'An hour and more with [Wordsworth] in bed – O agony!', he confided to his notebook. Whether or not this horrific vision was opium-induced, it served only to deepen his resentment.

Coleridge's last conversation poem is a final, valiant attempt to resist the various enemies that were destroying his ability to write poetry. 'To William Wordsworth', edited here from the earliest complete manuscript, is his immediate response to the 'Thirteen-Book Prelude', which he heard its author recite in January 1807. He was one of the few to know it in its entirety, as it would remain unpublished until after Wordsworth's death in 1850. He was profoundly impressed by it, and poured his energy into this celebration of poetic vigour, wanting to do justice to 'A tale divine of high and passionate thoughts / To their own music chaunted!' (ll. 39–40). 'The Prelude' is hailed as ultimate proof, were any needed, that Wordsworth was truly the author of 'The Recluse'. But Coleridge could not have been more wrong. Wordsworth had probably never been capable of writing 'The Recluse', except perhaps for a few optimistic months in 1798.

Given the complications that crept into their friendship, it is remarkable they remained on close terms for so long. In 1810 a mutual friend, Basil Montagu, falsely told Coleridge that Wordsworth had 'commissioned' him to say he had been a complete nuisance to his family because he was a 'rotten drunkard'.

## Notes

[1] George Berkeley (1685–1753), Bishop of Cloyne, was a philosopher famous for his denial of materiality in favour of the notion that all perceived objects are ideas in the brain. David Hartley (1705–7) provided Coleridge with the concepts to build his own theory that proposed a progressive view of the human race leading ultimately to millenarian self-realization.

Wordsworth disclaimed the remark as soon as he heard it, but Coleridge could neither forget nor forgive. Wordsworth visited London in 1812 to effect a reconciliation, but without success. Despite the intercession of mutual acquaintances, frequent meetings in London and a joint tour of the Continent in 1822, they would never recapture their former closeness.

Coleridge's later years were mitigated by the generosity of James Gillman, a doctor, and his wife, who took him in as a house guest at their London Highgate home from April 1816 until his death in 1834. Their aim was to manage his opium consumption, help him become more productive and perhaps prolong his life. They succeeded in all these tasks. A series of long prose works followed, many dictated to amanuenses: 'The Statesman's Manual' (1816), lectures on Shakespeare, Milton, Dante, Spenser, Ariosto and Cervantes (1819), lectures on philosophy (1818–19), *Aids to Reflection* (1825) and *On the Constitution of Church and State* (1829). This was a remarkable achievement for someone whose health was fragile. In addition, Coleridge continued his correspondence and notebooks, and found time to dictate his extensive *Opus Maximum*, the crowning achievement of his later years. Amidst all this, he managed to compose short poems including some that rank with his best, such as 'Constancy to an Ideal Object'. Far from being the underachiever ridiculed by Hazlitt, Coleridge managed to produce numerous works of prose and poetry on a scale manifested only with completion of the Collected Coleridge Edition in 2002.

## *To the River Otter*[1] (composed between 1793 and 1796)

Dear native brook, wild streamlet of the west![2]
  How many various-fated years have passed,
  What blissful and what anguished hours, since last
I skimmed the smooth thin stone along thy breast,
  Numbering its light leaps! Yet so deep impressed
  Sink the sweet scenes of childhood, that mine eyes
I never shut amid the sunny blaze,
  But straight with all their tints thy waters rise,
Thy crossing plank, thy margin's willowy maze,
  And bedded sand that, veined with various dyes,
Gleamed through thy bright transparence to the gaze!
  Visions of childhood, oft have ye beguiled
Lone manhood's cares, yet waking fondest sighs –
  Ah, that once more I were a careless child!

## Notes

To the River Otter

[1] Coleridge was born at Ottery St Mary in Devon on the River Otter.

[2] *the west* i.e. the west of England.

## *Letter from S.T. Coleridge to George Dyer,*[1] *10 March 1795* (extract)

There is one sentence in your last letter which affected me greatly: 'I feel a degree of languor, etc. etc., and, by seeing and frequently feeling much illiberality, acquire something of misanthropy'! It is melancholy to think that the best of us are liable to be shaped and coloured by surrounding objects – and a demonstrative proof that man was not made to live in great cities![2] Almost all the physical evil in the world depends on the existence of moral evil, and the long-continued contemplation of the latter does not tend to meliorate[3] the human heart. The pleasures which we receive from rural beauties are of little consequence compared with the moral effect of these pleasures;[4] beholding constantly the best possible, we at last become ourselves the best possible. In the country, all around us smile good and beauty, and the images of this divine *kaλoka' γaθou*[5] are miniatured on the mind of the beholder as a landscape on a convex mirror.[6] Thomson,[7] in that most lovely poem, *The Castle of Indolence*, says,

> I care not, Fortune, what you me deny –
> You cannot rob me of free nature's grace!
> You cannot shut the windows of the sky
> Through which the morning shows her dewy face;
> You cannot bar my constant feet to rove
> Through wood and vale by living stream at eve...[8]

Alas, alas! She *can* deny us all this, and can force us, fettered and handcuffed by our dependencies and wants, to *wish* and *wish* away the bitter little of life in the feloncrowded dungeon of a great city!

God love you, my very dear sir! I would that we could form a pantisocracy[9] in England and that you could be one of us! The finely-fibred heart that, like the statue of Memnon,[10] trembles into melody on the sunbeam touch of benevolence, is most easily jarred into the dissonance of misanthropy. But you will never suffer your feelings to be benumbed by the torpedo touch of that fiend – I know you, and know that you will drink of every mourner's sorrows even while your own cup is trembling over its brink!

## Notes

Letter from S.T. Coleridge to George Dyer

[1] Coleridge met Dyer in London in August 1794, when he persuaded him of the merits of pantisocracy ('he was enraptured – pronounced it impregnable'.

[2] *man was not made...cities* Dyer lived in London.

[3] *meliorate* improve.

[4] *The pleasures...pleasures* It was always important to Coleridge that love of nature had an improving moral effect on the individual. It would be amplified and reworked by Wordsworth into the central principle of 'The Recluse': that love of nature leads to love of mankind.

[5] *kaλoka' γaθou* nobility and beauty.

[6] *as a landscape on a convex mirror* The Claude Lorraine Glass was a dark or coloured hand-mirror, used by picturesque tourists to reflect the features of the landscape in subdued tones.

[7] James Thomson (1700–48), author of 'The Seasons', a loco-descriptive poem.

[8] *The Castle of Indolence* ii 19–24.

[9] *pantisocracy* Coleridge and Southey wished to go to America and set up an ideal society in which everyone was equal and all possessions were shared.

[10] *like the statue of Memnon* The statue of Memnon at Thebes in Egypt was believed to give forth a musical sound when touched by the dawn or the setting sun.

## *The Eolian Harp. Composed at Clevedon, Somersetshire* (1834)[1]

My pensive Sara,[2] thy soft cheek reclined
Thus on mine arm, most soothing sweet it is
To sit beside our cot, our cot o'ergrown
With white-flowered jasmine and the broad-leaved myrtle[3]
(Meet emblems they of innocence and love),
And watch the clouds that late were rich with light
Slow-sad'ning round, and mark the star of eve
Serenely brilliant (such should wisdom be)
Shine opposite! How exquisite the scents
Snatched from yon bean-field! And the world so hushed!
The stilly murmur of the distant sea
Tells us of silence.
And that simplest lute
Placed lengthways in the clasping casement – hark
How by the desultory breeze caressed![4]
Like some coy maid half-yielding to her lover,
It pours such sweet upbraidings as must needs
Tempt to repeat the wrong. And now its strings
Boldlier swept, the long sequacious notes
Over delicious surges sink and rise,
Such a soft floating witchery of sound
As twilight elfins make when they at eve
Voyage on gentle gales from fairyland,
Where melodies round honey-dropping flowers
Footless and wild, like birds of paradise,
Nor pause nor perch, hovering on untamed wing.
Oh the one life within us and abroad,
Which meets all motion and becomes its soul,
A light in sound, a sound-like power in light,
Rhythm in all thought, and joyance everywhere –
Methinks it should have been impossible
Not to love all things in a world so filled,
Where the breeze warbles, and the mute still air
Is Music slumbering on its instrument!

## Notes

The Eolian Harp

[1] The first of the conversation poems. When first published in 1796 it was called 'Effusion XXXV' because Coleridge wanted to number his poems as 'effusions' (inspired outpourings); it was not published under that title again.

[2] *Sara* Sara Fricker, with whom Coleridge was in love. He was to marry her less than two months after this poem was composed, on 4 October 1795.

[3] *white-flowered jasmine and the broad-leaved myrtle* In *Paradise Lost* Adam and Eve's 'blissful bower' also contains jasmine and myrtle.

[4] The Aeolian harp is a stringed instrument placed in front of an open window so as to catch the breeze; it is not unlike modern wind-chimes.

And thus, my love, as on the midway slope
Of yonder hill I stretch my limbs at noon,
Whilst through my half-closed eyelids I behold
The sunbeams dance, like diamonds, on the main,
And tranquil muse upon tranquillity,
Full many a thought uncalled and undetained,
And many idle flitting fantasies
Traverse my indolent and passive brain –
As wild and various as the random gales
That swell and flutter on this subject lute!
And what if all of animated nature
Be but organic harps diversely framed,
That tremble into thought, as o'er them sweeps,
Plastic[5] and vast, one intellectual[6] breeze,
At once the soul of each, and God of all?
But thy more serious eye a mild reproof
Darts, oh beloved woman! – nor such thoughts
Dim and unhallowed dost thou not reject,
And biddest me walk humbly with my God.
Meek daughter in the family of Christ,
Well hast thou said and holily dispraised
These shapings of the unregenerate mind,
Bubbles that glitter as they rise and break
On vain philosophy's aye-babbling spring.
For never guiltless may I speak of Him,
Th' Incomprehensible! save when with awe
I praise him, and with faith that inly[7] *feels* –
Who with his saving mercies healed me,
A sinful and most miserable man
Wildered and dark, and gave me to possess
Peace, and this cot, and thee, heart-honoured maid!

## Notes

[5] *Plastic* shaping, formative, creative. It is important to Coleridge that God's spiritual influence shape the sensibility of the beings it enters.

[6] *intellectual* spiritual.

[7] In 1796, Coleridge appended this note to the word 'inly': '"L'athée n'est point à mes yeux un faux esprit; je puis vivre avec lui aussi bien et mieux qu'avec le dévot, car il raisonne davantage, mais il lui manque un sens, et mon âme ne se fond point entièrement avec la sienne: il est froid au spectacle le plus ravissant, et il cherche un syllogisme lorsque je rends une action de grâce." *Appel à l'impartiale postérité, par la Citoyenne Roland*, troisième partie, p. 67' (Coleridge's note to the 1796 text). (The atheist is not, to my eyes, deceived; I can live with him as well as – if not better than with – the zealot, because he reasons more. But he is lacking in a certain sense, and my soul does not entirely combine with his: he is untouched by the most ravishing spectacle, and searches for a syllogism when I thank God.)

## *Reflections on Having Left a Place of Retirement* (composed March–April 1796)

*'Sermoni propiora'. – Horace.*[1]

Low was our pretty cot;[2] our tallest rose
Peeped at the chamber-window. We could hear
At silent noon, and eve, and early morn,
The sea's faint murmur. In the open air
Our myrtles blossomed, and across the porch
Thick jasmines twined; the little landscape round
Was green and woody and refreshed the eye.
It was a spot which you might aptly call
The Valley of Seclusion. Once I saw
(Hallowing his sabbath-day by quietness)
A wealthy son of commerce saunter by,
Bristowa's[3] citizen; methought it calmed
His thirst of idle gold, and made him muse
With wiser feelings – for he paused and looked
With a pleased sadness, and gazed all around,
Then eyed our cottage, and gazed round again,
And sighed, and said it was a blessed place.
And we *were* blessed. Oft with patient ear,
Long-listening to the viewless skylark's note
(Viewless, or haply for a moment seen
Gleaming on sunny wing), in whispered tones
I've said to my beloved, 'Such,[4] sweet girl,
The inobtrusive song of happiness,
Unearthly minstrelsy – then only heard
When the soul seeks to hear, when all is hushed
And the heart listens!'
But the time when first

### Notes

Reflections on Having Left a Place of Retirement

[1] From *Satires* I iv 42. In a note to 'Fears in Solitude' (1798), Coleridge was to write: 'The above is perhaps not poetry but rather a sort of middle thing between poetry and oratory – *sermoni propiora*. Some parts are, I am conscious, too tame even for animated prose.'

[2] *cot* cottage.

[3] *Bristowa's* Bristol's.

[4] *Such* i.e. similar to this (the skylark's song).

From that low dell, steep up the stony mount
I climbed with perilous toil and reached the top –
Oh, what a goodly scene! *Here* the bleak mount,
The bare bleak mountain speckled thin with sheep;
Grey clouds, that shadowing spot the sunny fields;
And river, now with bushy rocks o'erbrowed,
Now winding bright and full with naked banks;
And seats, and lawns, the abbey and the wood,
And cots, and hamlets, and faint city-spire;
The channel *there*, the islands and white sails,
Dim coasts, and cloudlike hills, and shoreless ocean –
It seemed like Omnipresence! God, methought,
Had built him there a temple: the whole world
Seemed *imaged* in its vast circumference.
No wish profaned my overwhelmed heart –
Blessed hour! It was a luxury – to be!
   Ah, quiet dell, dear cot, and mount sublime!
I was constrained to quit you. Was it right,
While my unnumbered brethren toiled and bled,[5]
That I should dream away the trusted hours
On rose-leaf beds, pamp'ring the coward heart
With feelings all too delicate for use?
Sweet is the tear that from some Howard's[6] eye
Drops on the cheek of one he lifts from earth;
And he that works me good with unmoved face
Does it but half – he chills me while he aids –
My benefactor, not my brother man.
Yet even this, this cold beneficence
Seizes my praise, when I reflect on those
(The sluggard pity's vision-weaving tribe!)
Who sigh for wretchedness, yet shun the wretched,
Nursing in some delicious solitude
Their slothful loves and dainty sympathies!
I therefore go and join head, heart and hand,
Active and firm, to fight the bloodless fight
Of Science,[7] Freedom, and the Truth in Christ.
   Yet oft when after honourable toil
Rests the tired mind, and waking loves to dream,
My spirit shall revisit thee, dear cot!
Thy jasmine and thy window-peeping rose,
And myrtles fearless of the mild sea-air;
And I shall sigh fond wishes, sweet abode!
Ah, had none greater, and that all had such!
It might be so, but the time is not yet:
Speed it, oh Father! Let thy Kingdom come!

## Notes

[5] *While my…bled* Britain had been at war with France since 1793.

[6] John Howard (1726–90), prison reformer and philanthropist.

[7] *Science* Knowledge, which would have included such things as chemistry.

## *Religious Musings* (extract) (composed 1794–6)[1]

There is one Mind,[2] one omnipresent Mind
Omnific.[3] His most holy name is Love –
Truth of subliming[4] import! with the which
Who feeds and saturates his constant soul,
He from his small particular orbit flies
With blessed outstarting![5] From himself he flies,
Stands in the sun, and with no partial gaze[6]
Views all creation, and he loves it all
And blesses it, and calls it very good!
This is indeed to dwell with the most high –
Cherubs and rapture-trembling seraphim
Can press no nearer to th' Almighty's throne.
But that we roam unconscious, or with hearts
Unfeeling of our universal Sire,
And that in his vast family no Cain[7]
Injures uninjured (in her best-aimed blow
Victorious murder a blind suicide),[8]
Haply for this some younger angel now
Looks down on human nature – and behold!
A sea of blood bestrewed with wrecks where mad
Embattling interests on each other rush
With unhelmed rage![9]
'Tis the sublime of man,
Our noontide majesty,[10] to know ourselves
Parts and proportions of one wondrous whole;
This fraternizes[11] man, this constitutes
Our charities and bearings – but 'tis God
Diffused through all that doth make all one whole.[12]
This the worst superstition: Him except,

## Notes

Religious Musings

[1] In this important poem the young Coleridge set out, though in very dense and frequently obscure terms, his central beliefs. He presents the French Revolution in terms of his expectation of the millennium (Christ's thousand-year rule on earth, thought to be nigh) and in this important extract explicates his Unitarian principles.

[2] *There is one Mind* Coleridge was a fervent Unitarian, and this opening remark expresses the central Unitarian belief in the absolute unity of the godhead.

[3] *Omnific* all-creating.

[4] *subliming* exalting.

[5] *Who feeds...outstarting* He who feeds and saturates his soul in the truth that God is Love may transcend (outstart) his earthly state ('particular orbit').

[6] *with no partial gaze* i.e. with a vision as universal and all-embracing as that of God.

[7] *Cain* The son of Adam and Eve, who killed his brother Abel and brought murder into the world; see Genesis 4:8.

[8] *Victorious murder a blind suicide* Because we are united in a common humanity, murder is almost as destructive of the aggressor as it is of the victim.

[9] *A sea of blood...rage* During the period in which this poem was written, the Reign of Terror had come to an end with Robespierre's execution, and given way to full-scale war as France had taken on the European allies (1793 onwards). A committed republican, Coleridge was horrified.

[10] *Our noontide majesty* the height of our spiritual existence.

[11] *fraternizes* *Fraternité'* was one of the ideals of the French Revolution.

[12] *'tis God...whole* a reiteration of the pantheist belief in a single divinity diffused through the universe.

Aught to desire,[13] supreme reality,
The plenitude and permanence of bliss!
Oh fiends of superstition![14] – not that oft
Your pitiless rites have floated with man's blood
The skull-piled temple, not for this shall wrath
Thunder against you from the Holy One!
But (whether ye, th' unclimbing bigot, mock
With secondary gods, or if more pleased
Ye petrify th' imbrothelled atheist's heart[15] –
The atheist your worst slave) I o'er some plain
Peopled with death, and to the silent sun
Steaming with tyrant-murdered multitudes,
Or where mid groans and shrieks loud-laughing trade[16]
More hideous packs his bales of living anguish –
I will raise up a mourning, oh ye fiends,
And curse your spells that film the eye of faith,[17]
Hiding the present God, whose presence lost,
The moral world's cohesion, we become
An anarchy of spirits! Toy-bewitched,[18]
Made blind by lusts, disherited of soul,
No common centre man, no common sire
Knoweth![19] A sordid solitary thing,
Mid countless brethren with a lonely heart,
Through courts and cities the smooth savage roams
Feeling himself, his own low self the whole,
When he by sacred sympathy might make
The whole one self![20] Self, that no alien knows!
Self, far diffused as fancy's wing can travel!
Self, spreading still, oblivious of its own,
Yet all of all possessing! This is faith![21]
This the Messiah's destined victory!

## Notes

[13] *This the...desire* i.e. the worst superstition is to desire anything except Him.

[14] *fiends of superstition* An attack on European Christians, who are responsible for using superstition as a means of perpetuating the slave trade.

[15] *th' imbrothelled atheist's heart* The atheist is, effectively, in the brothel of hell.

[16] *trade* the slave trade.

[17] *I o'er some plain...faith* It is not clear whether Coleridge has some specific event in mind, but in general terms he is saying the war between France and the allies is leading people to lose faith in God.

[18] *Toy-bewitched* seduced by idle pastimes.

[19] *An anarchy...Knoweth* Coleridge is attacking Godwinian thought, which he despised for its atheism and disapproval of marriage.

[20] *A sordid...self* Instead of enjoying the Unitarian perception of himself as part of the godhead, the Godwinian is a selfish moral degenerate.

[21] *Self, far diffused...Faith* Faith consists of self diffused through the world, integrated with the Unitarian God.

## *Letter from S.T. Coleridge to John Thelwall, 19 November 1796* (extract)

Your portrait of yourself interested me. As to me, my face, unless when animated by immediate eloquence, expresses great sloth and great (indeed almost idiotic) good nature. 'Tis a mere carcass of a face – fat, flabby, and expressive chiefly of inexpression. Yet I am told that my eyes, eyebrows, and forehead are physiognomically good,[1] but of this the deponent[2] knoweth not. As to my shape, 'tis a good shape enough if measured – but my gait is awkward, and the walk and the whole man indicates *indolence capable of energies*. I am, and ever have been, a great reader, and have read almost everything – a library-cormorant. I am deep in all out of the way books, whether of the monkish times or of the puritanical era.[3] I have read and digested most of the historical writers but I do not *like* history. Metaphysics and poetry and 'facts of mind' (i.e. accounts of all the strange phantasms that ever possessed your philosophy-dreamers[4] from Thoth the Egyptian[5] to Taylor the English pagan)[6] are my darling studies.

In short, I seldom read except to amuse myself, and I am almost always reading. Of useful knowledge, I am a so-so chemist, and I love chemistry.[7] All else is blank, but I *will* be (please God) an horticulturist and a farmer.[8] I compose very little and I absolutely hate composition. Such is my dislike that even a sense of duty is sometimes too weak to overpower it.

I cannot breathe through my nose, so my mouth, with sensual thick lips, is almost always open. In conversation I am impassioned, and oppose what I deem error with an eagerness which is often mistaken for personal asperity[9] – but I am ever so swallowed up in the *thing*, that I perfectly forget my opponent. Such am I.

## *This Lime-Tree Bower My Prison* (1834)[1]

In the June of 1797, some long-expected friends[2] paid a visit to the author's cottage, and on the morning of their arrival he met with an accident which disabled him from walking during the whole time of their stay. One evening, when they had left him for a few hours, he composed the following lines in the garden bower.

### Notes

Letter from S.T. Coleridge to John Thelwall

[1] *physiognomically good* i.e. that they indicate good character traits.

[2] *deponent* witness.

[3] *monkish times…era* i.e. from the Middle Ages to the seventeenth century.

[4] *philosophy-dreamers* visionaries.

[5] *Thoth the Egyptian* Thoth is the Greek name for Hermes Trismegistus, a mythological figure said to have founded the art of alchemy.

[6] *Taylor the English pagan* Thomas Taylor (1758–1835), classical scholar and Neoplatonist.

[7] *chemistry* One of Coleridge's mentors, Joseph Priestley (1733–1804), founder of modern Unitarianism, was an accomplished chemist.

[8] *an horticulturalist and a farmer* Coleridge enjoyed the theory, rather than the practice, of farming.

[9] *asperity* roughness, boisterousness.

This Lime-Tree Bower My Prison

[1] This poem was first published in Southey's *Annual Anthology* (1800), as 'This Lime-Tree Bower My Prison, A Poem Addressed to Charles Lamb of the India House, London', but probably the best-known version is this one, which appeared in Coleridge's collected poetical works of 1834.

[2] Charles Lamb and William and Dorothy Wordsworth.

Well, they are gone, and here must I remain,
This lime-tree bower my prison![3] I have lost
Beauties and feelings, such as would have been
Most sweet to my remembrance even when age
Had dimmed mine eyes to blindness! They, meanwhile,
Friends whom I never more may meet again,[4]
On springy[5] heath, along the hilltop edge,[6]
Wander in gladness, and wind down, perchance,
To that still roaring dell of which I told;
The roaring dell, o'erwooded, narrow, deep,
And only speckled by the midday sun;
Where its slim trunk the ash from rock to rock
Flings arching like a bridge – that branchless ash,
Unsunned and damp, whose few poor yellow leaves
Ne'er tremble in the gale, yet tremble still,
Fanned by the waterfall! And there my friends
Behold the dark green file of long lank weeds,[7]
That all at once (a most fantastic sight!)
Still nod and drip beneath the dripping edge
Of the blue clay-stone.
Now, my friends emerge
Beneath the wide wide heaven – and view again
The many-steepled tract magnificent
Of hilly fields and meadows, and the sea,
With some fair bark, perhaps, whose sails light up
The slip of smooth clear blue betwixt two isles
Of purple shadow! Yes, they wander on
In gladness all – but thou, methinks, most glad,
My gentle-hearted Charles![8] For thou hast pined
And hungered after nature many a year
In the great city pent, winning thy way,
With sad yet patient soul, through evil and pain
And strange calamity![9] Ah, slowly sink
Behind the western ridge, thou glorious sun!
Shine in the slant beams of the sinking orb,
Ye purple heath-flowers! Richlier burn, ye clouds!

## Notes

[3] At this point in the earliest version of the poem, Coleridge described himself as 'Lamed by the scathe of fire, lonely and faint'. This was explained in a letter where he writes that 'dear Sara accidentally emptied a skillet of boiling milk on my foot'.

[4] An exaggeration: Wordsworth and his sister had moved into Alfoxden House, not far from Coleridge's cottage, days before. They would remain for the next year.

[5] 'Elastic, I mean' (Coleridge's note) – meaning that the furze and heather reassumes its original shape after having been trodden on. In the course of the poem the poet will reassume his original mood, having been depressed by the 'accident' and its consequences.

[6] *the hilltop edge* The Wordsworths and Lamb would have climbed up the Quantock Hills near Coleridge's cottage.

[7] 'The Asplenium scolopendrium, called in some countries the Adder's tongue, in others the Hart's tongue; but Withering gives the Adder's tongue as the trivial name of the Ophioglossum only' (Coleridge's note). Coleridge and Wordsworth acquired William Withering's *Arrangement of British Plants* (4 vols., 1796) in August 1800.

[8] *My gentle-hearted Charles!* 'For God's sake', Lamb wrote to Coleridge, when the poem was published in 1800, 'don't make me ridiculous any more by terming me gentle-hearted in print, or do it in better verses … the meaning of "gentle" is equivocal at best, and almost always means "poor-spirited"'.

[9] *strange calamity* In September 1796 Lamb arrived home from his office job at East India House to find his mother stabbed to death, his father wandering round the house with a serving fork in his forehead, and his sister Mary screaming, covered in blood, with a knife in her hands. Both Lamb and his sister Mary spent time in lunatic asylums.

Live in the yellow light, ye distant groves!
And kindle, thou blue ocean! So my friend,
Struck with deep joy, may stand, as I have stood,
Silent with swimming sense; yea, gazing round
On the wide landscape, gaze till all doth seem
Less gross than bodily, and of such hues
As veil the Almighty Spirit, when yet he makes
Spirits perceive His presence.[10]
A delight
Comes sudden on my heart, and I am glad
As I myself were there! Nor in this bower,
This little lime-tree bower, have I not marked
Much that has soothed me. Pale beneath the blaze
Hung the transparent foliage; and I watched
Some broad and sunny leaf, and loved to see
The shadow of the leaf and stem above
Dappling its sunshine! And that walnut tree
Was richly tinged, and a deep radiance lay
Full on the ancient ivy which *usurps*
Those fronting elms, and now with blackest mass
Makes their dark branches gleam a lighter hue
Through the late twilight; and though now the bat
Wheels silent by, and not a swallow twitters,
Yet still the solitary humble-bee[11]
Sings in the bean-flower! Henceforth I shall know
That nature ne'er deserts the wise and pure –
No scene so narrow but may well employ
Each faculty of sense, and keep the heart
Awake to love and beauty! And sometimes
'Tis well to be bereaved of promised good,
That we may lift the soul, and contemplate
With lively joy the joys we cannot share.
My gentle-hearted Charles! when the last rook
Beat its straight path along the dusky air
Homewards, I blessed it, deeming its black wing
(Now a dim speck, now vanishing in the light)
Had crossed the mighty orb's dilated glory
While thou stoodst gazing; or, when all was still,
Flew creaking[12] o'er thy head, and had a charm
For thee, my gentle-hearted Charles! to whom
No sound is dissonant which tells of Life.

## Notes

[10] 'You remember, I am a Berkeleian' (Coleridge's note). George Berkeley, Bishop of Cloyne (1685–1753), denied the existence of the material world in favour of an invisible world created by God, perceptible by human beings in moments of heightened vision.

[11] *humble-bee* Against a copy of the 1817 printed text, Coleridge entered the following note: 'Cows without horns are called Hummel cows, in the country as the Hummel bee, as stingless (unless it be a corruption of *humming*, from the sound observable).'

[12] 'Some months after I had written this line, it gave me pleasure to find that Bartram had observed the same circumstance of the Savannah crane. "When these birds move their wings in flight, their strokes are slow, moderate and regular; and even when at a considerable distance or high above us, we plainly hear the quill-feathers; their shafts and webs upon one another creak as the joints or working of a vessel in a tempestuous sea"' (Coleridge's note). Coleridge was reading William Bartram's *Travels through North and South Carolina* (1794) by summer 1797.

## *Letter from S.T. Coleridge to John Thelwall, 14 October 1797* (extract)

I can at times feel strongly the beauties you describe – in themselves and for themselves. But more frequently all things appear little – all the knowledge that can be acquired, child's play; the universe itself, what but an immense heap of *little* things? I can contemplate nothing but parts, and parts are all little! My mind feels as if it ached to behold and know something *great*, something *one* and *indivisible*[1] – and it is only in the faith of this that rocks or waterfalls, mountains or caverns, give me the sense of sublimity or majesty! But in this faith *all things* counterfeit infinity! 'Struck with the deepest calm of joy', I stand

> Silent, with swimming sense, and gazing round
> On the wide landscape, gaze till all doth seem
> Less gross than bodily, a living thing
> Which acts upon the mind, and with such hues
> As clothe th' Almighty Spirit, when he makes
> Spirits perceive his presence!

## *Letter from S.T. Coleridge to Thomas Poole, 16 October 1797* (extract)

I read every book that came in my way without distinction. And my father was fond of me, and used to take me on his knee, and hold long conversations with me.[1] I remember that at eight years old I walked with him one winter evening from a farmer's house a mile from Ottery, and he told me the names of the stars, and how Jupiter was a thousand times larger than our world, and that the other twinkling stars were suns that had worlds rolling round them. And when I came home, he showed me how they rolled round. I heard him with a profound delight and admiration, but without the least mixture of wonder or incredulity. For, from my early reading of fairy tales and genii etc. etc., my mind had been habituated *to the Vast* – and I never regarded my senses in any way as the criteria of my belief. I regulated all my creeds by my conceptions – not by my sight, even at that age.

Should children be permitted to read romances, and relations of giants and magicians and genii? I know all that has been said against it, but I have formed my faith in the affirmative. I know no other way of giving the mind a love of 'the Great' and 'the Whole'. Those who have been led to the same truths step by step through the constant testimony of their senses, seem to me to want a sense which I possess: they contemplate nothing but *parts*, and all parts are necessarily little. And the universe to them is but a mass of *little things*. It is true that the mind *may* become credulous and prone to superstition by the former method – but are not the experimentalists[2] credulous even to madness in believing any absurdity rather than believe the grandest truths, if they have not the testimony of their own senses in their favour? I have known some who have been *rationally* educated, as it is styled. They were marked by a microscopic acuteness, but when they looked at great things, all became a blank and they saw nothing – and denied (very illogically) that anything could be seen, and uniformly put the negation of a power for the possession of a power, and called the want of imagination 'judgement', and the never being moved to rapture 'philosophy'!

### Notes

LETTER FROM S.T. COLERIDGE TO JOHN THELWALL

[1] *My mind feels…indivisible* Coleridge yearns for the transcendental experience described in 'Religious Musings' 140–2.

LETTER FROM S.T. COLERIDGE TO THOMAS POOLE

[1] *And my father…me* Coleridge was the youngest of John Coleridge's many children, and probably the favourite. John Coleridge was headmaster of the King Henry VII Grammar School at Ottery St Mary and vicar of St Mary's, until his death in 1781.

[2] *experimentalists* those who base their religious faith and beliefs only on what is perceived by the five senses, and on the reason.

## *Of the Fragment of 'Kubla Khan'* (1816)[1]

The following fragment is here published at the request of a poet of great and deserved celebrity,[2] and as far as the author's own opinions are concerned, rather as a psychological curiosity than on the ground of any supposed *poetic* merits.

In the summer of the year 1797,[3] the author, then in ill health, had retired to a lonely farmhouse between Porlock and Lynton on the Exmoor confines of Somerset and Devonshire. In consequence of a slight indisposition, an anodyne had been prescribed,[4] from the effects of which he fell asleep in his chair at the moment that he was reading the following sentence, or words of the same substance, in *Purchas's Pilgrimage*: 'Here the Khan Kubla commanded a palace to be built, and a stately garden thereunto. And thus ten miles of fertile ground were enclosed with a wall.'[5]

The author continued for about three hours in a profound sleep (at least of the external senses) during which time he has the most vivid confidence that he could not have composed less than from two to three hundred lines – if that indeed can be called composition in which all the images rose up before him as *things*, with a parallel production of the correspondent expressions, without any sensation or consciousness of effort. On awaking he appeared to himself to have a distinct recollection of the whole, and taking his pen, ink, and paper, instantly and eagerly wrote down the lines that are here preserved. At this moment he was unfortunately called out by a person on business from Porlock and detained by him above an hour, and on his return to his room, found to his no small surprise and mortification that though he still retained some vague and dim recollection of the general purpose of the vision, yet, with the exception of some eight or ten scattered lines and images, all the rest had passed away like the images on the surface of a stream into which a stone has been cast – but, alas! without the after-restoration of the latter:

> Then all the charm
> Is broken – all that phantom-world so fair
> Vanishes, and a thousand circlets spread,
> And each misshapes the other. Stay awhile,
> Poor youth, who scarcely dar'st lift up thine eyes –
> The stream will soon renew its smoothness, soon
> The visions will return! And lo, he stays,
> And soon the fragments dim of lovely forms
> Come trembling back, unite, and now once more
> The pool becomes a mirror.[6]

Yet from the still-surviving recollections in his mind, the author has frequently purposed to finish for himself what had been originally, as it were, given to him. *Αὔριον ἅδιον ᾄσω*,[7] but the tomorrow is yet to come.

As a contrast to this vision, I have annexed a fragment of a very different character, describing with equal fidelity the dream of pain and disease.[8]

### Notes

Of the Fragment of 'Kubla Khan'

1 This short essay was prefaced to 'Kubla Khan' on its first publication in 1816.

2 *a poet of great and deserved celebrity* Lord Byron, who described it as 'a fine wild poem'. 'Kubla Khan' and 'Christabel' circulated in literary circles for years before they were formally published.

3 *In the summer...1797* The exact date of composition is unknown. If, as seems likely, Coleridge's retirement to a farmhouse occurred during the walking tour to the Valley of the Rocks with the Wordsworths, the probable date is early November 1797.

4 *an anodyne...prescribed* Opium was generally used for the treatment of dysentery at this time. In a manuscript version of the poem, *c.*1804, Coleridge noted 'This fragment with a good deal more, not recoverable, composed in a sort of reverie brought on by two grains of opium taken to check a dysentery, at a farm-house between Porlock and Lynton, a quarter of a mile from Culbone Church, in the fall of the year 1797. S.T. Coleridge'.

5 'In Xaindu did Cublai Can build a stately pallace, encompassing sixteene miles of plaine ground with a wall, wherein are fertile meddowes, pleasant springs, delightfull streames, and all sorts of beasts of chase and game, and in the middest thereof a sumptuous house of pleasure, which may be removed from place to place' (Samuel Purchas, *Purchas his Pilgrimage* (1613), p. 350).

6 Coleridge quotes his own *The Picture* 69–78.

7 *Αὔριον ἅδιον ᾄσω* 'Tomorrow I shall sing more sweetly'; Theocritus, *Idyll* i 145.

8 *a fragment...disease* 'The Pains of Sleep'.

## *Kubla Khan* (1816)

In Xanadu[1] did Kubla Khan
A stately pleasure-dome decree,
Where Alph, the sacred river, ran
Through caverns measureless to man
    Down to a sunless sea.
So twice five miles of fertile ground
With walls and towers were girdled round;
And here were gardens bright with sinuous rills
Where blossomed many an incense-bearing tree;
And here were forests ancient as the hills,
And folding sunny spots of greenery.

But oh, that deep romantic chasm which slanted
Down the green hill athwart a cedarn cover!
A savage place, as holy and enchanted
As e'er beneath a waning moon was haunted
By woman wailing for her demon-lover!
And from this chasm, with ceaseless turmoil seething,
As if this earth in fast thick pants were breathing,
A mighty fountain momently was forced
Amid whose swift half-intermitted burst
Huge fragments vaulted like rebounding hail,
Or chaffy grain beneath the thresher's flail!
And mid these dancing rocks at once and ever,
It flung up momently the sacred river.
Five miles meandering with a mazy motion
Through wood and dale the sacred river ran,
Then reached the caverns measureless to man
And sank in tumult to a lifeless ocean.
And mid this tumult Kubla heard from far
Ancestral voices prophesying war!

    The shadow of the dome of pleasure
    Floated midway on the waves,
    Where was heard the mingled measure
    From the fountain and the caves;
It was a miracle of rare device,
A sunny pleasure-dome with caves of ice!

    A damsel with a dulcimer
    In a vision once I saw:
    It was an Abyssinian maid
    And on her dulcimer she played,

## Notes

Kubla Khan

[1] The manuscript text gives 'Xannadù', with a stress marked on the final syllable.

Singing of Mount Abora.[2]
Could I revive within me
Her symphony and song,
To such a deep delight 'twould win me
That with music loud and long,
I would build that dome in air,
That sunny dome, those caves of ice!
And all who heard should see them there,
And all should cry, 'Beware, beware!
His flashing eyes, his floating hair!
Weave a circle round him thrice,
And close your eyes with holy dread –
For he on honey-dew hath fed
And drank the milk of paradise.'

## *Frost at Midnight* (1834)

The frost performs its secret ministry
Unhelped by any wind. The owlet's cry
Came loud – and hark, again! loud as before.
The inmates of my cottage, all at rest,
Have left me to that solitude which suits
Abstruser musings, save that at my side
My cradled infant[1] slumbers peacefully.
'Tis calm indeed! – so calm that it disturbs
And vexes meditation with its strange
And extreme silentness. Sea, hill, and wood,
This populous village! Sea, and hill, and wood,
With all the numberless goings-on of life,
Inaudible as dreams! The thin blue flame
Lies on my low-burnt fire, and quivers not;
Only that film which fluttered on the grate
Still flutters there, the sole unquiet thing.[2]
Methinks its motion in this hush of nature
Gives it dim sympathies with me who live,
Making it a companionable form
Whose puny flaps and freaks the idling spirit
By its own moods interprets, everywhere
Echo or mirror seeking of itself,
And makes a toy of thought.
But oh, how oft,

## Notes

[2] *Mount Abora* Coleridge originally wrote 'Amora' in the MS. Mount Amara alludes to *Purchas his Pilgrimage*, in which it is said to be 'situate as the navel of the Ethopian body, and centre of their empire, under the equinoctial line where the sun may take his best view thereof, as not encountering in all his long journey with the like theatre ... the sun himself so in love with the sight, that the first and last thing he vieweth in all those parts is this hill.'

FROST AT MIDNIGHT

[1] *My cradled infant* Hartley Coleridge, born 19 September 1796. He was one and a half years old. This is the first of his numerous appearances in the poetry of Wordsworth and Coleridge, including 'The Nightingale' 91–105, 'Christabel' 644–65, 'To H.C., Six Years Old' and 'Ode' 85–131.

[2] 'In all parts of the kingdom these films are called "strangers", and supposed to portend the arrival of some absent friend' (Coleridge's note).

How oft at school,[3] with most believing mind,
Presageful, have I gazed upon the bars,
To watch that fluttering stranger! And as oft
With unclosed lids, already had I dreamt
Of my sweet birthplace, and the old church-tower
Whose bells, the poor man's only music, rang
From morn to evening all the hot fair-day,
So sweetly that they stirred and haunted me
With a wild pleasure, falling on mine ear
Most like articulate sounds of things to come!
So gazed I till the soothing things I dreamt
Lulled me to sleep, and sleep prolonged my dreams!
And so I brooded all the following morn,
Awed by the stern preceptor's[4] face, mine eye
Fixed with mock study on my swimming book;
Save if the door half opened, and I snatched
A hasty glance, and still my heart leaped up,
For still I hoped to see the stranger's face –
Townsman, or aunt, or sister more beloved,
My playmate when we both were clothed alike![5]
    Dear babe,[6] that sleepest cradled by my side,
Whose gentle breathings heard in this deep calm
Fill up the interspersed vacancies
And momentary pauses of the thought;
My babe so beautiful, it fills my heart
With tender gladness thus to look at thee,
And think that thou shalt learn far other lore
And in far other scenes! For I was reared
In the great city, pent mid cloisters dim,
And saw nought lovely but the sky and stars.
But thou, my babe, shalt wander like a breeze
By lakes and sandy shores, beneath the crags
Of ancient mountain, and beneath the clouds
Which image in their bulk both lakes and shores
And mountain crags;[7] so shalt thou see and hear
The lovely shapes and sounds intelligible
Of that eternal language which thy God
Utters, who from eternity doth teach
Himself in all, and all things in himself.
Great universal teacher! He shall mould
Thy spirit, and by giving make it ask.
    Therefore all seasons shall be sweet to thee,
Whether the summer clothe the general earth

## Notes

[3] *school* a reference to Coleridge's time at Christ's Hospital in the City of London, 1782–91.

[4] *preceptor* teacher.

[5] *sister…alike* Until well into the nineteenth century, small boys and girls were dressed in frocks until boys were breeched. Coleridge was deeply attached to his sister Anne (1767–91), whose early death from consumption distressed him greatly.

[6] *Dear babe* Coleridge turns again to his son Hartley.

[7] *But thou…crags* Coleridge had not actually seen the Lake District in February 1798, when these lines were written; he had heard about them from Wordsworth. Cumbrian lakes do not have 'sandy shores'.

With greenness, or the redbreast sit and sing
Betwixt the tufts of snow on the bare branch
Of mossy apple-tree, while the nigh thatch
Smokes in the sun-thaw; whether the eave-drops fall
Heard only in the trances of the blast,
Or if the secret ministry of frost
Shall hang them up in silent icicles,
Quietly shining to the quiet moon.

## 'Christabel' (Part I composed February–April 1798; Part II composed by August–October 1800; Conclusion to Part II composed *c.*6 May 1801)[1]

### *Preface*

The first part of the following poem was written in the year 1797, at Stowey, in the county of Somerset. The second part, after my return from Germany, in the year 1800, at Keswick, Cumberland. It is probable that if the poem had been finished at either of the former periods, or if even the first and second part had been published in the year 1800, the impression of its originality would have been much greater than I dare at present expect. But for this I have only my own indolence to blame. The dates are mentioned for the exclusive purpose of precluding charges of plagiarism or servile imitation from myself.[2] For there is amongst us a set of critics, who seem to hold that every possible thought and image is traditional; who have no notion that there are such things as fountains in the world, small as well as great; and who would therefore charitably derive every rill they behold flowing, from a perforation made in some other man's tank. I am confident, however, that as far as the present poem is concerned, the celebrated poets whose writings I might be suspected of having imitated, either in particular passages, or in the tone and the spirit of the whole, would be among the first to vindicate me from the charge, and who, on any striking coincidence, would permit me to address them in this doggerel version of two monkish Latin hexameters.

'Tis mine and it is likewise yours;
But an if this will not do;
Let it be mine, good friend! for I
Am the poorer of the two.

I have only to add that the metre of 'Christabel' is not, properly speaking, irregular, though it may seem so from its being founded on a new principle: namely, that of counting in each line the accents, not the syllables. Though the latter may vary from seven to twelve, yet in each line the accents will be found to be only four. Nevertheless, this occasional variation in number of syllables is not introduced wantonly, nor for the mere ends of convenience, but in correspondence with some transition in the nature of the imagery or passion.

## Notes

CHRISTABEL

[1] 'Christabel' was not published until 1816, but came close to appearing in *Lyrical Ballads* (1800). Coleridge even sent a copy of Part I to the printers in early September 1800; it seems to have been his inability to complete the poem that led to its being cancelled from the volume.

[2] *plagiarism or servile imitation from myself* Walter Scott's poem 'The Lay of the Last Minstrel' (1805) borrowed from 'Christabel', Scott having been shown a manuscript copy by a mutual acquaintance, John Stoddart, in September–October 1802.

*Part I*

'Tis the middle of night by the castle clock,
And the owls have awakened the crowing cock;
Tu-whit!——Tu-whoo!
And hark, again! the crowing cock,
How drowsily it crew.

Sir Leoline, the Baron rich,
Hath a toothless mastiff bitch;
From her kennel beneath the rock
She makes answer to the clock,
Four for the quarters and twelve for the hour,
Ever and aye, moonshine or shower,
Sixteen short howls, not overloud;
Some say she sees my lady's shroud.

Is the night chilly and dark?
The night is chilly but not dark.
The thin grey cloud is spread on high,
It covers but not hides the sky.
The moon is behind, and at the full,
And yet she looks both small and dull.
The night is chill, the cloud is grey:
'Tis a month before the month of May,
And the spring comes slowly up this way.

The lovely lady, Christabel,
Whom her father loves so well,
What makes her in the wood so late
A furlong[3] from the castle gate?
She had dreams all yesternight
Of her own betrothed knight –
Dreams that made her moan and leap
As on her bed she lay in sleep;
And she in the midnight wood will pray
For the weal[4] of her lover that's far away.

She stole along, she nothing spoke,
The breezes they were still also;
And nought was green upon the oak
But moss and rarest mistletoe;
She kneels beneath the huge oak tree
And in silence prayeth she.
The lady leaps up suddenly,
The lovely lady, Christabel!
It moaned as near as near can be,
But what it is, she cannot tell:
On the other side it seems to be
Of the huge, broad-breasted, old oak tree.

Notes

[3] *A furlong* an eighth of a mile (220 yards).

[4] *weal* welfare.

The night is chill, the forest bare –
Is it the wind that moaneth bleak?
There is not wind enough in the air
To move away the ringlet curl
From the lovely lady's cheek;
There is not wind enough to twirl
The one red leaf, the last of its clan,
That dances as often as dance it can,
Hanging so light and hanging so high
On the topmost twig that looks up at the sky.

Hush, beating heart of Christabel!
Jesu Maria,[5] shield her well!

She folded her arms beneath her cloak
And stole to the other side of the oak:
  What sees she there?

There she sees a damsel bright
Dressed in a silken robe of white;
Her neck, her feet, her arms were bare,
And the jewels disordered in her hair.
I guess 'twas frightful there to see
A lady so richly clad as she –
   Beautiful exceedingly!

'Mary mother, save me now!'
Said Christabel, 'And who art thou?'

The lady strange made answer meet
And her voice was faint and sweet.
'Have pity on my sore distress,
I scarce can speak for weariness!
Stretch forth thy hand, and have no fear –'

Said Christabel, 'How cam'st thou here?'
And the lady, whose voice was faint and sweet,
Did thus pursue her answer meet:

'My sire is of a noble line
And my name is Geraldine.
Five warriors seized me yestermorn –
Me, even me, a maid forlorn;
They choked my cries with force and fright
And tied me on a palfrey[6] white.
The palfrey was as fleet as wind,
And they rode furiously behind.
They spurred amain,[7] their steeds were white,

## Notes

[5] *Jesu Maria* An oath used by Friar Lawrence at *Romeo and Juliet* II iii 69.

[6] *palfrey* A saddle-horse for ordinary riding, as opposed to a war-horse.

[7] *amain* at full speed.

And once we crossed the shade of night.
As sure as Heaven shall rescue me,
I have no thought what men they be;
Nor do I know how long it is
(For I have lain in fits, I wis)
Since one, the tallest of the five,
Took me from the palfrey's back,
A weary woman scarce alive.
Some muttered words his comrades spoke,
He placed me underneath this oak,
He swore they would return with haste;
Whither they went I cannot tell –
I thought I heard, some minutes past,
Sounds as of a castle-bell.
Stretch forth thy hand (thus ended she)
And help a wretched maid to flee.'

Then Christabel stretched forth her hand
And comforted fair Geraldine,
Saying that she should command
The service of Sir Leoline,
And straight be convoyed,[8] free from thrall,[9]
Back to her noble father's hall.

So up she rose and forth they passed
With hurrying steps, yet nothing fast;
Her lucky stars the lady blessed,
And Christabel, she sweetly said,
'All our household are at rest,
Each one sleeping in his bed.
Sir Leoline is weak in health
And may not well awakened be,
So to my room we'll creep in stealth
And you tonight must sleep with me.'

They crossed the moat, and Christabel
Took the key that fitted well –
A little door she opened straight
All in the middle of the gate,
The gate that was ironed[10] within and without
Where an army in battle array had marched out.
The lady sank, belike through pain,
And Christabel with might and main
Lifted her up, a weary weight,
Over the threshold of the gate;
Then the lady rose again
And moved as she were not in pain.

## Notes

[8] *convoyed* escorted.
[9] *thrall* captivity.
[10] *ironed* reinforced with iron.

So free from danger, free from fear,
They crossed the court – right glad they were.
And Christabel devoutly cried
To the lady by her side,
'Praise we the Virgin all divine
Who hath rescued thee from thy distress!'
'Alas, alas,' said Geraldine,
'I cannot speak for weariness.'
So free from danger, free from fear,
They crossed the court – right glad they were.

Outside her kennel, the mastiff old
Lay fast asleep in moonshine cold.
The mastiff old did not awake,
Yet she an angry moan did make.
And what can ail the mastiff bitch?
Never till now she uttered yell
Beneath the eye of Christabel.
Perhaps it is the owlet's scritch,
For what can ail the mastiff bitch?

They passed the hall that echoes still,
Pass as lightly as you will.
The brands[11] were flat, the brands were dying,
Amid their own white ashes lying;
But when the lady passed, there came
A tongue of light, a fit of flame,
And Christabel saw the lady's eye,
And nothing else saw she thereby
Save the boss of the shield of Sir Leoline tall
Which hung in a murky old nitch[12] in the wall.
'Oh softly tread', said Christabel,
'My father seldom sleepeth well.'

Sweet Christabel, her feet she bares
And they are creeping up the stairs,
Now in glimmer and now in gloom,
And now they pass the Baron's room,
As still as death with stifled breath;
And now have reached her chamber door,
And now with eager feet press down
The rushes of her chamber floor.

The moon shines dim in the open air
And not a moonbeam enters here.
But they without its light can see
The chamber carved so curiously,

## Notes

[11] *brands* wood burnt in the hearth.

[12] *nitch* niche.

Carved with figures strange and sweet
All made out of the carver's brain
For a lady's chamber meet;
The lamp with twofold silver chain
Is fastened to an angel's feet.
The silver lamp burns dead and dim,
But Christabel the lamp will trim.[13]
She trimmed the lamp and made it bright
And left it swinging to and fro,
While Geraldine in wretched plight
Sank down upon the floor below.

'Oh weary lady Geraldine,
I pray you, drink this cordial[14] wine.
It is a wine of virtuous powers –
My mother made it of wild-flowers.'

'And will your mother pity me,
Who am a maiden most forlorn?'

Christabel answered, 'Woe is me!
She died the hour that I was born.
I have heard the grey-haired friar tell
How on her deathbed she did say
That she should hear the castle bell
Strike twelve upon my wedding day.
Oh mother dear, that thou wert here!'
'I would', said Geraldine, 'she were.'

But soon with altered voice said she,
'Off, wandering mother! Peak and pine!
I have power to bid thee flee.'[15]
Alas, what ails poor Geraldine?
Why stares she with unsettled eye?
Can she the bodiless dead espy?
And why with hollow voice cries she,
'Off, woman, off! this hour is mine –

Though thou her guardian spirit be,
Off, woman, off! – 'tis given to me'?
Then Christabel knelt by the lady's side,
And raised to heaven her eyes so blue;
'Alas!' said she, 'this ghastly ride –
Dear lady, it hath wildered[16] you!'
The lady wiped her moist cold brow,
And faintly said, ''Tis over now!'

## Notes

[13] *trim* to clean the wick of a lamp for fresh burning.

[14] *cordial* reviving, restorative.

[15] *Off...flee* In a marginal note entered in a copy of the 1816 printed text, Coleridge explained: 'The mother of Christabel, who is now her guardian spirit, appears to Geraldine, as in answer to her wish. Geraldine fears the spirit, but yet has power over it for a time.'

[16] *wildered* perplexed, bewildered.

Again the wild-flower wine she drank;
Her fair large eyes 'gan[17] glitter bright,
And from the floor whereon she sank,
The lofty lady stood upright:
She was most beautiful to see,
Like a lady of a far countrée.

And thus the lofty lady spake:
'All they who live in the upper sky
Do love you, holy Christabel!
And you love them, and for their sake,
And for the good which me befell,
Even I, in my degree will try,
Fair maiden, to requite you well.
But now unrobe yourself, for I
Must pray, ere yet in bed I lie.'

Quoth Christabel, 'So let it be!'
And as the lady bade, did she.
Her gentle limbs did she undress,
And lay down in her loveliness.

But through her brain, of weal and woe
So many thoughts moved to and fro
That vain it were her lids to close;
So halfway from the bed she rose,
And on her elbow did recline
To look at the lady Geraldine.

Beneath the lamp the lady bowed
And slowly rolled her eyes around;
Then drawing in her breath aloud
Like one that shuddered, she unbound
The cincture[18] from beneath her breast:
Her silken robe and inner vest
Dropped to her feet, and full in view,
Behold! her bosom and half her side –
A sight to dream of, not to tell!
And she is to sleep by Christabel.[19]

She took two paces and a stride,
And lay down by the maiden's side;
And in her arms the maid she took,
  Ah wel-a-day!
And with low voice and doleful look
  These words did say:

## Notes

[17] *'gan* began to.

[18] *cincture* belt.

[19] *Behold...Christabel* The MS text of 1800, in the Christabel notebook at the Wordsworth Library, Grasmere, makes Geraldine less human:

Behold! her bosom and half her side
Are lean and old and foul of hue –
A sight to dream of, not to tell,
And she is to sleep with Christabel.

In a MS version of 1816, Geraldine's side is 'dark and rough as the sea-wolf 's hide'.

'In the touch of this bosom there worketh a spell
Which is lord of thy utterance, Christabel![20]
Thou knowest tonight, and wilt know tomorrow,
This mark of my shame, this seal of my sorrow;
But vainly thou warrest,
For this is alone in
Thy power to declare,
That in the dim forest
Thou heard'st a low moaning,
And found'st a bright lady surpassingly fair,
And didst bring her home with thee in love and in charity,
To shield her and shelter her from the damp air.'

### *The Conclusion to Part I*

It was a lovely sight to see
The lady Christabel, when she
Was praying at the old oak tree.
Amid the jagged shadows
Of mossy leafless boughs,
Kneeling in the moonlight
To make her gentle vows;
Her slender palms together pressed,
Heaving sometimes on her breast;
Her face resigned to bliss or bale,
Her face – oh call it fair, not pale!
And both blue eyes more bright than clear,
Each about to have a tear.

With open eyes (ah woe is me!)
Asleep, and dreaming fearfully,
Fearfully dreaming, yet I wis,
Dreaming that alone, which is –
Oh sorrow and shame! Can this be she,
The lady who knelt at the old oak tree?
And lo! the worker of these harms
That holds the maiden in her arms,
Seems to slumber still and mild,
As a mother with her child.

A star hath set, a star hath risen,
Oh Geraldine, since arms of thine
Have been the lovely lady's prison!
Oh Geraldine, one hour was thine –
Thou'st had thy will! By tairn[21] and rill

## Notes

[20] *In the touch...Christabel* A marginal note to a copy of the 1816 printed text by Coleridge reads: 'As soon as the wicked bosom, with the mysterious sign of evil stamped thereby, touches Christabel, she is deprived of the power of disclosing what had occurred.'

[21] *tairn* The earliest MS version of the poem has a note: 'Tairn or tarn (derived by Lye from the Icelandic *tiorn*, stagnum, palus) is rendered in our dictionaries as synonymous with mere or lake; but it is properly a large pool or reservoir in the mountains, commonly the feeder of some mere in the valleys. Tarn Watling and Blellum Tarn, though on lower ground than other tarns, are yet not exceptions – for both are on elevations, and Blellum Tarn feeds the Winander mere.' This is the first indication that the poem is set in the Lake District.

The night-birds all that hour were still;
But now they are jubilant anew,
From cliff and tower, tu-whoo! tu-whoo!
Tu-whoo! tu-whoo! from wood and fell!

And see! the lady Christabel
Gathers herself from out her trance;
Her limbs relax, her countenance
Grows sad and soft; the smooth thin lids
Close o'er her eyes, and tears she sheds –
Large tears that leave the lashes bright;
And oft the while she seems to smile
As infants at a sudden light!

Yea she doth smile and she doth weep
Like a youthful hermitess
Beauteous in a wilderness,
Who praying always, prays in sleep.

And if she move unquietly,
Perchance 'tis but the blood so free
Comes back and tingles in her feet.
No doubt she hath a vision sweet:
What if her guardian spirit 'twere?
What if she knew her mother near?
But this she knows – in joys and woes,
That saints will aid if men will call,
For the blue sky bends over all!

## *Part II*

'Each matin bell',[22] the Baron saith,
'Knells us back to a world of death.'
These words Sir Leoline first said
When he rose and found his lady dead;
These words Sir Leoline will say
Many a morn to his dying day.

And hence the custom and law began
That still at dawn the sacristan[23]
Who duly pulls the heavy bell
Five and forty beads must tell[24]
Between each stroke – a warning knell
Which not a soul can choose but hear
From Bratha Head[25] to Windermere.[26]

Notes

[22] *matin bell* sounded at midnight or 2 a.m.

[23] *sacristan* (or sexton) officer responsible for the fabric of the parish church; his main duties were ringing bells and digging graves.

[24] *tell* count.

[25] *Bratha Head* i.e. the length of Langdale, through which the River Brathay runs until it reaches Windermere.

[26] *Windermere* Windermere lake.

Saith Bracy the bard, 'So let it knell!
And let the drowsy sacristan
Still count as slowly as he can!
There is no lack of such, I ween,
As well fill up the space between.
In Langdale Pike[27] and Witch's Lair[28]
And Dungeon Ghyll[29] (so foully rent),
With ropes of rock and bells of air
Three sinful sextons' ghosts are pent,
Who all give back, one after t'other,
The death-note to their living brother;
And oft too, by the knell offended,
Just as their one! – two! – three! is ended,
The Devil mocks the doleful tale
With a merry peal from Borrowdale.'[30]

The air is still – through mist and cloud
That merry peal comes ringing loud;
And Geraldine shakes off her dread
And rises lightly from the bed,
Puts on her silken vestments white
And tricks her hair in lovely plight,[31]
And nothing doubting of her spell
Awakens the lady Christabel.

'Sleep you, sweet lady Christabel?
I trust that you have rested well.'

And Christabel awoke and spied
The same who lay down by her side –
Oh rather say, the same whom she
Raised up beneath the old oak tree!
Nay, fairer yet, and yet more fair,
For she belike hath drunken deep
Of all the blessedness of sleep!
And while she spake, her looks, her air
Such gentle thankfulness declare,
That (so it seemed) her girded vests
Grew tight beneath her heaving breasts.
'Sure I have sinned!' said Christabel,
'Now heaven be praised if all be well!'

## Notes

[27] *Langdale Pike* Consists of two mountains of over 2,300 ft each, called Harrison Stickle and Pike of Stickle.

[28] *Witch's Lair* Probably the cave on Pike of Stickle.

[29] *Dungeon Ghyll* Stream going up between the two Langdale Pikes to a height of 2,400 ft.

[30] *Borrowdale* The valley of Borrowdale is due north of the Langdale Pikes.

[31] *plight* fashion.

And in low faltering tones, yet sweet,
Did she the lofty lady greet
With such perplexity of mind
As dreams too lively leave behind.[32]

So quickly she rose, and quickly arrayed
Her maiden limbs, and having prayed
That He who on the cross did groan
Might wash away her sins unknown,
She forthwith led fair Geraldine
To meet her sire, Sir Leoline.

The lovely maid and the lady tall
Are pacing both into the hall,
And pacing on through page and groom,
Enter the Baron's presence-room.[33]

The Baron rose, and while he pressed
His gentle daughter to his breast,
With cheerful wonder in his eyes
The lady Geraldine espies,
And gave such welcome to the same,
As might beseem so bright a dame!

But when he heard the lady's tale,
And when she told her father's name,
Why waxed[34] Sir Leoline so pale,
Murmuring o'er the name again –
Lord Roland de Vaux of Tryermaine?

Alas, they had been friends in youth,
But whispering tongues can poison truth,
And constancy lives in realms above;
And life is thorny, and youth is vain,
And to be wroth[35] with one we love
Doth work like madness in the brain.
And thus it chanced, as I divine,
With Roland and Sir Leoline;
Each spake words of high disdain
And insult to his heart's best brother –
They parted, ne'er to meet again!
But never either found another
To free the hollow heart from paining –
They stood aloof, the scars remaining
Like cliffs which had been rent asunder.

## Notes

[32] *With such...behind* In a MS marginal note to a copy of the 1816 printed text, Coleridge wrote: 'Christabel is made to believe that the fearful sight had taken place only in a dream.'

[33] *presence-room* room where Sir Leoline receives guests; reception room.

[34] *waxed* became.

[35] *wroth* angry.

A dreary sea now flows between,
But neither heat, nor frost, nor thunder
Shall wholly do away, I ween,
The marks of that which once hath been.

Sir Leoline a moment's space
Stood gazing on the damsel's face,
And the youthful Lord of Tryermaine
Came back upon his heart again.

Oh then the Baron forgot his age,
His noble heart swelled high with rage;
He swore by the wounds in Jesu's side
He would proclaim it far and wide
With trump and solemn heraldry,
That they who thus had wronged the dame
Were base as spotted infamy!
'And if they dare deny the same,
My herald shall appoint a week,
And let the recreant traitors seek
My tournay court[36] – that there and then
I may dislodge their reptile souls
From the bodies and forms of men!'
He spake – his eye in lightning rolls!
For the lady was ruthlessly seized, and he kenned[37]
In the beautiful lady the child of his friend!

And now the tears were on his face,
And fondly in his arms he took
Fair Geraldine, who met th' embrace,
Prolonging it with joyous look,
Which when she viewed, a vision fell
Upon the soul of Christabel –
The vision of fear, the touch and pain!
She shrunk and shuddered, and saw again
(Ah woe is me! Was it for thee,
Thou gentle maid, such sights to see?)[38] –
Again she saw that bosom old,
Again she felt that bosom cold,
And drew in her breath with a hissing sound.
Whereat the knight turned wildly round,
And nothing saw but his own sweet maid
With eyes upraised, as one that prayed.

The touch, the sight, had passed away,
And in its stead that vision blessed,

## Notes

[36] *My tournay court* The sheriff 's county court usually met twice a year.

[37] *kenned* recognized.

[38] *Which when she viewed…to see* Coleridge's MS note in a copy of the 1816 volume reads: 'Christabel then recollects the whole, and knows that it was not a dream, but yet cannot disclose the fact that the strange lady is a supernatural being with the stamp of the Evil Ones on her.'

Which comforted her after rest,[39]
While in the lady's arms she lay,
Had put a rapture in her breast,
And on her lips and o'er her eyes
Spread smiles like light!
With new surprise,

'What ails then my beloved child?'
The Baron said. His daughter mild
Made answer, 'All will yet be well!'
I ween she had no power to tell
Aught else, so mighty was the spell.

Yet he who saw this Geraldine
Had deemed her sure a thing divine,
Such sorrow with such grace she blended,
As if she feared she had offended
Sweet Christabel, that gentle maid!
And with such lowly tones she prayed
She might be sent without delay
Home to her father's mansion.
'Nay,

Nay, by my soul!' said Leoline.
'Ho! Bracy the bard, the charge be thine!
Go thou with music sweet and loud,
And take two steeds with trappings proud,
And take the youth whom thou lov'st best
To bear thy harp and learn thy song,
And clothe you both in solemn vest,
And over the mountains haste along,
Lest wand'ring folk that are abroad
Detain you on the valley road.

And when he has crossed the Irthing flood,
My merry bard, he hastes, he hastes
Up Knorren Moor, through Halegarth Wood,[40]
And reaches soon that castle good
Which stands and threatens Scotland's wastes.

Bard Bracy! Bard Bracy! Your horses are fleet,
Ye must ride up the hall, your music so sweet,
More loud than your horses' echoing feet!
And loud and loud to Lord Roland call,
"Thy daughter is safe in Langdale hall!

## Notes

[39] *The touch…after rest* In a MS marginal note to a copy of the 1816 printed text, Coleridge wrote: 'Christabel for a moment sees her mother's spirit.'

[40] *Irthing flood…Halegarth Wood* In a MS marginal note to a copy of the 1816 printed text, Coleridge wrote: 'How gladly Sir Leoline repeats the names and shows how familarly he had once been acquainted with all the spots and paths in the neighbourhood of his former friend's castle and residence.'

Thy beautiful daughter is safe and free –
Sir Leoline greets thee thus through me.
He bids thee come without delay
With all thy numerous array,
And take thy lovely daughter home;
And he will meet thee on the way
With all his numerous array,
White with their panting palfreys' foam!"
And, by mine honour, I will say
That I repent me of the day
When I spake words of fierce disdain
To Roland de Vaux of Tryermaine!
For since that evil hour hath flown,
Many a summer's sun have shone;
Yet ne'er found I a friend again
Like Roland de Vaux of Tryermaine.'

The lady fell and clasped his knees,
Her face upraised, her eyes o'erflowing;
And Bracy replied, with faltering voice,
His gracious hail[41] on all bestowing:
'Thy words, thou sire of Christabel,
Are sweeter than my harp can tell;
Yet might I gain a boon[42] of thee,
This day my journey should not be,
So strange a dream hath come to me,
That I had vowed with music loud
To clear yon wood from thing unblessed,
Warned by a vision in my rest!

For in my sleep I saw that dove,
That gentle bird whom thou dost love,
And call'st by thy own daughter's name –
Sir Leoline! I saw the same
Fluttering and uttering fearful moan
Among the green herbs[43] in the forest alone;
Which when I saw, and when I heard,
I wondered what might ail the bird,
For nothing near it could I see
Save the grass and green herbs underneath the old tree.

And in my dream methought I went
To search out what might there be found,
And what the sweet bird's trouble meant
That thus lay fluttering on the ground.
I went, and peered, and could descry
No cause for her distressful cry;

## Notes

[41] *hail* greeting.
[42] *boon* favour.
[43] *herbs* plants.

But yet for her dear lady's sake
I stooped, methought the dove to take,
When lo! I saw a bright green snake
Coiled around its wings and neck.
Green as the herbs on which it couched,
Close by the dove's its head it crouched,
And with the dove it heaves and stirs,
Swelling its neck as she swelled hers!

I woke; it was the midnight hour,
The clock was echoing in the tower;
But though my slumber was gone by,
This dream it would not pass away –
It seems to live upon my eye!
And thence I vowed this self-same day,
With music strong and saintly song,
To wander through the forest bare
Lest aught unholy loiter there.'

Thus Bracy said: the Baron the while,
Half-listening heard him with a smile,
Then turned to Lady Geraldine,
His eyes made up of wonder and love;
And said, in courtly accents fine,
'Sweet maid, Lord Roland's beauteous dove,
With arms more strong than harp or song,
Thy sire and I will crush the snake!'
He kissed her forehead as he spake,
And Geraldine, in maiden wise,
Casting down her large bright eyes,
With blushing cheek and courtesy fine
She turned her from Sir Leoline,
Softly gathering up her train
That o'er her right arm fell again,
And folded her arms across her chest,
And couched her head upon her breast,
And looked askance at Christabel –
Jesu Maria, shield her well!

A snake's small eye blinks dull and shy,
And the lady's eyes they shrunk in her head,
Each shrunk up to a serpent's eye;
And with somewhat of malice and more of dread
At Christabel she looked askance!
One moment and the sight was fled;
But Christabel, in dizzy trance,
Stumbling on the unsteady ground,
Shuddered aloud with a hissing sound;
And Geraldine again turned round
And like a thing that sought relief,
Full of wonder and full of grief,
She rolled her large bright eyes divine
Wildly on Sir Leoline.

The maid, alas! her thoughts are gone,
She nothing sees, no sight but one!
The maid, devoid of guile and sin,
I know not how, in fearful wise
So deeply had she drunken in
That look, those shrunken serpent eyes,
That all her features were resigned
To this sole image in her mind,
And passively did imitate
That look of dull and treacherous hate.
And thus she stood in dizzy trance,
Still picturing that look askance
With forced unconscious sympathy
Full before her father's view –
As far as such a look could be,
In eyes so innocent and blue!

But when the trance was o'er, the maid
Paused awhile and inly prayed,
Then falling at her father's feet,
'By my mother's soul do I entreat
That thou this woman send away!'
She said – and more she could not say,
For what she knew she could not tell,
O'er-mastered by the mighty spell.

Why is thy cheek so wan and wild,
Sir Leoline? Thy only child
Lies at thy feet, thy joy, thy pride,
So fair, so innocent, so mild –
The same for whom thy lady died!
Oh by the pangs of her dear mother,
Think thou no evil of thy child!
For her and thee, and for no other
She prayed the moment ere she died,
Prayed that the babe for whom she died
Might prove her dear lord's joy and pride!
That prayer her deadly pangs beguiled,
  Sir Leoline!
And would'st thou wrong thy only child,
  Her child and thine!

Within the Baron's heart and brain,
If thoughts like these had any share,
They only swelled his rage and pain
And did but work confusion there;
His heart was cleft with pain and rage,
His cheeks they quivered, his eyes were wild –
Dishonoured thus in his old age,
Dishonoured by his only child,
And all his hospitality
To th' insulted daughter of his friend
By more than woman's jealousy

Brought thus to a disgraceful end.
He rolled his eye with stern regard
Upon the gentle minstrel bard,
And said in tones abrupt, austere,
'Why, Bracy, dost thou loiter here?
I bade thee hence!' The bard obeyed;
And, turning from his own sweet maid,
The aged knight, Sir Leoline,
Led forth the lady Geraldine![44]

### *The Conclusion to Part II* [45]

A little child,[46] a limber elf,
Singing, dancing to itself,
A fairy thing with red round cheeks
That always finds and never seeks,
Makes such a vision to the sight
As fills a father's eyes with light,
And pleasures flow in so thick and fast
Upon his heart, that he[47] at last
Must needs express his love's excess
With words of unmeant bitterness.
Perhaps 'tis pretty to force together
Thoughts so all unlike each other,
To mutter and mock a broken charm,
To dally with wrong that does no harm.
Perhaps 'tis tender too and pretty
At each wild word to feel within
A sweet recoil of love and pity.
And what if, in a world of sin
(Oh sorrow and shame should this be true!),
Such giddiness of heart and brain
Comes seldom save from rage and pain,
So talks as it's most used to do.

## Notes

[44] The poem was never concluded, and partly for this reason was not included in *Lyrical Ballads* (1800). In later years Coleridge gave varying accounts of how it might have ended, including this, the most extensive, recorded by James Gillman: 'Over the mountains, the Bard, as directed by Sir Leoline, "hastes" with his disciple; but in consequence of one of those inundations supposed to be common in this country, the spot only where the castle once stood is discovered, the edifice itself being washed away. He determines to return. Geraldine being acquainted with all that is passing, like the Weird Sisters in *Macbeth*, vanishes. Reappearing, however, she waits the return of the Bard, exciting in the meantime, by her wily arts, all the anger she could rouse in the Baron's breast, as well as the jealousy of which he is described to have been susceptible. The old Bard and the youth at length arrive, and therefore she can no longer personate the character of Geraldine, the daughter of Lord Roland de Vaux, but changes her appearance to that of the accepted though absent lover of Christabel. Next ensues a courtship most distressing to Christabel, who feels (she knows not why) great disgust for her once favoured knight. This coldness is very painful to the Baron, who has no more conception than herself of the supernatural transformation. She at last yields to her father's entreaties, and consents to approach the altar with this hated suitor. The real lover returning, enters at this moment, and produces the ring which she once had given him in sign of her betrothment. Thus defeated, the supernatural being Geraldine disappears. As predicted, the castle bell tolls, the mother's voice is heard, and to the exceeding great joy of the parties, the rightful marriage takes place, after which follows a reconciliation and explanation between the father and daughter.'

[45] These lines were sent as a fragment to Southey in a letter of 6 May 1801 (Griggs ii 728); it is not clear whether they were at that time considered to form part of 'Christabel'. They appeared as the conclusion to Part II in the printed text of 1816.

[46] *A little child* Hartley Coleridge.

[47] *he* i.e. Hartley.

## *Letter from S.T. Coleridge to Thomas Poole, 6 April 1799*[1] (extract)

My baby has not lived in vain! This life has been to him what it is to all of us – education and development! Fling yourself forward into your immortality only a few thousand years, and how small will not the difference between one year old and sixty years appear! Consciousness! It is not otherwise necessary to our conceptions of future continuance than as connecting the *present link* of our being with the one *immediately* preceding it – and *that* degree of consciousness, *that* small portion of *memory*, it would not only be arrogant, but in the highest degree absurd, to deny even to a much younger infant.

'Tis a strange assertion that the essence of identity lies in *recollective* consciousness; 'twere scarcely less ridiculous to affirm that the 8 miles from Stowey to Bridgwater consist in the 8 milestones. Death in a doting old age falls upon my feelings ever as a more hopeless phenomenon than death in infancy – but *nothing* is hopeless.

What if the vital force which I sent from my arm into the stone, as I flung it in the air and skimmed it upon the water – what if even that did not perish? It was *Life*! It was a particle of *Being*! It was *Power*! – and *how could* it perish? *Life, Power, Being*! – organization may be and probably *is* their *effect*; their *cause* it *cannot* be! I have indulged very curious fancies concerning that force, that *swarm* of motive powers which I sent out of my body into that stone – and which, one by one, left the untractable or already possessed mass, and – but the German ocean lies between us. It is all too far to send you such fancies as these! Grief indeed,

Doth love to dally with fantastic thoughts,
And smiling, like a sickly moralist,
Finds some resemblance to her own concerns
In the straws of chance, and things inanimate![2]

But I cannot truly say that I grieve. I am perplexed, I am sad – and a little thing, a very trifle, would make me weep. But for the death of the baby I have *not* wept! Oh, this strange, strange, strange scene-shifter, death! – that giddies one with insecurity, and so unsubstantiates the living things that one has grasped and handled! Some months ago Wordsworth transmitted to me a most sublime epitaph;[3] whether it had any reality, I cannot say. Most probably, in some gloomier moment he had fancied the moment in which his sister might die.

## *The Day-Dream* (composed March 1802, published *The Morning Post* 19 October 1802)[1]

I

If thou wert here, these tears were 'tears of light'![2]
But from as sweet a day-dream did I start
As ever made these eyes grow idly bright;

### Notes

LETTER FROM S.T. COLERIDGE TO THOMAS POOLE

[1] Coleridge's son, Berkeley (born 14 May 1798), died 10 February 1799 during his father's stay in Germany. At first the news was kept from Coleridge, but later Poole thought it better to let him know. This letter is Coleridge's first written response to the news, from Göttingen.

[2] Coleridge quotes himself: *Osorio* V i 11–14.

[3] *a most sublime epitaph* 'A Slumber did my Spirit Seal'.

THE DAY-DREAM

[1] The date of composition is conjectural, based on George Whalley's argument that the poem was written prior to 'A Letter to Sara Hutchinson', probably at Greta Hall. When published in *The Morning Post*, in somewhat revised form, it appeared under the title, 'The Day-Dream, from an Emigrant to his Absent Wife'.

[2] *tears of light* The phrase is borrowed from Wordsworth, 'Matthew' 23–4: 'The tears which came to Matthew's eyes / Were tears of light, the oil of gladness.'

And though I weep, yet still about the heart
A dear and playful tenderness doth linger,
Touching my heart as with a baby's finger.

2

My mouth half-open like a witless man,
I saw the couch, I saw the quiet room,
The heaving shadows and the firelight gloom;
And on my lips I know not what there ran –
On my unmoving lips a subtile[3] feeling;
I know not what, but had the same been stealing

3

Upon a sleeping mother's lips, I guess
It would have made the loving mother dream
That she was softly stooping down to kiss
Her babe, that something more than babe did seem –
An obscure presence of its darling father,
Yet still its own sweet baby self far rather!

4

Across my chest there lived a weight so warm
As if some bird had taken shelter there;
And lo, upon the couch, a woman's form! –
Thine, Sara,[4] thine! Oh joy, if thine it were!
I gazed with anxious hope, and feared to stir it –
A deeper trance ne'er rapt a yearning spirit!

5

And now, when I seemed *sure* my love to see,
Her very self in her own quiet home,
There came an elfish laugh, and wakened me!
'Twas Hartley,[5] who behind my chair had clomb,[6]
And with his bright eyes at my face was peeping;
I blessed him, tried to laugh – and fell a-weeping.

## *The Picture; or, The Lover's Resolution* (composed March 1802; published in *The Morning Post*, 6 September 1802)[1]

Through weeds and thorns, and matted underwood
I force my way; now climb, and now descend
O'er rocks, or bare or mossy, with blind foot
Crushing the purple whorts;[2] while oft unseen,

## Notes

[3] *subtile* delicate, fine.

[4] Sara Hutchinson (1775–1835), Coleridge's 'Asra', was Wordsworth's sister-in-law. Coleridge's unconsummated love for her lasted until his break with Wordsworth led him to reside in London.

[5] Hartley Coleridge (b. 1796).

[6] *clomb* climbed.

The Picture; or, The Lover's Resolution

[1] In March 1802 Coleridge made the following entry in a notebook: 'A poem on the endeavour to emancipate the soul from day-dreams and note the different attempts and the vain ones' (*Notebooks* i 1153). The poem was 'The Picture'.

[2] *whorts* whortleberries.

Hurrying along the drifted forest leaves,
The scared snake rustles. Onward still I toil,
I know not, ask not whither. A new joy
Lovely as light, sudden as summer gust
And gladsome as the first-born of the spring,
Beckons me on, or follows from behind,
Playmate or guide. The master-passion quelled,
I feel that I am free. With dun-red bark
The fir-trees and th' unfrequent slender oak
Forth from this tangle wild of bush and brake
Soar up, and form a melancholy vault
High o'er me, murm'ring like a distant sea.
No myrtle-walks are here![3] These are no groves
For Love[4] to dwell in; the low stumps would gore
His dainty feet; the briar and the thorn
Make his plumes haggard; till, like wounded bird,
Easily caught, the dusky dryads,[5]
With prickles sharper than his darts, would mock
His little godship, making him perforce
Creep through a thorn-bush on yon hedgehog's back.
This is my hour of triumph! I can now
With my own fancies play the merry fool,
And laugh away worse folly, being free.
Here will I seat myself beside this old,
Hollow, and woody oak, which ivy-twine
Clothes, as with network;[6] here will couch my limbs
Close by this river, in this silent shade,
As safe and sacred from the step of man
As an invisible world – unheard, unseen,[7]
And list'ning only to the pebbly stream
That murmurs with a dead yet bell-like sound
Tinkling, or bees, that in the neighb'ring trunk
Make honey-hoards. This breeze that visits me
Was never Love's accomplice, never raised
The tendril ringlets from the maiden's brow,
And the blue, delicate veins above her cheek;
Ne'er played the wanton, never half-disclosed
The maiden's snowy bosom, scatt'ring thence
Eye-poisons for some love-distempered youth,
Who ne'er, henceforth, may see an aspen-grove
Shiver in sunshine, but his feeble heart
Shall flow away like a dissolving thing.
Sweet breeze! thou only, if I guess aright,
Liftest the feathers of the robin's breast,
Who swells his little breast, so full of song,

## Notes

[3] *No myrtle-walks are here* Coleridge may be recalling the myrtle at Clevedon, mentioned at 'Eolian Harp' (1795) 4–5 and 'Reflections on Having Left a Place of Retirement' 5.

[4] *Love* cupid.

[5] *dryads* wood-nymphs.

[6] *network* light fabric made of netted threads.

[7] *Close by…unseen* cf. Coleridge's notebook entry, March 1802: 'A river, so translucent as not to be seen – and yet murmuring – shadowy world – and these a dream / Enchanted river.'

Singing above me on the mountain ash.
And thou too, desert stream! No pool of thine,
Though clear as lake in latest summer eve,
Did e'er reflect the stately virgin's robe,
The face, the form divine, her downcast look
Contemplative, her cheek upon her palm
Supported; the white arm and elbow rest
On the bare branch of half-uprooted tree,
That leans towards its mirror! He, meanwhile,
Who from her count'nance turned, or looked by stealth
(For fear is true love's cruel nurse), he now,
With steadfast gaze and unoffending eye,
Worships the wat'ry idol, dreaming hopes
Delicious to the soul – but fleeting, vain
Ev'n as that phantom-world on which he gazed!
She (sportive tyrant) with her left hand plucks
The heads of tall flow'rs that behind her grow –
Lychnis, and willow-herb, and foxglove-bells;
And suddenly, as one that toys with time,
Scatters them on the pool! Then all the charm
Is broken – all that phantom world so fair
Vanishes, and a thousand circlets spread,
And each misshape the other. Stay awhile,
Poor youth, who scarcely dar'st lift up thine eyes –
The stream will soon renew its smoothness, soon
The visions will return! And lo, he stays,
And soon the fragments dim of lovely forms
Come trembling back, unite, and now once more
The pool becomes a mirror;[8] and behold
Each wild-flow'r on the marge inverted there,
And there the half-uprooted tree – but where,
Oh where the virgin's snowy arm, that leaned
On its bare branch? He turns, and she is gone!
Homeward she steals through many a woodland maze
Which he shall seek in vain. Ill-fated youth,
Go, day by day, and waste thy manly prime
In mad love-gazing on the vacant brook,
Till sickly thoughts bewitch thine eyes, and thou
Behold'st her shadow still abiding there,
The naiad of the mirror![9]
Not to thee,
Oh wild and desert stream, belongs this tale.
Gloomy and dark art thou; the crowded firs
Tow'r from thy shores, and stretch across thy bed,
Making thee doleful as a cavern well!
Save when the shy kingfishers build their nest
On thy steep banks, no loves hast thou, wild stream!

## Notes

[8] Lines 69–78 are quoted by Coleridge in the introduction to the printed text of 'Kubla Khan' (1816), p. 640.

[9] *naiad of the mirror* nymph of the pond.

This be my chosen haunt – emancipate[10]
From passion's dreams, a freeman, and alone,
I rise and trace its devious course. Oh lead,
Lead me to deeper shades, to lonelier glooms.
Lo! stealing through the canopy of firs,
How fair the sunshine spots that mossy rock,
Isle of the river, whose disparted[11] waters
Dart off asunder with an angry sound,
How soon to reunite! They meet, they join
In deep embrace, and open to the sun
Lie calm and smooth. Such the delicious hour
Of deep enjoyment, foll'wing love's brief quarrels!
And hark, the noise of a near waterfall!
I come out into light – I find myself
Beneath a weeping birch (most beautiful
Of forest trees, the lady of the woods)
Hard by the brink of a tall weedy rock
That overbrows the cataract. How bursts
The landscape on my sight! Two crescent hills
Fold in behind each other, and so make
A circular vale, and landlocked, as might seem,
With brook and bridge, and grey-stone cottages,
Half hid by rocks and fruit-trees. Beneath my feet
The whortleberries are bedewed with spray,
Dashed upwards by the furious waterfall.
How solemnly the pendent ivy mass
Swings in its winnow![12] All the air is calm,
The smoke from cottage chimneys, tinged with light,
Rises in columns; from this house alone
Close by the waterfall, the column slants
And feels its ceaseless breeze. But what is this?
That cottage, with its slanting chimney smoke,
And close beside its porch a sleeping child,
His dear head pillowed on a sleeping dog,
One arm between its forelegs, and the hand
Holds loosely its small handful of wild-flow'rs,
Unfilletted,[13] and of unequal lengths –
A curious picture, with a master's haste
Sketched on a strip of pinky-silver skin
Peeled from the birchen bark! Divinest maid –
Yon bark her canvas, and these purple berries
Her pencil! See, the juice is scarcely dried
On the fine skin! She has been newly here,
And lo! Yon patch of heath has been her couch –
The pressure still remains! Oh blessed couch,

## Notes

[10] *emancipate* free (i.e. from romantic entanglement).

[11] *disparted* divided (by the rock).

[12] *winnow* swinging motion caused by the spray of the waterfall.

[13] *Unfilletted* i.e. the stems of the bunch of flowers are not tied up together.

For this may'st thou flow'r early, and the sun
Slanting, at eve rest bright, and linger long
Upon thy purple bells! Oh Isabel,
Daughter of genius, stateliest of our maids,
More beautiful than whom Alcaeus wooed,
The Lesbian woman of immortal song,[14]
Oh child of genius, stately, beautiful,
And full of love to all, save only one,
And not ungentle ev'n to me! My heart,
Why beats it thus? Through yonder coppice-wood
Needs must the pathway turn, that leads away
On to her father's house. She is alone!
The night draws on – such ways are hard to hit –
And fit it is I should restore this sketch
Dropped unawares, no doubt. Why should I yearn
To keep the relic? 'Twill but idly feed
The passion that consumes me. Let me haste!
This picture in my hand, which she has left;
She cannot blame me, that I followed her,
And I may be her guide the long wood through!

## *A Letter to Sara Hutchinson, 4 April 1802. Sunday Evening*[1]

I

Well! if the bard was weather-wise who made
The dear old ballad of Sir Patrick Spence,
This night, so tranquil now, will not go hence
Unroused by winds that ply a busier trade
Than that which moulds yon clouds in lazy flakes,
Or the dull sobbing draught that drones and rakes
Upon the strings of this Eolian lute,[2]
Which better far were mute.
For lo! the new moon, winter-bright,
And all suffused[3] with phantom light
(With swimming phantom light o'erspread,
But rimmed and circled with a silver thread);
I see the old moon in her lap, foretelling
The coming-on of rain and squally blast.
Ah Sara![4] that the gust ev'n now were swelling,
And the slant night-shower driving loud and fast.

## Notes

[14] *whom Alcaeus…song* Sappho.

A Letter to Sara Hutchinson

[1] In the MS the title actually reads 'A Letter to ——', but there can be no doubt that the addressee was Sara Hutchinson. 4 April 1802 was the day before Wordsworth set out to propose marriage to Mary Hutchinson. This is the poem from which Coleridge derived 'Dejection: An Ode'.

[2] *Eolian lute* Aeolian harps were placed lengthways in front of open windows, where their strings were 'played' by the wind.

[3] *suffused* overspread.

[4] Sara Hutchinson (1775–1835), Wordsworth's sister-in-law.

2

A grief without a pang – void, dark, and drear;
A stifling, drowsy, unimpassioned grief
That finds no natural outlet, no relief
In word, or sigh, or tear –
This, Sara, well thou know'st,
Is that sore evil which I dread the most
And oft'nest suffer in this heartless mood,
To other thoughts by yonder throstle wooed,
That pipes within the larch-tree not unseen
(The larch which pushes out in tassels green
Its bundled leafits), wooed to mild delights
By all the tender sounds and gentle sights
Of this sweet primrose-month – and *vainly* wooed,
Oh dearest Sara, in this heartless[5] mood.

3

All this long eve so balmy and serene
Have I been gazing on the western sky
And its peculiar tint of yellow-green;
And still I gaze, and with how blank an eye!
And those thin clouds above, in flakes and bars,
That give away their motion to the stars,
Those stars that glide behind them and between,
Now sparkling, now bedimmed, but always seen;
Yon crescent moon, as fixed as if it grew
In its own cloudless, starless lake of blue –
A boat becalmed! Dear William's sky canoe![6]
I see them all, so excellently fair;
I *see*, not *feel*, how beautiful they are!

4

My genial spirits fail,[7]
And what can these avail
To lift the smoth'ring weight from off my breast?
It were a vain endeavour,
Though I should gaze forever
On that green light that lingers in the west:[8]
I may not hope from outward forms to win
The passion and the life, whose fountains are within;
These lifeless shapes, around, below, above –
Oh dearest Sara, what can they impart?
Even when the gentle thought that thou, my love,
Art gazing now like me
And see'st the heaven I see –
Sweet thought it is, yet feebly stirs my heart!

## Notes

[5] *heartless* depressed, discouraged.

[6] *Dear William's sky canoe* As featured in the prologue to Wordsworth's 'Peter Bell' (composed 1798, published 1819).

[7] *My genial spirits fail* An echo of Milton, 'Samson Agonistes' 594: 'my genial spirits droop.'

[8] *that green light that lingers in the west* Borrowed from Southey, 'Madoc' (1805) II xxxvi 260: 'The last green light that lingers in the west.'

5

Feebly, oh feebly! Yet
(I well remember it)
In my first dawn of youth, that fancy stole
With many gentle yearnings on my soul.
At eve, sky-gazing in 'ecstatic fit'[9]
(Alas, far-cloistered in a city school,[10]
The sky was all I knew of beautiful),
At the barred window often did I sit,
And often on the leaded school-roof lay,
    And to myself would say,
'There does not live the man so stripped of good affections
As not to love to see a maiden's quiet eyes
Upraised and linking on sweet dreams by dim connections
To moon, or evening star, or glorious western skies!'
While yet a boy, this thought would so pursue me,
That often it became a kind of vision to me.

6

Sweet thought, and dear of old
To hearts of finer mould![11]
Ten thousand times by friends and lovers blessed!
    I spake with rash despair,
    And ere I was aware,
The weight was somewhat lifted from my breast!
Dear Sara! in the weather-fended wood,[12]
Thy loved haunt where the stock-doves coo at noon,
    I guess that thou hast stood
And watched yon crescent and that ghost-like moon;
    And yet far rather, in my present mood,
I would that thou'dst been sitting all this while
Upon the sod-built seat of camomile,[13]
And though thy robin may have ceased to sing,
Yet needs for *my* sake must thou love to hear
The beehive murmuring near –
That ever-busy and most quiet thing
Which I have heard at midnight murmuring.

7

    I feel my spirit moved:
    And wheresoe'er thou be,
    Oh sister, oh beloved!
Thy dear mild eyes that see
The very heaven *I* see –
There is a prayer in them, it is for *me*!
And I, dear Sara, *I* am blessing *thee*![14]

## Notes

[9] Milton, 'The Passion' 42.

[10] *a city school* Christ's Hospital in the City of London.

[11] *mould* form.

[12] *the weather-fended wood* The wood provides cover from wind and rain, and is therefore weather (de)fended. The phrase 'weather-fends' is from Shakespeare, *The Tempest* V i 10.

[13] *the sod-built seat of camomile* 'Sara's seat' was built by Coleridge and the Wordsworths on White Moss Common, Rydal, 10 October 1801.

[14] *I am blessing thee* One in a long line of benedictions; cf. those of Hartley in 'Frost at Midnight' and Charles Lamb in 'This Lime-Tree Bower My Prison'.

8

It was as calm as this, the happy night[15]
When Mary, thou and I together were,
The low decaying fire our only light,
And listened to the stillness of the air!
Oh, that affectionate and blameless maid,
Dear Mary, on her lap my head she laid –
    Her hand was on my brow
    Even as my own is now,
And on my cheek I felt thy eyelash play.[16]
Such joy I had that I may truly say
My spirit was awe-stricken with the excess
And trance-like depth of its brief happiness.

9

Ah fair remembrances that so revive
My heart and fill it with a living power –
Where were they, Sara? Or did I not strive
To win them to me on the fretting hour
Then when I wrote thee that complaining scroll,[17]
Which even to bodily sickness bruised thy soul?
And yet thou blam'st thyself alone, and yet
    Forbidd'st me all regret.[18]

10

And must I not *regret* that I distressed
Thee, best beloved, who lovest me the best?
My better mind had fled I know not whither –
For oh! was this an absent friend's employ,
To send from far both pain and sorrow thither,
Where still his blessings should have called down joy?
I read thy guileless letter o'er again,
I hear thee of thy blameless self complain,
And only this I learn – and this, alas, I know –
That thou art weak and pale with sickness, grief, and pain,
And *I* – *I* made thee so!

11

Oh, *for my own sake*, I regret *perforce*
Whatever turns *thee*, Sara, from the course
Of calm well-being and a heart at rest.
When thou and, with thee, those whom thou lov'st best
Shall dwell together in one quiet home,

## Notes

[15] *the happy night* The exact date is not known, but it was during Coleridge's visit to Gallow Hill, 2–13 March 1802. It is recalled also in 'The Day-Dream' and 'A Day-Dream'.

[16] *And on my cheek...play* cf. 'A Day-Dream' 31–2: 'Thine eyelash on my cheek doth play – / 'Tis Mary's hand upon my brow!'

[17] *that complaining scroll* A letter to Sara. The 'bodily sickness' of l. 116 may be the sickness into which she had fallen by 29 February 1802, which drew Coleridge back to Gallow Hill from London. He remained at Gallow Hill from 2 to 13 March, weeping aloud when he left for Keswick.

[18] Coleridge's letters not infrequently caused Sara distress.

One home the sure *abiding* home of all,
I too will crown me with a coronal;[19]
Nor shall this heart in idle wishes roam
    Morbidly soft!
No, let me trust that I shall wear away
In no inglorious toils the manly day;
And only now and then, and not too oft,
Some dear and memorable eve shall bless,
Dreaming of all your love and happiness.

12

Be happy, and I need thee not in sight!
Peace in thy heart, and quiet in thy dwelling,
Health in thy limbs, and in thy eyes the light
Of love, and hope, and honourable feeling;
Where'er I am, I needs must be content –
Not near thee, haply shall be more content!
To all things I prefer the permanent.[20]
And better seems it for a heart like mine
Always to *know*, than sometimes to *behold*
    Their happiness and thine:
For change doth trouble me with pangs untold!
To see thee, hear thee, feel thee, then to part –
    Oh, it weighs down the heart!
To visit those I love, as I love *thee*,
Mary, William, and dear Dorothy,
It is but a temptation to repine!
The transientness is poison in the wine,
Eats out the pith of joy, makes all joy hollow,
All pleasure a dim dream of pain to follow!
My own peculiar lot, my household life,
It is (and will remain) indifference or strife;
While ye are well and happy, 'twould but wrong you
If I should fondly yearn to be among you –
Wherefore, oh wherefore, should I wish to be
A withered branch upon a blossoming tree?

13

But (let me say it, for I vainly strive
To beat away the thought) – but if thou pined,
Whate'er the cause, in body or in mind,
I were the miserablest man alive
To know it and be absent! Thy delights
Far off or near, alike shall I partake –
But oh! to mourn for thee, and to forsake
All power, all hope of giving comfort to thee;
To know that thou art weak and worn with pain

## Notes

[19] *I too…coronal* An allusion to Wordsworth's 'Ode': 'My heart is at your festival, / My head hath its coronal' (ll. 39–40).

[20] *To all things…permanent* cf. Wordsworth's reference to the 'beautiful and permanent forms of nature', Preface to *Lyrical Ballads*, p. 508.

And not to hear thee, Sara, not to view thee,
    Not sit beside thy bed,
    Not press thy aching head,
    Not bring thee health again,
    At least to hope, to try
By this voice which thou lov'st, and by this earnest eye –

14

Nay, wherefore did I let it haunt my mind,
    This dark distressful dream?
I turn from it and listen to the wind
Which long has howled unnoticed! What a scream
Of agony, by torture lengthened out,
That lute sent forth! Oh thou wild storm without!
Or crag, or tairn,[21] or lightning-blasted tree,
Or pine-grove whither woodman never clomb,[22]
Or lonely house long held the witches' home,
Methinks were fitter instruments for thee,
Mad lutanist, that in this month of showers,
Of dark-brown gardens and of peeping flowers,
Mak'st devil's yule,[23] with worse than wintry song,
The blooms and buds and timorous leaves among!
Thou actor, perfect in all tragic sounds,
Thou mighty poet, even to frenzy bold,
    What tell'st thou now about?
'Tis of a rushing of an host[24] in rout,
And many groans from men with smarting wounds,[25]
That groan at once from smart, and shudder with the cold!
But hush, there is a break of deepest silence –
Again! But that dread sound, as of a rushing crowd,
And groans and tremulous shuddering – all are over.
And it has other sounds, and all less deep, less loud;
        A tale of less affright,
    And tempered with delight,
As William's self had made the tender lay!
        'Tis of a little child
    Upon a heathy wild[26]
Not far from home, but it has lost its way,
And now moans low in utter grief and fear,
And now screams loud, and hopes to make its mother hear!

15

'Tis midnight, and small thought have I of sleep –
Full seldom may my friend[27] such vigils keep –

## Notes

[21] *tairn* expanse of water high among the mountains.

[22] *clomb* climbed.

[23] *yule* festival; yule was the pagan festival that became Christmas. This is the devil's yule because it is April rather than December.

[24] *host* army.

[25] *an host…wounds* Coleridge was very conscious of the war against France, which had been going on since 1793 and which had halted (temporarily) after signing of the Treaty of Amiens, just a week before.

[26] *a little child…wild* Coleridge has in mind Wordsworth's 'Lucy Gray', published in *Lyrical Ballads* (1800).

[27] *my friend* Sara Hutchinson.

Oh breathe she softly in her gentle sleep!
Cover her, gentle sleep, with wings of healing,
And be this tempest but a mountain birth!
May all the stars hang bright above her dwelling,
Silent, as though they watched the sleeping earth,
Like elder sisters with love-twinkling eyes!
Healthful and light, my darling, may'st thou rise,
And of the same good tidings to me send –
For oh, beloved friend!
I am not the buoyant thing I was of yore,
When like an own child, I to joy belonged;
For others mourning oft, myself oft sorely wronged,
Yet bearing all things then as if I nothing bore.

16

Ere I was wedded,[28] though my path was rough,
The joy within me dallied with distress,
And all misfortunes were but as the stuff
Whence fancy made me dreams of happiness;
For hope grew round me like the climbing vine,
And leaves and fruitage not my own, seemed mine!
But now ill tidings bow me down to earth,
Nor care I that they rob me of my mirth;
    But oh! each visitation
Suspends what nature gave me at my birth –
My shaping spirit of imagination!
I speak not now of those habitual ills
That wear out life, when two unequal minds
Meet in one house, and two discordant wills –
    This leaves me where it finds,
Past cure and past complaint – a fate austere
Too fixed and hopeless to partake of fear!

17

But thou, *dear* Sara (dear indeed thou art,
My comforter, a heart within my heart!),
Thou and the few we love, though few ye be,
Make up a world of hopes and fears for me.
And when affliction or distempering pain
Or wayward chance befall you, I complain
Not that I mourn – oh friends most dear, most true!
    Methinks to weep with you
Were better far than to rejoice alone –
But that my coarse domestic life[29] has known
No griefs but such as dull and deaden me,
No habits of heart-nursing sympathy,
No mutual mild enjoyments of its own,

## Notes

[28] *Ere I was wedded* Before Coleridge married Sara Fricker in 1795 he had enjoyed a career as a political lecturer and pamphleteer.

[29] *my coarse domestic life* Coleridge's marriage was disintegrating.

No hopes of its own vintage – none, oh none! –
Whence, when I mourn for you, my heart must borrow
Fair forms and living motions for its sorrow.
For not to think of what I needs must feel,
But to be still and patient all I can,
And haply by abstruse research to steal
From my own nature all the natural man –
This was my sole resource, my wisest plan;
And that which suits a part infects the whole,
And now is almost grown the temper of my soul.[30]

18

My little children[31] are a joy, a love,
    A good gift from above!
But what is bliss, that ever calls up woe,
  And makes it doubly keen,
Compelling me to feel what well I know –
What a most blessed lot mine *might* have been.
Those little angel children (woe is me!),
There have been hours when, feeling how they bind
And pluck out the wing-feathers of my mind,
Turning my error to necessity,
I have half-wished they never had been born![32]
That, seldom; but sad thought they always bring,
And, like the poet's nightingale,[33] I sing
My love-song with my breast against a thorn.

19

With no unthankful spirit I confess
This clinging grief, too, in its turn awakes
That love and father's joy – but oh! it makes
The love the greater, and the joy far less.
These mountains too, these vales, these woods, these lakes,
Scenes full of beauty and of loftiness
Where all my life I fondly hope to live –
I were sunk low indeed, did they *no* solace give.
But oft I seem to feel, and evermore to fear,
They are not to me now the things which once they were.[34]

20

Oh Sara, we receive but what we give,
And in *our* life alone does nature live;

## Notes

[30] *For not…soul* These lines were not included in 'Dejection: An Ode' in 1802, but were readmitted to the 1817 text.

[31] *My little children* Hartley (b. 1796) and Derwent (b. 1800). Sara would be born 23 December 1802.

[32] *I have…born* The unsatisfactoriness of his marriage was largely the cause of these guilty feelings about his children, with whom he was spending less and less time; cf. 'The Day-Dream' 25–30, and his comment to his wife in a letter of Christmas Day 1801: 'Oh my dear Hartley, my Derwent! My children! The night before last I dreamt I saw them so vividly, that I was quite ill in the morning and wept my eyes red.'

[33] *the poet's nightingale* Philomela, one of the subjects of Ovid's *Metamorphoses*. She was seduced by her brother-in-law, Tereus King of Thrace, who cut out her tongue to prevent her from incriminating him. She was finally turned into a nightingale, her sad song said to derive from the thorn in her breast.

[34] *They are not…were* A reworking of Wordsworth, 'Ode' 9: 'The things which I have seen I now can see no more.'

Ours is her wedding-garment, ours her shroud!
And would we aught behold of higher worth
Than that inanimate cold world allowed
To the poor, loveless, ever-anxious crowd –
Ah! from the soul itself must issue forth
A light, a glory,[35] and a luminous cloud
Enveloping the earth!
And from the soul itself must there be sent
A sweet and potent voice, of its own birth,
Of all sweet sounds the life and element.
Oh pure of heart![36] thou need'st not ask of me
What this strange music in the soul may be,
What and wherein it doth exist,
This light, this glory, this fair luminous mist,
This beautiful and beauty-making power!
Joy,[37] innocent Sara! Joy that ne'er was given
Save to the pure and in their purest hour,
Joy, Sara, is the spirit and the power
That, wedding nature to us, gives in dower[38]
A new earth and new heaven
Undreamt of by the sensual and the proud!
Joy is that sweet voice, joy that luminous cloud –
We, we ourselves rejoice!
And thence flows all that charms or ear or sight,
All melodies the echoes of that voice,
All colours a suffusion from that light.
Sister and friend[39] of my devoutest[40] choice!
Thou being innocent and full of love,
And nested with the darlings of thy love;
And feeling in thy soul, heart, lips, and arms
Even what the conjugal and mother dove
That borrows genial warmth from these she warms
Feels in her thrilled wings, blessedly outspread[41] –
Thou, freed awhile from cares and human dread
By the immenseness of the good and fair
Which thou seest everywhere –
Thus, thus would'st thou rejoice!
To thee would all things *live* from pole to pole,
Their life the eddying of thy living soul.
Oh dear! Oh innocent! Oh full of love!
Sara, thou friend of my devoutest[42] choice,
As dear as light and impulse from above –
So may'st thou ever, evermore rejoice!

## Notes

[35] *glory* divine effulgence of light, as at Wordsworth, 'Ode' 18.

[36] *Oh pure of heart* Sara Hutchinson.

[37] *Joy* In a notebook entry Coleridge glossed joy as 'when the heart is full as of a deep and quiet fountain overflowing insensibly, or the gladness of joy, when the fountain becomes ebullient'.

[38] *dower* a wedding-gift.

[39] *Sister and friend* i.e. Sara Hutchinson.

[40] *devoutest* most devoted, most attached.

[41] *Even what…outspread* Coleridge has in mind the moment of creation, *Paradise Lost* i 21–2, where the Holy Spirit 'Dove-like sat'st brooding on the vast abyss / And madest it pregnant'.

[42] *devoutest* most devoted, most attached.

## *A Day-Dream* (composed June 1802; published 1828)

My eyes make pictures, when they are shut:
I see a fountain, large and fair,
A willow and a ruined hut,[1]
And thee,[2] and me, and Mary[3] there.
Oh Mary, make thy gentle lap our pillow!
Bend o'er us, like a bower, my beautiful green willow!

A wild rose roofs the ruined shed,
And that and summer well agree;
And lo! where Mary leans her head –
Two dear names carved upon the tree!
And Mary's tears, they are not tears of sorrow:
Our sister and our friend[4] will both be here tomorrow.
'Twas day! But now few, large, and bright
The stars are round the crescent moon!
And now it is a dark warm night,
The balmiest of the month of June!
A glow-worm fallen, and on the marge remounting
Shines, and its shadow[5] shines, fit stars for our sweet fountain.

Oh ever, ever be thou blessed!
For dearly, Asra, love I thee!
This brooding warmth across my breast,[6]
This depth of tranquil bliss – ah me!
Fount, tree and shed are gone, I know not whither,
But in one quiet room we three are still together.

The shadows dance upon the wall
By the still dancing fire-flames made;
And now they slumber, moveless all,
And now they melt to one deep shade!
But not from me shall this mild darkness steal thee;
I dream thee with mine eyes, and at my heart I feel thee.

Thine eyelash on my cheek doth play –
'Tis Mary's hand upon my brow![7]
But let me check this tender lay
Which none may hear but she and thou!
Like the still hive at quiet midnight humming,
Murmur it to yourselves, ye two beloved women!

## Notes

A DAY-DREAM

[1] *hut* cottage.

[2] *thee* Sara Hutchinson (1775–1835), Wordsworth's sister-in-law.

[3] Mary Hutchinson (1770–1859), who married Wordsworth on 4 October 1802.

[4] *Our sister and our friend* Dorothy and William Wordsworth.

[5] *shadow* reflection (in the fountain).

[6] *This brooding warmth…breast* Sara has become the 'the conjugal and mother dove' of 'A Letter to Sara Hutchinson' 327–9.

[7] *Thine eyelash…brow* cf. 'A Letter to Sara Hutchinson' 104–7.

## *Dejection: An Ode* (composed *c.*July 1802)[1]

*Late, late yestreen I saw the new moon*
*With the old moon in her arms;*
*And I fear, I fear, my master dear,*
*We shall have a deadly storm.*
(*Ballad of Sir Patrick Spence*)

I

Well! if the bard was weather-wise who made
The grand old ballad of Sir Patrick Spence,
This night, so tranquil now, will not go hence
Unroused by winds that ply a busier trade
Than those which mould yon clouds in lazy flakes,
Or the dull sobbing draught that moans and rakes
Upon the strings of this Eolian lute,[2]
Which better far were mute.
For lo! the new moon, winter-bright,
And overspread with phantom light
(With swimming phantom light o'erspread,
But rimmed and circled by a silver thread);
I see the old moon in her lap, foretelling
The coming-on of rain and squally blast.
And oh, that even now the gust were swelling,
And the slant night-shower driving loud and fast.
Those sounds which oft have raised me whilst they awed
And sent my soul abroad,
Might now perhaps their wonted[3] impulse give,
Might startle this dull pain, and make it move and live!

II

A grief without a pang – void, dark, and drear;
A stifled, drowsy, unimpassioned grief
Which finds no natural outlet, no relief
In word, or sigh, or tear –
Oh Lady![4] in this wan and heartless mood,
To other thoughts by yonder throstle wooed
All this long eve so balmy and serene,
Have I been gazing on the western sky
And its peculiar tint of yellow-green;
And still I gaze, and with how blank an eye!
And those thin clouds above, in flakes and bars,
That give away their motion to the stars,

## Notes

DEJECTION: AN ODE

[1] Coleridge first published this poem in *The Morning Post*, 4 October 1802, as a sort of gift to Wordsworth, whose wedding-day it was (as well as being the seventh anniversary of Coleridge's own unhappy marriage). In that version he addressed it to 'Edmund'; in this text the addressee is a 'Lady'.

[2] *Eolian lute* Aeolian harps were placed lengthways in front of open windows, where their strings were 'played' by the wind; see Coleridge's 'The Eolian Harp'.

[3] *wonted* expected, usual.

[4] *Lady* Coleridge has in mind the original addressee of this work, Sara Hutchinson.

Those stars that glide behind them or between,
Now sparkling, now bedimmed, but always seen;
Yon crescent moon, as fixed as if it grew
In its own cloudless, starless lake of blue –
I see them all, so excellently fair;
I see, not feel, how beautiful they are!

III

My genial spirits fail,[5]
And what can these avail
To lift the smoth'ring weight from off my breast?
It were a vain endeavour,
Though I should gaze for ever
On that green light that lingers in the west:
I may not hope from outward forms to win
The passion and the life, whose fountains are within!

IV

Oh Lady, we receive but what we give,
And in our life alone does nature live;
Ours is her wedding-garment, ours her shroud!
And would we aught behold of higher worth
Than that inanimate cold world allowed
To the poor loveless ever-anxious crowd –
Ah! from the soul itself must issue forth
A light, a glory,[6] a fair luminous cloud
Enveloping the earth!
And from the soul itself must there be sent
A sweet and potent voice, of its own birth,
Of all sweet sounds the life and element.

V

Oh pure of heart![7] thou need'st not ask of me
What this strong music in the soul may be,
What and wherein it doth exist,
This light, this glory, this fair luminous mist,
This beautiful and beauty-making power!
Joy, virtuous Lady! Joy that ne'er was given
Save to the pure and in their purest hour,
Life, and life's effluence,[8] cloud at once and shower,
Joy, Lady, is the spirit and the power
Which, wedding nature to us, gives in dower[9]
A new earth and new heaven
Undreamt of by the sensual and the proud!
Joy is the sweet voice, joy the luminous cloud –
We in ourselves rejoice!

## Notes

[5] *My genial spirits fail* An echo of Milton, 'Samson Agonistes' 594: 'my genial spirits droop.'
[6] *glory* divine effulgence of light.
[7] *Oh pure of heart* the addressee of the poem, in this case, 'Lady'.
[8] *effluence* emanation, radiating energies.
[9] *dower* wedding-gift.

And thence flows all that charms or ear or sight,
    All melodies the echoes of that voice,
All colours a suffusion from that light.

VI

There was a time[10] when, though my path was rough,
    This joy within me dallied with distress,
And all misfortunes were but as the stuff
    Whence fancy made me dreams of happiness;
For hope grew round me like the twining vine,
And fruits and foliage not my own, seemed mine!
But now afflictions bow me down to earth,
Nor care I that they rob me of my mirth;
        But oh! each visitation
Suspends what nature gave me at my birth –
    My shaping spirit of imagination!
For not to think of what I needs must feel,
    But to be still and patient all I can,
And haply by abstruse research to steal
    From my own nature all the natural man –
    This was my sole resource, my only plan;
Till that which suits a part infects the whole,
And now is almost grown the habit of my soul.

VII

Hence, viper thoughts, that coil around my mind,
    Reality's dark dream!
I turn from you, and listen to the wind,
    Which long has raved unnoticed. What a scream
Of agony, by torture lengthened out,
That lute sent forth! Thou wind, that rav'st without!
    Bare crag, or mountain tairn,[11] or blasted tree,
Or pine-grove whither woodman never clomb,[12]
Or lonely house long held the witches' home,
    Methinks were fitter instruments for thee,
Mad lutanist, who in this month of show'rs,
Of dark-brown gardens and of peeping flow'rs,
Mak'st devil's yule,[13] with worse than wintry song,
The blossoms, buds, and tim'rous leaves among!
    Thou actor, perfect in all tragic sounds,
Thou mighty poet,[14] e'en to frenzy bold,
            What tell'st thou now about?
            'Tis of the rushing of an host[15] in rout,

## Notes

[10] *There was a time* Echoes Wordsworth, 'Ode' 1. In the 'Letter to Sara Hutchinson', this was the time 'Ere I was wedded' (l. 231).

[11] 'Tairn is a small lake, generally if not always applied to the lakes up in the mountains, and which are the feeders of those in the valleys. This address to the storm-wind will not appear extravagant to those who have heard it at night, and in a mountainous country' (Coleridge's note).

[12] *clomb* climbed.

[13] *yule* festival; yule was the pagan festival that became Christmas. This is the devil's yule because it is April rather than December.

[14] *Thou mighty poet* i.e. the wind of line 96.

[15] *host* army.

With groans of trampled men with smarting wounds[16] –
At once they groan with pain, and shudder with the cold!
But hush, there is a pause of deepest silence!
And all that noise, as of a rushing crowd,
With groans and tremulous shudderings – all is over.
It tells another tale, with sounds less deep and loud,
A tale of less affright
And tempered with delight,
As Otway's[17] self had framed the tender lay –
'Tis of a little child
Upon a lonesome wild
Not far from home, but she hath lost her way,
And now moans low in bitter grief and fear,
And now screams loud, and hopes to make her mother hear.

VIII

'Tis midnight, but small thoughts have I of sleep;
Full seldom may my friend such vigils keep!
Visit her, gentle sleep, with wings of healing,
And may this storm be but a mountain birth;
May all the stars hang bright above her dwelling,
Silent, as though they watched the sleeping earth!
With light heart may she rise,
Gay fancy, cheerful eyes,
Joy lift her spirit, joy attune her voice:
To her may all things live, from pole to pole,
Their life the eddying of her living soul!
Oh simple spirit, guided from above;
Dear Lady, friend devoutest[18] of my choice,
Thus may'st thou ever, evermore rejoice.

## *The Pains of Sleep* (1816)[1]

Ere on my bed my limbs I lay,
It hath not been my use to pray
With moving lips or bended knees;

## Notes

[16] *an host…wounds*, In 1815, Britain's long war with France (which had begun in 1793) had come to an end.

[17] This reference to Thomas Otway (1652–85), who, according to Johnson, died in penury after wandering across a heath in a state of near-nakedness, further veils the reference to Wordsworth, whose 'Lucy Gray' tells the story of a lost child.

[18] *devoutest* most devoted, most attached.

THE PAINS OF SLEEP

[1] Coleridge had embarked on 15 August 1803 on a tour of Scotland with the Wordsworths. Badly depressed, he accompanied them as far as Loch Lomond, but departed from them at Arrochar. Attempting to withdraw from opium, he embarked on a marathon walk, covering 263 miles in eight days before reaching Perth on 11 September. It was there he wrote a letter to Southey, containing this poem. He introduced it by saying 'I have been on a wild journey – taken up for a spy and clapped into Fort Augustus – and I am afraid they may have frightened poor Sara by sending her off a scrap of a letter I was writing to her. I have walked 263 miles in eight days, so I must have strength somewhere, but my spirits are dreadful, owing entirely to the horrors of every night. I truly dread to sleep; it is no shadow with me, but substantial misery foot-thick that makes me sit by my bedside of a morning and cry. I have abandoned all opiates except ether be one, and that only in fits – and that is a blessed medicine! and when you see me drink a glass of spirit and water, except by prescription of a physician, you shall despise me – but I still cannot get quiet rest –'.

But silently, by slow degrees,
My spirit I to love compose,
In humble trust mine eyelids close
With reverential resignation;
No wish conceived, no thought expressed!
Only a *sense* of supplication,
A sense o'er all my soul impressed
That I am weak, yet not unblessed –
Since in me, round me, everywhere,
Eternal strength and wisdom are.

But yesternight I prayed aloud
In anguish and in agony,
Upstarting from the fiendish crowd
Of shapes and thoughts that tortured me;
A lurid light, a trampling throng,
Sense of intolerable wrong,
And whom I scorned, those only strong!
Thirst of revenge, the powerless will
Still baffled, and yet burning still!
Desire with loathing strangely mixed,
On wild or hateful objects fixed.
Fantastic passions! Mad'ning brawl!
And shame and terror over all!
Deeds to be hid which were not hid,
Which all confused I could not know,
Whether I suffered or I did –
For all seemed guilt, remorse or woe,
My own or others, still the same
Life-stifling fear, soul-stifling shame!

Thus two nights passed: the night's dismay
Saddened and stunned the coming day.
Sleep, the wide blessing, seemed to me
Distemper's worst calamity.
The third night when my own loud scream
Had waked me from the fiendish dream,
O'ercome with sufferings strange and wild,
I wept as I had been a child –
And having thus by tears subdued
My anguish to a milder mood,
Such punishments, I said, were dues
To natures deepliest stained with sin:
For aye entempesting anew
Th' unfathomable hell within,
The horror of their deeds to view,
To know and loathe, yet wish and do!
Such griefs with such men well agree,
But wherefore, wherefore fall on me?
To be beloved is all I need,
And whom I love, I love indeed.

## *Letter from S.T. Coleridge to Thomas Poole, 14 October 1803* (extract)[1]

Wordsworth is in good health, and all his family. He has one LARGE boy, christened John. He has made a beginning to his *Recluse*.[2] He was here on Sunday last. His wife's sister, who is on a visit at Grasmere, was in a bad hysterical way, and he rode in to consult our excellent medical men.[3] I now see very little of Wordsworth. My own health makes it inconvenient and unfit for me to go thither one third as often, as I used to do – and Wordsworth's indolence, etc., keeps him at home. Indeed, were I an irritable man (and an unthinking one), I should probably have considered myself as having been very unkindly used by him in this respect, for I was at one time confined for two months, and he never came in to see me – me, who had ever paid such unremitting attentions to him!

But we must take the good and the ill together – and by seriously and habitually reflecting on our own faults and endeavouring to amend them, we shall then find little difficulty in confining our attention (as far as it acts on our friends' characters) to their good qualities. Indeed, I owe it to truth and justice, as well as to myself, to say that the concern which I have felt in this instance (and one or two other more *crying* instances) of self-involution in Wordsworth, has been almost wholly a feeling of friendly regret and disinterested apprehension. I saw him more and more benetted in hypochondriacal fancies, living wholly among *devotees*, having every the minutest thing, almost his very eating and drinking, done for him by his sister or wife – and I trembled lest a film should rise and thicken on his moral eye.

The habit too of writing such a multitude of small poems was in this instance hurtful to him – such things as that sonnet of his in Monday's *Morning Post* about Simonides and the ghost.[4] I rejoice, therefore, with a deep and true joy, that he has at length yielded to my urgent and repeated (almost unremitting) requests and remonstrances, and will go on with *The Recluse* exclusively – a great work in which he will sail on an open ocean and a steady wind, unfretted by short tacks, reefing and hauling and disentangling the ropes; great work necessarily comprehending his attention and feelings within the circle of great objects and elevated conceptions. This is his natural element. The having been out of it has been his disease; to return into it is the specific remedy – both remedy and health. It is what food is to famine.

I have seen enough positively to give me feelings of hostility towards the plan of several of the poems in the *Lyrical Ballads*, and I really consider it as a misfortune that Wordsworth ever deserted his former mountain-track to wander in lanes and alleys – though in the event it may prove to have been a great benefit to him. He will steer, I trust, the middle course.

## *Letter from S.T. Coleridge to Richard Sharp, 15 January 1804* (extract)[1]

Wordsworth is a poet, a most original poet. He no more resembles Milton than Milton resembles Shakespeare – no more resembles Shakespeare than Shakespeare resembles Milton: he is himself. And I dare affirm that he will hereafter be admitted as the first and greatest philosophical

## Notes

Letter from S.T. Coleridge to Thomas Poole

[1] This letter, written from Greta Hall, Keswick, where Coleridge's family were now living with Southey, indicates something of the strain that had crept into the relationship with Wordsworth.

[2] 'The Recluse' was the epic poem planned in 1798, which Coleridge and Wordsworth believed, would help precipitate the millennium (Christ's thousand-year rule on earth predicted in the Bible, as in Revelation 20:6). Coleridge was becoming increasingly impatient at Wordsworth's failure to write it.

[3] Joanna Hutchinson suffered a 'hysteric and fainting fit' at Dove Cottage on the evening of 7 October 1803. Wordsworth rode to Keswick to consult Mr Edmondson about it the next day, meeting Southey and Coleridge on 9 October before returning to Grasmere that evening.

[4] 'I find it written of Simonides', composed by 7 October 1803, published in *The Morning Post*, 10 October 1803. Coleridge may also have in mind some of the poems which were to appear in *Poems in Two Volumes* (1807).

Letter from S.T. Coleridge to Richard Sharp

[1] The euphoric tone of this letter may owe something to Coleridge's opium addiction, as well as to the fact that, in the week preceding, Wordsworth read 'The Two-Part Prelude' to him, and they had agreed that it would comprise part of 'The Recluse'. Wordsworth promised Coleridge he would begin work on 'The Recluse' immediately, and in return Coleridge had promised to send him 'notes' on its contents. Unfortunately those 'notes' never arrived in Grasmere (and it may be doubted whether they ever existed).

poet – the only man who has effected a complete and constant synthesis of thought and feeling, and combined them with poetic forms, with the music of pleasurable passion and with imagination, or the *modifying* power in that highest sense of the word in which I have ventured to oppose it to fancy, or the *aggregating* power (in that sense in which it is a dim analogue of creation – not all that we can *believe* but all that we can *conceive* of creation). Wordsworth is a poet, and I feel myself a better poet, in knowing how to honour *him*, than in all my own poetic compositions – all I have done or hope to do. And I prophesy immortality to his *Recluse*, as the first and finest philosophical poem, if only it be (as it undoubtedly will be) a faithful transcript of his own most august and innocent life, of his own habitual feelings and modes of seeing and hearing.

## *To William Wordsworth. Lines Composed, for the Greater Part, on the Night on which He Finished the Recitation of His Poem in Thirteen Books, Concerning the Growth and History of His Own Mind, January 1807, Coleorton, near Ashby-de-la-Zouch* (composed January 1807; first published 1817)[1]

Oh friend! Oh teacher! God's great gift to me!
Into my heart have I received that lay
More than historic, that prophetic lay
Wherein (high theme by thee first sung aright)
Of the foundations and the building-up
Of thy own spirit, thou hast loved to tell
What may be told, to th' understanding mind
Revealable; and what within the mind
May rise enkindled. Theme as hard as high!
Of smiles spontaneous, and mysterious fear
(The first-born they of reason, and twin-birth);
Of tides obedient to external force,
And currents self-determined, as might seem,
Or by interior power; of moments awful,[2]
Now in thy hidden life, and now abroad,
Mid festive crowds, *thy* brows too garlanded,
A brother of the feast; of fancies fair,
Hyblaean[3] murmurs of poetic thought,
Industrious in its joy, by lilied streams
Native or outland, lakes and famous hills!
Of more than fancy – of the hope of man
Amid the tremor of a realm aglow,[4]
Where France in all her towns lay vibrating,
Ev'n as a bark becalmed on sultry seas
Beneath the voice from heaven, the bursting crash
Of heaven's immediate thunder, when no cloud

## Notes

To William Wordsworth

[1] This poem is one of the earliest literary responses to Wordsworth's great poem. Wordsworth, Dorothy, Mary, Coleridge, Hartley and Sara Hutchinson, all spent the Christmas of 1806 at Coleorton, the country seat of Sir George Beaumont, and in the New Year, 7 January 1807, Wordsworth read them the 'Thirteen-Book Prelude'. It remained unpublished until 1850.

[2] *awful* i.e. full of awe.

[3] *Hyblaean* honeyed; Hybla was a Sicilian town near Syracuse, known for honey and herbs.

[4] *of the hope...aglow* a reference to Books IX and X of 'The Prelude', in which Wordsworth describes his residence in France, 1791–2.

Is visible, or shadow on the main!
Ah, soon night rolled on night, and every cloud
Opened its eye of fire; and hope aloft
Now fluttered, and now tossed upon the storm
Floating![5] Of hope afflicted, and struck down,
Thence summoned homeward – homeward to thy heart,
Oft from the watchtower of man's absolute self,
With light unwaning on her eyes, to look
Far on – herself a glory to behold,
The angel of the vision! Then (last strain!)
Of duty, chosen laws controlling[6] choice,
Virtue and love! An Orphic[7] tale indeed,
A tale divine of high and passionate thoughts
To their own music chaunted!
                                        Ah great bard!
Ere yet that last swell dying awed the air,
With steadfast ken[8] I viewed thee in the choir
Of ever-enduring men. The truly great
Have all one age, and from one visible space
Shed influence;[9] for they, both power and act,
Are permanent, and time is now with them,
Save as it worketh for them, they in it.
Nor less a sacred roll, than those of old,
And to be placed, as they, with gradual fame
Among the archives of mankind, thy work
Makes audible a linked song of truth,
Of truth profound a sweet continuous song
Not learnt but native, her own natural notes!
Dear shall it be to every human heart,
To me how more than dearest! Me, on whom
Comfort from thee and utterance of thy love
Came with such heights and depths of harmony,
Such sense of wings uplifting, that the storm
Scattered and whirled me, till my thoughts became
A bodily tumult! And thy faithful hopes,
Thy hopes of me, dear friend, by me unfelt
Were troublous[10] to me, almost as a voice
Familiar once and more than musical
To one cast forth, whose hope had seemed to die,
A wanderer with a worn-out heart,
Mid strangers pining with untended wounds!
    Oh friend, too well thou know'st, of what sad years
The long suppression had benumbed my soul,[11]

## Notes

[5] *and hope aloft…Floating* a reference to the Reign of Terror, which led radicals in England to lose hope in the French Revolution.

[6] In the MS Coleridge writes: 'Impelling? Directing?'

[7] *Orphic* oracular; communicated by God.

[8] *ken* gaze.

[9] *Shed influence* Coleridge is thinking of Milton's description of the Pleiades 'shedding sweet influence' (*Paradise Lost* vii 375).

[10] *troublous* confusing (because Coleridge had lost hope in himself).

[11] *benumbed my soul* as at 'Letter to Sara Hutchinson' 43: 'I *see*, not *feel*, how beautiful they are!'

That even as life returns upon the drowned,
Th' unusual joy awoke a throng of pains –
Keen pangs of *love*, awakening, as a babe,
Turbulent, with an outcry in the heart;
And fears self-willed, that shunned the eye of hope,
And hope, that would not know itself from fear;
Sense of passed youth, and manhood come in vain;
And genius given, and knowledge won in vain;
And all which I had culled in wood-walks wild,
And all which patient toil had reared, and all
Commune with thee had opened out, but[12] flowers
Strewed on my corse, and borne upon my bier,
In the same coffin, for the self-same grave!
That way no more! And ill beseems it me,
Who came a welcomer in herald's guise,
Singing of glory and futurity,
To wander back on such unhealthful road
Plucking the poisons of self-harm! And ill
Such intertwine beseems triumphal wreaths
Strewed before thy advancing! Thou too, friend!
Oh injure not the memory of that hour
Of thy communion with my nobler mind[13]
By pity or grief,[14] already felt too long!
Nor let my words import more blame than needs.
The tumult rose and ceased; for peace is nigh
Where Wisdom's voice has found a list'ning heart.
Amid the howl of more than wintry storms
The halcyon[15] hears the voice of vernal hours,
Already on the wing!
Eve following eve,[16]
Dear tranquil time, when the sweet sense of home
Becomes most sweet! Hours for their own sake hailed,
And more desired, more precious, for thy song! isn't this line 100?
In silence list'ning, like a devout child,
My soul lay passive, by thy various strain[17]
Driven as in surges now, beneath the stars,
With momentary stars of my own birth,
Fair constellated foam still darting off
Into the darkness! – now a tranquil sea
Outspread and bright, yet swelling to the moon!
And when, oh friend, my comforter, my guide,
Strong in thyself and powerful to give strength,
Thy long-sustained lay finally closed,
And thy deep voice had ceased (yet thou thyself

## Notes

[12] *but* i.e. [nothing] but.
[13] *that hour…mind* a reference to the *annus mirabilis* of 1797–8.
[14] *pity or grief* i.e. felt for Coleridge in his present, miserable state.
[15] *halcyon* kingfisher which, according to classical legend, brought the seas and winds to a calm when it bred in a nest which floated on the ocean.
[16] *Eve following eve* the evenings when Wordsworth recited 'The Thirteen-Book Prelude' to Coleridge at Coleorton.
[17] *thy various strain* 'varied in tone and subject matter' i.e. 'The Prelude'.

Wert still before mine eyes, and round us both
That happy vision of beloved faces,
All whom I deepliest love, in one room all!),
Scarce conscious and yet conscious of its close,
I sat, my being blended in one thought
(Thought was it? Or aspiration? Or resolve?)
Absorbed, yet hanging still upon the sound:
And when I rose, I found myself in prayer!

## *Letter from S.T. Coleridge to William Wordsworth, 30 May 1815* (extract)[1]

What did my criticism amount to, reduced to its full and naked sense? This: that, *comparatively* with the former poem, *The Excursion*, as far as it was new to me, had disappointed my expectations; that the excellences were so many and of so high a class, that it was impossible to attribute the inferiority (if any such really existed) to any flagging of the writer's own genius; and that I conjectured that it might have been occasioned by the influence of self-established convictions having given to certain thoughts and expressions a depth and force which they had not for readers in general. In order, therefore, to explain the *disappointment*, I must recall to your mind what my *expectations* were; and as these again were founded on the supposition that (in whatever order it might be published) the poem on the growth of your own mind[2] was as the ground-plat[3] and the roots out of which *The Recluse* was to have sprung up as the tree. As far as the same sap in both, I expected them doubtless to have formed one complete whole, but in matter, form, and product to be different, each not only a distinct but a different work. In the first I had found 'theme by thee first sung aright'[4]:

Of smiles spontaneous, and mysterious fears
(The first-born they of reason, and twin-birth);
Of tides obedient to external force,
And currents self-determined, as might seem,
Or by some central breath; of moments awful,
Now in thy inner life, and now abroad,
When power streamed from thee, and thy soul received
The light reflected as a light bestowed!
Of fancies fair, and milder hours of youth,

## Notes

Letter from S.T. Coleridge to Wordsworth

[1] Wordsworth and Coleridge's friendship had soured in 1810, when a mutual friend, Basil Montagu, told Coleridge of a thoughtless remark Wordsworth made about his opium addiction. Despite repeated attempts to patch things up, both men were aware of a rift that would never heal. Wordsworth had published 'The Excursion' in 1814, for which he had high hopes, but it was greeted by some of the worst reviews he would ever receive. Then, on 3 April 1815, Coleridge confided to another mutual friend, Lady Beaumont, that he thought 'The Excursion' less good than 'The Prelude' and that its chief fault was that

> having by the conjoint operation of his own experiences, feelings, and reason *himself* convinced *himself* of truths, which the generality of persons have either taken for granted from their infancy, or at least adopted in early life, he has attached all their own depth and weight to doctrines and words, which come almost as truisms or commonplaces to others.

Word of this got back to Wordsworth, and on 22 May he wrote to Coleridge to say that he was more 'perplexed than enlightened by your *comparative* censure'. On reading that, Coleridge composed this reply, explaining his disappointment in detail. As with many of Coleridge's retrospective comments on 'The Recluse', the reader should read it with caution. It was written over seventeen years after 'The Recluse' was formulated, and provides a plan that may be more detailed than anything ever written by Coleridge in 1798. He had been able to develop (and perhaps embroider) his ambitions for it over the years, without necessarily communicating them to Wordsworth.

[2] *the poem...mind* i.e. 'The Prelude'.

[3] *ground-plat* plot of ground on which the edifice of 'The Recluse' would be built.

[4] *theme by thee...aright* Coleridge's 'To William Wordsworth' 4; he goes on to quote ll. 10–40.

Hyblaean[5] murmurs of poetic thought,
Industrious in its joy, in vales and glens
Native or outland, lakes and famous hills!
Or on the lonely high-road, when the stars
Were rising, or by secret mountain streams,
The guides and the companions of thy way;
Of more than fancy – of the social sense
Distending wide, and man beloved as man,
Where France in all her towns lay vibrating,
Ev'n as a bark becalmed beneath the burst
Of heaven's immediate thunder, when no cloud
Is visible, or shadow on the main!
For thou wert there,[6] thy own brows garlanded
Amid the tremor of a realm aglow,
Amid a mighty nation jubilant,
When from the general heart of humankind
Hope sprang forth, like a full-born deity!
Of that dear hope afflicted, and amazed,
So homeward summoned! Thenceforth calm and sure
From the dread watchtower of man's absolute self,
With light unwaning on her eyes, to look
Far on – herself a glory[7] to behold,
The angel of the vision! Then (last strain!)
Of duty! Chosen laws controlling choice!
Action and joy! – AN ORPHIC[8] SONG INDEED,
A SONG DIVINE OF HIGH AND PASSIONATE TRUTHS
TO THEIR OWN MUSIC CHAUNTED!

Indeed through the whole of that poem *Αὔρα τις εἰσεπνὲυσε μυστικωτάτη*.[9] *This* I considered as *The Excursion*, and the second as *The Recluse* I had (from what I had at different times gathered from your conversation on the plan) anticipated as commencing with you set down and settled in an abiding home, and that with the description of that home you were to begin a *Philosophical Poem*, the result and fruits of a spirit so framed and so disciplined, as had been told in the former.

Whatever in Lucretius[10] is poetry is not philosophical; whatever is philosophical is not poetry – and in the very pride of confident hope I looked forward to *The Recluse* as the *first* and *only* true philosophical poem in existence. Of course, I expected the colours, music, imaginative life, and passion of *poetry*, but the matter and arrangement of *philosophy* – not doubting from the advantages of the subject that the totality of a system was not only capable of being harmonized with, but even calculated to aid, the unity (beginning, middle, and end) of a *poem*. Thus, whatever the length of the work might be, still it was a *determinate* length.

Of the subjects announced each would have its own appointed place and, excluding repetitions, each would relieve and rise in interest above the other. I supposed you first to have meditated the faculties of man in the abstract; in their correspondence with his sphere of action – and first, in the feeling, touch, and taste, then in the eye, and last in the ear; to have laid a solid and immovable

## Notes

[5] *Hyblaean* honeyed; Hybla was a Sicilian town near Syracuse known for honey and herbs.

[6] *For thou wert there* i.e. in Revolutionary France, 1791–2.

[7] *a glory* an effulgent light.

[8] *Orphic* oracular; communicated by God.

[9] 'a certain most mystical breeze blew into me' (Aristophanes, *The Frogs* 313–14).

[10] Lucretius, *De rerum natura*, philosophical poem in six books.

foundation for the edifice by removing the sandy sophisms[11] of Locke and the mechanic dogmatists;[12] and demonstrating that the senses were living growths and developments of the mind and spirit in a much juster as well as higher sense than the mind can be said to be formed by the senses. Next I understood that you would take the human race in the concrete, have exploded the absurd notion of Pope's *Essay on Man*,[13] Darwin,[14] and all the countless believers (even, strange to say, among Christians) of man's having progressed from an orang-utan state – so contrary to all history, to all religion, nay, to all possibility; to have affirmed a fall, in some sense, as a fact the possibility of which cannot be understood from the nature of the will, but the reality of which is attested by experience and conscience; fallen men contemplated in the different ages of the world, and in the different states – savage – barbarous – civilized – the lonely cot or borderer's wigwam – the village – the manufacturing town – sea-port – city – universities – and, not disguising the sore evils under which the whole creation groans, to point out, however, a manifest scheme of redemption from this slavery, of reconciliation from this enmity with nature (What are the obstacles? The Antichrist that must be and already is); and to conclude by a grand didactic swell on the necessary identity of a true philosophy with true religion, agreeing in the results and differing only as the analytic and synthetic process, as discursive from intuitive,[15] the former chiefly useful as perfecting the latter.

In short, the necessity of a general revolution in the modes of developing and disciplining the human mind by the substitution of life and intelligence (considered in its different powers, from the plant up to that state in which the difference of degree becomes a new kind – man, self-consciousness – but yet not by essential opposition), for the philosophy of mechanism which in everything that is needworthy of the human intellect strikes *death*, and cheats itself by mistaking clear images for distinct conceptions, and which idly demands conceptions where intuitions alone are possible or adequate to the majesty of the truth. In short, facts elevated into theory, theory into laws, and laws into living and intelligent powers – true idealism necessarily perfecting itself in realism, and realism refining itself into idealism.

Such or something like this was the plan I had supposed that you were engaged on.

## From *Biographia Literaria* (1817)

### *Chapter 13 (extract)*[1]

The imagination then I consider either as primary or secondary. The primary imagination I hold to be the living power and prime agent of all human perception, and as a repetition in the finite mind of the eternal act of creation in the infinite I AM. The secondary imagination I consider as an echo of the former, coexisting with the conscious will, yet still as identical with the primary in the *kind* of its agency, and differing only in *degree*, and in the *mode* of its operation. It dissolves, diffuses, dissipates, in order to recreate; or, where this process is rendered impossible, yet still at all events it struggles to idealize and to unify. It is essentially *vital*, even as all objects (*as* objects) are essentially fixed and dead.

## Notes

[11] *sandy sophisms* dry and specious arguments.

[12] *Locke...mechanic dogmatists* John Locke (1632–1704), author of the *Essay Concerning Human Understanding* (1690); other 'dogmatists' probably include Isaac Newton (1642–1727) and Francis Bacon (1561–1626).

[13] *Essay on Man* (1732–4), a philosophical poem, part of a larger work never completed by Pope, in which he seeks to vindicate the ways of God to man and prove that the universe is the best of all possible schemes.

[14] Erasmus Darwin (1731–1802), grandfather of Charles Darwin, author of *The Botanic Garden* (1789–91) and *Zoönomia* (1794–6).

[15] *discursive or intuitive* The same distinction is mentioned by Wordsworth in 'Thirteen-Book Prelude' xiii 113. Milton had differentiated discursive reason (belonging to man), from a higher, 'intuitive' reason, to which man may aspire, and which is possessed by angels (*Paradise Lost* v 487–90).

From Biographia Literaria

[1] The first of the extracts from *Biographia* consists of the famous definition of the primary and secondary imagination. Coleridge began dictating the volume in July 1815, and it was intended to be a combination of autobiography, a defence of Wordsworth against reviewers such as Jeffrey, and a treatise on philosophy and religion.

Fancy, on the contrary, has no other counters to play with but fixities and definites. The fancy is indeed no other than a mode of memory emancipated from the order of time and space – while it is blended with, and modified by, that empirical phenomenon of the will which we express by the word 'choice'. But equally with the ordinary memory the fancy must receive all its materials ready-made from the law of association.

## *The Rime of the Ancient Mariner. In Seven Parts*[1] (1817)

*Facile credo, plures esse Naturas invisibiles quam visibiles in rerum universitate. Sed harum omnium familiam quis nobis enarrabit? et gradus et cognationes et discrimina et singularum munera? Quid agunt? quae loca habitant? Harum rerum notitiam semper ambivit ingenium humanum, nunquam attigit. Juvat, interea, non diffiteor, quandoque in animo, tanquam in Tabulâ, majoris et melioris mundi imaginem contemplari: ne mens assuefecta hodiernae vitae minutiis se contrahat nimis, et tota subsidat in pusillas cogitationes. Sed veritati interea invigilandum est, modusque servandus, ut certa ab incertis, diem a nocte, distinguamus.*[2]

(Thomas Burnet, *Archaeologiae Philosophicae* (London, 1692, pp. 68–9)

### *Part The First*

An ancient Mariner meeteth three gallants bidden to a wedding-feast, and detaineth one.

It is an ancient Mariner,
And he stoppeth one of three:
'By thy long grey beard and glittering eye
Now wherefore stopp'st thou me?

The Bridegroom's doors are opened wide
And I am next of kin;
The guests are met, the feast is set –
Mayst hear the merry din.'

He holds him with his skinny hand,
'There was a ship', quoth he;
'Hold off! Unhand me, grey-beard loon!'
Eftsoons his hand dropped he.

The Wedding-Guest is spellbound by the eye of the old seafaring man, and constrained to hear his tale.

He holds him with his glittering eye –
The Wedding-Guest stood still,
And listens like a three years' child:
The Mariner hath his will.

## Notes

THE RIME OF THE ANCIENT MARINER. IN SEVEN PARTS

[1] This was the fifth published text of 'The Ancient Mariner', and the first in which Coleridge was identified as the author. It is radically different from previous texts in containing the Latin epigraph, marginal glosses and numerous revisions to the poem itself.

[2] This adaptation from Burnet may be translated: 'I can easily believe that there are more invisible than visible beings in the universe. But who will describe to us their families, ranks, affinities, differences, and functions? What do they do? Where do they live? The human mind has always sought knowledge of these things, but has never attained it. I admit that it is good sometimes to contemplate in thought, as in a picture, the image of a greater and better world; otherwise the mind, used to the minor concerns of daily life, may contract itself too much, and concentrate entirely on trivia. But meanwhile we must be vigilant for truth and moderation, that we may distinguish certainty from doubt, day from night.'

The Wedding-Guest sat on a stone,
He cannot choose but hear;
And thus spake on that ancient man,
The bright-eyed mariner.

'The ship was cheered, the harbour cleared,
Merrily did we drop
Below the kirk, below the hill,
Below the lighthouse top.

The Mariner tells how the ship sailed southward with a good wind and fair weather till it reached the line.[3]

The Sun came up upon the left,
Out of the sea came he;
And he shone bright, and on the right
Went down into the sea.

Higher and higher every day,
Till over the mast at noon –'
The Wedding-Guest here beat his breast,
For he heard the loud bassoon.

The Wedding-Guest heareth the bridal music, but the Mariner continueth his tale.

The bride hath paced into the hall,
Red as a rose is she;
Nodding their heads before her goes
The merry minstrelsy.[4]

The Wedding-Guest he beat his breast,
Yet he cannot choose but hear;
And thus spake on that ancient man,
The bright-eyed Mariner.

The ship drawn by a storm toward the south pole.

'And now the STORM-BLAST came, and he
Was tyrannous and strong;
He struck with his o'ertaking wings,
And chased us south along.

With sloping masts and dipping prow,
As who pursued with yell and blow
Still treads the shadow of his foe
And forward bends his head,
The ship drove fast, loud roared the blast,
And southward aye we fled.

And now there came both mist and snow,
And it grew wonderous cold:
And ice, mast-high, came floating by,
As green as emerald.

Notes

[3] *line* equator.

[4] *before her…minstrelsy* cf. Chaucer, *Squire's Tale* 268: 'Toforn hym gooth the loud mynstralcye'.

The land of ice, and of fearful sounds where no living thing was to be seen.

And through the drifts[5] the snowy clift[6]
Did send a dismal sheen:
Nor shapes of men nor beasts we ken –
The ice was all between.

The ice was here, the ice was there,
The ice was all around:
It cracked and growled, and roared and howled
Like noises in a swound![7]

Till a great sea-bird, called the albatross, came through the snow-fog, and was received with great joy and hospitality.

At length did cross an albatross,
Thorough the fog it came;
As if it had been a Christian soul,[8]
We hailed it in God's name.

It ate the food it ne'er had eat,
And round and round it flew.
The ice did split with a thunder-fit;
The helmsman steered us through!

And lo! the Albatross proveth a bird of good omen, and followeth the ship as it returned northward through fog and floating ice.

And a good south wind sprung up behind,
The Albatross did follow;
And every day, for food or play,
Came to the Mariner's hollo!

In mist or cloud, on mast or shroud,
It perched for vespers[9] nine,
Whiles all the night, through fog-smoke white,
Glimmered the white Moonshine.'

The ancient Mariner inhospitably killeth the pious bird of good omen.

'God save thee, ancient Mariner!
From the fiends that plague thee thus!
Why look'st thou so?' 'With my crossbow
I shot the ALBATROSS![10]

## *Part The Second*

The sun now rose upon the right,
Out of the sea came he;
Still hid in mist, and on the left
Went down into the sea.

## Notes

[5] *drifts* floating ice.

[6] *clift* cleft.

[7] *swound* swoon.

[8] *a Christian soul* i.e. a human being.

[9] *vespers* evenings.

[10] The central event of the poem was suggested by a travel book which Wordsworth read, Shelvocke's *Voyage Round the World* (1726); see p. 341 n. 13.

And the good south wind still blew behind,
But no sweet bird did follow,
Nor any day for food or play
Came to the mariners' hollo!

His shipmates cry out against the ancient Mariner, for killing the bird of good luck.

And I had done an hellish thing
And it would work 'em woe:
For all averred[11] I had killed the bird
That made the breeze to blow.
"Ah wretch!" said they, "the bird to slay
That made the breeze to blow!"

But when the fog cleared off, they justify the same – and thus make themselves accomplices in the crime.

Nor dim nor red, like God's own head
The glorious Sun uprist:
Then all averred I had killed the bird
That brought the fog and mist.
"'Twas right", said they, "such birds to slay,
That bring the fog and mist."

The fair breeze continues; the ship enters the Pacific Ocean and sails northward, even till it reaches the line.

The fair breeze blew, the white foam flew,
The furrow[12] streamed off free:
We were the first that ever burst
Into that silent sea.

The ship hath been suddenly becalmed.

Down dropped the breeze, the sails dropped down, '
Twas sad as sad could be,
And we did speak only to break
The silence of the sea!

All in a hot and copper sky
The bloody Sun at noon
Right up above the mast did stand,
No bigger than the Moon.

Day after day, day after day,
We stuck, nor breath nor motion,
As idle as a painted ship
Upon a painted ocean.

And the albatross begins to be avenged.

Water, water, every where,
And all the boards did shrink;
Water, water, every where,
Nor any drop to drink.

## Notes

[11] *averred* maintained that.

[12] 'In the former edition the line was "The furrow followed free". But I had not been long on board a ship before I perceived that this was the image as seen by a spectator from the shore, or from another vessel. From the ship itself the wake appears like a brook flowing off from the stern' (Coleridge's note).

The very deeps did rot: O Christ!
That ever this should be!
Yea, slimy things did crawl with legs
Upon the slimy sea.

About, about, in reel and rout
The death-fires danced at night;
The water, like a witch's oils,
Burnt green and blue and white.

A spirit had followed them; one of the invisible inhabitants of this planet, neither departed souls nor angels; concerning whom the learned Jew, Josephus,[13] and the Platonic Constantinopolitan,[14] Michael Psellus,[15] may be consulted. They are very numerous, and there is no climate or element without one or more.

And some in dreams assured were
Of the spirit that plagued us so;
Nine fathom deep he had followed us
From the land of mist and snow.

And every tongue, through utter drought,
Was withered at the root;
We could not speak, no more than if
We had been choked with soot.

The shipmates in their sore distress would fain throw the whole guilt on the ancient Mariner: in sign whereof they hang the dead sea-bird round his neck.

Ah! wel-a-day! what evil looks
Had I from old and young!
Instead of the cross the Albatross
About my neck was hung.

## *Part The Third*

There passed a weary time. Each throat
Was parched, and glazed each eye.
A weary time! a weary time!
How glazed each weary eye!
When looking westward, I beheld
A something in the sky.

The ancient Mariner beholdeth a sign in the element afar off.

At first it seemed a little speck
And then it seemed a mist;
It moved and moved, and took at last
A certain shape, I wist.[16]

A speck, a mist, a shape, I wist!
And still it neared and neared:
And as if it dodged a water-sprite,
It plunged and tacked and veered.

## Notes

[13] Flavius Josephus (*c.*37–*c.*100), author of *Antiquitates Judaicae* and, more famously, *De bello Judaico*, which Coleridge read in November 1800 (*Notebooks* i 851).

[14] *Platonic Constantinopolitan* Neoplatonic philosopher from Constantinople (see note 15).

[15] Michael Constantine Psellus (*c.*1018–*c.*1078), whose commentary to the *Chaldaean Oracles*, as John Livingston Lowes has pointed out, informed both this poem and 'Kubla Khan'; see Lowes, *The Road to Xanadu* (1978), pp. 216–17.

[16] *wist* was aware of.

At its nearer approach, it seemeth him to be a ship; and at a dear ransom he freeth his speech from the bonds of thirst.

With throat unslaked, with black lips baked,
We could nor laugh nor wail;
Through utter drought all dumb we stood!
I bit my arm, I sucked the blood,
And cried, "A sail! A sail!"

A flash of joy.

With throat unslaked, with black lips baked,
Agape they heard me call:
Gramercy![17] they for joy did grin
And all at once their breath drew in
As they were drinking all.

And horror follows. For can it be without a *ship* that comes onward without wind or tide?

"See, see!" I cried, "She tacks no more,
Hither to work us weal;[18]
Without a breeze, without a tide,
She steadies with upright keel!"

The western wave was all a-flame,
The day was well nigh done!
Almost upon the western wave
Rested the broad bright Sun;
When that strange shape drove suddenly
Betwixt us and the Sun.

It seemeth him but the skeleton of a ship.

And straight the Sun was flecked with bars
(Heaven's Mother send us grace!)
As if through a dungeon-grate he peered
With broad and burning face.

Alas! thought I, and my heart beat loud,
How fast she nears and nears!
Are those *her* sails that glance in the Sun
Like restless gossameres?

And its ribs are seen as bars on the face of the setting sun.
The spectre-woman and her death-mate, and no other on board the skeleton-ship.

Are those *her* ribs through which the Sun
Did peer, as through a grate?
And is that Woman all her crew?
Is that a DEATH? And are there two?
Is DEATH that woman's mate?

Like vessel, like crew!

*Her* lips were red, *her* looks were free,
Her locks were yellow as gold;
Her skin was as white as leprosy,
The Nightmare LIFE-IN-DEATH was she
Who thicks man's blood with cold.

## Notes

[17] *Gramercy!* mercy on us!

[18] *weal* harm.

DEATH and LIFE-IN-DEATH have diced for the ship's crew, and she (the latter) winneth the ancient Mariner.

The naked hulk alongside came,
And the twain were casting dice;
"The game is done! I've won! I've won!"
Quoth she, and whistles thrice.

A gust of wind sterte up behind
And whistled through his bones;
Through the holes of his eyes and the hole of his mouth
Half whistles and half groans.

The Sun's rim dips, the stars rush out,
At one stride comes the dark;[19]
With far-heard whisper, o'er the sea,
Off shot the spectre-bark.

We listened and looked sideways up!
Fear at my heart, as at a cup,
My life-blood seemed to sip!
The stars were dim, and thick the night,
The steersman's face by his lamp gleamed white;

At the rising of the Moon,

From the sails the dews did drip –
Till clomb[20] above the eastern bar
The horned moon, with one bright star
Within the nether tip.[21]

One after another,

One after one, by the star-dogged Moon
Too quick for groan or sigh,
Each turned his face with a ghastly pang
And cursed me with his eye.

His shipmates drop down dead;

Four times fifty living men
(And I heard nor sigh nor groan)
With heavy thump, a lifeless lump,
They dropped down one by one.

But LIFE-IN-DEATH begins her work on the ancient Mariner.

The souls did from their bodies fly,
They fled to bliss or woe!
And every soul, it passed me by
Like the whiz of my crossbow.'

## Notes

[19] *The sun's rim…dark* Coleridge added a marginal gloss in the MS in copies of *Sibylline Leaves* to explain: 'Between the tropics there is no twilight. As the sun's last segment dips down, and the evening gun is fired, the constellations appear arrayed.' Subsequent printed texts included the terser gloss: 'No twilight within the courts of the sun.'

[20] *clomb* climbed.

[21] *with one bright star…tip* In one copy of *Sibylline Leaves*, Coleridge noted: 'It is a common superstition among sailors "that something evil is about to happen whenever a star dogs the moon."'

*Part The Fourth*

The Wedding-Guest feareth that a spirit is talking to him;

'I fear thee, ancient Mariner!
I fear thy skinny hand!
And thou art long and lank and brown
As is the ribbed sea-sand.[22]

I fear thee and thy glittering eye,
And thy skinny hand so brown.'

But the ancient Mariner assureth him of his bodily life, and proceedeth to relate his horrible penance.

'Fear not, fear not, thou Wedding-Guest!
This body dropped not down.

Alone, alone, all, all alone,
Alone on a wide wide sea!
And never a saint took pity on
My soul in agony.

He despiseth the creatures of the calm,

The many men so beautiful!
And they all dead did lie;
And a thousand thousand slimy things
Lived on; and so did I.

And envieth that *they* should live, and so many lie dead.

I looked upon the rotting sea
And drew my eyes away;
I looked upon the rotting deck,
And there the dead men lay.

I looked to Heaven and tried to pray,
But or ever a prayer had gushed,
A wicked whisper came and made
My heart as dry as dust.

I closed my lids, and kept them close,
And the balls like pulses beat;
For the sky and the sea, and the sea and the sky
Lay like a cloud on my weary eye,
And the dead were at my feet.

But the curse liveth for him in the eye of the dead men.

The cold sweat melted from their limbs,
Nor rot nor reek did they;
The look with which they looked on me
Had never passed away.

## Notes

[22] 'For the last two lines of this stanza I am indebted to Mr Wordsworth. It was on a delightful walk from Nether Stowey to Dulverton, with him and his sister, in the autumn of 1797, that this poem was planned and in part composed' (Coleridge's note).

An orphan's curse would drag to Hell
A spirit from on high;
But O! more horrible than that
Is the curse in a dead man's eye!
Seven days, seven nights, I saw that curse,
And yet I could not die.

In his loneliness and fixedness, he yearneth towards the journeying moon, and the stars that still sojourn, yet still move onward; and everywhere the blue sky belongs to them, and is their appointed rest, and their native country, and their own natural homes, which they enter unannounced, as lords that are certainly expected, and yet there is a silent joy at their arrival.

The moving Moon went up the sky
And nowhere did abide;
Softly she was going up,
And a star or two beside –

Her beams bemocked the sultry main,
Like April hoar-frost spread;
But where the ship's huge shadow lay
The charmed[23] water burnt alway
A still and awful red.

By the light of the moon he beholdeth God's creatures of the great calm.

Beyond the shadow of the ship,
I watched the water-snakes;
They moved in tracks of shining white,
And when they reared, the elfish light
Fell off in hoary flakes.

Within the shadow of the ship
I watched their rich attire:
Blue, glossy green, and velvet black,
They coiled and swam, and every track
Was a flash of golden fire.

Their beauty and their happiness.

He blesseth them in his heart.

O happy living things! no tongue
Their beauty might declare:
A spring of love gushed from my heart
And I blessed them unaware!
Sure my kind saint took pity on me,
And I blessed them unaware.

The spell begins to break.

The self-same moment I could pray,
And from my neck so free
The Albatross fell off and sank
Like lead into the sea.

## *Part The Fifth*

O sleep! It is a gentle thing
Beloved from pole to pole!
To Mary Queen[24] the praise be given;
She sent the gentle sleep from Heaven
That slid into my soul.

Notes

[23] *charmed* dead calm.

[24] *Mary Queen* the Virgin Mary.

By grace of the holy Mother, the ancient Mariner is refreshed with rain.

The silly[25] buckets on the deck,
That had so long remained,
I dreamt that they were filled with dew;
And when I awoke, it rained.

My lips were wet, my throat was cold,
My garments all were dank;
Sure I had drunken in my dreams
And still my body drank.

I moved and could not feel my limbs;
I was so light – almost
I thought that I had died in sleep
And was a blessed ghost.

He heareth sounds, and seeth strange sights and commotions in the sky and the element.

And soon I heard a roaring wind;
It did not come anear,
But with its sound it shook the sails
That were so thin and sere.[26]

The upper air bursts into life!
And a hundred fire-flags sheen,[27]
To and fro they were hurried about;
And to and fro, and in and out
The wan stars danced between.[28]

And the coming wind did roar more loud,
And the sails did sigh like sedge;
And the rain poured down from one black cloud,
The Moon was at its edge.

The thick black cloud was cleft, and still
The Moon was at its side;
Like waters shot from some high crag,
The lightning fell with never a jag,
A river steep and wide.

The bodies of the ship's crew are inspirited,[29] and the ship moves on;

The loud wind never reached the ship,
Yet now the ship moved on!
Beneath the lightning and the Moon
The dead men gave a groan.

They groaned, they stirred, they all uprose,
Nor spake, nor moved their eyes;
It had been strange, even in a dream,
To have seen those dead men rise.

## Notes

[25] *silly* plain, rustic, homely.
[26] *sere* worn.
[27] *sheen* shining.
[28] *The upper air…between* the aurora borealis.
[29] *inspirited* quickened, animated.

The helmsman steered, the ship moved on,
Yet never a breeze up-blew;
The mariners all 'gan work the ropes
Where they were wont to do;
They raised their limbs like lifeless tools –
We were a ghastly crew.

The body of my brother's son
Stood by me, knee to knee;
The body and I pulled at one rope
But he said nought to me.'

But not by the souls of the men, nor by dæmons of earth or the middle air, but by a blessed troop of angelic spirits, sent down by the invocation of the guardian saint.

'I fear thee, ancient Mariner!'
'Be calm, thou Wedding-Guest!
'Twas not those souls that fled in pain,
Which to their corses came again,
But a troop of spirits blessed;

For when it dawned, they dropped their arms,
And clustered round the mast;
Sweet sounds rose slowly through their mouths
And from their bodies passed.

Around, around, flew each sweet sound,
Then darted to the Sun;
Slowly the sounds came back again,
Now mixed, now one by one.

Sometimes a-dropping from the sky
I heard the skylark sing;
Sometimes all little birds that are,
How they seemed to fill the sea and air
With their sweet jargoning![30]

And now 'twas like all instruments,
Now like a lonely flute,
And now it is an angel's song
That makes the Heavens be mute.

It ceased, yet still the sails made on
A pleasant noise till noon,
A noise like of a hidden brook
In the leafy month of June,
That to the sleeping woods all night
Singeth a quiet tune.

## Notes

[30] *jargoning* birdsong.

Till noon we quietly sailed on,
Yet never a breeze did breathe;
Slowly and smoothly went the ship,
Moved onward from beneath.

The lonesome spirit from the South Pole carries on the ship as far as the line, in obedience to the angelic troop, but still requireth vengeance.

Under the keel nine fathom deep,
From the land of mist and snow,
The spirit slid; and it was he
That made the ship to go.
The sails at noon left off their tune,
And the ship stood still also.

The sun right up above the mast
Had fixed her to the ocean;
But in a minute she 'gan stir
With a short uneasy motion –
Backwards and forwards half her length,
With a short uneasy motion.

Then like a pawing horse let go,
She made a sudden bound;
It flung the blood into my head,
And I fell down in a swound.

The Polar Spirit's fellow-dæmons, the invisible inhabitants of the element, take part in his wrong; and two of them relate, one to the other, that penance long and heavy for the ancient Mariner hath been accorded to the Polar Spirit, who returneth southward.

How long in that same fit I lay,
I have not to declare;
But ere my living life returned,
I heard and in my soul discerned
Two VOICES in the air.

"Is it he?" quoth one, "Is this the man?
By him who died on cross,
With his cruel bow he laid full low
The harmless Albatross.

The spirit who bideth by himself
In the land of mist and snow,
He loved the bird that loved the man
Who shot him with his bow."

The other was a softer voice,
As soft as honey-dew;
Quoth he, "The man hath penance done,
And penance more will do."'

## *Part The Sixth*

FIRST VOICE
But tell me, tell me! speak again,
Thy soft response renewing –
What makes that ship drive on so fast?
What is the OCEAN doing?

SECOND VOICE
Still as a slave before his lord,
The OCEAN hath no blast;
His great bright eye most silently
Up to the Moon is cast –

If he may know which way to go,
For she guides him smooth or grim.
See, brother, see! how graciously
She looketh down on him!

The Mariner hath been cast into a trance; for the angelic power causeth the vessel to drive northward, faster than human life could endure.

FIRST VOICE
But why drives on that ship so fast
Without or wave or wind?
SECOND VOICE
The air is cut away before,
And closes from behind.

Fly, brother, fly! more high, more high!
Or we shall be belated;
For slow and slow that ship will go
When the Mariner's trance is abated.

The supernatural motion is retarded; the Mariner awakes, and his penance begins anew.

'I woke, and we were sailing on
As in a gentle weather;
'Twas night, calm night, the Moon was high;
The dead men stood together.

All stood together on the deck,
For a charnel-dungeon[31] fitter;
All fixed on me their stony eyes
That in the moon did glitter.

The pang, the curse, with which they died
Had never passed away;
I could not draw my eyes from theirs,
Nor turn them up to pray.

The curse is finally expiated.

And now this spell was snapped; once more
I viewed the ocean green,
And looked far forth, yet little saw
Of what had else been seen –

Like one that on a lonesome road
Doth walk in fear and dread,
And having once turned round walks on
And turns no more his head;
Because he knows a frightful fiend
Doth close behind him tread.

## Notes

[31] *charnel-dungeon* dungeon containing dead bodies.

But soon there breathed a wind on me,
Nor sound nor motion made;
Its path was not upon the sea,
In ripple or in shade.

It raised my hair, it fanned my cheek
Like a meadow-gale of spring –
It mingled strangely with my fears,
Yet it felt like a welcoming.

Swiftly, swiftly flew the ship,
Yet she sailed softly too;
Sweetly, sweetly blew the breeze –
On me alone it blew.

And the ancient Mariner beholdeth his native country.

O dream of joy! Is this indeed
The lighthouse top I see?
Is this the hill? Is this the kirk?
Is this mine own countree?

We drifted o'er the harbour-bar,[32]
And I with sobs did pray –
"O let me be awake, my God!
Or let me sleep alway!"

The harbour-bay was clear as glass,
So smoothly it was strewn![33]
And on the bay the moonlight lay
And the shadow of the moon.

The rock shone bright, the kirk no less
That stands above the rock;
The moonlight steeped in silentness
The steady weathercock.

The angelic spirits leave the dead bodies,

And the bay was white with silent light,
Till rising from the same,
Full many shapes that shadows were
In crimson colours came.

And appear in their own forms of light.

A little distance from the prow
Those crimson shadows were;
I turned my eyes upon the deck –
O, Christ! what saw I there!

## Notes

[32] *bar* bank of silt across the mouth of the harbour.

[33] *strewn* levelled.

Each corse lay flat, lifeless and flat,
And by the holy rood![34]
A man all light, a seraph-man[35]
On every corse there stood.

This seraph-band, each waved his hand –
It was a heavenly sight!
They stood as signals to the land,
Each one a lovely light;

This seraph-band, each waved his hand,
No voice did they impart –
No voice, but O! the silence sank
Like music on my heart.

But soon I heard the dash of oars,
I heard the Pilot's cheer;
My head was turned perforce away
And I saw a boat appear.

The Pilot and the Pilot's boy,
I heard them coming fast –
Dear Lord in Heaven! it was a joy
The dead men could not blast.

I saw a third – I heard his voice;
It is the Hermit good!
He singeth loud his godly hymns
That he makes in the wood.
He'll shrieve my soul, he'll wash away
The albatross's blood.

## *Part The Seventh*

The Hermit of the Wood

This Hermit good lives in that wood
Which slopes down to the sea;
How loudly his sweet voice he rears!
He loves to talk with marineres
That come from a far countree.

He kneels at morn, and noon and eve—
He hath a cushion plump;
It is the moss that wholly hides
The rotted old oak-stump.

Notes

[34] *rood* cross.

[35] *seraph-man* The seraphim were the highest order of angels, whose purpose was to glow with the love of God.

The Skiff-boat neared, I heard them talk:
"Why, this is strange, I trow!
Where are those lights so many and fair,
That signal made but now?"

Approacheth the ship with wonder.

"Strange, by my faith!" the Hermit said,
"And they answered not our cheer!
The planks look warped, and see those sails,
How thin they are and sere!
I never saw aught like to them
Unless perchance it were

The skeletons of leaves that lag
My forest-brook along;
When the ivy-tod[36] is heavy with snow
And the owlet whoops to the wolf below
That eats the she-wolf 's young."

"Dear Lord! it hath a fiendish look",
The Pilot made reply,
"I am a-feared." "Push on, push on!"
Said the Hermit cheerily.
The boat came closer to the ship
But I nor spake nor stirred;
The boat came close beneath the ship
And straight a sound was heard!

The ship suddenly sinketh.

Under the water it rumbled on,
Still louder and more dread;
It reached the ship, it split the bay –
The ship went down like lead.

The ancient Mariner is saved in the Pilot's boat.

Stunned by that loud and dreadful sound
Which sky and ocean smote,
Like one that hath been seven days drowned,
My body lay afloat;
But swift as dreams, myself I found
Within the Pilot's boat.

Upon the whirl where sank the ship,
The boat spun round and round;
And all was still, save that the hill
Was telling of the sound.

## Notes

[36] *ivy-tod* ivy-bush.

I moved my lips – the Pilot shrieked
And fell down in a fit;
The holy Hermit raised his eyes,
And prayed where he did sit.

I took the oars; the Pilot's boy
Who now doth crazy go,
Laughed loud and long, and all the while
His eyes went to and fro.
"Ha! ha!" quoth he, "full plain I see,
The Devil knows how to row."

And now all in my own countrée
I stood on the firm land!
The Hermit stepped forth from the boat,
And scarcely he could stand.

The ancient Mariner earnestly entreateth the Hermit to shrieve him; and the penance of life falls on him.

"O shrieve me, shrieve me, holy man!"
The Hermit crossed his brow.
"Say quick", quoth he, "I bid thee say –
What manner of man art thou?"

Forthwith this frame of mine was wrenched
With a woeful agony,
Which forced me to begin my tale;
And then it left me free.

And ever and anon throughout his future life an agony constraineth him to travel from land to land,

Since then, at an uncertain hour,
That agony returns,
And till my ghastly tale is told,
This heart within me burns.

I pass, like night, from land to land,
I have strange power of speech;
The moment that his face I see,
I know the man that must hear me;
To him my tale I teach.

What loud uproar bursts from that door!
The wedding-guests are there;
But in the garden-bower the bride
And bridemaids singing are;
And hark, the little vesper-bell[37]
Which biddeth me to prayer!

## Notes

[37] *vesper-bell* bell used to summon the congregation for vespers, evensong.

O Wedding-Guest! this soul hath been
Alone on a wide wide sea;
So lonely 'twas, that God himself
Scarce seemed there to be.

O sweeter than the marriage-feast,
'Tis sweeter far to me
To walk together to the kirk
With a goodly company! –

To walk together to the kirk,
And all together pray,
While each to his great Father bends,
Old men, and babes, and loving friends,
And youths and maidens gay!

And to teach by his own example love and reverence to all things that God made and loveth.

Farewell, farewell! but this I tell
To thee, thou wedding-guest!
He prayeth well who loveth well
Both man and bird and beast.

He prayeth best who loveth best
All things both great and small,
For the dear God who loveth us,
He made and loveth all.'

The Mariner, whose eye is bright,
Whose beard with age is hoar,
Is gone; and now the Wedding-Guest
Turned from the bridegroom's door.

He went like one that hath been stunned
And is of sense forlorn:
A sadder and a wiser man,
He rose the morrow morn.

## *From* Table Talk

### *The Ancient Mariner* (dictated 31 May 1830)

The fault of 'The Ancient Mariner' consists in making the moral sentiment too apparent and bringing it in too much as a principle or cause in a work of such pure imagination.

### *The True Way for a Poet* (dictated 19 September 1830)

Southey picked nature's pockets as a poet, instead of borrowing from her. He went out and took some particular image, for example a water-insect – and then exactly copied its make, colours and motions. This he put in a poem. The true way for a poet is to examine nature, but write from your recollection, and trust more to your imagination than your memory.

## *The Recluse*[1] (dictated 21 July 1832)

Wordsworth should have first published his Thirteen Books on the growth of an individual mind, far superior to any part of *The Excursion*. Then the plan suggested and laid out by me was that he should assume the station of a man in repose, whose mind was made up, and so prepared to deliver upon authority a system of philosophy. He was to treat man as man – a subject of eye, ear, touch, taste, in contact with external nature, informing the senses from the mind and not compounding a mind out of the senses; then the pastoral and other states, assuming a satiric or Juvenalian spirit as he approached the high civilization of cities and towns; and then opening a melancholy picture of the present state of degeneracy and vice; thence revealing the necessity for and proof of the whole state of man and society being subject to and illustrative of a redemptive process in operation, showing how this idea reconciled all the anomalies, and how it promised future glory and restoration. Something of this sort I suggested, and it was agreed on. It is what in substance I have been all my life doing in my system of philosophy.

Wordsworth spoilt many of his best poems by abandoning the contemplative position, which is alone fitted for him, and introducing the object in a dramatic way. This is seen in 'The Leech-Gatherer'[2] and 'Ruth'. Wordsworth had more materials for the great philosophic poet than any man I ever knew or (as I think) has existed in this country for a long time – but he was utterly unfitted for the epic or narrative style. His mental-internal action is always so excessively disproportionate to the actual business that the latter either goes to sleep or becomes ridiculous. In his reasoning you will find no progression: it eddies, it comes round and round again, perhaps with a wider circle, but it is repetition still.

## *Keats*[1] (dictated 11 August 1832)

A loose, not well-dressed youth, met Mr Green and me in Mansfield Lane.[2] Green knew him and spoke. It was Keats. He was introduced to me, and stayed a minute or so. After he had gone a little, he came back and said, 'Let me carry away the memory, Coleridge, of having pressed your hand.' There is death in *his* hand, said I to Green when he was gone. Yet this was before the consumption showed itself.[3]

### Notes

The Recluse

[1] This account of 'The Recluse' should be regarded as a supplement to Coleridge's longer and more detailed account of the poem in his letter to Wordsworth of May 1815. As with that document, it should be approached with caution. 'The Recluse' was conceived in 1797–8, and may not have been conceived as Coleridge suggested.

[2] i.e. 'Resolution and Independence'.

Keats

[1] This meeting took place probably on 11 April 1819. Joseph Henry Green (1791–1863) performed a number of services for Coleridge, including that of amanuensis, confidant, friend and literary executor. Like Keats, he had grown up close to the Swan and Hoop in Moorgate, and was one of Keats's lecturers in anatomy at Guy's Hospital.

[2] *Mansfield Lane* ran adjacent to Kenwood House on Hampstead Heath.

[3] Keats knew he was fatally infected with tuberculosis by early February 1820.

# George Gordon Byron, 6th Baron Byron (1788–1824)

George Gordon, Lord Byron, that most image-conscious of poets (and one of the biggest-selling of his day), was born 22 January 1788, to Catherine Gordon and Captain John 'Mad Jack' Byron, in poor lodgings in London. He had a deformed right foot from birth and, despite several failed operations, was lame for the rest of his life. Abandoned by her husband (who, having spent his wife's inheritance, died in mysterious circumstances in France in 1791), his mother took her son to Aberdeen in her native Scotland, where she brought him up as best she could, though in considerable poverty. Here he came to love the Scottish countryside – and, at the age of 7, his cousin, Mary Duff.

He was only 10 years old when, on the death of his great-uncle in 1798, he succeeded to the barony, becoming sixth Lord Byron. At that point he and his mother moved to Newstead Abbey in Nottinghamshire, and he began to receive private tuition in preparation for entrance to a public school. At this period, his nurse May Gray beat and sexually abused him. This went on for about two years before it was discovered and she was dismissed.

At home, he fell in love with another cousin, Margaret Parker, who inspired Byron's 'first dash into poetry'. He entered Harrow School in 1801. Among his contemporaries were a future marquess, two actual and five future earls and viscounts, four other lords, four baronets, two future Prime Ministers (Lord Palmerston and Robert Peel), and the Duke of Dorset, who became Byron's 'fag' (or servant). At the age of 15 he fell in love with yet another cousin, Mary Chaworth, refusing to go back to Harrow because of his feelings for her. This gave way to an intense friendship with the 23-year-old Lord Grey de Ruthyn, who had taken a lease on Newstead Abbey until Byron's coming of age five years hence. Their association came to an abrupt halt in January 1804 when Grey seduced Byron, who returned to Harrow soon after.

He fell in love with other boys in his remaining year and a half there; Lady Caroline Lamb later claimed he slept with three of them. In spite of his obvious brilliance, he was never a diligent student but read voraciously, noting at the age of 19 he had digested 'about four thousand novels, including the works of Cervantes, Fielding, Smollett, Richardson, Mackenzie, Sterne, Rabelais and Rousseau'. In 1805 he led a rebellion against the new headmaster, the Reverend Dr George Butler, whom he found affected, ingratiating, overbearing, boastful, pedantic and (worst of all) socially inadequate. He organized the dragging of Butler's desk into the middle of the School House where it was set on fire, and composed scurrilous verses about him. Other triumphs included his performance of King Lear's address to the storm at the 1805 Speech Day, followed by the scoring of eighteen runs in the Eton–Harrow cricket match – no mean feat for someone with a club foot.

He left Harrow having incurred numerous debts, and took every opportunity, after going up to Trinity College, Cambridge, in October 1805, to increase them, living on the highest of hogs. By January 1808 his debts amounted to over £5,000 – a huge sum. Cambridge brought out his lordliness: the keeping of dogs being prohibited, he kept a tame bear in a turret at the top of a staircase. He struck up a passionate friendship with the choirboy John Edleston, 'the only being I esteem', who inspired the 'Thyrza' poems. In 1806 he gathered his juvenile poetry as *Fugitive Pieces* but suppressed it at the last moment; in January 1807 he privately printed his juvenilia as *Poems on Various Occasions*; and in the summer of 1807 published a third volume, *Hours of Idleness*. It drew damning criticism from Henry Brougham (anonymously) in the *Edinburgh Review* for January 1808, whose opening remarks set the tone for what was to come: 'His effusions are spread over a dead flat, and can no more get above or below the level, than if they were so much stagnant water.' Byron downed three bottles of claret after dinner and contemplated suicide.

The following day he decided to take revenge with a vigorous satire on literary life, *English Bards and Scotch Reviewers* (1809), the chief butt of which was Francis Jeffrey, editor of the *Edinburgh Review*, whom he held responsible for the attack. He laboured over it for more than a year before it was published anonymously, by which time it had grown to the point at which it lambasted virtually everyone in the literary world – the 'dunces', as he put it, which included his guardian, the Earl of Carlisle, who nurtured the ambition of being a verse-dramatist: 'No muse will cheer, with renovating smile, / The paralytic puking of Carlisle.'

The only writers of whom he had anything good to say were Thomas Campbell, Thomas Moore, Samuel Rogers and William Gifford. He saw them as faithful to the Augustan tradition of Pope, Dryden and Swift, rejected by Wordsworth, Coleridge and Southey for misguided poetic and philosophical systems. That was why he sniffed at Wordsworth's *Poems in Two Volumes* when he reviewed it in 1807, dismissing its author's 'namby-pamby' weakness for 'the most commonplace ideas'. Even his own poetry failed sufficiently to conform to the Augustan tradition, as he noted in correspondence with his publisher, John Murray, in September 1817:

> With regard to poetry in general I am convinced, the more I think of it, that he [Thomas Moore] and all of us – Scott, Southey, Wordsworth, Moore, Campbell, I – are all in the wrong, one as much as another – that we are upon a wrong revolutionary poetical system (or systems) not worth a damn in itself – and from which none but Rogers and Crabbe are free – and that the present and next generations will finally be of this opinion. I am the more confirmed in this by having lately gone over some of our classics, particularly Pope, whom I tried in this way: I took Moore's poems and my own and some others, and went over them side by side with Pope's, and I was really astonished (I ought not to have been so) and mortified at the ineffable distance in point of sense, harmony, effect, and even Imagination, passion, and invention, between the little Queen Anne's man [Pope] and us of the lower Empire.

This was the position from which Byron attacked his contemporaries throughout his life, and which was to inform his criticism of the Lake poets in 'Don Juan'. Whatever the rights and wrongs of that, *English Bards and Scotch Reviewers*, a satire in Popean couplets, enjoyed huge popularity, going through numerous editions, and attracting favourable coverage.

Having graduated from Cambridge in July 1808, he became a man about town, known liaisons including his adolescent page, Robert Rushton; Caroline Cameron, a 16-year-old Brighton prostitute who dressed as his pageboy; 'a famous French "Entremetteuse" who assisted young gentlemen in their youthful pastimes'; and at least three regular mistresses. It was as a supporter of Napoleon (who now, as Emperor, ruled most of Europe) that he took his seat in the House of Lords on 13 March 1809 on the Whig side, in opposition to the government. In July, more than £12,000 in debt, he eluded his creditors by embarking with Cambridge friend John Cam Hobhouse on a tour of Portugal, Spain, Gibraltar, Malta, Albania and Greece. In these countries homosexuality was less frowned upon than in England, and that may explain why he chose them. In the course of his travels he met the former robber baron Ali Pasha (Turkish despot of Albania and western Greece), swam the Hellespont, saved the life of a Turkish girl condemned to death, and met the woman he would celebrate in verse as the 'Maid of Athens'.

After two years and twelve days abroad, he landed at Sheerness in Kent on 14 July 1811, bringing with him the manuscript of 'Childe Harold's Pilgrimage', a semi-autobiographical poem about his travels. It was published by John Murray in March 1812 and became an instant success. All five hundred copies of the first edition sold out within three days of publication, and Byron became an overnight celebrity. As Samuel Rogers recalled: 'The genius which the poem exhibited, the youth, the rank of the author, his romantic wanderings in Greece, – these combined to make the world stark mad about Childe Harold and Byron.' In a favourable notice in the *Edinburgh Review*, Francis Jeffrey described the poem as follows:

> Childe Harold is a sated epicure – sickened with the very fullness of prosperity – oppressed with ennui, and stung by occasional remorse; – his heart hardened by a long course of sensual indulgence, and his opinion of mankind degraded by his acquaintance with the baser part of them. In this state he wanders over the fairest and most interesting parts of Europe, in the vain hope of stimulating his palsied sensibility by novelty, or at least of occasionally forgetting his mental anguish in the toils and perils of his journey.

The identification of Byron with his protagonist turbo-charged interest in the poem and its author. Female admirers wrote fan mail, enclosing their own verses, requesting signed copies of his works, samples of his handwriting and locks of his hair – a trend that continued unabated until his death. From this point onwards virtually everything he published sold in thousands, making him one of the bestselling writers of the day.

He delivered his maiden speech in the House of Lords on 27 February 1812 on behalf of the stocking-weavers of Nottingham (Luddites), in response to a vicious piece of legislation, the Tory Frame Work Bill, which proposed the death penalty as punishment for destruction of the new 'frames' that mechanized production. Byron sympathized with working people, and was proud to defend them in Parliament:

> How will you carry the bill into effect? Can you commit a whole county to their own prisons? Will you erect a gibbet in every field to hang up men like scarecrows? Or will you proceed ... by decimation, place the country under martial law, depopulate and lay waste all around you, and restore Sherwood forest as an acceptable gift to the crown in its former condition of a royal chase and an asylum for outlaws? Are these the remedies for a starving and desperate populace?

Byron was probably too much of a freethinker to have made a successful career within the constraints of the party system. Though welcomed into Whig circles at the highest levels, he seems not to have gained the trust Henry Richard Fox, third Lord Holland, who had observed the relish with which Byron castigated authority figures. 'I was born for opposition', Byron later wrote.

'Childe Harold' put an end to his political ambitions, but confirmed him as a writer – and with the tsunami of admirers came Lady Caroline Lamb, married to the Hon. William Lamb since 1805. In February 1812, she was handed the manuscript of 'Childe Harold' by Rogers, who told her to read it with the words: 'You should know the new poet.' As Lamb recalled,

> I read it, and that was enough. Rogers said, 'He has a club-foot, and bites his nails.' I said, 'If he was ugly as Aesop I must know him.' I was one night at Lady Westmoreland's; the women were all throwing their heads at him. Lady Westmoreland led me up to him. I looked earnestly at him, and turned on my heel. My opinion, in my journal was, 'mad – bad – and dangerous to know'. A day or two passed; I was sitting with Lord and Lady Holland, when he was announced. Lady Holland said, 'I must present Lord Byron to you'. Lord Byron said, 'That offer was made to you before; may I ask why you rejected it?' He begged permission to come and see me. He did so the next day. Rogers and Moore were standing by me: I was on the sofa. I had just come in from riding. I was filthy and heated. When Lord Byron was announced, I flew out of the room to wash myself. When I returned, Rogers said, 'Lord Byron, you are a happy man. Lady Caroline has been sitting here in all her dirt with us, but when you were announced, she flew to beautify herself.' Lord Byron wished to come and see me at eight o'clock, when I was alone; that was my dinner-hour. I said he might. From that moment, for more than nine months, he almost lived at Melbourne House. It was then the centre of all gaiety, at least in appearance.

Her husband knew of the affair but turned a blind eye. Perhaps he knew it would not last: it began in

March and ended in November – a comparatively long time for Byron, who was bored by women. Caroline kept him interested by being volatile and unpredictable – she was a 'volcano'. He outfitted her in pageboy gear, the thrill of seeing a woman cross-dress being a constant source of excitement. But the sword was bound to outwear its sheath, and he brought the relationship to a sudden end with a letter bearing the seal of his new conquest, Lady Oxford. Lady Caroline was not easily to be cast aside, however, and became what we would now describe as a 'stalker', following him wherever he went, loitering in the street when he was attending parties. 'You talked to me about keeping her out', Byron told Lady Melbourne in June 1814; 'it is impossible – she comes at all times – at any time – and the moment the door is open in she walks – I can't throw her out of the window.' Her revenge took the form of a novel, *Glenarvon* (1816), which portrayed Byron as the evil and depraved Earl of Glenarvon, and reprinted, word for word, the letter with which he ended their affair.

Byron consolidated his success with Oriental romances that reworked the successful formula of 'Childe Harold', in which the dark, brooding hero found himself in exotic locations: 'The Giaour' (1813), 'The Bride of Abydos' (1813), 'The Corsair' (1814) and 'Lara' (1814). Enormously popular, they were literary fantasies for an audience eager for escape – diverting enough for both author and reader, though not the great poetry for which he was destined. All the same, his stock was on the rise. By 1816 he had sufficient clout to order Murray to publish Coleridge's 'Christabel'; 'Kubla Khan: A Vision'; 'The Pains of Sleep' for the first time. Murray thought it doomed, but Byron was too important an author to displease.

During these years he became very close to Augusta Leigh, his half-sister, the child of his father's first marriage. Her mother had died only two days after her birth, and she had been brought up by a grandmother and various relatives. She did not meet Byron as a child; they first met when he was at Harrow, and began to correspond in 1804. In 1807 she married a cousin, Colonel George Leigh, and over the next six years gave birth to three daughters. In the summer of 1813 Byron visited the Leighs near Newmarket, fell passionately in love with her, and took her back to London, showing her off as his consort. A physical relationship developed, and it was thanks only to the counsel of Lady Melbourne that he was dissuaded from the plan of eloping with Augusta to the Continent. Generally speaking, Byron preferred men to women, but this was the great romance of his life; no one would mean so much to him as his half-sister. Yet he knew he was in danger of ruining her reputation, and that it had to end. Augusta was to become the subject of his most heartfelt love poems, the Stanzas and Epistle that bear her name, and their relationship is memorialized in 'Childe Harold's Pilgrimage' Canto III (stanza 55): '*That* love was pure ...'

Desperate that the bisexual half-brother with whom she had been involved should attain some measure of respectability, Augusta urged him to court Annabella Milbanke, a society heiress, whom he married on 2 January 1815. Made in haste, it was a match made in hell – though it is hard to imagine what kind of woman would have been suitable. Annabella was the opposite of her volatile husband, her skill at mathematics bespeaking a temperament that had little in common with his. Byron called her the Princess of Parallelograms. (The character of Don Juan's mother, Donna Inez, whose 'favourite science was the mathematical', is based on her.) Their daughter, Augusta Ada, was born on 10 December, by which time the marriage was on the rocks and debt-collectors on the doorstep.

They separated in February 1816 amidst accusations of infidelity and outright insanity. Caroline Lamb whipped Annabella into a frenzy by revealing details of Byron's homosexual liaisons, and in a short time London was buzzing with it. Ostracized from society, besieged by creditors, Byron decided to leave England – this time for ever. He ordered his coachmaker to make a replica of Napoleon's carriage and on 25 April 1816 set out with Hobhouse and his personal physician, John Polidori, on a whirlwind tour that took in Bruges, Antwerp, Brussels and Waterloo (already a tourist destination thanks to the battle the previous year).

The Byron ménage arrived at the Hotel Angleterre in Sécheron near Geneva on 25 May, where he amused himself by putting his age down in the hotel register as 100. Two days later on the hotel jetty he met Shelley, who arrived ten days before with Mary Godwin and her half-sister Claire Clairmont (with whom Byron had had an affair in London). Geneva remained his base until the end of September, and during that summer he and Shelley saw a great deal of each other. It was an important moment in literary history, not unlike the annus mirabilis of 1797–8 when Wordsworth and Coleridge inspired each other to ever greater heights of poetic achievement. Shelley's influence had an immediate effect: from this time onwards one senses a seriousness and commitment in Byron's poetry that was not there before.

The Shelleys moved to Maison Chappuis, a small house on the far side of the lake at Montalègre, while Byron moved into Villa Diodati at Cologny, on the bank above them. Diodati had pleasant associations because Milton stayed there with his friend Charles Diodati in 1639. Each day Byron and Shelley would sail across the lake and talk. Towards the end of June they set out on a week-long expedition round Lac Léman in a new boat Byron had purchased, taking with them an English translation of Rousseau's *Julie, ou La Nouvelle Héloïse* from which Shelley read aloud. In the evenings they read each other ghost stories. This led Byron to suggest the story-writing competition that inspired Mary Godwin's *Frankenstein*. Byron began, but did not finish, a fragment of a novel about an aristocratic vampire, Augustus Darvell; Polidori stole the idea for his own story, *The Vampyre*, featuring the evil Lord Ruthven, who bore more than a passing resemblance to his employer. For years to come, moneygrubbing publishers would publish Polidori's novel under Byron's name.

This was a hugely creative period. During the summer Byron composed much of 'Prometheus', 'Darkness' and 'Childe Harold' Canto III; Shelley wrote two of his most important poems, 'Hymn to Intellectual Beauty' and 'Mont Blanc'. 'Childe Harold' Canto III is included here, perhaps the most Wordsworthian of Byron's works. Though for much of his life contemptuous of Wordsworth (for his rejection of Pope), Byron during the summer of 1816 listened to Shelley's recitals of Wordsworth's *Poems* (1815) and 'The Excursion' (1814) – as he later remarked, Shelley 'used to dose me with Wordsworth physic even to nausea'. The medicine, however unpleasant, was to influence Byron's account of the Alpine landscape, and the effects were observed by Wordsworth when he remarked that Byron's 'poetical obligations to me' consisted 'not so much in particular expressions, though there is no want of these, as in the tone (assumed rather than natural) of enthusiastic admiration of nature, and a sensibility to her influences'. Wordsworth was right. When Byron says 'High mountains are a feeling, but the hum / Of human cities torture' (ll. 682–3), he is at his least persuasive. He preferred cities, whether London, Venice or Rome. The pose he strikes is modelled on Wordsworth's reference to 'the din / Of towns and cities' in 'Tintern Abbey'.

'Childe Harold' Canto III ranges across Europe, taking the same route as that followed by Byron in April–May 1816, visiting Waterloo (for melancholy reflections on war), sailing up the Rhine (for further reflections of a similar kind), into Switzerland, and arrival at Geneva, where Harold memorializes Rousseau and Voltaire. Perhaps the most impressive stanzas are those about Napoleon:

> There sunk the greatest, nor the worst of men,
> Whose spirit antithetically mixed
> One moment of the mightiest, and again
> On little objects with like firmness fixed,
> Extreme in all things!
>
> (ll. 316–20)

There is provocation in this: back home, Napoleon was public enemy no.1, and Byron knew such comments would scandalize his readers. All the same, his admiration was genuine. To be 'a god unto thyself' was a principal Byronic ambition, and as Napoleon had achieved precisely that, it was natural that he should have regarded him as a kindred spirit. In exile Byron may have identified with him more than ever; both had been hurled from their former eminences – Byron by disgrace, Napoleon by fortune. He goes on to cast Napoleon as a type of overreacher, possessing 'a fever at the core, / Fatal to him who bears, to all who ever bore' (ll. 377–8): a tragic hero condemned by circumstance and the injustice of his time.

You can't hold views like this and claim to subscribe to the central tenets of Christian theism, and neither Byron nor Shelley believed in God in anything like the conventional sense. In Canto III Byron goes out of his way to declare that 'I have not loved the world ... Nor coined my cheek to smiles, nor cried aloud / In worship of an echo' (ll. 1049, 1052–3). If he believes in anything, it is his own god-like potential. At his most credulous, Byron is willing to admit only the bare possibility of 'the Power which gave' (l.156) – and, even then, makes the point that it is responsible for having permitted the carnage of Waterloo.

Byron left Switzerland at the end of August and went south, arriving in Venice in November. Although he would continue to tour Italy, he was to be based, for the next three years, in Venice. Here, in 1818, he composed the fourth and final Canto of 'Childe Harold', and began experimenting with the Italian stanza form, *ottava rima*. It was a turning point in his poetic development, as he found it better suited to his purposes than the Spenserian stanza as it was geared to feminine rhymes and a rapid metre – ideal for comedy. He experimented with it in 'Beppo' and the 'Epistle to Augusta', then, in 1818, began his masterpiece: 'Don Juan'. This was originally to have been a single poem no longer than Canto I, but as he reached its end he realized the central character had more potential. He immediately set about a second Canto. Cantos I and II were the first to appear in print, and are presented here in their entirety with the Dedication, as Byron intended. The Dedication was written for the first edition of 1819, but in the event it was cancelled, not to be published until 1832, well after Byron's death. Why? Its forthright attack on the Lake Poets, especially Southey. Byron despised them for having forsaken the radical creed they espoused as young men: Wordsworth's patron was a Tory landowner, Southey had become a Tory journalist, and Coleridge had disappeared into the vortex of his own metaphysics. They had failed their promise, and in Byron's view Southey was the worst: 'A tinkering slavemaker who mends old chains' (l. 111).

Byron declared, 'I have no plan – I had no plan – but I had or have materials', and the manner in which Don Juan is written is just as important as the story; as he observed, 'I mean it for a poetical Tristram Shandy.' It is sufficiently copious to contain all the unpredictability and accumulated detritus of life as it is lived. 'Almost all Don Juan is real life', Byron declared, 'either my own, or from people I know.' He gave his remaining years to it, leaving it unfinished at the time of his death. It would run to sixteen Cantos, and there would be fourteen stanzas of a seventeenth.

Anxious about the content of the poem, John Murray issued Cantos I and II on 15 July 1819, omitting both his name and Byron's from the title-page. All the same, everyone knew who was the author, and despite (or perhaps because of) its risqué subject matter, it sold well.

In 'Don Juan', nothing is sacred; everything reduced to the same materialistic level and profaned. Take, for instance, the moment in the cave when, frying eggs for the emaciated Juan, Zoe notes that 'the best feelings must have victual' – love is dependent on being well-fed. Wordsworth did not see the joke; in late January 1820, he told Henry Crabb Robinson: 'I am persuaded that 'Don Juan' will do more harm to the English character than anything of our time.' That lack of respect for things sacred, besides being funny, was the secret of the poem's popularity.

It was one of Byron's more appalling boasts that, during his time in Venice, he made love to over 200 women – typical of the kind of claim he used to deflect public attention from his interest in adolescent boys. True or not, a degree of stability entered his private life when, in the year of Juan's appearance, he became *cavaliere servente* (lover of a married woman) to Contessa Teresa Guiccioli, whom he encountered at a *conversazione* at Palazzo Benzoni in Venice. Their first assignation took place the day after, and the 'essential part of the business' occupied them, according to Byron, 'four continuous days'. Their love affair would sustain him until the end of his life. He followed the Guicciolis to their home in Ravenna, then to their palace in Bologna. It was while on that journey he composed one of his most successful love poems, 'To the Po'.

He moved to Pisa to be near Shelley who, with him and Leigh Hunt, wished to set up a new periodical entitled *The Liberal*. Unfortunately, before it could begin publishing, Shelley went sailing in his new boat, the Ariel, and was drowned. Shelley's corpse was washed up several days later, and cremated on the beach at Viareggio with Byron in attendance. According to Trelawny, Shelley's heart 'would not take the flame', and in due course it would pass, as a relic, into the possession of Shelley's descendants. *The Liberal* struggled on for four numbers, attracting terrible reviews, until it was discontinued and Hunt returned with his family to England.

Byron prided himself on consistency in politics, and it was characteristic of him to join the fight for Greek independence. The massacre of Chios in spring 1822, in which 25,000 Greeks were slaughtered by the Turks, led to an outpouring of support for their plight. He was an eager recruit to the London Greek Committee, formed in January 1823. It was not merely the cause that drew him, but identification with the Suliotes, the exiled military caste of Orthodox Christian Albanians whom he thought of as similar to a Scottish clan. He decided he would not only donate funds, but form an elite private army to fight on the Greek side, which he would command. He parted with Teresa Guiccioli at Genoa and sailed for Cephalonia. By the time he landed at Missolonghi on 5 January 1824 he was in charge of up to a thousand Suliote warriors. But he would never reach the battlefield. He contracted a fever in early April and, weakened by repeated bleeding (the usual treatment for fever was to apply leeches to the forehead and arms), died on 19 April. He was in his thirty-seventh year.

He was already one of the most mythologized writers who had ever lived, thanks to his own poetry, and an early death consolidated his popularity. When his body was shipped back to England, it lay in state for two days at 20 Great George Street in London. So grief-stricken were those who came to view it that barriers had to be erected to hold them back. When the body was taken on the long journey to Hucknall Torkard churchyard in Nottinghamshire, crowds lined the streets, weeping openly as it passed. Most were working people, who remembered his defence of them in Parliament years before.

This was only the beginning. In no time at all Byron was a cult figure, a trend fuelled in part by publication of his conversations with such associates as Leigh Hunt, Thomas Medwin and Lady Blessington. His correspondence and journals flowed into print with the first attempt at a collected edition by Thomas Moore in 1830. It was an international bestseller, and the more recent edition (1973–93) by Leslie A. Marchand remains one of the great scholarly achievements of our time, as well as one of the more entertaining. For a while it was fashionable for artists to paint Byron during his final illness – 'The Death of Byron' by Joseph-Denis von Odevaere and 'Lord Byron on his Deathbed' by R.C. Moore are two of the most notable. His poetry attracted some of the most skilled illustrators of the day, including Thomas Stothard, Richard Westall, J.M.W. Turner, and George and I.R. Cruikshank; Ford Madox Brown produced some remarkable full-scale paintings based on *Sardanapalus* and 'The Prisoner of Chillon'. He was more famous still on the Continent, where Delacroix depicted scenes from 'The Corsair', 'Lara', 'Mazeppa' and 'The Prisoner of Chillon', while Berlioz composed music based on 'Childe Harold' Cantos III and IV. In Greece he remains a national hero, with streets and town squares named after him. Despite his propensity for 15-year-old boys, he remains the most popular personality of the Romantic period, exemplifying the myth of the poet who lived life to the full and died in his prime.

I am grateful to Dr Peter Cochran for invaluable advice on editorial conundrums in Byron's texts.

## *She Walks in Beauty* (composed *c.*12 June 1814)[1]

I

She walks in beauty like the night
Of cloudless climes and starry skies,
And all that's best of dark and bright
Meet in her aspect and her eyes,
Thus mellowed to that tender light
Which heaven to gaudy day denies.

II

One shade the more, one ray the less
Had half-impaired the nameless grace
Which waves in every raven tress
Or softly lightens o'er her face –
Where thoughts serenely sweet express
How pure, how dear their dwelling place.

III

And on that cheek and o'er that brow,
So soft, so calm, yet eloquent,
The smiles that win, the tints that glow,
But tell of days in goodness spent,
A mind at peace with all below,
A heart whose love is innocent.

## *Childe Harold's Pilgrimage: Canto III* (composed 25 April–4 July 1816; published 18 November 1816)

*Afin que cette application vous forçât à penser à autre chose. Il n'y a en vérité de remède que celui-là et le temps.*
Lettre du Roi de Prusse à D'Alembert, 7 Sept. 1776[1]

I

Is thy face like thy mother's, my fair child,[2]
Ada, sole daughter of my house and heart?
When last I saw thy young blue eyes, they smiled;
And then we parted – not as now we part,
But with a hope.
Awaking with a start,

## Notes

She Walks in Beauty

[1] Byron met Anne Wilmot (1784–1871) on 11 June 1814; she was the wife of his first cousin, Robert John Wilmot.

Childe Harold's Pilgrimage: Canto III

[1] 'So that this work will force you to think of something else. Truly, that and time are the only remedies.'

[2] *my fair child* Byron's only legitimate daughter Ada Augusta, born 10 December 1815. After Lady Byron left him five weeks later, he did not see her again.

The waters heave around me, and on high
The winds lift up their voices. I depart
Whither I know not, but the hour's gone by
When Albion's lessening shores could grieve or glad mine eye.[3]

2

Once more upon the waters, yet once more![4]
And the waves bound beneath me as a steed
That knows his rider – welcome to their roar!
Swift be their guidance, wheresoe'er it lead!
Though the strained mast should quiver as a reed
And the rent canvas fluttering strew the gale,
Still must I on – for I am as a weed
Flung from the rock on ocean's foam, to sail
Where'er the surge may sweep, the tempest's breath prevail.

3

In my youth's summer I did sing of one,[5]
The wandering outlaw of his own dark mind;
Again I seize the theme then but begun,
And bear it with me as the rushing wind
Bears the cloud onwards. In that tale I find
The furrows of long thought, and dried-up tears
Which, ebbing, leave a sterile track behind,
O'er which all heavily the journeying years
Plod the last sands of life, where not a flower appears.

4

Since my young days of passion[6] (joy or pain),
Perchance my heart and harp have lost a string
And both may jar; it may be that in vain
I would essay,[7] as I have sung, to sing.
Yet, though a dreary[8] strain, to this I cling,
So that it wean me from the weary dream
Of selfish grief or gladness; so it fling
Forgetfulness around me. It shall seem
To me (though to none else) a not ungrateful theme.

5

He, who grown aged in this world of woe
(In deeds not years), piercing the depths of life
So that no wonder waits him; nor below
Can love or sorrow, fame, ambition, strife,
Cut to his heart again with the keen knife

## Notes

[3] *the hour's gone by…mine eye* Byron began writing this Canto while at sea, 25 April 1816. He felt hounded out of England by the bad publicity whipped up by his wife.

[4] *Once more…once more* Byron echoes *Henry V* III i 1: 'Once more unto the breach, dear friends, once more.'

[5] *In my youth's summer…one* i.e. Childe Harold. Byron began Canto I on 31 October 1809, when he was 21.

[6] *Since my young days of passion* Byron was 28 at the time of writing.

[7] *essay* attempt.

[8] *dreary* melancholy.

Of silent sharp endurance – he can tell
Why thought seeks refuge in lone caves yet[9] rife
With airy images, and shapes which dwell
Still unimpaired, though old, in the soul's haunted cell.

6

'Tis to create, and in creating live
A being more intense, that we endow
With form our fancy, gaining as we give
The life we image – even as I do now.
What am I? Nothing. But not so art thou,
Soul of my thought,[10] with whom I traverse earth,
Invisible but gazing, as I glow
Mixed with thy spirit, blended with thy birth,
And feeling still with thee in my crushed feelings' dearth.

7

Yet must I think less wildly. I *have* thought
Too long and darkly till my brain became,
In its own eddy, boiling and o'erwrought,
A whirling gulf of fantasy and flame;
And thus, untaught in youth my heart to tame,
My springs of life were poisoned. 'Tis too late!
Yet am I changed, though still enough the same
In strength to bear what time cannot abate,
And feed on bitter fruits without accusing fate.

8

Something too much of this:[11] but now 'tis past,
And the spell closes with its silent seal.
Long absent Harold[12] reappears at last;
He of the breast which fain no more would feel,
Wrung with the wounds which kill not, but ne'er heal;
Yet Time, who changes all, had altered him
In soul and aspect as in age: years steal
Fire from the mind as vigour from the limb;
And Life's enchanted cup but sparkles near the brim.

9

His had been quaffed too quickly, and he found
The dregs were wormwood;[13] but he filled again,
And from a purer fount,[14] on holier ground,
And deemed its spring perpetual – but in vain!
Still round him clung invisibly a chain
Which galled for ever, fettering though unseen,

## Notes

[9] *yet* still.

[10] *Soul of my thought* Byron is still thinking of his daughter.

[11] *Something too much of this* borrowed from *Hamlet* III ii 74.

[12] *Harold* A late entrance for the hero of the poem, whose character was Byron's alter ego, embodying the deepest anxieties and preoccupations of his creator.

[13] *wormwood* plant known for its bitter taste.

[14] *a purer fount* Greece, where Harold had gone in Canto II.

And heavy though it clanked not; worn with pain,
Which pined although it spoke not, and grew keen,
Entering with every step he took, through many a scene.

10

Secure in guarded coldness, he had mixed
Again in fancied safety with his kind,
And deemed his spirit now so firmly fixed
And sheathed with an invulnerable mind,
That, if no joy, no sorrow lurked behind;
And he, as one, might midst the many stand
Unheeded, searching through the crowd to find
Fit speculation – such as in strange land
He found in wonder-works of God and Nature's hand.

11

But who can view the ripened rose, nor seek
To wear it? Who can curiously behold
The smoothness and the sheen of Beauty's cheek,
Nor feel the heart can never all grow old?
Who can contemplate fame through clouds unfold
The star which rises o'er her steep, nor climb?
Harold, once more within the vortex, rolled
On with the giddy circle, chasing Time,
Yet with a nobler aim than in his Youth's fond prime.

12

But soon he knew himself the most unfit
Of men to herd with man,[15] with whom he held
Little in common; untaught to submit
His thoughts to others, though his soul was quelled
In youth by his own thoughts; still uncompelled,
He would not yield dominion of his mind
To spirits against whom his own rebelled,
Proud though in desolation – which could find
A life within itself, to breathe without mankind.

13

Where rose the mountains, there to him were friends;
Where rolled the ocean, thereon was his home;
Where a blue sky, and glowing clime, extends,
He had the passion and the power to roam;
The desert, forest, cavern, breaker's foam,
Were unto him companionship; they spake
A mutual language, clearer than the tome
Of his land's tongue, which he would oft forsake
For nature's pages glassed by sunbeams on the lake.

Notes

[15] *man* i.e. mankind.

14

Like the Chaldean,[16] he could watch the stars
Till he had peopled them with beings bright
As their own beams; and earth, and earth-born jars,[17]
And human frailties, were forgotten quite:
Could he have kept his spirit to that flight
He had been happy; but this clay will sink
Its spark immortal, envying it the light
To which it mounts, as if to break the link
That keeps us from yon heaven which woos us to its brink.

15

But in Man's dwellings he became a thing
Restless and worn, and stern and wearisome,
Drooped as a wild-born falcon with clipped wing,
To whom the boundless air alone were home:
Then came his fit again, which to o'ercome,
As eagerly the barred-up bird will beat
His breast and beak against his wiry dome
Till the blood tinge his plumage – so the heat
Of his impeded soul would through his bosom eat.

16

Self-exiled Harold wanders forth again,
With nought of hope left, but with less of gloom;
The very knowledge that he lived in vain,
That all was over on this side the tomb,[18]
Had made Despair a smilingness[19] assume,
Which, though 'twere wild (as on the plundered wreck
When mariners would madly meet their doom
With draughts intemperate on the sinking deck),
Did yet inspire a cheer, which he forbore to check.

17

Stop! For thy tread is on an Empire's dust!
An earthquake's spoil is sepulchred below![20]
Is the spot marked with no colossal bust?
Nor column trophied for triumphal show?
None; but the moral's truth tells simpler so.
As the ground was before, thus let it be;
How that red rain[21] hath made the harvest grow!
And is this all the world has gained by thee,
Thou first and last of fields, king-making Victory?[22]

## Notes

[16] *Chaldean* the Chaldeans were renowned astronomers.

[17] *jars* quarrels.

[18] *That all was over…tomb* i.e. that there was no afterlife.

[19] *a smilingness* a smiling expression.

[20] *Stop!…below* Byron visited the battlefield at Waterloo on Saturday 4 May 1816. The 'earthquake's spoil' consists of thousands of people killed in battle.

[21] *red rain* blood shed on the fields in the battle.

[22] *king-making Victory* The Bourbon restoration of April–May 1814 strengthened monarchical power throughout Europe. In a letter written soon after his visit to Waterloo, Byron commented on the battle: 'I detest the cause and the victors – and the victory – including Blucher and the Bourbons'.

18

And Harold stands upon this place of skulls,
The grave of France, the deadly Waterloo!
How in an hour the Power which gave[23] annuls
Its gifts, transferring fame as fleeting too!
In 'pride of place'[24] here last the eagle flew,
Then tore with bloody talon the rent plain,
Pierced by the shaft[25] of banded nations through;
Ambition's life and labours all were vain;
He wears the shattered links of the world's broken chain.

19

Fit retribution! Gaul[26] may champ the bit
And foam in fetters – but is earth more free?
Did nations combat to make *one*[27] submit?
Or league[28] to teach all kings true sovereignty?
What? Shall reviving thraldom[29] again be
The patched-up idol of enlightened days?
Shall we, who struck the lion down, shall we
Pay the wolf homage? Proffering lowly gaze
And servile knees to thrones? No! Prove[30] before ye praise!

20

If not, o'er one fallen despot boast no more!
In vain fair cheeks were furrowed with hot tears
For Europe's flowers long rooted up before
The trampler of her vineyards; in vain, years
Of death, depopulation, bondage, fears,
Have all been borne, and broken by the accord
Of roused-up millions: all that most endears
Glory, is when the myrtle wreathes a sword,
Such as Harmodius drew on Athens' tyrant lord.[31]

21

There was a sound of revelry by night,[32]
And Belgium's capital had gathered then
Her beauty and her chivalry – and bright
The lamps shone o'er fair women and brave men;
A thousand hearts beat happily; and when
Music arose with its voluptuous swell,

## Notes

[23] *the Power which gave* Rather than say 'God', Byron uses the term employed by Shelley in 'Hymn to Intellectual Beauty' and 'Mont Blanc'.

[24] '"Pride of place" is a term of falconry, and means the highest pitch of flight. See *Macbeth*, etc.' (Byron's note). Byron refers to *Macbeth* II iv 12: 'A falcon, tow'ring in her pride of place.'

[25] *shaft* arrow.

[26] *Gaul* France.

[27] *one* Napoleon.

[28] *league* band together. The Battle of Waterloo was fought by an alliance of the British, Dutch, Austrians, Swedes and Prussians.

[29] *thraldom* slavery. Byron was no friend to monarchy.

[30] *Prove* i.e. establish the true value of the victory.

[31] *Such as Harmodius…tyrant lord* Byron alludes to Harmodius and Aristogeiton, their daggers wreathed in myrtle branches, who in 514 BCE attempted to kill Hippias and Hipparchus, tyrannical rulers of Athens. The sword wreathed in myrtle leaves is an emblem of the freedom fighter.

[32] *There was a sound…night* The stanza recalls the famous ball given by the Duchess of Richmond in Brussels on 15 June 1815, the night prior to the inconclusive Battle of Quatre Bras; Waterloo was fought three days later.

Soft eyes looked love to eyes which spake again,
And all went merry as a marriage bell;
But hush! hark! a deep sound strikes like a rising knell!

22

Did ye not hear it? No, 'twas but the wind,
Or the car rattling o'er the stony street;
On with the dance! Let joy be unconfined;
No sleep till morn, when Youth and Pleasure meet
To chase the glowing Hours with flying feet –
But hark! that heavy sound breaks in once more,
As if the clouds its echo would repeat;
And nearer – clearer – deadlier than before!
Arm! Arm! It is – it is – the cannon's opening roar![33]

23

Within a windowed niche of that high hall
Sate Brunswick's fated chieftain;[34] he did hear
That sound the first amidst the festival,
And caught its tone with Death's prophetic ear;
And when they smiled because he deemed it near,
His heart more truly knew that peal too well
Which stretched his father on a bloody bier,
And roused the vengeance blood alone could quell;
He rushed into the field, and, foremost fighting, fell.

24

Ah! then and there was hurrying to and fro,
And gathering tears, and tremblings of distress,
And cheeks all pale, which but an hour ago
Blushed at the praise of their own loveliness –
And there were sudden partings, such as press
The life from out young hearts, and choking sighs
Which ne'er might be repeated; who could guess
If ever more should meet those mutual eyes,
Since upon nights so sweet such awful morn could rise?

25

And there was mounting in hot haste: the steed,
The mustering squadron, and the clattering car,
Went pouring forward with impetuous speed,
And swiftly forming in the ranks of war;
And the deep thunder peal on peal afar;

## Notes

[33] *the cannon's opening roar!* Wellington discovered the approach of Napoleon not from the sound of cannon but from dispatches sent by the Prussian commander, Blücher.

[34] *Brunswick's fated chieftain* Frederick, Duke of Brunswick (1771–1815), nephew of George III, killed at Quatre Bras. His father, Charles William Ferdinand, was killed in 1806 at Auerstädt.

And near, the beat of the alarming drum[35]
Roused up the soldier ere the morning star;
While thronged the citizens with terror dumb,
Or whispering, with white lips, 'The foe! They come! They come!'

26

And wild and high the 'Cameron's gathering'[36] rose!
The war-note of Lochiel,[37] which Albyn's[38] hills
Have heard, and, heard, too, have her Saxon foes:
How in the noon of night that pibroch[39] thrills,
Savage and shrill! But with the breath which fills
Their mountain-pipe, so fill the mountaineers
With the fierce native daring which instils
The stirring memory of a thousand years,
And Evan's, Donald's fame rings in each clansman's ears![40]

27

And Ardennes[41] waves above them her green leaves,
Dewy with nature's tear-drops, as they pass,
Grieving, if aught inanimate e'er grieves,
Over the unreturning brave – alas!
Ere evening to be trodden like the grass
Which now beneath them, but above shall grow
In its next verdure, when this fiery mass
Of living valour, rolling on the foe
And burning with high hope, shall moulder cold and low.

28

Last noon beheld them full of lusty life,
Last eve in Beauty's circle proudly gay,
The midnight brought the signal-sound of strife,
The morn the marshalling in arms, the day
Battle's magnificently-stern array!
The thunder-clouds close o'er it, which when rent
The earth is covered thick with other clay,[42]
Which her own clay shall cover, heaped and pent,
Rider and horse, friend, foe, in one red burial blent![43]

## Notes

[35] *the alarming drum* The drum sounds an alarm to the soldiers.

[36] *Cameron's gathering* rallying cry of the Cameron clan.

[37] *Lochiel* title of the chief of the Camerons.

[38] *Albyn* Gaelic name for Scotland.

[39] *pibroch* Series of martial variations for the bagpipe, on a theme called the 'urlar'.

[40] *And Evan's…ears* Sir Evan or Ewen Cameron (1629–1719) resisted Cromwell 1652–8 and fought at Killiecrankie for James II in 1689. His grandson Donald Cameron (1695–1748) fought to restore the Stuarts in 1745 and was wounded at Culloden the following year. Byron spent his formative years in Scotland.

[41] *Ardennes* 'The woods of Soignies is supposed to be a remnant of the "forest of Ardennes", famous in Boiardo's *Orlando*, and immortal in Shakespeare's *As You Like It*. It is also celebrated in Tacitus as being the spot of successful defence by the Germans against the Roman encroachments. I have ventured to adopt the name connected with more noble associations than those of mere slaughter' (Byron's note). An error-strewn note: Soignies is between Waterloo and Brussels, Ardennes is in Luxembourg, and Arden is English.

[42] *other clay* corpses.

[43] *blent* blended.

29

Their praise is hymned by loftier harps than mine;[44]
Yet one I would select from that proud throng,
Partly because they blend me with his line,[45]
And partly that I did his sire some wrong,
And partly that bright names will hallow song;
And his was of the bravest, and when showered
The death-bolts deadliest the thinned files along,
Even where the thickest of war's tempest loured,
They reached no nobler breast than thine – young, gallant Howard![46]

30

There have been tears and breaking hearts for thee,
And mine were nothing, had I such to give;
But when I stood beneath the fresh green tree,
Which living waves where thou didst cease to live,[47]
And saw around me the wide field revive
With fruits and fertile promise, and the spring
Come forth her work of gladness to contrive,
With all her reckless[48] birds upon the wing,
I turned from all she brought to those she could not bring.[49]

31

I turned to thee, to thousands, of whom each
And one as all a ghastly gap did make
In his own kind and kindred, whom to teach
Forgetfulness were mercy for their sake;
The Archangel's trump, not Glory's, must awake
Those whom they thirst for; though the sound of Fame
May for a moment soothe, it cannot slake
The fever of vain longing, and the name
So honoured but assumes a stronger, bitterer claim.

## Notes

[44] *loftier harps than mine* Scott's, in 'The Field of Waterloo' (Edinburgh, 1815).

[45] *line* i.e. of descent.

[46] *young, gallant Howard!* The Hon. Frederick Howard (1785–1815), Byron's cousin, son of his guardian, the Earl of Carlisle, who he had criticized in *English Bards and Scotch Reviewers* (1809) for his ambitions as a verse-dramatist: 'So dull in youth, so drivelling in his age, / His scenes alone had damned our sinking stage' (ll. 733–4).

[47] *didst cease to live* i.e. died.

[48] *reckless* carefree.

[49] 'My guide from Mont St Jean over the field seemed intelligent and accurate. The place where Major Howard fell was not far from two tall and solitary trees (there was a third cut down, or shivered in the battle) which stand a few yards from each other at a pathway's side. Beneath these he died and was buried. The body has since been removed to England. A small hollow for the present marks where it lay, but will probably soon be effaced; the plough has been upon it, and the grain is.

After pointing our the different spots where Picton and other gallant men had perished, the guide said, "Here Major Howard lay; I was near him when wounded." I told him my relationship, and he seemed then still more anxious to point out the particular spot and circumstances. The place is one of the most marked in the field from the peculiarity of the two trees above mentioned.

I went on horseback twice over the field, comparing it with my recollection of similar scenes. As a plain, Waterloo seems marked out for the scene of some great action, though this may be mere imagination: I have viewed with attention those of Platea, Troy, Mantinea, Leuctra, Chaeronea, and Marathon; and the field around Mont St Jean and Hougoumont appears to want little but a better cause, and that undefinable but impressive halo which the lapse of ages throws around a celebrated spot, to vie in interest with any or all of these, except perhaps the last mentioned' (Byron's note).

32

They mourn, but smile at length – and, smiling, mourn:
The tree will wither long before it fall;
The hull drives on, though mast and sail be torn;
The roof-tree sinks, but moulders on the hall
In massy hoariness; the ruined wall
Stands when its wind-worn battlements are gone;
The bars survive the captive they enthrall;[50]
The day drags through though storms keep out the sun;
And thus the heart will break, yet brokenly live on:

33

Even as a broken mirror, which the glass
In every fragment multiplies; and makes
A thousand images of one that was,
The same, and still the more, the more it breaks;
And thus the heart will do which not forsakes,
Living in shattered guise; and still, and cold,
And bloodless, with its sleepless sorrow aches,
Yet withers on till all without is old,
Showing no visible sign, for such things are untold.

34

There is a very life in our despair,
Vitality of poison – a quick[51] root
Which feeds these deadly branches; for it were
As nothing did we die; but Life will suit
Itself to Sorrow's most detested fruit,
Like to the apples on the Dead Sea's shore,
All ashes to the taste.[52] Did man compute
Existence by enjoyment, and count o'er
Such hours 'gainst years of life, say, would he name threescore?

35

The Psalmist numbered out the years of man:[53]
They are enough; and if thy tale[54] be *true*,
Thou, who didst grudge him even that fleeting span,
More than enough, thou fatal Waterloo!
Millions of tongues record thee, and anew
Their children's lips shall echo them, and say,
'Here, where the sword united nations drew,
Our countrymen were warring on that day!'
And this is much, and all which will not pass away.

## Notes

[50] *enthrall* imprison.

[51] *quick* living.

[52] 'The (fabled) apples on the brink of the Lake Asphaltes were said to be fair without, and within ashes. – Vide Tacitus, *Historia* [Book 5, sec.7]' (Byron's note).

[53] *The Psalmist…years of man* Byron refers to Psalm 90:10: 'The days of our years are threescore years and ten; and if by reason of strength they be fourscore years, yet is their strength labour and sorrow; for it is soon cut off, and we fly away.'

[54] *tale* a pun, meaning both 'story' and 'counting'.

36

There sunk the greatest, nor the worst of men,[55]
Whose spirit antithetically mixed
One moment of the mightiest, and again
On little objects with like firmness fixed,
Extreme in all things! Hadst thou been betwixt,[56]
Thy throne[57] had still been thine, or never been;
For daring made thy rise as fall: thou seek'st
Even now to reassume the imperial mien,[58]
And shake again the world, the Thunderer of the scene!

37

Conqueror and captive of the earth art thou!
She trembles at thee still, and thy wild name
Was ne'er more bruited[59] in men's minds than now
That thou art nothing, save the jest of Fame,
Who wooed thee once, thy vassal, and became
The flatterer of thy fierceness – till thou wert
A god unto thyself; nor less the same
To the astounded kingdoms all inert,
Who deemed thee for a time whate'er thou didst assert.

38

Oh, more or less than man – in high or low,
Battling with nations, flying from the field;
Now making monarchs' necks thy footstool, now
More than thy meanest soldier taught to yield;[60]
An empire thou couldst crush, command, rebuild,
But govern not thy pettiest passion, nor,
However deeply in men's spirits skilled,
Look through thine own,[61] nor curb the lust of war,
Nor learn that tempted Fate will leave the loftiest star.

39

Yet well thy soul hath brooked[62] the turning tide
With that untaught innate philosophy,
Which, be it wisdom, coldness, or deep pride,
Is gall and wormwood[63] to an enemy.
When the whole host of hatred stood hard by
To watch and mock thee shrinking, thou hast smiled
With a sedate and all-enduring eye;
When Fortune fled her spoiled and favourite child,
He stood unbowed beneath the ills upon him piled.

## Notes

[55] *There sunk...men* Napoleon. Byron thought Napoleon no worse than the despots who had taken his place.

[56] *betwixt* i.e. between the mightiest and the meanest.

[57] *Thy throne* Napoleon crowned himself Emperor in December 1804.

[58] *thou seek'st...mien* Napoleon was at this time in exile on St Helena.

[59] *bruited* celebrated.

[60] *now / More than thy meanest soldier...yield* Napoleon has been taught to humble himself even more than the lowest of his soldiers.

[61] *thine own* i.e. spirit.

[62] *brooked* endured.

[63] *gall and wormwood* i.e. very bitter.

40

Sager than in thy fortunes; for in them
Ambition steeled thee on too far to show
That just habitual scorn, which could contemn
Men and their thoughts; 'twas wise to feel, not so
To wear it ever on thy lip and brow,
And spurn the instruments[64] thou wert to use
Till they were turned unto thine overthrow:
'Tis but a worthless world to win or lose;
So hath it proved to thee, and all such lot who choose.

41

If, like a tower upon a headlong rock,
Thou[65] hadst been made to stand or fall alone,
Such scorn of man had helped to brave the shock;
But men's thoughts were the steps which paved thy throne,
Their admiration thy best weapon shone;
The part of Philip's son[66] was thine, not then
(Unless aside thy purple[67] had been thrown)
Like stern Diogenes[68] to mock at men:
For sceptred cynics earth were far too wide a den.[69]

42

But quiet to quick[70] bosoms is a hell,
And *there* hath been thy bane: there is a fire
And motion of the soul which will not dwell
In its own narrow being, but aspire
Beyond the fitting medium of desire,
And, but once kindled, quenchless evermore,
Preys upon high adventure, nor can tire
Of aught but rest – a fever at the core,
Fatal to him who bears, to all who ever bore.

43

This makes the madmen who have made men mad
By their contagion: conquerors and kings,
Founders of sects and systems, to whom add
Sophists, bards, statesmen, all unquiet things
Which stir too strongly the soul's secret springs,
And are themselves the fools to those they fool –

## Notes

[64] *the instruments* i.e. other men.

[65] *Thou* Napoleon, at the time of writing imprisoned on St Helena in the wake of his final defeat at Waterloo.

[66] *Philip's son* Alexander the Great, son of Philip of Macedonia, who also conquered an empire.

[67] *thy purple* the colour worn by emperors. Napoleon crowned himself Emperor in 1804.

[68] *stern Diogenes* Greek, Cynic, philosopher of the fourth century BCE, known for austere habits, and choosing to live in the open.

[69] 'The great error of Napoleon, "if we have writ our annals true", was a continued obtrusion on mankind of his want of all community of feeling for or with them; perhaps more offensive to human vanity than the active cruelty of more trembling and suspicious tyranny.

Such were his speeches to public assemblies as well as individuals: and the single expression which he is said to have used on returning to Paris after the Russian winter had destroyed his army, rubbing his hands over a fire, "This is pleasanter than Moscow", would probably alienate more favour from his cause than the destruction and reverses which led to the remark' (Byron's note).

[70] *quick* vital, hasty.

Envied, yet how unenviable! What stings
Are theirs! One breast laid open were a school
Which would unteach mankind the lust to shine or rule:

44

Their breath is agitation, and their life
A storm whereon they ride, to sink at last;
And yet so nursed and bigoted to strife,
That, should their days (surviving perils passed)
Melt to calm twilight, they feel overcast
With sorrow and supineness, and so die;
Even as a flame unfed, which runs to waste
With its own flickering, or a sword laid by
Which eats into itself, and rusts ingloriously.

45

He who ascends to mountain-tops shall find
The loftiest peaks most wrapped in clouds and snow;
He who surpasses or subdues mankind
Must look down on the hate of those below.
Though high *above* the sun of glory glow
And far *beneath* the earth and ocean spread,
*Round* him are icy rocks, and loudly blow
Contending tempests on his naked head,
And thus reward the toils which to those summits led.

46

Away with these! True wisdom's world will be
Within its own creation, or in thine,
Maternal Nature![71] For who teems like thee,
Thus on the banks of thy majestic Rhine?[72]
There Harold gazes on a work divine,
A blending of all beauties; streams and dells,
Fruit, foliage, crag, wood, cornfield, mountain, vine,
And chiefless castles breathing stern farewells
From gray but leafy walls, where Ruin greenly dwells.

47

And there they[73] stand, as stands a lofty mind,
Worn, but unstooping to the baser crowd,
All tenantless, save to the crannying[74] wind,
Or holding dark communion with the cloud.
There was a day when they were young and proud;
Banners on high, and battles[75] passed below;

## Notes

[71] *Maternal Nature!* This owes much to the temporary influence of Wordsworth, whose poetry Shelley read Byron in Geneva in the summer of 1816, when this poem was composed.

[72] *thy majestic Rhine?* Byron travelled up the Rhine via Bonn, Koblenz and Mannheim, 10–16 May 1816.

[73] *they* i.e. ruined castles.

[74] *crannying* The wind is so strong it penetrates into nooks and crannies of the ruin.

[75] *battles* a pun, meaning both battalions and military engagements.

But they who fought are in a bloody shroud,
And those which waved[76] are shredless dust ere now,
And the bleak battlements shall bear no future blow.

48

Beneath these battlements, within those walls,
Power dwelt amidst her passions; in proud state
Each robber-chief upheld his armed halls,
Doing his evil will, nor less elate[77]
Than mightier heroes of a longer date.
What want these outlaws conquerors should have[78]
But history's purchased page to call them great?[79]
A wider space? An ornamented grave?
Their hopes were not less warm, their souls were full as brave.

49

In their baronial feuds and single fields,
What deeds of prowess unrecorded died!
And Love, which lent a blazon[80] to their shields,
With emblems well devised by amorous pride,
Through all the mail of iron hearts would glide;
But still their flame was fierceness, and drew on
Keen contest and destruction near allied,
And many a tower for some fair mischief won,
Saw the discoloured[81] Rhine beneath its ruin run.

50

But thou, exulting and abounding river!
Making thy waves a blessing as they flow
Through banks whose beauty would endure for ever
Could man but leave thy bright creation so,
Nor its fair promise from the surface mow
With the sharp scythe of conflict – then to see
Thy valley of sweet waters, were to know
Earth paved like heaven, and to seem such to me,
Even now what wants thy stream? – that it should Lethe[82] be.

51

A thousand battles have assailed thy banks,
But these and half their fame have passed away,
And Slaughter heaped on high his weltering ranks:

## Notes

[76] *those which waved* flags.

[77] *elate* proud.

[78] '"What wants that knave / That a king should have?" was King James's question on meeting Johnny Armstrong and his followers in full accoutrements. See the ballad' (Byron's note). Johnnie Armstrong, Laird of Gilnockie, surrendered to James V in such fine attire the king hanged him for insolence.

[79] *What want...great* i.e. if they have conquerors, what else do these outlaws need, except for a historian to write up their story and call them great?

[80] *a blazon* the device of a bleeding heart.

[81] *discoloured* i.e. with blood.

[82] *Lethe* river of forgetfulness in Hades, from which souls drank in order to forget their previous lives.

Their very graves are gone, and what are they?
Thy tide washed down the blood of yesterday,
And all was stainless, and on thy clear stream
Glassed, with its dancing light, the sunny ray;
But o'er the blackened memory's blighting dream
Thy waves would vainly roll, all sweeping as they seem.

52

Thus Harold inly said,[83] and passed along,
Yet not insensible[84] to all which here
Awoke the jocund birds to early song
In glens which might have made even exile[85] dear:
Though on his brow were graven lines austere,
And tranquil sternness, which had ta'en the place
Of feelings fierier far but less severe,
Joy was not always absent from his face,
But o'er it in such scenes would steal with transient trace.

53

Nor was all love shut from him, though his days
Of passion had consumed themselves to dust.
It is in vain that we would coldly gaze
On such as smile upon us; the heart must
Leap kindly back to kindness, though disgust
Hath weaned it from all worldlings: thus he felt,
For there was soft remembrance, and sweet trust
In one fond breast,[86] to which his own would melt,
And in its tenderer hour on that his bosom dwelt.

54

And he had learned to love – I know not why,
For this in such as him seems strange of mood,
The helpless looks of blooming infancy,
Even in its earliest nurture; what subdued,
To change like this, a mind so far imbued
With scorn of man, it little boots to know –
But thus it was; and though in solitude
Small power the nipped affections have to grow,
In him this glowed when all beside had ceased to glow.

55

And there was one soft breast, as hath been said,
Which unto his was bound by stronger ties
Than the church links withal; and, though unwed,
*That* love was pure, and, far above disguise,

## Notes

[83] *Thus Harold inly said* Stanzas 47–51 comprise Harold's inner thoughts.

[84] *insensible* unaware.

[85] *exile* Byron exiled himself from England permanently after separating from his wife in spring 1816.

[86] *one fond breast* Augusta Leigh, Byron's half-sister, to whom he was passionately attached, the subject of his 'Stanzas' and 'Epistle'.

Had stood the test of mortal enmities
Still undivided, and cemented more
By peril, dreaded most in female eyes;
But this was firm, and from a foreign shore
Well to that heart might his these absent greetings pour!

1

The castled crag of Drachenfels[87]
Frowns o'er the wide and winding Rhine,
Whose breast of waters broadly swells
Between the banks which bear the vine,
And hills all rich with blossomed trees,
And fields which promise corn and wine,
And scattered cities crowning these,
Whose far white walls along them shine,
Have strewed a scene, which I should see
With double joy wert *thou* with me.

2

And peasant girls, with deep blue eyes,
And hands which offer early flowers,
Walk smiling o'er this Paradise;
Above, the frequent feudal towers
Through green leaves lift their walls of gray;
And many a rock which steeply lours,
And noble arch in proud decay,
Look o'er this vale of vintage-bowers;
But one thing want these banks of Rhine –
Thy gentle hand to clasp in mine!

3

I send the lilies given to me;
Though long before thy hand they touch,
I know that they must withered be,
But yet reject them not as such;
For I have cherished them as dear,
Because they yet may meet thine eye,
And guide thy soul to mine even here,
When thou behold'st them drooping nigh,
And know'st them gathered by the Rhine,
And offered from my heart to thine!

4

The river nobly foams and flows,
The charm of this enchanted ground,

## Notes

[87] 'The castle of Drachenfels stands on the highest summit of "the Seven Mountains", over the Rhine banks; it is in ruins, and connected with some singular traditions. It is the first in view on the road from Bonn, but on the opposite side of the river; on this bank, nearly facing it, are the remains of another called the Jew's castle, and a large cross commemorative of the murder of a chief by his brother. The number of castles and cities along the course of the Rhine on both sides is very great, and their situations remarkably beautiful' (Byron's note).

And all its thousand turns disclose
Some fresher beauty varying round;
The haughtiest breast its wish might bound
Through life to dwell delighted here;
Nor could on earth a spot be found
To nature and to me so dear,
Could thy dear eyes in following mine
Still sweeten more these banks of Rhine!

56

By Coblentz, on a rise of gentle ground,
There is a small and simple pyramid,[88]
Crowning the summit of the verdant mound;
Beneath its base are heroes' ashes hid –
Our enemy's[89] – but let not that forbid
Honour to Marceau![90] o'er whose early tomb
Tears, big tears, gushed from the rough soldier's lid,[91]
Lamenting and yet envying such a doom,[92]
Falling for France, whose rights he battled to resume.[93]

57

Brief, brave, and glorious was his young career,
His mourners were two hosts,[94] his friends and foes;
And fitly may the stranger lingering here
Pray for his gallant spirit's bright repose;
For he was Freedom's champion, one of those,
The few in number, who had not o'erstepped
The charter to chastise[95] which she bestows
On such as wield her weapons; he had kept
The whiteness of his soul – and thus men o'er him wept.[96]

## Notes

[88] *pyramid* i.e. a memorial.

[89] *Our enemy's* i.e. those of French heroes.

[90] *Marceau* François Sévérin Desgravins Marceau (1769–96) died in a battle with the forces of the Archduke Charles of Austria.

[91] *lid* eyelid.

[92] *doom* fate.

[93] *resume* take back.

[94] *hosts* armies. Marceau was mourned by both forces: the French, retreating from Altenkirchen, had to leave him behind, and the Austrians buried him.

[95] *chastise* i.e. teach tyrants (enemies of Freedom) a lesson.

[96] 'The monument of the young and lamented General Marceau (killed by a rifle-ball at Altenkirchen on the last day of the fourth year of the French republic) still remains as described.

The inscriptions on his monument are rather too long, and not required; his name was enough. France adored, and her enemies admired; both wept over him. His funeral was attended by the generals and detachments from both armies. In the same grave General Hoche is interred, a gallant man also in every sense of the word, but though he distinguished himself greatly in battle, *he* had not the good fortune to die there; his death was attended by suspicions of poison.

A separate monument (not over his body, which is buried by Marceau's) is raised for him near Andernach, opposite to which one of his most memorable exploits was performed, in throwing a bridge to an island on the Rhine. The shape and style are different from that of Marceau's, and the inscription more simple and pleasing.

The Army of the Sambre and Meuse
to its Commander in Chief
Hoche

This is all, and as it should be. Hoche was esteemed among the first of France's earlier generals before Bonaparte monopolized her triumphs. He was the destined commander of the invading army of Ireland' (Byron's note). Lazare Hoche (1768–97) died of consumption, but the rapid deterioration of his health led to speculation he had been poisoned.

58

Here Ehrenbreitstein,[97] with her shattered wall
Black with the miner's blast,[98] upon her height
Yet shows of what she was, when shell and ball
Rebounding idly on her strength did light;
A tower of victory! from whence the flight
Of baffled foes was watched along the plain:
But peace destroyed what war could never blight,
And laid those proud roofs bare to Summer's rain –
On which the iron shower[99] for years had poured in vain.

59

Adieu to thee, fair Rhine! How long delighted
The stranger fain would linger on his way!
Thine is a scene alike where souls united
Or lonely Contemplation thus might stray;
And could the ceaseless vultures cease to prey
On self-condemning bosoms,[100] it were here,
Where nature, nor too sombre nor too gay,
Wild but not rude, awful yet not austere,
Is to the mellow earth as autumn to the year.

60

Adieu to thee again! A vain adieu!
There can be no farewell to scene like thine;
The mind is coloured by thy every hue;
And if reluctantly the eyes resign
Their cherished gaze upon thee, lovely Rhine,
'Tis with the thankful glance of parting praise;
More mighty spots may rise – more glaring shine,
But none unite in one attaching maze
The brilliant, fair, and soft – the glories of old days,

61

The negligently grand, the fruitful bloom
Of coming ripeness, the white city's sheen,
The rolling stream, the precipice's gloom,
The forest's growth, and gothic walls between,
The wild rocks shaped, as they had turrets been[101]

## Notes

[97] 'Ehrenbreitstein (i.e. "the broad stone of honour"), one of the strongest fortresses in Europe, was dismantled and blown up by the French at the Truce of Leoben. It had been and could only be reduced by famine or treachery. It yielded to the former, aided by surprise. After having seen the fortifications of Gibraltar and Malta, it did not much strike by comparison, but the situation is commanding. General Marceau besieged it in vain for some time, and I slept in a room where I was shown a window at which he is said to have been standing observing the progress of the siege by moonlight, when a ball struck immediately below it' (Byron's note). Marceau unsuccessfully besieged Ehrenbreitstein in 1795–6. It was finally taken, after a long siege, in 1799. It was blown up not after the Treaty of Leoben (1797), but after the Treaty of Lunéville (1801). Byron visited the ruins in mid-May 1816.

[98] *the miner's blast* The miner would dig tunnels under the walls of the fortresses, for the detonation of explosives – to 'undermine' the building.

[99] *the iron shower* i.e. artillery fire directed against the fortress.

[100] *ceaseless vultures…bosoms* Jupiter had Prometheus nailed to a rock for 30,000 years, with an eagle devouring his liver.

[101] *as they had turrets been* as if they had been turrets.

In mockery of man's art; and these withal
A race of faces happy as the scene,
Whose fertile bounties here extend to all,
Still springing o'er thy banks, though empires near them fall.

62

But these recede. Above me are the Alps,
The palaces of nature, whose vast walls
Have pinnacled in clouds their snowy scalps,
And throned Eternity in icy halls
Of cold sublimity, where forms and falls
The avalanche – the thunderbolt of snow!
All that expands the spirit, yet appals,
Gather around these summits, as to show
How earth may pierce to heaven, yet leave vain man below.

63

But ere these matchless heights I dare to scan,
There is a spot should not be passed in vain –
Morat,[102] the proud, the patriot field! where man
May gaze on ghastly trophies of the slain,
Nor blush for those who conquered on that plain;
Here Burgundy bequeathed his tombless host,
A bony heap, through ages to remain,
Themselves their monument; the Stygian coast
Unsepulchred they roamed, and shrieked each wandering ghost.[103]

64

While Waterloo with Cannae's carnage vies,
Morat and Marathon twin names shall stand;[104]
They were true Glory's stainless victories
Won by the unambitious heart and hand
Of a proud, brotherly, and civic band,
All unbought champions in no princely cause

## Notes

[102] *Morat* The Battle of Morat was the bloodiest of three battles fought by the Swiss against the French (under Charles the Bold, Duke of Burgundy) in 1476.

[103] 'The chapel is destroyed, and the pyramid of bones diminished to a small number by the Burgundian legion in the service of France, who anxiously effaced this record of their ancestors' less successful invasions. A few still remain notwithstanding the pains taken by the Burgundians for ages (all who passed that way removing a bone to their own country) and the less justifiable larcenies of the Swiss postillions, who carried them off to sell for knife-handles, a purpose for which the whiteness imbibed by the bleaching of years had rendered them in great request. Of these relics I ventured to bring away as much as may have made the quarter of a hero, for which the sole excuse is, that if I had not,the next passerby might have perverted them to worse uses than the careful preservation which I intend for them' (Byron's note).

[104] Morat and Marathon (490 BCE) were victories of men fighting for their freedom; Waterloo and Cannae (216 BCE) were battles between countries seeking power over each other.

Of vice-entailed Corruption;[105] they no land
Doomed to bewail the blasphemy of laws
Making kings' rights divine, by some Draconic[106] clause.[107]

65

By a lone wall a lonelier column rears
A gray and grief-worn aspect of old days;
'Tis the last remnant of the wreck of years,
And looks as with the wild-bewildered gaze
Of one to stone converted by amaze,
Yet still with consciousness; and there it stands
Making a marvel that it not decays,
When the coeval pride of human hands,
Levelled Aventicum,[108] hath strewed her subject lands.

66

And there – oh, sweet and sacred be the name! –
Julia – the daughter, the devoted – gave
Her youth to heaven; her heart, beneath a claim
Nearest to heaven's, broke o'er a father's grave.
Justice is sworn 'gainst tears, and hers would crave
The life she lived in; but the judge was just,
And then she died on him she could not save.
Their tomb was simple, and without a bust,
And held within their urn one mind, one heart, one dust.[109]

67

But these are deeds which should not pass away,
And names that must not wither, though the earth
Forgets her empires with a just decay,

## Notes

[105] *vice-entailed Corruption* i.e. corruption is inseparable from vice.

[106] *Draconic* harsh, cruel; after Draco, author of the notoriously severe penal code for Athens (621 BCE).

[107] Like many radicals of the day, Byron disagreed heartily with the divine right of kings. 'Draco, the author of the first red book on record, was an Athenian special pleader in great business. Hippias, the Athenian Bourbon, was in the Battle of Marathon, and did not keep at the respectful distance from danger of the Ghent refugees – but the English and Prussians resembled the Medes and Persians as little as Blucher and the British General did Datis and Artaphernes and Bonaparte was still more remote in cause and character from Miltiades – and a parallel "after the manner of Plutarch" might have still existed in the fortunes of the sons of Pisistratus and the reigning doctors of right-divinity' (Byron's note). Byron offers an ironic comparison between the principals at Waterloo and those at Marathon. The sons of Pisistratus, Hippias and Hipparchus died inglorious.

[108] 'Aventicum (near Morat) was the Roman capital of Helvetia, where Avenches now stands' (Byron's note).

[109] 'Julia Alpinula, a young Aventian priestess, died soon after a vain endeavour to save her father, condemned to death as a traitor by Aulus Caecina. Her epitaph was discovered many years ago; it is thus –

Julia Alpinula
Hic jaceo
Infelicis patris, infelix proles
Deae Aventiae Sacerdos;
Exorare patris necem non potui
Male mori in fatis ille erat.
Vixi annos XXIII.

I know of no human composition so affecting as this, nor a history of deeper interest. These are the names and actions which ought not to perish, and to which we turn with a true and healthy tenderness, from the wretched and glittering detail of a confused mass of conquests and battles, with which the mind is roused for a time to a false and feverish sympathy, from whence it recurs at length with all the nausea consequent on such intoxication' (Byron's note).

The enslavers and the enslaved, their death and birth;
The high, the mountain-majesty of worth
Should be, and shall, survivor of its woe,
And from its immortality look forth
In the sun's face, like yonder Alpine snow,
Imperishably pure beyond all things below.

68

Lake Leman[110] woos me with its crystal face,
The mirror where the stars and mountains view
The stillness of their aspect in each trace
Its clear depth yields of their far height and hue:
There is too much of man here to look through,
With a fit mind, the might which I behold;
But soon in me shall loneliness renew
Thoughts hid, but not less cherished than of old,
Ere mingling with the herd had penned me in their fold.

69

To fly from, need not be to hate, mankind;
All are not fit with them to stir and toil,
Nor is it discontent to keep the mind
Deep in its fountain, lest it overboil
In the hot throng, where we become the spoil[111]
Of our infection, till too late and long
We may deplore and struggle with the coil[112]
In wretched interchange of wrong for wrong
Midst a contentious world, striving where none are strong.

70

There in a moment we may plunge our years
In fatal penitence, and in the blight
Of our own soul turn all our blood to tears,
And colour things to come with hues of night;
The race of life becomes a hopeless flight
To those that walk in darkness: on the sea
The boldest steer but where their ports invite,
But there are wanderers o'er eternity
Whose bark drives on and on, and anchored ne'er shall be.

71

Is it not better, then, to be alone,
And love earth only for its earthly sake?
By the blue rushing of the arrowy Rhone[113]

Notes

[110] *Lake Leman* Lake Geneva.

[111] *spoil* prey.

[112] *coil* mortal coil; bustle of life.

[113] 'The colour of the Rhone at Geneva is blue, to a depth of tint which I have never seen equalled in water, salt or fresh, except in the Mediterranean and Archipelago' (Byron's note). The 'Archipelago' is the Aegean, in which he swam in May 1810.

Or the pure bosom of its nursing lake,
Which feeds it as a mother who doth make
A fair but froward[114] infant her own care,
Kissing its cries away as these awake?
Is it not better thus our lives to wear
Than join the crushing crowd, doomed to inflict or bear?

72

I live not in myself, but I become
Portion of that around me; and to me
High mountains are a feeling, but the hum
Of human cities torture.[115] I can see
Nothing to loathe in nature, save to be
A link reluctant in a fleshly chain,
Classed among creatures, when the soul can flee,
And with the sky, the peak, the heaving plain
Of ocean, or the stars, mingle, and not in vain.

73

And thus I am absorbed, and this is life.
I look upon the peopled desert past
As on a place of agony and strife
Where for some sin to sorrow I was cast
To act and suffer, but remount at last
With a fresh pinion, which I feel to spring
(Though young, yet waxing vigorous as the blast
Which it would cope with) on delighted wing,
Spurning the clay-cold bonds which round our being cling.[116]

74

And when at length the mind shall be all free
From what it hates in this degraded form,
Reft of its carnal life, save what shall be
Existent happier in the fly and worm;
When elements to elements conform
And dust is as it should be, shall I not
Feel all I see – less dazzling, but more warm?
The bodiless thought? The spirit of each spot –
Of which, even now, I share at times the immortal lot?

75

Are not the mountains, waves and skies a part
Of me and of my soul, as I of them?
Is not the love of these deep in my heart
With a pure passion? Should I not contemn

## Notes

[114] *froward* refractory.

[115] Here and in succeeding lines Byron repeats attitudes lifted from Wordsworth's 'Tintern Abbey'.

[116] *Spurning…cling* the attitude of the Byronic overreacher.

All objects if compared with these, and stem
A tide of suffering, rather than forego
Such feelings for the hard and worldly phlegm[117]
Of those whose eyes are only turned below,
Gazing upon the ground, with thoughts which dare not glow?

76

But this is not my theme, and I return
To that which is immediate – and require
Those who find contemplation in the urn
To look on one[118] whose dust was once all fire,
A native of the land where I respire[119]
The clear air for a while, a passing guest
Where he became a being whose desire
Was to be glorious ('twas a foolish quest,
The which to gain and keep, he sacrificed all rest).

77

Here the self-torturing sophist,[120] wild Rousseau,
The apostle of affliction, he who threw
Enchantment over passion, and from woe
Wrung overwhelming eloquence – first drew
The breath which made him wretched; yet he knew
How to make madness beautiful, and cast
O'er erring deeds and thoughts a heavenly hue
Of words like sunbeams, dazzling as they passed
The eyes, which o'er them shed tears feelingly and fast.

78

His love was passion's essence, as a tree
On fire by lightning;[121] with ethereal flame[122]
Kindled he was, and blasted – for to be
Thus, and enamoured, were in him the same.
But his was not the love of living dame,
Nor of the dead who rise upon our dreams,[123]
But of ideal beauty,[124] which became
In him existence, and o'erflowing teems
Along his burning page, distempered though it seems.

79

This breathed itself to life in Julie,[125] this
Invested her with all that's wild and sweet;

## Notes

[117] *phlegm* coldness, lack of passion.

[118] *one* Jean-Jacques Rousseau, born in Geneva 1712 (d. 1778), whose political, fictional and philosophical writings strongly influenced the outbreak of revolution at the end of the eighteenth century.

[119] *respire* inhale.

[120] *sophist* learned man.

[121] *a tree / On fire by lightning* An image used also by Shelley and Mary Shelley.

[122] *ethereal flame* fire from heaven.

[123] *But his…dreams* The comparison is with Dante's Beatrice and Petrarch's Laura.

[124] *ideal beauty* cf. Shelley's *Hymn to Intellectual Beauty*, which Byron would have known in manuscript.

[125] *Julie* Heroine of Rousseau's *Julie, ou la Nouvelle Héloïse* (1761), which Shelley and Byron read in 1816, and deals with the illicit love of Julie and her tutor Saint-Preux.

This hallowed, too, the memorable kiss
Which every morn his fevered lip would greet
From hers[126] who, but with friendship, his would meet:
But to that gentle touch, through brain and breast
Flashed the thrilled spirit's love-devouring heat –
In that absorbing sigh, perchance more blessed
Than vulgar minds may be with all they seek possessed.[127]

80

His life was one long war with self-sought foes
Or friends by him self-banished,[128] for his mind
Had grown suspicion's sanctuary, and chose,
For its own cruel sacrifice, the kind,
'Gainst whom he raged with fury strange and blind.
But he was frenzied – wherefore, who may know,
Since cause might be which skill could never find?
But he was frenzied by disease or woe
To that worst pitch of all, which wears a reasoning show.

81

For then he was inspired, and from him came,
As from the Pythian's mystic cave of yore,[129]
Those oracles[130] which set the world in flame,
Nor ceased to burn till kingdoms were no more.
Did he not this for France, which lay before
Bowed to the inborn tyranny of years?
Broken and trembling to the yoke she bore,
Till by the voice of him and his compeers
Roused up to too much wrath, which follows o'ergrown fears?

82

They made themselves a fearful monument!
The wreck of old opinions, things which grew
Breathed from the birth of time: the veil they rent,[131]
And what behind it lay, all earth shall view.
But good with ill they also overthrew,
Leaving but ruins, wherewith to rebuild

## Notes

[126] *hers* Rousseau describes his unrequited love of the Comtesse d'Houdetot in his *Confessions*.

[127] 'This refers to the account in his *Confessions* of his passion for the Comtesse d'Houdetot (the mistress of St Lambert) and his long walk every morning for the sake of the single kiss which was the common salutation of French acquaintance. Rousseau's description of his feelings on this occasion may be considered as the most passionate, yet not impure description and expression of love that ever kindled into words; which after all must be felt, from their very force, to be inadequate to the delineation: a painting can give no sufficient idea of the ocean' (Byron's note).

[128] *self-sought foes…self-banished* Including Madame de Warens, Madame d'Epinay, Diderot, Grimm, Voltaire, Hume and St Lambert.

[129] *the Pythian's mystic cave of yore* The Pythian was the priestess of the oracle at Delphi; she gave utterance in a state of frenzy and sat on a three-legged stool.

[130] *oracles* The *Discours* of 1750 and 1753 and *Le Contrat social* (1762) inspired the French Revolution.

[131] *the veil they rent* cf. the moment of Christ's death: 'And, behold, the veil of the temple was rent in twain from the top to the bottom' (Matthew 27:51).

Upon the same foundation, and renew
Dungeons[132] and thrones,[133] which the same hour refilled
As heretofore, because ambition was self-willed.

83

But this will not endure, nor be endured!
Mankind have felt their strength and made it felt.[134]
They might have used it better, but, allured
By their new vigour, sternly have they dealt
On one another; pity ceased to melt
With her once-natural charities. But they
Who in oppression's darkness caved had dwelt,
They were not eagles, nourished with the day;
What marvel then, at times, if they mistook their prey?

84

What deep wounds ever closed without a scar?
The heart's[135] bleed longest, and but heal to wear
That which disfigures it; and they who war
With their own hopes, and have been vanquished, bear
Silence but not submission. In his lair
Fixed Passion holds his breath until the hour
Which shall atone for years – none need despair:
It came, it cometh, and will come, the power
To punish or forgive; in *one* we shall be slower.

85

Clear placid Leman! thy contrasted lake,
With the wild world I dwelt in, is a thing
Which warns me, with its stillness, to forsake
Earth's troubled waters for a purer spring.
This quiet sail is as a noiseless wing
To waft me from distraction; once I loved
Torn ocean's roar, but thy soft murmuring
Sounds sweet as if a sister's voice reproved
That I with stern[136] delights should e'er have been so moved.

86

It is the hush of night, and all between
Thy margin and the mountains, dusk – yet clear,
Mellowed and mingling, yet distinctly seen
(Save darkened Jura, whose capped heights appear
Precipitously steep); and, drawing near,

## Notes

[132] *Dungeons* The Bastille prison in Paris, symbol of the *ancien régime*, was demolished soon after 14 July 1789 during the Revolution; it was not rebuilt.

[133] *thrones* Ferdinand VII of Spain and Louis XVIII of France were restored to their respective thrones in 1814 – not something that gave Byron much cheer.

[134] *Mankind have felt their strength and made it felt* this stanza picks up a subject that preoccupied all defenders of revolution: the necessity for violence in the cause of liberty.

[135] *The heart's* i.e. the heart's wounds.

[136] *stern* uncompromising.

There breathes a living fragrance from the shore
Of flowers yet fresh with childhood; on the ear
Drops the light drip of the suspended oar,[137]
Or chirps the grasshopper one goodnight carol more

87

(He is an evening reveller who makes
His life an infancy, and sings his fill);
At intervals, some bird from out the brakes[138]
Starts into voice a moment, then is still.
There seems a floating whisper on the hill,
But that is fancy, for the starlight dews
All silently their tears of love instil,
Weeping themselves away, till they infuse
Deep into nature's breast the spirit of her hues.

88

Ye stars which are the poetry of heaven!
If in your bright leaves we would read the fate
Of men and empires, 'tis to be forgiven
That in our aspirations to be great,
Our destinies o'erleap their mortal state,
And claim a kindred with you – for ye are
A beauty and a mystery, and create
In us such love and reverence from afar
That fortune, fame, power, life, have named themselves a star.

89

All heaven and earth are still – though not in sleep,
But breathless (as we grow when feeling most)
And silent (as we stand in thoughts too deep);[139]
All heaven and earth are still: from the high host
Of stars to the lulled lake and mountain-coast,
All is concentred in a life intense
Where not a beam, nor air, nor leaf is lost,
But hath a part of being,[140] and a sense
Of that which is of all creator and defence.

90

Then stirs the feeling infinite, so felt
In solitude, where we are least alone –
A truth which through our being then doth melt
And purifies from self; it is a tone,

## Notes

[137] *Drops the light…oar* An echo of Wordsworth's 'Lines Written near Richmond': 'Remembrance! as we glide along, / For him suspend the dashing oar' (ll. 33–4).

[138] *brakes* fern, bracken.

[139] *thoughts too deep* Byron echoes Wordsworth, 'Ode' 206: 'Thoughts that do often lie too deep for tears.'

[140] *Where not a beam…part of being* Virtually identical to the pantheism of Wordsworth's 'Tintern Abbey' 96–103.

The soul and source of music, which makes known
Eternal harmony, and sheds a charm
Like to the fabled Cytherea's zone,[141]
Binding all things with beauty – 'twould disarm
The spectre death, had he substantial power to harm.

91

Not vainly did the early Persian make
His altar the high places and the peak
Of earth-o'ergazing mountains,[142] and thus take
A fit and unwalled temple, there to seek
The spirit in whose honour shrines are weak,
Upreared of human hands. Come and compare
Columns and idol-dwellings, Goth[143] or Greek,
With nature's realms of worship, earth and air,[144]
Nor fix on fond[145] abodes to circumscribe thy prayer!

92

The sky is changed, and such a change![146] Oh night
And storm and darkness, ye are wondrous strong,
Yet lovely in your strength, as is the light
Of a dark eye in woman! Far along
From peak to peak, the rattling crags among,
Leaps the live thunder – not from one lone cloud
But every mountain now hath found a tongue,
And Jura answers through her misty shroud
Back to the joyous Alps, who call to her aloud!

## Notes

[141] *Cytherea's zone* Aphrodite's girdle ('zone') brought love to those wearing it.

[142] 'It is to be recollected that the most beautiful and impressive doctrines of the founder of Christianity were delivered not in the Temple, but on the mount.

To waive the question of devotion, and turn to human eloquence – the most effectual and splendid specimens were not pronounced within walls. Demosthenes addressed the public and popular assemblies. Cicero spoke in the forum. That this added to their effect on the mind of both orator and hearers, may be conceived from the difference between what we read of the emotions then and there produced, and those we ourselves experience in the perusal in the closet. It is one thing to read the *Iliad* at Sigaeum and on the tumuli, or by the springs with Mount Ida above, and the plain and rivers and Archipelago around you, and another to trim your taper over it in a snug library – *this* I know.

Were the early and rapid progress of what is called Methodism to be attributed to any cause beyond the enthusiasm excited by its vehement faith and doctrines (the truth or error of which I presume neither to canvas nor to question) I should venture to ascribe it to the practice of preaching in the *fields*, and the unstudied and extemporaneous effusions of its teachers.

The Musselmans, whose erroneous devotion (at least in the lower orders) is most sincere, and therefore impressive, are accustomed to repeat their prescribed orisons and prayers wherever they may be at the stated hours – of course frequently in the open air, kneeling upon a light mat (which they carry for the purpose of a bed or cushion as required); the ceremony lasts some minutes, during which they are totally absorbed, and only living in their supplication. Nothing can disturb them. On me the simple and entire sincerity of these men, and the spirit which appeared to be within and upon them, made a far greater impression than any general rite which was ever performed in places of worship, of which I have seen those of almost every persuasion under the sun: including most of our own sectaries, and the Greek, the Catholic, the Armenian, the Lutheran, the Jewish, and the Mahometan. Many of the negroes, of whom there are numbers in the Turkish empire, are idolators, and have free exercise of their belief and its rites. Some of these I had a distant view of at Patras, and from what I could make out of them, they appeared to be of a truly pagan description, and not very agreeable to a spectator' (Byron's note).

[143] *Goth* One of a Germanic tribe, who, in the third, fourth and fifth centuries, invaded both the Eastern and Western empires, and founded kingdoms in Italy, France and Spain.

[144] *earth and air* Once again, Byron is thinking of the pantheistic statement of faith in *Tintern Abbey*, in which Wordsworth seeks 'a sense sublime' in 'the round ocean, and the living air, / And the blue sky, and in the mind of man' (ll. 96–100).

[145] *fond* foolish.

[146] 'The thunder-storms to which these lines refer occurred on 13 June 1816 at midnight. I have seen among the Acroceraunian mountains of Chimari several more terrible, but none more beautiful' (Byron's note).

93

And this is in the night – most glorious night,
Thou wert not sent for slumber! Let me be
A sharer in thy fierce and far delight,
A portion of the tempest and of thee!
How the lit lake shines, a phosphoric sea,
And the big rain comes dancing to the earth!
And now again 'tis black, and now the glee
Of the loud hills shakes with its mountain-mirth,
As if they did rejoice o'er a young earthquake's birth.[147]

94

Now where the swift Rhone cleaves his way between
Heights which appear as lovers who have parted
In hate, whose mining depths so intervene
That they can meet no more, though broken-hearted,
Though in their souls (which thus each other thwarted)
Love was the very root of the fond rage
Which blighted their life's bloom, and then departed –
Itself expired, but leaving them an age
Of years all winters, war within themselves to wage;

95

Now where the quick Rhone thus hath cleft his way,
The mightiest of the storms hath ta'en his stand:
For here not one but many make their play,
And fling their thunderbolts from hand to hand,
Flashing and cast around; of all the band
The brightest through these parted hills hath forked
His lightnings, as if he did understand
That in such gaps as desolation worked,
There the hot shaft[148] should blast whatever therein lurked.

96

Sky, mountains, river, winds, lake, lightnings – ye
With night and clouds and thunder, and a soul
To make these felt and feeling, well may be
Things that have made me watchful; the far roll
Of your departing voices is the knoll[149]
Of what in me is sleepless – if I rest.
But where of ye, oh tempests, is the goal?
Are ye like those within the human breast?
Or do ye find, at length, like eagles, some high nest?

## Notes

[147] *a young earthquake's birth* Byron is probably echoing Shelley, 'Mont Blanc' 72–3.

[148] *the hot shaft* i.e. of lightning.

[149] *knoll* summit.

97

Could I embody and unbosom now
That which is most within me! Could I wreak[150]
My thoughts upon expression, and thus throw
Soul, heart, mind, passions, feelings (strong or weak),
All that I would have sought and all I seek,
Bear, know, feel, and yet breathe – into *one* word,
And that one word were lightning, I would speak!
But as it is, I live and die unheard
With a most voiceless thought, sheathing it as a sword.

98

The morn is up again, the dewy morn
With breath all incense, and with cheek all bloom,
Laughing the clouds away with playful scorn
And living as if earth contained no tomb,
And glowing into day: we may resume
The march of our existence. And thus I,
Still on thy shores, fair Leman, may find room
And food for meditation, nor pass by
Much that may give us pause, if pondered fittingly.

99

Clarens![151] Sweet Clarens, birthplace of deep Love!
Thine air is the young breath of passionate thought;
Thy trees take root in Love; the snows above,
The very glaciers have his colours caught,
And sunset into rose hues[152] sees them wrought

## Notes

[150] *wreak* vent.

[151] *Clarens!* Byron and Shelley sailed to Clarens, visiting the Castle of Chillon, on 26 June 1816. Shelley had just been reading *La Nouvelle Héloïse*; Byron had read it many times before.

[152] 'Rousseau's Heloise, Letter 17, part 4, note. "Ces montagnes sont si hautes qu'une demi-heure après le soleil couché, leurs sommets sont encore éclairés de ses rayons; dont le rouge forme sur ces cimes blanches *une belle couleur de rose* qu'on apperçoit de fort loin."

This applies more particularly to the heights over Meillerie. "J'allai à Vévay loger à la Clef, et pendant deux jours que j'y restai sans voir personne, je pris pour cette ville un amour qui m'a suivi dans tous mes voyages, et qui m'y a fait établir enfin les héros de mon roman. Je dirois volontiers à ceux qui ont du goût et qui sont sensibles: allez à Vévay – visitez le pays, examinez les sites, promenez-vous sur le lac, et dites si la Nature n'a pas fait ce beau pays pour une Julie, pour une Claire et pour un St Preux; mais ne les y cherchez pas." *Les Confessions*, livre iv. Page 306. Lyons ed. 1796.

In July 1816, I made a voyage round the Lake of Geneva; and, as far as my own observations have led me in a not uninterested nor inattentive survey of all the scenes most celebrated by Rousseau in his *Heloise*, I can safely say, that in this there is no exaggeration. It would be difficult to see Clarens (with the scenes around it, Vevay, Chillon, Bôveret, St Gingo, Meillerie, Evian, and the entrances of the Rhone), without being forcibly struck with its peculiar adaptation to the persons and events with which it has been peopled. But this is not all; the feeling with which all around Clarens, and the opposite rocks of Meillerie is invested, is of a still higher and more comprehensive order than the mere sympathy with individual passion; it is a sense of the existence of love in its most extended and sublime capacity, and of our own participation of its good and of its glory: it is the great principle of the universe, which is there more condensed, but not less manifested; and of which, though knowing ourselves a part, we lose our individuality, and mingle in the beauty of the whole.

If Rousseau had never written, nor lived, the same associations would not less have belonged to such scenes. He has added to the interest of his works by their adoption; he has shown his sense of their beauty by the selection; but they have done that for him which no human being could do for them.

I had the fortune (good or evil as it might be) to sail from Meillerie (where we landed for some time), to St Gingo during a lake storm, which added to the magnificence of all around, although occasionally accompanied by danger to the boat, which was small and overloaded. It was over this very part of the lake that Rousseau has driven the boat of St Preux and Madame Wolmar to Meillerie for shelter during a tempest.

On gaining the shore at St Gingo, I found that the wind had been sufficiently strong to blow down some fine old chestnut trees on the lower part of the mountains. On the opposite height of Clarens is a chateau.

By rays which sleep there lovingly: the rocks,
The permanent crags, tell here of Love, who sought
In them a refuge from the worldly shocks,
Which stir and sting the soul with hope that woos, then mocks.

100

Clarens! By heavenly feet thy paths are trod –
Undying Love's, who here ascends a throne
To which the steps are mountains;[153] where the god
Is a pervading life and light – so shown
Not on those summits solely, nor alone
In the still cave and forest; o'er the flower
His eye is sparkling, and his breath hath blown,
His soft and summer breath, whose tender power
Passes the strength of storms in their most desolate hour.

101

All things are here of *him*;[154] from the black pines,
Which are his shade on high, and the loud roar
Of torrents, where he listeneth, to the vines
Which slope his green path downward to the shore,
Where the bowed waters meet him, and adore,
Kissing his feet with murmurs; and the wood,
The covert of old trees, with trunks all hoar,
But light leaves, young as joy, stands where it stood,
Offering to him, and his, a populous solitude,

102

A populous solitude of bees and birds,
And fairy-formed and many-coloured things,
Who worship him with notes more sweet than words,
And innocently open their glad wings,
Fearless and full of life: the gush of springs,
And fall of lofty fountains, and the bend
Of stirring branches, and the bud which brings
The swiftest thought of beauty, here extend
Mingling, and made by Love, unto one mighty end.

## Notes

The hills are covered with vineyards, and interspersed with some small but beautiful woods; one of these was named the "Bosquet de Julie", and it is remarkable that, though long ago cut down by the brutal selfishness of the monks of St Bernard (to whom the land appertained), that the ground might be enclosed into a vineyard for the miserable drones of an execrable superstition, the inhabitants of Clarens still point out the spot where its trees stood, calling it by the name which consecrated and survived them.

Rousseau has not been particularly fortunate in the preservation of the "local habitations" he has given to "airy nothings". The Prior of Great St Bernard has cut down some of his woods for the sake of a few casks of wine, and Bonaparte has levelled part of the rocks of Meillerie in improving the road to the Simplon. The road is an excellent one, but I cannot quite agree with a remark which I heard made, that "La route vaut mieux que les souvenirs"' (Byron's note).

[153] *a throne...mountains* This image may be borrowed from Shelley, 'Mont Blanc' 15–17.

[154] *him* i.e. Love.

103

He who hath loved not, here would learn that lore,
And make his heart a spirit; he who knows
That tender mystery, will love the more,
For this is Love's recess, where vain men's woes,
And the world's waste, have driven him far from those,
For 'tis his nature to advance or die;
He stands not still, but or decays, or grows
Into a boundless blessing, which may vie
With the immortal lights, in its eternity!

104

'Twas not for fiction chose Rousseau this spot,
Peopling it with affections; but he found
It was the scene which passion must allot
To the mind's purified beings; 'twas the ground
Where early Love his Psyche's zone unbound,[155]
And hallowed it with loveliness: 'tis lone,
And wonderful, and deep, and hath a sound,
And sense, and sight of sweetness; here the Rhone
Hath spread himself a couch, the Alps have reared a throne.[156]

105

Lausanne, and Ferney! Ye have been the abodes
Of names[157] which unto you bequeathed a name;
Mortals who sought and found, by dangerous roads,
A path to perpetuity of fame:
They were gigantic minds, and their steep aim
Was, Titan-like, on daring doubts to pile[158]
Thoughts which should call down thunder, and the flame
Of heaven again assailed – if heaven the while
On man, and man's research, could deign do more than smile.

106

The one[159] was fire and fickleness, a child
Most mutable in wishes, but in mind
A wit as various – gay, grave, sage, or wild –
Historian, bard, philosopher, combined;
He multiplied himself among mankind,
The Proteus[160] of their talents: but his own

## Notes

[155] *Where early Love his Psyche's zone unbound* In Apuleius, *Metamorphoses*, Love undid Psyche's girdle when he made love to her, disobeying the orders of Venus, who was jealous of Psyche's beauty. Byron's point is that Rousseau chose Clarens for setting his novel's love-scenes because he wanted to project, through the novel, his own feelings for Madame d'Houdetot (one of the mind's 'purified beings').

[156] *throne* In 'Mont Blanc', Shelley describes the mountain as the 'secret throne' of Power (l. 17).

[157] *names* 'Voltaire and Gibbon' (Byron's note). Edward Gibbon (1737–94), author of *The Decline and Fall of the Roman Empire*, lived at Lausanne 1783–93. Voltaire resided at his estate at Ferney 1758–77. Both were freethinkers.

[158] *Titan-like...pile* The Titans and Giants piled Pelion upon Ossa in an attempt to gain heaven and overthrow Jupiter.

[159] *The one* i.e. Voltaire.

[160] *Proteus* sea-god with the ability to change his shape; Voltaire mastered different forms of intellectual endeavour.

Breathed most in ridicule – which, as the wind,
Blew where it listed,[161] laying all things prone –
Now to o'erthrow a fool, and now to shake a throne.[162]

107

The other,[163] deep and slow, exhausting thought,
And hiving[164] wisdom with each studious year,
In meditation dwelt, with learning wrought,[165]
And shaped his weapon with an edge severe,
Sapping a solemn creed with solemn sneer;
The lord of irony – that master-spell
Which stung his foes to wrath, which grew from fear,
And doomed him to the zealot's ready hell,
Which answers to all doubts so eloquently well.[166]

108

Yet peace be with their ashes – for by them,
If merited, the penalty is paid;
It is not ours to judge, far less condemn;
The hour must come when such things shall be made
Known unto all – or hope and dread allayed
By slumber, on one pillow, in the dust,
Which, thus much we are sure, must lie decayed;
And when it shall revive, as is our trust,
'Twill be to be forgiven, or suffer what is just.

109

But let me quit man's works, again to read
His maker's,[167] spread around me, and suspend
This page, which from my reveries[168] I feed,
Until it seems prolonging without end.
The clouds above me to the white Alps tend,
And I must pierce them, and survey whate'er
May be permitted, as my steps I bend
To their most great and growing region, where
The earth to her embrace compels the powers of air.

110

Italia too, Italia! Looking on thee,
Full flashes on the soul the light of ages,
Since the fierce Carthaginian[169] almost won thee,
To the last halo of the chiefs and sages

## Notes

[161] *listed* wanted.

[162] *now to shake a throne* Voltaire's writings helped bring about the French Revolution.

[163] *The other* i.e. Gibbon.

[164] *hiving* hoarding.

[165] *wrought* created (i.e. his history of the Roman Empire).

[166] Gibbon's work was controversial in its day because it effectively demolished the traditional, religiously slanted views of the later Roman period. He said that his history recorded the triumph of superstition and barbarism over culture and civilization.

[167] *His maker's* i.e. nature.

[168] *reveries* i.e. his sublime experiences in the midst of natural things (which inspire him).

[169] *the fierce Carthaginian* Hannibal, Carthaginian general who attempted to conquer Italy in the third century BCE, won many battles against the Romans, but finally failed.

Who glorify thy consecrated pages;
Thou wert the throne and grave of empires;[170] still,
The fount at which the panting mind assuages
Her thirst of knowledge, quaffing there her fill,
Flows from the eternal source of Rome's imperial hill.[171]

111

Thus far have I proceeded in a theme
Renewed with no kind auspices[172] – to feel
We are not what we have been, and to deem
We are not what we should be; and to steel
The heart against itself; and to conceal,
With a proud caution, love, or hate, or aught
(Passion or feeling, purpose, grief or zeal)
Which is the tyrant spirit of our thought,
Is a stern task of soul. No matter, it is taught.

112

And for these words, thus woven into song,
It may be that they are a harmless wile,
The colouring of the scenes which fleet along,
Which I would seize, in passing, to beguile
My breast, or that of others, for a while.
Fame is the thirst of youth – but I am not
So young as to regard men's frown or smile
As loss or guerdon[173] of a glorious lot;
I stood and stand alone, remembered or forgot.

113

I have not loved the world, nor the world me;
I have not flattered its rank breath, nor bowed
To its idolatries a patient knee,
Nor coined[174] my cheek to smiles, nor cried aloud
In worship of an echo;[175] in the crowd
They could not deem me one of such.[176] I stood
Among them, but not of them, in a shroud
Of thoughts which were not their thoughts, and still could
Had I not filed[177] my mind,[178] which thus itself subdued.

114

I have not loved the world, nor the world me,
But let us part fair foes; I do believe,
Though I have found them not, that there may be

## Notes

[170] *Thou wert the throne and grave of empires* Rome conquered the Etruscan and Carthaginian civilizations, and incorporated the Greek and Persian empires.

[171] *Flows…hill* a reference to the founding of the Roman Empire.

[172] *auspices* i.e. prospect of success.

[173] *guerdon* reward.

[174] *coined* counterfeited.

[175] *In worship of an echo* To Byron, God is no more than an echo.

[176] *such* i.e. a worshipper of God.

[177] *filed* debased.

[178] *Had I not filed my mind* Byron notes the allusion to *Macbeth* III i 63–4: 'If 't be so, / For Banquo's issue have I filed my mind.'

Words which are things, hopes which will not deceive,
And virtues which are merciful, nor weave
Snares for the failing. I would also deem
O'er others' griefs that some sincerely grieve,[179]
That two, or one, are almost what they seem,
That goodness is no name, and happiness no dream.

115

My daughter! with thy name this song begun!
My daughter! with thy name thus much shall end!
I see thee not – I hear thee not – but none
Can be so wrapped in thee; thou art the friend
To whom the shadows of far years extend:
Albeit my brow thou never should'st behold,
My voice shall with thy future visions blend
And reach into thy heart – when mine is cold –
A token and a tone, even from thy father's mould.[180]

116

To aid thy mind's development, to watch
Thy dawn of little joys, to sit and see
Almost thy very growth, to view thee catch
Knowledge of objects (wonders yet to thee!),
To hold thee lightly on a gentle knee,
And print on thy soft cheek a parent's kiss –
This, it should seem, was not reserved for me,
Yet this was in my nature. As it is,
I know not what is there, yet something like to this.

117

Yet though dull hate as duty should be taught,
I know that thou wilt love me, though my name
Should be shut from thee, as a spell still fraught[181]
With desolation, and a broken claim.
Though the grave closed between us, 'twere the same,
I know that thou wilt love me, though to drain
*My* blood from out thy being were an aim
And an attainment, all would be in vain:
Still thou would'st love me, still that more than life retain.

118

The child of love, though born in bitterness
And nurtured in convulsion,[182] of thy sire
These were the elements – and thine no less.
As yet such are around thee, but thy fire

## Notes

[179] 'It is said by Rochfoucault that "there is *always* something in the misfortunes of men's best friends not displeasing to them"' (Byron's note).

[180] *mould* body.

[181] *fraught* loaded.

[182] *convulsion* i.e. Byron's rancorous separation from his wife.

Shall be more tempered, and thy hope far higher.
Sweet be thy cradled slumbers! O'er the sea
And from the mountains where I now respire,
Fain would I waft such blessing upon thee,
As, with a sigh, I deem thou might'st have been to me!

## *Prometheus* (composed July or early August 1816)[1]

I

Titan![2] to whose immortal eye
The sufferings of mortality
Seen in their sad reality,
Were not as things that gods despise –
What was thy pity's recompense?
A silent suffering, and intense;
The rock, the vulture, and the chain,
All that the proud can feel of pain,
The agony they do not show,
The suffocating sense of woe
Which speaks but in its loneliness,
And then is jealous lest the sky
Should have a listener, nor will sigh
Until its voice is echoless.

II

Titan! to thee the strife was given
Between the suffering and the will,
Which torture where they cannot kill;
And the inexorable heaven,
And the deaf tyranny of fate,
The ruling principle of hate
Which for its pleasure doth create
The things it may annihilate,
Refused thee even the boon to die:
The wretched gift eternity
Was thine – and thou hast borne it well.
All that the thunderer[3] wrung from thee
Was but the menace which flung back
On him the torments of thy rack;[4]
The fate thou didst so well foresee

## Notes

PROMETHEUS

[1] When Jupiter took fire away from earth, Prometheus stole replacement fire from the chariot of the sun. In revenge, Jupiter had Prometheus nailed to a rock for 30,000 years, with an eagle incessantly devouring his liver. He was eventually freed, and the bird killed, by Hercules. Byron uses the story to reprise his concept of the overreacher. Prometheus was much on the minds of Shelley, Mary Godwin and Byron in the summer of 1816. He helped inspire Mary's *Frankenstein; or, the Modern Prometheus* (1818), and would be the subject of Shelley's *Prometheus Unbound* several years later.

[2] *Titan!* In classical literature, the Titans were the children of Uranus (heaven) and Ge (earth).

[3] *the thunderer* Jupiter, who was responsible for Prometheus's punishment, used the thunderbolt as his instrument of war.

[4] *rack* suffering.

But would not to appease him tell;
And in thy silence was his sentence,
And in his soul a vain repentance,
And evil dread so ill dissembled
That in his hand the lightnings trembled.

III

Thy godlike crime was to be kind,
To render with thy precepts less
The sum of human wretchedness,
And strengthen man with his own mind;
But baffled[5] as thou wert from high,
Still in thy patient energy,
In the endurance and repulse
Of thine impenetrable spirit,
Which earth and heaven could not convulse,
A mighty lesson we inherit:
Thou art a symbol and a sign
To mortals of their fate and force;
Like thee, man is in part divine,
A troubled stream from a pure source;
And man in portions can foresee
His own funereal destiny;
His wretchedness and his resistance,
And his sad unallied existence:
To which his spirit may oppose
Itself – an equal to all woes,
And a firm will, and a deep sense,
Which even in torture can descry
Its own concentred recompense,
Triumphant where it dares defy,
And making death a victory.

## *Stanzas to Augusta (composed 24 July 1816)*[1]

I

Though the day of my destiny's over,
    And the star of my fate hath declined,
Thy soft heart refused to discover
    The faults which so many could find;
Though thy soul with my grief was acquainted,
    It shrunk not to share it with me,
And the love which my spirit hath painted
    It never hath found but in *thee*.

Notes

[5] *baffled* obstructed, prevented.

Stanzas to Augusta

[1] Originally published as 'Stanzas to ———'. The relationship he had with Augusta Leigh, his half-sister, was always to be one of the most highly valued in Byron's life.

2

Then when nature around me is smiling
    The last smile which answers to mine,
I do not believe it beguiling
    Because it reminds me of thine;
And when winds are at war with the ocean,
    As the breasts I believed in with me,
If their billows excite an emotion
    It is that they bear me from *thee*.

3

Though the rock of my last hope is shivered[2]
    And its fragments are sunk in the wave,
Though I feel that my soul is delivered
    To pain – it shall not be its slave.
There is many a pang to pursue me –
    They may crush, but they shall not contemn;
They may torture, but shall not subdue me –
    'Tis of *thee* that I think, not of them.[3]

4

Though human, thou didst not deceive me;
    Though woman, thou didst not forsake;
Though loved, thou forborest to grieve me;
    Though slandered, thou never couldst shake;
Though trusted, thou didst not betray[4] me;
    Though parted, it was not to fly;
Though watchful, 'twas not to defame me,
    Nor, mute, that the world might belie.

5

Yet I blame not the world, nor despise it,
    Nor the war of the many with one –
If my soul was not fitted to prize it
    'Twas folly not sooner to shun:
And if dearly that error hath cost me,
    And more than I once could foresee,
I have found that, whatever it lost me,
    It could not deprive me of *thee*.

6

From the wreck of the past, which hath perished,
    Thus much I at least may recall,

## Notes

[2] *shivered* shattered.

[3] Byron felt persecuted by the unfavourable publicity arising from his separation from his wife; as he told Thomas Moore on 29 February 1816: 'I am at war "with all the world and his wife"; or, rather, "all the world and *my* wife" are at war with me, and have not yet crushed me – whatever they may do. I don't know that in the course of a hair-breadth existence I was ever, at home or abroad, in a situation so completely uprooting of present pleasure, or rational hope for the future, as this same' (Marchand v 35).

[4] *betray* All printed texts until McGann's Clarendon Press edition (1980–93) have 'disclaim'. McGann's emendation reinstates a reading attributable to Byron rather than his publisher.

It hath taught me that what I most cherished
    Deserved to be dearest of all:
In the desert a fountain is springing,[5]
    In the wide waste there still is a tree,
And a bird in the solitude singing,
    Which speaks to my spirit of *thee*.

## *Epistle to Augusta* (composed August 1816)[1]

I

My sister, my sweet sister – if a name
    Dearer and purer were, it should be thine.
Mountains and seas divide us,[2] but I claim
    No tears, but tenderness to answer mine:
Go where I will, to me thou art the same –
    A loved regret which I would not resign;
There yet are two things in my destiny:
A world to roam through,[3] and a home with thee.

2

The first were nothing – had I still the last
    It were the haven of my happiness;
But other claims and other ties thou hast,[4]
    And mine is not the wish to make them less.
A strange doom[5] was thy father's son's,[6] and past
    Recalling, as it lies beyond redress,
Reversed for him our grandsire's fate of yore[7] –
He had no rest at sea, nor I on shore.

3

If my inheritance of storms hath been
    In other elements, and on the rocks
Of perils overlooked or unforeseen,
    I have sustained my share of worldly shocks;

## Notes

[5] *In the desert a fountain is springing* the ultimate source is biblical (Judges 15:19), but Byron is probably recalling Milton, *Samson Agonistes* 581–2: 'But God who caused a fountain at thy prayer / From the dry ground to spring…'

Epistle to Augusta

[1] Originally published 1830, posthumously; this is Byron's first sustained composition in *ottava rima*.

[2] Byron was resident at the Villa Diodati on the shores of Lake Geneva (Lake Leman at l. 75).

[3] *A world to roam through* Byron had exiled himself from England in April 1816 after separating from his wife and daughter. There is a slight verbal echo of the exile of Adam and Eve from Eden in the final lines of 'Paradise Lost': 'The world was all before them …'; cf. l. 81 and note.

[4] *But other claims…hast* Augusta married Colonel George Leigh in 1807, and had by now given birth to three daughters.

[5] *doom* fate.

[6] *thy father's son's* i.e. Byron. They had the same father, Captain John (Mad Jack) Byron.

[7] The rough draft of the poem contains the following note in Byron's hand: 'Admiral Byron was remarkable for never making a voyage without a tempest: "But, though it were tempest-tossed, / Still his bark could not be lost." He returned safely from the wreck of the Wager (in Anson's voyage) and subsequently circumnavigated the world many years after, as commander of a similar expedition.' The quotation reworks *Macbeth* I iii 24–5.

The fault was mine – nor do I seek to screen
  My errors with defensive paradox:
I have been cunning in mine overthrow,[8]
The careful pilot of my proper woe.

4

Mine were my faults, and mine be their reward;
  My whole life was a contest, since the day
That gave me being gave me that which marred
  The gift – a fate or will that walked astray –
And I at times have found the struggle hard,
  And thought of shaking off my bonds of clay;[9]
But now I fain would for a time survive,
If but to see what next can well arrive.

5

Kingdoms and empires in my little day
  I have outlived and yet I am not old;
And when I look on this, the petty spray
  Of my own years of trouble, which have rolled
Like a wild bay of breakers, melts away:
  Something (I know not what) does still uphold
A spirit of slight patience; not in vain,
Even for its own sake, do we purchase pain.

6

Perhaps the workings of defiance stir
  Within me, or perhaps a cold despair
Brought on when ills habitually recur;
  Perhaps a harder clime or purer air –
For to all such may change of soul refer,
  And with light armour we may learn to bear –
Have taught me a strange quiet which was not
The chief companion of a calmer lot.

7

I feel almost at times as I have felt
  In happy childhood[10] – trees and flowers and brooks,
Which do remember me of where I dwelt
  Ere my young mind was sacrificed to books,
Come as of yore upon me, and can melt
  My heart with recognition of their looks –
And even at moments I could think I see
Some living things to love – but none like thee.

## Notes

[8] *overthrow* ruin; somewhat self-dramatizing, but Byron saw himself as having been ruined, at least in social terms, by his wife's campaign against him.

[9] *my bonds of clay* For the Byronic overreacher, who longs to fulfil his divine aspirations, the human body is a form of imprisonment; cf. Childe Harold, who spurns 'the clay-cold bonds which round our being cling' ('Childe Harold's Pilgrimage' iii 697).

[10] *In happy childhood* Byron did not know Augusta as a child, when he was brought up by his mother in the Scottish countryside.

8

Here are the Alpine landscapes, which create
  A fund for contemplation – to admire
Is a brief feeling of a trivial date –
  But something worthier do such scenes inspire:
Here to be lonely is not desolate,
  For much I view which I could most desire,
And above all a lake I can behold –
Lovelier, not dearer, than our own of old.[11]

9

Oh that thou wert but with me! – but I grow
  The fool of my own wishes, and forget;
The solitude which I have vaunted so
  Has lost its praise in this but one regret –
There may be others which I less may show;
  I am not of the plaintive mood – and yet
I feel an ebb in my philosophy
And the tide rising in my altered eye.

10

I did remind thee of our own dear lake
  By the old Hall which may be mine no more;[12]
Leman's is fair, but think not I forsake
  The sweet remembrance of a dearer shore:
Sad havoc time must with my memory make
  Ere *that* or *thou* can fade these eyes before –
Though like all things which I have loved, they[13] are
Resigned[14] for ever, or divided far.

11

The world is all before me[15] – I but ask
  Of Nature that with which she will comply:
It is but in her summer's sun to bask,
  To mingle in the quiet of her sky,[16]
To see her gentle face without a mask
  And never gaze on it with apathy.
She was my early friend, and now shall be
My sister – till I look again on thee.

12

I can reduce all feelings but this one,
  And that I would not – for at length I see
Such scenes as those wherein my life begun –
  The earliest – were the only paths for me.

## Notes

[11] *than our own of old* Byron refers to the lake at Newstead Abbey, where he had frolicked with Augusta in January and late August 1814.

[12] Byron had to sell Newstead Abbey to pay off his debts. At the time of writing, however, it was still on his hands; it was sold in late 1817 to his Harrow schoolfriend Major Thomas Wildman for £94,500.

[13] *they* i.e. the lake at Newstead and Augusta.

[14] *Resigned* surrendered.

[15] A sardonic echo of the more optimistic context of Adam and Eve leaving Eden, 'Paradise Lost' xii 646.

[16] *the quiet of her sky* a deliberate echo of Wordsworth, 'Tintern Abbey' 8.

Had I but sooner known the crowd to shun,
I had been better than I now can be;
The passions which have torn me would have slept –
*I* had not suffered, and *thou* hadst not wept.

13

With false ambition what had I to do?
Little with love, and least of all with fame!
And yet they came unsought and with me grew,
And made me all which they can make – a name.
Yet this was not the end I did pursue –
Surely I once beheld a nobler aim.
But all is over – I am one the more
To baffled millions which have gone before.

14

And for the future – this world's future may
From me demand but little from my care;
I have outlived myself by many a day,
Having survived so many things that were;
My years have been no slumber – but the prey
Of ceaseless vigils; for I had the share
Of life which might have filled a century
Before its fourth in time had passed me by.

15

And for the remnants which may be to come
I am content – and for the past I feel
Not thankless, for within the crowded sum
Of struggles happiness at times would steal;
And for the present, I would not benumb
My feelings farther – nor shall I conceal
That with all this I still can look around
And worship nature with a thought profound.

16

For thee, my own sweet sister, in thy heart
I know myself secure – as thou in mine
We were and are – I am – even as thou art –
Beings who ne'er each other can resign,
It is the same together or apart:
From life's commencement to its slow decline
We are entwined – let death come slow or fast,
The tie[17] which bound the first endures the last!

Notes

[17] *tie* Byron implicitly compares his blood tie to Augusta with the marriage tie to Annabella.

## *Darkness* (composed between 21 July and 25 August 1816)[1]

I had a dream, which was not all a dream.
The bright sun was extinguished, and the stars
Did wander darkling[2] in the eternal space,
Rayless, and pathless,[3] and the icy earth
Swung blind and blackening in the moonless air;
Morn came, and went – and came, and brought no day,
And men forgot their passions in the dread
Of this their desolation; and all hearts
Were chilled into a selfish prayer for light:
And they did live by watchfires – and the thrones,
The palaces of crowned kings – the huts,
The habitations of all things which dwell,
Were burnt for beacons;[4] cities were consumed,
And men were gathered round their blazing homes
To look once more into each other's face;
Happy were those who dwelt within the eye
Of the volcanoes, and their mountain-torch:
A fearful hope was all the world contained;
Forests were set on fire – but hour by hour
They fell and faded – and the crackling trunks
Extinguished with a crash – and all was black.
The brows of men by the despairing light
Wore an unearthly aspect, as by fits
The flashes fell upon them; some lay down
And hid their eyes and wept; and some did rest
Their chins upon their clenched hands, and smiled;
And others hurried to and fro, and fed
Their funeral piles with fuel, and looked up
With mad disquietude on the dull sky,
The pall of a past world; and then again
With curses cast them down upon the dust,
And gnashed their teeth and howled. The wild birds shrieked,
And, terrified, did flutter on the ground,[5]
And flap their useless wings; the wildest brutes
Came tame and tremulous;[6] and vipers crawled

## Notes

Darkness

[1] The end of the world was one of the topics discussed with Shelley and Mary Godwin in summer 1816; it is also the theme of Mary's novel *The Last Man* (1826). But the most obvious source for this poem is the weather system that prevailed across Europe in summer 1816. A series of disturbances, including the eruption of the Tambora volcano in Indonesia, caused an unusual incidence of mists, fogs and rains in Geneva. Byron is also indebted to various apocalyptic passages in the Bible, notably Jeremiah 4, Ezekiel 32 and 38, Joel 2:31, Matthew 25 and Revelation 6:12.

[2] *darkling* in the dark.

[3] *the stars…pathless* As McGann notes, there is an echo here of Milton's 'Il Penseroso' (appropriately, as the poem was written at the Villa Diodati, where Milton once resided), where the moon is compared with 'one that had been led astray / Through the heaven's wide pathless way' (ll. 69–70).

[4] *beacons* signals – of continuing life.

[5] *The wild birds…on the ground* A recollection of Coleridge's 'Christabel', where the sweet bird in Bracy's dream 'lay fluttering on the ground' (l. 532).

[6] *The wildest brutes…tremulous* An allusion to the famous apocalyptic prophecy, when 'The wolf also shall dwell with the lamb, and the leopard shall lie down with the kid; and the calf and the young lion and the fatling together; and a little child shall lead them' (Isaiah 11:6).

And twined themselves among the multitude,
Hissing, but stingless – they were slain for food:
And War, which for a moment was no more,
Did glut himself again; a meal was bought
With blood, and each sat sullenly apart
Gorging himself in gloom. No love was left;
All earth was but one thought – and that was death,
Immediate and inglorious; and the pang
Of famine fed upon all entrails – men
Died, and their bones were tombless as their flesh;
The meagre by the meagre were devoured,
Even dogs assailed their masters, all save one,
And he was faithful to a corpse, and kept
The birds and beasts and famished men at bay,
Till hunger clung[7] them, or the dropping dead
Lured their lank jaws; himself sought out no food,
But with a piteous and perpetual moan
And a quick desolate cry, licking the hand
Which answered not with a caress – he died.
The crowd was famished by degrees, but two
Of an enormous city did survive,
And they were enemies; they met beside
The dying embers of an altar-place
Where had been heaped a mass of holy things
For an unholy usage; they raked up,
And shivering scraped with their cold skeleton hands
The feeble ashes, and their feeble breath
Blew for a little life, and made a flame
Which was a mockery; then they lifted up
Their eyes as it grew lighter, and beheld
Each other's aspects – saw, and shrieked, and died –
Even of their mutual hideousness they died,
Unknowing who he was upon whose brow
Famine had written Fiend. The world was void,
The populous and the powerful – was a lump,
Seasonless, herbless, treeless, manless, lifeless –
A lump of death – a chaos of hard clay.
The rivers, lakes, and ocean all stood still,
And nothing stirred within their silent depths;
Ships sailorless lay rotting on the sea,
And their masts fell down piecemeal; as they dropped
They slept on the abyss without a surge –
The waves were dead; the tides were in their grave,
The moon their mistress had expired before;
The winds were withered in the stagnant air,
And the clouds perished; Darkness had no need
Of aid from them – she was the universe.

## Notes

[7] *clung* shrivelled, as at *Macbeth* V v 39: 'Till famine cling thee.'

## *Letter from Lord Byron to Thomas Moore, 28 February 1817* (extract; including 'So We'll Go No More a-Roving')[1]

I feel anxious to hear from you, even more than usual, because your last indicated that you were unwell. At present, I am on the invalid regimen myself. The Carnival – that is, the latter part of it – and sitting up late o' nights, had knocked me up a little. But it is over, and it is now Lent, with all its abstinence and Sacred Music.

The mumming[2] closed with a masked ball at the Fenice,[3] where I went, as also to most of the ridottos,[4] etc., etc. And, though I did not dissipate much upon the whole, yet I find 'the sword wearing out the scabbard', though I have but just turned the corner of twenty-nine.

So we'll go no more a-roving
    So late into the night,
Though the heart be still as loving,
    And the moon be still as bright.

For the sword outwears its sheath,
    And the soul wears out the breast,
And the heart must pause to breathe,
    And love itself have rest.

Though the night was made for loving,
    And the day returns too soon,
Yet we'll go no more a-roving
    By the light of the moon.

## Notes

Letter from Lord Byron to Thomas Moore

[1] This important letter was written from Venice, and presents Byron's famous poem, 'So we'll go no more a-roving',in the context in which it was first composed.

[2] *mumming* revelries conducted behind masks.

[3] *the Fenice* Venetian opera theatre, principal venue for the carnival, which closed on the evening of 18 February. It was destroyed by fire in summer 1996.

[4] *ridottos* entertainment or social assembly consisting of music and dancing.

# *Don Juan* (published 1819)[1]
## *Dedication* (composed 3 July–6 September 1818; first published 1832)

1

Bob Southey! You're a poet – Poet Laureate,[2]
And representative of all the race;[3]
Although 'tis true you turned out a Tory at
Last, yours has lately been a common case;
And now, my epic renegade, what are ye at,
With all the Lakers[4] in and out of place?
A nest of tuneful persons, to my eye
Like 'four and twenty blackbirds in a pie,

2

Which pie[5] being opened, they began to sing'
(This old song and new simile holds good),
'A dainty dish to set before the King'
Or Regent,[6] who admires such kind of food.
And Coleridge[7] too has lately taken wing,
But like a hawk encumbered with his hood,
Explaining metaphysics to the nation;[8]
I wish he would explain his explanation.

3

You, Bob, are rather insolent, you know,
At being disappointed in your wish
To supersede all warblers here below,
And be the only blackbird in the dish;
And then you overstrain yourself, or so,
And tumble downward like the flying fish
Gasping on deck, because you soar too high, Bob,
And fall for lack of moisture, quite a dry-bob![9]

## Notes

Don Juan

[1] 'Don Juan' is probably Byron's finest achievement in verse. It was the epic poem he was born to write. Cantos I and II appeared first, without the Dedication, in 1819; they are published here in their entirety.

[2] Southey was Poet Laureate 1813–43, a post that entailed the composition of occasional poems in honour of the King. For Byron and Shelley, this was conclusive proof, were any needed, that Southey had abandoned his early radicalism. In an unpublished Preface to 'Don Juan', Byron wrote that the Dedication 'may be further supposed to be produced by someone who may have a cause of aversion from the said Southey – for some personal reason – perhaps a gross calumny invented or circulated by this Pantisocratic apostle of apostasy, who is sometimes as unguarded in his assertions as atrocious in his conjectures, and feeds the cravings of his wretched vanity – disappointed in its nobler hopes, and reduced to prey upon such snatches of fame as his contributions to the *Quarterly Review*'. Byron's animus towards him was indeed personal: as he told Hobhouse on 11 November 1818, 'The son of a bitch on his return from Switzerland two years ago, said that Shelley and I "had formed a league of incest and practised our precepts with etc." He lied like a rascal, for *they were not sisters* – one being Godwin's daughter by Mary Wollstonecraft, and the other the daughter of the present Mrs Godwin by a *former* husband. The attack contains no allusion to the cause, but some good verses, and all political and poetical. He lied in another sense, for there was no promiscuous intercourse, my commerce being limited to the carnal knowledge of the Miss Clairmont'.

[3] *all the race* i.e. of poets.

[4] *Lakers* i.e. Southey, Wordsworth and Coleridge, who were first lumped together as the 'Lake School' by Jeffrey. By this time Coleridge was resident in London rather than Cumbria.

[5] *pie* There may be a pun on the name of Henry James Pye (1745–1813), Laureate prior to Southey.

[6] *Regent* George, Prince of Wales, governed as Prince Regent 1811–20, during his father's insanity.

[7] As recently as 1816, Byron had given Coleridge £100 to help him through a bad patch; enmity developed because, as Byron told Murray, 'Coleridge went about repeating Southey's lie with pleasure'. The lie was the rumour about the league of incest (see Note 2 above).

[8] *Explaining metaphysics to the nation* Byron is thinking of Coleridge's recent prose discourses, *The Statesman's Manual* (1816), *Biographia Literaria* and *Lay Sermon* (1817) and *The Friend* (1818).

[9] *a dry-bob!* To have sex without climaxing.

4

And Wordsworth, in a rather long *Excursion*
   (I think the quarto holds five hundred pages),[10]
Has given a sample from the vasty[11] version
   Of his new system to perplex the sages;
'Tis poetry (at least by his assertion),
   And may appear so when the dog-star rages;[12]
And he who understands it would be able
To add a story[13] to the Tower of Babel.[14]

5

You gentlemen, by dint of long seclusion
   From better company, have kept your own
At Keswick,[15] and, through still-continued fusion
   Of one another's minds, at last have grown
To deem as a most logical conclusion
   That poesy has wreaths for you alone;
There is a narrowness in such a notion
Which makes me wish you'd change your lakes for ocean.

6

I would not imitate the petty thought,
   Nor coin[16] my self-love to so base a vice,
For all the glory your conversion[17] brought,
   Since gold alone should not have been its price.
You have your salary – was't for that you wrought?[18]
   And Wordsworth has his place in the Excise.[19]
You're shabby fellows, true – but poets still,
And duly seated on the immortal hill.[20]

7

Your bays[21] may hide the baldness of your brows,
   Perhaps some virtuous blushes (let them go);
To you I envy neither fruit nor boughs,
   And for the fame you would engross[22] below
The field is universal, and allows

## Notes

[10] *five hundred pages* Jeffrey criticized 'The Excursion' (1814) for its length.

[11] *vasty* vast, enormous.

[12] *when the dog-star rages* The star Sirius, in the constellation of the Greater Dog, the brightest of the fixed stars, has been alleged to have all kinds of bad effects when its influence rises with the sun; the joke here is that it will distort everyone's judgement so much as to make 'The Excursion' appear to be poetry; cf. Pope, *Epistle to Dr Arbuthnot* 3–4: 'The dog-star rages! Nay 'tis past a doubt, / All Bedlam, or Parnassus, is let out.'

[13] *story* floor, level.

[14] *the Tower of Babel* the cause of God's decision to confound the language of men; Genesis II:1–9.

[15] *At Keswick* Only Southey lived at Keswick (as Byron well knew); Coleridge lived in London, and Wordsworth in Grasmere.

[16] *coin* 'fashion', effectively, 'convert'. The implication is that Southey's vanity has led him to relinquish his ideals for the pittance he is paid as Laureate.

[17] *conversion* a pun, meaning: (i) conversion of vanity to the gold Southey is paid as Laureate, and (ii) conversion from radical to Tory.

[18] *wrought* i.e. composed poetry.

[19] An unpublished note appears in the proofs: 'Wordsworth's place may be in the Customs; it is, I think, in that of the Excise – besides another at Lord Lonsdale's table, where this poetical charlatan and political parasite picks up the crumbs with a hardened alacrity, the converted Jacobin having long subsided into the clownish sycophant of the worst prejudices of aristocracy.' William Lowther, 1st Earl of Lonsdale, was Wordsworth's patron; he procured Wordsworth's job as Distributor of Stamps and was the dedicatee of 'The Excursion'.

[20] *the immortal hill* Parnassus, a mountain of Phocis (northwest of Athens), sacred to the muses.

[21] *bays* The leaves of the bay-tree or bay-laurel were, in classical times, the symbol of poetic excellence.

[22] *engross* monopolize. Byron was quite famous himself.

Scope to all such as feel the inherent glow –
Scott, Rogers, Campbell, Moore and Crabbe[23] will try
'Gainst you the question with posterity.

8

For me who, wandering with pedestrian[24] muses,
  Contend not with you on the winged steed,
I wish your fate may yield ye, when she chooses,
  The fame you envy[25] and the skill you need;[26]
And recollect a poet nothing loses
  In giving to his brethren their full meed
Of merit, and complaint of present days
Is not the *certain* path to future praise.[27]

9

He that reserves his laurels for posterity
  (Who does not often claim the bright reversion?)[28]
Has generally no great crop[29] to spare it, he
  Being only injured by his own assertion;
And although here and there some glorious rarity
  Arise like Titan from the sea's immersion,[30]
The major part of such appellants[31] go
To God knows where – for no one else can know.

10

If, fallen in evil days on evil tongues,[32]
  Milton appealed to the avenger, Time;
If Time, the avenger, execrates his wrongs,
  And makes the word 'Miltonic' mean 'sublime',
*He* deigned not to belie his soul in songs,
  Nor turn his very talent to a crime;
*He* did not loathe the sire to laud the son,[33]
But closed the tyrant-hater he begun.[34]

11

Think'st thou, could he, the blind old man,[35] arise
  Like Samuel from the grave,[36] to freeze once more
The blood of monarchs with his prophecies,
  Or be alive again, again all hoar

## Notes

[23] *Scott, Rogers, Campbell, Moore and Crabbe* Walter Scott, Samuel Rogers, Thomas Campbell, Thomas Moore and George Crabbe were well-known and respected poets in their day. Byron saw them as working, broadly speaking, within the neoclassical tradition stemming from Pope; as such, they were vastly preferable to the Lakers.

[24] *pedestrian* by implication, less metaphysical and more down to earth.

[25] *The fame you envy* In the Proem to *Carmen Nuptiale* (1816), Southey had written: 'There was a time when all my youthful thought / Was of the muse; and of the poet's fame' (ll. 1–2).

[26] *need* i.e. lack.

[27] *And recollect…praise* In the Proem to 'Carmen Nuptiale' (1816), Southey wrote that Fancy had told him to walk 'Far from the vain, the vicious, and the proud' (l. 27). Byron seems to have taken this as a reference to himself.

[28] *the bright reversion* the right of succession (i.e. to posthumous fame).

[29] *no great crop* i.e. of praise for other poets.

[30] *Arise like Titan from the sea's immersion* Byron has in mind Helios, son of Hyperion, god of the sun.

[31] *appellants* challengers, i.e. those who reserve their laurels for posterity.

[32] 'Paradise Lost' vii 25–6.

[33] *He did not loathe…son* Charles I and II. Byron's point is that Southey (a former republican) hated George III (in his radical youth) but praised his son (the Prince Regent); by contrast, Milton remained a republican throughout his life.

[34] *But closed the tyrant-hater he begun* As far as Byron was concerned, both George III and the Prince Regent were tyrants. At that time, the monarch (an inherited post) had enormous political power.

[35] *the blind old man* Milton.

[36] *Like Samuel from the grave* Samuel was raised from the grave by the Witch of Endor; I Samuel 28:13–14.

With time and trials, and those helpless eyes
   And heartless daughters,[37] worn and pale and poor –
Would *he* adore a sultan? – *he* obey
The intellectual eunuch Castlereagh?[38]

12

Cold-blooded, smooth-faced, placid miscreant!
   Dabbling its sleek young hands in Erin's[39] gore,
And thus for wider carnage taught to pant,
   Transferred to gorge upon a sister-shore;
The vulgarest tool that tyranny could want,
   With just enough of talent, and no more,
To lengthen fetters by another fixed,
And offer poison long already mixed.

13

An orator of such set trash of phrase[40]
   Ineffably, legitimately vile,
That even its grossest flatterers dare not praise,
   Nor foes (all nations) condescend to smile;
Not even a sprightly blunder's spark can blaze
   From that Ixion grindstone's[41] ceaseless toil,
That turns and turns, to give the world a notion
Of endless torments and perpetual motion.

14

A bungler even in its disgusting trade,
   And botching, patching, leaving still behind
Something of which its masters are afraid,
   States to be curbed[42] and thoughts to be confined,
Conspiracy or congress[43] to be made,
   Cobbling at manacles for all mankind –
A tinkering slavemaker who mends old chains,
With God and man's abhorrence for its gains.

15

If we may judge of matter by the mind,
   Emasculated to the marrow, *It*
Hath but two objects: how to serve and bind,
   Deeming the chain it wears even men may fit;
Eutropius[44] of its many masters – blind

## Notes

[37] *heartless daughters* said to have robbed Milton of his books.

[38] Robert Stewart, Viscount Castlereagh (1769–1822), Foreign Secretary 1812–22. As Secretary to the Lord Lieutenant of Ireland (1797–1801), he had been responsible for imprisoning the leaders of the United Irish rebellion.

[39] *Erin's* Ireland's.

[40] *such set trash of phrase* Castlereagh was renowned as an incompetent speaker.

[41] *Ixion grindstone's* Ixion, King of Thessaly, was banished from heaven and sentenced to be tied to a burning and spinning wheel in Hades.

[42] *States to be curbed* i.e. France under Napoleon; Castlereagh helped negotiate the alliance with Russia, Austria and Prussia that led to Napoleon's defeat.

[43] *congress* As Foreign Secretary, Castlereagh was instrumental in the Treaty of Paris (May 1814), which restored the Bourbon monarchy after Napoleon's abdication, and the Congress of Vienna (1814–15), which reorganized Europe after the Napoleonic Wars.

[44] *Eutropius* Roman eunuch raised to high office; see Gibbon, *Decline and Fall of the Roman Empire*, chapter 32.

To worth as freedom, wisdom as to wit –
Fearless, because *no* feeling dwells in ice,
Its very courage stagnates to a vice.

16
Where shall I turn me not to view its bonds
(For I will never feel them)? Italy,
Thy late-reviving Roman soul desponds
Beneath the lie this state-thing[45] breathed o'er thee;
Thy clanking chain and Erin's yet green wounds
Have voices, tongues to cry aloud for me.
Europe has slaves, allies, kings, armies still –
And Southey lives to sing them very ill.[46]

17
Meantime, Sir Laureate,[47] I proceed to dedicate,
In honest, simple verse, this song to you,
And if in flattering strains I do not predicate,[48]
'Tis that I still retain my 'buff and blue'[49]
(My politics, as yet, are all to educate);
Apostasy's so fashionable too,
To keep *one* creed's a task grown quite herculean –
Is it not so, my Tory ultra-Julian?[50]

## *Canto I*

1
I want a hero[1] – an uncommon want
When every year and month sends forth a new one,
Till after cloying the gazettes with cant,
The age discovers he is not the true one;
Of such as these I should not care to vaunt,
I'll therefore take our ancient friend Don Juan;[2]
We all have seen him in the pantomime[3]
Sent to the devil,[4] somewhat ere his time.

2
Vernon, the butcher Cumberland, Wolfe, Hawke,
Prince Ferdinand, Granby, Burgoyne, Keppel, Howe,[5]

## Notes

[45] *this state-thing* The Congress of Vienna ('this state-thing') restored papal power.

[46] This stanza provides an overview of Castlereagh's misdeeds. In 1798 he had helped to defeat the Irish insurrection and establish the Union of 1801; as a chief negotiator of the Treaty of Vienna, 1814–15, he had been responsible for suppressing the revival of free Italian cities, instead placing Italy under Austrian rule. Southey celebrated his deeds in 'Carmen Triumphale' (1814) and 'The Poet's Pilgrimage to Waterloo' (1816).

[47] *Sir Laureate* Southey.

[48] *predicate* extol, commend (i.e. Southey and his poetry).

[49] *buff and blue* colours of the Whig Club. The comparison is with Southey, who has relinquished all his liberal credentials.

[50] 'I allude not to our friend Landor's hero, the traitor Count Julian, but to Gibbon's hero, vulgarly yclept "The Apostate"' (Byron's note). Julian was brought up as a Christian, but secretly worshipped Roman gods before he became Emperor in 361 CE. During his brief reign he attempted to restore pagan worship (he died 363).

### Canto I

[1] *I want a hero* Byron's lack of a hero is a witty variation on Virgil's epic opening, 'Of arms and the man I sing …'

[2] *Juan* Pronounced with a hard 'J', to rhyme with 'new one' and 'true one'.

[3] *pantomime* musical drama without words. In London, only Drury Lane Theatre and Covent Garden Theatre were allowed to perform 'spoken drama'; other theatres were confined to plays without words. Byron may well have seen Don Juan portrayed in Italian.

[4] *Sent to the devil* By contrast, Byron's poem will humanize Juan, and redeem him from the accusations commonly levelled against him.

[5] *Vernon…Howe* Celebrated eighteenth-century military and naval commanders.

Evil and good, have had their tithe of talk,
  And filled their signposts then, like Wellesley now;[6]
Each in their turn like Banquo's monarchs stalk,[7]
  Followers of fame, 'nine farrow' of that sow;[8]
France, too, had Buonaparté and Dumourier,[9]
Recorded in the *Moniteur* and *Courier*.[10]

3

Barnave, Brissot, Condorcet, Mirabeau,
  Petion, Clootz, Danton, Marat, La Fayette
Were French, and famous people as we know;
  And there were others, scarce forgotten yet –
Joubert, Hoche, Marceau, Lannes, Dessaix, Moreau,[11]
  With many of the military set,
Exceedingly remarkable at times,
But not at all adapted to my rhymes.

4

Nelson[12] was once Britannia's god of war,
  And still should be so, but the tide is turned;
There's no more to be said of Trafalgar –
  'Tis with our hero quietly inurned
Because the army's grown more popular,[13]
  At which the naval people are concerned;
Besides, the Prince is all for the land-service,
Forgetting Duncan, Nelson, Howe, and Jervis.[14]

5

Brave men were living before Agamemnon[15]
  And since, exceeding valorous and sage –
A good deal like him too, though quite the same none;
  But then they shone not on the poet's page,
And so have been forgotten. I condemn none,
  But can't find any in the present age
Fit for my poem (that is, for my new one),
So as I said, I'll take my friend Don Juan.

6

Most epic poets plunge *in medias res*[16]
  (Horace makes this the heroic turnpike road),[17]

## Notes

[6] *And filled their signposts then, like Wellesley now* Wellington Street and Waterloo Bridge were opened and dedicated on the anniversary of Waterloo in 1817.

[7] *like Banquo's monarchs stalk* An allusion to the vision granted Macbeth at *Macbeth* IV ii 112–24.

[8] *'nine farrow' of that sow* An allusion to the witches' spell in *Macbeth* IV i 64–5: 'Pour in sow's blood, that hath eaten / Her nine farrow.'

[9] Charles Dumouriez (1729–1823) defeated the Austrian army in 1792 at Jemappes.

[10] *the Moniteur and Courier* French official newspapers: *Gazette Nationale; ou le moniteur universel* and *Courier Républicain*.

[11] These are politicians and military leaders involved with the French Revolution.

[12] Horatio, Lord Nelson (1758–1805), killed at the Battle of Trafalgar, with Napoleon's forces, 21 October 1805.

[13] *Because the army's grown more popular* i.e. since Waterloo.

[14] These are all distinguished admirals.

[15] Agamemnon commanded the Greeks in the Trojan wars.

[16] *in medias res* into the middle of things; i.e. start in midstory. This is the recommendation of Horace, *Ars Poetica* 148.

[17] *the heroic turnpike road* i.e. the initial step in the writing of an epic poem. A 'turnpike road' is one on which turnpikes are or were erected for the collection of tolls; hence, a main road or highway.

And then your hero tells, whene'er you please,
  What went before by way of episode,
While seated after dinner at his ease
  Beside his mistress in some soft abode –
Palace or garden, paradise or cavern,
Which serves the happy couple for a tavern.

7

That is the usual method, but not mine;
  My way is to begin with the beginning.
The regularity of my design
  Forbids all wandering as the worst of sinning,
And therefore I shall open with a line
  (Although it cost me half an hour in spinning)
Narrating somewhat of Don Juan's father
And also of his mother, if you'd rather.

8

In Seville was he born, a pleasant city
  Famous for oranges and women; he
Who has not seen it will be much to pity,
  So says the proverb – and I quite agree:[18]
Of all the Spanish towns is none more pretty
  (Cadiz perhaps,[19] but that you soon may see).
Don Juan's parents lived beside the river,
A noble stream, and called the Guadalquivir.

9

His father's name was Jóse (Don, of course) –
  A true hidalgo,[20] free from every stain
Of Moor or Hebrew blood, he traced his source
  Through the most Gothic gentlemen of Spain;
A better cavalier ne'er mounted horse
  (Or, being mounted, e'er got down again)
Than Jóse, who begot our hero, who
Begot – but that's to come. Well, to renew:

10

His mother was a learned lady famed
  For every branch of every science known,[21]
In every Christian language ever named,
  With virtues equalled by her wit alone;
She made the cleverest people quite ashamed,

## Notes

[18] *and I quite agree* Byron was in Seville, 25–29 July 1809. The 'proverb' runs: 'Quien no ha visto Sevilla / No ha visto maravilla' ('Whoever has not seen Seville has not seen a marvel').

[19] Byron was in Cadiz, 29 July–3 August 1809.

[20] *hidalgo* a gentleman by birth, one of the lower nobility.

[21] *His mother…known* Byron always denied that Donna Inez was supposed to be a caricature of his wife, but friends recognized the similarities, and advised him not to publish the poem on that account. Lady Byron was renowned for her expertise at mathematics, classical literature and philosophy.

And even the good with inward envy groan,
Finding themselves so very much exceeded
In their own way by all the things that she did.

11

Her memory was a mine – she knew by heart
All Calderon and greater part of Lopé,[22]
So that if any actor missed his part
She could have served him for the prompter's copy;
For her Feinagle's[23] were an useless art,
And he himself obliged to shut up shop – he
Could never make a memory so fine as
That which adorned the brain of Donna Inez.

12

Her favourite science was the mathematical,[24]
Her noblest virtue was her magnanimity,
Her wit (she sometimes tried at wit) was Attic[25] all,
Her serious sayings darkened to sublimity;
In short, in all things she was fairly what I call
A prodigy – her morning dress was dimity,[26]
Her evening silk or, in the summer, muslin
(And other stuffs with which I won't stay puzzling).

13

She knew the Latin – that is, the Lord's prayer,
And Greek – the alphabet, I'm nearly sure;
She read some French romances here and there,
Although her mode of speaking was not pure;
For native Spanish she had no great care
(At least her conversation was obscure);
Her thoughts were theorems, her words a problem,
As if she deemed that mystery would ennoble 'em.

14

She liked the English and the Hebrew tongue,
And said there was analogy between 'em;
She proved it somehow out of sacred song,
But I must leave the proofs to those who've seen 'em;
But this I heard her say, and can't be wrong,
And all may think which way their judgments lean 'em,
''Tis strange; the Hebrew noun which means "I am",
The English always use to govern damn.'[27]

## Notes

[22] *All Calderon…Lopé* Pedro Calderón de la Barca (1600–81) and Lopé de Vega (1562–1635) were Spanish playwrights.

[23] Gregor von Feinagle (1765–1819) devised a system of mnemonics, on which he lectured in England and Scotland in 1811.

[24] *Her favourite science…mathematical* Byron used to call his wife the Princess of Parallelograms.

[25] Attic wit is refined, delicate, and piquant.

[26] *dimity* stout cotton fabric; said by Thomas Moore to have been Lady Byron's favourite dress material.

[27] *'Tis strange…damn* 'damn' was spelt 'd–n' in the first edition. Yahweh ('I am' in Hebrew) indicates God; see Exodus 3:13–14.

15

Some women use their tongues; she looked a lecture,
  Each eye a sermon, and her brow a homily,
An all-in-all-sufficient self-director
  Like the lamented late Sir Samuel Romilly,[28]
The law's expounder and the state's corrector[29]
  Whose suicide was almost an anomaly –
One sad example more that 'All is vanity';[30]
The jury brought their verdict in: insanity.

16

In short, she was a walking calculation,
  Miss Edgeworth's[31] novels stepping from their covers,
Or Mrs Trimmer's books on education,[32]
  Or 'Coeleb's Wife' set out in search of lovers,[33]
Morality's prim personification
  In which not envy's self a flaw discovers:
To others' share let 'female errors fall',[34]
For she had not even one – the worst of all.

17

Oh she was perfect past all parallel
  Of any modern female saint's comparison;
So far beyond the cunning powers of hell,
  Her guardian angel had given up his garrison;
Even her minutest motions went as well
  As those of the best timepiece made by Harrison;[35]
In virtues nothing earthly could surpass her,
Save thine 'incomparable oil', Macassar![36]

18

Perfect she was, but as perfection is
  Insipid in this naughty world of ours,
Where our first parents[37] never learned to kiss
  Till they were exiled from their earlier bowers,[38]

## Notes

[28] *the lamented late Sir Samuel Romilly* bitterly ironic. Romilly (1757–1818) sided with Lady Byron when she separated from her husband, earning Byron's lasting hatred. After Romilly's suicide, Byron commented: 'I still loathe him as much as we can hate dust – but that is nothing.'

[29] *the state's corrector* Romilly had been MP for Westminster.

[30] *All is vanity* Ecelesiastes I:2: 'Vanity of vanities, saith the Preacher, vanity of vanities; all is vanity.

[31] Maria Edgeworth (1767–1849) wrote educational volumes for children, including *The Parent's Assistant* (1796) and *Practical Education* (co-authored with her father, Richard Lovell Edgeworth) (1798). She was also a distinguished novelist.

[32] Sarah Trimmer (1741–1810) wrote a number of exemplary tales and moral lessons for children, including *An Easy Introduction to the Knowledge of Nature* (1790) and *Instructive Tales* (1810).

[33] Hannah More was famous in 1819 as the author of a monstrously successful didactic novel, *Coelebs in Search of a Wife* (1808), which had gone to a twelfth edition by the end of 1809.

[34] *female errors fall* An allusion to Pope, *The Rape of the Lock* ii 17–18: 'If to her share some female errors fall, / Look on her face, and you'll forget 'em all.'

[35] John Harrison (1693–1776), eminent horologist of the day.

[36] *thine 'incomparable oil', Macassar* Macassar oil was a tonic for the follicles advertised in hyperbolic terms that gave Byron and his cronies much amusement; see, for example, the front page of *The Courier*, 2 January 1809: 'Macassar oil, for the growth of HAIR. The virtues of this oil, extracted from a tree in the island of Macassar, are proudly pre-eminent to anything ever produced in this or any other country, for improving and accelerating the growth of hair, preventing it falling off, or turning grey, giving it an incomparable gloss, and producing wonderful effects on children's hair. Its virtues need only the test of experience to evince its extraordinary effects.' Byron was using Macassar oil as he composed 'Don Juan'.

[37] *our first parents* Adam and Eve.

[38] Adam and Eve had children only after being cast out of Paradise.

Where all was peace and innocence and bliss
(I wonder how they got through the twelve hours) –
Don Jóse, like a lineal son of Eve,
Went plucking various fruit without her leave.

19

He was a mortal of the careless kind
With no great love for learning or the learned,
Who chose to go where'er he had a mind,
And never dreamed his lady was concerned;
The world, as usual, wickedly inclined
To see a kingdom or a house o'erturned,
Whispered he had a mistress, some said *two* –
But for domestic quarrels *one* will do.

20

Now Donna Inez had, with all her merit,
A great opinion of her own good qualities;
Neglect, indeed, requires a saint to bear it –
And so indeed, she was in her moralities;
But then she had a devil of a spirit,
And sometimes mixed up fancies with realities,
And let few opportunities escape
Of getting her liege-lord into a scrape.

21

This was an easy matter with a man
Oft in the wrong and never on his guard;
And even the wisest, do the best they can,
Have moments, hours, and days, so unprepared
That you might 'brain them with their lady's fan',[39]
And sometimes ladies hit exceeding hard,
And fans turn into falchions[40] in fair hands,
And why and wherefore no one understands.

22

'Tis pity learned virgins ever wed
With persons of no sort of education,
Or gentlemen who, though well-born and bred,
Grow tired of scientific conversation.
I don't choose to say much upon this head;
I'm a plain man and in a single station,
But oh, ye lords of ladies intellectual,[41]
Inform us truly, have they not hen-pecked you all?

## Notes

[39] *brain them with their lady's fan* Hotspur's comment at *1 Henry IV* II iii 22–3: 'Zounds, and I were now by this rascal, I could brain him with his lady's fan.'

[40] *falchions* broad swords.

[41] *ladies intellectual* A reference to Bluestocking circles of Byron's day, which included Lady Caroline Lamb, Lady Oxford and Annabella Milbanke.

23

Don Jóse and his lady quarrelled – *why*
Not any of the many could divine,
Though several thousand people chose to try,
'Twas surely no concern of theirs nor mine;
I loathe that low vice curiosity,
But if there's anything in which I shine,
'Tis in arranging all my friends' affairs –
Not having, of my own, domestic cares.

24

And so I interfered, and with the best
Intentions, but their treatment was not kind;
I think the foolish people were possessed,
For neither of them could I ever find,
Although their porter afterwards confessed –
But that's no matter, and the worst's behind,
For little Juan o'er me threw, downstairs,
A pail of housemaid's water, unawares.

25

A little curly-headed, good-for-nothing,
And mischief-making monkey from his birth;
His parents ne'er agreed except in doting
Upon the most unquiet imp on earth;
Instead of quarrelling, had they been but both in
Their senses, they'd have sent young master forth
To school, or had him soundly whipped at home
To teach him manners for the time to come.

26

Don Jóse and the Donna Inez led
For some time an unhappy sort of life,
Wishing each other not divorced but dead;
They lived respectably as man and wife,
Their conduct was exceedingly well-bred,
And gave no outward signs of inward strife –
Until at length the smothered fire broke out,
And put the business past all kind of doubt.

27

For Inez called some druggists and physicians[42]
And tried to prove her loving lord was mad,[43]
But as he had some lucid intermissions,
She next decided he was only bad;
Yet when they asked her for her depositions,[44]
No sort of explanation could be had,

Notes

[42] *druggists and physicians* chemists and doctors.

[43] *And tried to prove...was mad* Byron believed his wife had tried to prove him mad.

[44] *depositions* statements, testimony (that he was mad).

Save that her duty both to man and God
Required this conduct (which seemed very odd).

28

She kept a journal where his faults were noted
And opened certain trunks of books and letters –
All which might, if occasion served, be quoted;
And then she had all Seville for abettors,
Besides her good old grandmother (who doted);
The hearers of her case became repeaters,
Then advocates, inquisitors, and judges –
Some for amusement, others for old grudges.[45]

29

And then this best and meekest woman bore
With such serenity her husband's woes,
Just as the Spartan ladies did of yore
Who saw their spouses killed, and nobly chose
Never to say a word about them more;
Calmly she heard each calumny that rose,
And saw his agonies with such sublimity
That all the world exclaimed 'What magnanimity!'

30

No doubt this patience, when the world is damning us,
Is philosophic in our former friends;
'Tis also pleasant to be deemed magnanimous
(The more so in obtaining our own ends);
And what the lawyers call a *malus animus*,[46]
Conduct like this by no means comprehends:[47]
Revenge in person's certainly no virtue,
But then 'tis not *my* fault, if *others* hurt you.

31

And if our quarrels should rip up old stories
And help them with a lie or two additional,
I'm not to blame, as you well know, no more is
Anyone else – they were become traditional;
Besides, their resurrection aids our glories
By contrast, which is what we just were wishing all:
And science profits by this resurrection –
Dead scandals form good subjects for dissection.

32

Their friends[48] had tried at reconciliation,
Then their relations[49] who made matters worse

## Notes

[45] This is a description of the whispering campaign conducted against Byron by his wife.

[46] *malus animus* bad intent.

[47] *comprehends* comprises.

[48] *friends* In Byron's case, Hobhouse, Rogers and Madame de Staël.

[49] *relations* In Byron's case, his sister Augusta, and cousin George Anson Byron (who ended up supporting Lady Byron).

('Twere hard to say upon a like occasion
To whom it may be best to have recourse;
I can't say much for friend or yet relation);
The lawyers did their utmost for divorce
But scarce a fee was paid on either side
Before, unluckily, Don Jóse died.

33

He died – and most unluckily, because,
According to all hints I could collect
From counsel[50] learned in those kinds of laws
(Although their talk's obscure and circumspect),
His death contrived to spoil a charming cause:
A thousand pities also with respect
To public feeling, which on this occasion
Was manifested in a great sensation.

34

But ah, he died – and buried with him lay
The public feeling and the lawyers' fees;
His house was sold, his servants sent away,
A Jew took one of his two mistresses,
A priest the other (at least so they say).
I asked the doctors after his disease:
He died of the slow fever called the tertian[51]
And left his widow to her own aversion.

35

Yes, Jóse was an honourable man[52] –
That I must say, who knew him very well;
Therefore his frailties I'll no further scan
(Indeed there were not many more to tell),
And if his passions now and then outran
Discretion, and were not so peaceable
As Numa's (who was also named Pompilius),[53]
He had been ill brought up, and was born bilious.[54]

36

Whate'er might be his worthlessness or worth,
Poor fellow, he had many things to wound him,
Let's own, since it can do no good on earth;
It was a trying moment that which found him
Standing alone beside his desolate hearth
Where all his household gods lay shivered[55] round him;

## Notes

[50] *counsel* body of legal advisers.

[51] *the slow fever called the tertian* Tertian fever progresses slowly because it strikes only every other day.

[52] *an honourable man* An echo of Antony's attack on Brutus and the assassins of Caesar, *Julius Caesar* III ii 82–3.

[53] The 43-year reign of Numa, second king of Rome, was known for its peaceability.

[54] *bilious* ill-tempered.

[55] *shivered* shattered.

No choice was left his feelings or his pride
Save death or Doctors' Commons[56] – so he died.

37

Dying intestate, Juan was sole heir
To a chancery-suit[57] and messuages[58] and lands
Which, with a long minority and care,
Promised to turn out well in proper hands;
Inez became sole guardian (which was fair)
And answered but to nature's just demands;
An only son left with an only mother
Is brought up much more wisely than another.

38

Sagest of women, even of widows, she
Resolved that Juan should be quite a paragon
And worthy of the noblest pedigree
(His sire was of Castile, his dam from Aragon).
Then for accomplishments of chivalry,
In case our lord the king should go to war again,
He learned the arts of riding, fencing, gunnery,
And how to scale a fortress – or a nunnery.

39

But that which Donna Inez most desired,
And saw into herself each day before all
The learned tutors whom for him she hired,
Was that his breeding should be strictly moral;
Much into all his studies she enquired,
And so they were submitted first to her, all,
Arts, sciences – no branch was made a mystery
To Juan's eyes, excepting natural history.

40

The languages (especially the dead),[59]
The sciences (and most of all the abstruse),
The arts (at least all such as could be said
To be the most remote from common use) –
In all these he was much and deeply read;
But not a page of anything that's loose[60]
Or hints continuation of the species
Was ever suffered, lest he should grow vicious.[61]

41

His classic studies made a little puzzle
Because of filthy loves of gods and goddesses

## Notes

[56] *Doctors' Commons* divorce courts.

[57] *chancery-suit* legal claim for property.

[58] *messuages* dwelling-place with adjoining lands.

[59] *The languages (especially the dead)* i.e. Latin and Greek.

[60] *loose* wanton, immoral.

[61] *vicious* immoral, depraved.

Who in the earlier ages made a bustle,
 But never put on pantaloons or bodices;
His reverend tutors had at times a tussle,
 And for their *Aeneids*, *Iliads*, and *Odysseys*,
Were forced to make an odd sort of apology –
For Donna Inez dreaded the mythology.

42

Ovid's a rake, as half his verses show him,
 Anacreon's morals are a still worse sample,
Catullus scarcely has a decent poem,
 I don't think Sappho's 'Ode' a good example,
Although Longinus tells us there is no hymn
 Where the sublime soars forth on wings more ample;
But Virgil's songs are pure, except that horrid one
Beginning with *Formosum pastor Corydon*.[62]

43

Lucretius' irreligion[63] is too strong
 For early stomachs, to prove wholesome food;
I can't help thinking Juvenal was wrong
 (Although no doubt his real intent was good)
For speaking out so plainly in his song –
 So much indeed as to be downright rude;[64]
And then what proper person can be partial
To all those nauseous epigrams of Martial?[65]

44

Juan was taught from out the best edition,
 Expurgated by learned men who place
Judiciously, from out the schoolboy's vision,
 The grosser parts; but fearful to deface
Too much their modest bard by this omission,
 And pitying sore his mutilated case,
They only add them all in an appendix[66] –
Which saves, in fact, the trouble of an index;

45

For there we have them all at one fell swoop,
 Instead of being scattered through the pages;
They stand forth marshalled in a handsome troop
 To meet the ingenuous youth of future ages,

## Notes

[62] *Ovid's a rake…Corydon* Byron lists erotic poets and poems, including Sappho's 'Ode to Aphrodite', Ovid's *Amores* and *Ars Amatoria*, the love-songs of Anacreon and Catullus, and Virgil's *Eclogue* ii (dealing with pederastic love).

[63] *Lucretius' irreligion* In *De rerum natura*, Lucretius attempted to show that the course of world history had taken place without divine intervention.

[64] *downright rude* Juvenal portrayed the vices and depravities of Roman society.

[65] *Martial* Roman epigrammatist, witty and indecent.

[66] 'Fact. There is, or was, such an edition, with all the obnoxious epigrams of Martial placed by themselves at the end' (Byron's note).

Till some less rigid editor shall stoop
    To call them back into their separate cages,
Instead of standing staring altogether
Like garden gods – and not so decent either.

46

The missal[67] too (it was the family missal)
    Was ornamented in a sort of way
Which ancient mass-books often are, and this all
    Kinds of grotesques illumined; and how they,
Who saw those figures on the margin kiss all,
    Could turn their optics[68] to the text and pray
Is more than I know – but Don Juan's mother
Kept this herself, and gave her son another.

47

Sermons he read and lectures he endured,
    And homilies and lives of all the saints;
To Jerome and to Chrysostom[69] inured,
    He did not take such studies for restraints;
But how faith is acquired and then insured,
    So well not one of the aforesaid paints
As St Augustine in his fine *Confessions* –
Which make the reader envy his transgressions.[70]

48

This too was a sealed book to little Juan –
    I can't but say that his mamma was right,
If such an education was the true one.
    She scarcely trusted him from out her sight;
Her maids were old, and if she took a new one
    You might be sure she was a perfect fright;
She did this during even her husband's life –
I recommend as much to every wife.

49

Young Juan waxed[71] in goodliness and grace;
    At six a charming child, and at eleven
With all the promise of as fine a face
    As e'er to man's maturer growth was given.
He studied steadily and grew apace
    And seemed, at least, in the right road to heaven –
For half his days were passed at church, the other
Between his tutors, confessor, and mother.

## Notes

[67] *missal* Roman Catholic prayer book containing masses for each day of the year.

[68] *optics* eyes.

[69] Jerome and Chrysostom were early Christian theologians.

[70] *his transgressions* i.e. as committed in his early life.

[71] *waxed* grew. There seems to be an echo of Christ: 'And the child grew, and waxed strong in spirit, filled with wisdom: and the grace of God was upon him' (Luke 2:40).

50

At six, I said, he was a charming child,
At twelve he was a fine but quiet boy;
Although in infancy a little wild,
They tamed him down amongst them; to destroy
His natural spirit not in vain they toiled
(At least it seemed so); and his mother's joy
Was to declare how sage and still and steady
Her young philosopher was grown already.

51

I had my doubts – perhaps I have them still,
But what I say is neither here nor there;
I knew his father well, and have some skill
In character, but it would not be fair
From sire to son to augur good or ill;
He and his wife were an ill-sorted pair –
But scandal's my aversion, I protest
Against all evil speaking, even in jest.

52

For my part I say nothing – nothing – but
*This* I will say (my reasons are my own):
That if I had an only son to put
To school (as God be praised that I have none),
'Tis not with Donna Inez I would shut
Him up to learn his catechism alone –
No, no; I'd send him out betimes to college,
For there it was I picked up my own knowledge.

53

For there one learns – 'tis not for me to boast,
Though I acquired – but I pass over *that*,
As well as all the Greek I since have lost;
I say that there's the place – but *Verbum sat*;[72]
I think I picked up too, as well as most,
Knowledge of matters – but no matter *what* –
I never married – but I think, I know,
That sons should not be educated so.

54

Young Juan now was sixteen years of age –
Tall, handsome, slender, but well-knit; he seemed
Active, though not so sprightly, as a page,
And everybody but his mother deemed
Him almost man. But she flew in a rage
And bit her lips (for else she might have screamed)

## Notes

[72] *Verbum sat* 'a word [to the wise] is enough'.

If any said so – for to be precocious
Was in her eyes a thing the most atrocious.

55

Amongst her numerous acquaintance, all
Selected for discretion and devotion,
There was the Donna Julia, whom to call
Pretty were but to give a feeble notion
Of many charms in her as natural
As sweetness to the flower, or salt to ocean,
Her zone to Venus,[73] or his bow to Cupid
(But this last simile is trite and stupid).

56

The darkness of her oriental eye
Accorded with her Moorish origin
(Her blood was not all Spanish, by the by –
In Spain, you know, this is a sort of sin);
When proud Granada fell and, forced to fly,
Boabdil wept,[74] of Donna Julia's kin
Some went to Africa, some stayed in Spain;
Her great-great-grandmamma chose to remain.

57

She married (I forget the pedigree)
With an hidalgo, who transmitted down
His blood less noble than such blood should be;
At such alliances his sires would frown,
In that point so precise in each degree
That they bred *in and in*, as might be shown,
Marrying their cousins – nay, their aunts and nieces,
Which always spoils the breed, if it increases.

58

This heathenish cross restored the breed again,
Ruined its blood, but much improved its flesh;
For from a root the ugliest in old Spain
Sprung up a branch as beautiful as fresh –
The sons no more were short, the daughters plain
(But there's a rumour which I fain would hush:
'Tis said that Donna Julia's grandmamma
Produced her Don more heirs at love than law).

59

However this might be, the race[75] went on
Improving still through every generation

## Notes

[73] Venus's girdle ('zone') would make the wearer fall in love.

[74] *Boabdil wept* Mohamed XI, last Moorish king of Granada, wept when the city was besieged and surrendered to Spain, 1492.

[75] *race* family.

Until it centred in an only son
  Who left an only daughter; my narration
May have suggested that this single one
  Could be but Julia (whom on this occasion
I shall have much to speak about), and she
Was married, charming, chaste, and twenty-three.

60

Her eye (I'm very fond of handsome eyes)
  Was large and dark, suppressing half its fire
Until she spoke, then through its soft disguise
  Flashed an expression more of pride than ire,
And love than either; and there would arise
  A something in them which was not desire,
But would have been, perhaps – but for the soul
Which struggled through and chastened down the whole.

61

Her glossy hair was clustered o'er a brow
  Bright with intelligence, and fair and smooth;
Her eyebrow's shape was like the aerial bow,[76]
  Her cheek all purple with the beam of youth
Mounting, at times, to a transparent glow
  As if her veins ran lightning; she, in sooth,
Possessed an air and grace by no means common,
Her stature tall – I hate a dumpy woman.

62

Wedded she was some years, and to a man
  Of fifty – and such husbands are in plenty;
And yet, I think, instead of such a ONE
  'Twere better to have TWO of five and twenty,
Especially in countries near the sun;
  And now I think on't, 'mi vien in mente',[77]
Ladies even of the most uneasy virtue
Prefer a spouse whose age is short of thirty.

63

'Tis a sad thing, I cannot choose but say,
  And all the fault of that indecent sun
Who cannot leave alone our helpless clay,[78]
  But will keep baking, broiling, burning on,
That howsoever people fast and pray
  The flesh is frail,[79] and so the soul undone;
What men call gallantry, and gods adultery,
Is much more common where the climate's sultry.

## Notes

[76] *the aerial bow* rainbow.

[77] *mi vien in mente* 'it comes into my mind that…'.

[78] *clay* i.e. flesh.

[79] *The flesh is frail* Matthew 26:41: 'the spirit indeed is willing, but the flesh is weak.'

64

Happy the nations of the moral north!
    Where all is virtue, and the winter season
Sends sin, without a rag on, shivering forth
    ('Twas snow that brought St Francis back to reason);[80]
Where juries cast up what a wife is worth
    By laying whate'er sum, in mulct,[81] they please on
The lover, who must pay a handsome price,
Because it is a marketable vice.

65

Alfonso was the name of Julia's lord –
    A man well looking for his years and who
Was neither much beloved nor yet abhorred;
    They lived together as most people do,
Suffering each other's foibles by accord,
    And not exactly either *one* or *two*;
Yet he was jealous, though he did not show it,
For jealousy dislikes the world to know it.

66

Julia was (yet I never could see why)
    With Donna Inez quite a favourite friend;
Between their tastes there was small sympathy,
    For not a line had Julia ever penned;
Some people whisper (but no doubt they lie,
    For malice still imputes some private end)
That Inez had, ere Don Alfonso's marriage,
Forgot with him her very prudent carriage,[82]

67

And that still keeping up the old connection,
    Which time had lately rendered much more chaste,
She took his lady also in affection,
    And certainly this course was much the best.
She flattered Julia with her sage protection
    And complimented Don Alfonso's taste,
And if she could not (who can?) silence scandal,
At least she left it a more slender handle.

68

I can't tell whether Julia saw the affair
    With other people's eyes, or if her own
Discoveries made, but none could be aware
    Of this; at least no symptom e'er was shown.

## Notes

[80] St Francis had a 'wife of snow', according to Jacobus de Voragine's *Golden Legend*, containing the 'Life of St Francis'.

[81] *mulct* penalty.

[82] *carriage* social behaviour, conduct.

Perhaps she did not know, or did not care,
    Indifferent from the first, or callous grown;
I'm really puzzled what to think or say –
She kept her counsel in so close a way.

69

Juan she saw and, as a pretty child,
    Caressed him often – such a thing might be
Quite innocently done, and harmless styled,
    When she had twenty years and thirteen he;
But I am not so sure I should have smiled
    When he was sixteen, Julia twenty-three
(These few short years make wondrous alterations,
Particularly amongst sunburnt nations).

70

Whate'er the cause might be, they had become
    Changed; for the dame grew distant, the youth shy,
Their looks cast down, their greetings almost dumb,
    And much embarrassment in either eye.
There surely will be little doubt with some
    That Donna Julia knew the reason why;
But as for Juan, he had no more notion
Than he who never saw the sea of ocean.

71

Yet Julia's very coldness still was kind,
    And tremulously gentle her small hand
Withdrew itself from his, but left behind
    A little pressure, thrilling, and so bland[83]
And slight, so very slight, that to the mind
    'Twas but a doubt – but ne'er magician's wand
Wrought change with all Armida's[84] fairy art
Like what this light touch left on Juan's heart.

72

And if she met him, though she smiled no more,
    She looked a sadness sweeter than her smile,
As if her heart had deeper thoughts in store
    She must not own, but cherished more the while,
For that compression in its burning core;
    Even innocence itself has many a wile
And will not dare to trust itself with truth –
And love is taught hypocrisy from youth.

Notes

[83] *bland* soothing.

[84] Armida is the sorceress in Tasso, *Jerusalem Delivered*, who ensnares the hero, Rinaldo.

73

But passion most dissembles yet betrays
  Even by its darkness; as the blackest sky
Foretells the heaviest tempest, it displays
  Its workings through the vainly guarded eye,
And in whatever aspect it arrays
  Itself, 'tis still the same hypocrisy;
Coldness or anger, even disdain or hate
Are masks it often wears, and still too late.

74

Then there were sighs, the deeper for suppression,
  And stolen glances, sweeter for the theft,
And burning blushes, though for no transgression,
  Tremblings when met, and restlessness when left;
All these are little preludes to possession
  Of which young passion cannot be bereft,
And merely tend to show how greatly love is
Embarrassed at first starting with a novice.

75

Poor Julia's heart was in an awkward state –
  She felt it going, and resolved to make
The noblest efforts for herself and mate,
  For honour's, pride's, religion's, virtue's sake;
Her resolutions were most truly great
  And almost might have made a Tarquin quake;[85]
She prayed the Virgin Mary for her grace,
As being the best judge of a lady's case.

76

She vowed she never would see Juan more
  And next day paid a visit to his mother,
And looked extremely at the opening door
  Which, by the Virgin's grace, let in another;
Grateful she was, and yet a little sore;
  Again it opens, it can be no other,
'Tis surely Juan now – no! I'm afraid
That night the Virgin was no further prayed.

77

She now determined that a virtuous woman
  Should rather face and overcome temptation,
That flight was base and dastardly, and no man
  Should ever give her heart the least sensation –
That is to say, a thought beyond the common
  Preference, that we must feel upon occasion

## Notes

[85] *Her resolutions…quake* The comparison is with Lucretia, legendary heroine of ancient Rome, the beautiful and virtuous wife of the nobleman Lucius Tarquinius Collatinus. She was raped by Sextus Tarquinus, and later stabbed herself to death.

For people who are pleasanter than others,
But then they only seem so many brothers.

78

And even if by chance (and who can tell?
The Devil's so very sly) she should discover
That all within was not so very well,
And if still free, that such or such a lover
Might please perhaps, a virtuous wife can quell
Such thoughts and be the better when they're over
And if the man should ask, 'tis but denial:
I recommend young ladies to make trial.

79

And then there are things such as love divine,
Bright and immaculate, unmixed and pure,
Such as the angels think so very fine,
And matrons who would be no less secure,
Platonic, perfect, 'just such love as mine',
Thus Julia said, and thought so, to be sure –
And so I'd have her think, were I the man
On whom her reveries celestial ran.

80

Such love is innocent, and may exist
Between young persons without any danger;
A hand may first, and then a lip be kissed –
For my part, to such doings I'm a stranger,
But *hear* these freedoms form the utmost list[86]
Of all o'er which such love may be a ranger;
If people go beyond, 'tis quite a crime
But not my fault – I tell them all in time.

81

Love then, but love within its proper limits
Was Julia's innocent determination
In young Don Juan's favour, and to him its
Exertion might be useful on occasion;
And lighted at too pure a shrine to dim its
Ethereal lustre, with what sweet persuasion
He might be taught by love and her together –
I really don't know what, nor Julia either.

82

Fraught with this fine intention, and well-fenced[87]
In mail of proof[88] – her purity of soul,

Notes

[86] *list* territory.

[87] *well-fenced* well-protected.

[88] *mail of proof* good-quality chain mail; but the usage is metaphorical.

She, for the future of her strength convinced,
And that her honour was a rock, or mole,[89]
Exceeding sagely from that hour dispensed
With any kind of troublesome control;
But whether Julia to the task was equal
Is that which must be mentioned in the sequel.[90]

83

Her plan she deemed both innocent and feasible,
And surely with a stripling of sixteen
Not scandal's fangs could fix on much that's seizable,
Or if they did so, satisfied to mean
Nothing but what was good, her breast was peaceable –
A quiet conscience makes one so serene!
Christians have burnt each other, quite persuaded
That all the Apostles would have done as they did.

84

And if in the meantime her husband died –
But heaven forbid that such a thought should cross
Her brain, though in a dream! And then she sighed;
Never could she survive that common loss,
But just suppose that moment should betide –
I only say suppose it, *inter nos*[91]
(This should be *entre nous*, for Julia thought
In French, but then the rhyme would go for nought),

85

I only say suppose this supposition:
Juan being then grown up to man's estate[92]
Would fully suit a widow of condition[93] –
Even seven years hence it would not be too late;
And in the interim (to pursue this vision)
The mischief, after all, could not be great,
For he would learn the rudiments of love
(I mean the seraph[94] way of those above).

86

So much for Julia. Now we'll turn to Juan –
Poor little fellow, he had no idea
Of his own case, and never hit the true one;
In feelings quick as Ovid's Miss Medea,[95]
He puzzled over what he found a new one,
But not as yet imagined it could be a

## Notes

[89] *mole* great immovable mass.

[90] *the sequel* i.e. what follows.

[91] *inter nos* between us.

[92] *man's estate* i.e. manhood.

[93] *of condition* of quality.

[94] Seraphs are angels whose purpose is to adore God.

[95] *Ovid's Miss Medea* Medea felt a sudden, overpowering love for Jason, leader of the famous Argonauts, in Ovid, *Metamorphoses* vii 9–10.

Thing quite in course, and not at all alarming
Which, with a little patience, might grow charming.

87

Silent and pensive, idle, restless, slow,
His home deserted for the lonely wood,
Tormented with a wound he could not know,
His, like all deep grief, plunged in solitude;
I'm fond myself of solitude or so,
But then I beg it may be understood –
By solitude I mean a sultan's, not
A hermit's, with a harem for a grot.

88

'Oh love, in such a wilderness as this,
Where transport and security entwine,
Here is the empire of thy perfect bliss,
And here thou art a god indeed divine!'[96]
The bard I quote from does not sing amiss,
With the exception of the second line –
For that same twining 'transport and security'
Are twisted to a phrase of some obscurity.

89

The poet meant, no doubt (and thus appeals
To the good sense and senses of mankind),
The very thing which everybody feels,
As all have found on trial, or may find –
That no one likes to be disturbed at meals
Or love. I won't say more about 'entwined'
Or 'transport', as we knew all that before,
But beg 'security' will bolt the door.

90

Young Juan wandered by the glassy brooks
Thinking unutterable things; he threw
Himself at length within the leafy nooks
Where the wild branch of the cork forest grew;
There poets find materials for their books,
And every now and then we read them through
So that[97] their plan and prosody are eligible –
Unless, like Wordsworth, they prove unintelligible.[98]

91

He, Juan (and not Wordsworth),[99] so pursued
His self-communion with his own high soul,

## Notes

[96] Campbell, 'Gertrude of Wyoming' iii 1–4. Campbell was one of the few poets of his time that Byron admired.

[97] *So that* so long as.

[98] *Unlike…unintelligible* Another gibe at 'The Excursion' (1814), mocked for incomprehensibility in the Dedication, stanza 4, above.

[99] *and not Wordsworth* Somewhat disingenuous, as Byron is using Juan's love-sickness to burlesque Wordsworthian responses to nature.

Until his mighty heart[100] in its great mood
   Had mitigated part (though not the whole)
Of its disease; he did the best he could
   With things not very subject to control,
And turned, without perceiving his condition,
Like Coleridge, into a metaphysician.

92

He thought about himself, and the whole earth,
   Of man the wonderful, and of the stars,
And how the deuce they ever could have birth;
   And then he thought of earthquakes and of wars,
How many miles the moon might have in girth,
   Of air-balloons,[101] and of the many bars[102]
To perfect knowledge of the boundless skies –
And then he thought of Donna Julia's eyes.

93

In thoughts like these true wisdom may discern
   Longings sublime and aspirations high,
Which some are born with, but the most part learn
   To plague themselves withal, they know not why;
'Twas strange that one so young should thus concern
   His brain about the action of the sky:
If you think 'twas philosophy that this did,
I can't help thinking puberty assisted.

94

He pored upon the leaves and on the flowers,
   And heard a voice in all the winds; and then
He thought of wood-nymphs and immortal bowers,
   And how the goddesses came down to men:
He missed the pathway, he forgot the hours,
   And when he looked upon his watch again,
He found how much old Time had been a winner –
He also found that he had lost his dinner.

95

Sometimes he turned to gaze upon his book,
   Boscan or Garcilasso;[103] by the wind
Even as the page is rustled while we look,
   So by the poesy of his own mind
Over the mystic leaf his soul was shook,
   As if 'twere one whereon magicians bind

## Notes

[100] *mighty heart* The phrase is borrowed from Wordsworth, 'Composed upon Westminster Bridge, 3 September 1802' 14: 'And all that mighty heart is lying still.'

[101] *air-balloons* Hot-air balloons were the invention of Joseph Michel Montgolfier, 1783. They were all the rage across Europe at this time.

[102] *bars* barriers.

[103] *Boscan or Garcilasso* Juan Boscán Almogáver (d. c.1543) and Garcilaso de la Vega, sixteenth-century Spanish poets who introduced Italian features into their literature through their imitations of Petrarch.

Their spells, and give them to the passing gale,
According to some good old woman's tale.

96

Thus would he while his lonely hours away
    Dissatisfied, nor knowing what he wanted;
Nor[104] glowing reverie, nor poet's lay
    Could yield his spirit that for which it panted,
A bosom whereon he his head might lay,
    And hear the heart beat with the love it granted,
With – several other things which I forget,
Or which, at least, I need not mention yet.

97

Those lonely walks and lengthening reveries
    Could not escape the gentle Julia's eyes;
She saw that Juan was not at his ease;
    But that which chiefly may, and must surprise
Is that the Donna Inez did not tease
    Her only son with question or surmise –
Whether it was she did not see or would not,
Or like all very clever people, could not.

98

This may seem strange, but yet 'tis very common;
    For instance, gentlemen, whose ladies take
Leave to o'erstep the written rights of woman,
    And break the – which commandment is't they break?[105]
I have forgot the number, and think no man
    Should rashly quote, for fear of a mistake.
I say, when these same gentlemen are jealous,
They make some blunder which their ladies tell us.

99

A real husband always is suspicious,
    But still no less suspects in the wrong place,
Jealous of someone who had no such wishes,[106]
    Or pandering blindly to his own disgrace
By harbouring some dear friend extremely vicious[107] –
    The last indeed's infallibly the case,
And when the spouse and friend are gone off wholly,[108]
He wonders at their vice, and not his folly.

## Notes

[104] *Nor* neither.
[105] *which commandment is't they break* 'Thou shalt not commit adultery' (Exodus 20:14).
[106] *no such wishes* i.e. to commit adultery.
[107] *vicious* immoral. The husband makes the mistake of unwittingly welcoming a friend who is having an affair with his wife.
[108] *are gone off wholly* i.e. have run away together.

100

Thus parents also are at times short-sighted;
    Though watchful as the lynx, they ne'er discover
(The while the wicked world beholds delighted)
    Young Hopeful's mistress or Miss Fanny's lover,
Till some confounded escapade has blighted
    The plan of twenty years, and all is over;
And then the mother cries, the father swears,
And wonders why the devil he got[109] heirs.

101

But Inez was so anxious and so clear
    Of sight, that I must think on this occasion
She had some other motive much more near
    For leaving Juan to this new temptation;
But what that motive was I shan't say here –
    Perhaps to finish Juan's education,
Perhaps to open Don Alfonso's eyes
In case he thought his wife too great a prize.

102

It was upon a day, a summer's day –
    Summer's indeed a very dangerous season,
And so is spring about the end of May;
    The sun, no doubt, is the prevailing reason;
But whatsoe'er the cause is, one may say
    (And stand convicted of more truth than treason),
That there are months which nature grows more merry in;
March has its hares, and May must have its heroine.

103

'Twas on a summer's day, the sixth of June –
    I like to be particular in dates,
Not only of the age and year, but moon;
    They are a sort of post-house[110] where the Fates[111]
Change horses, making history change its tune,
    Then spur away o'er empires and o'er states,
Leaving at last not much besides chronology,
Excepting the post-obits[112] of theology.

104

'Twas on the sixth of June, about the hour
    Of half-past six – perhaps still nearer seven,
When Julia sat within as pretty a bower
    As e'er held houri[113] in that heathenish heaven

## Notes

[109] *got* conceived.

[110] *post-house* inn where horses are kept for the use of travellers.

[111] In Greek myth, the Fates were three goddesses who determined the course of human life.

[112] *post-obits* legacies.

[113] *houri* nymph of the Muslim heaven.

Described by Mahomet and 'Anacreon' Moore[114] –
To whom the lyre and laurels have been given
With all the trophies of triumphant song;
He won them well, and may he wear them long!

105

She sat, but not alone; I know not well
How this same interview had taken place,
And even if I knew, I should not tell –
People should hold their tongues in any case;
No matter how or why the thing befell,
But there were she and Juan, face to face –
When two such faces are so, 'twould be wise
(But very difficult) to shut their eyes.

106

How beautiful she looked! Her conscious heart
Glowed in her cheek, and yet she felt no wrong.
Oh love, how perfect is thy mystic art,
Strengthening the weak, and trampling on the strong;
How self-deceitful is the sagest part
Of mortals whom thy lure hath led along;
The precipice she stood on was immense –
So was her creed[115] in her own innocence.

107

She thought of her own strength,[116] and Juan's youth,
And of the folly of all prudish fears,
Victorious virtue and domestic truth –
And then of Don Alfonso's fifty years:
I wish these last had not occurred, in sooth,
Because that number rarely much endears,
And through all climes, the snowy and the sunny,
Sounds ill in love, whate'er it may in money.

108

When people say, 'I've told you *fifty* times',
They mean to scold, and very often do;
When poets say, 'I've written *fifty* rhymes',
They make you dread that they'll recite them too;
In gangs of *fifty*, thieves commit their crimes;
At *fifty* love for love is rare, 'tis true –
But then, no doubt, it equally as true is,
A good deal may be bought for *fifty* louis.[117]

## Notes

[114] *'Anacreon' Moore* Thomas Moore translated a set of 'anacreontic' poems (first printed in 1554) of unknown origin. It was one of his most successful publications.

[115] *creed* belief.

[116] *strength* i.e. moral strength.

[117] *louis* gold coin issued in the reign of Louis XIII and subsequently till that of Louis XVI.

109

Julia had honour, virtue, truth and love
    For Don Alfonso, and she inly swore
By all the vows below to powers above
    She never would disgrace the ring she wore,
Nor leave a wish which wisdom might reprove;
    And while she pondered this, besides much more,
One hand on Juan's carelessly was thrown
Quite by mistake – she thought it was her own;

110

Unconsciously she leaned upon the other
    Which played within the tangles of her hair;[118]
And to contend with thoughts she could not smother,
    She seemed by the distraction of her air.
'Twas surely very wrong in Juan's mother
    To leave together this imprudent pair,
She who for many years had watched her son so –
I'm very certain *mine* would not have done so.

111

The hand which still held Juan's, by degrees
    Gently but palpably confirmed its grasp,
As if it said 'detain me, if you please';
    Yet there's no doubt she only meant to clasp
His fingers with a pure Platonic squeeze;
    She would have shrunk as from a toad or asp
Had she imagined such a thing could rouse
A feeling dangerous to a prudent spouse.

112

I cannot know what Juan thought of this,
    But what he did is much what you would do;
His young lip thanked it with a grateful kiss,
    And then, abashed at its own joy, withdrew
In deep despair lest he had done amiss –
    Love is so very timid when 'tis new;
She blushed and frowned not, but she strove to speak
And held her tongue, her voice was grown so weak.

113

The sun set and uprose the yellow moon –
    The devil's in the moon for mischief; they
Who called her chaste, methinks began too soon
    Their nomenclature;[119] there is not a day,

## Notes

[118] *Which played…hair* Byron is recalling 'Lycidas' 68–9: 'To sport with Amaryllis in the shade, / Or with the tangles of Neaera's hair?'

[119] *nomenclature* act of naming things.

The longest, not the twenty-first of June,
  Sees half the business in a wicked way
On which three single hours of moonshine smile –
And then she looks so modest all the while.

114

There is a dangerous silence in that hour,
  A stillness which leaves room for the full soul
To open all itself, without the power
  Of calling wholly back its self-control;
The silver light which, hallowing tree and tower,
  Sheds beauty and deep softness o'er the whole,
Breathes also to the heart, and o'er it throws
A loving languor which is not repose.

115

And Julia sat with Juan, half-embraced
  And half-retiring from the glowing arm,
Which trembled like the bosom where 'twas placed;
  Yet still she must have thought there was no harm,
Or else 'twere easy to withdraw her waist;
  But then the situation had its charm,
And then – God knows what next – I can't go on;
I'm almost sorry that I e'er begun.

116

Oh Plato, Plato! You have paved the way,
  With your confounded fantasies, to more
Immoral conduct by the fancied sway
  Your system feigns o'er the controlless core
Of human hearts, than all the long array
  Of poets and romancers – you're a bore,
A charlatan, a coxcomb, and have been
At best no better than a go-between.

117

And Julia's voice was lost except in sighs,
  Until too late for useful conversation;
The tears were gushing from her gentle eyes –
  I wish, indeed, they had not had occasion,
But who, alas, can love, and then be wise?
  Not that remorse did not oppose temptation,
A little still she strove, and much repented,
And whispering 'I will ne'er consent' – consented.

118

'Tis said that Xerxes[120] offered a reward
  To those who could invent him a new pleasure –

Notes

[120] Xerxes I, king who fought in the Persian Wars, 485–479 BCE. Montaigne wrote that he was 'wrapped in all human pleasures … [and] offered a prize to anyone who would find him others' ('Of Experience').

Methinks the requisition's rather hard
And must have cost his majesty a treasure;
For my part, I'm a moderate-minded bard,
Fond of a little love (which I call leisure);
I care not for new pleasures, as the old
Are quite enough for me, so they but hold.

119

Oh pleasure, you're indeed a pleasant thing,
Although one must be damned for you, no doubt;
I make a resolution every spring
Of reformation, ere the year run out;
But somehow, this my vestal vow[121] takes wing,
Yet still, I trust, it may be kept throughout:
I'm very sorry, very much ashamed,
And mean, next winter, to be quite reclaimed.

120

Here my chaste muse a liberty must take –
Start not, still chaster reader! She'll be nice hence-
Forward, and there is no great cause to quake;
This liberty is a poetic licence,
Which some irregularity may make
In the design, and as I have a high sense
Of Aristotle and the rules,[122] 'tis fit
To beg his pardon when I err a bit.

121

This licence is to hope the reader will
Suppose from June the sixth (the fatal day
Without whose epoch my poetic skill
For want of facts would all be thrown away),
But keeping Julia and Don Juan still
In sight, that several months have passed; we'll say
'Twas in November, but I'm not so sure
About the day – the era's more obscure.

122

We'll talk of that anon. 'Tis sweet to hear
At midnight on the blue and moonlit deep
The song and oar of Adria's[123] gondolier
By distance mellowed, o'er the waters sweep;
'Tis sweet to see the evening star appear;
'Tis sweet to listen as the nightwinds creep
From leaf to leaf; 'tis sweet to view on high
The rainbow, based on ocean, span the sky;

## Notes

[121] *vestal vow* i.e. of chastity.

[122] *the rules* Byron is thinking of the *Poetics* (the 'unities'), as suggested by stanza 121.

[123] *Adria* Venice.

123

'Tis sweet to hear the watchdog's honest bark
Bay deep-mouthed welcome as we draw near home;
'Tis sweet to know there is an eye will mark
Our coming, and look brighter when we come;
'Tis sweet to be awkened by the lark
Or lulled by falling waters; sweet the hum
Of bees, the voice of girls, the song of birds,
The lisp of children and their earliest words;

124

Sweet is the vintage, when the showering grapes
In Bacchanal profusion[124] reel to earth
Purple and gushing; sweet are our escapes
From civic revelry to rural mirth;
Sweet to the miser are his glittering heaps;
Sweet to the father is his first-born's birth;
Sweet is revenge – especially to women;
Pillage to soldiers, prize-money[125] to seamen;

125

Sweet is a legacy, and passing sweet
The unexpected death of some old lady
Or gentleman of seventy years complete,
Who've made 'us youth'[126] wait too too long already
For an estate or cash or country-seat,
Still breaking, but with stamina so steady,
That all the Israelites[127] are fit to mob its
Next owner for their double-damned post-obits.[128]

126

'Tis sweet to win (no matter how) one's laurels
By blood or ink; 'tis sweet to put an end
To strife; 'tis sometimes sweet to have our quarrels,
Particularly with a tiresome friend;
Sweet is old wine in bottles, ale in barrels;
Dear is the helpless creature we defend
Against the world; and dear the schoolboy spot
We ne'er forget, though there we are forgot.

127

But sweeter still than this, than these, than all,
Is first and passionate love – it stands alone
Like Adam's recollection of his fall;
The tree of knowledge has been plucked, all's known,

## Notes

[124] *Bacchanal profusion* Bacchus was the Roman name for the god of wine. The individual grapes are, by implication, like drunken revellers.

[125] *prize-money* proceeds from the sale of a captured ship, distributed among the captors.

[126] *us youth* 'They hate us youth'; Falstaff, *1 Henry IV* II ii 93.

[127] *Israelites* i.e. money-lenders.

[128] *post-obits* in this case, money owed to them by the deceased, for which the heir is liable.

And life yields nothing further to recall
Worthy of this ambrosial[129] sin, so shown
No doubt in fable, as the unforgiven
Fire which Prometheus filched for us from heaven.

128

Man's a strange animal, and makes strange use
Of his own nature and the various arts,[130]
And likes particularly to produce
Some new experiment to show his parts;[131]
This is the age of oddities let loose,
Where different talents find their different marts;
You'd best begin with truth, and when you've lost your
Labour, there's a sure market for imposture.

129

What opposite discoveries we have seen
(Signs of true genius, and of empty pockets)!
One makes new noses, one a guillotine,
One breaks your bones, one sets them in their sockets;
But vaccination certainly has been
A kind antithesis to Congreve's rockets,
With which the doctor paid off an old pox
By borrowing a new one from an ox.[132]

130

Bread has been made (indifferent) from potatoes,
And galvanism has set some corpses grinning,
But has not answered like the apparatus
Of the Humane Society's beginning,
By which men are unsuffocated gratis;
What wondrous new machines have late been spinning![133]
I said the smallpox has gone out of late,
Perhaps it may be followed by the great.[134]

131

'Tis said the great came from America,
Perhaps it may set out on its return;
The population there so spreads, they say,
'Tis grown high time to thin it in its turn
With war or plague or famine, any way,
So that civilization they may learn,

## Notes

[129] *ambrosial* divine; Prometheus was a demigod.

[130] *arts* skills, abilities.

[131] *parts* as McGann notes, an obscene pun.

[132] This stanza is a catalogue of recent scientific developments. The American quack doctor Benjamin Charles Perkins made new noses; Sir William Congreve (1772–1828) invented an artillery shell, first used against the French in the Battle of Leipzig (1813); Edward Jenner (1749–1823) first vaccinated against smallpox in 1796.

[133] Luigi Galvani used electricity to attempt to restore corpses to life (an inspiration for Mary Shelley's *Frankenstein*), as well as for therapeutic purposes (first described 1792); the Humane Society was founded 1774, for the rescue of drowning persons (the 'apparatus' is a resuscitator); the spinning-jenny was patented by James Hargreaves, 1770.

[134] *the great* syphilis.

And which in ravage the more loathsome evil is:
Their real lues,[135] or our pseudo-syphilis?

132

This is the patent-age of new inventions
  For killing bodies and for saving souls,[136]
All propagated with the best intentions:
  Sir Humphry Davy's lantern,[137] by which coals
Are safely mined for in the mode he mentions;
  Tombuctoo travels, voyages to the Poles
Are ways to benefit mankind, as true,
Perhaps, as shooting them at Waterloo.

133

Man's a phenomenon, one knows not what,
  And wonderful beyond all wondrous measure;
'Tis pity though, in this sublime world, that
  Pleasure's a sin, and sometimes sin's a pleasure;
Few mortals know what end[138] they would be at,
  But whether glory, power, or love or treasure,
The path is through perplexing ways, and when
The goal is gained, we die, you know – and then –

134

What then? I do not know, no more do you –
  And so goodnight. Return we to our story:
'Twas in November when fine days are few,
  And the far mountains wax[139] a little hoary
And clap a white cape on their mantles blue;
  And the sea dashes round the promontory,
And the loud breaker boils against the rock,
And sober suns must set at five o'clock.

135

'Twas, as the watchmen say, a cloudy night;
  No moon, no stars, the wind was low or loud
By gusts, and many a sparkling hearth was bright
  With the piled wood round which the family crowd;
There's something cheerful in that sort of light,
  Even as a summer sky's without a cloud –
I'm fond of fire and crickets, and all that,
A lobster-salad, and champagne, and chat.

## Notes

[135] *lues* syphilis.

[136] *saving souls* Probably a reference to the British and Foreign Bible Society, founded 1804, which published and distributed cheap Bibles around the world. It is still going strong.

[137] Davy (1778–1829), friend of Wordsworth, Coleridge, Scott and Byron, not only wrote poetry but invented the miner's safety-lamp, 1815.

[138] *end* an obscene pun.

[139] *wax* become.

136

'Twas midnight; Donna Julia was in bed –
Sleeping, most probably – when at her door
Arose a clatter might awake the dead[140]
(If they had never been awoke before,
And that they have been so we all have read,
And are to be so, at the least, once more);
The door was fastened, but with voice and fist
First knocks were heard, then 'Madam, madam – hist!

137

For God's sake, madam – madam, here's my master
With more than half the city at his back;
Was ever heard of such a cursed disaster!
'Tis not my fault, I kept good watch – alack!
Do pray undo the bolt a little faster;
They're on the stair just now, and in a crack[141]
Will all be here – perhaps he yet may fly;
Surely the window's not so *very* high!'

138

By this time Don Alfonso was arrived
With torches, friends and servants in great number;
The major part of them had long been wived,
And therefore paused not[142] to disturb the slumber
Of any wicked woman who contrived
By stealth her husband's temples to encumber;[143]
Examples of this kind are so contagious,
Were *one* not punished, *all* would be outrageous.

139

I can't tell how or why or what suspicion
Could enter into Don Alfonso's head,
But for a cavalier of his condition[144]
It surely was exceedingly ill-bred,
Without a word of previous admonition,
To hold a levee[145] round his lady's bed
And summon lackeys armed with fire and sword,
To prove himself the thing he most abhorred.[146]

140

Poor Donna Julia! Starting as from sleep
(Mind that I do not say she had not slept)

## Notes

[140] *awake the dead* A reference to I Corinthians 15:51–2, which prophesies that 'the dead shall be raised incorruptible.'

[141] *in a crack* immediately.

[142] *paused not* did not hesitate.

[143] *her husband's temples to encumber* Horns sprout on the foreheads of cuckolded husbands.

[144] *a cavalier of his condition* a gentleman of his rank.

[145] *levee* a social meeting held immediately on rising from bed; Don Alfonso has not even allowed his wife the opportunity to get up.

[146] *the thing he most abhorred* i.e. a cuckold.

Began at once to scream and yawn and weep;
 Her maid Antonia, who was an adept,
Contrived to fling the bedclothes in a heap,
 As if she had just now from out them crept –
I can't tell why she should take all this trouble
To prove her mistress had been sleeping double.

141

But Julia mistress, and Antonia maid,
 Appeared like two poor harmless women who
Of goblins, but still more of men afraid,
 Had thought one man might be deterred by two,
And therefore side by side were gently laid
 Until the hours of absence should run through,
And truant husband should return and say,
'My dear, I was the first who came away.'

142

Now Julia found at length a voice, and cried,
 'In Heaven's name, Don Alfonso, what d'ye mean?
Has madness seized you? Would that I had died
 Ere such a monster's victim I had been!
What may this midnight violence betide?
 A sudden fit of drunkenness or spleen?
Dare you suspect me, whom the thought would kill?
Search then the room!' Alfonso said, 'I will.'

143

*He* searched, *they* searched, and rummaged everywhere,
 Closet and clothes-press, chest and window-seat,
And found much linen, lace, and several pair
 Of stockings, slippers, brushes, combs, complete
With other articles of ladies fair,
 To keep them beautiful or leave them neat;
Arras they pricked,[147] and curtains with their swords,
And wounded several shutters and some boards.

144

Under the bed they searched, and there they found –
 No matter what, it was not that they sought;
They opened windows, gazing if the ground
 Had signs or footmarks, but the earth said nought;
And then they stared each others' faces round:
 'Tis odd not one of all these seekers thought
(And seems to me almost a sort of blunder)
Of looking *in* the bed as well as under.

Notes

[147] *Arras they pricked* i.e. they poked the hanging tapestry with their swords.

145

During this inquisition Julia's tongue
    Was not asleep: 'Yes, search and search', she cried,
'Insult on insult heap, and wrong on wrong!
    It was for this that I became a bride!
For this in silence I have suffered long
    A husband like Alfonso at my side;
But now I'll bear no more, nor here remain,
If there be law or lawyers in all Spain.

146

Yes, Don Alfonso, husband now no more
    (If ever you indeed deserved the name)!
Is't worthy of your years? You have threescore,
    Fifty or sixty (it is all the same),
Is't wise or fitting causeless to explore
    For facts against a virtuous woman's fame?
Ungrateful, perjured, barbarous Don Alfonso –
How dare you think your lady would go on so?

147

Is it for this I have disdained to hold
    The common privileges of my sex?[148] –
That I have chosen a confessor so old
    And deaf, that any other it would vex,
And never once he has had cause to scold,
    But found my very innocence perplex
So much, he always doubted I was married?
How sorry you will be when I've miscarried![149]

148

Was it for this that no cortejo ere
    I yet have chosen from out the youth of Seville?
Is it for this I scarce went anywhere
    Except to bullfights, mass, play, rout[150] and revel?
Is it for this, whate'er my suitors were,
    I favoured none – nay, was almost uncivil?
Is it for this that General Count O'Reilly,
Who took Algiers,[151] declares I used him vilely?

149

Did not the Italian musico Cazzani[152]
    Sing at my heart six months at least in vain?

## Notes

[148] *The common privileges of my sex* i.e. to take a lover (or 'cortejo').

[149] *when I've miscarried* i.e. when you've lost me.

[150] *rout* party.

[151] 'Donna Julia here made a mistake. Count O'Reilly did not take Algiers – but Algiers very nearly took him. He and his army and fleet retreated with great loss, and not much credit, from before that city in the year 1775' (Byron's note). The Irish-born Spanish general Alexander O'Reilly (?1722–94) was governor of Madrid and later Cadiz. The unsuccessful assault on Algiers was mounted in 1775.

[152] *musico* musician. Cazzani is an obscene pun on 'cazzo' (penis).

Did not his countryman, Count Corniani,[153]
  Call me the only virtuous wife in Spain?
Were there not also Russians, English, many?
  The Count Strongstroganoff[154] I put in pain,
And Lord Mount Coffeehouse, the Irish peer,[155]
Who killed himself for love (with wine) last year.

150

Have I not had two bishops at my feet,
  The Duke of Ichar, and Don Fernan Nunez?
And is it thus a faithful wife you treat?
  I wonder in what quarter now the moon is;[156]
I praise your vast forbearance not to beat
  Me also, since the time so opportune is –
Oh valiant man, with sword drawn and cocked trigger,
Now tell me, don't you cut a pretty figure?

151

Was it for this you took your sudden journey
  Under pretence of business indispensable
With that sublime of rascals, your attorney,
  Whom I see standing there, and looking sensible[157]
Of having played the fool? Though both I spurn, he
  Deserves the worst, his conduct's less defensible,
Because, no doubt, 'twas for his dirty fee,
And not from any love to you nor me.

152

If he comes here to take a deposition,[158]
  By all means let the gentleman proceed –
You've made the apartment in a fit condition!
  There's pen and ink for you, sir, when you need;
Let everything be noted with precision
  (I would not you for nothing should be feed);[159]
But as my maid's undressed, pray turn your spies out.'
'Oh!' sobbed Antonia, 'I could tear their eyes out!'

153

'There is the closet,[160] there the toilet,[161] there
  The antechamber[162] – search them under, over;
There is the sofa, there the great armchair,
  The chimney (which would really hold a lover).

## Notes

[153] Corniani derives from 'cornuto' (horned, cuckolded).

[154] *Count Strongstroganoff* Count Alexander Stroganov was a fellow-reveller of Byron's in Venice.

[155] This is a disdainful reference to the peerages created by the Act of Union between Ireland and England in 1801, for which Byron's *bête noire*, Castlereagh, had been largely responsible. The Mount was a coffeehouse near Grosvenor Square, London.

[156] *I wonder in what quarter now the moon is* i.e. because a full moon would explain why Don Alfonso is behaving like a lunatic.

[157] *sensible* aware.

[158] *deposition* statement for use as evidence.

[159] *I would not you for nothing should be feed* I would not want you to be paid ('feed') for doing nothing.

[160] *closet* private apartment.

[161] *toilet* table on which toilet articles are placed.

[162] *antechamber* waiting-room.

I wish to sleep, and beg you will take care
And make no further noise, till you discover
The secret cavern of this lurking treasure –
And when 'tis found, let me, too, have that pleasure.

154

And now, hidalgo, now that you have thrown
Doubt upon me, confusion over all,[163]
Pray have the courtesy to make it known
*Who* is the man you search for? How d'ye call
Him? What's his lineage? Let him but be shown;
I hope he's young and handsome – is he tall?
Tell me, and be assured that since you stain
My honour thus, it shall not be in vain.

155

At least, perhaps, he has not sixty years –
At that age he would be too old for slaughter
Or for so young a husband's jealous fears!
Antonia, let me have a glass of water;
I am ashamed of having shed these tears,
They are unworthy of my father's daughter;
My mother dreamed not in my natal hour[164]
That I should fall into a monster's power.

156

Perhaps 'tis of Antonia you are jealous –
You saw that she was sleeping by my side
When you broke in upon us with your fellows;
Look where you please, we've nothing, sir, to hide;
Only another time, I trust, you'll tell us,
Or for the sake of decency abide
A moment at the door, that we may be
Dressed to receive so much good company.

157

And now, sir, I have done, and say no more;
The little I have said may serve to show
The guileless heart in silence may grieve o'er
The wrongs to whose exposure it is slow;
I leave you to your conscience as before –
'Twill one day ask you *why* you used me so?
God grant you feel not then the bitterest grief!
Antonia, where's my pocket-handkerchief ?'

158

She ceased, and turned upon her pillow; pale
She lay, her dark eyes flashing through their tears

## Notes

[163] *confusion over all* An echo of the final line of Pope's *Dunciad*: 'And universal darkness buries all.'

[164] *my natal hour* hour of my birth.

Like skies that rain and lighten; as a veil,
Waved and o'ershading her wan cheek, appears
Her streaming hair; the black curls strive but fail
To hide the glossy shoulder, which uprears
Its snow through all; her soft lips lie apart,
And louder than her breathing beats her heart.

159

The *señor* Don Alfonso stood confused;
Antonia bustled round the ransacked room
And, turning up her nose, with looks abused
Her master and his myrmidons,[165] of whom
Not one, except the attorney, was amused;
He, like Achates,[166] faithful to the tomb,
So[167] there were quarrels, cared not for the cause,
Knowing they must be settled by the laws.

160

With prying snubnose and small eyes he stood,
Following Antonia's motions here and there
With much suspicion in his attitude;
For reputations he had little care,
So that a suit or action were made good;
Small pity had he for the young and fair,
And ne'er believed in negatives, till these
Were proved by competent false witnesses.

161

But Don Alfonso stood with downcast looks,
And, truth to say, he made a foolish figure –
When after searching in five hundred nooks,
And treating a young wife with so much rigour,
He gained no point except some self-rebukes,
Added to those his lady with such vigour
Had poured upon him for the last half-hour,
Quick, thick, and heavy, as a thunder-shower.

162

At first he tried to hammer an excuse
To which the sole reply were tears and sobs
And indications of hysterics, whose
Prologue is always certain throes and throbs,
Gasps and whatever else the owners choose;
Alfonso saw his wife and thought of Job's;[168]
He saw too, in perspective,[169] her relations,
And then he tried to muster all his patience.

## Notes

[165] *myrmidons* base unscrupulous henchmen.

[166] Achates was Aeneas's proverbially faithful companion.

[167] *So* if.

[168] Job's wife berated him: 'Dost thou still retain thine integrity? Curse God, and die' (Job 2:9).

[169] *in perspective* i.e. stretching into the distance.

163

He stood in act to speak, or rather stammer,
  But sage Antonia cut him short before
The anvil of his speech received the hammer,
  With, 'Pray sir, leave the room, and say no more,
Or madam dies.' Alfonso muttered, 'Damn her!'
  But nothing else – the time of words was o'er;
He cast a rueful look or two, and did
(He knew not wherefore) that which he was bid.

164

With him retired his *posse comitatus*[170] –
  The attorney last, who lingered near the door
Reluctantly, still tarrying there as late as
  Antonia let him, not a little sore
At this most strange and unexplained hiatus[171]
  In Don Alfonso's facts, which just now wore
An awkward look; as he resolved the case
The door was fastened in his legal face.

165

No sooner was it bolted than – oh shame!
  Oh sin! Oh sorrow! And oh womankind!
How can you do such things and keep your fame,
  Unless this world (and t'other too) be blind?
Nothing so dear as an unfilched good name![172]
  But to proceed, for there is more behind;
With much heartfelt reluctance be it said,
Young Juan slipped, half-smothered, from the bed.

166

He had been hid – I don't pretend to say
  How, nor can I indeed describe the where;
Young, slender, and packed easily, he lay
  No doubt, in little compass, round or square;
But pity him I neither must nor may
  His suffocation by that pretty pair;
'Twere better, sure, to die so, than be shut
With maudlin Clarence in his Malmsey butt.[173]

167

And secondly, I pity not, because
  He had no business to commit a sin
Forbid by heavenly, fined by human laws
  (At least 'twas rather early to begin);

## Notes

[170] *posse comitatus* 'the force of the county'; armed posse.

[171] *hiatus* i.e. missing piece of evidence.

[172] *Nothing so dear as an unfilched good name* A lighthearted echo of *Othello* III iii 159: 'But he that filches from me my good name …'

[173] George, Duke of Clarence, brother of Richard III, is drowned in a barrel of malmsey wine in Shakespeare's play (*Richard III* I iv 270).

But at sixteen the conscience rarely gnaws
  So much as when we call our old debts in
At sixty years, and draw the accompts of evil,
And find a deuced balance with the Devil.

168

Of his position I can give no notion;
  'Tis written in the Hebrew chronicle
How the physicians, leaving pill and potion,
  Prescribed by way of blister, a young belle,
When old King David's blood grew dull in motion,
  And that the medicine answered very well;[174]
Perhaps 'twas in a different way applied,
For David lived, but Juan nearly died.

169

What's to be done? Alfonso will be back
  The moment he has sent his fools away.
Antonia's skill was put upon the rack,
  But no device could be brought into play –
And how to parry the renewed attack?
  Besides, it wanted but few hours of day;
Antonia puzzled, Julia did not speak
But pressed her bloodless lip to Juan's cheek.

170

He turned his lip to hers, and with his hand
  Called back the tangles of her wandering hair;
Even then their love they could not all command,
  And half forgot their danger and despair.
Antonia's patience now was at a stand[175] –
  'Come, come, 'tis no time now for fooling there',
She whispered in great wrath, 'I must deposit
This pretty gentleman within the closet:

171

Pray keep your nonsense for some luckier night –
  *Who* can have put my master in this mood?
What will become on't? I'm in such a fright,
  The Devil's in the urchin, and no good –
Is this a time for giggling? this a plight?
  Why, don't you know that it may end in blood?
You'll lose your life, and I shall lose my place,[176]
My mistress, all, for that half-girlish face.

Notes

[174] *'Tis written…very well* see I Kings:1–3. King David was revived by 'a young virgin'.

[175] *at a stand* i.e. at an end.

[176] *place* job.

172

Had it but been for a stout cavalier
  Of twenty-five or thirty (come, make haste!) –
But for a child, what piece of work is here![177]
  I really, madam, wonder at your taste –
Come sir, get in; my master must be near.
  There for the present, at the least he's fast,
And if we can but till the morning keep
Our counsel – Juan, mind, you must not sleep!'

173

Now Don Alfonso entering, but alone,
  Closed the oration of the trusty maid;
She loitered, and he told her to be gone –
  An order somewhat sullenly obeyed;
However, present remedy was none,
  And no great good seemed answered if she stayed;
Regarding both with slow and sidelong view,
She snuffed the candle, curtsied and withdrew.

174

Alfonso paused a minute, then begun
  Some strange excuses for his late proceeding;
He would not justify what he had done –
  To say the best, it was extreme ill-breeding;
But there were ample reasons for it, none
  Of which he specified in this his pleading:
His speech was a fine sample, on the whole,
Of rhetoric which the learned call *rigmarole*.

175

Julia said nought, though all the while there rose
  A ready answer – which at once enables
A matron (who her husband's foible knows)
  By a few timely words to turn the tables,
Which, if it does not silence, still must pose,
  Even if it should comprise a pack of fables;
'Tis to retort with firmness, and when he
Suspects with *one*, do you reproach with *three*.

176

Julia in fact had tolerable grounds:
  Alfonso's loves with Inez were well-known;
But whether 'twas that one's own guilt confounds –
  But that can't be, as has been often shown,

## Notes

[177] *what piece of work is here!* an ironic reworking of *Hamlet* II ii 303–4: 'What a piece of work is a man ...'

A lady with apologies abounds;
    It might be that her silence sprang alone
From delicacy to Don Juan's ear,
To whom she knew his mother's fame was dear.

177

There might be one more motive (which makes two):
    Alfonso ne'er to Juan had alluded –
Mentioned his jealousy, but never who
    Had been the happy lover he concluded
Concealed amongst his premises; 'tis true
    His mind the more o'er this its mystery brooded;
To speak of Inez now were, one may say,
Like throwing Juan in Alfonso's way.

178

A hint, in tender cases, is enough;
    Silence is best – besides there is a *tact*[178]
(That modern phrase appears to me sad stuff,
    But it will serve to keep my verse compact)
Which keeps, when pushed by questions rather rough,
    A lady always distant from the fact –
The charming creatures lie with such a grace,
There's nothing so becoming to the face.

179

They blush, and we believe them – at least I
    Have always done so; 'tis of no great use
In any case attempting a reply,
    For then their eloquence grows quite profuse;
And when at length they're out of breath, they sigh
    And cast their languid eyes down, and let loose
A tear or two, and then we make it up,
And then – and then – and then – sit down and sup.

180

Alfonso closed his speech and begged her pardon,
    Which Julia half-withheld, and then half-granted,
And laid conditions, he thought, very hard on,
    Denying several little things he wanted;
He stood like Adam lingering near his garden,[179]
    With useless penitence perplexed and haunted,
Beseeching she no further would refuse –
When lo! he stumbled o'er a pair of shoes.

## Notes

[178] *tact* a keen faculty of perception or discrimination likened to the sense of touch.

[179] *Adam lingering near his garden* While being cast out of Eden in Milton's poem, Adam and Eve lingered near the eastern gate ('Paradise Lost' xii 636–9).

181

A pair of shoes! What then? Not much, if they
Are such as fit with lady's feet, but these
(No one can tell how much I grieve to say)
Were masculine: to see them and to seize
Was but a moment's act – ah wel-a-day![180]
My teeth begin to chatter, my veins freeze;
Alfonso first examined well their fashion,
And then flew out into another passion.

182

He left the room for his relinquished sword
And Julia instant to the closet flew,
'Fly, Juan, fly! For Heaven's sake, not a word –
The door is open, you may yet slip through
The passage you so often have explored;
Here is the garden-key – fly – fly – adieu!
Haste, haste! I hear Alfonso's hurrying feet –
Day has not broke; there's no one in the street.'

183

None can say that this was not good advice,
The only mischief was it came too late;
Of all experience 'tis the usual price,
A sort of income tax[181] laid on by fate:
Juan had reached the room-door in a trice
And might have done so by the garden-gate,
But met Alfonso in his dressing-gown,
Who threatened death – so Juan knocked him down.

184

Dire was the scuffle, and out went the light,
Antonia cried out 'Rape!' and Julia, 'Fire!'
But not a servant stirred to aid the fight.
Alfonso, pommelled to his heart's desire,
Swore lustily he'd be revenged this night;
And Juan too blasphemed an octave higher,
His blood was up – though young, he was a Tartar,[182]
And not at all disposed to prove a martyr.

185

Alfonso's sword had dropped ere he could draw it,
And they continued battling hand to hand,
For Juan very luckily ne'er saw it;
His temper not being under great command,
If at that moment he had chanced to claw it,
Alfonso's days had not been in the land

## Notes

[180] *ah wel-a-day* cf. Coleridge, 'Christabel' 252.

[181] *income tax* introduced in England as a war tax in 1799.

[182] *a Tartar* i.e. a young savage.

Much longer. Think of husbands', lovers', lives,
And how ye may be doubly widows, wives!

186

Alfonso grappled to detain the foe
And Juan throttled him to get away,
And blood ('twas from the nose) began to flow;
At last, as they more faintly wrestling lay,
Juan contrived to give an awkward blow,
And then his only garment quite gave way;
He fled, like Joseph,[183] leaving it – but there,
I doubt, all likeness ends between the pair.

187

Lights came at length, and men and maids who found
An awkward spectacle their eyes before:
Antonia in hysterics, Julia swooned,
Alfonso leaning breathless by the door;
Some half-torn drapery scattered on the ground,
Some blood and several footsteps, but no more –
Juan the gate gained, turned the key about,
And liking not the inside, locked the out.

188

Here ends this canto. Need I sing, or say,
How Juan, naked, favoured by the night
(Who favours what she should not), found his way,
And reached his home in an unseemly plight?
The pleasant scandal which arose next day,
The nine days' wonder which was brought to light,
And how Alfonso sued for a divorce,
Were in the English newspapers, of course.

189

If you would like to see the whole proceedings,
The depositions, and the cause at full,
The names of all the witnesses, the pleadings
Of counsel to nonsuit or to annul,[184]
There's more than one edition, and the readings
Are various, but they none of them are dull;
The best is that in shorthand ta'en by Gurney,[185]
Who to Madrid on purpose made a journey.

## Notes

[183] *like Joseph* When Joseph refused to commit adultery with Potiphar's wife, she claimed that he had tried to rape her, and that, 'when he heard that I lifted up my voice and cried, that he left his garment with me, and fled, and got him out' (Genesis 39:14).

[184] *to nonsuit or to annul* i.e. to bring the case to an end through lack of sufficient evidence.

[185] William Brodie Gurney (1777–1855), shorthand clerk in Parliament, famous for transcripts of trials and speeches of the day.

190

But Donna Inez, to divert the train[186]
Of one of the most circulating scandals
That had for centuries been known in Spain
Since Roderic's Goths or older Genseric's Vandals,[187]
First vowed (and never had she vowed in vain)
To Virgin Mary several pounds of candles;
And then by the advice of some old ladies,
She sent her son to be embarked[188] at Cadiz.

191

She had resolved that he should travel through
All European climes by land or sea
To mend his former morals, or get new,
Especially in France and Italy –
At least this is the thing most people do.
Julia was sent into a nunnery,
And there perhaps her feelings may be better
Shown in the following copy of her letter:

192

'They tell me 'tis decided – you depart.
'Tis wise, 'tis well, but not the less a pain;
I have no further claim on your young heart –
Mine was the victim, and would be again;
To love too much has been the only art
I used; I write in haste, and if a stain
Be on this sheet, 'tis not what it appears –
My eyeballs burn and throb, but have no tears.

193

I loved, I love you, for that love have lost
State, station, heaven, mankind's, my own esteem,
And yet cannot regret what it hath cost,
So dear is still the memory of that dream;
Yet if I name my guilt, 'tis not to boast –
None can deem harshlier of me than I deem:
I trace this scrawl because I cannot rest,
I've nothing to reproach, nor to request.

194

Man's love is of his life a thing apart,
'Tis woman's whole existence; man may range
The court, camp, church, the vessel and the mart,
Sword, gown, gain, glory, offer in exchange

## Notes

[186] *train* progress.

[187] Don Roderick was the last of Spain's Gothic kings, and ruled in the eighth century. In the year 455 the Vandal King Genseric led a marauding expedition against Rome, which he took and completely sacked.

[188] *embarked* put on board ship.

Pride, fame, ambition, to fill up his heart,
And few there are whom these cannot estrange;
Man has all these resources, we but one –
To love again, and be again undone.

195

My breast has been all weakness, is so yet;
I struggle, but cannot collect my mind;
My blood still rushes where my spirit's set
As roll the waves before the settled wind;
My brain is feminine, nor can forget –
To all, except your image, madly blind;
As turns the needle trembling to the pole
It ne'er can reach, so turns to you, my soul.

196

You will proceed in beauty and in pride,
Beloved and loving many; all is o'er
For me on earth, except some years to hide
My shame and sorrow deep in my heart's core;
These I could bear, but cannot cast aside
The passion which still rends it as before,
And so farewell; forgive me, love me – no,
That word is idle now, but let it go.

197

I have no more to say, but linger still,
And dare not set my seal upon this sheet,
And yet I may as well the task fulfil –
My misery can scarce be more complete;
I had not lived till now, could sorrow kill;
Death flies the wretch who fain the blow would meet,
And I must even survive this last adieu,
And bear with life, to love and pray for you!'

198

This note was written upon gilt-edged paper
With a neat crow-quill – rather hard, but new;
Her small white fingers scarce could reach the taper
But trembled as magnetic needles do,
And yet she did not let one tear escape her;
The seal a sunflower, 'Elle vous suit partout'[189]
The motto, cut upon a white cornelian;[190]
The wax was superfine, its hue vermilion.

199

This was Don Juan's earliest scrape – but whether
I shall proceed with his adventures is

Notes

[189] She follows you everywhere.' Byron owned a seal bearing this motto.

[190] *cornelian* stone used for making seals (for letters).

Dependent on the public altogether;
We'll see, however, what they say to this;
Their favour in an author's cap's a feather,
And no great mischief 's done by their caprice;
And if their approbation we experience,
Perhaps they'll have some more about a year hence.

200

My poem's epic, and is meant to be
Divided in twelve books, each book containing,
With love and war, a heavy gale at sea,
A list of ships and captains, and kings reigning,
New characters; the episodes are three:
A panorama view of hell's in training[191]
After the style of Virgil and of Homer,
So that my name of epic's no misnomer.

201

All these things will be specified in time
With strict regard to Aristotle's rules,
The vade-mecum[192] of the true sublime
Which makes so many poets, and some fools;
Prose poets like blank verse, I'm fond of rhyme –
Good workmen never quarrel with their tools;
I've got new mythological machinery
And very handsome supernatural scenery.

202

There's only one slight difference between
Me and my epic brethren gone before
And here the advantage is my own, I ween[193]
(Not that I have no several merits more,
But this will more peculiarly be seen) –
They so embellish that 'tis quite a bore
Their labyrinth of fables to thread through,
Whereas this story's actually true.

203

If any person doubt it, I appeal
To history, tradition, and to facts,
To newspapers (whose truth all know and feel),
To plays in five, and operas in three acts –
All these confirm my statement a good deal,
But that which more completely faith exacts
Is that myself, and several now in Seville,
Saw Juan's last elopement with the Devil.[194]

## Notes

[191] *training* preparation.

[192] *vade-mecum* handbook.

[193] *ween* believe.

[194] When in Seville in 1809, Byron saw a performance of *El Burlador de Sevilla o el Convidado de Piedra* ('The Trickster of Seville, or the Guest Made of Stone'), by Tirso de Molina (1583–1648).

204

If ever I should condescend to prose,
  I'll write poetical commandments[195] which
Shall supersede beyond all doubt all those
  That went before; in these I shall enrich
My text with many things that no one knows,
  And carry precept to the highest pitch:
I'll call the work 'Longinus o'er a bottle,
Or, Every poet his *own* Aristotle'.

205

Thou shalt believe in Milton, Dryden, Pope;
  Thou shalt not set up Wordsworth, Coleridge, Southey,
Because the first is crazed beyond all hope,
  The second drunk,[196] the third so quaint and mouthy;[197]
With Crabbe it may be difficult to cope,
  And Campbell's Hippocrene[198] is somewhat drouthy;[199]
Thou shalt not steal from Samuel Rogers, nor
Commit...flirtation with the muse of Moore.[200]

206

Thou shalt not covet Mr Sotheby's[201] muse,
  His Pegasus,[202] nor anything that's his;
Thou shalt not bear false witness like the Blues[203]
  (There's one, at least, is very fond of this);
Thou shalt not write, in short, but what I choose:
  This is true criticism, and you may kiss
Exactly as you please, or not, the rod –
But if you don't, I'll lay it on, by God!

207

If any person should presume to assert
  This story is not moral, first I pray
That they will not cry out before they're hurt,
  Then that they'll read it o'er again, and say
(But, doubtless, nobody will be so pert)
  That this is not a moral tale, though gay;
Besides, in Canto Twelfth I mean to show
The very place where wicked people go.

## Notes

195 *poetical commandments* The parody of the ten commandments in the following stanzas caused uproar in England when 'Don Juan' was first published.

196 *drunk* stupefied by opium.

197 *quaint and mouthy* affected and bombastic (in language).

198 *Hippocrene* fountain of Mt Helicon, sacred to the muses.

199 *drouthy* dry.

200 Byron thought of George Crabbe, Samuel Rogers, Thomas Moore and Thomas Campbell as among the few decent poets of his own time. Byron's comment about Campbell refers to the fact that he had recently given up poetry for the writing of prose criticism.

201 William Sotheby (1757–1833), most famous for his translation of Wieland's *Oberon* (1798), and for his plays, *The Death of Darnley* (1814) and *Ivan* (1816).

202 Pegasus was the winged horse who created Hippocrene, the fountain of Mt Helicon, with his hoof; he is generally referred to as a symbol of poetic inspiration.

203 *the Blues* i.e. the Bluestockings, many of whom were acquainted with Byron (Lady Blessington, Lady Oxford, Lady Caroline Lamb).

208
If, after all, there should be some so blind
To their own good this warning to despise,
Led by some tortuosity[204] of mind
Not to believe my verse and their own eyes,
And cry that they 'the moral cannot find',
I tell him, if a clergyman, he lies;
Should captains the remark or critics make,
They also lie too – under a mistake.

209
The public approbation I expect,
And beg they'll take my word about the moral,
Which I with their amusement will connect
(So children cutting teeth receive a coral);
Meantime, they'll doubtless please to recollect
My epical pretensions to the laurel:
For fear some prudish readers should grow skittish
I've bribed my grandmother's review – the *British*.[205]

210
I sent it in a letter to the editor
Who thanked me duly by return of post –
I'm for a handsome article his creditor;
Yet if my gentle muse he please to roast,
And break a promise after having made it her,
Denying the receipt of what it cost
And smear his page with gall[206] instead of honey,
All I can say is – that he had the money.

211
I think that with this holy new alliance
I may ensure the public, and defy
All other magazines of art or science –
Daily or monthly or three-monthly; I
Have not essayed[207] to multiply their clients
Because they tell me 'twere in vain to try,
And that the *Edinburgh Review* and *Quarterly*
Treat a dissenting author very martyrly.

212
'Non ego hoc ferrem calida juventa
Consule Planco',[208] Horace said, and so

## Notes

[204] *tortuosity* crookedness.

[205] The *British Review* was outraged by *Don Juan*, and particularly this line; its editor, William Roberts, in his review of the poem, solemnly denied the 'accusation', provoking Byron's 'Letter to the Editor of my Grandmother's Review' in the *Liberal* (1822).

[206] *gall* i.e. bitterness.

[207] *essayed* attempted.

[208] *Non ego…Consule Planco* from Horace, *Odes* III xiv 27–8; translated (roughly) at lines 1695–6.

Say I; by which quotation there is meant a
Hint that some six or seven good years ago
(Long ere I dreamt of dating from the Brenta)[209]
I was most ready to return a blow,
And would not brook at all this sort of thing
In my hot youth – when George the third was King.

213

But now at thirty years my hair is gray
(I wonder what it will be like at forty?
I thought of a peruke[210] the other day),
My heart is not much greener, and, in short, I
Have squandered my whole summer while 'twas May,
And feel no more the spirit to retort; I
Have spent my life, both interest and principal,
And deem not what I deemed, my soul invincible.

214

No more, no more – oh never more on me
The freshness of the heart can fall like dew,
Which out of all the lovely things we see
Extracts emotions beautiful and new,
Hived[211] in our bosoms like the bag o' the bee:
Think'st thou the honey with those objects grew?
Alas, 'twas not in them, but in thy power
To double even the sweetness of a flower.

215

No more, no more – oh never more, my heart,
Canst thou be my sole world, my universe!
Once all in all, but now a thing apart,
Thou canst not be my blessing or my curse;
The illusion's gone forever, and thou art
Insensible, I trust, but none the worse,
And in thy stead I've got a deal of judgement –
Though heaven knows how it ever found a lodgement.

216

My days of love are over, me no more
The charms of maid, wife, and still less of widow,
Can make the fool of which they made before;
In short, I must not lead the life I did do;
The credulous hope of mutual minds is o'er,
The copious use of claret is forbid too –
So, for a good old gentlemanly vice,
I think I must take up with avarice.

## Notes

[209] *the Brenta* The Brenta Riviera is several kilometres from Venice.

[210] *peruke* wig.

[211] *Hived* stored.

217

Ambition was my idol, which was broken
 Before the shrines of sorrow and of pleasure;
And the two last have left me many a token
 O'er which reflection may be made at leisure;
Now like Friar Bacon's brazen[212] head I've spoken,
 'Time is, time was, time's past';[213] a chemic[214] treasure
Is glittering youth, which I have spent betimes –
My heart in passion, and my head on rhymes.

218

What is the end of fame?[215] 'Tis but to fill
 A certain portion of uncertain paper;
Some liken it to climbing up a hill
 Whose summit, like all hills', is lost in vapour;
For this men write, speak, preach, and heroes kill,
 And bards burn what they call their 'midnight taper' –
To have, when the original is dust,
A name, a wretched picture, and worse bust.[216]

219

What are the hopes of man? Old Egypt's King
 Cheops erected the first pyramid
And largest, thinking it was just the thing
 To keep his memory whole, and mummy hid;
But somebody or other rummaging,
 Burglariously broke his coffin's lid:
Let not a monument give you or me hopes,
Since not a pinch of dust remains of Cheops.

220

But I, being fond of true philosophy,
 Say very often to myself, 'Alas!
All things that have been born were born to die,
 And flesh (which death mows down to hay) is grass;[217]
You've passed your youth not so unpleasantly,
 And if you had it o'er again, 'twould pass;
So thank your stars that matters are no worse
And read your Bible, sir, and mind your purse.'

221

But for the present, gentle reader and
 Still gentler purchaser, the bard (that's I)

## Notes

[212] *brazen* brass.

[213] *Time is, time was, time's past* The words of the brass head in Robert Greene's play, *Friar Bacon and Friar Bungay* (1594), IV i 1584, 1595, 1604.

[214] *chemic* i.e. transforming; alchemists attempted to convert base metals into gold.

[215] *What is the end of fame?* Byron was disdainful of literary fame; see for instance his remarks about Southey, Dedication, l. 60.

[216] *and worse bust* Bertel Thorwaldsen, the Danish sculptor, made a bust of Byron during his stay in Rome, summer 1817. Byron found it embarrassing, and commented, 'It is not at all like me; my expression is more unhappy.'

[217] *And flesh…is grass* cf. Isaiah 40:6.

Must with permission shake you by the hand;
And so your humble servant, and goodbye!
We meet again, if we should understand
Each other – and if not, I shall not try
Your patience further than by this short sample
('Twere well if others followed my example).

222

'Go, little book, from this my solitude!
I cast thee on the waters, go thy ways!
And if, as I believe, thy vein be good,
The world will find thee after many days.'[218]
When Southey's read, and Wordsworth understood,
I can't help putting in my claim to praise;
The four first rhymes are Southey's every line –
For God's sake, reader, take them not for mine!

## *Canto II*
## *(composed 13 December 1818–mid January 1819)*

I

Oh ye who teach the ingenuous youth of nations –
Holland, France, England, Germany, or Spain –
I pray ye flog them upon all occasions:
It mends their morals, never mind the pain!
The best of mothers and of educations
In Juan's case were but employed in vain,
Since, in a way that's rather of the oddest, he
Became divested of his native modesty.[1]

2

Had he but been placed at a public school,[2]
In the third form, or even in the fourth,
His daily task had kept his fancy cool,
At least, had he been nurtured in the north;
Spain may prove an exception to the rule,
But then exceptions always prove its worth –
A lad of sixteen causing a divorce
Puzzled his tutors very much, of course.

3

I can't say that it puzzles me at all,
If all things be considered: first there was
His lady-mother, mathematical,
A – never mind; his tutor, an old ass;

### Notes

[218] *Go, little book…many days* A cheeky recycling of Southey, 'L'Envoy', 'Carmen Nuptiale' (1816).

Canto II

[1] *native modesty* i.e. the modesty he was born with.

[2] *a public school* in England, one of the old-established fee-paying schools, such as Eton or Harrow (where Byron was educated).

A pretty woman (that's quite natural,
  Or else the thing had hardly come to pass);
A husband rather old, not much in unity
With his young wife; a time, and opportunity.

4

Well – well, the world must turn upon its axis,
  And all mankind turn with it, heads or tails,
And live and die, make love and pay our taxes,
  And, as the veering wind shifts, shift our sails;
The king commands us, and the doctor quacks us,[3]
  The priest instructs, and so our life exhales
A little breath, love, wine, ambition, fame,
Fighting, devotion, dust, perhaps a name.

5

I said that Juan had been sent to Cadiz –
  A pretty town, I recollect it well –
'Tis there the mart of the colonial trade is
  (Or was, before Peru learned to rebel);[4]
And such sweet girls – I mean, such graceful ladies,
  Their very walk would make your bosom swell;
I can't describe it, though so much it strike,
Nor liken it – I never saw the like:

6

An Arab horse, a stately stag, a barb[5]
  New broke, a cameleopard,[6] a gazelle –
No, none of these will do – and then their garb,
  Their veil and petticoat! (Alas, to dwell
Upon such things would very near absorb
  A canto!) Then their feet and ankles – well,
Thank heaven I've got no metaphor quite ready
(And so, my sober muse, come, let's be steady,

7

Chaste Muse! – Well, if you must, you must); the veil
  Thrown back a moment with the glancing hand,
While the o'erpowering eye that turns you pale
  Flashes into the heart. All sunny land
Of love, when I forget you, may I fail
  To – say my prayers; but never was there planned
A dress through which the eyes give such a volley,
Excepting the Venetian *fazzioli*.[7]

## Notes

[3] *quacks us* administers quack medicines to us.

[4] *before Peru learned to rebel* The Peruvian struggle for independence had begun in 1813, and after many obstacles was won in 1824, under Bolivar's leadership.

[5] *barb* a horse from the Barbary coast.

[6] *cameleopard* giraffe.

[7] *fazzioli* white kerchiefs used as a veil by the lower ranks.

8

But to our tale: the Donna Inez sent
Her son to Cadiz only to embark;
To stay there had not answered her intent,
But why? We leave the reader in the dark –
'Twas for a voyage that the young man was meant,
As if a Spanish ship were Noah's ark,
To wean him from the wickedness of earth
And send him like a dove of promise forth.

9

Don Juan bade his valet pack his things
According to direction, then received
A lecture and some money: for four springs
He was to travel, and though Inez grieved
(As every kind of parting has its stings),
She hoped he would improve – perhaps believed:
A letter, too, she gave (he never read it)
Of good advice – and two or three of credit.

10

In the meantime, to pass her hours away,
Brave Inez now set up a Sunday school
For naughty children, who would rather play
(Like truant rogues) the devil or the fool;
Infants of three years old were taught that day,
Dunces were whipped, or set upon a stool:
The great success of Juan's education[8]
Spurred her to teach another generation.

11

Juan embarked, the ship got under way,
The wind was fair, the water passing rough;
A devil of a sea rolls in that bay,
As I, who've crossed it oft,[9] know well enough;
And, standing upon deck, the dashing spray
Flies in one's face, and makes it weather-tough:
And there he stood to take, and take again,
His first, perhaps his last, farewell of Spain.

12

I can't but say it is an awkward sight
To see one's native land receding through
The growing waters;[10] it unmans one quite,
Especially when life is rather new.

## Notes

[8] *The great success of Juan's education* Ironic, of course. His education has been a complete failure.

[9] *As I, who've crossed it oft* Byron sailed from Cadiz on 3 August 1809, travelling to Gibraltar.

[10] *I can't but say...waters* Byron draws on his own experience of self-exile.

I recollect Great Britain's coast looks white,
    But almost every other country's blue,
When gazing on them, mystified by distance,
We enter on our nautical existence.

13

So Juan stood, bewildered, on the deck:
    The wind sung, cordage[11] strained, and sailors swore,
And the ship creaked, the town became a speck,
    From which away so fair and fast they bore.
The best of remedies is a beefsteak
    Against seasickness; try it, sir, before
You sneer, and I assure you this is true,
For I have found it answer – so may you.

14

Don Juan stood and, gazing from the stern,
    Beheld his native Spain receding far.
First partings form a lesson hard to learn,
    Even nations feel this when they go to war;
There is a sort of unexpressed concern,
    A kind of shock that sets one's heart ajar:[12]
At leaving even the most unpleasant people
And places, one keeps looking at the steeple.

15

But Juan had got many things to leave,
    His mother, and a mistress, and no wife,
So that he had much better cause to grieve
    Than many persons more advanced in life;
And if we now and then a sigh must heave
    At quitting even those we quit in strife,
No doubt we weep for those the heart endears –
That is, till deeper griefs congeal our tears.

16

So Juan wept, as wept the captive Jews
    By Babel's waters, still remembering Zion:[13]
I'd weep, but mine is not a weeping muse,
    And such light griefs are not a thing to die on;
Young men should travel, if but to amuse
    Themselves – and the next time their servants tie on
Behind their carriages their new portmanteau,[14]
Perhaps it may be lined with this my canto.

## Notes

[11] *cordage* the ship's rigging.

[12] *ajar* out of harmony.

[13] *By Babel's waters…Zion* Byron alludes to Psalm 137:1: 'By the rivers of Babylon, there we sat down, yea, we wept, when we remembered Zion.'

[14] *portmanteau* travelling bag.

17

And Juan wept, and much he sighed and thought,
While his salt tears dropped into the salt sea,
'Sweets to the sweet'[15] (I like so much to quote;
You must excuse this extract – 'tis where she,
The Queen of Denmark, for Ophelia brought
Flowers to the grave), and, sobbing often, he
Reflected on his present situation,
And seriously resolved on reformation.

18

'Farewell, my Spain, a long farewell!' he cried,
'Perhaps I may revisit thee no more,
But die, as many an exiled heart hath died,
Of its own thirst to see again thy shore;
Farewell, where Guadalquivir's waters glide!
Farewell, my mother! And, since all is o'er,
Farewell, too dearest Julia!' (Here he drew
Her letter out again, and read it through.)

19

'And oh, if e'er I should forget, I swear –
But that's impossible, and cannot be –
Sooner shall this blue ocean melt to air,
Sooner shall earth resolve itself to sea,
Than I resign thine image, oh my fair!
Or think of anything excepting thee;
A mind diseased no remedy can physic[16] –'
(Here the ship gave a lurch, and he grew seasick.)

20

'Sooner shall heaven kiss earth –' (Here he fell sicker)
'Oh Julia, what is every other woe?
(For God's sake let me have a glass of liquor,
Pedro, Battista,[17] help me down below!)
Julia, my love! – you rascal, Pedro, quicker –
Oh Julia! – this cursed vessel pitches so –
Beloved Julia, hear me still beseeching!'
(Here he grew inarticulate with reaching.)[18]

21

He felt that chilling heaviness of heart,
Or rather stomach – which, alas, attends,
Beyond the best apothecary's[19] art,
The loss of love, the treachery of friends,

## Notes

[15] *Sweets to the sweet* from *Hamlet* V i 243.

[16] *physic* cure. The line recalls *Macbeth* V iii 40: 'Canst thou not minister to a mind diseased …?'

[17] Byron's own servant was a former gondolier called Giovanni Battista Lusieri (1798–1874). He remained with him until his death at Missolonghi.

[18] *reaching* retching.

[19] *apothecary* one who prepared and sold drugs for medicinal purposes – the business now (since about 1800) conducted by a chemist.

Or death of those we dote on, when a part
  Of us dies with them as each fond hope ends:
No doubt he would have been much more pathetic,
But the sea acted as a strong emetic.[20]

22

Love's a capricious power; I've known it hold
  Out through a fever caused by its own heat,
But be much puzzled by a cough and cold,
  And find a quinsy[21] very hard to treat;
Against all noble maladies he's bold,
  But vulgar illnesses don't like to meet –
Nor that a sneeze should interrupt his sigh,
Nor inflammations redden his blind eye.

23

But worst of all is nausea, or a pain
  About the lower region of the bowels;
Love, who heroically breathes a vein,[22]
  Shrinks from the application of hot towels,
And purgatives are dangerous to his reign,
  Seasickness death: his love was perfect, how else
Could Juan's passion, while the billows roar,
Resist his stomach, ne'er at sea before?

24

The ship, called the most holy *Trinidada*,
  Was steering duly for the port Leghorn,
For there the Spanish family Moncada[23]
  Were settled long ere Juan's sire was born:
They were relations, and for them he had a
  Letter of introduction, which the morn
Of his departure had been sent him by
His Spanish friends for those in Italy.

25

His suite consisted of three servants and
  A tutor – the licentiate[24] Pedrillo,
Who several languages did understand,
  But now lay sick and speechless on his pillow,
And, rocking in his hammock, longed for land,
  His headache being increased by every billow;
And the waves oozing through the porthole made
His berth a little damp, and him afraid.

## Notes

[20] *emetic* medicine designed to induce vomiting.

[21] *a quinsy* tonsillitis.

[22] *breathes a vein* Lancing the veins was in Byron's day a frequently used method of treatment.

[23] *Moncada* A family of this name lived next door to Byron at La Mira, Venice, in 1818.

[24] *licentiate* Pedrillo was licensed in one or both of two ways: either he held a degree from the University of Salamanca (stanza 37) or he was authorized to teach and perform religious rites.

26

'Twas not without some reason, for the wind
 Increased at night until it blew a gale;
And though 'twas not much to a naval mind,
 Some landsmen would have looked a little pale –
For sailors are, in fact, a different kind.
 At sunset they began to take in sail,
For the sky showed it would come on to blow,
And carry away, perhaps, a mast or so.

27

At one o'clock the wind with sudden shift
 Threw the ship right into the trough of the sea,[25]
Which struck her aft, and made an awkward rift,
 Started the stern-post,[26] also shattered the
Whole of her stern-frame, and ere she could lift
 Herself from out her present jeopardy
The rudder tore away: 'twas time to sound[27]
The pumps, and there were four feet water found.

28

One gang of people instantly was put
 Upon the pumps, and the remainder set
To get up part of the cargo, and what-not,
 But they could not come at the leak as yet;
At last they did get at it really, but
 Still their salvation was an even bet.
The water rushed through in a way quite puzzling,
While they thrust sheets, shirts, jackets, bales of muslin

29

Into the opening – but all such ingredients
 Would have been vain, and they must have gone down,
Despite of all their efforts and expedients,
 But for the pumps: I'm glad to make them known
To all the brother tars who may have need hence,
 For fifty tons of water were upthrown
By them per hour, and they had all been undone
But for their maker, Mr Mann, of London.[28]

30

As day advanced the weather seemed to abate,
 And then the leak they reckoned to reduce,
And keep the ship afloat, though three feet yet
 Kept two hand- and one chain-pump[29] still in use.

## Notes

[25] *the trough of the sea* the hollow between waves.

[26] *Started the stern-post* displaced or loosened the upright beam at the stern of the ship, which supported the rudder.

[27] *sound* i.e. use the pumps to find out how much water the ship had taken in.

[28] *Mr Mann, of London* This detail derives from Byron's source, Sir John Graham Dalyell's *Shipwrecks and Disasters at Sea* (3 vols, 1812).

[29] *chain-pump* machine for raising water by means of an endless chain.

The wind blew fresh again: as it grew late
 A squall came on, and while some guns broke loose,
A gust, which all descriptive power transcends,
Laid with one blast the ship on her beam-ends.[30]

31

There she lay, motionless, and seemed upset;
 The water left the hold, and washed the decks,
And made a scene men do not soon forget;
 For they remember battles, fires, and wrecks,
Or any other thing that brings regret,
 Or breaks their hopes, or hearts, or heads, or necks:
Thus drownings are much talked of by the divers
And swimmers who may chance to be survivors.

32

Immediately the masts were cut away,
 Both main and mizen; first the mizen went,
The mainmast followed. But the ship still lay
 Like a mere log, and baffled our intent.
Foremast and bowsprit were cut down, and they
 Eased her at last (although we never meant
To part with all till every hope was blighted),
And then with violence the old ship righted.

33

It may be easily supposed, while this
 Was going on, some people were unquiet,
That passengers would find it much amiss
 To lose their lives as well as spoil their diet;
That even the able seaman, deeming his
 Days nearly o'er, might be disposed to riot,
As upon such occasions tars will ask
For grog, and sometimes drink rum from the cask.

34

There's nought, no doubt, so much the spirit calms
 As rum and true religion; thus it was
Some plundered, some drank spirits, some sung psalms,
 The high wind made the treble, and as bass
The hoarse harsh waves kept time; fright cured the qualms
 Of all the luckless landsmen's seasick maws:
Strange sounds of wailing, blasphemy, devotion,
Clamoured in chorus to the roaring ocean.

35

Perhaps more mischief had been done, but for
 Our Juan who, with sense beyond his years,

## Notes

[30] *Laid…beam-ends* When the ends of a ship's beams touch the water, the vessel lies on its side, in imminent danger of capsizing.

Got to the spirit-room,[31] and stood before
It with a pair of pistols; and their fears,
As if Death were more dreadful by his door
Of fire than water, spite of oaths and tears,
Kept still aloof the crew who, ere they sunk,
Thought it would be becoming to die drunk.

36

'Give us more grog', they cried, 'for it will be
All one an hour hence.' Juan answered, 'No!
'Tis true that death awaits both you and me,
But let us die like men, not sink below
Like brutes.' And thus his dangerous post kept he,
And none liked to anticipate the blow;
And even Pedrillo, his most reverend tutor,
Was for some rum a disappointed suitor.

37

The good old gentleman was quite aghast
And made a loud and a pious lamentation,
Repented all his sins, and made a last
Irrevocable vow of reformation;
Nothing should tempt him more (this peril past)
To quit his academic occupation
In cloisters of the classic Salamanca,[32]
To follow Juan's wake like Sancho Panza.[33]

38

But now there came a flash of hope once more:
Day broke, and the wind lulled – the masts were gone,
The leak increased; shoals round her, but no shore,
The vessel swam, yet still she held her own.
They tried the pumps again, and though before
Their desperate efforts seemed all useless grown,
A glimpse of sunshine set some hands to bale –
The stronger pumped, the weaker thrummed a sail.[34]

39

Under the vessel's keel the sail was past,
And for the moment it had some effect;
But with a leak, and not a stick of mast,
Nor rag of canvas, what could they expect?
But still 'tis best to struggle to the last,
'Tis never too late to be wholly wrecked –
And though 'tis true that man can only die once,
'Tis not so pleasant in the Gulf of Lyons.

## Notes

[31] *spirit-room* cabin where alcohol was stored.

[32] *the classic Salamanca* Spanish university founded in the thirteenth century.

[33] Sancho Panza was Don Quixote's sidekick in Cervantes's famous novel.

[34] *thrummed a sail* They fastened bunches of rope-yarn over a sail so as to produce a shaggy surface, suitable to stop the leak.

40

There winds and waves had hurled them, and from thence,
Without their will, they carried them away;
For they were forced with steering to dispense,
And never had as yet a quiet day
On which they might repose, or even commence
A jury-mast[35] or rudder, or could say
The ship would swim an hour, which, by good luck,
Still swam – though not exactly like a duck.

41

The wind, in fact, perhaps, was rather less,
But the ship laboured so, they scarce could hope
To weather out much longer; the distress
Was also great with which they had to cope
For want of water, and their solid mess
Was scant enough: in vain the telescope
Was used – nor sail nor shore appeared in sight,
Nought but the heavy sea, and coming night.

42

Again the weather threatened; again blew
A gale, and in the fore- and after-hold
Water appeared – yet, though the people knew
All this, the most were patient, and some bold,
Until the chains and leathers were worn through
Of all our pumps: a wreck complete she rolled
At mercy of the waves, whose mercies are
Like human beings during civil war.

43

Then came the carpenter at last, with tears
In his rough eyes, and told the captain he
Could do no more; he was a man in years,
And long had voyaged through many a stormy sea,
And if he wept at length, they were not fears
That made his eyelids as a woman's be,
But he, poor fellow, had a wife and children,
Two things for dying people quite bewildering.

44

The ship was evidently settling now
Fast by the head;[36] and, all distinction gone,
Some went to prayers again, and made a vow
Of candles to their saints – but there were none

Notes

[35] *jury-mast* temporary replacement mast.

[36] *head* the fore-part of the ship, the bow.

To pay them with; and some looked o'er the bow;
Some hoisted out the boats; and there was one
That begged Pedrillo for an absolution,
Who told him to be damned – in his confusion.

45

Some lashed them in their hammocks, some put on
Their best clothes, as if going to a fair;
Some cursed the day on which they saw the sun,[37]
And gnashed their teeth and, howling, tore their hair;
And others went on as they had begun,
Getting the boats out, being well aware
That a tight boat will live in a rough sea,
Unless with breakers close beneath her lee.[38]

46

The worst of all was that, in their condition,
Having been several days in great distress,
'Twas difficult to get out such provision
As now might render their long suffering less –
Men, even when dying, dislike inanition.
Their stock was damaged by the weather's stress:
Two casks of biscuit and a keg of butter
Were all that could be thrown into the cutter.[39]

47

But in the longboat they contrived to stow
Some pounds of bread, though injured by the wet;
Water, a twenty gallon cask or so;
Six flasks of wine; and they contrived to get
A portion of their beef up from below,
And with a piece of pork, moreover, met,
But scarce enough to serve them for a luncheon –
Then there was rum, eight gallons in a puncheon.[40]

48

The other boats, the yawl and pinnace, had
Been stove[41] in the beginning of the gale;
And the longboat's condition was but bad,
As there were but two blankets for a sail
And one oar for a mast, which a young lad
Threw in by good luck over the ship's rail –
And two boats could not hold, far less be stored,
To save one half the people then on board.

## Notes

[37] *Some cursed...the sun* As at Jeremiah 20:14: 'Cursed be the day wherein I was born.'

[38] *lee* side of the boat sheltered from the wind. The line means 'unless the boat could be driven by the wind against breakers to the lee-side'.

[39] *cutter* lifeboat.

[40] *puncheon* large cask.

[41] *had / Been stove* had a hole made in the side.

49

'Twas twilight, and the sunless day went down
    Over the waste of waters, like a veil
Which, if withdrawn, would but disclose the frown
    Of one whose hate is masked but to assail;
Thus to their hopeless eyes the night was shown
    And grimly darkled o'er their faces pale,
And the dim desolate deep; twelve days had Fear
Been their familiar, and now Death was here.

50

Some trial had been making at a raft
    With little hope in such a rolling sea –
A sort of thing at which one would have laughed,
    If any laughter at such times could be,
Unless with people who too much have quaffed,
    And have a kind of wild and horrid glee,
Half-epileptical, and half-hysterical:
Their preservation would have been a miracle.

51

At half-past eight o'clock, booms, hencoops, spars,
    And all things, for a chance, had been cast loose,
That still could keep afloat the struggling tars –
    For yet[42] they strove, although of no great use.
There was no light in heaven but a few stars,
    The boats put off o'ercrowded with their crews;
She gave a heel, and then a lurch to port,
And, going down head foremost – sunk, in short.

52

Then rose from sea to sky the wild farewell,
    Then shrieked the timid, and stood still the brave,
Then some leaped overboard with dreadful yell,
    As eager to anticipate their grave;
And the sea yawned around her like a hell,
    And down she sucked with her the whirling wave,
Like one who grapples with his enemy,
And strives to strangle him before he die.

53

And first one universal shriek there rushed,
    Louder than the loud ocean, like a crash
Of echoing thunder; and then all was hushed
    Save the wild wind and the remorseless dash
Of billows; but at intervals there gushed,
    Accompanied with a convulsive splash,

Notes

[42] *yet* still.

A solitary shriek, the bubbling cry
Of some strong swimmer in his agony.

54

The boats, as stated, had got off before,
And in them crowded several of the crew;
And yet their present hope was hardly more
Than what it had been, for so strong it blew
There was slight chance of reaching any shore;
And then they were too many, though so few –
Nine in the cutter, thirty in the boat
Were counted in them when they got afloat.

55

All the rest perished; near two hundred souls
Had left their bodies – and, what's worse, alas!
When over Catholics the ocean rolls,
They must wait several weeks before a mass
Takes off one peck[43] of purgatorial coals,
Because, till people know what's come to pass,
They won't lay out their money on the dead:
It costs three francs for every mass that's said.

56

Juan got into the longboat, and there
Contrived to help Pedrillo to a place;
It seemed as if they had exchanged their care,
For Juan wore the magisterial face
Which courage gives, while poor Pedrillo's pair
Of eyes were crying for their owner's case:
Battista, though (a name called shortly Tita),
Was lost by getting at some aqua vita.[44]

57

Pedro, his valet, too, he tried to save,
But the same cause, conducive to his loss,
Left him so drunk, he jumped into the wave
As o'er the cutter's edge he tried to cross,
And so he found a wine-and-watery grave;
They could not rescue him although so close,
Because the sea ran higher every minute,
And for the boat – the crew kept crowding in it.

58

A small old spaniel which had been Don Jóse's,
His father's, whom he loved, as ye may think
(For on such things the memory reposes
With tenderness), stood howling on the brink,

## Notes

[43] *peck* small quantity (technically, the fourth part of a bushel, or two gallons).

[44] *aqua vita* spirits (probably brandy).

Knowing (dogs have such intellectual noses!),
No doubt, the vessel was about to sink;
And Juan caught him up, and ere he stepped
Off, threw him in, then after him he leapt.

59

He also stuffed his money where he could
About his person, and Pedrillo's too –
Who let him do, in fact, whate'er he would,
Not knowing what himself to say or do,
As every rising wave his dread renewed;
But Juan, trusting they might still get through,
And deeming there were remedies for any ill,
Thus re-embarked[45] his tutor and his spaniel.

60

'Twas a rough night, and blew so stiffly yet,
That the sail was becalmed between the seas,
Though on the wave's high top too much to set,
They dared not take it in for all the breeze;
Each sea curled o'er the stern, and kept them wet,
And made them bale without a moment's ease,
So that themselves as well as hopes were damped,
And the poor little cutter quickly swamped.

61

Nine souls more went in her: the longboat still
Kept above water, with an oar for mast;
Two blankets stitched together, answering ill
Instead of sail, were to the oar made fast –
Though every wave rolled menacing to fill,
And present peril all before surpassed,
They grieved for those who perished with the cutter,
And also for the biscuit casks and butter.

62

The sun rose red and fiery, a sure sign
Of the continuance of the gale: to run
Before the sea, until it should grow fine,
Was all that for the present could be done.
A few teaspoonfuls of their rum and wine
Was served out to the people, who begun
To faint, and damaged bread wet through the bags,
And most of them had little clothes but rags.

63

They counted thirty, crowded in a space
Which left scarce room for motion or exertion.

Notes

[45] *re-embarked* again put on board a boat.

They did their best to modify their case:
    One half sat up, though numbed with the immersion,
While t'other half were laid down in their place
    At watch and watch; thus, shivering like the tertian
Ague[46] in its cold fit, they filled their boat,
With nothing but the sky for a greatcoat.

64

'Tis very certain the desire of life
    Prolongs it; this is obvious to physicians
When patients, neither plagued with friends nor wife,
    Survive through very desperate conditions,
Because they still can hope, nor shines the knife
    Nor shears of Atropos[47] before their visions:
Despair of all recovery spoils longevity,
And makes men's miseries of alarming brevity.

65

'Tis said that persons living on annuities
    Are longer lived than others – God knows why,
Unless to plague the grantors;[48] yet so true it is,
    That some, I really think, *do* never die.
Of any creditors the worst a Jew it is,
    And *that's* their mode of furnishing supply:
In my young days they lent me cash that way,
Which I found very troublesome to pay.[49]

66

'Tis thus with people in an open boat,
    They live upon the love of life, and bear
More than can be believed, or even thought,
    And stand like rocks the tempest's wear and tear;
And hardship still has been the sailor's lot
    Since Noah's ark went cruising here and there;
She had a curious crew as well as cargo,
Like the first old Greek privateer, the Argo.[50]

67

But man is a carnivorous production
    And must have meals, at least one meal a day;
He cannot live, like woodcocks, upon suction,[51]
    But, like the shark and tiger, must have prey –
Although his anatomical construction
    Bears vegetables in a grumbling way,

## Notes

[46] *the tertian / Ague* a fever that recurs every other day.

[47] *shears of Atropos* Atropos, eldest of the three Fates, is represented blind, with a pair of scissors with which she cuts the thread of life.

[48] *the grantors* those who set up the annuity.

[49] *In my young days…to pay* By 1816, when he left England, Byron had amassed £30,000 in debts.

[50] *Argo* the ship (named after the city of Argos) which carried Jason and his companions to capture the golden fleece.

[51] *like woodcocks, upon suction* Woodcocks appear to be sucking as they probe with their long bills in the turf.

Your labouring people think beyond all question
Beef, veal, and mutton, better for digestion.

68

And thus it was with this our hapless crew,
   For on the third day there came on a calm,
And though at first their strength it might renew,
   And lying on their weariness like balm,
Lulled them like turtles sleeping on the blue
   Of ocean, when they woke they felt a qualm,
And fell all ravenously on their provision,
Instead of hoarding it with due precision.

69

The consequence was easily foreseen:
   They ate up all they had, and drank their wine
In spite of all remonstrances, and then –
   On what, in fact, next day were they to dine?
They hoped the wind would rise, these foolish men,
   And carry them to shore! These hopes were fine,
But as they had but one oar, and that brittle,
It would have been more wise to save their victual.[52]

70

The fourth day came, but not a breath of air,
   And ocean slumbered like an unweaned child;
The fifth day, and their boat lay floating there,
   The sea and sky were blue, and clear, and mild –
With their one oar (I wish they had had a pair)
   What could they do? And hunger's rage grew wild;
So Juan's spaniel, spite of his entreating,
Was killed, and portioned out for present eating.

71

On the sixth day they fed upon his hide,
   And Juan, who had still refused, because
The creature was his father's dog that died,
   Now feeling all the vulture[53] in his jaws,
With some remorse received (though first denied)
   As a great favour one of the forepaws,
Which he divided with Pedrillo, who
Devoured it, longing for the other too.

72

The seventh day, and no wind; the burning sun
   Blistered and scorched, and, stagnant on the sea,

## Notes

[52] *victual* food (pronounced 'vittle').

[53] *feeling all the vulture* i.e. feeling as hungry as a vulture.

They lay like carcasses; and hope was none,
Save in the breeze that came not. Savagely
They glared upon each other – all was done,
Water, and wine, and food; and you might see
The longings of the cannibal arise
(Although they spoke not) in their wolfish eyes.

73

At length one whispered his companion, who
Whispered another, and thus it went round,
And then into a hoarser murmur grew –
An ominous, and wild, and desperate sound;
And when his comrade's thought each sufferer knew,
'Twas but his own, suppressed till now, he found.
And out they spoke of lots for flesh and blood,
And who should die to be his fellow's food.

74

But ere they came to this, they that day shared
Some leathern caps, and what remained of shoes;
And then they looked around them and despaired,
And none to be the sacrifice would choose;
At length the lots were torn up and prepared,
But of materials that much shock the muse –
Having no paper, for the want of better,
They took by force from Juan Julia's letter.

75

The lots were made, and marked, and mixed and handed
In silent horror, and their distribution
Lulled even the savage hunger which demanded,
Like the Promethean vulture,[54] this pollution;[55]
None in particular had sought or planned it,
'Twas nature gnawed them to this resolution
By which none were permitted to be neuter[56] –
And the lot fell on Juan's luckless tutor.

76

He but requested to be bled to death:
The surgeon had his instruments, and bled
Pedrillo, and so gently ebbed his breath,
You hardly could perceive when he was dead.
He died as born, a Catholic in faith,
Like most in the belief in which they're bred,
And first a little crucifix he kissed,
And then held out his jugular and wrist.

## Notes

[54] *the Promethean vulture* Prometheus was nailed to the rock of the Caucasus for 30,000 years while an eagle (in some versions a vulture) feasted on his liver.

[55] *pollution* defilement (of Julia's love-letter). Nothing is sacred in the face of starvation.

[56] *neuter* exempt.

77

The surgeon, as there was no other fee,
Had his first choice of morsels for his pains;
But being thirstiest at the moment, he
Preferred a draught from the fast-flowing veins:
Part was divided, part thrown in the sea,
And such things as the entrails and the brains
Regaled two sharks, who followed o'er the billow –
The sailors ate the rest of poor Pedrillo.

78

The sailors ate him, all save three or four
Who were not quite so fond of animal food;
To these was added Juan who, before
Refusing his own spaniel, hardly could
Feel now his appetite increased much more;
'Twas not to be expected that he should,
Even in extremity of their disaster,
Dine with them on his pastor and his master.

79

'Twas better that he did not, for, in fact,
The consequence was awful in the extreme;
For they who were most ravenous in the act
Went raging mad – Lord, how they did blaspheme,
And foam and roll, with strange convulsions racked,
Drinking salt-water like a mountain-stream,
Tearing and grinning, howling, screeching, swearing,
And, with hyena laughter, died despairing.

80

Their numbers were much thinned by this infliction,
And all the rest were thin enough, Heaven knows;
And some of them had lost their recollection,
Happier than they who still perceived their woes;
But others pondered on a new dissection,
As if not warned sufficiently by those
Who had already perished, suffering madly,
For having used their appetites so sadly.

81

And next they thought upon the master's mate
As fattest – but he saved himself because,
Besides being much averse from such a fate,
There were some other reasons: the first was
He had been rather indisposed of late;
And that which chiefly proved his saving clause
Was a small present made to him at Cadiz,
By general subscription of the ladies.[57]

Notes

[57] *a small present…ladies* i.e. he was suffering from syphilis.

82

Of poor Pedrillo something still remained,
But was used sparingly – some were afraid,
And others still their appetites constrained,
Or but at times a little supper made;
All except Juan, who throughout abstained,
Chewing a piece of bamboo, and some lead:
At length they caught two boobies and a noddy,[58]
And then they left off eating the dead body.

83

And if Pedrillo's fate should shocking be,
Remember Ugolino condescends
To eat the head of his arch-enemy
The moment after he politely ends
His tale;[59] if foes be food in hell, at sea
'Tis surely fair to dine upon our friends
When shipwreck's short allowance grows too scanty,
Without being much more horrible than Dante.

84

And the same night there fell a shower of rain
For which their mouths gaped, like the cracks of earth
When dried to summer dust; till taught by pain,
Men really know not what good water's worth:
If you had been in Turkey or in Spain,
Or with a famished boat's-crew had your berth,
Or in the desert heard the camel's bell,
You'd wish yourself where Truth is – in a well.

85

It poured down torrents, but they were no richer
Until they found a ragged piece of sheet
Which served them as a sort of spongy pitcher,
And when they deemed its moisture was complete,
They wrung it out, and though a thirsty ditcher[60]
Might not have thought the scanty draught so sweet
As a full pot of porter, to their thinking
They ne'er till now had known the joys of drinking.

86

And their baked lips,[61] with many a bloody crack,
Sucked in the moisture, which like nectar streamed;
Their throats were ovens, their swoln tongues were black
As the rich man's in hell,[62] who vainly screamed

## Notes

[58] *boobies…noddy* species of sea-bird.

[59] *Remember Ugolino…His tale* In his *Inferno*, Dante relates how Count Ugolino was imprisoned with his two sons and two grandsons and starved to death with them. In Hell, Ugolino is seen chewing on the skull of the man responsible for the atrocity (*Inferno* xxxiii 76–8).

[60] *ditcher* one who makes and repairs ditches.

[61] *baked lips* apparently an echo of Coleridge, 'Ancient Mariner' (1817) 149: 'With throat unslaked, with black lips baked.'

[62] *As the rich man's in hell* an allusion to the parable of Dives and Lazarus, Luke 16:19–26.

To beg the beggar, who could not rain back
  A drop of dew, when every drop had seemed
To taste of heaven (if this be true, indeed,
Some Christians have a comfortable creed).

87

There were two fathers in this ghastly crew,
  And with them their two sons, of whom the one
Was more robust and hardy to the view,
  But he died early; and when he was gone,
His nearest messmate[63] told his sire, who threw
  One glance on him, and said, 'Heaven's will be done!
I can do nothing', and he saw him thrown
Into the deep without a tear or groan.

88

The other father had a weaklier child,
  Of a soft cheek, and aspect delicate;
But the boy bore up long, and with a mild
  And patient spirit held aloof his fate;
Little he said, and now and then he smiled,
  As if to win a part from off the weight
He saw increasing on his father's heart,
With the deep deadly thought that they must part.

89

And o'er him bent his sire, and never raised
  His eyes from off his face, but wiped the foam
From his pale lips, and ever on him gazed,
  And when the wished-for shower at length was come,
And the boy's eyes, which the dull film half glazed,
  Brightened, and for a moment seemed to roam,
He squeezed from out a rag some drops of rain
Into his dying child's mouth – but in vain.

90

The boy expired; the father held the clay,[64]
  And looked upon it long, and when at last
Death left no doubt, and the dead burden lay
  Stiff on his heart, and pulse and hope were past,
He watched it wistfully, until away
  'Twas borne by the rude wave wherein 'twas cast.
Then he himself sunk down all dumb and shivering,
And gave no sign of life, save his limbs quivering.

91

Now overhead a rainbow, bursting through
  The scattering clouds, shone, spanning the dark sea,

## Notes

[63] *messmate* companion at mealtimes; a sardonic joke.

[64] *clay* body.

Resting its bright base on the quivering blue;
    And all within its arch appeared to be
Clearer than that without, and its wide hue
    Waxed[65] broad and waving, like a banner free,
Then changed like to a bow that's bent, and then
Forsook the dim eyes of these shipwrecked men.

92

It changed, of course; a heavenly chameleon,
    The airy child of vapour and the sun,
Brought forth in purple, cradled in vermilion,
    Baptized in molten gold, and swathed in dun,[66]
Glittering like crescents o'er a Turk's pavilion,
    And blending every colour into one,
Just like a black eye in a recent scuffle[67]
(For sometimes we must box without the muffle).[68]

93

Our shipwrecked seamen thought it a good omen –
    It is as well to think so, now and then;
'Twas an old custom of the Greek and Roman,
    And may become of great advantage when
Folks are discouraged; and most surely no men
    Had greater need to nerve themselves again
Than these, and so this rainbow looked like hope –
Quite a celestial kaleidoscope.[69]

94

About this time a beautiful white bird,
    Webfooted, not unlike a dove in size
And plumage (probably it might have erred
    Upon its course), passed oft before their eyes
And tried to perch, although it saw and heard
    The men within the boat, and in this guise
It came and went, and fluttered round them till
Night fell – this seemed a better omen still.

95

But in this case I also must remark
    'Twas well this bird of promise did not perch,
Because the tackle of our shattered bark
    Was not so safe for roosting as a church;
And had it been the dove from Noah's ark,
    Returning there from her successful search,

## Notes

[65] *Waxed* became.

[66] *dun* dull brown.

[67] Byron is deliberately profaning the image celebrated in Wordsworth's 'The Rainbow'.

[68] *muffle* boxing-glove. Bare-knuckle boxing was fashionable in the early nineteenth century; Byron himself trained with 'Gentleman' Jackson.

[69] *kaleidoscope* invented as recently as 1817 by Sir David Brewster; Byron was sent one by John Murray in November 1818.

Which in their way that moment chanced to fall,
They would have eat[70] her, olive-branch and all.[71]

96

With twilight it again came on to blow,
  But not with violence; the stars shone out,
The boat made way; yet now they were so low,
  They knew not where nor what they were about;
Some fancied they saw land, and some said 'No!'
  The frequent fog-banks gave them cause to doubt –
Some swore that they heard breakers,[72] others guns,
And all mistook about the latter once.

97

As morning broke the light wind died away,
  When he who had the watch sung out and swore
If 'twas not land that rose with the sun's ray,
  He wished that land he never might see more;
And the rest rubbed their eyes, and saw a bay,
  Or thought they saw, and shaped their course for shore –
For shore it was,[73] and gradually grew
Distinct, and high, and palpable to view.

98

And then of these some part burst into tears,
  And others, looking with a stupid stare,
Could not yet separate their hopes from fears,
  And seemed as if they had no further care;
While a few prayed (the first time for some years),
  And at the bottom of the boat three were
Asleep; they shook them by the hand and head,
And tried to awaken them, but found them dead.

99

The day before, fast sleeping on the water,
  They found a turtle of the hawk's-bill kind,
And by good fortune gliding softly, caught her,
  Which yielded a day's life, and to their mind
Proved even still a more nutritious matter
  Because it left encouragement behind:
They thought that in such perils, more than chance
Had sent them this for their deliverance.

## Notes

[70] *eat* pronounced 'ett' by Byron.

[71] See Genesis 8:6–11. In a useful note, Peter Cochran suggests that Byron has in mind a narrative of the shipwreck of the *Medusa*; see 'Byron's *Don Juan*, Canto II, Stanza 95: A Previously Unnoted Source in the *Medusa* Narrative', *N&Q* NS 39 (1992) 172–3.

[72] *breakers* waves breaking against the shore.

[73] *For shore it was* that of one of the smaller Cyclades (l. 1010); as the *Trinidada* went down near the Golfe du Lion, that would mean that the survivors had drifted an improbable 2,000 kilometres.

100

The land appeared a high and rocky coast,
And higher grew the mountains as they drew,
Set by a current, toward it: they were lost
In various conjectures, for none knew
To what part of the earth they had been tossed,
So changeable had been the winds that blew;
Some thought it was Mount Etna, some the highlands
Of Candia,[74] Cyprus, Rhodes, or other islands.

101

Meantime the current, with a rising gale,
Still set them onwards to the welcome shore
Like Charon's bark of spectres,[75] dull and pale.
Their living freight was now reduced to four,
And three dead, whom their strength could not avail
To heave into the deep with those before –
Though the two sharks still followed them, and dashed
The spray into their faces as they splashed.

102

Famine, despair, cold, thirst and heat, had done
Their work on them by turns, and thinned them to
Such things a mother had not known her son
Amidst the skeletons of that gaunt crew;
By night chilled, by day scorched – thus one by one
They perished, until withered to these few,
But chiefly by a species of self-slaughter,
In washing down Pedrillo with salt water.

103

As they drew nigh the land, which now was seen
Unequal in its aspect here and there,
They felt the freshness of its growing green
That waved in forest-tops and smoothed the air,
And fell upon their glazed eyes like a screen
From glistening waves, and skies so hot and bare –
Lovely seemed any object that should sweep
Away the vast, salt, dread, eternal deep.

104

The shore looked wild, without a trace of man,
And girt by formidable waves; but they
Were mad for land, and thus their course they ran,
Though right ahead the roaring breakers lay:
A reef between them also now began
To show its boiling surf and bounding spray –

Notes

[74] *Candia* Crete.

[75] *Like Charon's bark of spectres* The grim ferryman Charon took the ghosts of the dead across the rivers of the underworld.

But finding no place for their landing better,
They ran the boat for shore, and overset[76] her.

105

But in his native stream, the Guadalquivir,
  Juan to lave his youthful limbs was wont;
And having learnt to swim in that sweet river,
  Had often turned the art to some account:
A better swimmer you could scarce see ever,
  He could, perhaps, have passed the Hellespont,
As once (a feat on which ourselves we prided)
Leander, Mr Ekenhead, and I did.[77]

106

So here, though faint, emaciated, and stark,
  He buoyed his boyish limbs, and strove to ply
With the quick wave, and gain, ere it was dark,
  The beach which lay before him, high and dry:
The greatest danger here was from a shark
  That carried off his neighbour by the thigh;
As for the other two they could not swim,
So nobody arrived on shore but him.

107

Nor yet had he arrived but for the oar,
  Which, providentially for him, was washed
Just as his feeble arms could strike no more,
  And the hard wave o'erwhelmed him as 'twas dashed
Within his grasp; he clung to it, and sore
  The waters beat while he thereto was lashed;
At last, with swimming, wading, scrambling, he
Rolled on the beach, half-senseless, from the sea.

108

There, breathless, with his digging nails he clung
  Fast to the sand, lest the returning wave,
From whose reluctant[78] roar his life he wrung,
  Should suck him back to her insatiate grave:
And there he lay, full-length, where he was flung,
  Before the entrance of a cliff-worn cave,
With just enough of life to feel its pain,
And deem that it was saved, perhaps, in vain.

## Notes

[76] *overset* capsized.

[77] An MS note by Byron reads: 'Mr Ekenhead, Lieutenant of Marines on board of the Salsette (then commanded by Capt Bathurst) swam across the Dardanelles May 10th (I think) 1810. See the account in Hobhouse's travels.' Byron actually swam the Hellespont on 3 May 1810, and it was described in detail in 'Extract from Lord Byron's Journal', *London Magazine* I (1820) 295–6.

[78] *reluctant* opposing; Byron is also punning on the Latin root, *reluctari*, 'to struggle against'.

109

With slow and staggering effort he arose,
  But sunk again upon his bleeding knee
And quivering hand; and then he looked for those
  Who long had been his mates upon the sea,
But none of them appeared to share his woes
  Save one, a corpse from out the famished three,
Who died two days before, and now had found
An unknown barren beach for burial ground.

110

And as he gazed, his dizzy brain spun fast,
  And down he sunk; and as he sunk, the sand
Swam round and round, and all his senses passed:
  He fell upon his side, and his stretched hand
Drooped dripping on the oar (their jury-mast),[79]
  And, like a withered lily, on the land
His slender frame and pallid aspect lay,
As fair a thing as e'er was formed of clay.[80]

111

How long in his damp trance young Juan lay[81]
  He knew not, for the earth was gone for him,
And Time had nothing more of night nor day
  For his congealing blood, and senses dim;
And how this heavy faintness passed away
  He knew not, till each painful pulse and limb
And tingling vein seemed throbbing back to life –
For Death, though vanquished, still retired with strife.

112

His eyes he opened, shut, again unclosed,
  For all was doubt and dizziness; methought
He still was in the boat, and had but dozed,
  And felt again with his despair o'erwrought,
And wished it death in which he had reposed,
  And then once more his feelings back were brought;
And slowly by his swimming eyes was seen
A lovely female face of seventeen.

113

'Twas bending close o'er his, and the small mouth
  Seemed almost prying into his for breath;
And chafing him, the soft warm hand of youth
  Recalled his answering spirits back from death;

## Notes

[79] *jury-mast* replacement mast.

[80] *clay* flesh.

[81] *How long in his damp trance young Juan lay* An echo of Coleridge, 'Ancient Mariner' (1817) 398–9: 'How long in that same fit I lay, / I have not to declare.'

And, bathing his chill temples, tried to soothe
Each pulse to animation, till beneath
Its gentle touch and trembling care, a sigh
To these kind efforts made a low reply.

114

Then was the cordial poured, and mantle flung
Around his scarce-clad limbs; and the fair arm
Raised higher the faint head which o'er it hung;
And her transparent cheek, all pure and warm,
Pillowed his death-like forehead; then she wrung
His dewy curls, long drenched by every storm;
And watched with eagerness each throb that drew
A sigh from his heaved bosom – and hers too.

115

And lifting him with care into the cave,
The gentle girl, and her attendant – one
Young, yet her elder, and of brow less grave,
And more robust of figure – then begun
To kindle fire, and as the new flames gave
Light to the rocks that roofed them, which the sun
Had never seen, the maid, or whatsoe'er
She was, appeared distinct, and tall, and fair.

116

Her brow was overhung with coins of gold
That sparkled o'er the auburn of her hair,
Her clustering hair, whose longer locks were rolled
In braids behind, and though her stature were
Even of the highest for a female mould,
They nearly reached her heel; and in her air
There was a something which bespoke command,
As one who was a lady in the land.

117

Her hair, I said, was auburn; but her eyes
Were black as death, their lashes the same hue,
Of downcast length, in whose silk shadow lies
Deepest attraction – for when to the view
Forth from its raven fringe the full glance flies,
Ne'er with such force the swiftest arrow flew;
'Tis as the snake late coiled, who pours his length,
And hurls at once his venom and his strength.

118

Her brow was white and low, her cheek's pure dye
Like twilight rosy still with the set sun;
Short upper lip, sweet lips! – that make us sigh
Ever to have seen such, for she was one
Fit for the model of a statuary
(A race of mere impostors, when all's done;

I've seen much finer women, ripe and real,
Than all the nonsense of their stone[82] ideal).

119

I'll tell you why I say so, for 'tis just
One should not rail without a decent cause:
There was an Irish lady,[83] to whose bust
I ne'er saw justice done, and yet she was
A frequent model; and if e'er she must
Yield to stern Time and Nature's wrinkling laws,
They will destroy a face which mortal thought
Ne'er compassed, nor less mortal chisel wrought.

120

And such was she, the lady of the cave:
Her dress was very different from the Spanish –
Simpler, and yet of colours not so grave;
For, as you know, the Spanish women banish
Bright hues when out of doors, and yet, while wave
Around them (what I hope will never vanish)
The basquiña[84] and the mantilla,[85] they
Seem at the same time mystical[86] and gay.

121

But with our damsel this was not the case:
Her dress was many-coloured, finely spun;
Her locks curled negligently round her face,
But through them gold and gems profusely shone;
Her girdle sparkled, and the richest lace
Flowed in her veil, and many a precious stone
Flashed on her little hand; but, what was shocking,
Her small snow feet had slippers, but no stocking.

122

The other female's dress was not unlike,
But of inferior materials; she
Had not so many ornaments to strike[87] –
Her hair had silver only, bound to be
Her dowry; and her veil, in form alike,
Was coarser; and her air, though firm, less free;
Her hair was thicker, but less long; her eyes
As black, but quicker, and of smaller size.

123

And these two tended him, and cheered him both
With food and raiment, and those soft attentions

## Notes

[82] *stone* An early MS reading is 'damned'.

[83] *an Irish lady* Probably, as commentators have noted, Lady Adelaide Forbes (1789–1858); 'The Apollo Belvidere is the image of Lady Adelaide Forbes', he told Moore, 12 May 1817 (Marchand v 227).

[84] *basquiña* an outer skirt placed over indoor dress when going out.

[85] *mantilla* light cloak.

[86] *mystical* solemn.

[87] *strike* remove, take off.

Which are (as I must own) of female growth,
And have ten thousand delicate inventions:
They made a most superior mess of broth,
A thing which poesy but seldom mentions,
But the best dish that e'er was cooked since Homer's
Achilles ordered dinner for newcomers.[88]

124

I'll tell you who they were, this female pair,
Lest they should seem princesses in disguise;
Besides, I hate all mystery, and that air
Of claptrap, which your recent poets prize;
And so, in short, the girls they really were
They shall appear before your curious eyes –
Mistress and maid; the first was only daughter
Of an old man, who lived upon the water.

125

A fisherman he had been in his youth,
And still a sort of fisherman was he;
But other speculations were, in sooth,
Added to his connection with the sea –
Perhaps not so respectable, in truth:
A little smuggling, and some piracy
Left him, at last, the sole of many masters
Of an ill-gotten million of piastres.[89]

126

A fisher, therefore, was he – though of men,
Like Peter the Apostle[90] – and he fished
For wandering merchant vessels, now and then,
And sometimes caught as many as he wished;
The cargoes he confiscated, and gain
He sought in the slave-market too, and dished
Full many a morsel for that Turkish trade,
By which, no doubt, a good deal may be made.

127

He was a Greek, and on his isle had built
(One of the wild and smaller Cyclades)[91]
A very handsome house from out his guilt,
And there he lived exceedingly at ease;
Heaven knows what cash he got, or blood he spilt –
A sad[92] old fellow was he, if you please,
But this I know: it was a spacious building,
Full of barbaric carving, paint, and gilding.

## Notes

[88] *But the best dish...newcomers* Homer describes in the *Iliad* ix how Patroclus, Achilles and Automedon ate a sheep, a goat and a pig.

[89] *piastres* small Turkish coins.

[90] *though of men...Apostle* see Matthew 4:18–19.

[91] *Cyclades* Group of islands in the Aegean between the Peloponnese and the Dodecanese.

[92] *sad* appallingly bad.

128

He had an only daughter called Haidee,[93]
The greatest heiress of the Eastern Isles;
Besides, so very beautiful was she,
Her dowry was as nothing to her smiles:
Still in her teens, and like a lovely tree
She grew to womanhood, and between whiles
Rejected several suitors, just to learn
How to accept a better in his turn.

129

And walking out upon the beach below
The cliff, towards sunset, on that day she found,
Insensible – not dead, but nearly so –
Don Juan, almost famished, and half-drowned;
But being naked, she was shocked, you know,
Yet deemed herself in common pity bound,
As far as in her lay, 'to take him in,
A stranger',[94] dying, with so white a skin.

130

But taking him into her father's house
Was not exactly the best way to save,
But like conveying to the cat the mouse,
Or people in a trance into their grave;
Because the good old man had so much νοῦς,[95]
Unlike the honest Arab thieves so brave,
He would have hospitably cured the stranger,
And sold him instantly when out of danger.

131

And therefore, with her maid, she thought it best
(A virgin always on her maid relies)
To place him in the cave for present rest;
And when, at last, he opened his black eyes,
Their charity increased about their guest,
And their compassion grew to such a size,
It opened half the turnpike-gates to heaven
(St Paul says 'tis the toll which must be given).[96]

132

They made a fire, but such a fire as they
Upon the moment could contrive with such
Materials as were cast up round the bay –
Some broken planks, and oars, that to the touch

## Notes

[93] *Haidee* 'a caress' or 'the caressed one'; Byron would have encountered the name in popular Greek songs of the time.

[94] Matthew 25:35.

[95] νοῦς pronounced 'nouse' (rhyme with 'mouse'); sense, intelligence.

[96] 'And above all these things put on charity, which is the bond of perfectness' (Colossians 3:14).

Were nearly tinder, since so long they lay,
  A mast was almost crumbled to a crutch;
But, by God's grace, here wrecks were in such plenty,
That there was fuel to have furnished twenty.

133

He had a bed of furs, and a pelisse,[97]
  For Haidee stripped her sables off to make
His couch; and, that he might be more at ease
  And warm, in case by chance he should awake,
They also gave a petticoat apiece,
  She and her maid, and promised by daybreak
To pay him a fresh visit, with a dish
For breakfast, of eggs, coffee, bread, and fish.

134

And thus they left him to his lone repose.
  Juan slept like a top,[98] or like the dead
Who sleep at last, perhaps (God only knows),
  Just for the present; and in his lulled head
Not even a vision of his former woes
  Throbbed in accursed dreams, which sometimes spread
Unwelcome visions of our former years,
Till the eye, cheated, opens thick with tears.

135

Young Juan slept all dreamless, but the maid
  Who smoothed his pillow as she left the den
Looked back upon him, and a moment stayed,
  And turned, believing that he called again.
He slumbered; yet she thought, at least she said
  (The heart will slip even as the tongue and pen),
He had pronounced her name – but she forgot
That at this moment Juan knew it not.

136

And pensive to her father's house she went,
  Enjoining silence strict to Zoe,[99] who
Better than her knew what, in fact, she meant,
  She being wiser by a year or two:
A year or two's an age when rightly spent,
  And Zoe spent hers, as most women do,
In gaining all that useful sort of knowledge
Which is acquired in nature's good old college.

## Notes

[97] *pelisse* long cloak reaching the ankles, with sleeves or armholes.
[98] *Juan slept like a top* A reference to the apparent stillness of a spinning top when its axis of rotation is vertical.
[99] *Zoe* 'life'.

137

The morn broke, and found Juan slumbering still
Fast in his cave, and nothing clashed upon
His rest; the rushing of the neighbouring rill
And the young beams of the excluded sun
Troubled him not, and he might sleep his fill;
And need he had of slumber yet, for none
Had suffered more – his hardships were comparative
To those related in my granddad's *Narrative*.[100]

138

Not so Haidee: she sadly tossed and tumbled,
And started from her sleep, and, turning o'er,
Dreamed of a thousand wrecks o'er which she stumbled,
And handsome corpses strewed upon the shore;
And woke her maid so early that she grumbled,
And called her father's old slaves up, who swore
In several oaths – Armenian, Turk, and Greek;
They knew not what to think of such a freak.[101]

139

But up she got, and up she made them get
With some pretence about the sun, that makes
Sweet skies just when he rises, or is set;
And 'tis, no doubt, a sight to see when breaks
Bright Phoebus, while the mountains still are wet
With mist, and every bird with him awakes,
And night is flung off like a mourning suit
Worn for a husband, or some other brute.

140

I say, the sun is a most glorious sight;
I've seen him rise full oft, indeed of late
I have sat up on purpose all the night,
Which hastens, as physicians say, one's fate –
And so all ye, who would be in the right
In health and purse, begin your day to date
From daybreak, and when coffined at fourscore,[102]
Engrave upon the plate, you rose at four.

141

And Haidee met the morning face to face;
Her own was freshest, though a feverish flush
Had dyed it with the headlong blood, whose race
From heart to cheek is curbed into a blush,

## Notes

[100] *my granddad's Narrative* i.e. *A Narrative of the Hon. John Byron, containing an account of the great distress suffered by himself and his companions on the coast of Patagonia, from the year 1740, till their arrival in England, 1746* (1768) – a popular volume which went through eleven editions before 1825, reprinted intermittently until 1925.

[101] *a freak* i.e. freakish behaviour.

[102] *fourscore* eighty.

Like to a torrent which a mountain's base,
   That overpowers some alpine river's rush,
Checks to a lake, whose waves in circles spread,
Or the Red Sea – but the sea is not red.

142

And down the cliff the island virgin came,
   And near the cave her quick light footsteps drew,
While the sun smiled on her with his first flame,
   And young Aurora[103] kissed her lips with dew,
Taking her for a sister; just the same
   Mistake you would have made on seeing the two,
Although the mortal, quite as fresh and fair,
Had all the advantage too of not being air.

143

And when into the cavern Haidee stepped
   All timidly, yet rapidly, she saw
That like an infant Juan sweetly slept;
   And then she stopped, and stood as if in awe
(For sleep is awful),[104] and on tiptoe crept
   And wrapped him closer, lest the air, too raw,
Should reach his blood, then o'er him still as death
Bent, with hushed lips, that drank his scarce-drawn breath.

144

And thus like to an angel o'er the dying
   Who die in righteousness,[105] she leaned; and there
All tranquilly the shipwrecked boy was lying,
   As o'er him lay the calm and stirless air.
But Zoe the meantime some eggs was frying,
   Since, after all, no doubt the youthful pair
Must breakfast, and betimes; lest they should ask it,
She drew out her provision from the basket.

145

She knew that the best feelings must have victual
   And that a shipwrecked youth would hungry be;
Besides, being less in love, she yawned a little,
   And felt her veins chilled by the neighbouring sea.
And so she cooked their breakfast to a tittle;[106]
   I can't say that she gave them any tea,
But there were eggs, fruit, coffee, bread, fish, honey,
With Scio[107] wine – and all for love, not money.

## Notes

[103] *Aurora* goddess of dawn and morning.

[104] *awful* awe-inspiring.

[105] *the dying…righteousness* A profane reference to Matthew 25:46.

[106] *to a tittle* with minute exactness.

[107] *Scio* Italian form of Chios (island off the Ionian coast between Lesbos and Samos, known for the high quality of its wines).

146

And Zoe, when the eggs were ready, and
The coffee made, would fain have wakened Juan,
But Haidee stopped her with her quick small hand,
And without a word, a sign her finger drew on
Her lip, which Zoe needs must understand;
And, the first breakfast spoilt, prepared a new one,
Because her mistress would not let her break
That sleep which seemed as it would ne'er awake.

147

For still he lay, and on his thin worn cheek
A purple hectic[108] played like dying day
On the snow-tops of distant hills; the streak
Of sufferance yet upon his forehead lay,
Where the blue veins looked shadowy, shrunk, and weak;
And his black curls were dewy with the spray
Which weighed upon them yet, all damp and salt,
Mixed with the stony vapours of the vault.

148

And she bent o'er him, and he lay beneath,
Hushed as the babe upon its mother's breast,
Drooped as the willow when no winds can breathe,
Lulled like the depth of ocean when at rest,
Fair as the crowning rose of the whole wreath,
Soft as the callow cygnet[109] in its nest;
In short, he was a very pretty fellow,
Although his woes had turned him rather yellow.

149

He woke and gazed, and would have slept again,
But the fair face which met his eyes forbade
Those eyes to close, though weariness and pain
Had further sleep a further pleasure made;
For woman's face was never formed in vain
For Juan, so that, even when he prayed,
He turned from grisly saints and martyrs hairy
To the sweet portraits of the Virgin Mary.

150

And thus upon his elbow he arose,
And looked upon the lady, in whose cheek
The pale contended with the purple rose,
As with an effort she began to speak;

Notes

108 *purple hectic* purple flush.

109 *cygnet* young swan.

Her eyes were eloquent, her words would pose,[110]
   Although she told him, in good modern Greek,
With an Ionian accent, low and sweet,
That he was faint, and must not talk, but eat.

151

Now Juan could not understand a word,
   Being no Grecian; but he had an ear,
And her voice was the warble of a bird,
   So soft, so sweet, so delicately clear,
That finer, simpler music ne'er was heard;
   The sort of sound we echo with a tear
Without knowing why – an overpowering tone
Whence melody descends as from a throne.

152

And Juan gazed as one who is awoke
   By a distant organ, doubting if he be
Not yet a dreamer, till the spell is broke
   By the watchman, or some such reality,
Or by one's early valet's cursed knock –
   At least it is a heavy sound to me
Who like a morning slumber, for the night
Shows stars and women in a better light.

153

And Juan, too, was helped out from his dream
   Or sleep, or whatsoe'er it was, by feeling
A most prodigious appetite: the steam
   Of Zoe's cookery no doubt was stealing
Upon his senses, and the kindling beam
   Of the new fire, which Zoe kept up, kneeling,
To stir her viands, made him quite awake
And long for food, but chiefly a beefsteak.

154

But beef is rare within these oxless isles;
   Goat's flesh there is, no doubt, and kid, and mutton;
And, when a holiday upon them smiles,
   A joint upon their barbarous spits they put on:
But this occurs but seldom, between whiles,
   For some of these are rocks with scarce a hut on;
Others are fair and fertile, among which
This, though not large, was one of the most rich.

155

I say that beef is rare, and can't help thinking
   That the old fable of the Minotaur –

Notes

[110] *pose* puzzle, confuse.

From which our modern morals, rightly shrinking,
Condemn the royal lady's taste who wore
A cow's shape for a mask – was only (sinking
The allegory) a mere type, no more;
That Pasiphae promoted breeding cattle
To make the Cretans bloodier in battle.[111]

156

For we all know that English people are
Fed upon beef (I won't say much of beer
Because 'tis liquor only, and being far
From this my subject, has no business here);
We know, too, they are very fond of war,
A pleasure (like all pleasures) rather dear;
So were the Cretans – from which I infer
That beef and battles both were owing to her.[112]

157

But to resume. The languid Juan raised
His head upon his elbow, and he saw
A sight on which he had not lately gazed,
As all his latter meals had been quite raw –
Three or four things, for which the Lord he praised,
And, feeling still the famished vulture gnaw,
He fell upon whate'er was offered, like
A priest, a shark, an alderman,[113] or pike.

158

He ate, and he was well supplied; and she
Who watched him like a mother, would have fed
Him past all bounds, because she smiled to see
Such an appetite in one she had deemed dead:
But Zoe, being older than Haidee,
Knew (by tradition, for she ne'er had read)
That famished people must be slowly nursed,
And fed by spoonfuls, else they always burst.

159

And so she took the liberty to state,
Rather by deeds than words, because the case
Was urgent, that the gentleman whose fate
Had made her mistress quit her bed to trace[114]

## Notes

[111] Minos of Crete challenged Poseidon, god of the sea, to produce a bull from the ocean. So beautiful was it, that he could not sacrifice it, and substituted another, incurring Poseidon's wrath. After Minos's marriage to Pasiphaë, Poseidon made her fall in love with the bull, with which she had intercourse, giving birth to the Minotaur – half bull, half man. It became a scourge, devouring the Cretans, until Daedalus built a labyrinth to contain it.

[112] *her* Pasiphaë. As a result of the imprisonment of the Minotaur in the labyrinth, Minos waged war on Athens; having defeated it, he fed the Minotaur a yearly tribute of seven young men and seven maidens.

[113] *alderman* in London, the chief officer of a ward. Aldermen were a byword for greed in their levying of fines.

[114] *trace* tread.

The seashore at this hour, must leave his plate
Unless he wished to die upon the place –
She snatched it and refused another morsel,
Saying he had gorged enough to make a horse ill.

160

Next they – he being naked, save a tattered
Pair of scarce decent trousers – went to work,
And in the fire his recent rags they scattered
And dressed him, for the present, like a Turk
Or Greek; that is (although it not much mattered),
Omitting turban, slippers, pistols, dirk,[115]
They furnished him, entire except some stitches,
With a clean shirt and very spacious breeches.

161

And then fair Haidee tried her tongue at speaking,
But not a word could Juan comprehend,
Although he listened so that the young Greek in
Her earnestness would ne'er have made an end;
And, as he interrupted not, went ekeing
Her speech out to her protégé and friend,
Till pausing at the last her breath to take,
She saw he did not understand Romaic.[116]

162

And then she had recourse to nods and signs,
And smiles, and sparkles of the speaking eye,
And read (the only book she could) the lines
Of his fair face, and found, by sympathy,
The answer eloquent, where the soul shines
And darts in one quick glance a long reply;
And thus in every look she saw expressed
A world of words, and things at which she guessed.

163

And now, by dint of fingers and of eyes,
And words repeated after her, he took
A lesson in her tongue – but by surmise,
No doubt, less of her language than her look;
As he who studies fervently the skies
Turns oftener to the stars than to his book,
Thus Juan learned his alpha beta better
From Haidee's glance than any graven letter.

Notes

[115] *dirk* dagger.

[116] *Romaic* modern Greek vernacular, some of which Byron learnt on his visit to Athens in 1810–11.

164

'Tis pleasing to be schooled in a strange tongue
By female lips and eyes;[117] that is, I mean,
When both the teacher and the taught are young,
As was the case, at least, where I have been;
They smile so when one's right, and when one's wrong
They smile still more, and then there intervene
Pressure of hands, perhaps even a chaste kiss;
I learned the little that I know by this –

165

That is, some words of Spanish, Turk, and Greek,
Italian not at all, having no teachers;
Much English I cannot pretend to speak,
Learning that language chiefly from its preachers,
Barrow, South, Tillotson, whom every week
I study, also Blair[118] – the highest reachers
Of eloquence in piety and prose;
I hate your poets, so read none of those.[119]

166

As for the ladies, I have nought to say,
A wanderer from the British world of fashion,[120]
Where I, like other 'dogs, have had my day';[121]
Like other men too, may have had my passion –
But that, like other things, has passed away,
And all her fools whom I *could* lay the lash on:
Foes, friends, men, women, now are nought to me
But dreams of what has been, no more to be.

167

Return we to Don Juan. He begun
To hear new words, and to repeat them, but
Some feelings, universal as the sun,
Were such as could not in his breast be shut
More than within the bosom of a nun;
He was in love – as you would be, no doubt,
With a young benefactress; so was she,
Just in the way we very often see.

168

And every day by daybreak – rather early
For Juan, who was somewhat fond of rest,
She came into the cave, but it was merely
To see her bird reposing in his nest;

## Notes

[117] *'Tis pleasing...eyes* Byron learned Spanish in Seville from a female tutor, Greek from Teresa Macri in Athens, and Italian from Marianna Segati in Venice.

[118] Isaac Barrow (1630–77), Robert South (1634–1716), John Tillotson (1630–94) and Hugh Blair (1718–1800), distinguished sermonists.

[119] *I hate your poets, so read none of those* An overstatement designed to emphasize Byron's dislike of the Lake poets and admiration of Pope.

[120] *the British world of fashion* in which Byron had been a very big fish, 1812–16.

[121] *Hamlet* V i 292: 'The cat will mew, and dog will have his day.'

And she would softly stir his locks so curly,
Without disturbing her yet-slumbering guest,
Breathing all gently o'er his cheek and mouth,
As o'er a bed of roses the sweet south.[122]

169

And every morn his colour freshlier came,
And every day helped on his convalescence;
'Twas well, because health in the human frame
Is pleasant, besides being true love's essence;
For health and idleness to passion's flame
Are oil and gunpowder, and some good lessons
Are also learnt from Ceres and from Bacchus,[123]
Without whom Venus will not long attack us.[124]

170

While Venus fills the heart (without heart really
Love, though good always, is not quite so good),
Ceres presents a plate of vermicelli;[125]
For love must be sustained like flesh and blood,
While Bacchus pours out wine, or hands a jelly.[126]
Eggs, oysters too, are amatory food;[127]
But who is their purveyor from above
Heaven knows – it may be Neptune, Pan, or Jove.

171

When Juan woke he found some good things ready;
A bath, a breakfast, and the finest eyes
That ever made a youthful heart less steady,
Besides her maid's, as pretty for their size –
But I have spoken of all this already,
And repetition's tiresome and unwise;
Well, Juan, after bathing in the sea,
Came always back to coffee and Haidee.

172

Both were so young, and one so innocent,
That bathing passed for nothing; Juan seemed
To her, as 'twere, the kind of being sent,
Of whom these two years she had nightly dreamed:
A something to be loved, a creature meant
To be her happiness, and whom she deemed
To render happy; all who joy would win
Must share it – Happiness was born a twin.

## Notes

[122] *the sweet south* i.e. the warm south wind.

[123] *Ceres...Bacchus* corn (bread) and wine. Ceres is the goddess of corn and harvest; Bacchus the god of wine.

[124] *Are also learnt...attack us* A reworking of Terence, *Eunuchus* iv 5,6: 'sine Cerere et Libero friget Venus' (without Ceres and Bacchus, Venus freezes).

[125] *vermicelli* pasta is made of wheat.

[126] *a jelly* partly made of wine.

[127] *amatory food* aphrodisiacs (containing protein).

173
It was such pleasure to behold him, such
Enlargement of existence to partake
Nature with him, to thrill beneath his touch,
To watch him slumbering, and to see him wake:
To live with him for ever were too much,
But then the thought of parting made her quake;
He was her own, her ocean-treasure, cast
Like a rich wreck – her first love, and her last.[128]

174
And thus a moon rolled on, and fair Haidee
Paid daily visits to her boy, and took
Such plentiful precautions, that still he
Remained unknown within his craggy nook;
At last her father's prows put out to sea,
For certain merchantmen upon the look,
Not as of yore to carry off an Io,[129]
But three Ragusan[130] vessels, bound for Scio.

175
Then came her freedom, for she had no mother,
So that, her father being at sea, she was
Free as a married woman, or such other
Female, as where she likes may freely pass,
Without even the encumbrance of a brother –
The freest she that ever gazed on glass
(I speak of Christian lands in this comparison,
Where wives, at least, are seldom kept in garrison).

176
Now she prolonged her visits and her talk
(For they must talk), and he had learnt to say
So much as to propose to take a walk –
For little had he wandered since the day
On which, like a young flower snapped from the stalk,
Drooping and dewy on the beach he lay;
And thus they walked out in the afternoon,
And saw the sun set opposite the moon.

177
It was a wild and breaker-beaten coast,
With cliffs above, and a broad sandy shore
Guarded by shoals and rocks as by an host,[131]
With here and there a creek whose aspect wore

## Notes

[128] *her first love, and her last* A claim Byron himself made in a letter to Countess Teresa Guiccioli on 22 April 1819: 'You who are my only and last love, who are my only joy.'

[129] *Io* Io, a priestess at Argos, was kidnapped by Phoenicians (Herodotus I i 4–5).

[130] Ragusa was in Byron's day the name for Dubrovnik, an ancient seaport still flourishing on the Adriatic coast of Croatia.

[131] *host* army.

A better welcome to the tempest-tossed;
    And rarely ceased the haughty billow's roar,
Save on the dead long summer days, which make
The outstretched ocean glitter like a lake.

178

And the small ripple spilt upon the beach
    Scarcely o'erpassed the cream of your champagne,
When o'er the brim the sparkling bumpers reach,
    That spring-dew of the spirit, the heart's rain!
Few things surpass old wine – and they may preach
    Who please (the more because they preach in vain) –
Let us have wine and woman, mirth and laughter,
Sermons and soda-water the day after.

179

Man, being reasonable, must get drunk;
    The best of life is but intoxication:
Glory, the grape, love, gold – in these are sunk
    The hopes of all men, and of every nation;
Without their sap, how branchless were the trunk
    Of life's strange tree, so fruitful on occasion.
But to return; get very drunk, and when
You wake with headache, you shall see what then.

180

Ring for your valet, bid him quickly bring
    Some hock[132] and soda-water[133] – then you'll know
A pleasure worthy Xerxes the great king;[134]
    For not the blessed sherbet, sublimed[135] with snow,
Nor the first sparkle of the desert-spring,
    Nor Burgundy in all its sunset glow,
After long travel, ennui,[136] love, or slaughter,
Vie with that draught of hock and soda-water.

181

The coast (I think it was the coast that I
    Was just describing; yes, it *was* the coast)
Lay at this period quiet as the sky,
    The sands untumbled, the blue waves untossed,

## Notes

[132] *hock* white German wine.

[133] *hock and soda-water* cf. the stanza used as a headpiece to the poem in editions from 1832 onwards. Byron never intended it as a headpiece, and in fact scribbled it in the MS and then deleted it:

I would to Heaven that I were so much clay –
    As I am blood – bone – marrow, passion –
                                        feeling –
Because at least the past were past away –
    And for the future (but I write this reeling,
Having got drunk exceedingly today
    So that I seem to stand upon the ceiling)
I say, the future is a serious matter –
And so, for godsake, hock and soda-water.

[134] Xerxes I, Persian king who in 480 BCE assembled a great navy and army to avenge his father Darius for the loss of the Battle of Marathon in 490 BCE. He was eventually defeated at Salamis.

[135] *sublimed* chilled.

[136] *ennui* feeling of mental weariness and dissatisfaction produced by want of occupation.

And all was stillness save the sea-bird's cry
And dolphin's leap, and little billow crossed
By some low rock or shelf, that made it fret[137]
Against the boundary it scarcely wet.

182

And forth they wandered, her sire being gone,
As I have said, upon an expedition;
And mother, brother, guardian, she had none,
Save Zoe, who, although with due precision
She waited on her lady with the sun,
Thought daily service was her only mission,
Bringing warm water, wreathing her long tresses,
And asking now and then for cast-off dresses.

183

It was the cooling hour, just when the rounded
Red sun sinks down behind the azure hill,
Which then seems as if the whole earth it bounded,
Circling all nature, hushed, and dim, and still,
With the far mountain-crescent half surrounded
On one side, and the deep sea calm and chill
Upon the other, and the rosy sky,
With one star sparkling through it like an eye.

184

And thus they wandered forth, and, hand in hand,
Over the shining pebbles and the shells
Glided along the smooth and hardened sand,
And in the worn and wild receptacles
Worked by the storms, yet worked as it were planned,
In hollow halls, with sparry[138] roofs and cells,
They turned to rest; and, each clasped by an arm,
Yielded to the deep twilight's purple charm.

185

They looked up to the sky, whose floating glow
Spread like a rosy ocean, vast and bright;
They gazed upon the glittering sea below,
Whence the broad moon rose circling into sight;
They heard the wave's splash, and the wind so low,
And saw each other's dark eyes darting light
Into each other; and, beholding this,
Their lips drew near, and clung into a kiss –

Notes

[137] *fret* chafe.

[138] *sparry* Spar is an opaque crystalline mineral, which is embedded in the roofs and cells of the rocks.

186

A long, long kiss, a kiss of youth and love
And beauty, all concentrating like rays
Into one focus, kindled from above;
Such kisses as belong to early days
Where heart and soul and sense in concert[139] move,
And the blood's lava, and the pulse ablaze,
Each kiss a heartquake – for a kiss's strength,
I think, it must be reckoned by its length.

187

By length I mean duration; theirs endured
Heaven knows how long – no doubt they never reckoned,
And if they had, they could not have secured
The sum of their sensations to a second:
They had not spoken, but they felt allured
As if their souls and lips each other beckoned,
Which, being joined, like swarming bees they clung,
Their hearts the flowers from whence the honey sprung.

188

They were alone, but not alone as they
Who shut in chambers think it loneliness;
The silent ocean, and the starlight bay,
The twilight glow, which momently grew less,
The voiceless sands, and dropping caves that lay
Around them, made them to each other press,
As if there were no life beneath the sky
Save theirs, and that their life could never die.

189

They feared no eyes nor ears on that lone beach,
They felt no terrors from the night,[140] they were
All in all to each other; though their speech
Was broken words, they *thought* a language there,
And all the burning tongues the passions teach
Found in one sigh the best interpreter
Of nature's oracle – first love, that all
Which Eve has left her daughters since her fall.

190

Haidee spoke not of scruples, asked no vows,
Nor offered any; she had never heard
Of plight and promises to be a spouse,
Or perils by a loving maid incurred;

Notes

[139] *concert* unison.

[140] *They felt no terrors from the night* A profane allusion to Psalm 91:5, where the godly are told: 'Thou shalt not be afraid for the terror by night.'

She was all which pure ignorance allows,
  And flew to her young mate like a young bird;
And, never having dreamt of falsehood, she
Had not one word to say of constancy.

191

She loved, and was beloved; she adored,
  And she was worshipped; after nature's fashion,
Their intense souls, into each other poured,
  If souls could die, had perished in that passion;
But by degrees their senses were restored,
  Again to be o'ercome, again to dash on;
And, beating 'gainst *his* bosom, Haidee's heart
Felt as if never more to beat apart.

192

Alas, they were so young, so beautiful,
  So lonely, loving, helpless, and the hour
Was that in which the heart is always full,
  And, having o'er itself no further power,
Prompts deeds eternity cannot annul,
  But pays off moments in an endless shower
Of hellfire – all prepared for people giving
Pleasure or pain to one another living.

193

Alas for Juan and Haidee! They were
  So loving and so lovely – till then never,
Excepting our first parents, such a pair
  Had run the risk of being damned for ever;
And Haidee, being devout as well as fair,
  Had doubtless heard about the Stygian river,[141]
And hell and purgatory – but forgot
Just in the very crisis she should not.

194

They look upon each other, and their eyes
  Gleam in the moonlight; and her white arm clasps
Round Juan's head, and his around hers lies
  Half-buried in the tresses which it grasps;
She sits upon his knee, and drinks his sighs,
  He hers, until they end in broken gasps;
And thus they form a group that's quite antique –
Half-naked, loving, natural, and Greek.

## Notes

[141] *the Stygian river* The River Styx circled Hades nine times; those seeking to enter Hades had to be ferried across it by Charon.

195

And when those deep and burning moments passed,
    And Juan sunk to sleep within her arms,
She slept not, but all tenderly, though fast,
    Sustained his head upon her bosom's charms;
And now and then her eye to heaven is cast,
    And then on the pale cheek her breast now warms,
Pillowed on her o'erflowing heart, which pants
With all it granted, and with all it grants.

196

An infant when it gazes on a light,
    A child the moment when it drains the breast,
A devotee when soars the Host[142] in sight,
    An Arab with a stranger for a guest,
A sailor when the prize has struck in fight,[143]
    A miser filling his most hoarded chest,
Feel rapture; but not such true joy are reaping
As they who watch o'er what they love while sleeping.

197

For there it lies so tranquil, so beloved,
    All that it hath of life with us is living;
So gentle, stirless, helpless, and unmoved,
    And all unconscious of the joy 'tis giving;
All it hath felt, inflicted, passed, and proved,
    Hushed into depths beyond the watcher's diving;
There lies the thing we love with all its errors
And all its charms, like death without its terrors.

198

The lady watched her lover, and that hour
    Of love's, and night's, and ocean's solitude
O'erflowed her soul with their united power;
    Amidst the barren sand and rocks so rude
She and her wave-worn love had made their bower
    Where nought upon their passion could intrude,
And all the stars that crowded the blue space
Saw nothing happier than her glowing face.

199

Alas, the love of women! It is known
    To be a lovely and a fearful thing;
For all of theirs upon that die[144] is thrown,
    And if 'tis lost, life hath no more to bring

## Notes

[142] *Host* eucharistic wafer. The word 'soars' is distinctly comic.

[143] *when the prize has struck in fight* i.e. when the prize-ship (being attacked) has surrendered ('struck'). At this point it and its contents became booty, to be divided among the crew.

[144] *die* dice.

To them but mockeries of the past alone,
  And their revenge is as the tiger's spring,
Deadly, and quick, and crushing; yet as real
Torture is theirs – what they inflict they feel.

200

They are right; for man, to man so oft unjust,
  Is always so to women; one sole bond
Awaits them, treachery is all their trust;
  Taught to conceal, their bursting hearts despond
Over their idol, till some wealthier lust
  Buys them in marriage – and what rests beyond?
A thankless husband, next a faithless lover,
Then dressing, nursing, praying, and all's over.

201

Some take a lover, some take drams[145] or prayers,
  Some mind their household, others dissipation,
Some run away and but exchange their cares,
  Losing the advantage of a virtuous station;
Few changes e'er can better their affairs,
  Theirs being an unnatural situation
From the dull palace to the dirty hovel:
Some play the devil, and then write a novel.[146]

202

Haidee was Nature's bride, and knew not this;[147]
  Haidee was Passion's child, born where the sun
Showers triple light, and scorches even the kiss
  Of his gazelle-eyed daughters; she was one
Made but to love, to feel that she was his
  Who was her chosen: what was said or done
Elsewhere was nothing – she had nought to fear,
Hope, care, nor love beyond, her heart beat *here*.

203

And oh, that quickening of the heart, that beat!
  How much it costs us! Yet each rising throb
Is in its cause as its effect so sweet,
  That Wisdom, ever on the watch to rob
Joy of its alchemy,[148] and to repeat
  Fine truths, even Conscience, too, has a tough job
To make us understand each good old maxim,
So good – I wonder Castlereagh don't tax 'em.

## Notes

[145] *drams* A dram is a measure – in this case, of alcohol.

[146] *Some play the devil, and then write a novel* Lady Caroline Lamb, unceremoniously dumped by Byron after an affair of several months in 1812, took her revenge by fictionalizing their relationship in *Glenarvon* (1816).

[147] *this* i.e. the sufferings of the woman of the world, related in the previous three stanzas.

[148] *alchemy* magic.

204

And now 'twas done – on the lone shore were plighted
Their hearts; the stars, their nuptial torches, shed
Beauty upon the beautiful they lighted;
Ocean their witness, and the cave their bed,
By their own feelings hallowed and united,
Their priest was Solitude, and they were wed:
And they were happy, for to their young eyes
Each was an angel, and earth paradise.

205

Oh love, of whom great Caesar was the suitor,
Titus the master, Antony the slave,[149]
Horace, Catullus scholars, Ovid tutor,[150]
Sappho the sage bluestocking, in whose grave
All those may leap who rather would be neuter
(Leucadia's rock still overlooks the wave);[151]
Oh love, thou art the very god of evil –
For, after all, we cannot call thee devil.

206

Thou mak'st the chaste connubial[152] state precarious,
And jestest with the brows of mightiest men:
Caesar and Pompey, Mahomet, Belisarius,[153]
Have much employed the muse of history's pen;
Their lives and fortunes were extremely various,
Such worthies Time will never see again;
Yet to these four in three things the same luck holds –
They all were heroes, conquerors, and cuckolds.

207

Thou mak'st philosophers; there's Epicurus
And Aristippus,[154] a material crew!
Who to immoral courses would allure us
By theories quite practicable too;
If only from the devil they would insure us,
How pleasant were the maxim (not quite new),
'Eat, drink, and love, what can the rest avail us?' –
So said the royal sage Sardanapalus.[155]

## Notes

[149] Julius Caesar was Cleopatra's suitor; Mark Antony was her slave. Titus 'mastered' his love of Berenice and sent her away.

[150] Horace, Catullus and Ovid wrote about love. Ovid's *Ars Amatoria* is a textbook of lovemaking.

[151] Sappho was said to have thrown herself off the Leucadian rock into the sea when her love for Phaon was unrequited.

[152] *connubial* married.

[153] *Caesar and Pompey, Mahomet, Belisarius* Famous cuckolds: Caesar was cuckolded by his first wife, Pompeia; Pompey by his wife Mucia (who 'played the wanton' with Caesar); Mahomet by his wife Ayesha; and Belisarius (famous Byzantine general) by his wife Antonina (who seduced their adopted son).

[154] Aristippus (*c.*370 BCE) founded a hedonistic philosophy that offered pleasure as the goal of life; he lived luxuriously. Epicurus (342–270 BCE) said that happiness was the aim of life, achieved through virtuous living. Epicureanism was quickly devalued and became associated with sensual pleasures.

[155] Sardanapalus was an Assyrian of uncertain historical origin and character, renowned for being effeminate, slothful, and immersed in luxury and debauchery. He was the subject of a tragedy written by Byron in 1821.

208

But Juan! Had he quite forgotten Julia?
  And should he have forgotten her so soon?
I can't but say it seems to me most truly a
  Perplexing question; but, no doubt, the moon
Does these things for us, and whenever newly a
  Strong palpitation rises, 'tis her boon;
Else how the devil is it that fresh features
Have such a charm for us poor human creatures?

209

I hate inconstancy – I loathe, detest,
  Abhor, condemn, abjure the mortal made
Of such quicksilver[156] clay that in his breast
  No permanent foundation can be laid;
Love, constant love, has been my constant guest,
  And yet last night, being at a masquerade,
I saw the prettiest creature, fresh from Milan,
Which gave me some sensations like a villain.

210

But soon Philosophy came to my aid
  And whispered, 'Think of every sacred tie!'
'I will, my dear Philosophy!' I said,
  'But then her teeth, and then, oh heaven, her eye!
I'll just enquire if she be wife or maid,
  Or neither, out of curiosity.'
'Stop!' cried Philosophy, with air so Grecian
(Though she was masked then as a fair Venetian).

211

'Stop!' So I stopped. But to return: that which
  Men call inconstancy is nothing more
Than admiration due where nature's rich
  Profusion with young beauty covers o'er
Some favoured object; and as in the niche
  A lovely statue we almost adore,
This sort of adoration of the real
Is but a heightening of the *beau-ideal*.[157]

212

'Tis the perception of the beautiful,
  A fine extension of the faculties,

Notes

[156] *quicksilver* fast-changing.

[157] *beau-ideal* ideal beauty. Byron's argument (deliberately specious) is that admiration of a beautiful woman is no different from that of a beautiful work of art.

Platonic, universal, wonderful,
Drawn from the stars, and filtered through the skies,
Without which life would be extremely dull;
In short, it is the use of our own eyes,
With one or two small senses added, just
To hint that flesh is formed of fiery dust.

213

Yet 'tis a painful feeling, and unwilling,
For surely if we always could perceive
In the same object graces quite as killing[158]
As when she rose upon us like an Eve,
'Twould save us many a heartache, many a shilling[159]
(For we must get them anyhow, or grieve),
Whereas if one sole lady pleased for ever,
How pleasant for the heart, as well as liver![160]

214

The heart is like the sky, a part of heaven,
But changes night and day too, like the sky;
Now o'er it clouds and thunder must be driven,
And darkness and destruction as on high:
But when it hath been scorched, and pierced, and riven,
Its storms expire in water-drops; the eye
Pours forth at last the heart's-blood turned to tears,
Which make the English climate of our years.

215

The liver is the lazaret[161] of bile,[162]
But very rarely executes its function,
For the first passion stays there such a while,
That all the rest creep in and form a junction
Like knots of vipers on a dunghill's soil –
Rage, fear, hate, jealousy, revenge, compunction –
So that all mischiefs spring up from this entrail[163]
Like earthquakes from the hidden fire called 'central'.

216

In the meantime, without proceeding more
In this anatomy, I've finished now
Two hundred and odd stanzas as before,
That being about the number I'll allow

## Notes

[158] *killing* overpoweringly beautiful.

[159] *many a shilling* A typically Byronic twist, reducing everything to material terms. His point is that if he had loved only one woman, he would have saved the money he has spent on the many he has known in his life.

[160] *liver* seat of intense passion.

[161] *lazaret* lazaretto, hospital.

[162] *bile* intense passion, anger.

[163] *entrail* organ (i.e. the liver).

Each canto of the twelve, or twenty-four;
    And laying down my pen, I make my bow,
Leaving Don Juan and Haidee to plead
For them and theirs with all who deign to read.

## *Letter from Lord Byron to Douglas Kinnaird, 26 October 1819* (extract)

As to *Don Juan*, confess – confess, you dog (and be candid), that it is the sublime of *that there* sort of writing. It may be bawdy, but is it not good English? It may be profligate, but is it not *life*, is it not *the thing*? Could any man have written it who has not lived in the world? – and tooled in a post-chaise? In a hackney coach? In a gondola? Against a wall? In a court carriage? In a vis-à-vis?[1] On a table – and under it? I have written about a hundred stanzas of a third Canto, but it is damned modest – the outcry has frightened me.[2] I had such projects for the Don, but the *cant* is so much stronger than *cunt* nowadays, that the benefit of experience in a man who had well weighed the worth of both monosyllables must be lost to despairing posterity.[3]

## *Messalonghi, 22 January 1824. On This Day I Complete My Thirty-Sixth Year* (first published 1824)

1

'Tis time this heart should be unmoved,
    Since others it hath ceased to move;
Yet though I cannot be beloved,
        Still let me love.

2

My days are in the yellow leaf,
    The flowers and fruits of love are gone,
The worm, the canker and the grief
        Are mine alone.

3

The fire that on my bosom preys
    Is lone as some volcanic isle,
No torch is kindled at its blaze –
        A funeral pile!

## Notes

Letter from Lord Byron to Douglas Kinnaird

[1] *vis-à-vis* a light carriage for two people sitting face to face.

[2] *Don Juan* I–II was strongly attacked for 'degrading debauchery' and 'shameless indecency'.

[3] All the same, *Don Juan* III–V was published in August 1821.

4
The hope, the fear, the jealous care,
  The exalted portion of the pain,
And power of love I cannot share
    But wear the chain.

5
But 'tis not thus, and 'tis not here
  Such thoughts should shake my soul, nor now
Where glory decks the hero's bier
    Or binds his brow.

6
The sword, the banner, and the field,
  Glory and Greece about us see –
The Spartan borne upon his shield[1]
    Was not more free!

7
Awake (not Greece – she *is* awake),[2]
  Awake my spirit – think through whom
Thy life-blood tracks its parent lake
    And then strike home!

8
Tread those reviving passions down,
  Unworthy manhood; unto thee
Indifferent should the smile or frown
    Of beauty be.

9
If thou regret'st thy youth, why live?
  The land of honourable death
Is here: up to the field, and give
    Away thy breath!

10
Seek out (less often sought than found)
  A soldier's grave, for thee the best,
Then look around and choose thy ground
    And take thy rest.

## Notes

MESSALONGHI, 22 JANUARY 1824

[1] 'The slain were borne upon their shields' (Byron's MS note).

[2] The Greeks were waging a war of Independence against the Turks (see headnote).

# Percy Bysshe Shelley (1792–1822)

According to Hazlitt, Percy Bysshe Shelley

> has a fire in his eye, a fever in his blood, a maggot in his brain, a hectic flutter in his speech, which mark out the philosophic fanatic. He is sanguine complexioned, and shrill-voiced. ... He is clogged by no dull system of realities, no earth-bound feelings, no rooted prejudices, by nothing that belongs to the mighty trunk and hard husk of nature and habit, but is drawn up by irresistible levity to the regions of mere speculation and fancy, to the sphere of air and fire, where his delighted spirit floats in 'seas of pearl and clouds of amber'.

Some of Shelley's friends thought this crossed the line between praise and abuse, and reproached Hazlitt for having published it. But it still catches Shelley's strange combination of the visionary, the proselytizing and the hare-brained.

He was born on 4 August 1792 at Field Place, near Horsham in Sussex, the eldest child and only son of a baronet and Whig Member of Parliament. After two years at Syon House Academy in London, where he met his lifelong friend Thomas Medwin, he went up to Eton College, where he received a thorough grounding in the classics, became interested in science and radical politics, and wrote two Gothic novels – *Zastrozzi* and *St Irvyne* (both published 1810).

Such promise was expected to blossom at University College, Oxford, where he matriculated in October 1810 – and, in a sense, it did. His formal education came to an abrupt halt when he was expelled in March 1811 for refusing to answer questions concerning a pamphlet, *The Necessity of Atheism*, which he had written with his friend, Thomas Jefferson Hogg. It argued that God's existence could be proved only by reference to the senses, reason, and testimony of others: 'Truth has always been found to promote the best interests of mankind. Every reflecting mind must allow that there is no proof of the existence of a Deity. Q.E.D.' A contemporary who witnessed their sending down, recorded: 'The aforesaid two had made themselves as conspicuous as possible by great singularity of dress, and by walking up and down the centre of the quadrangle, as if proud of their anticipated fate. I believe no one regretted their departure, for there are but few, if any, who are not afraid of Shelley's strange and fantastic pranks, and the still stranger opinions he was known to entertain.'

Shelley's father, Sir Timothy, was horrified, not least by the looming possibility of legal action for blasphemous libel. He began communicating with his son through his solicitor in order 'to guard my character and honour in case of any prosecutions in the courts'. Shelley reacted by requesting that he be disinherited – the first step in the process of self-exile that overshadowed the rest of his life.

In the meantime he became involved with the 16-year-old Harriet Westbrook, daughter of a retired merchant and coffee-house proprietor, with whom in August 1811 he eloped to Edinburgh, where they married before settling in Keswick in the Lake District. Shelley hoped to meet Wordsworth and Coleridge there but instead met Southey. Southey was 37, Shelley 19. They got on well, Shelley going so far as to describe the older poet as 'an advocate of liberty and equality', a deist and 'a great man'. After one of their conversations, he noted that 'Southey says I am not an atheist but a pantheist'. But he became disillusioned with Southey when he realized he was a flat-out Tory. Shelley's time in Keswick culminated with an attempted house-breaking and robbery in which he was physically attacked.

In February 1812 he and Harriet sailed to Ireland, where he wanted to start a revolution. On arrival in Dublin he published and distributed his *Address to the Irish People*, arguing for Catholic emancipation and repeal of the Act of Union. He instructed his servant to give out copies at public houses, while he threw others into passing carriages and open windows, or gave them to beggars, drunks and prostitutes. 'Are you slaves, or are you men?' the pamphlet asked its readers, 'a real man is free.'

Invited to speak at the Fishamble Street Theatre by the Catholic Committee, Shelley came to the attention of Home Office spies. But the most important thing Shelley was to learn from his visit to Ireland was that revolution was unlikely to come from the oppressed majority. 'The poor of Dublin are assuredly the meanest and most miserable of all', he told the philosopher William Godwin, 'In their narrow streets thousands seem huddled together – one mass of animated filth! ... These were the persons to whom in my fancy I had addressed myself.'

By now Godwin was his hero. Godwin's philosophy, first articulated in *Political Justice* (1793), envisaged a society governed by reason. Human property and corrupt institutions such as 'government' and 'marriage' would wither away, leaving human beings free to do as they pleased, governed only by innate rationality. Such theories had an undeniable attraction for young radicals (in the early 1790s Wordsworth had been drawn to them) and by the time he arrived in Ireland Shelley was in correspondence with Godwin.

After returning to Wales in April, Shelley moved from one place to the next until settling in Lynmouth in Devon, where he founded a sort of commune consisting of females – Harriet, her sister Eliza and his friend Elizabeth Hitchener. He extended an invitation to Fanny Imlay (Mary Wollstonecraft's daughter by the traveller Gilbert Imlay), but her stepfather, William Godwin, wisely forbade it. In Lynmouth Shelley distributed revolutionary propaganda, putting messages in bottles and floating them out to sea, or sending them up in miniature hot-air balloons. This led the Home Office, under Viscount Sidmouth, to step up surveillance of him, thinking he was a French spy; on 19 August, his servant was caught pasting 'subversive' handbills on walls in Barnstaple and was arrested. It was time for Shelley to move on.

After a visit to London in early October 1812, where Shelley finally met the 56-year-old William Godwin, he settled at Tremadoc in Wales, where he continued to distribute revolutionary propaganda. There, on 26 February 1813, he was assaulted late in the evening by an 'assassin'. Shots were fired. A henchman returned early in the morning and a further skirmish took place. Though Shelley survived both attacks, the experience changed him: from now on he would no longer be an activist for revolution – instead, he would be a mouthpiece for it.

Back in London, Shelley published his first major poem, 'Queen Mab' (1813), which denounced the monarchy while putting the case for free love: 'Love is free: to promise for ever to love the same woman is not less absurd than to promise to believe the same creed: such a vow in both cases excludes us from all enquiry.' Perhaps not surprisingly, relations with Harriet were deteriorating, and Shelley separated from her in April 1814. 'I felt as if a dead and living body had been linked together in loathsome and horrible communion', he later told Hogg.

He met the 16-year-old Mary Godwin in May or June 1814, subsequently arranging clandestine meetings with her and her step-sister Jane at Mary Wollstonecraft's grave in St Pancras churchyard. 'I am thine, exclusively thine', Mary wrote in a copy of 'Queen Mab', 'I have pledged myself to thee and sacred is the gift.' When Godwin found out he banned further meetings. Shelley threatened suicide, brandishing a small pistol and a bottle of laudanum. 'His eyes were bloodshot, his hair and dress disordered', recalled his friend Thomas Love Peacock. 'He caught up a bottle of laudanum, and said: "I never part from this."'

On 28 July he eloped with Mary and Jane to the Continent. Typically, he wrote to Harriet from France, inviting her to join them in Switzerland. She didn't – and, after a whirlwind tour of France, Switzerland and Germany, a shortage of funds compelled the runaways to return to England in September.

On their return the ménage à trois settled in St Pancras, close to what is now Euston Road in central London, where they set off fireworks in the fields, discussed a further Irish trip and devised a plan to kidnap Shelley's two younger sisters from their school in Hackney. In the following months Jane changed her name to Claire (thus becoming Claire Clairmont), and Wordsworth's 'The Excursion' was published. Wordsworth was one of Shelley's favourite poets, but though Shelley continued to admire his spiritual aspirations, it was clear from this latest publication, dedicated to the Tory Lord Lowther, that he had abandoned his earlier radicalism. 'He is a slave', Mary wrote in her journal on 14 September 1814, adding that they were 'much disappointed' with 'The Excursion'. Shelley may not have composed his sonnet 'To Wordsworth' as early as this, but it marks the point at which he grew disillusioned with the Lake Poets generally.

In August 1815, after giving birth to a premature baby who died soon after, Mary moved with Shelley to Bishopsgate, Old Windsor. Shelley's first major poem, 'Alastor', was composed there after a lengthy expedition up the Thames, and the river is a constant presence in the poem. It seems to be driving him on, just as the Poet is driven by the spirit of solitude which Shelley thought dangerously self-involving, leading the Poet to his death. That visionary spirit, conjured up by the Poet from within, compels him to reject the Arab maiden and instead to feast on her visionary counterpart, the 'veiled maid' who dances through his dreams. Shelley's preoccupation with the Poet's unhealthy state of mind derives partly from his reading of Wordsworth's 'Lines Left upon a Seat in a Yew-Tree', also in blank verse.

Publication of 'Alastor' coincided roughly with the birth of a second child, William, in January 1816. Shortly after, Claire Clairmont had an affair with Byron in April and, pregnant by him, joined Percy and Mary for a second foray to the Continent in the summer. Journeying through Switzerland, Shelley amused himself by writing the word 'atheist' after his name in at least four hotel registers, thus fuelling the self-righteous outrage of such tourists as Southey, who would go home with unsavoury tales about Shelley and Byron's 'league of incest' with Mary and her stepsister.

Southey was right about one thing. Shelley's attitude to God was more complex than the word 'atheist' suggests. It is hardly surprising that the concept appealed to someone opposed to an established church implicated in the social and political oppression by which England was blighted. On the other hand, he was tremendously attracted to the pantheism of Wordsworth's 'Tintern Abbey':

> A motion and a spirit that impels
> All thinking things, all objects of all thought,
> And rolls through all things.
>
> ('Tintern Abbey' 101–3)

Rather than reject the concept of a deity, Shelley argues for existence of a 'Power' similar to Wordsworth's motion and spirit – at times identified with the tyrannical Jupiter in 'Prometheus Unbound', at others, closer to Demogorgon. Writing approvingly of Leigh Hunt's spiritual beliefs in 1811, Shelley noted his conviction in a God 'by no means perfect, but composed of good and evil like man'. From time to time this is what Shelley thought, but he could also contemplate the possibility of a universe without a creator. If any phrase were to encapsulate his position, it might be 'awful doubt' – awe for the natural world, mixed with scepticism as to existence of a divinity in the Christian sense.

Shelley met Byron for the first time on the jetty of l'Hôtel d'Angleterre on the shore of Lake Geneva, 27 May 1816. That momentous encounter marked the beginning of a summer of genius, reminiscent of the annus mirabilis of 1797–8, when William and Dorothy Wordsworth and Coleridge enjoyed a year of intellectual and creative collaboration. During its course, Shelley remained an enthusiastic, if critical, reader of Wordsworth, devouring his collected *Poems* of 1815, especially 'Tintern Abbey' and the 'Ode'. Byron later told Thomas Medwin that Shelley 'used to dose me with Wordsworth physic even to nausea'. As a result, Byron composed most of 'Childe Harold's Pilgrimage' Canto III, affecting (with varying success) a Wordsworthian enthusiasm for nature, and would go on, towards the end of the summer, to write 'Manfred', which also shows Wordsworth's influence.

As for Shelley, he composed two of his most important shorter poems in response to 'Tintern Abbey' – 'Mont Blanc' and the 'Hymn to Intellectual Beauty'. He liked Wordsworth's refusal to subscribe to conventional notions of the deity: the 'sense sublime / Of something far more deeply interfused' flows straight into his poetry. 'Mont Blanc' may be Shelley's masterpiece. It is an attempt to explain the function of poetry, where it comes from, and how it relates to the cosmos. It questions not just his vocation, but his entire belief-system. Its argument is that the poet is inspired by the same forces that produced the precipitous, violent landscape before him; they move him to speak ultimate truths capable of repealing 'Large codes of fraud and woe' – the injustices of governments such as those which had recently defeated Napoleon at Waterloo.

The weather was disappointingly wet, and the skies very dark, due to climate change triggered by the release into the atmosphere of volcanic ash from Mount Tambora the previous year. As a result, Byron and the Shelleys were often confined indoors. In order to pass the time, they read ghost stories, having obtained J.B.B. Eyriès's *Fantasmagoriana* (1812). In the evenings they shared these tales with Byron at his lodging, the villa Diodati, giving him the idea they should all try their hand at writing one. Shelley attempted one based on his childhood experience; Byron's personal physician, Dr Polidori, proposed a story about a lady punished for looking through a keyhole; and Mary Godwin would write *Frankenstein*.

Cooped up together, these highly intelligent young people developed relationships of unusual intensity. They were sitting in the long room at Diodati on 18 June when Byron recited Coleridge's description of Geraldine from 'Christabel' (recently published by John Murray at Byron's insistence): 'Behold! her bosom and half her side – Hideous, deformed, and pale of hue.' Shelley screamed in horror, put his hands to his head, and ran out of the room with a candle. He later said that the sight of Mary put him in mind of a woman 'who had eyes instead of nipples, which taking hold of his mind, horrified him'.

Four days later, Shelley and Byron set out on a boating expedition across Lake Leman, heading eastwards towards Evian. They visited places associated with Rousseau and Gibbon, freethinkers they admired, as Byron mentions in 'Childe Harold's Pilgrimage' Canto III, on which he was then working. They were nearly drowned when caught in a squall off the rocks of St Gingoux; by contrast with Byron, Shelley could not swim and remained in the boat until they were safe.

The summer with Byron came to an end and, having agreed to meet him again in Italy, Shelley returned to London with Mary and Claire. There followed two suicides – first that of Mary's half-sister Fanny Imlay, who may have recently discovered her parents had not been married (in those days a cause of disgrace), followed by that of Shelley's wife Harriet in November. Believing they would be able to assume custody of his two children by her, Shelley married Mary Godwin on 30 December. Much to his distress, it made no difference. Harriet's family disputed his suitability as a parent on the grounds of his being a revolutionary and an atheist, and the children were farmed out to foster-parents. The outcome was disastrous for Shelley, who would never again see his children by Harriet.

At this period Shelley and Mary socialized with other writers in London, particularly Leigh Hunt, Hazlitt, Haydon, Keats, and Charles and Mary Lamb. Meeting Shelley in January 1817, Haydon recorded that

> he could not bear the inhumanity of Wordsworth in talking about the beauty of the shining trout as they lay after being caught, that he had such a horror of torturing animals it was impossible to express it. Ah, thought I, you have more horror at putting a hook into a fish's mouth than giving a pang to a mother's bosom. He had seduced Mary Wollstonecraft's daughter and enticed away Mrs Godwin's own daughter, to her great misery.

Keats was wary of him too, and declined an invitation to visit him. With the failure of his longest and most ambitious poem to date, 'The Revolt of Islam', Shelley decided to travel to Italy. Passing through London, he engaged in a last sonnet-writing competition with Keats and Leigh Hunt, and, after a visit to the British Museum with the stockbroker poet Horace Smith, wrote 'Ozymandias'.

In March 1818 he set out across the Continent with Mary, William, Clara (their son and daughter), Claire, Allegra (Claire's daughter by Byron), their Swiss maid Elise and Milly Shields, their servant-girl from Marlow. Theirs was a nomadic life, travelling from Milan to Livorno, Venice, Rome, Naples, Livorno again, Florence and Pisa. Shelley was reunited with Byron in Venice in August 1818, where he was treated to a recitation of 'Childe Harold' Canto IV. Just over a month later he was seriously ill with dysentery and his daughter Clara died, partly through his own negligence. 'Stanzas Written in Dejection, near Naples' and 'Lines Written among the Euganean Hills' speak of his mood at the time.

They arrived in Rome on 5 March 1819 and took rooms on the Corso. Each day Shelley visited the Baths of Caracalla, ruins that in their heyday housed 1,500 people, and continued work on 'Prometheus Unbound', begun in Venice the previous year. It was finished in Rome in early April. (Joseph Severn's painting of Shelley writing at the Baths, now at the Keats–Shelley Memorial House in Rome, is an icon of the period.)

By now he was a controversial and despised figure among the English, and one day at the Post Office in Rome a man, hearing his name, approached him exclaiming, 'What, are you that damned atheist Shelley?' before striking him to the ground, for no reason other than his political reputation. In June the Shelleys prepared to head northwards to Livorno, but before their departure their beloved son William, 4 years old, died. He was buried in the Protestant Cemetery where, two years later, he was joined by Keats.

Shelley had been travelling for a year in Italy when a political event in England provoked a burst of intense creative activity. On 16 August 1819, at St Peter's Field, on the outskirts of Manchester, 60,000 working men and women met to listen to the orator Henry Hunt declare the need for universal suffrage, liberty and political rights; all came from a region of fifty miles' radius in orderly groups. The response of the local magistrates was to send in the Manchester and Salford yeomanry to arrest Hunt as he addressed the crowd. As they did so, they knocked down a woman and trampled her child to death. When the crowd surged, mounted hussars charged, sabres drawn. There was mass panic as people ran in all directions. In what became known as the Peterloo Massacre, eleven people were killed and over four hundred seriously injured, including over a hundred women and children, either wounded by sabres or trampled by horses. For decades, the atrocity was symbolic of everything unjust in British government. Lord Sidmouth, Lord Liverpool (the Prime Minister) and the Prince Regent publicly endorsed the action. The news reached Shelley within the week. A fortnight later he told his publisher, Charles Ollier, that 'the torrent of my indignation has not yet done boiling in my veins. I wait anxiously to hear how the country will express its sense of this bloody murderous oppression of its destroyers'.

Within twelve days he had composed the greatest poem of political protest in the language. 'The Mask of Anarchy' begins as satire, depicting the ministers of Lord Liverpool's government riding the horses which trample the crowd; then, from stanzas 34 to 63, a maid who has risen up to halt Anarchy (the idol of both the government and the people) addresses the crowd, telling them of false freedom and then of true freedom; and in the concluding section she tells them to stand up for their rights using passive, non-violent demonstration:

> Rise like lions after slumber
> In unvanquishable number;
> Shake your chains to earth like dew
> Which in sleep had fallen on you –
> Ye are many, they are few.
>
> (ll. 368–72)

The poem warns against Anarchy – it recognizes the appetite of the people for revenge, but warns them that were they to take it, the government would use it as the excuse for even more violent suppression.

Shelley sent the poem to Leigh Hunt for inclusion in *The Examiner* but, after much thought, Hunt chose not to publish. Instead he held on to it until 1832, well after Shelley's death, when he brought it out to coincide with the passing of the first Parliamentary Reform Bill. Had it been published in 1819, it could have made Shelley's name: the poem was designed for mass consumption, and would have had immediate impact. But it would also have led to Hunt's imprisonment for sedition, there being over seventy-five such prosecutions that year – and Hunt had no wish to return to prison (where he had been sent for libelling the Prince Regent in 1813). He was also less radical in his views than Shelley, and genuinely thought this a bad time to inflame the populace.

This was bad luck for Shelley, and typical of the fate of his best writing during his lifetime. Absence from England meant he was unlikely to get his work into print in the form he wished, if at all. He could not speak to publishers to argue his case, and on the rare occasions when it was published, it was ridiculed and attacked, often for political reasons. Shortly after completing 'The Mask of Anarchy' he happened to read a review of 'The Revolt of Islam' (1818) in the Tory *Quarterly Review*, which characterized him as someone who 'would overthrow the constitution ... he would pull down our churches, level our Establishment, and burn our bibles ... marriage he cannot endure.' It went on to attack him on personal grounds, preserving its worst mockery for his poem.

This kind of criticism must have hurt, but it further clarified his response to the Peterloo Massacre. He began to understand better his poetical aims and ambitions, and in order to articulate that renewed sense of purpose he composed 'Ode to the West Wind' (in *terza rima*) around 25 October 1819. Like the 'Mask', it is a statement of faith in the ability of human beings to resist the oppression of church and state, and realize their power of self-determination; thus, the 'Pestilence-stricken multitudes' are bidden to participate in the millennial vision of 'a new birth'. But the poem goes further than that. It insists on the primacy of the poet as the central agency, the saviour-like prophet, 'tameless, and swift, and proud', who will awaken the masses to their potential: 'Drive my dead thoughts over the universe / Like withered leaves to quicken a new birth!' (ll. 63–4).

In the essay 'On Love' he observed, 'I have found my language misunderstood like one in a distant and savage land', and in a letter of April 1819 he expressed his cynicism as to the reviewers' opinion of a collection of poems he had written, *Rosalind and Helen* (1819): 'As to the reviews, I suppose there is nothing but abuse.' It is moving to consider that a poet who during his lifetime was compelled to accept failure should have continued to believe in the power of his words to change the world for the better. What he could not know was that, for decades after his death, working-class people across the world would take inspiration from his poems in the struggle for their rights.

Mary Shelley's fourth child was born in November 1819 – Percy Florence (named after the city of his birth) was the only one that would survive. This was a period of remarkable artistic productivity for Shelley, and besides much else he composed 'England in 1819', a sonnet that glances back at the events of the past autumn. In a spirit of resignation, he sent it to Leigh Hunt for *The Examiner*, adding wisely, 'I do not expect you to publish it, but you may show it to whom you please'. Hunt decided not to publish.

The Shelleys moved to Pisa where, *c.*20 January 1821, he read an article by his old friend Thomas Love Peacock entitled 'The Four Ages of Poetry', in the first issue of Ollier's *Literary Miscellany*, arguing that English poetry was in terminal decline. To Shelley this was an attack on everything he stood for. It was impossible for him not to respond. The result was his *Defence of Poetry*, of which extracts are presented here, an amplification of the ideas found elsewhere in his writing. At its heart is a belief that the poet, a participant in 'the eternal, the infinite, and the one' – that is to say, a kind of priest or prophet – is the mouthpiece for cosmic, moral and political truths. It is Shelley's most important prose utterance, and was sent to Ollier for the next issue of his *Literary Miscellany*; it was not published.

In April 1821 Shelley heard of Keats's death. They had met at Hunt's in 1817, and he had become an admirer of his work, particularly 'Hyperion'. During his frequent boating expeditions Shelley devised a poem on Keats's death entitled 'Adonais'. Its starting-point was the belief that a 'savage criticism' of 'Endymion' in the *Quarterly Review* had exacerbated Keats's incipient tuberculosis, contracted while nursing his brother Tom. This had not been so, but Shelley became convinced of it. It turned Keats into yet another version of the prophet in the wilderness, which was how he saw himself. 'Adonais' is the occasion for some of the most persuasive Neoplatonic poetry Shelley was to compose:

He is made one with Nature: there is heard
His voice in all her music, from the moan
Of thunder, to the song of night's sweet bird;
He is a presence to be felt and known
In darkness and in light, from herb and stone,
Spreading itself where'er that Power may move
Which has withdrawn his being to its own,
Which wields the world with never-wearied love,
Sustains it from beneath, and kindles it above.
(ll. 370–8)

This is akin to the pantheist passages in 'Tintern Abbey'; both poems speak of the indefinable 'presence' that transcends the limitations of the human condition, coexistent with a universal consciousness that runs through nature. Shelley saw Keats as absorbed into that larger entity, just as the nameless woman of Wordsworth's 'A Slumber Did My Spirit Seal' was incorporated into the 'earth's diurnal course / With rocks and stones and trees!'

By now, strains had begun to sour Mary and Percy's marriage, due partly to mutual despondency at their children's deaths, and partly to an unfounded allegation that Claire had given birth to Shelley's child. In a letter of March 1820 Shelley complained that 'Mary considers me a portion of herself, and feels no more remorse in torturing me than in torturing her own mind. Could she suddenly know a person in every way my equal, and hold close and perpetual communion with him, as a distinct being from herself, as a friend instead of a husband, she would obtain empire over herself that she might not make him miserable.' There would be scant respite from these tensions during their last years together. In fact, the arrival in Pisa of Edward and Jane Williams brought another woman into Shelley's life. According to Mary, Jane 'has a very pretty voice, and a taste and ear for music which is almost miraculous. The harp is her favourite instrument; but we have none, and a very bad piano.'

Little wonder, then, that Shelley should have given Jane a guitar, enclosing the fair copy of 'With a Guitar, To Jane' – as naked a love poem as he ever wrote. The Shelleys moved to San Terenzo near Lerici in April 1822, where he received his boat, the *Ariel*, on 22 May. He sailed to Livorno with Edward Williams, but on the way back a storm blew up and the boat went down under full sail. Ten days later his body was washed up along the beach between Massa and Viareggio, the flesh of his arms and face entirely eaten away. It was identified by the copy of Keats's poems in his jacket pocket, and burnt on the beach in Byron's presence.

## *To Wordsworth* (composed probably September–October 1815)[1]

Poet of nature, thou hast wept to know
That things depart which never may return;
Childhood and youth, friendship and love's first glow
Have fled like sweet dreams,[2] leaving thee to mourn.
These common woes I feel. One loss is mine
Which thou too feel'st, yet I alone deplore.[3]
Thou wert as a lone star,[4] whose light did shine
On some frail bark in winter's midnight roar;
Thou hast like to a rock-built refuge stood
Above the blind and battling multitude;
In honoured poverty[5] thy voice did weave
Songs consecrate to truth and liberty –
Deserting these, thou leavest me to grieve,
Thus having been, that thou shouldst cease to be.

## *Alastor; or, The Spirit of Solitude* (composed 10 September and 14 December 1815)[1]

### *Preface*

The poem entitled 'Alastor' may be considered as allegorical of one of the most interesting situations of the human mind. It represents a youth[2] of uncorrupted feelings and adventurous genius led forth by an imagination inflamed and purified through familiarity with all that is

## Notes

To Wordsworth

[1] Shelley admired 'Tintern Abbey' and the 'Ode', but was disappointed by 'The Excursion' (1814), and despised Wordsworth for the conservatism of his middle age. He did not know 'The Prelude'.

[2] *Poet of nature ... dreams* a reference to Wordsworth's lament for the loss of his earlier intensity of vision in the 'Ode'.

[3] *deplore* lament.

[4] *Thou wert as a lone star* cf. Wordsworth's praise of Milton, 'London 1802' 9: 'Thy soul was like a star and dwelt apart.'

[5] *In honoured poverty* It cannot be said that Wordsworth was ever truly poor (although he and his siblings had known hard times after they were orphaned in 1783). Shelley is lamenting Wordsworth's acceptance of the job of Distributor for Stamps in Westmorland, which brought him a yearly salary of £400.

Alastor; or, The Spirit of Solitude

[1] Thomas Love Peacock recalled, in his *Memoirs of Shelley*: 'I proposed that [title] which he adopted: *Alastor; or, the Spirit of Solitude*. The Greek word *'Αλαϱστωρ* is an evil genius, A *κακοδαιϱμων*... The poem treated the spirit of solitude as a spirit of evil. I mention the true meaning of the word because many have supposed *Alastor* to be the name of the hero of the poem.'

[2] *a youth* not named in the poem, though obviously a version of Shelley himself.

excellent and majestic, to the contemplation of the universe. He drinks deep of the fountains of knowledge and is still insatiate. The magnificence and beauty of the external world sinks profoundly into the frame of his conceptions, and affords to their modifications a variety not to be exhausted. So long as it is possible for his desires to point towards objects thus infinite and unmeasured, he is joyous and tranquil and self-possessed. But the period arrives when these objects cease to suffice. His mind is at length suddenly awakened and thirsts for intercourse with an intelligence similar to itself. He images to himself the being whom he loves. Conversant with speculations of the sublimest and most perfect natures, the vision in which he embodies his own imaginations unites all of wonderful, or wise, or beautiful, which the poet, the philosopher, or the lover could depicture. The intellectual faculties, the imagination, the functions of sense, have their respective requisitions[3] on the sympathy of corresponding powers in other human beings. The poet is represented as uniting these requisitions, and attaching them to a single image. He seeks in vain for a prototype of his conception.[4] Blasted by his disappointment, he descends to an untimely grave.

The picture is not barren of instruction to actual men. The poet's self-centred seclusion was avenged by the furies of an irresistible passion pursuing him to speedy ruin. But that power which strikes the luminaries of the world with sudden darkness and extinction, by awakening them to too exquisite a perception of its influences, dooms to a slow and poisonous decay those meaner spirits that dare to abjure its dominion. Their destiny is more abject and inglorious as their delinquency is more contemptible and pernicious. They who, deluded by no generous error, instigated by no sacred thirst of doubtful knowledge, duped by no illustrious superstition, loving nothing on this earth, and cherishing no hopes beyond, yet keep aloof from sympathies with their kind, rejoicing neither in human joy nor mourning with human grief; these, and such as they, have their apportioned curse. They languish because none feel with them their common nature. They are morally dead. They are neither friends, nor lovers, nor fathers, nor citizens of the world, nor benefactors of their country. Among those who attempt to exist without human sympathy, the pure and tender-hearted perish through the intensity and passion of their search after its communities, when the vacancy of their spirit suddenly makes itself felt. All else,[5] selfish, blind, and torpid, are those unforeseeing multitudes who constitute, together with their own, the lasting misery and loneliness of the world. Those who love not their fellow-beings live unfruitful lives, and prepare for their old age a miserable grave.

The good die first,  
And those whose hearts are dry as summer dust,  
Burn to the socket![6]

14 December 1815

*Nondum amabam, et amare amabam, quaerebam quid amarem, amans amare.*[7]

Earth, ocean, air, beloved brotherhood!  
If our great mother[8] has imbued my soul  
With aught of natural piety[9] to feel

## Notes

[3] *requisitions* claims.

[4] *a prototype of his conception* An ideal embodiment of his imaginings. The essay 'On Love' refers to 'the ideal prototype of everything excellent or lovely that we are capable of conceiving as belonging to the nature of man'. See Shelley's letter to John Gisborne, 18 June 1822: 'I think one is always in love with something or other; the error (and I confess it is not easy for spirits cased in flesh and blood to avoid it) consists in seeking in a mortal image the likeness of what is perhaps eternal.'

[5] *All else* completely different.

[6] Shelley quoted these lines from Wordsworth, 'The Excursion' i 500–2, but they had originally been composed as 'Ruined Cottage' 96–8.

[7] 'I was not yet in love, and I loved to be in love, I sought what I might love, in love with loving'; St Augustine, *Confessions* III i.

[8] *our great mother* Cybele, goddess of the powers of nature.

[9] *natural piety* Wordsworth, 'The Rainbow' 8–9: 'And I could wish my days to be / Bound each to each by natural piety.'

Your love, and recompense the boon with mine;
If dewy morn, and odorous noon, and even,
With sunset and its gorgeous ministers,
And solemn midnight's tingling silentness;
If autumn's hollow sighs in the sere[10] wood,
And winter robing with pure snow and crowns
Of starry ice the grey grass and bare boughs;
If spring's voluptuous pantings when she breathes
Her first sweet kisses, have been dear to me;
If no bright bird, insect, or gentle beast
I consciously[11] have injured, but still loved
And cherished these my kindred – then forgive
This boast, beloved brethren, and withdraw
No portion of your wonted favour now.
Mother of this unfathomable world![12]
Favour my solemn song, for I have loved
Thee ever, and thee only; I have watched
Thy shadow and the darkness of thy steps,
And my heart ever gazes on the depth
Of thy deep mysteries. I have made my bed
In charnels[13] and on coffins, where black death
Keeps record of the trophies won from thee,
Hoping to still these obstinate questionings[14]
Of thee and thine, by forcing some lone ghost,
Thy messenger, to render up the tale
Of what we are.[15] In lone and silent hours,
When night makes a weird sound of its own stillness,
Like an inspired and desperate alchemist[16]
Staking his very life on some dark hope,
Have I mixed awful talk[17] and asking looks
With my most innocent love, until strange tears,
Uniting with those breathless kisses, made
Such magic as compels the charmed night
To render up thy charge – and though ne'er yet
Thou hast unveiled thy inmost sanctuary,
Enough from incommunicable dream,
And twilight phantasms, and deep noonday thought,
Has shone within me, that serenely now
And moveless, as a long-forgotten lyre[18]
Suspended in the solitary dome

## Notes

[10] *sere* dry, withered.

[11] *consciously* i.e. conscious of his culpability. Shelley used to go shooting, but became a vegetarian at the age of 19.

[12] *Mother of this unfathomable world* Nature, as well as Necessity; compare 'Queen Mab' vi 198: 'Necessity! Thou mother of the world!'

[13] *charnels* graveyards.

[14] *obstinate questionings* An allusion to Wordsworth, 'Ode' 144–5: 'those obstinate questionings / Of sense and outward things.'

[15] *I have made…what we are* Thomas Jefferson Hogg recalled that Shelley had, as a boy, frequented graveyards in the hope of meeting ghosts.

[16] *alchemist* Alchemists sought to turn base metals to gold – an impossibility.

[17] *awful talk* awe-inspired discussion.

[18] *a long-forgotten lyre* an Aeolian harp; with lines 42–9 compare Coleridge, 'Eolian Harp' 36–40.

Of some mysterious and deserted fane,[19]
I wait thy breath, Great Parent, that my strain
May modulate with murmurs of the air
And motions of the forests and the sea,
And voice of living beings, and woven hymns
Of night and day, and the deep heart of man.
 There was a poet whose untimely tomb
No human hands with pious reverence reared,
But the charmed eddies of autumnal winds
Built o'er his mouldering bones a pyramid
Of mouldering leaves in the waste wilderness;
A lovely youth – no mourning maiden decked
With weeping flowers or votive cypress[20] wreath
The lone couch of his everlasting sleep;
Gentle and brave and generous – no lorn[21] bard
Breathed o'er his dark fate one melodious sigh;
He lived, he died, he sung, in solitude.
Strangers have wept to hear his passionate notes,
And virgins, as unknown he passed, have pined
And wasted for fond love of his wild eyes.
The fire of those soft orbs has ceased to burn,
And silence, too enamoured of that voice,
Locks its mute music in her rugged cell.
 By solemn vision and bright silver dream
His infancy was nurtured;[22] every sight
And sound from the vast earth and ambient[23] air
Sent to his heart its choicest impulses.
The fountains of divine philosophy[24]
Fled not his thirsting lips, and all of great
Or good or lovely, which the sacred past
In truth or fable consecrates, he felt
And knew. When early youth had passed, he left
His cold fireside and alienated home[25]
To seek strange truths in undiscovered lands:
Many a wide waste and tangled wilderness
Has lured his fearless steps, and he has bought
With his sweet voice and eyes, from savage men,
His rest and food. Nature's most secret steps
He like her shadow has pursued, where'er
The red volcano overcanopies

## Notes

[19] *fane* temple.

[20] *cypress* symbol of death and mourning.

[21] *lorn* lonesome.

[22] *By solemn vision…nurtured* Shelley catches the tone of Wordsworth's account of the Wanderer's natural education in 'The Excursion', originally composed as 'The Pedlar' in 1798.

[23] *ambient* surrounding.

[24] *divine philosophy* cf. Milton, 'Comus' 475: 'How charming is divine philosophy!'

[25] *alienated home* Like Victor Frankenstein, the poet alienates his family. Shelley's relationship with his own father became strained during his undergraduate years and ended with a complete break in January 1812.

Its fields of snow and pinnacles of ice
With burning smoke, or where bitumen lakes[26]
On black bare pointed islets ever beat
With sluggish surge, or where the secret caves
Rugged and dark, winding among the springs
Of fire and poison, inaccessible
To avarice or pride, their starry domes
Of diamond and of gold expand above
Numberless and immeasurable halls,
Frequent[27] with crystal column, and clear shrines
Of pearl, and thrones radiant with chrysolite.[28]
Nor had that scene of ampler majesty
Than gems or gold, the varying roof of heaven
And the green earth lost in his heart its claims
To love and wonder; he would linger long
In lonesome vales, making the wild his home,
Until the doves and squirrels would partake
From his innocuous hand his bloodless food,[29]
Lured by the gentle meaning of his looks,
And the wild antelope that starts whene'er
The dry leaf rustles in the brake, suspend
Her timid steps to gaze upon a form
More graceful than her own.
                                        His wandering step,[30]
Obedient to high thoughts, has visited
The awful ruins of the days of old:
Athens, and Tyre, and Balbec,[31] and the waste
Where stood Jerusalem,[32] the fallen towers
Of Babylon,[33] the eternal pyramids,
Memphis and Thebes,[34] and whatsoe'er of strange
Sculptured on alabaster obelisk
Or jasper tomb, or mutilated sphinx,
Dark Ethiopia in her desert hills
Conceals. Among the ruined temples there,
Stupendous columns and wild images
Of more than man, where marble demons[35] watch
The Zodiac's brazen mystery[36] and dead men

## Notes

[26] *bitumen lakes* Lakes of mineral pitch, used in ancient times as mortar; cf. the 'lakes of bitumen' in Byron's Manfred I i 90.

[27] *Frequent* crowded.

[28] *chrysolite* olivine, a silicate of magnesia and iron found in lava. Its colour varies from pale yellowish-green (the precious stone) to dark bottle-green.

[29] *his bloodless food* Shelley was a vegetarian; see his 'Essay on the Vegetable System of Diet'.

[30] The poet's journey takes him back through human history to the birth of time (l. 128).

[31] *Tyre, and Balbec* ancient cities in the present-day Lebanon.

[32] Jerusalem was destroyed by the Emperor Titus in 70 CE; in 1867 it had a population of only 16,000.

[33] The ancient city of Babylon, home of the hanging gardens (one of the seven wonders of the ancient world), was in modern Iraq, south of Baghdad.

[34] *Memphis and Thebes* The youth goes up the Nile; these are ancient Egyptian cities.

[35] *demons* spirits, genii.

[36] *The Zodiac's brazen mystery* The Zodiac in the temple of Denderah, Upper Egypt, was renowned; mythological figures were arranged around the ceiling of its portico. The Zodiac was taken to Paris in 1822 and is now in the Bibliothèque Nationale de France.

Hang their mute thoughts on the mute walls around,
He lingered, poring on memorials
Of the world's youth, through the long burning day
Gazed on those speechless shapes, nor, when the moon
Filled the mysterious halls with floating shades,
Suspended he that task, but ever gazed
And gazed, till meaning on his vacant mind
Flashed[37] like strong inspiration, and he saw
The thrilling secrets of the birth of time.
Meanwhile an Arab maiden brought his food,
Her daily portion, from her father's tent,
And spread her matting for his couch, and stole
From duties and repose to tend his steps –
Enamoured, yet not daring for deep awe
To speak her love – and watched his nightly sleep,
Sleepless herself, to gaze upon his lips
Parted in slumber, whence the regular breath
Of innocent dreams arose. Then when red morn
Made paler the pale moon, to her cold home
Wildered, and wan, and panting, she returned.
   The poet wandering on, through Arabie
And Persia and the wild Carmanian waste,
And o'er the aerial mountains which pour down
Indus and Oxus from their icy caves,
In joy and exultation held his way;
Till in the Vale of Kashmir,[38] far within
Its loneliest dell, where odorous plants entwine
Beneath the hollow rocks a natural bower,
Beside a sparkling rivulet he stretched
His languid limbs.[39] A vision on his sleep
There came, a dream of hopes that never yet
Had flushed his cheek: he dreamed a veiled maid
Sat near him, talking in low solemn tones.
Her voice was like the voice of his own soul
Heard in the calm of thought; its music long,[40]
Like woven sounds of streams and breezes, held
His inmost sense suspended in its web
Of many-coloured woof and shifting hues.
Knowledge and truth and virtue were her theme,
And lofty hopes of divine liberty,
Thoughts the most dear to him, and poesy,
Herself a poet. Soon the solemn mood
Of her pure mind kindled through all her frame
A permeating fire – wild numbers[41] then

## Notes

[37] *on his vacant mind / Flashed* As in Wordsworth's 'Daffodils' 21–2: 'They flash upon that inward eye / Which is the bliss of solitude.'

[38] *through Arabie ... Kashmir* The poet's journey takes him through Arabia, Persia (modern Iran), through the Kerman desert in eastern Persia, over the Hindu Kush mountains (the 'Indian Caucasus'), and into Kashmir in northwest India.

[39] *he stretched ... limbs* A recollection of Gray, 'Elegy' 103–4: 'His listless length at noontide would he stretch / And pore upon the brook that babbles by.'

[40] *long* for a long time.

[41] *numbers* a song, with the accompaniment of a lute.

She raised, with voice stifled in tremulous sobs
Subdued by its own pathos;[42] her fair hands
Were bare alone, sweeping from some strange harp
Strange symphony,[43] and in their branching veins
The eloquent blood told an ineffable tale.
The beating of her heart was heard to fill
The pauses of her music, and her breath
Tumultuously accorded with those fits
Of intermitted song. Sudden she rose,
As if her heart impatiently endured
Its bursting burden: at the sound he turned,
And saw by the warm light of their own life
Her glowing limbs beneath the sinuous veil
Of woven wind, her outspread arms now bare,
Her dark locks floating in the breath of night,
Her beamy bending eyes, her parted lips
Outstretched and pale, and quivering eagerly.
His strong heart sunk and sickened with excess
Of love. He reared his shuddering limbs and quelled
His gasping breath, and spread his arms to meet
Her panting bosom; she drew back awhile,
Then, yielding to the irresistible joy,
With frantic gesture and short breathless cry
Folded his frame in her dissolving arms.
Now blackness veiled his dizzy eyes, and night
Involved[44] and swallowed up the vision; sleep,
Like a dark flood suspended in its course,
Rolled back its impulse on his vacant brain.
   Roused by the shock he started from his trance –
The cold white light of morning, the blue moon
Low in the west, the clear and garish[45] hills,
The distinct valley and the vacant woods,
Spread round him where he stood. Whither have fled
The hues of heaven that canopied his bower
Of yesternight? The sounds that soothed his sleep,
The mystery and the majesty of earth,
The joy, the exultation? His wan eyes
Gaze on the empty scene as vacantly
As ocean's moon looks on the moon in heaven.
The spirit of sweet human love has sent
A vision to the sleep of him who spurned
Her choicest gifts. He eagerly pursues
Beyond the realms of dream that fleeting shade;
He overleaps the bounds.[46] Alas, alas!
Were limbs and breath and being intertwined

## Notes

[42] *pathos* emotion.

[43] *Strange symphony* cf. Coleridge's 'Kubla Khan' 42–3: 'Could I revive within me / Her symphony and song.'

[44] *Involved* wrapped around.

[45] *garish* glaring.

[46] *the bounds* i.e. between illusion and reality, in trying to pursue the dream-image into the real world.

Thus treacherously? Lost, lost, forever lost
In the wide pathless desert of dim sleep,
That beautiful shape! Does the dark gate of death
Conduct to thy mysterious paradise,
Oh sleep? Does the bright arch of rainbow clouds
And pendent[47] mountains seen in the calm lake
Lead only to a black and watery depth,
While death's blue vault with loathliest[48] vapours hung,
Where every shade which the foul grave exhales
Hides its dead eye from the detested day,
Conducts, oh sleep, to thy delightful realms?[49]
This doubt with sudden tide flowed on his heart;
The insatiate hope which it awakened stung
His brain even like despair.[50]
While daylight held
The sky, the poet kept mute conference[51]
With his still soul. At night the passion came
Like the fierce fiend of a distempered dream,
And shook him from his rest, and led him forth
Into the darkness. As an eagle grasped
In folds of the green serpent, feels her breast
Burn with the poison, and precipitates[52]
Through night and day, tempest and calm and cloud,
Frantic with dizzying anguish, her blind flight
O'er the wide airy wilderness; thus driven
By the bright shadow[53] of that lovely dream,
Beneath the cold glare of the desolate night,
Through tangled swamps and deep precipitous dells,
Startling with careless step the moonlight snake,
He fled. Red morning dawned upon his flight,
Shedding the mockery of its vital hues
Upon his cheek of death. He wandered on
Till vast Aornos seen from Petra's steep[54]
Hung o'er the low horizon like a cloud;
Through Balk[55] and where the desolated tombs
Of Parthian kings scatter to every wind
Their wasting dust, wildly he wandered on
Day after day, a weary waste of hours,
Bearing within his life the brooding care
That ever fed on its decaying flame.
And now his limbs were lean: his scattered hair
Sered[56] by the autumn of strange suffering
Sung dirges in the wind; his listless hand

## Notes

[47] *pendent* overhanging.

[48] *loathliest* obnoxious.

[49] *Does the bright arch…delightful realms?* i.e. can it be that nature in all its beauty leads to nothing, while death, in all its horror, leads to the paradise revealed to the poet in sleep? The question is not answered.

[50] *despair* i.e. of ever being united with the ideal he has been allowed to see.

[51] *conference* communion; part of his inner being was at repose.

[52] *precipitates* hurries.

[53] *shadow* memory.

[54] *vast Aornos seen from Petra's steep* The poet returns from India, where the great rock Aornos stands by the Indus. There is no place called Petra in this area.

[55] The ancient city of Balkh was in modern-day Afghanistan. He is travelling through the area southeast of the Caspian Sea, where the Parthian kingdom used to be.

[56] *Sered* thinned, faded.

Hung like dead bone within its withered skin;
Life, and the lustre that consumed it, shone
As in a furnace burning secretly
From his dark eyes alone. The cottagers,
Who ministered with human charity
His human wants, beheld with wondering awe
Their fleeting visitant. The mountaineer,
Encountering on some dizzy precipice
That spectral form, deemed that the spirit of wind
With lightning eyes, and eager breath, and feet
Disturbing not the drifted snow, had paused
In its career; the infant would conceal
His troubled visage in his mother's robe
In terror at the glare of those wild eyes,
To remember their strange light in many a dream
Of after-times; but youthful maidens, taught
By nature, would interpret half the woe[57]
That wasted him, would call him with false names
Brother and friend, would press his pallid hand
At parting, and watch, dim through tears, the path
Of his departure from their father's door.
  At length upon the lone Chorasmian shore[58]
He paused, a wide and melancholy waste
Of putrid marshes. A strong impulse urged
His steps to the seashore; a swan[59] was there,
Beside a sluggish stream among the reeds.
It rose as he approached, and with strong wings
Scaling the upward sky, bent its bright course
High over the immeasurable main.
His eyes pursued its flight. 'Thou hast a home,
Beautiful bird; thou voyagest to thine home,
Where thy sweet mate will twine her downy neck
With thine, and welcome thy return with eyes
Bright in the lustre of their own fond joy.
And what am I that I should linger here,
With voice far sweeter than thy dying notes,
Spirit more vast than thine, frame more attuned
To beauty, wasting these surpassing powers
In the deaf air, to the blind earth, and heaven
That echoes not my thoughts?' A gloomy smile
Of desperate hope wrinkled his quivering lips –
For sleep, he knew, kept[60] most relentlessly
Its precious charge, and silent death exposed,
Faithless perhaps as sleep, a shadowy lure,[61]
With doubtful smile mocking its own strange charms.[62]
  Startled by his own thoughts he looked around.

## Notes

[57] *would interpret half the woe* i.e. they would guess that he was in love, but not that he was in love with an ideal.

[58] *Chorasmian shore* eastern shore of the Caspian Sea.

[59] *a swan* sacred to Apollo, god of poetry; it sang before dying.

[60] *kept* concealed, kept to itself.

[61] *lure* temptation.

[62] *For sleep…charms* The poet has not seen his vision in sleep; perhaps he will not see her in death.

There was no fair fiend near him, not a sight
Or sound of awe but in his own deep mind.
A little shallop[63] floating near the shore
Caught the impatient wandering of his gaze.
It had been long abandoned, for its sides
Gaped wide with many a rift, and its frail joints
Swayed with the undulations of the tide.
A restless impulse urged him to embark
And meet lone death on the drear ocean's waste,
For well he knew that mighty shadow loves
The slimy caverns of the populous deep.
   The day was fair and sunny, sea and sky
Drank its inspiring radiance, and the wind
Swept strongly from the shore, blackening the waves.
Following his eager soul, the wanderer
Leaped in the boat, he spread his cloak aloft
On the bare mast and took his lonely seat,
And felt the boat speed o'er the tranquil sea
Like a torn cloud before the hurricane.
   As one that in a silver vision floats
Obedient to the sweep of odorous winds
Upon resplendent clouds, so rapidly
Along the dark and ruffled waters fled
The straining boat. A whirlwind swept it on
With fierce gusts and precipitating force
Through the white ridges of the chafed sea.
The waves arose; higher and higher still
Their fierce necks writhed beneath the tempest's scourge
Like serpents struggling in a vulture's grasp.
Calm and rejoicing in the fearful war
Of wave ruining[64] on wave, and blast on blast
Descending, and black flood on whirlpool driven
With dark obliterating course, he sat:
As if their genii were the ministers
Appointed to conduct him to the light
Of those beloved eyes, the poet sat
Holding the steady helm. Evening came on,
The beams of sunset hung their rainbow hues[65]
High mid the shifting domes of sheeted spray
That canopied his path o'er the waste deep;
Twilight, ascending slowly from the east,
Entwined in duskier wreaths her braided locks
O'er the fair front and radiant eyes of day;
Night followed, clad with stars. On every side
More horribly the multitudinous streams
Of ocean's mountainous waste to mutual war
Rushed in dark tumult thundering, as to mock

## Notes

[63] *shallop* small open boat.

[64] *ruining* tumbling.

[65] *hung their rainbow hues* i.e. made rainbows in the spray.

The calm and spangled sky. The little boat
Still fled before the storm, still fled like foam
Down the steep cataract of a wintry river –
Now pausing on the edge of the riven[66] wave,
Now leaving far behind the bursting mass
That fell, convulsing ocean; safely fled –
As if that frail and wasted human form
Had been an elemental god.[67]
At midnight
The moon arose – and lo! the ethereal cliffs[68]
Of Caucasus,[69] whose icy summits shone
Among the stars like sunlight, and around
Whose caverned base the whirlpools and the waves,
Bursting and eddying irresistibly,
Rage and resound forever. Who shall save?
The boat fled on, the boiling torrent drove,
The crags closed round with black and jagged arms,
The shattered mountain overhung the sea,
And faster still, beyond all human speed,
Suspended on the sweep of the smooth wave,
The little boat was driven. A cavern there
Yawned, and amid its slant and winding depths
Engulfed the rushing sea. The boat fled on
With unrelaxing speed. 'Vision and love!'
The poet cried aloud, 'I have beheld
The path of thy departure. Sleep and death
Shall not divide us long!'
The boat pursued
The windings of the cavern. Daylight shone
At length upon that gloomy river's flow;
Now, where the fiercest war among the waves
Is calm, on the unfathomable stream
The boat moved slowly. Where the mountain, riven,
Exposed those black depths to the azure sky,
Ere yet the flood's enormous volume fell
Even to the base of Caucasus, with sound
That shook the everlasting rocks, the mass
Filled with one whirlpool all that ample chasm;
Stair above stair the eddying waters rose,[70]
Circling immeasurably fast, and laved
With alternating dash the gnarled roots
Of mighty trees that stretched their giant arms
In darkness over it. I' the midst was left,

## Notes

[66] *riven* split, torn asunder.

[67] *an elemental god* a god of the elements.

[68] *the ethereal cliffs* the cliffs reach into the ether.

[69] The boat has crossed the Caspian Sea to the mountains of the Caucasus, now in Georgia and Russia, on the western shore. Prometheus was nailed to the Caucasus by Jupiter.

[70] *Stair above stair the eddying waters rose* As it spins, the whirlpool lifts the boat up at its outer edge higher and higher ('stair above stair').

Reflecting yet distorting every cloud,
A pool of treacherous and tremendous calm.
Seized by the sway of the ascending stream,
With dizzy swiftness, round and round and round,
Ridge after ridge the straining boat arose,
Till on the verge of the extremest curve,
Where, through an opening of the rocky bank,
The waters overflow, and a smooth spot
Of glassy quiet mid those battling tides
Is left, the boat paused shuddering. Shall it sink
Down the abyss? Shall the reverting stress
Of that resistless gulf embosom it?
Now shall it fall? A wandering stream of wind,
Breathed from the west, has caught the expanded sail,
And lo! with gentle motion, between banks
Of mossy slope, and on a placid stream,
Beneath a woven grove it sails – and hark!
The ghastly torrent mingles its far roar
With the breeze murmuring in the musical woods.
Where the embowering trees recede, and leave
A little space of green expanse, the cove
Is closed by meeting banks, whose yellow flowers[71]
Forever gaze on their own drooping eyes,
Reflected in the crystal calm. The wave
Of the boat's motion marred their pensive task
Which nought but vagrant bird, or wanton wind,
Or falling spear-grass, or their own decay
Had e'er disturbed before. The poet longed
To deck with their bright hues his withered hair,
But on his heart its solitude returned
And he forbore. Not the strong impulse hid
In those flushed cheeks, bent eyes, and shadowy frame
Had yet performed its ministry;[72] it hung
Upon his life, as lightning in a cloud
Gleams, hovering ere it vanish, ere the floods
Of night close over it.
                                        The noonday sun
Now shone upon the forest, one vast mass
Of mingling shade whose brown[73] magnificence
A narrow vale embosoms; there huge caves,
Scooped in the dark base of their airy[74] rocks,
Mocking its moans,[75] respond and roar forever.
The meeting boughs and implicated[76] leaves

## Notes

[71] *yellow flowers* Narcissus was a beautiful youth who mistook his own image, reflected in the water, for a nymph. He fell in love with it, committed suicide, and was changed into the flower today named after him.

[72] *performed its ministry* An allusion to Coleridge, 'Frost at Midnight' 1: 'The frost performs its secret ministry.'

[73] *brown* dark.

[74] *airy* lofty, high.

[75] *Mocking its moans* echoing the moans of the wind in the forest.

[76] *implicated* intertwining.

Wove twilight o'er the poet's path as, led
By love, or dream, or god, or mightier death,
He sought in nature's dearest haunt some bank,
Her cradle,[77] and his sepulchre. More dark
And dark the shades accumulate. The oak,
Expanding its immense and knotty arms,
Embraces the light beech. The pyramids
Of the tall cedar overarching, frame
Most solemn domes within, and far below,
Like clouds suspended in an emerald sky,
The ash and the acacia floating hang
Tremulous and pale. Like restless serpents clothed
In rainbow and in fire, the parasites,[78]
Starred with ten thousand blossoms, flow around
The grey trunks, and, as gamesome[79] infants' eyes
With gentle meanings and most innocent wiles
Fold their beams round the hearts of those that love,
These twine their tendrils with the wedded boughs
Uniting their close union; the woven leaves
Make network of the dark blue light of day[80]
And the night's noontide clearness, mutable
As shapes in the weird clouds. Soft mossy lawns[81]
Beneath these canopies extend their swells,
Fragrant with perfumed herbs, and eyed with blooms
Minute yet beautiful. One darkest glen
Sends from its woods of musk-rose, twined with jasmine,
A soul-dissolving odour, to invite
To some more lovely mystery. Through the dell,
Silence and Twilight here, twin-sisters, keep
Their noonday watch, and sail among the shades
Like vaporous shapes half-seen; beyond, a well,
Dark, gleaming, and of most translucent wave,
Images[82] all the woven boughs above,
And each depending[83] leaf, and every speck
Of azure sky, darting between their chasms;
Nor aught else in the liquid mirror laves
Its portraiture,[84] but some inconstant star
Between one foliaged lattice[85] twinkling fair,
Or painted bird, sleeping beneath the moon,
Or gorgeous insect floating motionless,
Unconscious of the day ere yet his wings
Have spread their glories to the gaze of noon.[86]
Hither the poet came. His eyes beheld

## Notes

[77] *Her cradle* The poet travels back to the source of life.

[78] *parasites* climbing plants.

[79] *gamesome* playful.

[80] *Make network of the dark blue light of day* Daylight is seen as if through netted threads.

[81] *lawns* grassy clearings.

[82] *Images* reflects.

[83] *depending* hanging.

[84] *laves / Its portraiture* There is nothing else reflected in the well.

[85] *one foliaged lattice* a mass of interlaced leaves.

[86] *Or gorgeous insect…noon* The butterfly is unaware that outside the forest it is noon.

Their own wan light through the reflected lines
Of his thin hair, distinct in the dark depth
Of that still fountain; as the human heart,
Gazing in dreams over the gloomy grave,
Sees its own treacherous likeness there.[87] He heard
The motion of the leaves, the grass that sprung
Startled and glanced and trembled even to feel
An unaccustomed presence, and the sound
Of the sweet brook that from the secret springs
Of the dark fountain rose. A spirit[88] seemed
To stand beside him, clothed in no bright robes
Of shadowy silver or enshrining light
Borrowed from aught the visible world affords
Of grace, or majesty, or mystery –
But, undulating woods and silent well,
And leaping rivulet and evening gloom
Now deepening the dark shades, for speech assuming[89]
Held commune with him, as if he and it
Were all that was – only, when his regard
Was raised by intense pensiveness, two eyes,
Two starry eyes, hung in the gloom of thought
And seemed with their serene and azure smiles
To beckon him.
                    Obedient to the light
That shone within his soul, he went pursuing
The windings of the dell. The rivulet
Wanton and wild, through many a green ravine
Beneath the forest flowed. Sometimes it fell
Among the moss with hollow harmony
Dark and profound; now on the polished stones
It danced, like childhood laughing as it went;
Then through the plain in tranquil wanderings crept,
Reflecting every herb and drooping bud
That overhung its quietness. 'Oh stream!
Whose source is inaccessibly profound,
Whither do thy mysterious waters tend?
Thou imagest my life: thy darksome stillness,
Thy dazzling waves, thy loud and hollow gulfs,
Thy searchless fountain[90] and invisible course
Have each their type[91] in me. And the wide sky
And measureless ocean may declare as soon
What oozy[92] cavern or what wandering cloud
Contains thy waters, as the universe
Tell where these living thoughts reside, when stretched
Upon thy flowers my bloodless limbs shall waste

## Notes

[87] *Gazing in dreams…there* i.e. imagines its continued but uncertain (treacherous) life after death.

[88] *A spirit* probably nature.

[89] *for speech assuming* Nature used woods, well, rivulet and gloom as a means of communication.

[90] *searchless fountain* undiscoverable source.

[91] *type* i.e. corresponding idealized version.

[92] *oozy* damp.

I' the passing wind!'
Beside the grassy shore
Of the small stream he went; he did impress
On the green moss his tremulous step that caught
Strong shuddering from his burning limbs. As one
Roused by some joyous madness from the couch
Of fever, he did move, yet not like him
Forgetful of the grave,[93] where, when the flame
Of his frail exultation shall be spent,
He must descend. With rapid steps he went
Beneath the shade of trees, beside the flow
Of the wild babbling rivulet – and now
The forest's solemn canopies were changed
For the uniform and lightsome[94] evening sky.
Grey rocks did peep from the spare moss, and stemmed
The struggling brook; tall spires of windlestrae[95]
Threw their thin shadows down the rugged slope,
And nought but gnarled roots of ancient pines
Branchless and blasted, clenched with grasping roots
The unwilling soil. A gradual change was here,
Yet ghastly. For, as fast years flow away,
The smooth brow gathers, and the hair grows thin
And white, and where irradiate[96] dewy eyes
Had shone, gleam stony orbs: so from his steps
Bright flowers departed, and the beautiful shade
Of the green groves, with all their odorous winds
And musical motions. Calm, he still pursued
The stream, that with a larger volume[97] now
Rolled through the labyrinthine dell; and there
Fretted[98] a path through its descending curves
With its wintry speed. On every side now rose
Rocks which, in unimaginable forms,
Lifted their black and barren pinnacles
In the light of evening, and, its precipice
Obscuring, the ravine disclosed above,
Mid toppling stones, black gulfs and yawning caves,
Whose windings gave ten thousand various tongues
To the loud stream. Lo! where the pass expands
Its stony jaws, the abrupt mountain breaks
And seems, with its accumulated crags,
To overhang the world – for wide expand,
Beneath the wan stars and descending moon,
Islanded seas, blue mountains, mighty streams,
Dim tracts and vast, robed in the lustrous gloom
Of leaden-coloured[99] even, and fiery hills

## Notes

[93] *Forgetful of the grave* It is the fever-stricken man who, in his delirium, forgets the grave; the poet is all too mindful of death.
[94] *lightsome* illuminated.
[95] *windlestrae* dry stalks left by dead or dying plants.
[96] *irradiate* shining.
[97] *volume* of water.
[98] *Fretted* wore, ground.
[99] *leaden-coloured* dark grey.

Mingling their flames with twilight, on the verge
Of the remote horizon. The near scene,
In naked and severe simplicity,
Made contrast with the universe. A pine,
Rock-rooted, stretched athwart the vacancy
Its swinging boughs, to each inconstant blast
Yielding one only response, at each pause
In most familiar cadence, with the howl,
The thunder and the hiss of homeless streams
Mingling its solemn song, whilst the broad river,
Foaming and hurrying o'er its rugged path,
Fell into that immeasurable void,
Scattering its waters to the passing winds.
Yet the grey precipice and solemn pine
And torrent were not all; one silent nook
Was there. Even on the edge of that vast mountain,
Upheld by knotty roots and fallen rocks,
It overlooked in its serenity
The dark earth and the bending vault of stars.
It was a tranquil spot that seemed to smile
Even in the lap of horror. Ivy clasped
The fissured stones with its entwining arms,
And did embower with leaves forever green,
And berries dark, the smooth and even space
Of its inviolated floor; and here
The children of the autumnal whirlwind[100] bore,
In wanton sport, those bright leaves whose decay,
Red, yellow, or ethereally pale,
Rivals the pride of summer. 'Tis the haunt
Of every gentle wind whose breath can teach
The wilds to love tranquillity. One step,[101]
One human step alone, has ever broken
The stillness of its solitude; one voice
Alone[102] inspired its echoes – even that voice
Which hither came floating among the winds,
And led the loveliest among human forms[103]
To make their[104] wild haunts the depository
Of all the grace and beauty that endued[105]
Its motions, render up its majesty,
Scatter its music on the unfeeling storm,
And to the damp leaves and blue cavern mould,
Nurses of rainbow flowers and branching moss,
Commit[106] the colours of that varying cheek,

## Notes

[100] *The children of the autumnal whirlwind* i.e. gusts of wind.
[101] *One step* i.e. that of the poet.
[102] *one voice / Alone* i.e. that of the vision.
[103] *the loveliest among human forms* the poet.
[104] *their* i.e. the winds'.
[105] *endued* invested.
[106] *Commit* entrust.

That snowy breast, those dark and drooping eyes.
   The dim and horned moon hung low, and poured
A sea of lustre on the horizon's verge
That overflowed its mountains. Yellow mist
Filled the unbounded atmosphere, and drank
Wan moonlight even to fullness: not a star
Shone, not a sound was heard; the very winds,
Danger's grim playmates, on that precipice
Slept, clasped in his embrace. Oh storm of Death,
Whose sightless speed divides this sullen night,
And thou, colossal skeleton,[107] that, still
Guiding its irresistible career
In thy devastating omnipotence,
Art king of this frail world – from the red field
Of slaughter, from the reeking hospital,
The patriot's sacred couch, the snowy bed
Of innocence, the scaffold and the throne,
A mighty voice invokes thee: Ruin calls
His brother Death. A rare and regal prey
He hath prepared, prowling around the world –
Glutted with which thou mayst repose, and men
Go to their graves like flowers or creeping worms,
Nor ever more offer at thy dark shrine
The unheeded tribute of a broken heart.
   When on the threshold of the green recess
The wanderer's footsteps fell, he knew that death
Was on him. Yet a little, ere it fled,
Did he resign his high and holy soul
To images of the majestic past
That paused within his passive[108] being now,
Like winds that bear sweet music when they breathe
Through some dim latticed chamber. He did place
His pale lean hand upon the rugged trunk
Of the old pine; upon an ivied stone
Reclined his languid head; his limbs did rest,
Diffused and motionless, on the smooth brink
Of that obscurest chasm – and thus he lay,
Surrendering to their final impulses
The hovering powers of life. Hope and despair,
The torturers, slept;[109] no mortal pain or fear
Marred his repose, the influxes of sense[110]
And his own being unalloyed by pain,
Yet feebler and more feeble, calmly fed

## Notes

[107] *colossal skeleton* Death.

[108] *passive* an important detail; compare 'Mont Blanc' 37–8.

[109] *Hope and despair…slept* cf. Shelley's journal entry for 28 July 1814: 'I hope – but my hopes are not unmixed with fear for what will befall this inestimable spirit when we appear to die'.

[110] *the influxes of sense* his perceptions.

The stream of thought, till he lay breathing there
At peace, and faintly smiling. His last sight
Was the great moon, which o'er the western line
Of the wide world her mighty horn suspended,
With those dun beams inwoven darkness seemed
To mingle. Now upon the jagged hills
It rests, and still as[111] the divided frame
Of the vast meteor[112] sunk, the poet's blood,
That ever beat in mystic sympathy
With nature's ebb and flow, grew feebler still;
And when two lessening points of light[113] alone
Gleamed through the darkness, the alternate gasp
Of his faint respiration scarce did stir
The stagnate[114] night – till the minutest ray
Was quenched, the pulse yet lingered in his heart.
It paused, it fluttered. But when heaven remained
Utterly black, the murky shades involved
An image, silent, cold, and motionless,
As their own voiceless earth and vacant air.
Even as a vapour[115] fed with golden beams
That ministered on sunlight ere the west
Eclipses it, was now that wondrous frame –
No sense, no motion,[116] no divinity –
A fragile lute[117] on whose harmonious strings
The breath of heaven did wander, a bright stream
Once fed with many-voiced waves, a dream
Of youth, which night and time have quenched for ever –
Still, dark, and dry, and unremembered now.
   Oh for Medea's wondrous alchemy,
Which wheresoe'er it fell made the earth gleam
With bright flowers, and the wintry boughs exhale
From vernal blooms fresh fragrance![118] Oh that God,
Profuse[119] of poisons, would concede the chalice
Which but one living man[120] has drained – who now,
Vessel of deathless wrath, a slave that feels
No proud exemption in the blighting curse
He bears, over the world wanders for ever,
Lone as incarnate death! Oh that the dream
Of dark magician[121] in his visioned cave,
Raking the cinders of a crucible
For life and power, even when his feeble hand
Shakes in its last decay, were the true law

## Notes

[111] *still as* i.e. as still as.
[112] *meteor* at this period, a reference to any atmospheric occurrence.
[113] *two lessening points of light* tips of the setting moon's crescent.
[114] *stagnate* stagnant.
[115] *vapour* cloud.
[116] *No sense, no motion* Echoes Wordsworth, 'A Slumber Did My Spirit Seal' 5: 'No motion has she now, no force.'
[117] *A fragile lute* Once again, Shelley has in mind an Aeolian harp.
[118] *Oh for...fragrance* Medea, an enchantress in Greek mythology, brewed a potion to restore youth to Aeson, the father of her lover Jason; when spilt on the ground it had the effects described here.
[119] *Profuse* productive.
[120] *one living man* Ahasuerus, the wandering Jew, doomed to eternal life.
[121] *dark magician* The alchemist who, besides seeking to turn base metals into gold, seeks the elixir of eternal life.

Of this so lovely world! But thou art fled
Like some frail exhalation which the dawn
Robes in its golden beams – ah, thou hast fled! –
The brave, the gentle, and the beautiful,
The child of grace and genius. Heartless things
Are done and said i' the world, and many worms
And beasts and men live on, and mighty earth
From sea and mountain, city and wilderness,
In vesper low or joyous orison,[122]
Lifts still its solemn voice – but thou art fled;
Thou canst no longer know or love the shapes
Of this phantasmal scene,[123] who have to thee
Been purest ministers – who are, alas,
Now thou art not! Upon those pallid lips,
So sweet even in their silence, on those eyes
That image sleep in death, upon that form
Yet safe from the worm's outrage, let no tear
Be shed, not even in thought; nor – when those hues
Are gone, and those divinest lineaments
Worn by the senseless[124] wind – shall live alone
In the frail pauses of this simple strain.
Let not high verse, mourning the memory
Of that which is no more, or painting's woe
Or sculpture, speak in feeble imagery
Their own cold powers. Art and eloquence
And all the shows o' the world are frail and vain
To weep a loss that turns their lights to shade.
It is a woe too 'deep for tears',[125] when all
Is reft at once, when some surpassing spirit,
Whose light adorned the world around it, leaves
Those who remain behind not sobs or groans,
The passionate tumult of a clinging hope,
But pale despair and cold tranquillity,
Nature's vast frame, the web of human things,
Birth and the grave, that are not as they were.[126]

## *Journal-Letter from Percy Bysshe Shelley to Thomas Love Peacock, 22 July to 2 August 1816* (extract)[1]

*22 July 1816*. From Servox, three leagues remain to Chamounix. Mont Blanc was before us. The Alps with their innumerable glaciers on high, all around, closing in the complicated windings of the single vale; forests inexpressibly beautiful, but majestic in their beauty; interwoven beech

## Notes

[122] *vesper…orison* evensong … prayer – uttered, figuratively, by the earth.

[123] *this phantasmal scene* i.e. the transcendent, visionary world.

[124] *senseless* unfeeling.

[125] *It is a woe too 'deep for tears'* Wordsworth, 'Ode' 206: 'Thoughts that do often lie too deep for tears.'

[126] *that are not as they were* cf. Wordsworth, 'Ode' 6: 'It is not now as it has been of yore.'

Journal-Letter from Percy Bysshe Shelley to Thomas Love Peacock

[1] This important letter describes Shelley's initial response to the landscape which later provided an important setting for 'Mont Blanc' and *Frankenstein*. He had set off, with Mary Godwin and Claire Clairmont, on a tour of the vale of Chamounix, on 21 July; they would return to Maison Chappuis a week later.

and pine and oak overshadowed our road or receded whilst lawns of such verdure as I had never seen before occupied these openings, and, extending gradually, becoming darker into their recesses.

Mont Blanc was before us but was covered with cloud, and its base furrowed with dreadful gaps was seen alone. Pinnacles of snow, intolerably bright, part of the chain connected with Mont Blanc, shone through the clouds at intervals on high. I never knew I never imagined what mountains were before. The immensity of these aerial[2] summits excited, when they suddenly burst upon the sight, a sentiment of ecstatic wonder not unallied to madness. And remember this was all one scene. It all pressed home to our regard and to our imagination. Though it embraced a great number of miles, the snowy pyramids which shot into the bright blue sky seemed to overhang our path; the ravine, clothed with gigantic pines and black with its depth below (so deep that the very roaring of the untameable Arve which rolled through it could not be heard above), was close to our very footsteps. All was as much our own as if we had been the creators of such impressions in the minds of others, as now occupied our own. Nature was the poet whose harmony held our spirits more breathless than that of the divinest.

*25 July 1816*. We have returned from visiting this glacier – a scene, in truth, of dizzying wonder. The path that winds to it along the side of a mountain, now clothed with pines, now intersected with snowy hollows, is wide and steep. The cabin of Montanvert is three leagues from Chamounix, half of which distance is performed on mules – not so sure-footed but that, on the first day, the one which I rode fell in what the guides call a 'mauvais pas', so that I narrowly escaped being precipitated down the mountain. The guide continually held that which Mary rode.

We passed over a hollow covered with snow down which vast stones, detached from the rock above, are accustomed to roll. One had fallen the preceding day, a little time after we had returned. The guides desired us to pass quickly, for it is said that sometimes the least sound will accelerate their fall. We arrived at Montanvert, however, safe.

On all sides precipitous mountains, the abodes of unrelenting frost, surround this vale. Their sides are banked up with ice and snow, broken and heaped-up, and exhibiting terrific chasms. The summits are sharp and naked pinnacles whose overhanging steepness will not even permit snow to rest there. They pierce the clouds like things not belonging to this earth. The vale itself is filled with a mass of undulating ice, and has an ascent sufficiently gradual even to the remotest abysses of these horrible deserts. It is only half a league (about two miles) in breadth, and seems much less. It exhibits an appearance as if frost had suddenly bound up the waves and whirlpools of a mighty torrent.

We walked to some distance upon its surface. The waves are elevated about 12 or 15 feet from the surface of the mass, which is intersected with long gaps of unfathomable depth, the ice of whose sides is more beautifully azure than the sky. In these regions, everything changes and is in motion. This vast mass of ice has one general progress which ceases neither day nor night. It breaks and rises forever; its undulations sink whilst others rise. From the precipices which surround it, the echo of rocks which fall from their aerial summits, or of the ice and snow, scarcely ceases for one moment. One would think that Mont Blanc was a living being, and that the frozen blood forever circulated slowly through his stony veins.

## Notes

[2] *aerial* lofty.

## *Hymn to Intellectual Beauty* (composed between 22 June and 29 August 1816; edited from printed text corrected by Shelley)[1]

1

The awful[2] shadow of some unseen Power
Floats though unseen amongst us, visiting
This various world with as inconstant wing[3]
As summer winds that creep from flower to flower;
Like moonbeams that behind some piny mountain shower,[4]
It visits with inconstant glance
Each human heart and countenance;
Like hues and harmonies of evening,
Like clouds in starlight widely spread,
Like memory of music fled,
Like aught that for its grace may be
Dear, and yet dearer for its mystery.

2

Spirit of Beauty, that doth consecrate
With thine own hues all thou dost shine upon
Of human thought or form – where art thou gone?
Why dost thou pass away and leave our state,
This dim vast vale of tears, vacant and desolate?
Ask why the sunlight not forever
Weaves rainbows o'er yon mountain river,
Why aught should fail and fade that once is shown,
Why fear and dream, and death and birth
Cast on the daylight of this earth
Such gloom, why man has such a scope
For love and hate, despondency and hope?

3

No voice from some sublimer world hath ever
To sage or poet these responses given;
Therefore the name of God, and ghosts, and heaven[5]
Remain the records of their vain endeavour,

## Notes

HYMN TO INTELLECTUAL BEAUTY

[1] This poem should be read in the light of Wordsworth's 'Ode', by which it was inspired, also about the 'inconstancy' of the kind of intense vision Shelley celebrates.

[2] *awful* awesome.

[3] *with as inconstant wing* Shelley's point is that the 'awful Power' is not always perceptible.

[4] *some piny mountain shower* 'shower' is a verb. This poem was composed during Shelley's residence on the banks of Lake Geneva.

[5] *Therefore the name of God, and ghosts, and heaven* The original *Examiner* printed text reads: 'Therefore the names of Demon, Ghost, and Heaven'.

Frail spells, whose uttered charm might not avail to sever,
From all we hear and all we see,
Doubt, chance, and mutability.
Thy light alone, like mist o'er mountains driven,
Or music by the night wind sent
Through strings of some still instrument,[6]
Or moonlight on a midnight stream,
Gives grace and truth to life's unquiet dream.

4

Love, hope, and self-esteem, like clouds depart
And come, for some uncertain moments lent.
Man were immortal and omnipotent,
Didst thou,[7] unknown and awful as thou art,
Keep with thy glorious train firm state within his heart.
Thou messenger of sympathies
That wax and wane in lovers' eyes;
Thou that to human thought art nourishment,
Like darkness to a dying flame![8]
Depart not as thy shadow came,
Depart not lest the grave should be,
Like life and fear, a dark reality.

5

While yet a boy I sought for ghosts, and sped
Through many a listening chamber, cave and ruin
And starlight wood, with fearful steps pursuing
Hopes of high talk with the departed dead.[9]
I called on poisonous names[10] with which our youth is fed –
I was not heard – I saw them not –
When musing deeply on the lot
Of life, at that sweet time when winds are wooing
All vital things that wake to bring
News of buds and blossoming.
Sudden thy shadow fell on me –
I shrieked, and clasped my hands in ecstasy!

6

I vowed that I would dedicate my powers
To thee and thine; have I not kept the vow?
With beating heart and streaming eyes, even now
I call the phantoms of a thousand hours

## Notes

[6] *some still instrument* an Aeolian harp.

[7] *Man were...Didst thou* man would be ... if thou didst ...

[8] *nourishment, / Like darkness to a dying flame* Strong light was believed to stifle candlelight; conversely, darkness would feed it.

[9] As a boy, Shelley did go to cemeteries and woods at night, in the hope of meeting ghosts.

[10] *poisonous names* Presumably those of God and Christ. In earlier years Shelley did try prayer.

Each from his voiceless grave: they have in visioned bowers
Of studious zeal or love's delight
Outwatched with me the envious night;
They know that never joy illumed my brow
Unlinked with hope that thou wouldst free
This world from its dark slavery,
That thou, oh awful loveliness,
Wouldst give whate'er these words cannot express.

7

The day becomes more solemn and serene
When noon is past; there is a harmony
In autumn, and a lustre in its sky,
Which through the summer is not heard or seen,
As if it could not be, as if it had not been!
Thus let thy power, which like the truth
Of nature on my passive youth
Descended,[11] to my onward life supply
Its calm – to one who worships thee,
And every form containing thee,
Whom, spirit fair, thy spells did bind
To fear[12] himself, and love all humankind.

## *Mont Blanc. Lines Written in the Vale of Chamouni* (composed between 22 July and 29 August 1816)[1]

I

The everlasting universe of things
Flows through the mind, and rolls its rapid waves,
Now dark, now glittering, now reflecting gloom,
Now lending splendour, where from secret springs
The source of human thought its tribute[2] brings
Of waters, with a sound but half its own,[3]
Such as a feeble brook will oft assume
In the wild woods, among the mountains lone,
Where waterfalls around it leap forever,
Where woods and winds contend, and a vast river
Over its rocks ceaselessly bursts and raves.

## Notes

[11] *the truth / Of nature ... Descended* The passivity of the mind is equivalent to the psychological relaxation mentioned by De Quincey in his discussion of Wordsworth's 'There Was a Boy'. Shelley discusses it in his 'Essay on Christianity', written between 1813 and 1819: 'All that it [i.e. human life] contains of pure or of divine visits the passive mind in some serenest mood'.

[12] *fear* revere.

Mont Blanc. Lines Written in the Vale of Chamouni

[1] According to Mary Shelley, this poem 'was composed under the immediate impression of the deep and powerful feelings excited by the objects which it attempts to describe; and, as an undisciplined overflowing of the soul, rests its claim to approbation on an attempt to imitate the untamable wilderness and inaccessible solemnity from which those feelings sprang.'

[2] *tribute* tributary.

[3] *with a sound but half its own* cf. 'Tintern Abbey', in which Wordsworth refers to 'what they [the senses] half-create / And what perceive' (ll. 109–10).

II

Thus thou, ravine of Arve – dark, deep ravine –
Thou many-coloured, many-voicéd vale,
Over whose pines, and crags, and caverns sail
Fast cloud-shadows and sunbeams: awful[4] scene,
Where Power in likeness of the Arve comes down
From the ice gulfs that gird his secret throne,
Bursting through these dark mountains like the flame
Of lightning through the tempest; thou dost lie,
Thy giant brood of pines around thee clinging,
Children of elder time, in whose devotion
The chainless winds still come and ever came
To drink their odours, and their mighty swinging
To hear – an old and solemn harmony;
Thine earthly rainbows stretched across the sweep
Of the ethereal waterfall, whose veil
Robes some unsculptured image; the strange sleep
Which, when the voices of the desert fail,
Wraps all in its own deep eternity;
Thy caverns echoing to the Arve's commotion –
A loud, lone sound no other sound can tame;
Thou art pervaded with that ceaseless motion,
Thou art the path of that unresting sound,
Dizzy ravine! – and when I gaze on thee
I seem as in a trance sublime and strange
To muse on my own separate fantasy,
My own, my human mind, which passively
Now renders and receives fast influencings,
Holding an unremitting interchange[5]
With the clear universe of things around;
One legion of wild thoughts, whose wandering wings
Now float above thy darkness, and now rest
Where that[6] or thou[7] art no unbidden guest,
In the still cave of the witch Poesy,
Seeking among the shadows that pass by,
Ghosts of all things that are, some shade of thee,
Some phantom, some faint image; till the breast
From which they[8] fled recalls them, thou art there!

III

Some say that gleams of a remoter world
Visit the soul in sleep, that death is slumber,
And that its shapes the busy thoughts outnumber
Of those who wake and live. I look on high;
Has some unknown omnipotence unfurled[9]

## Notes

[4] *awful* awe-inspiring.

[5] *an unremitting interchange* the 'interchange' takes place because the mind does not merely perceive; it works on its perceptions, transforming them imaginatively.

[6] *that* the darkness of line 42.

[7] *thou* the ravine.

[8] *they* the 'legion of wild thoughts' (l. 41).

[9] *unfurled* drawn aside.

The veil of life and death? Or do I lie
In dream, and does the mightier world of sleep
Spread far around and inaccessibly
Its circles? For the very spirit fails,
Driven like a homeless cloud from steep to steep
That vanishes among the viewless gales!
Far, far above, piercing the infinite sky,
Mont Blanc appears, still, snowy, and serene.
Its subject mountains their unearthly forms
Pile around it, ice and rock; broad vales between
Of frozen floods, unfathomable deeps
Blue as the overhanging heaven, that spread
And wind among the accumulated steeps;
A desert peopled by the storms alone,
Save when the eagle brings some hunter's bone,
And the wolf tracks her there. How hideously
Its shapes are heaped around! – rude, bare, and high,
Ghastly, and scarred, and riven. Is this the scene
Where the old earthquake-demon taught her young
Ruin? Were these their toys? Or did a sea
Of fire envelop once this silent snow?
None can reply – all seems eternal now.
The wilderness has a mysterious tongue
Which teaches awful doubt,[10] or faith so mild,
So solemn, so serene, that man may be
But for such faith with nature reconciled.
Thou hast a voice, great mountain, to repeal
Large codes[11] of fraud and woe – not understood
By all, but which the wise, and great, and good
Interpret, or make felt, or deeply feel.

IV

The fields, the lakes, the forests, and the streams,
Ocean, and all the living things that dwell
Within the daedal[12] earth; lightning, and rain,
Earthquake, and fiery flood, and hurricane,
The torpor of the year[13] when feeble dreams
Visit the hidden buds, or dreamless sleep
Holds every future leaf and flower; the bound
With which from that detested trance they leap;
The works and ways of man, their death and birth,
And that of him and all that his may be;
All things that move and breathe[14] with toil and sound

## Notes

[10] *awful doubt* awe-inspired scepticism.

[11] *codes* laws.

[12] *daedal* varied, richly adorned.

[13] *The torpor of the year* i.e. winter.

[14] *All things that move and breathe* an echo of Wordsworth's pantheist statement of faith in 'Tintern Abbey' 103–5:

> A motion and a spirit that impels
> All thinking things, all objects of all thought,
> And rolls through all things.

Are born and die; revolve, subside and swell.
Power dwells apart in its tranquillity
Remote, serene, and inaccessible:[15]
And *this*, the naked countenance of earth
On which I gaze, even these primeval mountains
Teach the adverting[16] mind. The glaciers creep
Like snakes that watch their prey, from their far fountains
Slow rolling on; there, many a precipice,
Frost and the sun in scorn of mortal power
Have piled: dome, pyramid, and pinnacle,
A city of death, distinct[17] with many a tower
And wall impregnable of beaming ice.
Yet not a city, but a flood of ruin
Is there, that from the boundaries of the sky
Rolls its perpetual stream; vast pines are strewing
Its destined path, or in the mangled soil
Branchless and shattered stand; the rocks, drawn down
From yon remotest waste, have overthrown
The limits of the dead and living world,
Never to be reclaimed. The dwelling-place
Of insects, beasts, and birds, becomes its spoil;
Their food and their retreat for ever gone,
So much of life and joy is lost. The race
Of man flies far in dread; his work and dwelling
Vanish like smoke before the tempest's stream,
And their place is not known. Below, vast caves
Shine in the rushing torrents' restless gleam,
Which from those secret chasms in tumult welling[18]
Meet in the vale; and one majestic river,[19]
The breath and blood of distant lands, forever
Rolls its loud waters to the ocean waves,
Breathes its swift vapours to the circling air.

V

Mont Blanc yet gleams on high: the Power is there,
The still and solemn Power of many sights
And many sounds, and much of life and death.
In the calm darkness of the moonless nights,
In the lone glare of day, the snows descend
Upon that mountain; none beholds them there,
Nor when the flakes burn in the sinking sun,
Or the starbeams dart through them; winds contend

## Notes

[15] *inaccessible* At 4,810 metres, Mont Blanc is the highest mountain in Europe; it had been climbed only three times by 1816.

[16] *adverting* heedful, observant, thoughtful.

[17] *distinct* adorned.

[18] *Which from those secret chasms in tumult welling* an echo of Coleridge's recently published 'Kubla Khan' 17: 'And from this chasm, with ceaseless turmoil seething.' Shelley had seen Byron's copy of the printed text.

[19] *one majestic river* the Rhône, fed by Lake Geneva, into which flows the Arve.

Silently there, and heap the snow with breath
Rapid and strong, but silently! Its home
The voiceless lightning in these solitudes
Keeps innocently, and like vapour broods
Over the snow. The secret strength of things
Which governs thought, and to the infinite dome
Of heaven is as a law, inhabits thee!
And what were thou, and earth, and stars, and sea,
If to the human mind's imaginings
Silence and solitude were vacancy?

## *Ozymandias* (composed 26–28 December 1817)[1]

I met a traveller from an antique land
Who said, 'Two vast and trunkless legs of stone
Stand in the desert. Near them, on the sand
Half-sunk, a shattered visage lies, whose frown
And wrinkled lip, and sneer of cold command,
Tell that its sculptor well those passions read
Which yet survive, stamped on these lifeless things,
The hand that mocked them, and the heart that fed;
And on the pedestal these words appear:
"My name is Ozymandias, King of Kings,
Look on my works, ye mighty, and despair!"
Nothing beside remains. Round the decay
Of that colossal wreck, boundless and bare,
The lone and level sands stretch far away.'

## *On Love* (composed 20–25 July 1818)[1]

What is love? Ask him who lives, what is life; ask him who adores, what is God.

I know not the internal constitution of other men, or even of thine whom I now address. I see that in some external attributes they resemble me, but, when misled by that appearance I have thought to appeal to something in common and unburden my inmost soul to them, I have found

### Notes

Ozymandias

[1] Horace Smith (1779–1849), a banker and writer of light verse, met Shelley in London in December 1816. Together, Shelley and Smith visited the British Museum and their admiration of the newly acquired statue of Rameses II (thirteenth century BCE, also known as Ozymandias) prompted Smith to propose a sonnet-writing competition on the subject. Smith's sonnet was published on 1 February 1818 in *The Examiner*, and reads as follows:

In Egypt's sandy silence, all alone,
  Stands a gigantic leg, which far off throws
  The only shadow that the desert knows.
'I am great Ozymandias', saith the stone,
  'The King of Kings; this mighty city shows
The wonders of my hand.' The city's gone;
  Nought but the leg remaining to disclose
The site of this forgotten Babylon.
We wonder, and some hunter may express
Wonder like ours, when through the wilderness
  Where London stood, holding the wolf in chase,
He meets some fragment huge, and stops to guess
  What powerful but unrecorded race
  Once dwelt in that annihilated place.

On Love

[1] Scholars suggest this essay is a response to Plato. Shelley translated the *Symposium* 7–20 July 1818.

my language misunderstood like one in a distant and savage land. The more opportunities they have afforded me for experience, the wider has appeared the interval between us, and to a greater distance have the points of sympathy been withdrawn. With a spirit ill-fitted to sustain such proof,[2] trembling and feeble through its tenderness, I have everywhere sought, and have found only repulse and disappointment.

Thou demandest what is love. It is that powerful attraction towards all that we conceive, or fear, or hope beyond ourselves, when we find within our own thoughts the chasm of an insufficient void, and seek to awaken in all things that are, a community with what we experience within ourselves. If we reason, we would be understood; if we imagine, we would that the airy children of our brain were born anew within another's; if we feel, we would that another's nerves should vibrate to our own, that the beams of their eyes should kindle at once and mix and melt into our own, that lips of motionless ice should not reply to lips quivering and burning with the heart's best blood. This is love. This is the bond and the sanction which connects not only man with man, but with everything which exists. We are born into the world and there is something within us which, from the instant that we live and move, thirsts after its likeness; it is probably in correspondence with this law that the infant drains milk from the bosom of its mother. This propensity develops itself with the development of our nature.

We see dimly[3] within our intellectual nature a miniature, as it were, of our entire self, yet deprived of all that we condemn or despise: the ideal prototype of everything excellent or lovely that we are capable of conceiving as belonging to the nature of man – not only the portrait of our external being, but an assemblage of the minutest particulars of which our nature is composed; a mirror whose surface reflects only the forms of purity and brightness; a soul within our soul that describes a circle around its proper Paradise which pain and sorrow and evil dare not overleap.[4] To this we eagerly refer all sensations, thirsting that they should resemble or correspond with it.

The discovery of its antitype – the meeting with an understanding capable of clearly estimating the deductions of our own, an imagination which should enter into and seize upon the subtle and delicate peculiarities which we have delighted to cherish and unfold in secret, with a frame whose nerves, like the chords of two exquisite lyres strung to the accompaniment of one delightful voice, vibrate with the vibrations of our own, and of a combination of all these in such proportion as the type within demands: this is the invisible and unattainable point to which love tends, and to attain which it urges forth the powers of man to arrest the faintest shadow of that without the possession of which there is no rest or respite to the heart over which it rules.

Hence in solitude, or in that deserted state when we are surrounded by human beings and yet they sympathize not with us, we love the flowers, the grass, and the waters and the sky. In the motion of the very leaves of spring in the blue air there is then found a secret correspondence with our heart. There is eloquence in the tongueless wind and a melody in the flowing of brooks and the rustling of the reeds beside them, which by their inconceivable relation to something within the soul, awaken the spirits to a dance of breathless rapture, and bring tears of mysterious tenderness to the eyes like the enthusiasm of patriotic success or the voice of one beloved singing to you alone. Sterne says that if he were in a desert he would love some cypress[5] … So soon as this want or power is dead, man becomes the living sepulchre of himself, and what yet survives is the mere husk of what once he was.

## Notes

[2] *proof* trial.

[3] 'These words inefficient and metaphorical. Most words so. No help' (Shelley's note).

[4] *Paradise … overleap* Shelley recalls 'Paradise Lost' iv 181–2, where Satan 'overleaped all bound / Of hill or highest wall' in order to enter Eden.

[5] 'I declare, said I, clapping my hands cheerily together, that was I in a desert, I would find out wherewith in it to call forth my affections. If I could not do better, I would fasten them upon some sweet myrtle, or seek some melancholy cypress to connect myself to' (Sterne, *A Sentimental Journey* ed. Gardner D. Stout, Jr (Berkeley, 1967), pp. 115–16).

## *Lines Written among the Euganean Hills, October 1818*[1]

Many a green isle[2] needs must be
In the deep wide sea of misery,
Or the mariner, worn and wan,
Never thus could voyage on
Day and night, and night and day,
Drifting on his dreary way,
With the solid darkness black
Closing round his vessel's track;
Whilst above, the sunless sky,
Big with clouds, hangs heavily,
And behind the tempest fleet
Hurries on with lightning feet,
Riving[3] sail and cord and plank
Till the ship has almost drank
Death from the o'er-brimming deep,
And sinks down, down, like that sleep
When the dreamer seems to be
Weltering[4] through eternity;
And the dim low line before
Of a dark and distant shore
Still recedes, as ever still
Longing with divided will,
But no power to seek or shun,
He is ever drifted on
O'er the unreposing wave
To the haven of the grave.
What if there no friends will greet?[5]
What if there no heart will meet
His with love's impatient beat?
Wander wheresoe'er he may,
Can he dream before that day
To find refuge from distress
In friendship's smile, in love's caress?
Then 'twill wreak[6] him little woe
Whether such there be or no:

## Notes

Lines Written among the Euganean Hills

[1] This meditative poem was written at a difficult moment in Shelley's life. His baby daughter Clara had died at Venice in late September (barely a year old), and on their return to Byron's villa at Este, I Capuccini, a deep gloom pervaded the household. Clara's death depressed Mary, and Percy found himself in bad health. He sent this poem with a number of others to his publisher, prefacing them as follows: 'I do not know which of the few scattered poems I left in England will be selected by my bookseller, to add to this collection. One, which I sent from Italy, was written after a day's excursion among those lovely mountains which surround what was once the retreat, and where is now the sepulchre, of Petrarch. If anyone is inclined to condemn the insertion of the introductory lines, which image forth the sudden relief of a state of deep despondency by the radiant visions disclosed by the sudden burst of an Italian sunrise in autumn on the highest peak of those delightful mountains, I can only offer as my excuse, that they were not erased at the request of a dear friend, with whom added years of intercourse only add to my apprehension of its value, and who would have had more right than anyone to complain, that she has not been able to extinguish in me the very power of delineating sadness.' (The 'dear friend' is Mary Shelley.)

[2] *a green isle* The Euganean hills stand in the midst of a plain to the west of Padua.

[3] *Riving* tearing.

[4] *Weltering* tumbling.

[5] *What if there no friends will greet?* In Greek myth, friends were supposed to be reunited after death in the Elysian fields.

[6] *wreak* give.

Senseless[7] is the breast, and cold,
Which relenting love would fold;
Bloodless are the veins and chill
Which the pulse of pain did fill;
Every little living nerve
That from bitter words did swerve
Round the tortured lips and brow,
Are like sapless leaflets now
Frozen upon December's bough.

On the beach of a northern sea[8]
Which tempests shake eternally,
As once the wretch there lay to sleep,
Lies a solitary heap:
One white skull and seven dry bones,
On the margin of the stones
Where a few grey rushes stand,
Boundaries of the sea and land.
Nor is heard one voice of wail
But the sea-mews,[9] as they sail
O'er the billows of the gale;
Or the whirlwind up and down
Howling like a slaughtered town,
When a king in glory rides
Through the pomp of fratricides.[10]
Those unburied bones around
There is many a mournful sound;
There is no lament for him
Like a sunless vapour, dim,
Who once clothed with life and thought
What now moves nor murmurs not.

Aye, many flowering islands lie
In the waters of wide agony;
To such a one this morn was led
My bark, by soft winds piloted.
Mid the mountains Euganean[11]
I stood listening to the paean
With which the legioned rooks[12] did hail
The sun's uprise majestical;
Gathering round with wings all hoar,
Through the dewy mist they soar
Like grey shades, till th' eastern heaven

## Notes

[7] *Senseless* i.e. unperceiving (because dead).

[8] Shelley's daughter Clara was buried on the Lido, by the northern Adriatic.

[9] *sea-mews* seagulls.

[10] *a slaughtered town ... fratricides* A reference to the mass slaughter by the Danish King Christian II after he entered Stockholm, 1520.

[11] *Euganean* stressed on the third syllable.

[12] *rooks* Shelley may be referring to jackdaws, as there are no rooks in Italy. He may be thinking favourably of them because Coleridge had done so in *'This Lime-Tree Bower My Prison'*.

Bursts,[13] and then, as clouds of even[14]
Flecked with fire and azure lie
In the unfathomable sky,
So their plumes of purple grain,[15]
Starred with drops of golden rain,
Gleam above the sunlight woods,
As in silent multitudes
On the morning's fitful gale
Through the broken mist they sail,
And the vapours cloven and gleaming
Follow down the dark steep streaming,
Till all is bright and clear and still
Round the solitary hill.

Beneath is spread like a green sea
The waveless plain of Lombardy,[16]
Bounded by the vaporous air,
Islanded by cities fair;
Underneath day's azure eyes
Ocean's nursling, Venice,[17] lies,
A peopled labyrinth of walls,
Amphitrite's[18] destined halls
Which her hoary sire now paves
With his blue and beaming waves.
Lo! the sun upsprings behind,[19]
Broad, red, radiant, half-reclined
On the level quivering line
Of the waters crystalline;
And before that chasm of light,
As within a furnace bright,
Column, tower, and dome, and spire,
Shine like obelisks of fire,
Pointing with inconstant motion
From the altar of dark ocean
To the sapphire-tinted skies;
As the flames of sacrifice
From the marble shrines did rise,
As to pierce the dome of gold[20]
Where Apollo spoke of old.

## Notes

[13] *Bursts* i.e. into light – the sun rises in the east.

[14] *even* i.e. night.

[15] *their plumes of purple grain* their feathers were dyed purple by the light of the rising sun.

[16] *Beneath ... Lombardy* In a letter to Peacock of 8 October 1818 Shelley described the view from his villa in the Euganean Hills: 'We see before us the wide flat plains of Lombardy, in which we see the sun and moon rise and set, and the evening star, and all the golden magnificence of autumnal clouds.'

[17] Shelley was at Venice for a few days at the end of September 1818.

[18] Amphitrite was the daughter of Oceanus, god of the sea (her 'sire', line 98), and the wife of Poseidon. She will inherit the halls of Venice when they are swamped by the sea.

[19] *behind* i.e. behind Venice.

[20] *dome of gold* the Delphic oracle, through which Apollo (god of youth, poetry and music) was believed to speak.

Sun-girt city, thou hast been
Ocean's child, and then his queen;
Now is come a darker day,[21]
And thou soon must be his prey,
If the power that raised thee here
Hallow so thy watery bier.
A less drear ruin then than now,
With thy conquest-branded brow
Stooping to the slave of slaves
From thy throne, among the waves
Wilt thou be, when the sea-mew
Flies, as once before it flew,
O'er thine isles depopulate,[22]
And all is in its ancient state,
Save where many a palace gate
With green sea-flowers overgrown
Like a rock of ocean's own,
Topples o'er the abandoned sea
As the tides change sullenly.
The fisher on his watery way,
Wandering at the close of day,
Will spread his sail and seize his oar
Till he pass the gloomy shore,
Lest thy dead should, from their sleep
Bursting o'er the starlight[23] deep,
Lead a rapid masque[24] of death
O'er the waters of his path.

Those who alone thy towers behold
Quivering through aerial gold,
As I now behold them here,
Would imagine not they were
Sepulchres where human forms,
Like pollution-nourished worms,
To the corpse of greatness cling,
Murdered and now mouldering;[25]
But if Freedom should awake
In her omnipotence, and shake
From the Celtic Anarch's[26] hold
All the keys of dungeons[27] cold,
Where a hundred cities lie

## Notes

[21] *Now is come a darker day* Shelley's sorrow for Venice was due partly to the fact that, by the terms of the Congress of Vienna, 1815, it had been handed over to Austria; as he told Peacock on 8 October 1818: 'Venice, which was once a tyrant, is now the next worse thing – a slave.'

[22] *depopulate* laid waste.

[23] *starlight* i.e. starlit (an adjective).

[24] *masque* procession.

[25] Shelley was shocked by the degraded state of Venice under Austrian occupation: 'I had no conception of the excess to which avarice, cowardice, superstition, ignorance, passionless lust, and all the inexpressible brutalities which degrade human nature could be carried, until I had lived a few days among the Venetians.'

[26] *Celtic Anarch* Austrian tyrant, as at line 223.

[27] *dungeons* On his visit to Venice in September 1818 Shelley visited the dungeons in the Doge's palace 'where the prisoners were confined sometimes half up to their middles in stinking water.'

Chained like thee, ingloriously,
Thou and all thy sister band
Might adorn this sunny land,
Twining memories of old time
With new virtues more sublime:
If not, perish thou and they! –
Clouds which stain truth's rising day
By her sun consumed away,
Earth can spare ye, while like flowers
In the waste of years and hours,
From your dust new nations spring
With more kindly blossoming.

Perish! let there only be
Floating o'er thy hearthless sea,
As the garment of thy sky
Clothes the world immortally,
One remembrance more sublime
Than the tattered pall of time,
Which scarce hides thy visage wan –
That a tempest-cleaving swan[28]
Of the songs of Albion,[29]
Driven from his ancestral streams
By the might of evil dreams,[30]
Found a nest in thee; and Ocean
Welcomed him with such emotion
That its joy grew his,[31] and sprung
From his lips[32] like music flung
O'er a mighty thunder-fit,
Chastening terror. What though yet
Poesy's unfailing river,
Which through Albion winds forever,
Lashing with melodious wave
Many a sacred poet's grave,
Mourn its latest nursling fled?
What though thou with all thy dead
Scarce can for this fame repay
Aught thine own?[33] Oh rather say,
Though[34] thy sins and slaveries foul
Overcloud a sunlike soul?
As the ghost of Homer clings
Round Scamander's[35] wasting springs;

## Notes

[28] *a tempest-cleaving swan* Byron, then living at the Palazzo Mocenigo, Venice, where Shelley had met him the previous month.

[29] *Albion* England.

[30] *Driven … dreams* Byron was in self-exile, having been driven out of England by his wife's campaign against him after their separation.

[31] *its joy grew his* As Shelley reported to Peacock on 8 October 1818: '[Byron] is changed into the liveliest, and happiest looking man I ever met.'

[32] *sprung / From his lips* A reference to 'Don Juan' Canto I, which Byron had read to Shelley in late September 1818.

[33] *What though … own* Venice lacks a poet of its own as famous as Byron.

[34] *Though* i.e. '[What] Though thy sins …?'

[35] Scamander was a river near Troy, site of the wars described by Homer in the *Iliad*, but now neglected by poets (and therefore wasted).

As divinest Shakespeare's might
Fills Avon and the world with light,
Like omniscient power which he
Imaged mid mortality;
As the love from Petrarch's urn
Yet amid yon hills doth burn,[36]
A quenchless lamp by which the heart
Sees things unearthly – so thou art,
Mighty spirit;[37] so shall be
The city that did refuge thee.

Lo, the sun floats up the sky
Like thought-winged liberty,
Till the universal light
Seems to level plain and height;
From the sea a mist has spread,
And the beams of morn lie dead
On the towers of Venice now,
Like its glory long ago.
By the skirts of that grey cloud
Many-domed Padua[38] proud
Stands, a peopled solitude
Mid the harvest-shining plain,
Where the peasant heaps his grain
In the garner of his foe,[39]
And the milk-white oxen slow
With the purple vintage strain,
Heaped upon the creaking wain,
That the brutal Celt[40] may swill
Drunken sleep with savage will;
And the sickle to the sword
Lies unchanged, though many a lord,
Like a weed whose shade is poison,
Overgrows this region's foison,[41]
Sheaves of whom are ripe to come
To destruction's harvest home:
Men must reap the things they sow,
Force from force must ever flow
Or worse – but 'tis a bitter woe
That love or reason cannot change
The despot's rage, the slave's revenge.

Padua, thou within whose walls
Those mute guests at festivals,
Son and mother, Death and Sin,

## Notes

[36] *As the love ... burn* The house and grave of the great Italian poet Petrarch (1304–74) are at Arqua in the Euganean Hills.

[37] *Mighty spirit* Byron.

[38] Shelley was in Padua August 1818.

[39] *the garner of his foe* the granary of the Austrians. Shelley told Peacock, 'The Austrians take sixty percent in taxes'.

[40] *Celt* Austrian.

[41] *foison* harvest.

Played at dice for Ezzelin,[42]
Till Death cried, 'I win, I win!'
And Sin cursed to lose the wager,
But Death promised, to assuage her,
That he would petition for
Her to be made Vice-Emperor,
When the destined years were o'er,
Over all between the Po
And the eastern Alpine snow,
Under the mighty Austrian.
Sin smiled so as Sin only can,
And since that time, aye, long before,
Both have ruled from shore to shore –
That incestuous pair who follow
Tyrants as the sun the swallow,
As repentance follows crime,
And as changes follow time.

In thine halls the lamp of learning,
Padua, now no more is burning;[43]
Like a meteor, whose wild way
Is lost over the grave of day,
It gleams betrayed and to betray.
Once remotest nations came
To adore that sacred flame,
When it lit not many a hearth
On this cold and gloomy earth;
Now new fires from antique light
Spring beneath the wide world's might,
But their spark lies dead in thee,
Trampled out by tyranny.
As the Norway woodman quells,
In the depth of piny dells,[44]
One light flame among the brakes,[45]
While the boundless forest shakes,
And its mighty trunks are torn
By the fire thus lowly born;
The spark beneath his feet is dead,
He starts to see the flames it fed
Howling through the darkened sky
With a myriad tongues victoriously,
And sinks down in fear: so thou,
Oh tyranny, beholdest now
Light around thee, and thou hearest

## Notes

[42] Ezzelino da Romano (1194–1259), despot of Padua. Shelley is probably recalling Coleridge's 'Ancient Mariner', where Death and Life-in-Death cast dice for the mariner's soul.

[43] *In thine halls … burning* Padua University is one of the oldest in Europe, founded in the eleventh century.

[44] *piny dells* dells of pine trees.

[45] *brakes* ferns.

The loud flames ascend, and fearest –
Grovel on the earth! Aye, hide
In the dust thy purple[46] pride!

Noon descends around me now;
'Tis the noon of autumn's glow
When a soft and purple mist,
Like a vaporous amethyst,
Or an air-dissolved star[47]
Mingling light and fragrance, far
From the curved horizon's bound
To the point of heaven's profound,
Fills the overflowing sky;
And the plains that silent lie
Underneath, the leaves unsodden
Where the infant frost has trodden
With his morning-winged feet,
Whose bright print is gleaming yet;
And the red and golden vines,
Piercing with their trellised lines
The rough, dark-skirted wilderness;
The dun and bladed grass no less,
Pointing from this hoary tower[48]
In the windless air; the flower
Glimmering at my feet; the line
Of the olive-sandalled Apennine[49]
In the south dimly islanded;
And the Alps, whose snows are spread
High between the clouds and sun;
And of living things each one;
And my spirit which so long
Darkened this swift stream of song –
Interpenetrated lie
By the glory of the sky:
Be it love, light, harmony,
Odour, or the soul of all
Which from heaven like dew doth fall,
Or the mind which feeds this verse
Peopling the lone universe.

Noon descends, and after noon
Autumn's evening meets me soon,
Leading the infantine moon
And that one star,[50] which to her
Almost seems to minister
Half the crimson light she brings
From the sunset's radiant springs;

## Notes

[46] *purple* colour of imperial triumph.

[47] *an air-dissolved star* the star's light is diffused by the atmosphere.

[48] *this hoary tower* of the Benedictine monastery of the Olivetani on Monte Venda, the highest point in the Euganean Hills.

[49] *olive-sandalled Apennine* olive trees grow in the Apennines.

[50] *that one star* Hesper, the evening star.

And the soft dreams of the morn
(Which like winged winds had borne
To that silent isle, which lies
Mid remembered agonies,
The frail bark of this lone being)
Pass, to other sufferers fleeing,
And its ancient pilot, Pain,
Sits beside the helm again.

Other flowering isles must be
In the sea of life and agony;
Other spirits float and flee
O'er that gulf – even now, perhaps,
On some rock the wild wave wraps,
With folding wings they waiting sit
For my bark, to pilot it
To some calm and blooming cove,
Where for me and those I love,
May a windless bower be built
Far from passion, pain, and guilt,[51]
In a dell mid lawny hills
Which the wild sea-murmur fills,
And soft sunshine, and the sound
Of old forests echoing round,
And the light and smell divine
Of all flowers that breathe and shine.
We may live so happy there
That the spirits of the air,
Envying us, may even entice
To our healing paradise
The polluting multitude;
But their rage would be subdued
By that clime divine and calm,
And the winds whose wings rain balm
On the uplifted soul, and leaves
Under which the bright sea heaves;
While each breathless interval
In their whisperings musical
The inspired soul supplies
With its own deep melodies,
And the love which heals all strife
Circling like the breath of life,
All things in that sweet abode
With its own mild brotherhood:
They, not it, would change, and soon
Every sprite beneath the moon
Would repent its envy vain,
And the earth grow young again.

## Notes

[51] *guilt* This poem is inspired partly by guilt at the death of Shelley's baby daughter, Clara, due in part to his negligence.

## *Stanzas Written in Dejection, near Naples* (composed December 1818)[1]

The sun is warm, the sky is clear,
  The waves are dancing fast and bright,
Blue isles and snowy mountains wear
  The purple noon's transparent light:
The breath of the moist air is light
  Around its unexpanded buds;
Like many a voice of one delight
  The winds, the birds, the ocean floods,
The City's voice itself is soft like Solitude's.

I see the Deep's untrampled floor
  With green and purple seaweeds strown;
I see the waves upon the shore,
  Like light dissolved in star-showers, thrown:
I sit upon the sands alone,
  The lightning of the noontide ocean
Is flashing round me, and a tone
  Arises from its measured motion,
How sweet! did any heart now share in my emotion.

Alas! I have nor hope nor health,[2]
  Nor peace within nor calm around,
Nor that content surpassing wealth
  The sage in meditation found,
And walked with inward glory crowned –
  Nor fame, nor power, nor love, nor leisure.
Others I see whom these surround –
  Smiling they live, and call life pleasure;
To me that cup has been dealt in another measure.

Yet now despair itself is mild,
  Even as the winds and waters are;
I could lie down like a tired child,
  And weep away the life of care
Which I have borne and yet must bear,
  Till death like sleep might steal on me,
And I might feel in the warm air
  My cheek grow cold, and hear the sea
Breathe o'er my dying brain its last monotony.

## Notes

Stanzas Written in Dejection

[1] Shelley moved his family to Naples at the end of November 1818.

[2] *health* Mary Shelley recalled: 'At this time Shelley suffered greatly in health. He put himself under the care of a medical man, who promised great things, and made him endure severe bodily pain, without any good results. Constant and poignant physical pain exhausted him; and though he preserved the appearance of cheerfulness, and often greatly enjoyed our wanderings in the environs of Naples, and our excursions on the sunny sea, yet many hours were passed when his thoughts, shadowed by illness, became gloomy, and then he escaped to solitude, and in verses, which he hid from fear of wounding me, poured forth morbid but too natural bursts of discontent and sadness.'

Some might lament that I were cold,
As I when this sweet day is gone,
Which my lost heart, too soon grown old,
Insults with this untimely moan;
They might lament – for I am one
Whom men love not – and yet regret,
Unlike this day, which, when the sun
Shall on its stainless glory set,
Will linger, though enjoyed, like joy in memory yet.

## *The Mask of Anarchy. Written on the Occasion of the Massacre at Manchester* (composed 5–23 September 1819; edited from MS; published 1832)[1]

As I lay asleep in Italy[2]
There came a voice from over the Sea,
And with great power it forth led me
To walk in the visions of Poesy.

I met Murder on the way –
He had a mask like Castlereagh[3] –
Very smooth he looked, yet grim;
Seven bloodhounds followed him.[4]

All were fat; and well they might
Be in admirable plight,
For one by one, and two by two,
He tossed them human hearts to chew,
Which from his wide cloak he drew.

Next came Fraud, and he had on,
Like Eldon,[5] an ermined gown;
His big tears, for he wept well,
Turned to millstones as they fell.

And the little children, who
Round his feet played to and fro,
Thinking every tear a gem,
Had their brains knocked out by them.

## Notes

THE MASK OF ANARCHY

[1] On 16 August 1819, at St Peter's Field, on the outskirts of Manchester, a political meeting of 60,000 working men and women was dispersed by mounted dragoons, with a brutality that left eleven people dead and 421 cases of serious injury. The news reached Shelley within about a week, and he began meditating this poetic response to the event.

[2] Shelley was in Livorno when he heard of the Peterloo Massacre, 'and the torrent of my indignation has not yet done boiling in my veins', as he told Charles Ollier on 5 September 1819.

[3] Robert Stewart, Viscount Castlereagh (1769–1822), Foreign Secretary 1812–22. As Secretary to the Lord Lieutenant of Ireland (1797–1801), he had been responsible for imprisoning the leaders of the United Irish rebellion. Shelley would have been aware of Byron's stanzas attacking him, 'Don Juan' Dedication, stanzas 12–15.

[4] In 1815, Britain joined an alliance of seven other nations (Austria, France, Russia, Prussia, Portugal, Spain and Sweden) in an agreement to postpone final abolition of the slave trade.

[5] John Scott, Baron Eldon, Lord Chancellor, who, on 27 March 1817, was responsible for depriving Shelley of access to his children (Ianthe and Charles) by Harriet Westbrook. Shelley did not see Ianthe again, and Charles he never saw.

Clothed with the Bible, as with light,
And the shadows of the night,
Like Sidmouth,[6] next Hypocrisy
On a crocodile[7] rode by.

And many more Destructions played
In this ghastly masquerade,
All disguised, even to the eyes,
Like Bishops, lawyers, peers, or spies.

Last came Anarchy:[8] he rode
On a white horse, splashed with blood;
He was pale even to the lips,
Like Death in the Apocalypse.[9]

And he wore a kingly crown,
And in his grasp a sceptre shone;
On his brow this mark I saw –
'I am God, and King, and Law.'[10]

With a pace stately and fast,
Over English land he passed,
Trampling to a mire of blood
The adoring multitude.[11]

And a mighty troop around,
With their trampling shook the ground,
Waving each a bloody sword,
For the service of their Lord.[12]

And with glorious triumph, they
Rode through England proud and gay,
Drunk as with intoxication
Of the wine of desolation.

O'er fields and towns, from sea to sea,
Passed the Pageant[13] swift and free,
Tearing up, and trampling down,
Till they came to London town.

## Notes

[6] Henry Addington (1757–1844), created Viscount Sidmouth in 1805, had been Prime Minister and Chancellor of the Exchequer, and was in 1819 Home Secretary. He applauded the Peterloo Massacre in the House of Commons, as reported by Hazlitt.

[7] *a crocodile* Crocodiles were believed to weep as they devoured their prey, and the term 'crocodile tears' remains a byword for hypocrisy.

[8] *Anarchy* Shelley refers to the breakdown of order such as that which led to the Peterloo Massacre. He did not regard it as a good thing either for the government or for the victims.

[9] *He was pale ... Apocalypse* Revelation 6:8: 'And I looked, and behold a pale horse: and his name that sat on him was Death, and Hell followed with him.'

[10] *On his brow ... Law* a parody of the inscription borne by the messianic rider of Revelation: 'And he hath on his vesture and on his thigh a name written, KING OF KINGS, AND LORD OF LORDS' (Revelation 19:16).

[11] *The adoring multitude* The people admire Anarchy. Shelley's point is that to resort to violence is to justify the government's equally violent means of suppression.

[12] *their Lord* George III, the 'old, mad, blind, despised, and dying king' of 'England in 1819', although the term could also apply to the Christian God of the Church of England, part of what Shelley regarded as the corrupt political system responsible for the Peterloo Massacre.

[13] *Pageant* tableau, allegorical procession.

And each dweller, panic-stricken,
Felt his heart with terror sicken
Hearing the tempestuous cry
Of the triumph of Anarchy.

For with pomp to meet him came
Clothed in arms like blood and flame,
The hired murderers, who did sing
'Thou art God, and Law, and King.

We have waited, weak and lone,
For thy coming, Mighty One!
Our purses are empty, our swords are cold,
Give us glory, and blood, and gold.'

Lawyers and priests, a motley crowd,
To the earth their pale brows bowed;
Like a bad prayer, not overloud,
Whispering, 'Thou art Law and God.'

Then all cried with one accord,
'Thou art King, and God, and Lord;
Anarchy, to thee we bow,
By thy name made holy now!'

And Anarchy, the Skeleton,
Bowed and grinned to everyone,
As well as if his education
Had cost ten millions to the nation.

For he knew the Palaces
Of our Kings were rightly his;
His the sceptre, crown, and globe,[14]
And the gold-inwoven robe.

So he sent his slaves before
To seize upon the Bank and Tower,[15]
And was proceeding with intent
To meet his pensioned Parliament;[16]

When one fled past, a maniac maid,
And her name was Hope, she said;
But she looked more like Despair,
And she cried out in the air:

## Notes

[14] *globe* golden orb, symbol of kingly power.

[15] *the Bank and Tower* strongholds of power: the Bank of England, in London's Threadneedle Street since 1734, and the Tower of London, the most perfect medieval fortress in Britain, on Tower Hill since around 1066. They had been objects of an alleged plot in 1817, providing an excuse for the suspension of habeas corpus.

[16] *his pensioned Parliament* The politicians are in the pay of Anarchy, because his violent means enable them to retain power.

'My father Time is weak and grey
With waiting for a better day;
See how idiot-like he stands,
Fumbling with his palsied hands!

He has had child after child
And the dust of death is piled
Over everyone but me –
Misery, oh, misery!'

Then she lay down in the street,
Right before the horses' feet,
Expecting, with a patient eye,
Murder, Fraud and Anarchy.

When between her and her foes
A mist, a light, an image rose,
Small at first, and weak, and frail,
Like the vapour of a vale;

Till as clouds grow on the blast,
Like tower-crowned giants striding fast,
And glare with lightnings as they fly,
And speak in thunder to the sky,

It grew – a Shape arrayed in mail
Brighter than the viper's scale,
And upborne on wings whose grain[17]
Was as the light of sunny rain.

On its helm,[18] seen far away,
A planet, like the morning's,[19] lay;
And those plumes[20] its light rained through
Like a shower of crimson dew.

With step as soft as wind it passed
O'er the heads of men – so fast
That they knew the presence there,
And looked – and all was empty air.

As flowers beneath May's footstep waken,
As stars from night's loose hair are shaken,
As waves arise when loud winds call,
Thoughts sprung where'er that step did fall.

And the prostrate multitude
Looked – and ankle-deep in blood,
Hope, that maiden most serene,
Was walking with a quiet mien.

## Notes

[17] *grain* colour.
[18] *helm* helmet.
[19] *A planet, like the morning's* i.e. a star, like Venus (the morning star).
[20] *plumes* feathers in the helmet.

And Anarchy, the ghastly birth,
Lay dead earth upon the earth;
The Horse of Death, tameless as wind,
Fled, and with his hoofs did grind
To dust the murderers thronged behind.

A rushing light of clouds and splendour,
A sense awakening and yet tender,
Was heard and felt – and at its close
These words of joy and fear arose

(As if their own indignant Earth
Which gave the sons of England birth
Had felt their blood upon her brow,
And shuddering with a mother's throe

Had turned every drop of blood
By which her face had been bedewed
To an accent unwithstood;
As if her heart had cried aloud):

'Men of England, heirs of Glory,
Heroes of unwritten story,
Nurslings of one mighty Mother,
Hopes of her, and one another,

Rise like lions after slumber
In unvanquishable number,
Shake your chains to Earth like dew
Which in sleep had fallen on you –
Ye are many; they are few.

What is Freedom? Ye can tell
That which slavery is, too well –
For its very name has grown
To an echo of your own.

'Tis to work and have such pay
As just keeps life from day to day
In your limbs, as in a cell
For the tyrants' use to dwell.

So that ye for them are made
Loom, and plough, and sword, and spade,
With or without your own will bent
To their defence and nourishment.

'Tis to see your children weak
With their mothers pine and peak,[21]
When the winter winds are bleak –
They are dying whilst I speak.

## Notes

[21] *pine and peak* grow thin and emaciated; cf. *Macbeth* I iii 23.

'Tis to hunger for such diet
As the rich man in his riot[22]
Casts to the fat dogs that lie
Surfeiting beneath his eye.

'Tis to let the Ghost of Gold[23]
Take from toil a thousandfold –
More than ere its substance could
In the tyrannies of old.

Paper coin – that forgery
Of the title-deeds, which ye
Hold to something of the worth
Of the inheritance of Earth.

'Tis to be a slave in soul
And to hold no strong control
Over your own wills, but be
All that others make of ye.

And at length when ye complain
With a murmur weak and vain,
'Tis to see the Tyrant's crew
Ride over your wives and you –
Blood is on the grass like dew.

Then it is to feel revenge
Fiercely thirsting to exchange
Blood for blood and wrong for wrong –
Do not thus when ye are strong.

Birds find rest in narrow nest
When weary of their winged quest;
Beasts find fare in woody lair
When storm and snow are in the air.

Asses, swine, have litter spread
And with fitting food are fed;
All things have a home but one –
Thou, oh, Englishman, hast none![24]

This is slavery – savage men
Or wild beasts within a den
Would endure not as ye do;
But such ills they never knew.

## Notes

[22] *riot* extravagance.

[23] *the Ghost of Gold* paper money, which Shelley regarded as a trick to inflate the currency and depress the cost of labour.

[24] *Asses, swine … hast none* A reworking of Christ's words: 'The foxes have holes, and the birds of the air have nests; but the Son of man hath not where to lay his head' (Matthew 8:20).

What art thou Freedom? Oh, could slaves
Answer from their living graves
This demand, tyrants would flee
Like a dream's dim imagery.

Thou art not, as impostors say,
A shadow soon to pass away,
A superstition, and a name
Echoing from the cave of Fame.[25]

For the labourer thou art bread,
And a comely table spread
From his daily labour come
To a neat and happy home.

Thou art clothes, and fire, and food
For the trampled multitude;
No – in countries that are free
Such starvation cannot be
As in England now we see.

To the rich thou art a check,
When his foot is on the neck
Of his victim, thou dost make
That he treads upon a snake.

Thou art Justice; ne'er for gold
May thy righteous laws be sold
As laws are in England – thou
Shieldst alike the high and low.

Thou art Wisdom – Freemen never
Dream that God will damn for ever
All who think those things untrue
Of which Priests make such ado.

Thou art Peace – never by thee
Would blood and treasure wasted be,
As tyrants wasted them, when all
Leagued to quench thy flame in Gaul.[26]

What if English toil and blood
Was poured forth, even as a flood?
It availed, oh Liberty!
To dim, but not extinguish thee.

## Notes

[25] *Fame* rumour, gossip.

[26] *Gaul* Revolutionary France. England formed an alliance with Prussia and Austria in 1793, against France, following the execution of Louis XVI.

Thou art Love – the rich[27] have kissed
Thy feet, and like him following Christ,[28]
Give their substance to the free
And through the rough world follow thee;

Or turn their wealth to arms, and make
War for thy beloved sake
On wealth, and war, and fraud – whence they
Drew the power which is their prey.

Science,[29] Poetry, and Thought
Are thy lamps; they make the lot
Of the dwellers in a cot[30]
So serene, they curse it not.

Spirit, Patience, Gentleness,
All that can adorn and bless
Art thou – let deeds, not words, express
Thine exceeding loveliness.

Let a great Assembly be
Of the fearless and the free
On some spot of English ground
Where the plains stretch wide around.

Let the blue sky overhead
The green earth on which ye tread,
All that must eternal be
Witness the solemnity.

From the corners uttermost
Of the bounds of English coast;
From every hut, village and town
Where those who live and suffer moan
For others' misery or their own;

From the workhouse and the prison
Where pale as corpses newly risen,
Women, children, young and old,
Groan for pain, and weep for cold;

From the haunts of daily life
Where is waged the daily strife
With common wants and common cares
Which sows the human heart with tares;[31]

## Notes

[27] *the rich* i.e. those dedicated to liberty, such as Shelley.

[28] *like him following Christ* Shelley appears to have in mind the three disciples of Christ, Luke 9:57–62.

[29] *Science* knowledge.

[30] *cot* cottage.

[31] *tares* weeds – i.e. anxieties.

Lastly from the palaces
Where the murmur of distress
Echoes, like the distant sound
Of a wind alive around,

Those prison halls of wealth and fashion,
Where some few feel such compassion
For those who groan, and toil, and wail
As must make their brethren pale –

Ye who suffer woes untold,
Or to feel, or[32] to behold
Your lost country bought and sold
With a price of blood and gold –

Let a vast Assembly be,
And with great solemnity
Declare with measured words that ye
Are, as God has made ye, free.

Be your strong and simple words
Keen to wound as sharpened swords,
And wide as targes[33] let them be
With their shade to cover ye.

Let the tyrants pour around
With a quick and startling sound,
Like the loosening of a sea,
Troops of armed emblazonry.

Let the charged artillery drive
Till the dead air seems alive
With the clash of clanging wheels,
And the tramp of horses' heels.

Let the fixed bayonet
Gleam with sharp desire to wet
Its bright point in English blood,
Looking keen as one for food.

Let the horsemen's scimitars[34]
Wheel and flash, like sphereless stars
Thirsting to eclipse their burning
In a sea of death and mourning.

## Notes

[32] *Or … or* either … or.

[33] *targes* shields.

[34] *the horsemen's scimitars* Most of the wounded at Peterloo suffered sabre cuts.

Stand ye calm and resolute,
Like a forest close and mute,
With folded arms and looks which are
Weapons of an unvanquished war;

And let Panic, who outspeeds
The career of armed steeds
Pass, a disregarded shade
Through your phalanx undismayed.

Let the laws of your own land,
Good or ill, between ye stand
Hand to hand, and foot to foot,
Arbiters of the dispute,

The old laws of England – they
Whose reverend heads with age are grey,
Children of a wiser day;
And whose solemn voice must be
Thine own echo – Liberty!

On those who first should violate
Such sacred heralds in their state,
Rest the blood that must ensue,
And it will not rest on you.

And if then the tyrants dare,
Let them ride among you there,
Slash, and stab, and maim, and hew –
What they like, that let them do.

With folded arms and steady eyes,
And little fear, and less surprise,
Look upon them as they slay,
Till their rage has died away.

Then they will return with shame
To the place from which they came,
And the blood thus shed will speak
In hot blushes on their cheek.

Every woman in the land
Will point at them as they stand –
They will hardly dare to greet
Their acquaintance in the Street.

And the bold, true warriors
Who have hugged Danger in wars
Will turn to those who would be free,
Ashamed of such base company.

And that slaughter to the nation
Shall steam up like inspiration,
Eloquent, oracular –
A volcano heard afar.[35]

And these words shall then become
Like oppression's thundered doom
Ringing through each heart and brain,
Heard again – again – again.

Rise like lions after slumber
In unvanquishable number;
Shake your chains to earth like dew
Which in sleep had fallen on you –
Ye are many, they are few.'

## *Ode to the West Wind* (composed *c.*25 October 1819)[1]

I

Oh wild west wind, thou breath of autumn's being;
Thou from whose unseen presence the leaves dead
Are driven, like ghosts from an enchanter fleeing,

Yellow, and black, and pale, and hectic[2] red,
Pestilence-stricken multitudes; oh thou
Who chariotest to their dark wintry bed

The winged seeds, where they lie cold and low,
Each like a corpse within its grave, until
Thine azure sister of the spring shall blow

Her clarion[3] o'er the dreaming earth, and fill
(Driving sweet buds like flocks to feed in air)
With living hues and odours plain and hill –

Wild spirit, which art moving everywhere,
Destroyer and preserver, hear, oh hear!

## Notes

[35] *And that slaughter … afar* This image of revolution is comparable to the image of 'a volcano's meteor-breathing chasm, / Whence the oracular vapour is hurled up' ('Prometheus Unbound' II iii 3–4).

Ode to the West Wind

[1] 'This poem was conceived and chiefly written in a wood that skirts the Arno, near Florence, and on a day when that tempestuous wind, whose temperature is at once mild and animating, was collecting the vapours which pour down the autumnal rains. They began, as I foresaw, at sunset, with a violent tempest of hail and rain, attended by that magnificent thunder and lightning peculiar to the Cisalpine regions' (Shelley's note).

[2] *hectic* Shelley is thinking of the 'hectic' flush of a fever.

[3] *clarion* war-trumpet.

II

Thou on whose stream, mid the steep sky's commotion,
Loose clouds like earth's decaying leaves are shed,
Shook from the tangled boughs of heaven and ocean,

Angels[4] of rain and lightning; there are spread
On the blue surface of thine airy surge,
Like the bright hair uplifted from the head

Of some fierce maenad,[5] even from the dim verge
Of the horizon to the zenith's height,
The locks of the approaching storm. Thou dirge[6]

Of the dying year, to which this closing night
Will be the dome of a vast sepulchre,
Vaulted with all thy congregated might

Of vapours, from whose solid atmosphere
Black rain, and fire, and hail will burst[7] – oh hear!

III

Thou who didst waken from his summer dreams
The blue Mediterranean, where he lay,
Lulled by the coil of his crystalline streams,

Beside a pumice isle in Baiae's bay,
And saw in sleep old palaces and towers
Quivering within the wave's intenser day,[8]

All overgrown with azure moss and flowers
So sweet, the sense faints picturing them! Thou
For whose path the Atlantic's level powers

Cleave themselves into chasms, while far below
The sea-blooms and the oozy woods which wear
The sapless foliage of the ocean, know

Thy voice, and suddenly grow grey with fear,
And tremble and despoil themselves[9] – oh hear!

## Notes

[4] *Angels* messengers.

[5] *maenad* Bacchante, an inspired votary of Bacchus, god of wine.

[6] *dirge* lament for the dead.

[7] *Black rain, and fire, and hail will burst* weather conditions which prevailed on the day this poem was conceived.

[8] *Beside a pumice isle … day* In a letter to Peacock of 17 or 18 December 1818, Shelley described 'passing the Bay of Baiae and observing the ruins of its antique grandeur standing like rocks in the transparent sea under our boat'. In Roman times Baiae was the resort of emperors and the rich.

[9] 'The phenomenon alluded to at the conclusion of the third stanza is well known to naturalists. The vegetation at the bottom of the sea, of rivers, and of lakes, sympathizes with that of the land in the change of seasons, and is consequently influenced by the winds which announce it' (Shelley's note).

IV

If I were a dead leaf thou mightest bear;
If I were a swift cloud to fly with thee;
A wave to pant beneath thy power, and share

The impulse of thy strength, only less free
Than thou, oh uncontrollable! If even
I were as in my boyhood, and could be

The comrade of thy wanderings over heaven,
As then, when to outstrip thy skyey speed
Scarce seemed a vision; I would ne'er have striven

As thus with thee in prayer in my sore need.
Oh lift me as a wave, a leaf, a cloud!
I fall upon the thorns of life! I bleed!

A heavy weight of hours has chained and bowed
One too like thee[10] – tameless, and swift, and proud.

V

Make me thy lyre, even as the forest is:
What if my leaves are falling like its own?
The tumult of thy mighty harmonies

Will take from both a deep autumnal tone,
Sweet though in sadness. Be thou, spirit fierce,
My spirit! Be thou me, impetuous one!

Drive my dead thoughts over the universe
Like withered leaves to quicken a new birth!
And, by the incantation of this verse,

Scatter, as from an unextinguished hearth
Ashes and sparks, my words among mankind!
Be through my lips to unawakened earth

The trumpet of a prophecy! Oh wind,
If winter comes, can spring be far behind?

Notes

[10] *One too like thee* i.e. the poet.

## *England in 1819* (composed by 23 December 1819)[1]

An old, mad, blind, despised, and dying king;[2]
Princes,[3] the dregs of their dull race, who flow
Through public scorn – mud from a muddy spring;
Rulers who neither see, nor feel, nor know,
But leech-like to their fainting country cling,
Till they drop, blind in blood, without a blow.
A people starved and stabbed in th' untilled field;[4]
An army, which liberticide[5] and prey
Makes as a two-edged sword to all who wield;[6]
Golden and sanguine[7] laws which tempt and slay;
Religion Christless, Godless – a book sealed;
A senate, time's worst statute, unrepealed[8] –
Are graves from which a glorious phantom may
Burst, to illumine our tempestuous day.

## *Lift Not the Painted Veil* (composed 1819[1])

Lift not the painted veil which those who live
Call Life; though unreal shapes be pictured there
And it but mimic all we would believe
With colours idly spread – behind lurk Fear
And Hope, twin destinies, who ever weave
Their shadows o'er the chasm, sightless and drear.[2]
I knew one who had lifted it. He sought,
For his lost heart was tender, things to love
But found them not, alas; nor was there aught
The world contains, the which he could approve.
Through the unheeding many[3] he did move,
A splendour among shadows, a bright blot
Upon this gloomy scene, a Spirit that strove
For truth, and like the Preacher,[4] found it not.

## Notes

England in 1819

[1] Shelley sent this sonnet to Leigh Hunt for *The Examiner* on 23 December 1819. By now, he was becoming resigned to the fact that no one wanted to publish his poems. He sounds almost impatient in the letter to Hunt: 'What a state England is in! But you will never write politics. I don't wonder; but I wish then that you would write a paper in the *Examiner* on the actual state of the country, and what, under all the circumstances of the conflicting passions and interests of men, we are to expect.'

[2] George III, on the throne since 1760, was old and ill, and had been insane for years. He died on 29 January 1820.

[3] *Princes* George III's sons were prodigal, profligate and unstable to the point of madness.

[4] *A people ... field* A reference to the Peterloo Massacre, 16 August 1819.

[5] *liberticide* the killing of liberty.

[6] *Makes ... wield* the soldiers destroy their own freedom as they cut down the crowd.

[7] *Golden and sanguine* gold and blood are associated with tyranny.

[8] An early, deleted version of this line in the MS reads: 'A cloak of lies worn on Power's holiday.' The 'senate', or Houses of Parliament, was in Shelley's day representative only of aristocrats and the super-rich.

Lift Not the Painted Veil

[1] The dating of this sonnet is disputed.

[2] *sightless and drear* invisible and dark.

[3] *many* i.e. crowds, multitudes.

[4] *the Preacher* A reference to the Preacher in Ecclesiastes, who 'applied mine heart to know, and to search, and to seek out wisdom, and the reason of things, and to know the wickedness of folly, even of foolishness and madness ... but I find not' (Ecclesiastes 7:25, 28).

## *On Life* (composed late 1819)

Life and the world, or whatever we call that which we are and feel, is an astonishing thing. The mist of familiarity obscures from us the wonder of our being. We are struck with admiration at some of its transient modifications, but it is itself the great miracle. What are changes of empires, the wreck of dynasties, with the opinions which supported them; what is the birth and the extinction of religious and of political systems, to life? What are the revolutions of the globe which we inhabit, and the operations of the elements of which it is composed, compared with life? What is the universe of stars and suns (of which this inhabited earth is one), and their motions and their destiny, compared with life? Life, the great miracle, we admire not because it is so miraculous. It is well that we are so shielded by the familiarity of what is at once so certain and so unfathomable, from an astonishment which would otherwise absorb and overawe the functions of that which is its object.

If any artist, I do not say had executed, but had merely conceived in his mind the system of the sun, and the stars and planets, they not existing, and had painted to us in words or upon canvas the spectacle now afforded by the nightly cope of heaven, and illustrated it by the wisdom of astronomy, great would be our admiration. Or had he imagined the scenery of this earth, the mountains, the seas and the rivers, the grass and the flowers, and the variety of the forms and masses of the leaves of the woods, and the colours which attend the setting and the rising sun, and the hues of the atmosphere, turbid or serene, these things not before existing, truly we should have been astonished – and it would not have been a vain boast to have said of such a man, 'Non merita nome di creatore, sennon Iddio ed il Poeta'.[1] But now these things are looked on with little wonder, and to be conscious of them with intense delight is esteemed to be the distinguishing mark of a refined and extraordinary person. The multitude of men care not for them; it is thus with life – that which includes all.

What is life? Thoughts and feelings arise, with or without our will, and we employ words to express them. We are born, and our birth is unremembered, and our infancy remembered but in fragments. We live on, and in living we lose the apprehension of life. How vain is it to think that words can penetrate the mystery of our being! Rightly used they may make evident our ignorance to ourselves, and this is much. For what are we? Whence do we come, and whither do we go? Is birth the commencement, is death the conclusion of our being? What is birth and death?

The most refined abstractions of logic conduct to a view of life which, though startling to the apprehension, is in fact that which the habitual sense of its repeated combinations has extinguished in us. It strips, as it were, the painted curtain from this scene of things. I confess that I am one of those who am unable to refuse my assent to the conclusions of those philosophers who assert that nothing exists but as it is perceived.

It is a decision against which all our persuasions struggle, and we must be long convicted before we can be convinced that the solid universe of external things is 'such stuff as dreams are made of'.[2] The shocking absurdities of the popular philosophy of mind and matter, and its fatal consequences in morals, their violent dogmatism concerning the source of all things, had early conducted me to materialism.[3] This materialism is a seducing system to young and superficial minds; it allows its disciples to talk, and dispenses them from thinking. But I was discontented with such a view of things as it afforded; man is a being of high aspirations 'looking both before and after',[4] whose 'thoughts wander through eternity',[5] disclaiming alliance with transience and decay, incapable of imagining to himself annihilation, existing but in the future and the past, being not what he is, but what he has

## Notes

ON LIFE

[1] 'None deserves the name of creator except God and the poet'; from Pierantonio Serassi's *Life of Torquato Tasso* (1785).

[2] *such stuff as dreams are made of* from *The Tempest* IV i 156–7.

[3] *materialism* i.e. The philosophy of Locke, Hartley and Priestley, and of the French Enlightenment, particularly Holbach.

[4] *looking both before and after* from *Hamlet* IV iv 37.

[5] *thoughts wander through eternity* from 'Paradise Lost' ii 148: 'Those thoughts that wander through eternity.'

been and shall be. Whatever may be his true and final destination, there is a spirit within him at enmity with nothingness and dissolution. This is the character of all life and being. Each is at once the centre and the circumference, the point to which all things are referred, and the line in which all things are contained. Such contemplations as these, materialism and the popular philosophy of mind and matter alike forbid; they are only consistent with the intellectual system.

It is absurd to enter into a long recapitulation of arguments sufficiently familiar to those enquiring minds whom alone a writer on abstruse subjects can be conceived to address. Perhaps the most clear and vigorous statement of the intellectual system is to be found in Sir William Drummond's *Academical Questions*; after such an exposition it would be idle to translate into other words what could only lose its energy and fitness by the change. Examined point by point and word by word, the most discriminating intellects have been able to discern no train of thoughts in the process of reasoning, which does not conduct inevitably to the conclusion which has been stated.

What follows from the admission? It establishes no new truth, it gives us no additional insight into our hidden nature, neither its action, nor itself. Philosophy, impatient as it may be to build, has much work yet remaining as pioneer for the overgrowth of ages. It makes one step towards this object; it destroys error and the roots of error. It leaves what is too often the duty of the reformer in political and ethical questions to leave – a vacancy. It reduces the mind to that freedom in which it would have acted, but for the misuse of words and signs, the instruments of its own creation. By signs, I would be understood in a wide sense, including what is properly meant by that term, and what I peculiarly mean. In this latter sense, almost all familiar objects are signs, standing not for themselves but for others, in their capacity of suggesting one thought which shall lead to a train of thoughts. Our whole life is thus an education of error.

Let us recollect our sensations as children. What a distinct and intense apprehension had we of the world and of ourselves. Many of the circumstances of social life were then important to us, which are now no longer so. But that is not the point of comparison on which I mean to insist. We less habitually distinguished all that we saw and felt from ourselves. They seemed as it were to constitute one mass. There are some persons who in this respect are always children. Those who are subject to the state called reverie feel as if their nature were dissolved into the surrounding universe, or as if the surrounding universe were absorbed into their being. They are conscious of no distinction. And these are states which precede or accompany or follow an unusually intense and vivid apprehension of life. As men grow up, this power commonly decays, and they become mechanical and habitual agents. Thus feelings and then reasonings are the combined result of a multitude of entangled thoughts, and of a series of what are called impressions, planted by reiteration.

The view of life presented by the most refined deductions of the intellectual philosophy, is that of unity. Nothing exists but as it is perceived. The difference is merely nominal between those two classes of thought which are vulgarly distinguished by the names of ideas and of external objects. Pursuing the same thread of reasoning, the existence of distinct individual minds, similar to that which is employed in now questioning its own nature, is likewise found to be a delusion. The words, *I, you, they* are not signs of any actual difference subsisting between the assemblage of thoughts thus indicated, but are merely marks employed to denote the different modifications of the one mind.

Let it not be supposed that this doctrine conducts to the monstrous presumption that I, the person who now write and think, am that one mind. I am but a portion of it. The words *I*, and *you* and *they* are grammatical devices invented simply for arrangement and totally devoid of the intense and exclusive sense usually attached to them. It is difficult to find terms adequate to express so subtle a conception as that to which the intellectual philosophy has conducted us. We are on that verge where words abandon us, and what wonder if we grow dizzy to look down the dark abyss of how little we know!

The relations of *things* remain unchanged by whatever system. By the word *things* is to be understood any object of thought; that is, any thought upon which any other thought is employed, with an apprehension of distinction. The relations of these remain unchanged – and such is the material of our knowledge.

What is the cause of life? That is, how was it produced, or what agencies distinct from life, have acted or act upon life? All recorded generations of mankind have wearily busied themselves in inventing answers to this question. And the result has been religion. Yet that the basis of all things cannot be (as the popular philosophy alleges) mind, is sufficiently evident. Mind (as far as we have any experience of its properties, and, beyond that, experience how vain is argument) cannot create, it can only perceive. It is said also to be the cause; but cause is only a word expressing a certain state of the human mind with regard to the manner in which two thoughts are apprehended to be related to each other. If anyone desires to know how unsatisfactorily the popular philosophy employs itself upon this great question, they need only impartially reflect upon the manner in which thoughts develop themselves in their minds. It is infinitely improbable that the cause of mind – that is, of existence – is similar to mind.

## *To a Skylark* (composed late June 1820)[1]

Hail to thee, blithe spirit!
  Bird thou never wert –
That from heaven, or near it,
  Pourest thy full heart
In profuse strains of unpremeditated art.

Higher still and higher
  From the earth thou springest
Like a cloud of fire;
  The blue deep thou wingest,
And singing still dost soar, and soaring ever singest.

In the golden lightning
  Of the sunken sun
O'er which clouds are brightning,
  Thou dost float and run
Like an unbodied joy whose race is just begun.

The pale purple even
  Melts around thy flight;
Like a star of heaven
  In the broad daylight
Thou art unseen[2] – but yet I hear thy shrill delight,

Keen as are the arrows
  Of that silver sphere,[3]
Whose intense lamp narrows
  In the white dawn clear,
Until we hardly see – we feel that it is there.

## Notes

To a Skylark

[1] As Mary Shelley recalled, this poem was written at the Gisbornes' house at Livorno, probably on 22 June: 'It was on a beautiful summer evening, while wandering among the lanes whose myrtle hedges were the bowers of the fireflies, that we heard the carolling of the skylark which inspired one of the most beautiful of his poems.'

[2] *Thou art unseen* John Gisborne recalled how he and Shelley used to listen to the skylarks, which flew 'to a height at which the straining eye could scarcely ken the stationary and diminutive specks into which their soft and still receding forms had at length vanished' (Journal of John Gisborne, 20 October 1827).

[3] *that silver sphere* The morning star (Venus) is so bright that it can be seen even after sunrise.

All the earth and air
With thy voice is loud,
As when night is bare
From one lonely cloud
The moon rains out her beams – and heaven is overflowed.

What thou art we know not;
What is most like thee?
From rainbow clouds there flow not
Drops so bright to see
As from thy presence showers a rain of melody.

Like a poet hidden
In the light of thought,
Singing hymns unbidden,[4]
Till the world is wrought
To sympathy with hopes and fears it heeded not;

Like a high-born maiden
In a palace-tower,
Soothing her love-laden
Soul in secret hour,
With music sweet as love, which overflows her bower;

Like a glow-worm golden
In a dell of dew,
Scattering unbeholden
Its aerial hue
Among the flowers and grass which screen it from the view;

Like a rose embowered
In its own green leaves,
By warm winds deflowered
Till the scent it gives
Makes faint with too much sweet these heavy-winged thieves;

Sound of vernal showers
On the twinkling grass,
Rain-awakened flowers,
All that ever was
Joyous and clear and fresh, thy music doth surpass.

Teach us, sprite or bird,
What sweet thoughts are thine;
I have never heard
Praise of love or wine
That panted forth a flood of rapture so divine:

## Notes

[4] *hymns unbidden* i.e. poems that are the direct result of inspiration.

Chorus Hymeneal[5]
Or triumphal chaunt
Matched with thine would be all
But an empty vaunt,[6]
A thing wherein we feel there is some hidden want.

What objects are the fountains
Of thy happy strain?[7]
What fields or waves or mountains?
What shapes of sky or plain?
What love of thine own kind? What ignorance of pain?

With thy clear keen joyance
Languor cannot be –
Shadow of annoyance
Never came near thee;
Thou lovest, but ne'er knew love's sad satiety.

Waking or asleep,
Thou of death must deem
Things more true and deep
Than we mortals dream,
Or how could thy notes flow in such a crystal stream?

We look before and after,[8]
And pine for what is not;
Our sincerest laughter
With some pain is fraught –
Our sweetest songs are those that tell of saddest thought.

Yet if we could scorn
Hate and pride and fear;
If we were things born
Not to shed a tear,
I know not how thy joy we ever should come near.

Better than all measures
Of delightful sound;
Better than all treasures
That in books are found –
Thy skill to poet were, thou scorner of the ground!

Teach me half the gladness
That thy brain must know,
Such harmonious madness[9]
From my lips would flow
The world should listen then, as I am listening now.

## Notes

[5] *Chorus Hymeneal* wedding-song. Hymen was the Greek god of marriage.

[6] *vaunt* boast.

[7] *strain* song.

[8] *We look before and after* Hamlet speaks of how human beings were created 'with such large discourse, / Looking before and after' (*Hamlet* IV iv 36–7).

[9] *harmonious madness* inspiration to write beautiful poetry.

## *A Defence of Poetry; or, Remarks Suggested by an Essay Entitled 'The Four Ages of Poetry'* (extracts) (composed February–March 1821)[1]

According to one mode of regarding those two classes of mental action which are called reason and imagination, the former may be considered as mind contemplating the relations borne by one thought to another, however produced; and the latter, as mind acting upon those thoughts so as to colour them with its own light, and composing from them, as from elements, other thoughts, each containing within itself the principle of its own integrity. The one is the *to poiein*,[2] or the principle of synthesis, and has for its objects those forms which are common to universal nature and existence itself; the other is the *to logizein*,[3] or principle of analysis, and its action regards the relations of things simply as relations, considering thoughts not in their integral unity but as the algebraical representations which conduct to certain general results. Reason is the enumeration of quantities already known; imagination the perception of the value of those quantities, both separately and as a whole. Reason respects the differences, and imagination the similitudes of things. Reason is to imagination as the instrument to the agent, as the body to the spirit, as the shadow to the substance.

Poetry, in a general sense, may be defined to be 'the expression of the imagination'; and poetry is connate[4] with the origin of man. Man is an instrument over which a series of external and internal impressions are driven, like the alternations of an ever-changing wind over an Aeolian lyre, which move it, by their motion, to ever-changing melody.[5] But there is a principle within the human being (and perhaps within all sentient beings) which acts otherwise than in the lyre, and produces not melody alone, but harmony, by an internal adjustment of the sounds or motions thus excited to the impressions which excite them. It is as if the lyre could accommodate its chords to the motions of that which strikes them, in a determined proportion of sound – even as the musician can accommodate his voice to the sound of the lyre. A child at play by itself will express its delight by its voice and motions, and every inflection of tone and every gesture will bear exact relation to a corresponding antitype[6] in the pleasurable impressions which awakened it. It will be the reflected image of that impression – and as the lyre trembles and sounds after the wind has died away, so the child seeks, by prolonging in its voice and motions the duration of the effect, to prolong also a consciousness of the cause. In relation to the objects which delight a child, these expressions are what poetry is to higher objects.

The savage (for the savage is to ages what the child is to years) expresses the emotions produced in him by surrounding objects in a similar manner – and language and gesture, together with plastic or pictorial imitation, become the image of the combined effect of those objects, and of his apprehension of them. Man in society, with all his passions and his pleasures, next becomes

## Notes

A Defence of Poetry

[1] Inspired by Thomas Love Peacock's essay, 'The Four Ages of Poetry', published in *Ollier's Literary Miscellany* (1820). Peacock's argument was that classical poetry passed through four ages: (1) an iron age of warriors, heroes and gods; (2) a golden age of recollection (Homeric); (3) a silver age in which poetry took new forms and recreated itself (Virgilian); and (4) the brass age, a second childhood in which it regressed to the crudities of the iron age. Then came the dark ages, and then the 'four ages' of modern poetry. The romantic age, Peacock argued, is that of brass, in which the poet is half-barbarian, living in the past, with an outmoded way of thinking. Shelley had read it by 20 January 1821, and told Ollier (his and Peacock's publisher) that it 'has excited my polemical faculties so violently, that the moment I get rid of ophthalmia I mean to set about an answer to it, which I will send you, if you please. It is very clever, but, I think, very false'. Shelley began his response in late February; Part I was finished by 20 March. He sent it to Ollier, promising another two parts after its publication. Unfortunately, the *Literary Miscellany* failed, and Part I of the 'Defence' did not appear; Shelley was drowned in 1822 without completing it or seeing Part I into print. It was published in 1840.

[2] *to poiein* 'making' – the source of the word 'poet'.

[3] *to logizein* 'reasoning', 'calculating'.

[4] *connate* coeval, as old as.

[5] *Man is an instrument ... melody* cf. Shelley's 'Essay on Christianity': 'There is a power by which we are surrounded, like the atmosphere in which some motionless lyre is suspended, which visits with its breath our silent chords at will.'

[6] *antitype* 'that which is shadowed forth or represented by the "type" or symbol' (*Oxford English Dictionary*).

the object of the passions and pleasures of man; an additional class of emotions produces an augmented treasure of expressions; and language, gesture, and the imitative arts become at once the representation and the medium, the pencil and the picture, the chisel and the statue, the chord and the harmony. The social sympathies (or those laws from which as from its elements society results) begin to develop themselves from the moment that two human beings coexist; the future is contained within the present as the plant within the seed; and equality, diversity, unity, contrast, mutual dependence, become the principles alone capable of affording the motives according to which the will of a social being is determined to action (inasmuch as he is social), and constitute pleasure in sensation, virtue in sentiment, beauty in art, truth in reasoning, and love in the intercourse of kind. Hence men, even in the infancy of society, observe a certain order in their words and actions distinct from that of the objects and the impressions represented by them, all expression being subject to the laws of that from which it proceeds.

But let us dismiss those more general considerations which might involve an enquiry into the principles of society itself, and restrict our view to the manner in which the imagination is expressed upon its forms.

In the youth of the world, men dance and sing and imitate natural objects, observing in these actions (as in all others) a certain rhythm or order. And although all men observe a similar, they observe not the same order in the motions of the dance, in the melody of the song, in the combinations of language, in the series of their imitations of natural objects. For there is a certain order or rhythm belonging to each of these classes of mimetic representation, from which the hearer and the spectator receive an intenser and a purer pleasure than from any other. The sense of an approximation to this order has been called taste by modern writers.[7] Every man in the infancy of art observes an order which approximates more or less closely to that from which this highest delight results. But the diversity is not sufficiently marked as that its gradations should be sensible,[8] except in those instances where the predominance of this faculty of approximation to the beautiful (for so we may be permitted to name the relation between this highest pleasure and its cause) is very great. Those in whom it exists in excess are poets, in the most universal sense of the word – and the pleasure resulting from the manner in which they express the influence of society or nature upon their own minds, communicates itself to others, and gathers a sort of reduplication from that community. Their language is vitally metaphorical; that is, it marks the before unapprehended relations of things, and perpetuates their apprehension, until the words which represent them become through time signs for portions or classes of thoughts, instead of pictures of integral thoughts; and then if no new poets should arise to create afresh the associations which have been thus disorganized, language will be dead to all the nobler purposes of human intercourse.

These similitudes or relations are finely said by Lord Bacon[9] to be 'the same footsteps of nature impressed upon the various subjects of the world'[10] – and he considers the faculty which perceives them as the storehouse of axioms common to all knowledge. In the infancy of society every author is necessarily a poet, because language itself is poetry; and to be a poet is to apprehend the true and the beautiful, in a word the good which exists in the relation subsisting first between existence and perception, and secondly between perception and expression. Every original language

## Notes

[7] *has been called taste by modern writers* most notably Hazlitt, who, in his 'Essay on Taste' (1818), wrote: 'Genius is the power of producing excellence: taste is the power of perceiving the excellence thus produced in its several sorts and degrees, with all their force, refinement, distinctions, and connections.'

[8] *sensible* perceptible.

[9] Francis Bacon, Baron Verulam, Viscount St Albans (1561– 1626), Lord Chancellor of England, philosopher and essayist. His work appealed to Shelley because he was a Neoplatonist.

[10] *Of the Advancement of Learning* (1605), Book II, Chapter 5: 'Are not the organs of the senses of one kind with the organs of reflection, the eye with a glass ...? Neither are these only similitudes, as men of narrow observation may conceive them to be, but the same footsteps of Nature, treading or printing upon several subjects or matters.'

near to its source is in itself the chaos of a cyclic poem: the copiousness of lexicography and the distinctions of grammar are the works of a later age, and are merely the catalogue and the form of the creations of poetry.

But poets, or those who imagine and express this indestructible order, are not only the authors of language and of music, of the dance and architecture and statuary and painting; they are the institutors of laws, and the founders of civil society, and the inventors of the arts of life, and the teachers who draw into a certain propinquity with the beautiful and the true that partial apprehension of the agencies of the invisible world which is called religion. Hence all original religions are allegorical, or susceptible of allegory, and like Janus have a double face of false and true. Poets, according to the circumstances of the age and nation in which they appeared, were called in the earlier epochs of the world legislators or prophets.[11] A poet essentially comprises and unites both these characters. For he not only beholds intensely the present as it is, and discovers those laws according to which present things ought to be ordered, but he beholds the future in the present, and his thoughts are the germs of the flower and the fruit of latest time. Not that I assert poets to be prophets in the gross sense of the word, or that they can foretell the form as surely as they foreknow the spirit of events – such is the pretence of superstition which would make poetry an attribute of prophecy, rather than prophecy an attribute of poetry.

A poet participates in the eternal, the infinite, and the one; as far as relates to his conceptions, time and place and number are not. The grammatical forms which express the moods of time, and the difference of persons and the distinction of place are convertible with respect to the highest poetry without injuring it as poetry, and the choruses of Aeschylus, and the Book of Job, and Dante's *Paradise* would afford, more than any other writings, examples of this fact, if the limits of this paper did not forbid citation. The creations of sculpture, painting, and music, are illustrations still more decisive.

Language, colour, form, and religious and civil habits of action are all the instruments and the materials of poetry; they may be called poetry by that figure of speech which considers the effect as a synonym of the cause. But poetry in a more restricted sense expresses those arrangements of language, and especially metrical language, which are created by that imperial faculty whose throne is curtained within the invisible nature of man. And this springs from the nature itself of language, which is a more direct representation of the actions and passions of our internal being, and is susceptible of more various and delicate combinations, than colour, form, or motion, and is more plastic[12] and obedient to the control of that faculty of which it is the creation. For language is arbitrarily produced by the imagination and has relation to thoughts alone; but all other materials, instruments and conditions of art, have relations among each other which limit and interpose between conception and expression. The former is as a mirror which reflects, the latter as a cloud which enfeebles, the light of which both are mediums of communication. Hence the fame of sculptors, painters and musicians (although the intrinsic powers of the great masters of these arts may yield in no degree to that of those who have employed language as the hieroglyphic of their thoughts) has never equalled that of poets in the restricted sense of the term, as two performers of equal skill will produce unequal effects from a guitar and a harp. The fame of legislators and founders of religions (so long as their institutions last) alone seems to exceed that of poets in the restricted sense – but it can scarcely be a question whether, if we deduct the celebrity which their flattery of the gross opinions of the vulgar usually conciliates, together with that which belonged to them in their higher character of poets, any excess will remain.

## Notes

[11] *prophets* In his *Apologie for Poetrie*, Sir Philip Sidney had observed: 'Among the Romans a poet was called "Vates", which is as much as a diviner, foreseer, or prophet ... so heavenly a title did that excellent people bestow upon this heart-ravishing knowledge.'

[12] *plastic* susceptible to the artist's creative power.

We have thus circumscribed the word 'poetry' within the limits of that art which is the most familiar and the most perfect expression of the faculty itself. It is necessary however to make the circle still narrower, and to determine the distinction between measured and unmeasured language,[13] for the popular division into prose and verse is inadmissible in accurate philosophy.

Sounds as well as thoughts have relation both between each other and towards that which they represent, and a perception of the order of those relations has always been found connected with a perception of the order of the relations of thoughts. Hence the language of poets has ever affected a certain uniform and harmonious recurrence of sound, without which it were not poetry, and which is scarcely less indispensable to the communication of its influence than the words themselves, without reference to that peculiar order. Hence the vanity of translation: it were as wise to cast a violet into a crucible that you might discover the formal principle of its colour and odour, as seek to transfuse from one language into another the creations of a poet. The plant must spring again from its seed or it will bear no flower – and this is the burden of the curse of Babel.

An observation of the regular mode of the recurrence of this harmony in the language of poetical minds, together with its relation to music, produced metre, or a certain system of traditional forms of harmony and language. Yet it is by no means essential that a poet should accommodate his language to this traditional form, so that the harmony which is its spirit be observed. The practice is indeed convenient and popular, and to be preferred, especially in such composition as includes much action: but every great poet must inevitably innovate upon the example of his predecessors in the exact structure of his peculiar versification.

The distinction between poets and prose writers is a vulgar error. The distinction between philosophers and poets has been anticipated. Plato was essentially a poet[14] – the truth and splendour of his imagery and the melody of his language is the most intense that it is possible to conceive. He rejected the measure of the epic, dramatic, and lyrical forms, because he sought to kindle a harmony in thoughts divested of shape and action, and he forbore to invent any regular plan of rhythm which would include, under determinate forms, the varied pauses of his style. Cicero[15] sought to imitate the cadence of his periods but with little success. Lord Bacon was a poet.[16] His language has a sweet and majestic rhythm which satisfies the sense no less than the almost superhuman wisdom of his philosophy satisfies the intellect; it is a strain which distends,[17] and then bursts the circumference of the reader's mind, and pours itself forth together with it into the universal element with which it has perpetual sympathy. All the authors of revolutions in opinion are not only necessarily poets as they are inventors, nor even as their words unveil the permanent analogy of things by images which participate in the life of truth – but as their periods[18] are harmonious and rhythmical and contain in themselves the elements of verse, being the echo of the eternal music. Nor are those supreme poets who have employed traditional forms of rhythm on account of the form and action of their subjects, less capable of perceiving and teaching the truth of things, than those who have omitted that form. Shakespeare, Dante and Milton (to confine ourselves to modern writers) are philosophers of the very loftiest power.

A poem is the very image of life expressed in its eternal truth. There is this difference between a story and a poem: that a story is a catalogue of detached facts which have no other bond of connection than time, place, circumstance, cause and effect; the other is the creation of actions according to the unchangeable forms of human nature, as existing in the mind of the creator, which is itself the image of all other minds. The one is partial, and applies only to a definite period

## Notes

[13] *measured and unmeasured language* Shelley is looking for a more accurate definition of poetry and prose than that popularly conceived.

[14] *Plato was essentially a poet* again, Shelley follows Sidney, who wrote in his *Apologie*: 'Of all philosophers he [Plato] is the most poetical.'

[15] Marcus Tullius Cicero (106–43 BCE), Roman statesman and man of letters.

[16] 'see the Filium Labyrinthi, and the Essay on Death particularly' (Shelley's note).

[17] *distends* expands.

[18] *periods* sentences.

of time, and a certain combination of events which can never again recur; the other is universal, and contains within itself the germ of a relation to whatever motives or actions have place in the possible varieties of human nature. Time, which destroys the beauty and the use of the story of particular facts, stripped of the poetry which should invest them, augments that of poetry, and forever develops new and wonderful applications of the eternal truth which it contains. Hence epitomes[19] have been called the moths of just history;[20] they eat out the poetry of it. The story of particular facts is as a mirror which obscures and distorts that which should be beautiful: poetry is a mirror which makes beautiful that which is distorted.

The parts of a composition may be poetical, without the composition as a whole being a poem. A single sentence may be considered as a whole though it may be found in the midst of a series of unassimilated portions; a single word even may be a spark of inextinguishable thought. And thus all the great historians – Herodotus, Plutarch, Livy[21] – were poets; and although the plan of these writers, especially that of Livy, restrained them from developing this faculty in its highest degree, they make copious and ample amends for their subjection, by filling all the interstices of their subject with living images.

Having determined what is poetry and who are poets, let us proceed to estimate its effects upon society.

Poetry is ever accompanied with pleasure: all spirits on which it falls, open themselves to receive the wisdom which is mingled with its delight.[22] In the infancy of the world, neither poets themselves nor their auditors are fully aware of the excellency of poetry, for it acts in a divine and unapprehended manner, beyond and above consciousness – and it is reserved for future generations to contemplate and measure the mighty cause and effect in all the strength and splendour of their union. Even in modern times, no living poet ever arrived at the fullness of his fame. The jury which sits in judgement upon a poet, belonging as he does to all time, must be composed of his peers; it must be impanelled[23] by Time from the selectest of the wise of many generations. A poet is a nightingale who sits in darkness and sings to cheer its own solitude with sweet sounds; his auditors are as men entranced by the melody of an unseen musician, who feel that they are moved and softened, yet know not whence or why.[24] The poems of Homer and his contemporaries were the delight of infant Greece; they were the elements of that social system which is the column upon which all succeeding civilization has reposed. Homer embodied the ideal perfection of his age in human character – nor can we doubt that those who read his verses were awakened to an ambition of becoming like to Achilles, Hector and Ulysses.[25] The truth and beauty of friendship, patriotism and persevering devotion to an object, were unveiled to the depths in these immortal creations; the sentiments of the auditors must have been refined and enlarged by a sympathy with such great and lovely impersonations, until from admiring they imitated, and from imitation they identified themselves with the objects of their admiration. Nor let it be objected that these characters are remote from moral perfection, and that they can by no means be considered as edifying patterns

## Notes

[19] *epitomes* summary accounts.

[20] Bacon, *Of the Advancement of Learning* Book II, Chapter 2: 'As for the corruptions and moths of history, which are epitomes, the use of them deserveth to be banished, as all men of sound judgment have confessed, as those that have fretted and corroded the sound bodies of many excellent histories, and wrought them into base and unprofitable dregs.'

[21] *Herodotus, Plutarch, Livy* Historians of ancient Greece and Rome: Herodotus (*c.*480–*c.*425 BCE) wrote the first Greek history in nine books about the struggle between Asia and Greece, from Croesus to Xerxes; Plutarch (*c.*46–*c.*120 CE) wrote the *Parallel Lives* of eminent Romans and Greeks; Titus Livius (59 BCE–17 CE) wrote a history of Rome in 142 books, 35 of which are extant.

[22] *Poetry … delight* Shelley echoes Sidney's remark that the poet 'cometh to you with words set in delightful proportion, either accompanied with, or prepared for the well enchanting skill of music; and with a tale forsooth he cometh unto you, with a tale which holdeth children from play, and old men from the chimney corner; and, pretending no more, doth intend the winning of the mind from wickedness to virtue'.

[23] *impanelled* summoned, chosen.

[24] *A poet … or why* cf. 'To a Skylark' 36–40.

[25] *Achilles, Hector and Ulysses* heroes in the Trojan war.

for general imitation. Every epoch under names more or less specious has deified its peculiar errors; revenge is the naked idol of the worship of a semi-barbarous age, and self-deceit is the veiled image of unknown evil before which luxury and satiety[26] lie prostrate.

But a poet considers the vices of his contemporaries as the temporary dress in which his creations must be arrayed, and which cover without concealing the eternal proportions of their beauty.[27] An epic or dramatic personage is understood to wear them around his soul, as he may the ancient armour or the modern uniform around his body – whilst it is easy to conceive a dress more graceful than either. The beauty of the internal nature cannot be so far concealed by its accidental vesture,[28] but that the spirit of its form shall communicate itself to the very disguise, and indicate the shape it hides from the manner in which it is worn. A majestic form and graceful motions will express themselves through the most barbarous and tasteless costume. Few poets of the highest class have chosen to exhibit the beauty of their conceptions in its naked truth and splendour, and it is doubtful whether the alloy of costume, habit, etc., be not necessary to temper this planetary music for mortal ears.

The whole objection however of the immorality of poetry rests upon a misconception of the manner in which poetry acts to produce the moral improvement of man. Ethical science[29] arranges the elements which poetry has created, and propounds schemes and proposes examples of civil and domestic life. Nor is it for want of admirable doctrines that men hate, and despise, and censure, and deceive, and subjugate one another. But poetry acts in another and a diviner manner. It awakens and enlarges the mind itself by rendering it the receptacle of a thousand unapprehended combinations of thought. Poetry lifts the veil from the hidden beauty of the world, and makes familiar objects be as if they were not familiar; it re-produces all that it represents, and the impersonations clothed in its Elysian[30] light stand thenceforward in the minds of those who have once contemplated them as memorials of that gentle and exalted content which extends itself over all thoughts and actions with which it coexists. The great secret of morals is love, or a going out of our own nature, and an identification of ourselves with the beautiful which exists in thought, action, or person not our own. A man, to be greatly good, must imagine intensely and comprehensively; he must put himself in the place of another and of many others; the pains and pleasures of his species must become his own. The great instrument of moral good is the imagination – and poetry administers to the effect by acting upon the cause.[31]

Poetry enlarges the circumference of the imagination by replenishing it with thoughts of ever-new delight which have the power of attracting and assimilating to their own nature all other thoughts, and which form new intervals and interstices whose void forever craves fresh food. Poetry strengthens the faculty which is the organ of the moral nature of man, in the same manner as exercise strengthens a limb. A poet therefore would do ill to embody his own conceptions of right and wrong (which are usually those of his place and time) in his poetical creations (which participate in neither). By this assumption of the inferior office of interpreting the effect, in which perhaps after all he might acquit himself but imperfectly, he would resign a glory in a participation in the cause. There was little danger that Homer, or any of the eternal poets, should have so far misunderstood themselves as to have abdicated this throne of their widest dominion. Those in whom the poetical faculty, though great, is less intense (as Euripides, Lucan, Tasso)[32] have frequently affected a moral aim, and the effect of their poetry is diminished in exact proportion to the degree in which they compel us to advert to[33] this purpose....

## Notes

[26] *luxury and satiety* lust and excessive gratification.

[27] *But a poet ... beauty* cf. Shelley's remark in a letter to the Gisbornes of 13 July 1821: 'Poets, the best of them, are a very chameleonic race: they take the colour not only of what they feed on, but of the very leaves under which they pass.'

[28] *accidental vesture* i.e. outward appearance.

[29] *Ethical science* the science (or philosophy) of ethics.

[30] *Elysian* divine.

[31] *A man ... upon the cause* a fundamental principal in Shelley's philosophy.

[32] *Euripides, Lucan, Tasso* Euripides (*c*.480–406 BCE), one of the three great Attic tragedians, author of *Orestes, Medea, Bacchae*, among others; Marcus Annaeus Lucanus (39–65 CE), whose one surviving poem is the *Pharsalia*, the greatest Latin epic after the *Aeneid*; Torquato Tasso (1544–95) was the author of the epic *Gerusalemme Liberata* (1575).

[33] *advert to* take notice of.

The poetry of Dante[34] may be considered as the bridge thrown over the stream of time, which unites the modern and the ancient world. The distorted notions of invisible things which Dante and his rival Milton have idealized, are merely the mask and the mantle in which these great poets walk through eternity enveloped and disguised. It is a difficult question to determine how far they were conscious of the distinction which must have subsisted[35] in their minds between their own creed and that of the people. Dante at least appears to wish to mark the full extent of it by placing Riphaeus (whom Virgil calls 'justissimus unus')[36] in Paradise, and observing a most heretical caprice in his distribution of rewards and punishments. And Milton's poem contains within itself a philosophical refutation of that system of which, by a strange but natural antithesis, it has been a chief popular support.

Nothing can exceed the energy and magnificence of the character of Satan as expressed in *Paradise Lost*. It is a mistake to suppose that he could ever have been intended for the popular personification of evil. Implacable hate, patient cunning, and a sleepless refinement of device to inflict the extremest anguish on an enemy – these things are evil; and, although venial[37] in a slave, are not to be forgiven in a tyrant; although redeemed by much that ennobles his defeat in one subdued, are marked by all that dishonours his conquest in the victor. Milton's Devil as a moral being is as far superior to his God as one who perseveres in some purpose which he has conceived to be excellent in spite of adversity and torture, is to one who in the cold security of undoubted triumph inflicts the most horrible revenge upon his enemy, not from any mistaken notion of inducing him to repent of a perseverance in enmity, but with the alleged design of exasperating him to deserve new torments. Milton has so far violated the popular creed (if this shall be judged to be a violation) as to have alleged no superiority of moral virtue to his God over his Devil. And this bold neglect of a direct moral purpose is the most decisive proof of the supremacy of Milton's genius. He mingled, as it were, the elements of human nature as colours upon a single palette, and arranged them into the composition of his great picture according to the laws of epic truth; that is, according to the laws of that principle by which a series of actions of the external universe and of intelligent and ethical beings is calculated to excite the sympathy of succeeding generations of mankind. The *Divina Commedia* and *Paradise Lost* have conferred upon modern mythology a systematic form; and when change and time shall have added one more superstition to the mass of those which have arisen and decayed upon the earth, commentators will be learnedly employed in elucidating the religion of ancestral Europe, only not utterly forgotten because it will have been stamped with the eternity of genius.

Homer was the first, and Dante the second, epic poet – that is, the second poet the series of whose creations bore a defined and intelligible relation to the knowledge, and sentiment, and religion, and political conditions of the age in which he lived, and of the ages which followed it, developing itself in correspondence with their development. For Lucretius had limed[38] the wings of his swift spirit in the dregs of the sensible[39] world; and Virgil, with a modesty which ill became his genius, had affected the fame of an imitator even whilst he created anew all that he copied; and none among the flock of mock-birds, though their notes were sweet (Apollonius Rhodius, Quintus Calaber Smyrnaeus, Nonnus, Lucan, Statius, or Claudian),[40] have sought even to fulfil a single

## Notes

[34] *The poetry of Dante* Shelley read Dante in the original and in the blank verse translation of H.F. Cary (1775–1844), which began with the *Inferno* (1805), and continued in 1812 with *Purgatorio* and *Paradiso*. He visited Dante's tomb at Ravenna in August 1821.

[35] *subsisted* existed.

[36] 'The one man who was most just' (*Aeneid* ii 426). Dante places the Trojan Rhipheus in Paradise, even though he died before Christ's birth (*Paradiso* xx).

[37] *venial* pardonable.

[38] *limed* birds were caught by smearing bird-lime, a sticky substance, on twigs where they perched.

[39] *sensible* perceived.

[40] *Apollonius Rhodius ... Claudian* Minor classical poets: Apollonius Rhodius (*c*.295–215 BCE), author of *Argonautica*; Quintus Smyrnaeus (fourth century CE), called Calaber because of the discovery in Calabria of the only known MS of his *Posthomerica*, a 14-book sequel to Homer; Nonnus (*c*.400 CE), author of a Greek epic in 48 books on the adventures of the god Dionysus, *Dionysiaca*; Marcus Annaeus Lucanus (39 CE–65 CE), known for *Pharsalia*; Publius Papinius Statius (*c*.40–*c*.96 CE), author of the *Thebaid*; Claudius Claudianus, Roman poet of the fourth century CE, author of the epic *Rape of Proserpine*.

condition of epic truth. Milton was the third epic poet. For, if the title of epic in its highest sense is to be refused to the *Aeneid*, still less can it be conceded to the *Orlando Furioso*,[41] the *Gerusalemme Liberata, The Lusiad*,[42] or *The Faerie Queene*.

Dante and Milton were both deeply penetrated with the ancient religion of the civilized world – and its spirit exists in their poetry probably in the same proportion as its forms survived in the unreformed worship of modern Europe.[43] The one preceded and the other followed the Reformation at almost equal intervals. Dante was the first religious reformer, and Luther surpassed him rather in the rudeness and acrimony, than in the boldness of his censures of papal usurpation.[44] Dante was the first awakener of entranced Europe; he created a language in itself music and persuasion out of a chaos of inharmonious barbarisms; he was the congregator of those great spirits who presided over the resurrection of learning, the Lucifer[45] of that starry flock which in the thirteenth century shone forth from republican Italy, as from a heaven, into the darkness of the benighted world. His very words are instinct[46] with spirit – each is as a spark, a burning atom of inextinguishable thought, and many yet lie covered in the ashes of their birth, and pregnant with a lightning which has yet found no conductor. All high poetry is infinite; it is as the first acorn, which contained all oaks potentially. Veil after veil may be undrawn, and the inmost naked beauty of the meaning never exposed. A great poem is a fountain forever overflowing with the waters of wisdom and delight – and after one person or one age has exhausted all its divine effluence[47] which its peculiar relations enable them to share, another and yet another succeeds, and new relations are ever developed, the source of an unforeseen and an unconceived delight.

The age immediately succeeding to that of Dante, Petrarch, and Boccaccio, was characterized by a revival of painting, sculpture, music, and architecture. Chaucer caught the sacred inspiration, and the superstructure of English literature is based upon the materials of Italian invention.

But let us not be betrayed from a defence into a critical history of poetry and its influence on society. Be it enough to have pointed out the effects of poetry (in the large and true sense of the word) upon their own and all succeeding times, and to revert to the partial instances cited as illustrations of an opinion the reverse of that attempted to be established by the author of 'The Four Ages of Poetry'.[48]

But poets have been challenged to resign the civic crown[49] to reasoners and mechanists on another plea. It is admitted that the exercise of the imagination is more delightful, but it is alleged that that of the reason is more useful. Let us examine as the grounds of this distinction what is here meant by utility. Pleasure or good in a general sense is that which the consciousness of a sensitive and intelligent being seeks, and in which, when found, it acquiesces. There are two modes or degrees of pleasure – one durable, universal, and permanent; the other transitory and particular. Utility may either express the means of producing the former or the latter. In the former sense, whatever strengthens and purifies the affections, enlarges the imagination, and adds a spirit to sense, is useful. But the meaning in which the author of 'The Four Ages of Poetry' seems to have employed the word utility is the narrower one of banishing the importunity of the wants of our animal nature, the surrounding men with security of life, the dispersing the grosser delusions of superstition, and the conciliating such a degree of mutual forbearance among men as may consist with the motives of personal advantage.

## Notes

[41] *Orlando Furioso* epic by Ariosto.

[42] *The Lusiad* epic by Luiz de Camoëns.

[43] *the unreformed worship of modern Europe* i.e. the domination of the Roman Catholic Church.

[44] *papal usurpation* wrongful assumption of supreme authority of the Pope.

[45] *Lucifer* i.e. light-bearer.

[46] *instinct* imbued.

[47] *effluence* emanations.

[48] *the author of 'The Four Ages of Poetry'* Thomas Love Peacock.

[49] *civic crown* (*corona civica*) A garland of oak leaves and acorns, bestowed as a much-prized distinction upon one who saved the life of a fellow-citizen in war, here meant as the emblem of public utility.

Undoubtedly the promoters of utility in this limited sense have their appointed office in society. They follow the footsteps of poets, and copy the sketches of their creations into the book of common life. They make space, and give time. Their exertions are of the highest value so long as they confine their administration of the concerns of the inferior powers of our nature within the limits of what is due to the superior ones. But whilst the sceptic destroys gross superstitions, let him spare to deface, as some of the French writers have defaced, the eternal truths charactered[50] upon the imaginations of men. Whilst the mechanist abridges,[51] and the political economist combines labour,[52] let them beware that their speculations, for want of a correspondence with those first principles which belong to the imagination, do not tend, as they have in modern England, to exasperate at once the extremes of luxury and want.[53] They have exemplified the saying, 'To him that hath, more shall be given; and from him that hath not, the little that he hath shall be taken away'.[54] The rich have become richer, and the poor have become poorer; and the vessel of the state is driven between the Scylla and Charybdis[55] of anarchy and despotism. Such are the effects which must ever flow from an unmitigated exercise of the calculating faculty.

It is difficult to define pleasure in its highest sense, the definition involving a number of apparent paradoxes. For, from an inexplicable defect of harmony in the constitution of human nature, the pain of the inferior is frequently connected with the pleasure of the superior portions of our being. Sorrow, terror, anguish, despair itself are often the chosen expressions of an approximation to the highest good. Our sympathy in tragic fiction depends on this principle; tragedy delights by affording a shadow of the pleasure which exists in pain. This is the source also of the melancholy which is inseparable from the sweetest melody.[56] The pleasure that is in sorrow is sweeter than the pleasure of pleasure itself – and hence the saying, 'It is better to go to the house of mourning than to the house of mirth'.[57] Not that this highest species of pleasure is necessarily linked with pain. The delight of love and friendship, the ecstacy of the admiration of nature, the joy of the perception and still more of the creation of poetry is often wholly unalloyed.

The production and assurance of pleasure in this highest sense is true utility; those who produce and preserve this pleasure are poets or poetical philosophers.

The exertions of Locke, Hume, Gibbon, Voltaire, Rousseau,[58] and their disciples, in favour of oppressed and deluded humanity, are entitled to the gratitude of mankind. Yet it is easy to calculate the degree of moral and intellectual improvement which the world would have exhibited had they never lived. A little more nonsense would have been talked for a century or two, and perhaps a few more men, women and children burnt as heretics. We might not at this moment have been congratulating each other on the abolition of the Inquisition in Spain.[59] But it exceeds all imagination to conceive what would have been the moral condition of the world if neither Dante, Petrarch, Boccaccio, Chaucer, Shakespeare, Calderón,[60] Lord Bacon, nor Milton, had ever existed; if Raphael and Michelangelo had never been born; if the Hebrew poetry had never been translated; if a revival of a study of Greek literature had never taken place; if no monuments of ancient sculpture had been handed down to us; and if the poetry of the religion of the ancient world had been extinguished together with its belief. The human mind could never, except by the intervention of these excitements, have been awakened to the invention of those grosser[61] sciences, and that application

## Notes

[50] *charactered* represented.

[51] *the mechanist abridges* by inventing machines that reduce the need for labour.

[52] *the political economist combines labour* by organizing workers in the most efficient manner.

[53] *luxury and want* excessive overindulgence and desperate poverty.

[54] Matthew 25:29.

[55] *Scylla and Charybdis* dangerous cave of the monster Scylla, and a whirlpool, which demolished part of Ulysses's fleet in the *Odyssey*.

[56] *This is the source ... melody* cf. 'To a Skylark' 90: 'Our sweetest songs are those that tell of saddest thought.'

[57] Ecclesiastes 7:2.

[58] 'I follow the classification adopted by the author of "The Four Ages of Poetry", but Rousseau was essentially a poet. The others, even Voltaire, were mere reasoners' (Shelley's note).

[59] *We might not ... Spain* The Spanish Inquisition was suppressed in 1820, restored in 1823, and abolished finally in 1834.

[60] Pedro Calderón de la Barca (1600–81), whose plays Shelley was reading in Spanish in August 1819; as he told Peacock: 'A kind of Shakespeare is this Calderon, and I have some thoughts, if I find that I cannot do anything better, of translating some of his plays'.

[61] *grosser* more materialistic, to do with the physical world.

of analytical reasoning to the aberrations of society, which it is now attempted to exalt over the direct expression of the inventive and creative faculty itself.

We have more moral, political and historical wisdom than we know how to reduce into practice; we have more scientific and economical knowledge than can be accommodated to the just distribution of the produce which they multiply. The poetry in these systems of thought is concealed by the accumulation of facts and calculating processes. There is no want of knowledge respecting what is wisest and best in morals, government, and political economy – or at least, what is wiser and better than what men now practise and endure. But we let '*I dare not* wait upon *I would*, like the poor cat i' the adage.'[62] We want the creative faculty to imagine that which we know; we want the generous impulse to act that which we imagine; we want the poetry of life – our calculations have outrun conception; we have eaten more than we can digest. The cultivation of those sciences which have enlarged the limits of the empire of man over the external world, has, for want of the poetical faculty, proportionally circumscribed those of the internal world – and man, having enslaved the elements, remains himself a slave. To what but to a cultivation of the mechanical arts in a degree disproportioned to the presence of the creative faculty (which is the basis of all knowledge) is to be attributed the abuse of all inventions for abridging and combining labour, to the exasperation of the inequality of mankind? From what other cause has it arisen that these inventions which should have lightened, have added a weight to the curse imposed on Adam?[63] Thus, poetry, and the principle of self (of which money is the visible incarnation) are the God and the Mammon of the world.[64]

The functions of the poetical faculty are twofold: by one it creates new materials for knowledge and power and pleasure; by the other it engenders in the mind a desire to reproduce and arrange them according to a certain rhythm and order which may be called the beautiful and the good. The cultivation of poetry is never more to be desired than at periods when, from an excess of the selfish and calculating principle, the accumulation of the materials of external life exceed the quantity of the power of assimilating them to the internal laws of human nature. The body has then become too unwieldy for that which animates it.

Poetry is indeed something divine. It is at once the centre and the circumference of knowledge; it is that which comprehends all science, and that to which all science must be referred. It is at the same time the root and the blossom of all other systems of thought. It is that from which all spring, and that which adorns all – and that which, if blighted, denies the fruit and the seed, and withholds from the barren world the nourishment and the succession of the scions[65] of the tree of life. It is the perfect and consummate[66] surface and bloom of things; it is as the odour and the colour of the rose to the texture of the elements which compose it, as the form and the splendour of unfaded beauty to the secrets of anatomy and corruption. What were virtue, love, patriotism, friendship etc.; what were the scenery of this beautiful universe which we inhabit; what were our consolations on this side of the grave; and what were our aspirations beyond it – if poetry did not ascend to bring light and fire from those eternal regions where the owl-winged faculty of calculation dare not ever soar? Poetry is not like reasoning, a power to be exerted according to the determination of the will. A man cannot say, 'I will compose poetry'. The greatest poet even cannot say it: for the mind in creation is as a fading coal which some invisible influence, like an inconstant wind, awakens to transitory brightness. This power arises from within, like the colour of a flower which fades and changes as it is developed, and the conscious portions of our natures are unprophetic either of its approach or its departure. Could this influence be durable in its

## Notes

[62] *Macbeth* I vii 44–5.

[63] *the curse imposed on Adam* at Genesis 3:17–19.

[64] *the God and the Mammon of the world* 'No man can serve two masters: for either he will hate the one, and love the other; or else he will hold to the one, and despise the other. Ye cannot serve God and mammon' (Matthew 6:24).

[65] *scions* shoots, buds.

[66] *consummate* complete.

original purity and force, it is impossible to predict the greatness of the results – but when composition begins, inspiration is already on the decline, and the most glorious poetry that has ever been communicated to the world is probably a feeble shadow of the original conception of the poet. I appeal to the greatest poets of the present day, whether it be not an error to assert that the finest passages of poetry are produced by labour and study. The toil and the delay recommended by critics can be justly interpreted to mean no more than a careful observation of the inspired moments, and an artificial connection of the spaces between them by the intertexture of conventional expressions; a necessity only imposed by a limitedness of the poetical faculty itself. For Milton conceived the *Paradise Lost* as a whole before he executed it in portions. We have his own authority also for the muse having 'dictated' to him the 'unpremeditated song',[67] and let this be an answer to those who would allege the fiftysix various readings of the first line of the *Orlando Furioso*. Compositions so produced are to poetry what mosaic is to painting. This instinct and intuition of the poetical faculty is still more observable in the plastic and pictorial arts:[68] a great statue or picture grows under the power of the artist as a child in the mother's womb, and the very mind which directs the hands in formation is incapable of accounting to itself for the origin, the gradations, or the media of the process.

Poetry is the record of the best and happiest moments of the happiest and best minds. We are aware of evanescent visitations of thought and feeling sometimes associated with place or person, sometimes regarding our own mind alone, and always arising unforeseen and departing unbidden, but elevating and delightful beyond all expression – so that even in the desire and the regret they leave, there cannot but be pleasure, participating as it does in the nature of its object. It is, as it were, the interpenetration of a diviner nature through our own, but its footsteps are like those of a wind over a sea, which the coming calm erases, and whose traces remain only as on the wrinkled sand which paves it.

These, and corresponding conditions of being, are experienced principally by those of the most delicate sensibility and the most enlarged imagination – and the state of mind produced by them is at war with every base desire. The enthusiasm of virtue, love, patriotism and friendship, is essentially linked with these emotions; and whilst they last, self appears as what it is – an atom to a universe. Poets are not only subject to these experiences as spirits of the most refined organization, but they can colour all that they combine with the evanescent hues of this ethereal world; a word or a trait in the representation of a scene or a passion, will touch the enchanted chord, and reanimate, in those who have ever experienced these emotions, the sleeping, the cold, the buried image of the past. Poetry thus makes immortal all that which is best and most beautiful in the world; it arrests the vanishing apparitions which haunt the interlunations[69] of life, and veiling them in language or in form sends them forth among mankind, bearing sweet news of kindred joy to those with whom their sisters abide – abide, because there is no portal of expression from the caverns of the spirit which they inhabit, into the universe of things. Poetry redeems from decay the visitations of the divinity in man.

Poetry turns all things to loveliness: it exalts the beauty of that which is most beautiful, and it adds beauty to that which is most deformed; it marries exultation and horror, grief and pleasure, eternity and change; it subdues to union under its light yoke all irreconcilable things. It transmutes all that it touches, and every form moving within the radiance of its presence is changed by wondrous sympathy to an incarnation of the spirit which it breathes; its secret alchemy turns to potable gold[70] the poisonous waters which flow from death through life; it strips the veil of familiarity from the world, and lays bare the naked and sleeping beauty which is the spirit of its forms.

## Notes

[67] *We have ... song* A reference to 'Paradise Lost' ix 21–4, where Milton says that Urania, his 'celestial patroness', 'dictates to me slumbering, or inspires / Easy my unpremeditated verse'.

[68] *the plastic and pictorial arts* sculpture and painting.

[69] *interlunations* dark intervals.

[70] *potable gold* the elixir of life, potable (drinkable) gold, was the goal of the alchemist. There are rivers of it at 'Paradise Lost' iii 608–9.

All things exist as they are perceived, at least in relation to the percipient: 'The mind is its own place, and of itself can make a heaven of hell, a hell of heaven'.[71] But poetry defeats the curse which binds us to be subjected to the accident of surrounding impressions. And whether it spreads its own figured[72] curtain or withdraws life's dark veil from before the scene of things, it equally creates for us a being within our being. It makes us the inhabitants of a world to which the familiar world is a chaos. It reproduces the common universe of which we are portions and percipients, and it purges from our inward sight the film of familiarity which obscures from us the wonder of our being. It compels us to feel that which we perceive, and to imagine that which we know. It creates anew the universe after it has been annihilated in our minds by the recurrence of impressions blunted by reiteration. It justifies that bold and true word of Tasso: 'Non merita nome di creatore, sennon Iddio ed il Poeta'.[73]

A poet, as he is the author to others of the highest wisdom, pleasure, virtue and glory, so he ought personally to be the happiest, the best, the wisest, and the most illustrious of men. As to his glory, let time be challenged to declare whether the fame of any other institutor of human life be comparable to that of a poet. That he is the wisest, the happiest, and the best, inasmuch as he is a poet, is equally incontrovertible: the greatest poets have been men of the most spotless virtue, of the most consummate prudence, and (if we could look into the interior of their lives) the most fortunate of men. And the exceptions, as they regard those who possessed the imaginative faculty in a high yet an inferior degree, will be found on consideration to confirm rather than destroy the rule. Let us for a moment stoop to the arbitration[74] of popular breath, and usurping and uniting in our own persons the incompatible characters of accuser, witness, judge and executioner, let us without trial, testimony, or form, determine that certain motives of those who are 'there sitting where we dare not soar'[75] are reprehensible. Let us assume that Homer was a drunkard, that Virgil was a flatterer, that Horace was a coward, that Tasso was a madman, that Lord Bacon was a peculator,[76] that Raphael was a libertine, that Spenser was a Poet Laureate.[77] It is inconsistent with this division of our subject to cite living poets, but posterity has done ample justice to the great names now referred to. Their errors have been weighed and have been found as dust in the balance – if their sins 'were as scarlet, they are now white as snow';[78] they have been washed in the blood of the mediator and the redeemer Time. Observe in what a ludicrous chaos the imputations of real and of fictitious crime have been confused in the contemporary calumnies against poetry and poets; consider how little is as it appears – or appears as it is; look to your own motives, and judge not lest ye be judged.[79]

Poetry, as has been said, in this respect differs from logic: that it is not subject to the control of the active powers of the mind, and that its birth and recurrence has no necessary connection with consciousness or will. It is presumptuous to determine that these are the necessary conditions of all mental causation, when mental effects are experienced insusceptible of being referred to them. The frequent recurrence of the poetical power, it is obvious to suppose, may produce in the mind an habit of order and harmony correlative with its own nature and with its effects upon other minds. But in the intervals of inspiration (and they may be frequent without being durable) a poet becomes a man, and is abandoned to the sudden reflux[80] of the influences under which others habitually live. But as he is more delicately organized than other men, and sensible to pain and

## Notes

71 'Paradise Lost' i 254–5.

72 *figured* patterned.

73 'None deserves the name of creator except God and the poet'; from Pierantonio Serassi's *Life of Torquato Tasso* (1785).

74 *arbitration* judgement.

75 'Paradise Lost' iv 829.

76 *peculator* embezzler of public money.

77 *Poet Laureate* Although he liked him when he met him (see headnote above), Shelley thought that Southey's acceptance of the Laureateship marked his total abandonment of his youthful radicalism.

78 A paraphrase of Isaiah 1:18.

79 *judge not lest ye be judged* There are a number of scriptural echoes; see Daniel 5:27; Isaiah 40:15; Revelation 7:14; Hebrews 9:15; and Matthew 7:1.

80 *reflux* flowing back.

pleasure (both his own and that of others) in a degree unknown to them, he will avoid the one and pursue the other with an ardour proportioned to this difference. And he renders himself obnoxious to calumny, when he neglects to observe the circumstances under which these objects of universal pursuit and flight have disguised themselves in one another's garments.

But there is nothing necessarily evil in this error, and thus cruelty, envy, revenge, avarice, and the passions purely evil, have never formed any portion of the popular imputations on the lives of poets.

I have thought it most favourable to the cause of truth to set down these remarks according to the order in which they were suggested to my mind by a consideration of the subject itself, instead of following that of the treatise which excited me to make them public. Thus, although devoid of the formality of a polemical reply, if the views which they contain be just, they will be found to involve a refutation of the doctrines of 'The Four Ages of Poetry', so far at least as regards the first division of the subject. I can readily conjecture what should have moved the gall[81] of the learned and intelligent author of that paper; I confess myself, like him, unwilling to be stunned by the *Theseids* of the hoarse Codri of the day.[82] Bavius and Maevius undoubtedly are, as they ever were, insufferable persons.[83] But it belongs to a philosophical critic to distinguish rather than confound.

The first part of these remarks has related to poetry in its elements and principles; and it has been shown, as well as the narrow limits assigned them would permit, that what is called poetry in a restricted sense has a common source with all other forms of order and of beauty according to which the materials of human life are susceptible of being arranged, and which is poetry in an universal sense.

The second part[84] will have for its object an application of these principles to the present state of the cultivation of poetry, and a defence of the attempt to idealize the modern forms of manners and opinion, and compel them into a subordination to the imaginative and creative faculty. For the literature of England, an energetic development of which has ever preceded or accompanied a great and free development of the national will, has arisen, as it were, from a new birth. In spite of the low-thoughted envy which would undervalue contemporary merit, our own will be a memorable age in intellectual achievements, and we live among such philosophers and poets as surpass beyond comparison any who have appeared since the last national struggle for civil and religious liberty. The most unfailing herald, companion, or follower of the awakening of a great people to work a beneficial change in opinion or institution, is poetry. At such periods there is an accumulation of the power of communicating and receiving intense and impassioned conceptions respecting man and nature. The persons in whom this power resides may often (as far as regards many portions of their nature) have little apparent correspondence with that spirit of good of which they are the ministers.[85] But even whilst they deny and abjure,[86] they are yet compelled to serve the power which is seated upon the throne of their own soul. It is impossible to read the compositions of the most celebrated writers of the present day without being startled with the electric life which burns within their words. They measure the circumference and sound the depths of human nature with a comprehensive and all-penetrating spirit, and they are themselves perhaps the most sincerely

## Notes

[81] *gall* bitterness. Peacock had argued that the poets of the present day were barbarians.

[82] *unwilling to be stunned ... day* Codrus was the name applied by Roman poets to bad writers who annoyed others by reading aloud their feeble outpourings. Juvenal had criticized Codrus's *Theseid* in the first of his satires.

[83] *Bavius and Maevius ... persons* Bavius and Maevius were mediocre poets mocked by Virgil (*Eclogues* iii 90–1) and (Maevius only) Horace (*Epode* x). William Gifford was the author of *The Baviad* (1794) and *The Maeviad* (1795) in which he lampooned the Della Cruscans (mannered poetasters of the 1780s and 1790s) and their ilk. Shelley refers to the proliferation of bad poetry in his own day; as he told Peacock, 21 March 1821: 'The Bavii and Maevii of the day are very fertile.'

[84] *The second part* never written.

[85] *The persons ... ministers* Shelley may be thinking of Southey and Wordsworth, who had both, in Shelley's eyes, betrayed the cause of 'civil and religious liberty'; like Byron, he regarded both as traitors to the radical cause.

[86] *abjure* recant.

astonished at its manifestations, for it is less their own spirit than the spirit of the age. Poets are the hierophants[87] of an unapprehended inspiration, the mirrors of the gigantic shadows which futurity casts upon the present, the words which express what they understand not; the trumpets which sing to battle, and feel not what they inspire; the influence which is moved not, but moves. Poets are the unacknowledged legislators of the world.

## *Adonais: An Elegy on the Death of John Keats, Author of Endymion, Hyperion, etc.* (1821; composed between 11 April and 8 June 1821)[1]

Ἀστὴρ πρὶν μὲν ἐλαμπες ἐνὶ ςωοῖσιν Ἑῶος.
Νῦν δὲ θανὼν, λάμπεις Ἕσπεις Ἕσπερος ἐν φθιμένοις. (Plato)[2]

### *Preface*

Φάρμακον ἦλθε, Βίων, ποτὶ σὸν στόμα, φάρμακον εἶδες.
πῶς τευτοῖς χείλεσσι ποτέδραμε, κοὐκ; ἐγλυκάνθη;
τίς δὲ βροτὸς τοσσοῦτον ἀνάμερος, ἤκεράσι τοι,
ἤδοῦναι λαλέοντι τὸ φάρμακον; ἔκφυγεν ᾠδάν.

(Moschus, *Lament for Bion*)[3]

It is my intention to subjoin to the London edition of this poem,[4] a criticism upon the claims of its lamented object to be classed among the writers of the highest genius who have adorned our age. My known repugnance to the narrow principles of taste on which several of his earlier compositions were modelled, prove at least that I am an impartial judge. I consider the fragment of *Hyperion*[5] as second to nothing that was ever produced by a writer of the same years.

John Keats died at Rome of a consumption in his twenty-fourth year, on the —— of —— 1821,[6] and was buried in the romantic and lonely cemetery of the protestants in that city, under the pyramid which is the tomb of Cestius, and the massy walls and towers, now mouldering and desolate, which formed the circuit of ancient Rome. The cemetery is an open space among the ruins covered in winter with violets and daisies. It might make one in love with death[7] to think that one should be buried in so sweet a place.[8]

## Notes

[87] *hierophants* expounders.

ADONAIS: AN ELEGY ON THE DEATH OF JOHN KEATS PREFACE

[1] Shelley adapted the name from Adonis, the beautiful youth with whom Aphrodite, the Greek goddess of fertility, fell in love. He was killed by a wild boar, and from his blood sprang the rose, or from Aphrodite's tears the anemone. The poem was completed by 11 June 1821, and five days later Shelley told John Gisborne: 'this day I send it to the press at Pisa … I think it will please you: I have dipped my pen in consuming fire for his destroyers, otherwise the style is calm and solemn'.

[2] Shortly before composing 'Adonais', Shelley translated Plato's 'Epigram on Aster':

> Thou wert the morning star among the living,
> Ere thy fair light had fled;
> Now, having died, thou art as Hesperus, giving
> New splendour to the dead.

[3] 'Poison came, Bion, to thy mouth, thou didst know poison. To such lips as thine did it come, and was not sweetened? What mortal was so cruel that could mix poison for thee, or who could give thee the venom that heard thy voice? Surely, he had not music in his soul.'

[4] *the London edition of this poem* Shelley supervised the first publication of this poem in Pisa, 1821, but died before it could appear in London. The first English edition was published at Cambridge, 1829.

[5] *the fragment of Hyperion* i.e. 'Hyperion: A Fragment', published 1820 (see p. 1425), rather than 'The Fall of Hyperion' not published during Shelley's lifetime. When Shelley first received Keats's 1820 volume, he commented: 'The fragment called Hyperion promises for him that he is destined to become one of the first writers of the age' (letter of 29 October 1820).

[6] Keats died 23 February 1821, aged 25.

[7] *in love with death* Compare Keats, 'Ode to a Nightingale' 52.

[8] Shelley visited the Protestant (or, more correctly, the non-Catholic) Cemetery in Rome in late November 1818; his son William was buried there in 1819.

The genius[9] of the lamented person to whose memory I have dedicated these unworthy verses was not less delicate and fragile than it was beautiful; and where canker-worms abound, what wonder if its young flower was blighted in the bud? The savage criticism on his *Endymion*, which appeared in the *Quarterly Review*, produced the most violent effect on his susceptible mind; the agitation thus originated ended in the rupture of a blood-vessel in the lungs; a rapid consumption ensued, and the succeeding acknowledgements from more candid critics of the true greatness of his powers, were ineffectual to heal the wound thus wantonly inflicted.[10]

It may be well said that these wretched men know not what they do.[11] They scatter their insults and their slanders without heed as to whether the poisoned shaft lights on a heart made callous by many blows, or one like Keats', composed of more penetrable stuff.[12] One of their associates is, to my knowledge, a most base and unprincipled calumniator.[13] As to *Endymion* – was it a poem (whatever might be its defects) to be treated contemptuously by those who had celebrated with various degrees of complacency and panegyric, *Paris*, and *Woman*, and *A Syrian Tale*, and Mrs. Lefanu, and Mr. Barrett, and Mr Howard Payne,[14] and a long list of the illustrious obscure? Are these the men who, in their venal good nature, presumed to draw a parallel between the Revd. Mr Milman and Lord Byron?[15] What gnat did they strain at here, after having swallowed all those camels?[16] Against what woman taken in adultery, dares the fore-most of these literary prostitutes to cast his opprobrious stone?[17] Miserable man! You, one of the meanest, have wantonly defaced one of the noblest specimens of the work-manship of God. Nor shall it be your excuse that, murderer as you are, you have spoken daggers but used none.[18]

The circumstances of the closing scene of poor Keats' life were not made known to me until the *Elegy* was ready for the press. I am given to understand that the wound which his sensitive spirit had received from the criticism of *Endymion*, was exasperated by the bitter sense of unrequited benefits; the poor fellow seems to have been hooted from the stage of life, no less by those on whom he had wasted the promise of his genius, than those on whom he had lavished his fortune and his care. He was accompanied to Rome, and attended in his last illness by Mr Severn,[19] a young artist of the highest promise, who, I have been informed, 'almost risked his own life, and sacrificed every prospect to unwearied attendance upon his dying friend.'[20] Had I known these circumstances before the completion of my poem, I should have been tempted to add my feeble tribute of applause to the more solid recompense which the virtuous man finds in the recollection of his own motives. Mr Severn can dispense with a reward from 'such stuff as dreams are made of '.[21] His conduct is a golden augury of the success of his future career; may the unextinguished spirit of his illustrious friend animate the creations of his pencil, and plead against oblivion for his name!

## Notes

[9] *genius* spirit.

[10] *The savage criticism ... inflicted* This helped perpetuate the myth that Keats was 'killed' by a review – that of 'Endymion' in the *Quarterly Review* for April 1818, by Croker.

[11] *these wretched men know not what they do* An echo of Christ's comment on those who crucified him: 'Father, forgive them; for they know not what they do' (Luke 23:34).

[12] *penetrable stuff* cf. *Hamlet* III iv 35–6: 'And let me wring your heart, for so I shall / If it be made of penetrable stuff.'

[13] *One of their associates ... calumniator* Robert Southey, who Shelley thought had attacked his poem, 'The Revolt of Islam', in the *Quarterly Review* in 1817; the actual author was John Taylor Coleridge. Shelley has in mind Southey's part in the spreading of rumours about the 'league of incest'.

[14] Revd George Croly, *Paris in 1815* (1817); Eaton Stannard Barrett, *Woman* (1810); H. Galley Knight, *Ilderim: A Syrian Tale* (1816): all these works were reviewed in the *Quarterly*, 1817–20. Mrs Alicia Lefanu (*c.*1795–*c.*1826) was the author of *The Flowers* (1809). John Howard Payne was an American dramatist, whose *Brutus* was reviewed harshly by the *Quarterly Review*.

[15] Revd Henry Hart Milman's *Saviour, Lord of the Bright City* and *Fall of Jerusalem* were praised by the *Quarterly*, 1818–20.

[16] *What gnat ... camels* cf. Christ's criticism of the Pharisees, Matthew 23:24: 'Ye blind guides, which strain at a gnat, and swallow a camel.'

[17] *Against what woman ... stone* see John 8:7.

[18] *you have spoken daggers but used none* cf. *Hamlet* III ii 396: 'I will speak daggers to her, but use none.'

[19] Joseph Severn (1793–1879), a young artist who accompanied Keats to Rome, and nursed him until his death. Severn remained in Rome, became British Consul there in 1860, and was buried next to Keats.

[20] This information was in a letter from the Revd Robert Finch to John Gisborne, and was passed on to Shelley on 13 June 1821.

[21] *such stuff as dreams are made of* from *The Tempest* IV i 156–7.

## *Elegy*

I

I weep for Adonais – he is dead!
Oh weep for Adonais, though our tears
Thaw not the frost which binds so dear a head!
And thou, sad Hour, selected from all years
To mourn our loss, rouse thy obscure compeers,
And teach them thine own sorrow, say: 'With me
Died Adonais; till the Future dares
Forget the Past, his fate and fame shall be
An echo and a light unto eternity!'

II

Where wert thou, mighty Mother,[1] when he lay,
When thy Son lay, pierced by the shaft[2] which flies
In darkness?[3] Where was lorn Urania
When Adonais died? With veiled eyes,
Mid listening Echoes, in her Paradise
She sat, while one,[4] with soft enamoured breath,
Rekindled all the fading melodies,
With which, like flowers that mock the corpse beneath,
He had adorned and hid the coming bulk of death.

III

Oh weep for Adonais – he is dead!
Wake, melancholy Mother, wake and weep!
Yet wherefore? Quench within their burning bed
Thy fiery tears, and let thy loud heart keep,
Like his, a mute and uncomplaining sleep;
For he is gone, where all things wise and fair
Descend. Oh dream not that the amorous Deep
Will yet restore him to the vital air –
Death feeds on his mute voice, and laughs at our despair.

IV

Most musical of mourners, weep again!
Lament anew, Urania! He died,[5]
Who was the Sire of an immortal strain,
Blind, old, and lonely, when his country's pride,

## Notes

ELEGY

[1] *mighty Mother* Urania, muse of astronomy, whom Shelley makes the mother of Adonais. She is forsaken ('lorn') in line 12.

[2] *the shaft* i.e. of an arrow. Shelley is writing figuratively of Croker's hostile review of 'Endymion' in the *Quarterly Review*. He is also recalling Psalm 91:5: 'Thou shalt not be afraid for the terror by night; nor for the arrow that flieth by day.'

[3] *Where wert thou ... darkness* the appeal is an essential part of formal elegy; cf. Milton's 'Lycidas' 50–1: 'Where were ye nymphs when the remorseless deep / Closed o'er the head of your loved Lycidas?'

[4] *one* i.e. an Echo.

[5] *He died* Milton, whose muse was also Urania. He died on 8 November 1674 in Bunhill House, London.

The priest, the slave, and the liberticide,[6]
Trampled and mocked with many a loathed rite
Of lust and blood;[7] he went, unterrified,
Into the gulf of death, but his clear Sprite[8]
Yet reigns o'er earth – the third among the sons of light.[9]

V

Most musical of mourners, weep anew!
Not all to that bright station dared to climb –
And happier they their happiness who knew,
Whose tapers yet burn through that night of time
In which suns perished;[10] others more sublime,
Struck by the envious wrath of man or God,
Have sunk, extinct in their refulgent[11] prime;
And some yet live, treading the thorny road
Which leads, through toil and hate, to Fame's serene abode.

VI

But now, thy youngest, dearest one, has perished
The nursling of thy widowhood,[12] who grew,
Like a pale flower by some sad maiden cherished,
And fed with true love tears instead of dew[13] –
Most musical of mourners, weep anew!
Thy extreme hope, the loveliest and the last,
The bloom, whose petals nipped before they blew[14]
Died on the promise of the fruit, is waste;
The broken lily lies – the storm is overpast.

VII

To that high Capital,[15] where kingly Death
Keeps his pale court[16] in beauty and decay,
He came; and bought, with price of purest breath,
A grave among the eternal.[17] Come away![18]
Haste, while the vault of blue Italian day
Is yet his fitting charnel-roof![19] while still

## Notes

[6] *liberticide* destroyer of liberty.

[7] When the Stuart monarchy was restored with Charles II in 1660, some of those responsible for the execution of Charles I were beheaded. Milton escaped punishment, partly through the efforts of his friend and former colleague, Andrew Marvell.

[8] *Sprite* spirit.

[9] *the third among the sons of light* a reference to Shelley's discussion of epic poets in 'A Defence of Poetry', where Milton is ranked alongside Homer and Dante. In a MS note, Shelley lists the poets who would mourn Keats: 'It is difficult to assign any order of precedence except that founded on fame; thence, why (the Scriptures excepted), Virgil, Anacreon, Petrarch, Homer, Sophocles, Aeschylus, Dante, Petrarch, Lucretius, Virgil, Calderon, Shakespeare, Milton.'

[10] *And happier they ... perished* minor poets ('tapers') whose works survive are happier than major poets ('suns') whose work is lost.

[11] *refulgent* glorious, radiant.

[12] *The nursling of thy widowhood* Keats is presented as Milton's heir. Shelley was an admirer of Keats's Miltonic 'Hyperion'.

[13] Lines 48–9 recall Keats's 'Isabella' 424.

[14] *blew* blossomed.

[15] *that high Capital* Rome; Keats died at 26, Piazza di Spagna, today a museum devoted to him, Shelley and Byron.

[16] *Death ... court* an echo of *Richard II* III ii 160–2:

> for within the hollow crown
> That rounds the mortal temples of a king
> Keeps Death his court ...

[17] *the eternal* i.e. both Rome, the eternal city, and the many illustrious people buried there.

[18] *Come away!* addressed to those gathered round the body of Adonais.

[19] *charnel-roof* the roof of a tomb.

He lies, as if in dewy sleep he lay;
Awake him not! surely he takes his fill
Of deep and liquid[20] rest, forgetful of all ill.

VIII

He will awake no more, oh never more!
Within the twilight chamber spreads apace
The shadow of white Death, and at the door
Invisible Corruption waits to trace
His extreme way to her dim dwelling-place;
The eternal Hunger sits, but pity and awe
Soothe her pale rage, nor dares she to deface
So fair a prey, till darkness, and the law
Of mortal change, shall fill the grave which is her maw.

IX

Oh weep for Adonais! The quick Dreams,[21]
The passion-winged Ministers of thought
Who were his flocks, whom near the living streams
Of his young spirit he fed, and whom he taught
The love which was its music, wander not –
Wander no more from kindling brain to brain,
But droop there, whence they sprung; and mourn their lot
Round the cold heart, where, after their sweet pain,[22]
They ne'er will gather strength, or find a home again.

X

And one with trembling hands clasps his cold head,
And fans him with his moonlight wings, and cries,
'Our love, our hope, our sorrow, is not dead;[23]
See, on the silken fringe of his faint eyes,
Like dew upon a sleeping flower, there lies
A tear some Dream has loosened from his brain.'
Lost Angel of a ruined Paradise![24]
She knew not 'twas her own; as with no stain
She faded, like a cloud which had outwept its rain.[25]

## Notes

[20] *liquid* undisturbed, perfect.

[21] *quick Dreams* Keats's living ('quick') poems, which grieve for him.

[22] *sweet pain* Curiously, this appears in Keats's manuscript draft of 'Hyperion: A Fragment' Book III (starting at line 125 of the published text):

> Soon wild commotions shook him, and made flush
> All the immortal fairness of his limbs
> Into a hue more roseate than sweet pain
> Gives to a ravish'd Nymph when her warm tears
> Gush luscious with no sob ...

It is unlikely that Shelley knew Keats's unpublished manuscript; 'sweet pain' is just a typical Keatsian formulation.

[23] *our sorrow, is not dead* cf. 'Lycidas' 166: 'For Lycidas your sorrow is not dead.'

[24] *a ruined Paradise* Adonais's creative imagination.

[25] *like a cloud that had outwept its rain* i.e. like a cloud that had more grief than it could express through its available moisture.

XI

One from a lucid urn of starry dew
Washed his light limbs as if embalming them;
Another clipped her profuse locks, and threw
The wreath upon him, like an anadem,[26]
Which frozen tears instead of pearls begem;
Another in her wilful grief would break
Her bow and winged reeds,[27] as if to stem
A greater loss with one which was more weak,
And dull the barbed fire[28] against his frozen cheek.

XII

Another Splendour on his mouth alit[29] –
That mouth, whence it was wont to draw the breath
Which gave it strength to pierce the guarded wit,
And pass into the panting heart beneath
With lightning and with music: the damp death
Quenched its caress upon his icy lips,
And, as a dying meteor stains a wreath
Of moonlight vapour, which the cold night clips,[30]
It flushed through his pale limbs, and passed to its eclipse.

XIII

And others came – Desires and Adorations,
Winged Persuasions and veiled Destinies,
Splendours, and Glooms, and glimmering Incarnations
Of hopes and fears, and twilight Fantasies;
And Sorrow, with her family of Sighs,
And Pleasure, blind with tears, led by the gleam
Of her own dying smile instead of eyes,
Came in slow pomp – the moving pomp might seem
Like pageantry of mist on an autumnal stream.[31]

XIV

All he had loved, and moulded into thought,
From shape, and hue, and odour, and sweet sound,
Lamented Adonais. Morning sought
Her eastern watchtower, and her hair unbound,
Wet with the tears which should adorn the ground,
Dimmed the aerial eyes that kindle day;
Afar the melancholy thunder moaned,
Pale Ocean in unquiet slumber lay,
And the wild winds flew round, sobbing in their dismay.

## Notes

[26] *anadem* garland of flowers.

[27] *winged reeds* arrows.

[28] *barbed fire* A peculiar image that refers to the hooks or barbs on arrows that makes them difficult to remove from the wound. Shelley is almost certainly thinking of the 'storm of arrows barbed with fire' at 'Paradise Lost' vi 546.

[29] *alit* alighted.

[30] *clips* means both 'embraces' and 'cuts off '.

[31] *the moving pomp … autumnal stream* Shelley has in mind Keats's 'Season of mists and mellow fruitfulness' ('To Autumn' 1).

XV

Lost Echo[32] sits amid the voiceless mountains
And feeds her grief with his remembered lay,[33]
And will no more reply to winds or fountains,
Or amorous birds perched on the young green spray,
Or herdsman's horn, or bell at closing day;
Since she can mimic not his lips, more dear
Than those for whose disdain she pined away
Into a shadow of all sounds – a drear
Murmur, between their songs, is all the woodmen hear.

XVI

Grief made the young Spring wild, and she threw down
Her kindling buds, as if she Autumn were,
Or they dead leaves; since her delight is flown
For whom should she have waked the sullen year?
To Phoebus was not Hyacinth so dear[34]
Nor to himself Narcissus, as to both
Thou Adonais: wan they stand and sere[35]
Amid the drooping comrades of their youth,
With dew all turned to tears; odour, to sighing ruth.[36]

XVII

Thy spirit's sister, the lorn nightingale,[37]
Mourns not her mate with such melodious pain;
Not so the eagle, who like thee could scale
Heaven, and could nourish in the sun's domain
Her mighty youth with morning,[38] doth complain,
Soaring and screaming round her empty nest,
As Albion[39] wails for thee: the curse of Cain[40]
Light on his head[41] who pierced thy innocent breast,
And scared the angel soul that was its earthly guest!

XVIII

Ah woe is me! Winter is come and gone,
But grief returns with the revolving year;
The airs and streams renew their joyous tone;
The ants, the bees, the swallows reappear;
Fresh leaves and flowers deck the dead Seasons' bier;

## Notes

[32] The nymph Echo faded into an echo of sound when Narcissus rejected her; Narcissus fell in love with his own reflection and was transformed into a flower.

[33] *lay* Keats's poetry.

[34] Hyacinth, loved by Phoebus Apollo, was killed out of jealousy by Zephyrus and then turned into a flower by Apollo.

[35] *sere* withered.

[36] *ruth* pity.

[37] *the lorn nightingale* A reference to Keats's 'Ode to a Nightingale'.

[38] The eagle was believed to be able to replenish its youthful vision by flying into the sun and then diving into a fountain.

[39] *Albion* England.

[40] *the curse of Cain* Cain, who killed his brother Abel and brought murder into the world, was cursed as 'a fugitive and a vagabond ... in the earth' (Genesis 4:12, 14).

[41] *his head* i.e. that of the critic held responsible by Shelley for Keats's death – John Wilson Croker (although Shelley was unaware of his identity, the review having been published anonymously).

The amorous birds now pair in every brake,[42]
And build their mossy homes in field and brere;[43]
And the green lizard, and the golden snake,
Like unimprisoned flames, out of their trance awake.

XIX

Through wood and stream and field and hill and Ocean
A quickening life from the Earth's heart has burst
As it has ever done, with change and motion,
From the great morning of the world when first
God dawned on Chaos; in its steam immersed
The lamps of Heaven flash with a softer light;
All baser things pant with life's sacred thirst,
Diffuse themselves, and spend in love's delight,
The beauty and the joy of their renewed might.

XX

The leprous corpse touched by this spirit tender
Exhales itself in flowers of gentle breath;[44]
Like incarnations of the stars, when splendour
Is changed to fragrance, they illumine death
And mock the merry worm that wakes beneath;
Nought we know, dies. Shall that alone which knows[45]
Be as a sword consumed before the sheath[46]
By sightless[47] lightning? – th' intense atom glows
A moment, then is quenched in a most cold repose.

XXI

Alas! that all we loved of him should be,
But for our grief, as if it had not been,
And grief itself be mortal! Woe is me!
Whence are we, and why are we? Of what scene
The actors or spectators? Great and mean
Meet massed in death, who lends what life must borrow.
As long as skies are blue, and fields are green,
Evening must usher night, night urge the morrow,
Month follow month with woe, and year wake year to sorrow.

XXII

*He* will awake no more, oh never more!
'Wake thou,' cried Misery, 'childless Mother, rise
Out of thy sleep, and slake,[48] in thy heart's core,

## Notes

[42] *brake* thicket.

[43] *brere* archaic spelling of 'briar'.

[44] *flowers of gentle breath* anemones, thought to have sprung from Adonis's blood when he was killed by a boar.

[45] *that alone which knows* the human mind.

[46] *a sword consumed before the sheath* Shelley would have known Byron's variations on this image: 'Childe Harold's Pilgrimage' iii 913, and 'So We'll Go No More A-Roving' 5: 'For the sword outwears its sheath.'

[47] *sightless* invisible.

[48] *slake* soothe.

A wound more fierce than his with tears and sighs.'
And all the Dreams that watched Urania's eyes,
And all the Echoes whom their sister's song[49]
Had held in holy silence, cried: 'Arise!'
Swift as a Thought by the snake Memory stung,
From her ambrosial[50] rest the fading Splendour sprung.[51]

XXIII

She rose like an autumnal Night, that springs
Out of the East, and follows wild and drear
The golden Day, which, on eternal wings,
Even as a ghost abandoning a bier,
Had left the Earth a corpse. Sorrow and fear
So struck, so roused, so rapt[52] Urania;
So saddened round her like an atmosphere
Of stormy mist; so swept her on her way
Even to the mournful place where Adonais lay.

XXIV

Out of her secret Paradise she sped,
Through camps and cities rough with stone, and steel,
And human hearts, which to her airy tread
Yielding not, wounded the invisible
Palms[53] of her tender feet where'er they fell:
And barbed tongues,[54] and thoughts more sharp than they
Rent the soft Form they never could repel,
Whose sacred blood, like the young tears of May,
Paved with eternal flowers that undeserving way.

XXV

In the death-chamber for a moment Death,
Shamed by the presence of that living Might,
Blushed to annihilation, and the breath
Revisited those lips, and life's pale light
Flashed through those limbs, so late her dear delight.
'Leave me not wild and drear and comfortless,
As silent lightning leaves the starless night!
Leave me not!' cried Urania. Her distress
Roused Death: Death rose and smiled, and met her vain caress.

## Notes

[49] *And all the Echoes … song* Echo repeated Keats's poem at line 15.
[50] *ambrosial* heavenly.
[51] *the fading Splendour sprung* the Splendour was fading from grief.
[52] *rapt* enchanted.
[53] *Palms* soles.
[54] *barbed tongues* i.e. hostile critics.

XXVI

'Stay yet awhile! speak to me once again;
Kiss me, so long but as a kiss may live;
And in my heartless[55] breast and burning brain
That word, that kiss shall all thoughts else survive,
With food of saddest memory kept alive,
Now thou art dead, as if it were a part
Of thee, my Adonais! I would give
All that I am to be as thou now art!
But I am chained to Time, and cannot thence depart!

XXVII

Oh gentle child, beautiful as thou wert,
Why didst thou leave the trodden paths of men
Too soon, and with weak hands[56] though mighty heart
Dare the unpastured dragon[57] in his den?
Defenceless as thou wert, oh where was then
Wisdom the mirrored shield,[58] or scorn the spear?
Or hadst thou waited the full cycle, when
Thy spirit should have filled its crescent sphere,
The monsters of life's waste had fled from thee like deer.

XXVIII

The herded wolves, bold only to pursue;
The obscene ravens, clamorous o'er the dead;
The vultures to the conqueror's banner true
Who feed where Desolation first has fed,
And whose wings rain contagion – how they fled,
When, like Apollo, from his golden bow,
The Pythian of the age one arrow sped
And smiled![59] The spoilers[60] tempt no second blow,
They fawn on the proud feet that spurn them lying low.

XXIX

The sun comes forth, and many reptiles spawn;
He sets, and each ephemeral insect then
Is gathered into death without a dawn,
And the immortal stars awake again;[61]

## Notes

[55] *heartless* disheartened, dejected.

[56] *with weak hands* A reference to the weakness of Keats's early verse. Keats wrote to Shelley, 16 August 1820: 'I remember you advising me not to publish my first-blights, on Hampstead Heath'. In fact, Keats's first volume, *Poems* (1817), received generally favourable reviews; it was 'Endymion' (1818) that attracted criticism.

[57] *the unpastured dragon* the critic blamed by Shelley for Keats's death.

[58] *the mirrored shield* Perseus used a mirrored shield to slay the Medusa.

[59] *The Pythian … smiled* Byron's 'English Bards and Scotch Reviewers' (1809) attacked those responsible for the harsh review of his *Hours of Idleness*. Apollo killed a python with an arrow and established the Pythian games in celebration.

[60] *spoilers* ravagers, barbarians (i.e. the reviewers).

[61] *The sun … awake again* In Shelley's metaphor, the sun is the great poet during his lifetime; the reptiles are the critics; the ephemeral insects imitate the great poet's works; the stars are great poets of the past.

So is it in the world of living men:
A godlike mind soars forth, in its delight
Making earth bare and veiling heaven, and when
It sinks, the swarms that dimmed or shared its light
Leave to its kindred lamps[62] the spirit's awful night.'

XXX

Thus ceased she: and the mountain shepherds came
Their garlands sere, their magic mantles rent;
The Pilgrim of Eternity[63] (whose fame
Over his living head like Heaven is bent,
An early but enduring monument)
Came, veiling all the lightnings of his song
In sorrow; from her wilds Ierne sent
The sweetest lyrist[64] of her saddest wrong,
And love taught grief to fall like music from his tongue.

XXXI

Midst others of less note came one frail Form,[65]
A phantom among men, companionless
As the last cloud of an expiring storm
Whose thunder is its knell. He, as I guess,
Had gazed on Nature's naked loveliness,
Actaeon-like,[66] and now he fled astray
With feeble steps o'er the world's wilderness,
And his own thoughts, along that rugged way,
Pursued, like raging hounds, their father and their prey.

XXXII

A pardlike[67] Spirit beautiful and swift,
A Love in desolation masked, a Power
Girt round with weakness – it can scarce uplift
The weight of the superincumbent hour:[68]
It is a dying lamp, a falling shower,
A breaking billow; even whilst we speak,
Is it not broken? On the withering flower
The killing sun smiles brightly: on a cheek
The life can burn in blood, even while the heart may break.

## Notes

[62] *its kindred lamps* stars (i.e. other creative spirits).

[63] *The Pilgrim of Eternity* Byron; the reference is to 'Childe Harold's Pilgrimage'.

[64] *Ierne sent ... lyrist* Thomas Moore, from Ireland (Ierne) – popular poet, author of ballads and songs. Shelley forwarded a copy of 'Adonais' to Moore through Horace Smith, who reported, 3 October 1821: 'I gave Moore your copy of "Adonais" and he was very much pleased with it, particularly with the allusion to himself'.

[65] *one frail Form* Shelley.

[66] Actaeon, seeing Diana bathing, was turned into a stag and torn to pieces by his own dogs.

[67] *pardlike* A pard is a leopard or panther; in an early draft, Shelley has 'Pantherlike'.

[68] *the superincumbent hour* The overhanging ('superincumbent') hour is that of Adonais's death.

XXXIII

His head was bound with pansies overblown,
And faded violets, white, and pied, and blue;
And a light spear topped with a cypress cone,
Round whose rude shaft dark ivy tresses grew[69]
Yet dripping with the forest's noonday dew,
Vibrated, as the ever-beating heart
Shook the weak hand that grasped it: of that crew
He came the last, neglected and apart –
A herd-abandoned deer struck by the hunter's dart.

XXXIV

All stood aloof, and at his partial moan
Smiled through their tears; well knew that gentle band
Who in another's fate now wept his own;
As in the accents of an unknown land,
He sung new sorrow; sad Urania scanned
The Stranger's mien, and murmured, 'Who art thou?'
He answered not, but with a sudden hand
Made bare his branded and ensanguined brow,
Which was like Cain's or Christ's[70] – oh that it should be so!

XXXV

What softer voice is hushed over the dead?
Athwart what brow is that dark mantle thrown?
What form leans sadly o'er the white deathbed
In mockery[71] of monumental stone,
The heavy heart heaving without a moan?
If it be He[72] who, gentlest of the wise,
Taught, soothed, loved, honoured the departed one,
Let me not vex, with inharmonious sighs,
The silence of that heart's accepted sacrifice.

XXXVI

Our Adonais has drunk poison – oh!
What deaf and viperous murderer could crown
Life's early cup with such a draught of woe?[73]
The nameless worm would now itself disown:
It felt, yet could escape the magic tone

## Notes

[69] *a light spear ... grew* A thyrsus, a staff or spear tipped with an ornament like a pine-cone, and sometimes wreathed with ivy or vine branches, was carried, in Greek myth, by Dionysus (Bacchus) and his votaries. Ivy was the emblem of the poet in Latin poetry.

[70] Shelley's comparison of himself with Christ enraged early reviewers, although it had already been made, implicitly at least, in 'Prometheus Unbound' and 'Ode to the West Wind'. In particular, the Revd George Croly, in *Blackwood's Edinburgh Magazine* (December 1821), quoted this line and remarked: 'We have heard it mentioned as the only apology for the predominant irreligion and nonsense of this person's works, that his understanding is unsettled.'

[71] *mockery* imitation; the 'form' is alive, but is so still it appears to be a statue.

[72] *He* Leigh Hunt, a crucial influence on Keats.

[73] *What deaf ... woe* Stanzas 36–7 attack the reviewer responsible for Keats's death. Shelley thought him to be Southey, though the actual culprit was John Wilson Croker.

Whose prelude held all envy, hate, and wrong,
But what was howling in one breast alone,
Silent with expectation of the song,
Whose master's hand is cold, whose silver lyre unstrung.

XXXVII

Live thou whose infamy is not thy fame!
Live! Fear no heavier chastisement from me,
Thou noteless[74] blot on a remembered name!
But be thyself, and know thyself to be!
And ever at thy season[75] be thou free
To spill the venom when thy fangs o'erflow –
Remorse and self-contempt shall cling to thee;
Hot Shame shall burn upon thy secret brow,
And like a beaten hound tremble thou shalt – as now.

XXXVIII

Nor let us weep that our delight is fled
Far from these carrion kites that scream below –
He wakes or sleeps with the enduring dead;
Thou canst not soar where he is sitting now.
Dust to the dust! But the pure spirit shall flow
Back to the burning fountain whence it came,
A portion of the Eternal, which must glow
Through time and change, unquenchably the same,
Whilst thy cold embers choke the sordid hearth of shame.

XXXIX

Peace, peace! He is not dead, he doth not sleep –
He hath awakened from the dream of life –
'Tis we who, lost in stormy visions, keep
With phantoms an unprofitable strife,
And in mad trance, strike with our spirit's knife
Invulnerable nothings. *We* decay
Like corpses in a charnel;[76] fear and grief
Convulse us and consume us day by day,
And cold hopes swarm like worms within our living clay.

XL

He has outsoared the shadow of our night;[77]
Envy and calumny and hate and pain,
And that unrest which men miscall delight,
Can touch him not and torture not again;

Notes

[74] *noteless* not worth noting, undistinguished.

[75] *at thy season* every quarter, when the *Quarterly Review* was published.

[76] *charnel* tomb.

[77] *the shadow of our night* The shadow cast by the earth away from the sun.

From the contagion of the world's slow stain
He is secure, and now can never mourn
A heart grown cold, a head grown grey in vain;
Nor, when the spirit's self has ceased to burn,
With sparkless ashes load an unlamented urn.

XLI

He lives, he wakes – 'tis Death is dead, not he;
Mourn not for Adonais. Thou young Dawn
Turn all thy dew to splendour, for from thee
The spirit thou lamentest is not gone;
Ye caverns and ye forests, cease to moan!
Cease ye faint flowers and fountains, and thou Air
Which like a mourning veil thy scarf hadst thrown
O'er the abandoned Earth, now leave it bare
Even to the joyous stars which smile on its despair!

XLII

He is made one with Nature: there is heard
His voice in all her music, from the moan
Of thunder, to the song of night's sweet bird;[78]
He is a presence to be felt and known
In darkness and in light, from herb and stone,
Spreading itself where'er that Power[79] may move
Which has withdrawn his being to its own,
Which wields the world with never-wearied love,
Sustains it from beneath, and kindles it above.

XLIII

He is a portion of the loveliness
Which once he made more lovely: he doth bear
His part, while the one Spirit's plastic stress[80]
Sweeps through the dull dense world, compelling there
All new successions to the forms they wear;
Torturing th' unwilling dross that checks its flight
To its own likeness, as each mass may bear;
And bursting in its beauty and its might
From trees and beasts and men into the Heaven's light.

## Notes

[78] *night's sweet bird* the nightingale. Shelley refers, again, to Keats's 'Ode to a Nightingale'.

[79] *Power* cf. 'Mont Blanc' and 'Hymn to Intellectual Beauty'.

[80] *plastic stress* shaping, moulding power. Shelley is almost ertainly thinking of the pantheism of Coleridge's 'Eolian Harp', where the divine 'intellectual breeze' is 'Plastic and vast' (l. 39).

XLIV

The splendours of the firmament of time[81]
May be eclipsed, but are extinguished not;
Like stars to their appointed height they climb,
And death is a low mist which cannot blot
The brightness it may veil. When lofty thought
Lifts a young heart above its mortal lair,
And love and life contend in it for what
Shall be its earthly doom,[82] the dead live there
And move like winds of light on dark and stormy air.[83]

XLV

The inheritors of unfulfilled renown[84]
Rose from their thrones, built beyond mortal thought,
Far in the Unapparent. Chatterton
Rose pale, his solemn agony had not
Yet faded from him; Sidney, as he fought
And as he fell and as he lived and loved
Sublimely mild, a Spirit without spot,
Arose; and Lucan, by his death approved:
Oblivion as they rose shrank like a thing reproved.

XLVI

And many more whose names on Earth are dark,
But whose transmitted effluence[85] cannot die
So long as fire outlives the parent spark,
Rose, robed in dazzling immortality.
'Thou art become as one of us', they cry,
'It was for thee yon kingless sphere has long
Swung blind in unascended majesty,
Silent alone amid an Heaven of song.
Assume thy winged throne, thou Vesper of our throng!'[86]

XLVII

Who mourns for Adonais? Oh come forth
Fond[87] wretch, and know thyself and him aright!
Clasp with thy panting soul the pendulous Earth;[88]
As from a centre, dart thy spirit's light

## Notes

[81] *The splendours ... time* i.e. Keats and other poets.

[82] *doom* destiny.

[83] *When lofty thought ... air* The creative minds of the dead influence the hearts of the young.

[84] *inheritors of unfulfilled renown* Poets who died before they could realize their full potential. Shelley goes on to specify Thomas Chatterton, who committed suicide at the age of 17 in 1770; Sir Philip Sidney, who died in 1586 at the age of 32, from a wound sustained in the Netherlands in their fight against Spain; and Lucan, who committed suicide in 65 BCE at the age of 25. (Having been a flatterer of Nero, Lucan joined a conspiracy against him; his suicide served to redeem his reputation.)

[85] *effluence* i.e. power.

[86] In the Ptolemaic system of astronomy, the songs of concentric whirling spheres around the earth blended into a harmony. Adonais is to be the genius of the third sphere of Venus.

[87] *Fond* It is foolish ('Fond') to mourn Adonais.

[88] *the pendulous Earth* An allusion to 'The pendulous round earth' of 'Paradise Lost' iv 1000, where 'pendulous' means 'suspended' (in space).

Beyond all worlds, until its spacious might
Satiate the void circumference; then shrink
Even to a point within our day and night –
And keep thy heart light lest it make thee sink
When hope has kindled hope, and lured thee to the brink.[89]

XLVIII

Or go to Rome, which is the sepulchre
Oh not of him, but of our joy: 'tis nought
That ages, empires, and religions there
Lie buried in the ravage they have wrought;
For such as he[90] can lend – they[91] borrow not
Glory from those who made the world their prey;
And he is gathered to the kings of thought[92]
Who waged contention with their time's decay,
And of the past are all that cannot pass away.

XLIX

Go thou to Rome – at once the Paradise,
The grave, the city, and the wilderness;
And where its wrecks like shattered mountains rise,
And flowering weeds, and fragrant copses dress
The bones of Desolation's nakedness,
Pass, till the Spirit of the spot shall lead
Thy footsteps to a slope of green access[93]
Where, like an infant's smile,[94] over the dead,
A light of laughing flowers along the grass is spread.

L

And grey walls[95] moulder round, on which dull Time
Feeds, like slow fire upon a hoary brand;[96]
And one keen pyramid with wedge sublime,[97]
Pavilioning the dust of him who planned
This refuge for his memory, doth stand
Like flame transformed to marble; and beneath,
A field is spread, on which a newer band
Have pitched in Heaven's smile their camp of death
Welcoming him we lose with scarce extinguished breath.

## Notes

[89] *And keep … brink* Shelley tells the 'Fond wretch' to keep his heart light so that when death is near, he has not built too much hope on immortality.

[90] *he* Adonais.

[91] *they* 'such as he'; creative spirits like Keats.

[92] *kings of thought* including Chatterton, Sidney and Lucan.

[93] *a slope of green access* the Protestant Cemetery in Rome, where Keats was buried.

[94] *like an infant's smile* Shelley's son William died suddenly at the age of three in June 1819; he was also buried in the Protestant Cemetery in Rome.

[95] *grey walls* of Rome, begun by Aurelian (emperor, 270–5), which bound one side of the cemetery.

[96] *a hoary brand* a log in the fireplace, nearly burnt up.

[97] The pyramid is a monument to a Roman tribune, Gaius Cestius, who died about 12 BCE, incorporated into the city walls.

LI

Here pause: these graves are all too young as yet
To have outgrown the sorrow which consigned
Its charge to each; and if the seal is set,
Here, on one fountain of a mourning mind,
Break it not thou![98] Too surely shalt thou find
Thine own well full, if thou returnest home,
Of tears and gall.[99] From the world's bitter wind[100]
Seek shelter in the shadow of the tomb.
What Adonais is, why fear we to become?

LII

The One remains, the many change and pass;
Heaven's light forever shines, Earth's shadows fly;
Life, like a dome of many-coloured glass,
Stains the white radiance of Eternity,[101]
Until Death tramples it to fragments. Die,
If thou wouldst be with that which thou dost seek!
Follow where all is fled! Rome's azure sky,
Flowers, ruins, statues, music, words, are weak
The glory they transfuse with fitting truth to speak.

LIII

Why linger, why turn back, why shrink, my Heart?[102]
Thy hopes are gone before: from all things here
They have departed – thou shouldst now depart!
A light is passed from the revolving year,
And man, and woman; and what still is dear
Attracts to crush, repels to make thee wither.
The soft sky smiles, the low wind whispers near:
'Tis Adonais calls! Oh, hasten thither,
No more let Life divide what Death can join together.

LIV

That Light whose smile kindles the Universe,
That Beauty in which all things work and move,
That Benediction which the eclipsing Curse
Of birth can quench not, that sustaining Love
Which through the web of being blindly wove

Notes

[98] *on one fountain ... thou* The mourner is told not to break the seal on the fountain of Shelley's grief for his son William.

[99] *gall* bitter grief.

[100] *bitter wind* a wry pun on 'malaria', the disease from which William Shelley died (meaning 'bad air' in Italian).

[101] *Life ... Eternity* Just as sunlight shining through stained glass separates into different colours, so eternal unity is distributed among different people and things on earth.

[102] Shelley is addressing himself.

By man and beast and earth and air and sea,
Burns bright or dim, as each are mirrors of
The fire for which all thirst – now beams on me,
Consuming the last clouds of cold mortality.

LV

The breath whose might I have invoked in song
Descends on me; my spirit's bark is driven
Far from the shore, far from the trembling throng
Whose sails were never to the tempest given;
The massy earth and sphered skies are riven!
I am borne darkly, fearfully, afar;
Whilst burning through the inmost veil of Heaven,
The soul of Adonais, like a star,
Beacons from the abode where the Eternal are.

## *Music, When Soft Voices Die*

Music, when soft voices die,
Vibrates in the memory –
Odours, when sweet violets sicken,
Live within the sense they quicken.
Rose leaves, when the rose is dead,
Are heaped for the beloved's bed;
And so thy thoughts, when thou art gone,
Love itself shall slumber on.

## *When Passion's Trance Is Overpast* (composed 1821)[1]

When passion's trance is overpast,
If tenderness and truth could last
Or live, whilst all wild feelings keep
Some mortal slumber, dark and deep,
I should not weep, I should not weep!

It were enough to feel, to see
Thy soft eyes gazing tenderly,
And dream the rest – and burn and be
The secret food of fires unseen,
Couldst thou but be as thou hast been.

After the slumber of the year
The woodland violets reappear;
All things revive in field or grove,

Notes

When Passion's Trance Is Overpast

[1] Strains had formed within the Shelleys' marriage during the months prior to composition of this poem.

And sky and sea; but two, which move,
And for all others, life and love.

## *To Edward Williams* (composed 26 January 1822; edited from MS)[1]

I

The serpent[2] is shut out from Paradise –
The wounded deer must seek the herb no more
In which its heart's cure lies;
The widowed dove must cease to haunt a bower
Like that from which its mate with feigned sighs
Fled in the April hour;
I too must seldom seek again
Near happy friends a mitigated pain.

2

Of hatred I am proud; with scorn, content;
Indifference, which once hurt me, is now grown
Itself indifferent.
But not to speak of love, Pity alone
Can break a spirit already more than bent.
The miserable one
Turns the mind's poison into food:
Its medicine is tears, its evil, good.[3]

3

Therefore if now I see you seldomer
Dear friends, dear *friend*,[4] know that I only fly
Yours looks, because they stir
Griefs that should sleep, and hopes that cannot die.
The very comfort which they minister
I scarce can bear; yet I
(So deeply is the arrow gone)
Should quickly perish if it were withdrawn.

4

When I return to my cold home,[5] you ask
Why I am not as I have lately been?
You spoil me for the task

### Notes

To Edward Williams

[1] Edward and Jane Williams were friends of Thomas Medwin, Shelley's boyhood friend, who brought them to meet the Shelleys in Pisa in January 1821. By January 1822 Shelley had become somewhat estranged from Mary and soon developed feelings for Jane. He gave a copy of this poem to Edward Williams on 26 January 1822, saying: 'If any of these stanzas should please you, you may read them to Jane, but to no one else – and yet on second thoughts I had rather you would not.' On the same day, Williams recorded in his journal that 'Shelley sent us some beautiful but too melancholy lines'.

[2] *The serpent* Byron's nickname for Shelley was 'The Snake'.

[3] *its evil good* Shelley is recalling Satan: 'Evil be thou my good' ('Paradise Lost' iv 110).

[4] *dear friend* presumably a reference to Jane Williams.

[5] *my cold home* a reference to his strained marriage.

Of acting a forced part in life's dull scene.
Of wearing on my brow the idle mask
Of author, great or mean,
In the world's carnival. I sought
Peace thus, and but in you I found it not.

5

Full half an hour today I tried my lot
With various flowers, and every one still said
'She loves me, loves me not'.
And if this meant a vision long since fled –
If it meant Fortune, Fame, or Peace of thought,
If it meant – (but I dread
To speak what you may know too well);
Still there was truth in the sad oracle.

6

The crane o'er seas and forests seeks her home.
No bird so wild but has its quiet nest
When it no more would roam.
The sleepless billows on the ocean's breast
Break like a bursting heart, and die in foam
And thus, at length, find rest.
Doubtless there is a place of peace
Where *my* weak heart and all its throbs will cease.

7

I asked her yesterday if she believed
That I had resolution; one who *had*
Would ne'er have thus relieved
His heart with words, but what his judgement bad
Would do, and leave the scorner unrelieved.
These verses were too sad
To send to you, but that I know,
Happy yourself you feel another's woe.

## *With a Guitar, to Jane* (composed April 1822)[1]

*Ariel* to *Miranda* – Take
This slave of music for the sake
Of him who is the slave of thee;
And teach it all the harmony
In which thou canst, and only thou,

## Notes

WITH A GUITAR, TO JANE

[1] By the time this was written, the Shelleys' relationship had broken down, and Shelley had become attached to Jane Williams. He bought her a beautiful guitar in April 1822 and gave it to her with a fair copy draft of this poem, from which my text is taken. Both the guitar and manuscript survive today in the Bodleian Library, Oxford.

Make the delighted spirit glow,
Till joy denies itself again
And, too intense, is turned to pain;
For by permission and command
Of thine own Prince Ferdinand[2]
Poor Ariel[3] sends this silent token
Of more than ever can be spoken;
Your guardian spirit Ariel, who
From life to life must still pursue
Your happiness, for thus alone
Can Ariel ever find his own;
From Prospero's enchanted cell,
As the mighty verses tell,
To the throne of Naples he
Lit you o'er the trackless sea,[4]
Flitting on, your prow before,
Like a living meteor.
When you die, the silent moon
In her interlunar swoon[5]
Is not sadder in her cell
Than deserted Ariel;
When you live again on earth[6]
Like an unseen star of birth[7]
Ariel guides you o'er the sea
Of life from your nativity.
Many changes have been run
Since Ferdinand and you begun
Your course of love, and Ariel still
Has tracked your steps and served your will;
Now in humbler, happier lot
This is all remembered not;
And now, alas! the poor sprite[8] is
Imprisoned for some fault of his
In a body like a grave –
From you he only dares to crave,
For his service and his sorrow,
A smile today, a song tomorrow.

The artist who this idol[9] wrought
To echo all harmonious thought

## Notes

[2] *Ferdinand* A reference to Edward Williams. By coincidence, the maker of the guitar given to Jane was Ferdinando Bottari.

[3] *Poor Ariel* Shelley casts himself in the role of Jane's guardian spirit.

[4] *To the throne ... sea* In Shakespeare's play, Ariel conducts Prospero and Miranda back to Naples, from where they were once banished.

[5] *In her interlunar swoon* a recollection of Milton's '*Samson Agonistes*':

> The sun to me is dark
> And silent as the moon,
> When she deserts the night
> Hid in her vacant interlunar cave. (ll. 86–9)

Pliny writes that the time when the moon is in conjunction with the sun is called the interlunar day.

[6] *When you live again on earth* a reference to reincarnation.

[7] *star of birth* Astrologers believe that we are born under particular stars that govern our fates.

[8] *the poor sprite* Ariel (Shelley).

[9] *this idol* the guitar, made by Ferdinando Bottari in Pisa.

Felled a tree, while on the steep
The woods were in their winter sleep
Rocked in that repose divine
On the windswept Apennine;
And dreaming, some of autumn past,
And some of spring approaching fast,
And some of April buds and showers,
And some of songs in July bowers,
And all of love; and so this tree –
Oh that such our death may be –
Died in sleep, and felt no pain,
To live in happier form again,
From which, beneath Heaven's fairest star,[10]
The artist wrought this loved guitar
And taught it justly to reply
To all who question skilfully
In language gentle as thine own;
Whispering in enamoured tone
Sweet oracles of woods and dells
And summer winds in sylvan cells;
For it had learnt all harmonies
Of the plains and of the skies,
Of the forests and the mountains,
And the many-voiced fountains,
The clearest echoes of the hills,
The softest notes of falling rills,
The melodies of birds and bees,
The murmuring of summer seas,
And pattering rain and breathing dew,
And airs of evening; and it knew
That seldom-heard mysterious sound[11]
Which, driven on its diurnal round[12]
As it floats through boundless day,
Our world enkindles on its way –
All this it knows, but will not tell
To those who cannot question well
The Spirit that inhabits it;
It talks according to the wit
Of its companions; and no more
Is heard than has been felt before
By those who tempt it to betray
These secrets of an elder day.
But, sweetly as its answers will
Flatter hands of perfect skill,
It keeps its highest holiest tone
For one beloved Jane alone.

## Notes

[10] *Heaven's fairest star* Venus, which is the brightest 'star' in the sky, and that of love.

[11] *mysterious sound* the music of the spheres.

[12] *its diurnal round* Shelley's phrasing is Wordsworthian, recalling Lucy: 'Rolled round in earth's diurnal course' ('A Slumber Did My Spirit Seal' 7). 'Diurnal' means 'daily'.

# John Keats (1795–1821)

Of the major Romantic poets, Keats was the last to be born and the first to die, at the early age of 25. Had any other writer in this volume ceased to write at such an early age, they would be seen as little more than promising, and not eligible for inclusion in a volume such as this: poets mature late, often around the age of 30. In achieving what he did within his all-too-brief lifetime, Keats demonstrated an almost unparalleled precocity. He worked hard, developed with abnormal rapidity and produced some of the finest poetry in the language.

He was born on 29 October 1795, in Finsbury, north London, the eldest child of Thomas Keats, Head Ostler at the Swan and Hoop Inn, Moorgate, and Frances Jennings. They were not working class, as is sometimes suggested, but fairly well-to-do, respectable and middle-class. From the very beginning Keats knew he wanted to be a poet, declaring as much from the time he could speak. Brothers George and Tom were born in 1797 and 1799, his sister Fanny in 1803. But like many of their time, they were soon orphaned, for in 1804 their father died after falling from his horse, and in 1810 their mother died of a 'decline', which biographers interpret as a reference to consumption, an ailment that would afflict her children.

From 1803 Keats attended the Enfield school run by John Clarke whose son, Charles Cowden Clarke, became a lifelong friend. Clarke recalled Keats as having a highly retentive memory, and as reading the entire contents of the school library, 'which consisted principally of abridgements of all the voyages and travels of any note; Mavor's collection, also his "Universal History"; Robertson's histories of Scotland, America, and Charles the Fifth; all Miss Edgeworth's productions, together with many other works equally well calculated for youth'.

With the deaths of his parents it became imperative that Keats find a trade, and in summer 1811 he left school to become a physician. He was 14 when he began an apprenticeship with Thomas Hammond, a doctor in Edmonton (two miles to the south of Enfield), who taught him how to give vaccinations for smallpox, bleed patients with a lancet or leeches, dress wounds, set bones, pull teeth, diagnose illnesses, and make up pills, ointments, poultices and other medicines. He did well enough to register as a student at Guy's Hospital on 1 October 1815, a month short of his twentieth birthday. He made rapid progress: four weeks into his studies he was appointed dresser to Mr Lucas, one of the hospital surgeons, and on 25 July 1816 examination success made him licentiate of the Society of Apothecaries, giving him the right to practise as apothecary, physician and surgeon. During this period he continued to write; a fellow student at Guy's recalled that in the lecture room 'I have seen Keats in a deep poetic dream: his mind was on Parnassus with the muses.'

In mid-October 1816, he began the long climb up Parnassus when introduced to Leigh Hunt on the gentle slopes of Hampstead Heath. It was an encounter that changed his life. 'We became intimate on the spot', Hunt recalled, 'and I found the young poet's heart as warm as his imagination.' More than a decade older than Keats, Hunt was an established writer eager to form a coterie of like-minded souls with shared ideological convictions, prepared to engage in intellectual discourse both in person and in print. They enjoyed soirées, sonnet-writing competitions, and vigorous debates on political topics. Keats's need for a mentor – someone to help him refine, develop and promote his talent – was satisfied, at least for the moment. Friendship with Hunt gave Keats access to the bohemian London: Shelley, Lamb, Hazlitt, John Scott (who would become editor of the *London Magazine*), Charles and James Ollier (who would publish Keats's first book of poems) and Benjamin Robert Haydon, among others.

Hunt lived in the Vale of Health in Hampstead, in a white cottage full of music, pictures, busts of poets, flowers and books. Keats was soon a 'familiar of the household, and was always welcomed'. He fell into the habit of sleeping on the sofa in Hunt's library where, awakening one morning, he began to compose 'Sleep and Poetry', probably in October or November 1816:

> What is more gentle than a wind in summer?
> What is more soothing than the pretty hummer
> That stays one moment in an open flower
> And buzzes cheerily from bower to bower?
> (ll. 1–4)

The weaknesses of these lines are traceable to Hunt, whose poetry also contained feminine rhymes, fey diction (the 'hummer' is a bee) and unashamed use of such adjectives as 'pretty'. Hunt believed poetry to be the vehicle of pleasure – or, to use his term, 'luxuries'. 'We should consider ourselves as what we really are: creatures made to enjoy more than to know', he wrote in *Foliage* (1818), adding, 'I write to enjoy myself.' Commitment to the ornamental, pleasure-giving function of poetry was a powerful influence on young Keats, and although he would outgrow it, it remained part of his thinking to the end.

Keats had arrived at the point where he had to make the choice between medicine and poetry. In autumn 1816 he broke the news to his guardian, Richard Abbey. 'Not intend to be a surgeon!' said Abbey. 'Why, what do you mean to be?' 'I mean to rely on my abilities as a poet.' 'John, you are either mad or a fool to talk in so absurd a manner.' 'My mind is made up. I know that I possess abilities greater than most men, and therefore I am determined to gain my living by exercising them.' Abbey is said to have called him a 'silly boy', and prophesied a 'speedy termination to his inconsiderate enterprise'.

But there was encouragement too. On 1 December 1816 *The Examiner* published an article by Hunt entitled 'Young Poets', which praised Keats alongside Shelley: 'He has not yet published anything except in a newspaper; but a set of his manuscripts was handed us the other day, and fairly surprised us with the truth of their ambition, and ardent grappling with Nature.' It concluded with the complete text of 'On First Looking into Chapman's Homer'. Having read it on the day of its appearance, Hunt was inspired to compose 'To John Keats'.

Keats met Shelley at Hunt's cottage in December 1816, and shortly after read his 'Hymn to Intellectual Beauty' in manuscript, which Hunt was to publish in *The Examiner* early the following year. At this point, Shelley was living in Bath with Mary Godwin, in the wake of the death of his first wife, Harriet Westbrook. When he moved to Marlow in Buckinghamshire in February 1817, he invited Keats to visit, but Keats declined in order that 'I might have my own unfettered scope'. Evidently, he feared Shelley might prove too strong an influence, perhaps because feeling that one mentor was ample. Keats and Shelley engaged in a last sonnet-writing competition before Shelley departed for the Continent in February 1818.

Hunt and Keats celebrated the publication of Keats's *Poems* on 3 March 1817 by breaking open a bottle of wine in Hunt's garden and crowning each other with garlands of ivy (Hunt) and laurel (Keats). They then wrote commemorative sonnets; Hunt was sufficiently unashamed to publish them in *Foliage*. But first, his opinion of Keats's first book was called for, and in June and July he published a three-part review in *The Examiner*, which hailed Keats as 'a young poet indeed' before pointing out his faults ('a tendency to notice everything too indiscriminately and without an eye to natural proportion and effect; and second, a sense of the proper variety of versification without a due consideration of its principles') and 'beauties', to which the third instalment was dedicated. 'Happy Poetry Preferred', reads the heading given by Hunt to an extract from 'Sleep and Poetry'. Though ostensibly a publicity exercise, the entire thing was hugely patronizing. Perhaps the most galling thing about the article was Hunt's use of Keats's 'smiling Muse' as a means of criticizing 'the morbidity that taints the productions of the Lake Poets'. As an admirer of Wordsworth and Coleridge, Keats cannot have approved.

The friendship began to cool. Wordsworth's influence is evident in 'Endymion', on which Keats worked throughout the spring and summer of 1817, which shows him exploring the heroic couplet in ways that reveal a seriousness derived from Wordsworth and Shakespeare. Its 'Hymn to Pan' was the strongest evidence thus far that Keats would turn into the author of the 1819 Odes. Shelley was among those who recognized its quality, but not Wordsworth, who expressed his opinion of it when introduced to Keats in London, as Haydon recalled:

> Wordsworth received him kindly, and after a few minutes Wordsworth asked him what he had been lately doing. I said, 'He has just finished an exquisite Ode to Pan', and as he had not a copy I begged Keats to repeat it, which he did in his usual half-chant (most touching), walking up and down the room. When he had done I felt, really, as if I had heard a young Apollo. Wordsworth drily said, 'a very pretty piece of Paganism'.

Biographers continue to dispute Keats's reaction to this. He saw a good deal of Wordsworth at this period, and it seems unlikely he took it to heart. Their encounter at the 'immortal dinner' at the end of the year seems to have been friendly and cordial.

While working on 'Endymion', Keats developed his ideas about creativity, which were influenced by Hazlitt's essay 'On Gusto', reprinted from *The Examiner* in Hazlitt and Hunt's *The Round Table* (1817). Hazlitt's starting point is that 'Gusto in art is power or passion defining any object'. For him, works of art are ratified by the artist's ability to transcend the barriers of the self and embody another object or being. This is close to what Keats terms 'imagination', which gives the artist access to a heightened reality he called 'truth'. That reality was intensified beyond the level of everyday experience – idealized and exemplary (or 'true'). Where Keats differed from Hazlitt was in regarding the artist as a chameleon, capable of abnegating the self and assuming the emotions and character of other things. Hazlitt, who was a great believer in the egotistical sublime of Wordsworth – in 'genius' – does not license this, for he thought of genius and gusto as identical. Keats's reservations about egotism are related to increasing ambivalence about Hunt, whose claims to genius he found absurd. For Keats, the imagination worked where the self was submerged in an act of what he called 'negative capability':

> A poet is the most unpoetical of any thing in existence, because he has no identity, he is continually in for – and filling – some other body. The sun, the moon, the sea, and men and women who are creatures of impulse, are poetical, and have about them an unchangeable attribute; the poet has none, no identity – he is certainly the most unpoetical of all God's creatures.

It is crucial to Keats that the poet lose all sense of self in imaginative engagement with his subject. And he goes further:

> What the imagination seizes as beauty must be truth, whether it existed before or not. For I have the same idea of all our passions as of love: they are all in their sublime, creative of essential beauty.... The imagination may be compared to Adam's dream: he awoke and found it truth.

Emerging from an imaginative experience in which he has 'lost' awareness of the self, the poet 'awakens' to an apprehension he would not otherwise have been granted – the 'essential beauty' of the thing created by his negatively capable imagination. The point about 'essential beauty' (equivalent to 'truth') is that it derives from the otherness of something distinct and separate from the artist's ego; it's akin to a revelation.

Keats states that the artist who negates himself in the act of creation is 'capable of being in uncertainties, mysteries, doubts, without any irritable reaching after fact and reason'. Coleridge had once been such a poet, but the ill, middle-aged man Keats encountered on Hampstead Heath was in thrall to logical trains of thought ('consequitive reasoning', in Keats's words), discoursing at length on 'a thousand things' with barely a glance in his direction: 'I heard his voice as he came towards me – I heard it as he moved away – I had heard it all the interval'.

'Isabella', written during the spring of 1818, is the first great narrative work of Keats's maturity. It translates a story he found in Boccaccio's *Decameron,* probably at the suggestion of Hazlitt, and was intended for a volume of translations, to have been written jointly with Keats's friend John Hamilton Reynolds, which in the end did not materialize. Keats's handling of *ottava rima,* the Italian stanza he knew from Fairfax's translation of Tasso's *Gerusalemme Liberata,* is assured. That he should have chosen to versify such a macabre tale – one focused, moreover, on psychological disturbance – shows he was trying to break free of the Huntian emphasis on 'luxuries'. Even so, he thought the poem 'too smokeable.... There is too much inexperience of life, and simplicity of knowledge in it – which might do very well after one's death, but not while one is alive'.

The 'Cockney School' attacks, initiated by John Gibson Lockhart, began the previous year, and were making Keats question Hunt's ideas about poetry even more. He must have known he would soon be singled out by Lockhart for special attention. Rather than brood on it, he went on a walking tour of the Lake District and Scotland with his friend Charles Brown in the summer of 1818. One of his aims was to visit Wordsworth at Rydal Mount, but he was shaken to discover the great man was not at home because of the general election, in which he was campaigning on behalf of his patron – Lord Lowther, who was a Tory. It was a disappointing reminder that the middle-aged poet had sold out. He left a brief note on Wordsworth's mantelpiece and continued on his way.

Keats and Brown walked round Derwentwater and climbed Skiddaw before crossing the border into Dumfries, then headed north to Inverary and Oban, and the western Highlands where the dominant language was Gaelic. But the weather was variable, and after climbing Ben Nevis on 2 August Keats realized he was suffering from tonsillitis and decided to return home. He arrived in London to find his brother Tom suffering from tuberculosis in its advanced stages. As he nursed him, Keats composed 'Hyperion', work on which came to an abrupt halt when Tom died on 1 December.

The new poem aspired, Keats said, to 'a more naked and grecian manner'. He wanted to purge his poetry of Huntian mannerism, which he now saw as a crucial weakness. Instead, his new theme was loss and suffering, which he believed would draw him closer to Wordsworth and Milton. 'Hyperion' followed the exile of the Titans, pre-Hellenic gods, by their children, led by Jupiter. As the poem opens, Saturn and the Titans are already defeated and in despair, except for Hyperion, god of the sun, who is still in power and in Books I and II attempts to rouse them to action. In Book III Apollo enters, in the midst of being transformed into god of the sun, music, healing and prophecy, by the Titan goddess, Mnemosyne (who has changed sides): 'Knowledge enormous makes a god of me', Apollo tells her (iii 113). Keats's friend Richard Woodhouse noted that 'the poem, if completed, would have treated of the dethronement of Hyperion, the former god of the sun, by Apollo (and incidentally of those of Oceanus by Neptune, of Saturn by Jupiter, etc., and of the war of the giants for Saturn's re-establishment), with other events of which we have but very dark hints in the mythological poets of Greece and Rome. In fact, the incidents would have been pure creations of the poet's brain.' For Keats, the story's appeal was that Apollo's painful emergence and the despondency of the fallen Titans illustrated aspects of his artistic self.

Shelley recognized its achievement as soon as he saw it. He approved especially of the way it rewrote 'Paradise Lost' *in* non-Christian terms: on 29 October 1820 he told Marianne Hunt 'the fragment called "Hyperion" promises for him that he is destined to become one of the first writers of the age'. Never one of Keats's admirers, Byron moderated his usual severity when assessing 'Hyperion', partly because Keats had just died when he read it, and partly because he was writing to Shelley: 'The impression of "Hyperion" upon my mind was that it was the best of his works.'

In late September 1818 the Tory *Quarterly Review* published a highly critical review of 'Endymion' by John Wilson Croker. It was a destructive analysis of Keats's diction and style, which began by arguing he was 'a copyist of Mr Hunt, but he is more unintelligible, almost as rugged, twice as diffuse, and ten times more tiresome and absurd than his prototype who, though he impudently presumed to seat himself in the chair of criticism, and to measure his own poetry by his own standard, yet generally had a meaning'. Croker went on to suggest that Keats had adopted Hunt's aesthetic system, which stifled what little talent he possessed. Keats cannot have been pleased at being aligned with Hunt, but it would not be long before he dismissed the critics' animus with the hope that 'I shall be among the English Poets after my death'. This disproves Shelley's claim that Croker's review led directly to the disease from which Keats was to die: Keats was hurt, but he had the confidence to rise above it.

At this period he met the 18-year-old Fanny Brawne, who later recalled that 'his conversation was in the highest degree interesting, and his spirits good, excepting at moments when anxiety regarding his brother's health dejected them'. Keats spent Christmas with her and her family, before going to Chichester in January 1819. Its medieval cathedral inspired a poem he had just begun – 'The Eve of St Agnes'. Although complete by 2 February, he revised it again in September: few episodes illustrate so vividly the speed with which he was developing. The problem with the first version, as Keats saw it, was its sentimentality – the Huntian quality attacked by reviewers. He wanted to make it less obviously a vehicle of 'luxuries' by emphasizing the sense of physical suffering, death and the intensity of love. To that end he revised the last stanza so as to kill off Angela – 'dead, stiff and ugly' (as Woodhouse complained), and added a stanza to the bedroom scene so that 'as soon as Madeline has confessed her love, Porphyro winds by degrees his arm round her, presses breast to breast, and acts all the acts of a *bona fide* husband, while she fancies she is only playing the part of a wife in a dream'.

His publishers balked at the indecency, and dropped the new stanza for the 1820 printed text (though readers of this volume will find it in a footnote). Woodhouse says he challenged Keats over these alterations, saying that ladies would not wish to read such things (an important consideration, as most poetry readers were women), to which Keats replied he wrote only for men. It was not that he sought to be offensive for its own sake, but was striving to emerge from under Hunt's shadow, by incorporating into his poetry such un-Huntian subjects as death, disease and sex.

Love and death-like suffering converge in 'La Belle Dame Sans Merci: A Ballad', a poem of April 1819 that may reflect Keats's increasingly frustrated feelings for Fanny Brawne, not to mention his reaction to the letters sent to his dying brother by a friend, Charles Wells, under the fictitious identity of a woman, Amena. Writing as Amena, Wells had tantalized Tom with thoughts that he, as her Knight, might be soothed by her. It was a cruel deception by which, so Keats believed, Tom's death had been hastened, and it may have shaped the nightmarish view of love in 'La Belle Dame'. In the end the Knight is trapped forever on the cold hill's side in a landscape that speaks of sterility and unfulfilled desire.

The darkness of 'La Belle Dame' shows how far Keats had travelled since being cast as Hunt's acolyte eighteen months before; it speaks of the proximity of death, the awareness of which suffuses the great poetry on which he was about to embark. 'Ode to Psyche' was written in the days following its completion. Keats said that it

> is the first and the only one with which I have taken even moderate pains. I have for the most part dashed off my lines in a hurry; this I have done leisurely. I think it reads the more richly for it, and will I hope encourage me to write other things in even a more peaceable and healthy spirit. You must recollect that Psyche was not embodied as a goddess before the time of Apuleius the Platonist, who lived after the Augustan age, and consequently the goddess was never worshipped or sacrificed to with any of the ancient fervour, and perhaps never thought of in the old religion. I am more orthodox than to let a heathen goddess be so neglected.

Keats approaches the Psyche myth in his own way, anglicizing it through the literary genre of pastoral. The most Keatsian element is the dream-vision with which it begins, of two lovers 'couched side by side / In deepest grass' – exactly the kind of thing he might have seen while wandering the lanes of Hampstead. These human figures become, in the transforming imagination, Psyche and Cupid. Having noted that Psyche has no temple or retinue of her own, the poet devotes himself to her ('Yes, I will be thy priest') and declares his intention of building a temple to her in his mind. In some ways its most significant achievement is its stanza form, derived from experiments with the sonnet, and used throughout the remaining Odes.

It is not certain which poem Keats composed next. 'Ode to a Nightingale' is usually placed before 'Ode on a Grecian Urn' (as here), though John Barnard has argued for the reverse order. The 'Ode to a Nightingale' (written at Charles Brown's house in Hampstead, now a museum) may represent the summit of Keats's achievement. Poets before and after Keats chose the nightingale as their subject, but none so memorably as him. As the Ode begins, the poet stands, listening to the nightingale in the depths of the night, somewhere in the fields of Hampstead; it is so dark he cannot see the ground clearly, but can smell the flowers that surround him. The aching of his heart (presumably he is love-sick) is soothed, and he is tempted to a luxurious death accompanied by the nightingale's song. In the grip of that fancy, he reflects that, as the inhabitant of other eras and worlds, the bird aspires to the status of immortal being. With that, he emerges from the inner recesses of reverie to the threshold of full consciousness. Keats is inspired partly by Hazlitt's comment on the author of 'The Faerie Queene': 'Spenser was the poet of our waking dreams; and he has invented not only a language, but a music of his own for them. The undulations are infinite, like those of the waves of the sea: but the effect is still the same, lulling the senses into a deep oblivion of the jarring noises of the world, from which we have no wish ever to be recalled.'

'Ode on a Grecian Urn' begins in the midst of a meditation on the object mentioned in its title – one that depicts images the poet has, as the poem begins, already transformed into an alternative reality. The world of the urn becomes, in the negatively capable imagination of the poet, one in which human frailties such as sickness, age and death are transcended; in which human passion never fades; in which creativity continues indefinitely, unthreatened by time. In other words, the idealized reality created by a long-dead Greek artist transports the poet to a place of perfection. It is important, from Keats's perspective, that the artist speaks to all who see his work: 'Beauty is truth, truth beauty.' Critics have laboured across many decades to explicate that remark, though it is surely not obscure. In his letters he wrote that the imagination is like Adam's dream; he awoke and found it truth. The elevated apprehensions of the imagination – the heightened insights into the world granted at those moments when the imagination 'sees into the life of things' – are visions of reality, a reality that exists not merely in the imagination, but in the real world. And that reality is, by its nature, a thing of beauty, a revelation of what was always there, but which we could not otherwise have seen in its true colours. So it is with the depictions on the urn: they are of a perfect, timeless universe, a heightened depiction of earthly things, preserved forever.

Critics tend to find the 'Ode on Melancholy' problematic. Again, the drama behind the poem is important. As it starts, the poet has descended into depression – real, psychological depression, a state of mind that lurks behind several of these poems. He tells himself, 'No, no, go not to Lethe', meaning that it would be a mistake to kill himself, and the rest of the poem attempts to understand why he should live. The answer seems to be that melancholy is an inescapable aspect of human experience – even the most joyous, as when two lovers devote themselves to each other. Again, Keats is reacting against Hunt's dictum that poetry is designed only for pleasure. The poem's final conceit is that 'Joy's grape' can be tasted at its fullest only by those who have known the 'might' of Melancholy.

By this time it should be clear that Keats's great Odes are inspired by moods of his own mind, and the 'Ode on Indolence' is typical in that regard. It is set during 'My idle days', when 'The blissful cloud of summer indolence / Benumbed my eyes'. Like anyone else, Keats seems at certain periods to have wished not to exert himself in any way – simply to relax, shut his eyes, and think of nothing. In that mood he is assailed three times by three allegorical figures, who represent things capable of rousing him from his inertia and causing him 'annoy': Love, Ambition and Poesy. Keats gives them all due consideration, but bids them adieu, so preserving his 'idle sprite' for the pleasures of 'nothingness'. It is the last thing we might expect a young poet to do but Keats's response is based on a profound conviction in the visionary power by which he is invested, and which he knows will guarantee his place in the pantheon.

By the end of June 1819, Keats had reached some kind of understanding with Fanny Brawne – not an engagement, exactly, more an expression of intent – before leaving for the Isle of Wight, where he began 'Lamia', which he would complete at Winchester in early autumn. Based on a story he encountered in Burton's *Anatomy of Melancholy*, it heralded a fresh attempt to escape the 'smokeability' of his early work. The defect of 'The Eve of St Agnes', he feared, was identification with its characters. In 'Lamia' he would strive to tell the story as 'coldly' as he could.

He knew Coleridge's 'Christabel' (published 1816), as well as the definition of the lamia from Lemprière's classical dictionary: 'Certain monsters of Africa, who had the face and breast of a woman, and the rest of the body like that of a serpent. They allured strangers to them, that they might devour them, and though they were not endowed with the faculty of speech, yet their hissings were pleasing and agreeable.' Keats makes his Lamia sympathetic; she does not eat small children and possesses something of the glamour of Coleridge's Geraldine. The appeal of the narrative borrowed from Burton lay in that it permitted Keats further to explore the difference between the 'consequitive' reasoner, and the artist or lover – in this case, Apollonius the philosopher, and Lycius. Apollonius is therefore less agreeable than in Burton, where he is the instigator of a successful witch-hunt. Furthermore, Keats adds Lycius's death which makes his fatal passion more than merely poignant; it is almost tragic. He was satisfied with 'Lamia', as he wrote in September 1819: 'I am certain there is that sort of fire in it which must take hold of people in some way – give them either pleasant or unpleasant sensation. What they want is a sensation of some sort.' Keats's friend Woodhouse admired 'Lamia' when he heard it, as he told John Taylor: 'You may suppose all these events have given Keats scope for some beautiful poetry which, even in this cursory hearing of it, came every now and then upon me, and made me "start, as though a sea-nymph quired".'

Keats's last great ode, 'To Autumn', was written in mid-September in Winchester, shortly after completion of 'Lamia'. Many would regard it as the greatest thing he ever composed. In a letter to Reynolds, he described the weather and the countryside by which he was surrounded:

> How beautiful the season is now, how fine the air. A temperate sharpness about it. Really, without joking, chaste weather – Dian skies. I never liked stubble fields so much as now. Aye better than the chilly green of the spring. Somehow a stubble plain looks warm – in the same way that some pictures look warm. This struck me so much in my Sunday's walk that I composed upon it.

The letter tells us everything we need to know about Keats's state of mind at this moment. As in the other Odes, he finds his mood reflected in his surroundings. The very season is embodied in the persona of a farm labourer sitting on the floor of a granary, or a half-reaped furrow – like the many rustic folk Keats must have seen on his walks around the countryside. And as that figure becomes the agent of plenitude and ripeness, it becomes also the agent of maturity – not merely that of the natural world but of Keats's own talents as he achieves his finest poetic utterance to date. The third stanza of the poem takes the form of a valediction to the fullness of the harvest and bounty of the natural world, containing the dim awareness of darker times to come.

The two parts of 'Lamia' were interrupted so Keats could work on a revised version of 'Hyperion', influenced by Milton ('Paradise Lost') and Dante ('Inferno'). This time it was framed within a dream-vision, whereby Moneta would relate the Titans' fall, picking up the original narrative at line 294 of Canto I with the entrance of Saturn and Thea. 'The Fall of Hyperion' would not be published until 1857, and during the nineteenth century it gained few admirers – but it is now accepted that the passages written for it reveal the development in Keats's thinking since composition of 'Hyperion: A Fragment' a year before. They show how critical he had become of the self-indulgent dreamer, instead favouring the poet for whom 'the miseries of the world / Are misery' (Canto I, ll. 148–9). This was part of Keats's disillusionment with Byron, now classed among 'mock lyrists, large self-worshippers / And careless hectorers in proud bad verse' (Canto I, ll. 207–8).

Keats would write more, but nothing that would surpass the achievements of 1818–19. His enemy was time. In early February 1820, he collapsed on arrival at Wentworth Place in Hampstead, with a haemorrhage of the lungs. 'I know the colour of that blood', he told Charles Brown, 'it is arterial blood. I cannot be deceived in that colour. That drop of blood is my death-warrant. I must die.' The story of what happened next is well known. He would release Fanny Brawne from their 'understanding' and commence a drawn-out physical decline. His last lifetime volume, *Lamia, Isabella, The Eve of St Agnes, and Other Poems,* was published in July 1820.

In September he travelled to Italy with Joseph Severn in search of a warmer climate, which it was hoped would prolong his life. But the journey and its tribulations damaged his health further and, after arriving in Rome on 15 November, where he and Severn found lodgings at 26 Piazza di Spagna, he had only weeks before his final relapse. Writing to his old friend Charles Brown, he spoke of the 'habitual feeling of my real life having past, and that I am leading a posthumous existence'. After weeks of suffering, he died on 23 February 1821, to be buried in the non-Catholic cemetery three days later. Unaware his old friend was already dead, Leigh Hunt wrote to Severn at Rome, with a last request:

> Tell him – tell that great poet and noblehearted man – that we shall all bear his memory in the most precious part of our hearts, and that the world shall bow their heads to it, as our loves do. Or if this, again, will trouble his spirit, tell him that we shall never cease to remember and love him; and that the most sceptical of us has faith enough in the high things that nature puts into our heads to think all who are of one accord in mind or heart are journeying to one and the same place, and shall unite somewhere or other again, face to face, mutually conscious, mutually delighted. Tell him he is only before us on the road, as he was in everything else; or whether you tell him the latter or no, tell him the former, and add that we shall never forget that he was so, and that we are coming after…

Within three years both Shelley and Byron would follow; the next thirteen years saw the deaths of Hazlitt, Lamb and Coleridge. Keats's death marked the beginning of the end of Romanticism.

## *On First Looking into Chapman's Homer* (composed October 1816)[1]

Much have I travelled in the realms of gold,
And many goodly states and kingdoms seen;
Round many western islands have I been
Which bards in fealty to Apollo[2] hold.
Oft of one wide expanse had I been told
That deep-browed Homer ruled as his demesne,[3]
Yet did I never breathe its pure serene[4]
Till I heard Chapman speak out loud and bold:
Then felt I like some watcher of the skies
When a new planet swims into his ken;
Or like stout Cortez[5] when with eagle eyes
He stared at the Pacific – and all his men
Looked at each other with a wild surmise –
Silent, upon a peak in Darien.[6]

## Notes

On First Looking into Chapman's Homer

[1] George Chapman (1559–1634) translated *The Whole Works of Homer* (1614). In October 1816 Charles Cowden Clarke read through it with Keats one night. Keats returned to his lodgings in Dean Street at dawn the following morning, and had composed this poem by 10 o'clock. It was first published in *The Examiner*, 1 December 1816.

[2] Apollo is the god of poetry; bards are therefore bound in fealty to him.

[3] *demesne* domain, kingdom.

[4] *serene* clear, bright sky (Latin *serenum* means a clear or bright sky).

[5] *Cortez* It was in fact Vasco Nunez de Balboa (1475–1519) who was the first European to stand, in 1513, on that peak and see the Pacific (which he claimed for Spain). In 1519 Hernán Cortés (1485–1547) conquered Mexico for Spain and entered Mexico City for the first time.

[6] *Darien* is the region that connects Panama to Colombia.

## *Addressed to Haydon*[1] (composed 19 November 1816)

Great spirits now on earth are sojourning:[2]
He of the cloud, the cataract, the lake,
Who on Helvellyn's[3] summit, wide awake,
Catches his freshness from archangel's wing;
He of the rose, the violet, the spring,
The social smile, the chain for freedom's sake;[4]
And lo! whose steadfastness would never take
A meaner sound than Raphael's whispering.[5]
And other spirits there are standing apart
Upon the forehead of the age to come;
These, these will give the world another heart
And other pulses: hear ye not the hum
Of mighty workings?[6] ______________
Listen awhile ye nations, and be dumb.

## *On the Grasshopper and the Cricket* (composed 30 December 1816)[1]

The poetry of earth is never dead:[2]
When all the birds are faint with the hot sun,
And hide in cooling trees, a voice will run
From hedge to hedge about the new-mown mead;
That is the Grasshopper's – he takes the lead
In summer luxury, he has never done
With his delights; for when tired out with fun
He rests at ease beneath some pleasant weed.
The poetry of earth is ceasing never:
On a lone winter evening, when the frost
Has wrought a silence,[3] from the stove there shrills
The Cricket's song, in warmth increasing ever,
And seems to one in drowsiness half lost,
The Grasshopper's among some grassy hills.

## Notes

ADDRESSED TO HAYDON

[1] *Haydon* the artist Benjamin Robert Haydon. Keats sent this poem to him in a letter, 20 November 1816, having dined with him the previous evening.

[2] Keats celebrates the achievement of Wordsworth (lines 2–4), Leigh Hunt (lines 5–6) and Haydon (lines 7–8).

[3] Helvellyn mountain towers over Grasmere (3,116 ft), though Keats had not at this stage seen it.

[4] *the chain for freedom's sake* a reference to Hunt's spell in jail for libelling the Prince Regent.

[5] *whose steadfastness…Raphael's whispering* The overall meaning seems to be that Haydon's artistic ability rivals that of Raphael.

[6] The incompleteness of the line is deliberate, and was suggested by Haydon. It originally read: 'Of mighty workings in a distant mart?'

ON THE GRASSHOPPER AND THE CRICKET

[1] This poem was the product of a sonnet-writing competition with Leigh Hunt. Charles Cowden Clarke, who umpired the competition, said that 'Keats won as to time'.

[2] According to Charles Cowden Clarke, Leigh Hunt thought the first line was 'a preposterous opening'.

[3] *On a lone winter…a silence* When he first heard this line and a half, Hunt exclaimed 'Ah! That's perfect! Bravo Keats!'

## *From 'Endymion: A Poetic Romance', Book I* (extracts; composed April–November 1817; published 1818)

### *A Thing of Beauty Is a Joy for Ever*

A thing of beauty is a joy for ever:[1]
Its loveliness increases; it will never
Pass into nothingness, but still will keep
A bower quiet for us, and a sleep
Full of sweet dreams, and health, and quiet breathing.
Therefore, on every morrow, are we wreathing
A flowery band to bind us to the earth,
Spite of despondence, of the inhuman dearth
Of noble natures, of the gloomy days,
Of all the unhealthy and o'er-darkened ways
Made for our searching – yes, in spite of all,
Some shape of beauty moves away the pall
From our dark spirits. Such the sun, the moon,
Trees old and young, sprouting a shady boon
For simple sheep; and such are daffodils
With the green world they live in; and clear rills
That for themselves a cooling covert make
'Gainst the hot season; the mid-forest brake,
Rich with a sprinkling of fair musk-rose[2] blooms;
And such too is the grandeur of the dooms[3]
We have imagined for the mighty dead,
All lovely tales that we have heard or read –
An endless fountain of immortal drink,
Pouring unto us from the heaven's brink.

### *Hymn to Pan*[1]

Oh thou, whose mighty palace roof doth hang
From jagged trunks, and overshadoweth
Eternal whispers, glooms, the birth, life, death
Of unseen flowers in heavy peacefulness;
Who lov'st to see the hamadryads[2] dress
Their ruffled locks where meeting hazels darken,
And through whole solemn hours dost sit, and hearken
The dreary melody of bedded reeds
In desolate places, where dank moisture breeds

## Notes

Endymion: A Thing of Beauty Is a Joy for Ever

[1] *A thing of beauty is a joy for ever* Keats's fellow-student at Guy's Hospital, Henry Stephens, who was present when this line was composed, recalled that it originally read: 'A thing of beauty is a constant joy.'

[2] *musk-rose* a rambling rose with white flowers and a characteristic scent.

[3] *dooms* destinies.

Endymion: Hymn to Pan

[1] In spite of the fact that Wordsworth disparagingly told Keats the 'Hymn to Pan' was 'a very pretty piece of Paganism', it looks forward to the mature style of the major 1819 Odes. Pan is the god of universal nature. The 'Hymn' was composed on 26 April 1817.

[2] *hamadryads* wood-nymphs fabled to live and die with the trees they inhabited.

The pipy hemlock[3] to strange overgrowth;
Bethinking thee, how melancholy loath
Thou wast to lose fair Syrinx[4] – do thou now,
By thy love's milky brow,
By all the trembling mazes that she ran,
Hear us, great Pan!

Oh thou, for whose soul-soothing quiet, turtles[5]
Passion their voices[6] cooingly 'mong myrtles,[7]
What time thou wanderest at eventide
Through sunny meadows that outskirt the side
Of thine enmossed realms; oh thou, to whom
Broad-leaved fig trees even now foredoom[8]
Their ripened fruitage, yellow-girted bees
Their golden honeycombs, our village leas
Their fairest-blossomed beans and poppied corn,
The chuckling[9] linnet its five young unborn
To sing for thee, low-creeping strawberries
Their summer coolness, pent-up butterflies[10]
Their freckled wings – yea, the fresh-budding year
All its completions; be quickly near,
By every wind that nods the mountain pine,[11]
Oh forester divine!

Thou, to whom every faun and satyr flies
For willing service, whether to surprise
The squatted hare[12] while in half-sleeping fit;
Or upward ragged precipices flit
To save poor lambkins from the eagle's maw;
Or by mysterious enticement draw
Bewildered shepherds to their path again;
Or to tread breathless round the frothy main,
And gather up all fancifullest shells
For thee to tumble into naiads'[13] cells,
And, being hidden, laugh at their out-peeping;
Or to delight thee with fantastic leaping,
The while they pelt each other on the crown
With silvery oak-apples, and fir-cones brown –
By all the echoes that about thee ring,
Hear us, oh satyr king!

## Notes

[3] *pipy hemlock* poison hemlock has tall hollow stems.

[4] When Pan pursued Syrinx, she changed into a reed.

[5] *turtles* turtle-doves.

[6] *Passion their voices* fill their voices with passion. The use of 'passion' as a verb follows Spenser's *Faerie Queene*, but was taken by reviewers as an example of Cockney affectation.

[7] *myrtles* shrubs with shiny evergreen leaves and white sweet-scented flowers, sacred to Venus and used as an emblem of love.

[8] *foredoom* anticipate.

[9] *chuckling* clucking.

[10] *pent-up butterflies* butterflies still in chrysalis form.

[11] *pine* emblem of Pan.

[12] *squatted hare* the hare in its form.

[13] *naiad* water-nymph.

Oh hearkener to the loud-clapping shears,
While ever and anon to his shorn peers
A ram goes bleating; winder of the horn,[14]
When snouted wild-boars routing[15] tender corn
Anger our huntsmen; breather round our farms,
To keep off mildews and all weather harms;
Strange ministrant of undescribed sounds,
That come a-swooning over hollow grounds
And wither drearily on barren moors;
Dread opener of the mysterious doors
Leading to universal knowledge – see,
Great son of Dryope,[16]
The many that are come to pay their vows
With leaves about their brows!

Be still the unimaginable lodge
For solitary thinkings; such as dodge
Conception to the very bourne[17] of heaven,
Then leave the naked brain; be still the leaven
That spreading in this dull and clodded earth
Gives it a touch ethereal,[18] a new birth;[19]
Be still a symbol of immensity,
A firmament reflected in a sea,
An element filling the space between,
An unknown – but no more. We humbly screen
With uplift hands our foreheads, lowly bending,
And giving out a shout most heaven-rending,
Conjure thee to receive our humble paean,[20]
Upon thy Mount Lycean![21]

### *The Pleasure Thermometer*[1]

Wherein lies happiness? In that which becks[2]
Our ready minds to fellowship divine,
A fellowship with essence,[3] till we shine

## Notes

[14] *winder of the horn* one who blows the horn.
[15] *routing* digging up (with the snout).
[16] Keats follows Chapman's 'Hymn to Pan' which represents Pan as the son of Dryope and Hermes.
[17] *bourne* boundary.
[18] *ethereal* divine.
[19] *Be still the unimaginable lodge…new birth* In his hostile review of 'Endymion' in the *Quarterly Review* (April 1818), John Wilson Croker quoted these lines to support his charge that Keats 'seems to us to write a line at random, and then he follows not the thought excited by this line, but that suggested by the *rhyme* with which it concludes.… *Lodge, dodge – heaven, leaven – earth, birth*; such, in six words, is the sum and substance of six lines'.
[20] *paean* hymn of praise.
[21] Lycaeus was a mountain of Arcadia sacred to Pan.

Endymion: The Pleasure Thermometer
[1] The 'thermometer' measures happiness by its intensity and selfless involvement; the four 'degrees', in ascending order, are (i) sensual enjoyment of nature (line 782); (ii) music (lines 783–94); (iii) friendship (lines 803–5); (iv) passion (lines 805–42). This passage is spoken by Endymion. Keats commented on it in his letter to John Taylor of 30 January 1818: 'The whole thing must, I think, have appeared to you, who are a consequitive man, as a thing almost of mere words. But I assure you that when I wrote it, it was a regular stepping of the Imagination towards a Truth. My having written that argument will perhaps be of the greatest service to me of anything I ever did. It set before me at once the gradations of happiness even like a kind of Pleasure Thermometer.'
[2] *becks* beckons.
[3] *essence* used as synonym for 'a thing of beauty'.

Full alchemized,[4] and free of space. Behold
The clear religion[5] of heaven! Fold
A rose-leaf round thy finger's taperness
And soothe thy lips; hist, when the airy stress
Of music's kiss impregnates the free winds,
And with a sympathetic touch unbinds
Aeolian magic from their lucid wombs;[6]
Then old songs waken from enclouded[7] tombs,
Old ditties sigh above their father's grave,
Ghosts of melodious prophecyings rave
Round every spot where trod Apollo's foot;
Bronze clarions awake and faintly bruit[8]
Where long ago a giant battle[9] was;
And from the turf, a lullaby doth pass
In every place where infant Orpheus[10] slept.
Feel we these things? That moment have we stepped
Into a sort of oneness, and our state
Is like a floating spirit's. But there are
Richer entanglements, enthralments far
More self-destroying,[11] leading, by degrees,
To the chief intensity: the crown of these
Is made of love and friendship, and sits high
Upon the forehead of humanity.
All its more ponderous and bulky worth
Is friendship, whence there ever issues forth
A steady splendour; but at the tip-top
There hangs by unseen film an orbed drop
Of light, and that is love. Its influence,
Thrown in our eyes, genders[12] a novel sense
At which we start and fret; till in the end,
Melting into its radiance, we blend,
Mingle, and so become a part of it –
Nor with aught else can our souls interknit
So wingedly. When we combine therewith,
Life's self is nourished by its proper pith,[13]
And we are nurtured like a pelican brood.[14]
Aye, so delicious is the unsating[15] food,
That men who might have towered in the van[16]
Of all the congregated world, to fan
And winnow from the coming step of time

## Notes

[4] *alchemized* transformed, spiritualized.
[5] *religion* pronounced as four syllables.
[6] *when the airy stress…wombs* Keats is thinking of an Aeolian harp.
[7] *enclouded* dim, obscure.
[8] *bruit* proclaim.
[9] *a giant battle* between the Titans and the gods of Olympus, the background to 'Hyperion'.
[10] Orpheus was taught to play the lyre by Apollo, his father, and reached such skill that he could influence animate and inanimate nature by his music.
[11] *self-destroying* capable of negating our sense of self (a good thing in Keats).
[12] *genders* creates.
[13] *proper pith* own substance.
[14] *a pelican brood* the pelican was said to feed its young with its own blood.
[15] *unsating* uncloying.
[16] *towered in the van* A military metaphor; had been foremost at the front of an attacking army.

All chaff of custom, wipe away all slime
Left by men-slugs and human serpentry,
Have been content to let occasion[17] die
Whilst they did sleep in love's Elysium.
And truly, I would rather be struck dumb
Than speak against this ardent listlessness;[18]
For I have ever thought that it might bless
The world with benefits unknowingly,
As does the nightingale, up-perched high,
And cloistered among cool and bunched leaves –
She sings but to her love, nor e'er conceives
How tiptoe night holds back her dark-grey hood.
Just so may love, although 'tis understood
The mere commingling[19] of passionate breath,
Produce more than our searching witnesseth:
What I know not – but who of men can tell
That flowers would bloom, or that green fruit would swell
To melting pulp, that fish would have bright mail,[20]
The earth its dower[21] of river, wood, and vale,
The meadows runnels,[22] runnels pebble-stones,
The seed its harvest, or the lute its tones,
Tones ravishment, or ravishment its sweet,
If human souls did never kiss and greet?

## *Letter from John Keats to Benjamin Bailey, 22 November 1817* (extract)[1]

I wish you knew all that I think about genius and the heart – and yet I think you are thoroughly acquainted with my innermost breast in that respect, or you could not have known me even thus long and still hold me worthy to be your dear friend. In passing, however, I must say of one thing that has pressed upon me lately and increased my humility and capability of submission, and that is this truth: men of genius are great as certain ethereal chemicals operating on the mass of neutral intellect – but they have not any individuality, any determined character. I would call the top and head of those who have a proper self, men of power.

But I am running my head into a subject which I am certain I could not do justice to under five years' study and 3 vols. octavo – and moreover long to be talking about the imagination. So, my dear Bailey, do not think of this unpleasant affair if possible – do not – I defy any harm to come of it – I defy – I shall write to Crips this week and request him to tell me all his goings-on from time to time by letter wherever I may be – it will all go on well. So don't, because you have suddenly discovered a coldness in Haydon,[2] suffer yourself to be teased. Do not, my dear fellow.

## Notes

[17] *occasion* ephemeral circumstance.

[18] *ardent listlessness* passionate suspension of self-consciousness, mystic trance.

[19] *commingling* intermingling.

[20] *bright mail* i.e. scales.

[21] *dower* gift.

[22] *runnels* streams.

Letter from John Keats to Benjamin Bailey

[1] This letter contains one of Keats's earliest, and most important, statements on the imagination. Benjamin Bailey (1791–1853) was an undergraduate at Oxford when John Hamilton Reynolds introduced him to Keats in spring 1817. Throughout September 1817 Keats shared Bailey's college quarters, and composed 'Endymion' Book III there.

[2] Benjamin Robert Haydon, artist and friend of Keats.

Oh, I wish I was as certain of the end of all your troubles as that of your momentary start about the authenticity of the imagination. I am certain of nothing but of the holiness of the heart's affections[3] and the truth of imagination. What the imagination seizes as beauty must be truth, whether it existed before or not. For I have the same idea of all our passions as of love: they are all, in their sublime, creative of essential beauty.[4] In a word, you may know my favourite speculation by my first book and the little song I sent in my last – which is a representation from the fancy of the probable mode of operating in these matters. The imagination may be compared to Adam's dream: he awoke and found it truth.[5] I am the more zealous in this affair because I have never yet been able to perceive how anything can be known for truth by consequitive[6] reasoning – and yet it must be. Can it be that even the greatest philosopher ever arrived at his goal without putting aside numerous objections? However it may be, oh for a life of sensations rather than of thoughts! It is 'a vision in the form of youth', a shadow of reality to come. And this consideration has further convinced me, for it has come as auxiliary to another favourite speculation of mine – that we shall enjoy ourselves hereafter by having what we called happiness on earth repeated in a finer tone and so repeated. And yet such a fate can only befall those who delight in sensation, rather than hunger as you do after truth; Adam's dream will do here, and seems to be a conviction that imagination and its empyreal reflection is the same as human life and its spiritual repetition. But as I was saying, the simple imaginative mind may have its rewards in the repetition of its own silent working coming continually on the spirit with a fine suddenness. To compare great things with small, have you never, by being surprised with an old melody in a delicious place by a delicious voice, felt over again your very speculations and surmises at the time it first operated on your soul? Do you not remember forming to yourself the singer's face more beautiful than it was possible, and yet with the elevation of the moment you did not think so? Even then, you were mounted on the wings of imagination so high that the prototype must be hereafter – that delicious face you will see! What a time!

I am continually running away from the subject. Sure this cannot be exactly the case with a complex mind, one that is imaginative and at the same time careful of its fruits, who would exist partly on sensation, partly on thought – to whom it is necessary that years should bring the philosophic mind.[7] Such an one I consider yours and therefore it is necessary to your eternal happiness that you not only drink this old wine of heaven, which I shall call the redigestion of our most ethereal musings on earth, but also increase in knowledge and know all things.

## *Letter from John Keats to George and Tom Keats, 21 December 1817* (extract)

I spent Friday evening with Wells[1] and went the next morning to see 'Death on the Pale Horse'.[2] It is a wonderful picture when West's age is considered, but there is nothing to be intense upon – no women one feels mad to kiss, no face swelling into reality.[3] The excellence of every art is its intensity, capable of making all disagreeables evaporate, from their being in close relationship with

## Notes

[3] *affections* feelings.

[4] *For I have…beauty* at their most sublime (i.e. intense and powerful), human emotions ('passions') apprehend the inherent beauty of the 'essences' they perceive.

[5] *The imagination…truth* Genesis 2:21–2: 'And the Lord God caused a deep sleep to fall upon Adam, and he slept: and he took one of his ribs, and closed up the flesh instead thereof; And the rib, which the Lord God had taken from man, made he a woman, and brought her unto the man.' This episode was reworked in one of the most impressive passages of 'Paradise Lost' viii 452–86.

[6] *consequitive* consecutive, logical, rational.

[7] *the philosophic mind* Wordsworth, 'Ode' 189.

Letter from John Keats to George and Tom Keats

[1] Charles Jeremiah Wells (1800–79), a schoolfriend of Tom Keats.

[2] Painting by Benjamin West (1738–1820), President of the Royal Academy. His exhibition was at 125 Pall Mall.

[3] *It is…reality* Keats follows the opinions expressed by Hazlitt in his article, 'West's Picture of Death on the Pale Horse', in the *Edinburgh Magazine* for December 1817: 'There is no gusto, no imagination in Mr West's colouring.'

beauty and truth. Examine *King Lear* and you will find this exemplified throughout, but in this picture we have unpleasantness without any momentous depth of speculation excited, in which to bury its repulsiveness. The picture is larger than 'Christ Rejected'.[4]

I dined with Haydon the Sunday after you left, and had a very pleasant day. I dined too (for I have been out too much lately) with Horace Smith, and met his two brothers[5] with Hill and Kingston and one Dubois. They only served to convince me how superior humour is to wit in respect to enjoyment. These men say things which make one start without making one feel. They are all alike; their manners are alike; they all know fashionables; they have a mannerism in their very eating and drinking, in their mere handling a decanter. They talked of Kean[6] and his low company. Would I were with that company instead of yours, said I to myself! I know suchlike acquaintance will never do for me, and yet I am going to Reynolds[7] on Wednesday.

Brown and Dilke[8] walked with me and back from the Christmas pantomime. I had not a dispute but a disquisition with Dilke, on various subjects. Several things dovetailed in my mind, and at once it struck me what quality went to form a man of achievement, especially in literature, and which Shakespeare possessed so enormously. I mean *negative capability*; that is, when man is capable of being in uncertainties, mysteries, doubts, without any irritable reaching after fact and reason. Coleridge, for instance, would let go by a fine isolated verisimilitude[9] caught from the penetralium[10] of mystery, from being incapable of remaining content with half-knowledge. This pursued through volumes would perhaps take us no further than this: that with a great poet the sense of beauty overcomes every other consideration, or rather obliterates all consideration.

## *On Sitting Down to Read* King Lear *Once Again* (composed 22 January 1818)

Oh golden-tongued Romance, with serene lute!
Fair plumèd siren,[1] queen of far away!
Leave melodizing on this wintry day,
Shut up thine olden pages, and be mute.
Adieu! for, once again, the fierce dispute
Betwixt damnation and impassioned clay[2]
Must I burn through; once more humbly assay[3]
The bitter-sweet of this Shakespearian fruit.
Chief poet, and ye clouds of Albion,[4]
Begetters of our deep eternal theme!
When through the old oak forest I am gone,[5]
Let me not wander in a barren dream;
But when I am consumed in the fire,
Give me new phoenix wings to fly at my desire.

### Notes

[4] West painted *Christ Rejected* 1812–14; it had been exhibited in the autumn of 1814 in Pall Mall, and attracted almost a quarter of a million visitors.

[5] Horace (1779–1849) and James Smith (1775–1839) were responsible for the parodic *Rejected Addresses* (1812). Their brother was Leonard Smith (1778–1837).

[6] Edmund Kean (1787–1833), after Kemble the most celebrated Shakespearean actor of his day.

[7] John Hamilton Reynolds (1794–1852), friend of Keats and poet.

[8] Charles Armitage Brown (1786–1842), one of Keats's closest friends; Charles Wentworth Dilke (1789–1864), with whose family Keats was close, and who introduced Keats to the love of his life, Fanny Brawne.

[9] *verisimilitude* revelation.

[10] *penetralium* interior, depth.

On Sitting Down to Read King Lear Once Again

[1] *Fair plumèd siren* Romance is imagined as a fair-haired, Spenserian heroine.

[2] *clay* i.e. flesh.

[3] *assay* test.

[4] *Albion* England.

[5] *When through the old oak forest I am gone* i.e. when I have finished reading this play

## *When I Have Fears that I May Cease to Be* (composed 22–31 January 1818)

When I have fears that I may cease to be
Before my pen has gleaned my teeming brain,
Before high-piled books, in charact'ry,[1]
Hold like rich garners[2] the full-ripened grain;
When I behold, upon the night's starred face,
Huge cloudy symbols of a high romance,
And think that I may never live to trace
Their shadows, with the magic hand of chance;
And when I feel, fair creature of an hour,[3]
That I shall never look upon thee more,
Never have relish in the fairy power
Of unreflecting love – then on the shore
Of the wide world I stand alone and think,
Till love and fame to nothingness do sink.

## *Letter from John Keats to John Hamilton Reynolds, 3 February 1818* (extract)

It may be said that we ought to read our contemporaries, that Wordsworth etc. should have their due from us. But, for the sake of a few fine imaginative or domestic passages, are we to be bullied into a certain philosophy engendered in the whims of an egotist?[1] Every man has his speculations, but every man does not brood and peacock[2] over them till he makes a false coinage and deceives himself. Many a man can travel to the very bourne of heaven,[3] and yet want confidence to put down his half-seeing. Sancho[4] will invent a journey heavenward as well as anybody. We hate poetry that has a palpable design upon us – and if we do not agree, seems to put its hand in its breeches' pocket.[5] Poetry should be great and unobtrusive, a thing which enters into one's soul, and does not startle it or amaze it with itself but with its subject. How beautiful are the retired flowers! How would they lose their beauty were they to throng into the highway crying out, 'Admire me, I am a violet!', 'Dote upon me, I am a primrose!' Modern poets differ from the Elizabethans in this: each of the moderns, like an Elector[6] of Hanover, governs his petty state, and knows how many straws are swept daily from the causeways in all his dominions, and has a continual itching that all the housewives should have their coppers[7] well-scoured. The ancients were emperors of vast provinces – they had only heard of the remote ones and scarcely cared to visit them. I will cut all this – I will have no more of Wordsworth or Hunt in particular. Why should we be of the tribe of Manasseh, when we can wander with Esau?[8] Why should we kick against the pricks,[9] when we can walk on roses? Why should we be owls, when we can be eagles? Why be teased with 'nice-eyed

### Notes

WHEN I HAVE FEARS THAT I MAY CEASE TO BE

[1] *charact'ry* words.

[2] *garners* storehouses for grain.

[3] *fair creature of an hour* According to Woodhouse, Keats was remembering a beautiful woman he had seen at Vauxhall pleasure-gardens.

LETTER FROM JOHN KEATS TO JOHN HAMILTON REYNOLDS

[1] Keats, like Hazlitt, regarded Wordsworth as too preoccupied with the workings of his own mind.

[2] *peacock* preen himself.

[3] *the very bourne of heaven* the gateway to heaven; Keats alludes to himself, 'Endymion' Book I, 295.

[4] Sancho Panza, the comic buffoon who accompanies Don Quixote on his adventures.

[5] *seems to put its hand…pocket* apparently a gesture of defiant hostility.

[6] *Elector* one of the princes of Germany formerly entitled to take part in the election of the emperor.

[7] *coppers* copper fittings (on their front doors, etc.).

[8] *Why should we…Esau* Keats may be thinking of Gideon's comment, 'my family is poor in Manasseh, and I am the least in my father's house' (Judges 6:15). The point is that Manasseh's lands are small, while Esau was a nomad, free to go where he liked. See also Genesis 48:5–20.

[9] *Why should we…pricks* Keats alludes to Acts 9:5: 'I am Jesus whom thou persecutest: it is hard for thee to kick against the pricks.'

wagtails',[10] when we have in sight 'The cherub Contemplation'?[11] Why with Wordsworth's Matthew, 'with a bough of wilding in his hand',[12] when we can have Jaques 'under an oak',[13] etc. The secret of the bough of wilding will run through your head faster than I can write it. Old Matthew spoke to him some years ago on some nothing, and because he happens in an evening walk to imagine the figure of the old man, he must stamp it down in black and white, and it is henceforth sacred. I don't mean to deny Wordsworth's grandeur and Hunt's merit, but I mean to say we need not be teased with grandeur and merit, when we can have them uncontaminated and unobtrusive. Let us have the old poets and Robin Hood!

## *Isabella; or, The Pot of Basil: A Story from Boccaccio*[1] (composed *c.*March–27 April 1818)

1

Fair Isabel, poor simple Isabel!
  Lorenzo, a young palmer[2] in Love's eye!
They could not in the self-same mansion dwell
  Without some stir of heart, some malady;
They could not sit at meals but feel how well
  It soothed each to be the other by;
They could not, sure, beneath the same roof sleep
But to each other dream, and nightly weep.

2

With every morn their love grew tenderer,
  With every eve deeper and tenderer still;
He might not in house, field, or garden stir,
  But her full shape would all his seeing fill;
And his continual voice was pleasanter
  To her, than noise of trees or hidden rill;
Her lute-string gave an echo of his name,
She spoilt her half-done broidery with the same.

3

He knew whose gentle hand was at the latch
  Before the door had given her to his eyes;
And from her chamber-window he would catch
  Her beauty farther than the falcon spies;
And constant as her vespers[3] would he watch
  Because her face was turned to the same skies;
And with sick longing all the night outwear,
To hear her morning-step upon the stair.

## Notes

[10] *nice-eyed wagtails* an allusion to Leigh Hunt, 'The Nymphs' (1818) ii 169–71:

> Little ponds that hold the rains,
> Where the nice-eyed wagtails glance,
> Sipping 'twixt their jerking dance.

[11] *The cherub Contemplation* from Milton, 'Il Penseroso' 54.

[12] *with a bough of wilding in his hand!* An allusion to Wordsworth, 'The Two April Mornings' 59–60.

[13] *under an oak* Keats alludes to *As You Like It*, where Jaques is described 'Under an oak, whose antique root peeps out / Upon the brook that brawls along this wood' (II i 31–2).

Isabella

[1] Keats based his poem on the fifth novel of the fourth day in Boccaccio's *Decameron*. He sticks fairly closely to the original.

[2] *palmer* pilgrim.

[3] *vespers* evening prayers.

4

A whole long month of May in this sad plight
   Made their cheeks paler by the break[4] of June:
'Tomorrow will I bow to my delight,
   Tomorrow will I ask my lady's boon.'[5]
'Oh may I never see another night,
   Lorenzo, if thy lips breathe not love's tune.'
So spake they to their pillows; but, alas,
Honeyless days and days did he let pass

5

Until sweet Isabella's untouched cheek
   Fell sick within the rose's just domain,[6]
Fell thin as a young mother's, who doth seek
   By every lull to cool her infant's pain:
'How ill she is,' said he, 'I may not speak,
   And yet I will, and tell my love all plain:
If looks speak love-laws, I will drink her tears,
And at the least 'twill startle off her cares.'

6

So said he one fair morning, and all day
   His heart beat awfully against his side;
And to his heart he inwardly did pray
   For power to speak, but still the ruddy tide
Stifled his voice, and pulsed[7] resolve away,
   Fevered his high conceit of such a bride,
Yet brought him to the meekness of a child –
Alas, when passion is both meek and wild!

7

So once more he had waked and anguished
   A dreary night of love and misery,
If Isabel's quick eye had not been wed
   To every symbol[8] on his forehead high;
She saw it waxing very pale and dead,
   And straight all flushed; so, lisped tenderly,
'Lorenzo!' – here she ceased her timid quest,
But in her tone and look he read the rest.

## Notes

[4] *break* beginning.

[5] *boon* favour.

[6] *within the rose's just domain* the part of the cheek that is pink.

[7] *pulsed* drove.

[8] *symbol* indication (of his lovesickness), which Isabella is quick to notice.

8

'Oh Isabella, I can half perceive
  That I may speak my grief into thine ear;
If thou didst ever anything believe,
  Believe how I love thee, believe how near
My soul is to its doom; I would not grieve
  Thy hand by unwelcome pressing, would not fear
Thine eyes[9] by gazing, but I cannot live
Another night, and not my passion shrive.[10]

9

Love, thou art leading me from wintry cold;
  Lady, thou leadest me to summer clime,
And I must taste the blossoms that unfold
  In its ripe warmth this gracious morning time.'
So said, his erewhile timid lips grew bold,
  And poesied with hers in dewy rhyme;[11]
Great bliss was with them, and great happiness
Grew, like a lusty flower in June's caress.

10

Parting they seemed to tread upon the air,
  Twin roses by the zephyr blown apart
Only to meet again more close, and share
  The inward fragrance of each other's heart.
She, to her chamber gone, a ditty fair
  Sang, of delicious love and honeyed dart;[12]
He with light steps went up a western hill
And bade the sun farewell, and joyed his fill.[13]

11

All close they met again, before the dusk
  Had taken from the stars its pleasant veil,
All close they met, all eves, before the dusk
  Had taken from the stars its pleasant veil,
Close in a bower of hyacinth and musk,
  Unknown of any, free from whispering tale.
Ah, better had it been for ever so,
Than idle ears should pleasure in their woe!

## Notes

[9] *would not fear Thine eyes* Lorenzo does not want to make her fearful by gazing devotedly at her.

[10] *shrive* confess.

[11] *And poesied with hers in dewy rhyme* that is, they kissed.

[12] *honeyed dart* Cupid's arrows were believed to be tipped with gall and honey.

[13] *joyed his fill* felt completely joyful.

12

Were they unhappy then? It cannot be.
  Too many tears for lovers have been shed,
Too many sighs give we to them in fee,[14]
  Too much of pity after they are dead,
Too many doleful stories do we see
  Whose matter in bright gold were best be read –
Except in such a page where Theseus' spouse[15]
Over the pathless waves towards him bows.

13

But for the general award of love,
  The little sweet doth kill much bitterness;
Though Dido silent is in under-grove,[16]
  And Isabella's was a great distress,
Though young Lorenzo in warm Indian clove
  Was not embalmed, this truth is not the less –
Even bees, the little almsmen of spring-bowers,
Know there is richest juice in poison-flowers.

14

With her two brothers[17] this fair lady dwelt,
  Enriched from ancestral merchandize,
And for them many a weary hand did swelt[18]
  In torched mines and noisy factories,
And many once proud-quivered loins did melt
  In blood from stinging whip; with hollow eyes
Many all day in dazzling river stood
To take the rich-ored driftings of the flood.[19]

15

For them the Ceylon diver held his breath,
  And went all naked to the hungry shark;
For them his ears gushed blood; for them in death
  The seal on the cold ice with piteous bark
Lay full of darts; for them alone did seethe
  A thousand men in troubles wide and dark:
Half-ignorant, they turned an easy wheel
That set sharp racks at work, to pinch and peel.

## Notes

[14] *in fee* as their rightful due.

[15] *Theseus' spouse* Ariadne fell in love with Theseus at first sight, and helped him find his way out of the minotaur's labyrinth.

[16] *Though Dido silent is in under-grove* Dido, Queen of Carthage, loved Aeneas but was abandoned by him, and committed suicide. The wanderings of her forlorn ghost are described by Virgil, *Aeneid* vi 451.

[17] *two brothers* There are three in Boccaccio, and they are not exploitative businessmen, as here.

[18] *swelt* sweltered, suffered oppressive heat.

[19] *To take the rich-ored driftings of the flood* that is, they panned for gold.

16

Why were they proud? Because their marble founts
Gushed with more pride than do a wretch's tears?
Why were they proud? Because fair orange mounts[20]
Were of more soft ascent than lazar stairs?[21]
Why were they proud? Because red-lined accounts
Were richer than the songs of Grecian years?
Why were they proud? – again we ask aloud,
Why in the name of glory were they proud?

17

Yet were these Florentines as self-retired
In hungry pride and gainful cowardice
As two close Hebrews in that land inspired,[22]
Paled in and vineyarded from beggar-spies[23] –
The hawks of ship-mast forests, the untired
And panniered mules for ducats and old lies,
Quick cat's-paws on the generous stray-away,[24]
Great wits in Spanish, Tuscan, and Malay.

18

How was it these same ledger-men could spy
Fair Isabella in her downy nest?
How could they find out in Lorenzo's eye
A straying from his toil? Hot Egypt's pest[25]
Into their vision covetous and sly!
How could these moneybags see east and west?
Yet so they did – and every dealer fair
Must see behind, as doth the hunted hare.

19

Oh eloquent and famed Boccaccio!
Of thee we now should ask forgiving boon,[26]
And of thy spicy myrtles as they blow,
And of thy roses amorous of the moon,
And of thy lilies, that do paler grow
Now they can no more hear thy gittern's[27] tune,
For venturing syllables that ill beseem
The quiet glooms of such a piteous theme.

## Notes

[20] *orange-mounts* hills with orange trees on them.

[21] *lazar stairs* a staircase in a lazar-house (house for diseased people, especially those suffering from leprosy).

[22] *that land inspired* Palestine.

[23] *beggar-spies* those who, were they to have contact with the brothers, might reveal to them the pains and sufferings of poverty, from which the brothers have insulated themselves.

[24] *Quick cat's-paws on the generous stray-away* The alert ruffian cons money out of the innocent runaway.

[25] *Hot Egypt's pest* The plague of darkness visited upon the Egyptians (Exodus 10:21–3).

[26] *forgiving boon* the blessing of forgiveness.

[27] *gittern's* A cithern is a sort of guitar dating back to the sixteenth century.

20

Grant thou a pardon here, and then the tale
Shall move on soberly, as it is meet;
There is no other crime, no mad assail
To make old prose in modern rhyme more sweet:
But it is done (succeed the verse or fail)
To honour thee, and thy gone spirit greet;
To stead[28] thee as a verse in English tongue,
An echo of thee in the north-wind sung.

21

These brethren having found by many signs
What love Lorenzo for their sister had,
And how she loved him too, each unconfines
His bitter thoughts to other, well nigh mad
That he, the servant of their trade designs,
Should in their sister's love be blithe and glad,
When 'twas their plan to coax her by degrees
To some high noble and his olive-trees.[29]

22

And many a jealous conference had they,
And many times they bit their lips alone
Before they fixed upon a surest way
To make the youngster for his crime atone;
And at the last, these men of cruel clay
Cut Mercy with a sharp knife to the bone –
For they resolved in some forest dim
To kill Lorenzo, and there bury him.

23

So on a pleasant morning, as he leant
Into the sunrise, o'er the balustrade
Of the garden-terrace, towards him they bent
Their footing through the dews, and to him said,
'You seem there in the quiet of content,
Lorenzo, and we are most loath to invade
Calm speculation; but if you are wise,
Bestride your steed while cold is in the skies:

Notes

[28] *stead* serve.

[29] *olive-trees* i.e. estates.

24

Today we purpose, aye, this hour we mount
To spur three leagues towards the Apennine.
Come down, we pray thee, ere the hot sun count
His dewy rosary on the eglantine.'
Lorenzo, courteously as he was wont,
Bowed a fair greeting to these serpents' whine,
And went in haste, to get in readiness
With belt, and spur, and bracing huntsman's dress.

25

And as he to the courtyard passed along,
Each third step did he pause, and listened oft
If he could hear his lady's matin-song
Or the light whisper of her footstep soft;
And as he thus over his passion hung,
He heard a laugh full musical aloft,
When, looking up, he saw her features bright
Smile through an in-door lattice,[30] all delight.

26

'Love, Isabel!' said he, 'I was in pain
Lest I should miss to bid thee a good morrow;
Ah, what if I should lose thee, when so fain
I am to stifle all the heavy sorrow
Of a poor three hours' absence? But we'll gain
Out of the amorous dark what day doth borrow.
Goodbye! I'll soon be back.' 'Goodbye!' said she,
And as he went she chanted merrily.

27

So the two brothers and their murdered man[31]
Rode past fair Florence, to where Arno's stream
Gurgles through straitened banks, and still doth fan
Itself with dancing bulrush, and the bream
Keeps head against the freshets.[32] Sick and wan
The brothers' faces in the ford did seem;
Lorenzo's flush with love. They passed the water
Into a forest quiet for the slaughter.

## Notes

[30] *in-door lattice* Barnard suggests that this refers to a door with a lattice window set into it, rather than a lattice window in one of the building's outside walls.

[31] *their murdered man* This line is famous as an example of 'prolepsis', the figure of speech whereby a future action is anticipated. It was first praised by Charles Lamb: 'The anticipation of the assassination is wonderfully conceived in one epithet.'

[32] *freshets* fresh water streams.

28

There was Lorenzo slain and buried in,
There in that forest did his great love cease.
Ah, when a soul doth thus its freedom win,
It aches in loneliness – is ill at peace
As the break-covert bloodhounds[33] of such sin:
They dipped their swords in the water, and did tease
Their horses homeward with convulsed spur,
Each richer by his being a murderer.

29

They told their sister how, with sudden speed,
Lorenzo had ta'en ship for foreign lands
Because of some great urgency and need
In their affairs, requiring trusty hands.
Poor girl, put on thy stifling widow's weed,
And 'scape at once from hope's accursed bands!
Today thou wilt not see him, nor tomorrow,
And the next day will be a day of sorrow.

30

She weeps alone for pleasures not to be;
Sorely she wept until the night came on,
And then, instead of love – oh misery! –
She brooded o'er the luxury[34] alone:
His image in the dusk she seemed to see,
And to the silence made a gentle moan,
Spreading her perfect arms upon the air,
And on her couch low murmuring, 'Where, oh where?'

31

But Selfishness, Love's cousin, held not long
Its fiery vigil in her single breast;
She fretted for the golden hour, and hung
Upon the time with feverish unrest
Not long – for soon into her heart a throng
Of higher occupants, a richer zest,
Came tragic: passion not to be subdued,
And sorrow for her love in travels rude.

## Notes

[33] *break-covert bloodhounds* hunting-dogs breaking cover in pursuit of their prey. Keats means that the victim's soul is as uneasy ('ill at peace') as those of his murderers ('the break-covert bloodhounds').

[34] *the luxury* It is typical of Keats that Isabella's mounting grief should be a 'luxury'; that is, something intensely, keenly and painfully experienced.

32

In the middays of autumn, on their eves,
The breath of winter comes from far away,
And the sick west[35] continually bereaves
Of some gold tinge, and plays a roundelay
Of death among the bushes and the leaves,
To make all bare before he dares to stray
From his north cavern. So sweet Isabel
By gradual decay from beauty fell

33

Because Lorenzo came not. Oftentimes
She asked her brothers, with an eye all pale,
Striving to be itself, what dungeon climes
Could keep him off so long? They spake a tale
Time after time, to quiet her. Their crimes
Came on them like a smoke from Hinnom's vale,[36]
And every night in dreams they groaned aloud
To see their sister in her snowy shroud.

34

And she had died in drowsy ignorance,
But for a thing more deadly dark than all;
It came like a fierce potion drunk by chance
Which saves a sick man from the feathered pall
For some few gasping moments; like a lance
Waking an Indian from his cloudy hall
With cruel pierce, and bringing him again
Sense of the gnawing fire at heart and brain.

35

It was a vision. In the drowsy gloom,
The dull of midnight, at her couch's foot
Lorenzo stood and wept: the forest tomb
Had marred his glossy hair which once could shoot
Lustre into the sun, and put cold doom
Upon his lips, and taken the soft lute
From his lorn[37] voice, and past his loamed ears
Had made a miry channel for his tears.

## Notes

[35] *the sick west* the west wind.

[36] *Hinnom's vale* Keats knew of this valley, to the south of Jerusalem, from the Bible: 'He burnt incense in the valley of the son of Hinnom, and burnt his children in the fire, after the abominations of the heathen' (2 Chronicles 28:3).

[37] *lorn* ruined.

36

Strange sound it was when the pale shadow spake;
For there was striving in its piteous tongue
To speak as when on earth it was awake,
And Isabella on its music hung:
Languor there was in it, and tremulous shake,
As in a palsied Druid's harp unstrung;
And through it moaned a ghostly undersong
Like hoarse night-gusts sepulchral briars among.

37

Its eyes, though wild, were still all dewy bright
With love, and kept all phantom fear aloof
From the poor girl by magic of their light,
The while it did unthread the horrid woof[38]
Of the late darkened time, the murderous spite
Of pride and avarice, the dark pine roof
In the forest, and the sodden turfed dell
Where, without any word, from stabs he fell –

38

Saying moreover, 'Isabel, my sweet!
Red whortleberries droop above my head,
And a large flintstone weighs upon my feet;
Around me beeches and high chestnuts shed
Their leaves and prickly nuts; a sheepfold bleat
Comes from beyond the river to my bed:
Go, shed one tear upon my heather-bloom,
And it shall comfort me within the tomb.

39

I am a shadow now – alas, alas! –
Upon the skirts of human nature dwelling
Alone. I chant alone the holy mass
While little sounds of life are round me knelling,
And glossy bees at noon do fieldward pass,
And many a chapel bell the hour is telling,
Paining me through; those sounds grow strange to me,
And thou art distant in humanity.

Notes

[38] *woof* fabric. Keats uses the term metaphorically: the ghost reveals to Isabella the substance of what happened to him.

40

I know what was, I feel full well what is,
   And I should rage, if spirits could go mad;
Though I forget the taste of earthly bliss,
   That paleness[39] warms my grave, as though I had
A seraph chosen from the bright abyss
   To be my spouse: thy paleness makes me glad;
Thy beauty grows upon me, and I feel
A greater love through all my essence steal.'[40]

41

The spirit mourned 'Adieu!', dissolved, and left
   The atom darkness in a slow turmoil,
As when of healthful midnight sleep bereft,
   Thinking on rugged hours and fruitless toil,
We put our eyes into a pillowy cleft,
   And see the spangly gloom froth up and boil:
It made sad Isabella's eyelids ache,
And in the dawn she started up awake.

42

'Ha ha!' said she, 'I knew not this hard life,
   I thought the worst was simple misery;
I thought some fate with pleasure or with strife
   Portioned us – happy days or else to die!
But there is crime: a brother's bloody knife.
   Sweet spirit, thou hast schooled my infancy:
I'll visit thee for this, and kiss thine eyes,
And greet thee morn and even in the skies.'

43

When the full morning came, she had devised
   How she might secret to the forest hie;
How she might find the clay, so dearly prized,
   And sing to it one latest lullaby;
How her short absence might be unsurmised[41]
   While she the inmost of the dream would try.
Resolved, she took with her an aged nurse,
And went into that dismal forest-hearse.[42]

## Notes

[39] *That paleness* Isabella is pale-skinned.

[40] *Thy beauty grows upon me…my essence steal* Keats quoted this couplet in his letter to Fanny Brawne of February 1820: 'In my present state of health I feel too much separated from you and could almost speak to you in the words of Lorenzo's ghost to Isabella.'

[41] *unsurmised* unnoticed.

[42] *forest-hearse* forest-tomb; the forest where Lorenzo was buried.

44

See, as they creep along the riverside,
How she doth whisper to that aged dame,
And after looking round the champaign[43] wide
Shows her a knife. 'What feverous hectic flame
Burns in thee, child? What good can thee betide,
That thou shouldst smile again?' The evening came,
And they had found Lorenzo's earthly bed:
The flint was there, the berries at his head.

45

Who hath not loitered in a green churchyard
And let his spirit, like a demon-mole,
Work through the clayey soil and gravel hard
To see skull, coffined bones, and funeral stole,[44]
Pitying each form that hungry death hath marred,
And filling it once more with human soul?
Ah, this is holiday to what was felt
When Isabella by Lorenzo knelt!

46

She gazed into the fresh-thrown mould as though
One glance did fully all its secrets tell;
Clearly she saw, as other eyes would know
Pale limbs at bottom of a crystal well;
Upon the murderous spot she seemed to grow,
Like to a native lily of the dell –
Then with her knife, all sudden, she began
To dig more fervently than misers can.

47

Soon she turned up a soiled glove whereon
Her silk had played in purple fantasies;[45]
She kissed it with a lip more chill than stone
And put it in her bosom, where it dries
And freezes utterly unto the bone
Those dainties made to still an infant's cries.[46]
Then 'gan she work again, nor stayed her care,
But to throw back at times her veiling hair.

Notes

[43] *champaign* level, open countryside.

[44] *stole* robe.

[45] *Her silk had played in purple fantasies* she had embroidered the glove in purple silk.

[46] *Those dainties made to still an infant's cries* i.e. her breasts.

48

That old nurse stood beside her wondering
  Until her heart felt pity to the core
At sight of such a dismal labouring,
  And so she kneeled, with her locks all hoar,[47]
And put her lean hands to the horrid thing:
  Three hours they laboured at this travail sore.[48]
At last they felt the kernel of the grave,
And Isabella did not stamp and rave.

49

Ah, wherefore all this wormy circumstance?
  Why linger at the yawning tomb so long?
Oh for the gentleness of old romance,
  The simple plaining of a minstrel's song!
Fair reader, at the old tale take a glance,
  For here, in truth, it doth not well belong
To speak; oh turn thee to the very tale,
And taste the music of that vision pale.

50

With duller steel than the Perséan sword[49]
  They cut away no formless monster's head,
But one whose gentleness did well accord
  With death, as life. The ancient harps have said
Love never dies but lives, immortal Lord:
  If Love impersonate was ever dead,
Pale Isabella kissed it and low moaned;
'Twas love, cold – dead indeed, but not dethroned.

51

In anxious secrecy they took it home,
  And then the prize was all for Isabel:
She calmed its wild hair with a golden comb,
  And all around each eye's sepulchral cell
Pointed each fringed lash; the smeared loam
  With tears, as chilly as a dripping well,
She drenched away – and still she combed, and kept
Sighing all day, and still she kissed and wept.

## Notes

[47] *hoar* grey.

[48] *travail sore* difficult task.

[49] *the Perséan sword* Perseus was given a scythe-shaped sword with which to cut off the Gorgon's head.

52

Then in a silken scarf, sweet with the dews
Of precious flowers plucked in Araby,
And divine liquids come with odorous ooze
Through the cold serpent-pipe[50] refreshfully,
She wrapped it up and for its tomb did choose
A garden-pot wherein she laid it by,
And covered it with mould, and o'er it set
Sweet basil, which her tears kept ever wet.

53

And she forgot the stars, the moon and sun,
And she forgot the blue above the trees,
And she forgot the dells where waters run,
And she forgot the chilly autumn breeze;
She had no knowledge when the day was done,
And the new morn she saw not, but in peace
Hung over her sweet basil evermore,
And moistened it with tears unto the core.

54

And so she ever fed it with thin tears,
Whence thick and green and beautiful it grew,
So that it smelt more balmy than its peers
Of basil-tufts in Florence; for it drew
Nurture besides, and life, from human fears,
From the fast-mouldering head there shut from view;
So that the jewel, safely casketed,
Came forth, and in perfumed leafits spread.

55

Oh Melancholy, linger here awhile!
Oh Music, Music, breathe despondingly!
Oh Echo, Echo, from some sombre isle
Unknown, Lethean,[51] sigh to us, oh sigh!
Spirits in grief, lift up your heads and smile –
Lift up your heads, sweet spirits, heavily,
And make a pale light in your cypress glooms,
Tinting with silver wan your marble tombs.

## Notes

[50] *cold serpent-pipe* pipes coiled like snakes, through which the perfumes ('divine liquids') were distilled from 'precious flowers plucked in Araby'.

[51] *Lethean* forgotten.

56

Moan hither, all ye syllables of woe,
  From the deep throat of sad Melpomene![52]
Through bronzed lyre in tragic order go
  And touch the strings into a mystery;
Sound mournfully upon the winds and low –
  For simple Isabel is soon to be
Among the dead: she withers like a palm
Cut by an Indian for its juicy balm.

57

Oh leave the palm to wither by itself,
  Let not quick winter chill its dying hour!
It may not be – those Baälites of pelf,[53]
  Her brethren, noted the continual shower
From her dead eyes, and many a curious elf
  Among her kindred wondered that such dower
Of youth and beauty should be thrown aside
By one marked out to be a noble's bride.

58

And furthermore her brethren wondered much
  Why she sat drooping by the basil green,
And why it flourished as by magic touch –
  Greatly they wondered what the thing might mean!
They could not surely give belief, that such
  A very nothing would have power to wean
Her from her own fair youth and pleasures gay,
And even remembrance of her love's delay.

59

Therefore they watched a time when they might sift
  This hidden whim – and long they watched in vain,
For seldom did she go to chapel-shrift,[54]
  And seldom felt she any hunger-pain;
And when she left, she hurried back as swift
  As bird on wing to breast its eggs again,
And, patient as a hen-bird, sat her there
Beside her basil, weeping through her hair.

## Notes

[52] *sad Melpomene* Muse of Tragedy.

[53] *Baälites of pelf* worshippers of money.

[54] *chapel-shrift* confession.

60

Yet they contrived to steal the basil-pot,
   And to examine it in secret place:
The thing was vile with green and livid spot,
   And yet they knew it was Lorenzo's face.
The guerdon[55] of their murder they had got,
   And so left Florence in a moment's space,
Never to turn again. Away they went,
With blood upon their heads, to banishment.

61

Oh Melancholy, turn thine eyes away!
   Oh Music, Music, breathe despondingly!
Oh Echo, Echo, on some other day,
   From isles Lethean, sigh to us, oh sigh!
Spirits of grief, sing not your 'Well-a-way!',
   For Isabel, sweet Isabel, will die –
Will die a death too lone and incomplete
Now they have ta'en away her basil sweet.

62

Piteous she looked on dead and senseless things,
   Asking for her lost basil amorously;
And with melodious chuckle in the strings
   Of her lorn voice,[56] she oftentimes would cry
After the pilgrim in his wanderings
   To ask him where her basil was, and why
'Twas hid from her – 'For cruel 'tis', said she,
'To steal my basil-pot away from me.'

63

And so she pined, and so she died forlorn,
   Imploring for her basil to the last;
No heart was there in Florence but did mourn
   In pity of her love, so overcast.
And a sad ditty of this story borne
   From mouth to mouth through all the country passed;
Still is the burthen sung: 'O cruelty,
To steal my basil-pot away from me!'

## Notes

[55] *guerdon* reward, benefit.

[56] *her lorn voice* Like that of Lorenzo, Isabella's voice is also now ruined ('lorn'), so that she can do no more than 'chuckle' with the music.

## Letter from John Keats to John Hamilton Reynolds, 3 May 1818 (extract)

I will return to Wordsworth, whether or no he has an extended vision or a circumscribed grandeur, whether he is an eagle in his nest or on the wing. And to be more explicit and to show you how tall I stand by the giant, I will put down a simile of human life as far as I now perceive it – that is, to the point to which I say we both have arrived at. Well, I compare human life to a large mansion of many apartments,[1] two of which I can only describe, the doors of the rest being as yet shut upon me. The first we step into we call the infant or thoughtless chamber, in which we remain as long as we do not think. We remain there a long while, and, notwithstanding the doors of the second chamber remain wide open, showing a bright appearance, we care not to hasten to it, but are at length imperceptibly impelled by the awakening of the thinking principle within us. We no sooner get into the second chamber, which I shall call the chamber of maiden thought, than we become intoxicated with the light and the atmosphere, we see nothing but pleasant wonders, and think of delaying there forever in delight. However, among the effects this breathing[2] is father of, is that tremendous one of sharpening one's vision into the heart and nature of man, of convincing one's nerves that the world is full of misery and heartbreak, pain, sickness, and oppression – whereby this chamber of maiden thought becomes gradually darkened and, at the same time, on all sides of it many doors are set open – but all dark, all leading to dark passages. We see not the balance of good and evil. We are in a mist. *We* are now in that state. We feel the 'burden of the mystery'.[3] To this point was Wordsworth come, as far as I can conceive, when he wrote 'Tintern Abbey', and it seems to me that his genius is explorative of those dark passages. Now if we live, and go on thinking, we too shall explore them. He is a genius and superior to us, insofar as he can, more than we, make discoveries, and shed a light in them. Here I must think Wordsworth is deeper than Milton, though I think it has depended more upon the general and gregarious advance of intellect, than individual greatness of mind. From the *Paradise Lost* and the other works of Milton, I hope it is not too presuming (even between ourselves) to say, his philosophy, human and divine, may be tolerably understood by one not much advanced in years. In his time, Englishmen were just emancipated from a great superstition[4] – and men had got hold of certain points and resting-places in reasoning which were too newly born to be doubted, and too much opposed by the mass of Europe not to be thought ethereal and authentically divine. Who could gainsay his ideas on virtue, vice, and chastity in *Comus*, just at the time of the dismissal of codpieces,[5] and a hundred other disgraces? Who would not rest satisfied with his hintings at good and evil in the *Paradise Lost*, when just free from the Inquisition[6] and burning in Smithfield?[7] The Reformation produced such immediate and great benefits, that Protestantism was considered under the immediate eye of heaven, and its own remaining dogmas and superstitions then, as it were, regenerated, constituted those resting-places and seeming sure points of reasoning. From that I have mentioned, Milton, whatever he may have thought in the sequel, appears to have been content with

## Notes

LETTER FROM JOHN KEATS TO JOHN HAMILTON REYNOLDS

[1] *a large mansion…apartments* cf. John 14:2: 'In my Father's house are many mansions.'

[2] *breathing* influence.

[3] *burden of the mystery* from 'Tintern Abbey' 39.

[4] *a great superstition* the Roman Catholic Church.

[5] *the dismissal of codpieces* Codpieces (bagged appendages, often highly ornamented, worn by men on the front of breeches), went out of fashion in the last half of the seventeenth century. Milton's *Comus* was written in 1634.

[6] *the Inquisition* Ecclesiastical tribunal (officially styled the Holy Office) for the suppression of heresy and punishment of heretics, organized in the thirteenth century under Pope Innocent III, with a central governing body at Rome called the Congregation of the Holy Office. The Inquisition existed in Italy, France, the Netherlands, Spain, Portugal, and the Spanish and Portuguese colonies. The Spanish Inquisition, reorganized 1478–83, became notorious in the sixteenth century for its severities. It was abolished in France in 1772, and in Spain finally in 1834. The Congregation of the Holy Office still exists, but is chiefly concerned with heretical literature.

[7] *burning in Smithfield* Many Protestants were burned, roasted or boiled alive in Smithfield in the City of London during Mary's reign.

these by his writings. He did not think into the human heart, as Wordsworth has done; yet Milton as a philosopher had sure as great powers as Wordsworth. What is then to be inferred? Oh, many things. It proves there is really a grand march of intellect; it proves that a mighty providence subdues the mightiest minds to the service of the time being, whether it be in human knowledge or religion…

## Letter from John Keats to Richard Woodhouse, 27 October 1818

My dear Woodhouse,

Your letter gave me a great satisfaction, more on account of its friendliness than any relish of that matter in it which is accounted so acceptable in the 'genus irritabile'.[1] The best answer I can give you is, in a clerk-like manner, to make some observations on two principal points, which seem to point like indices into the midst of the whole pro and con, about genius, and views, and achievements, and ambition, etc.

First: as to the poetical character itself (I mean that sort of which, if I am anything, I am a member – that sort distinguished from the Wordsworthian or egotistical sublime, which is a thing *per se* and stands alone),[2] it is not itself – it has no self – it is everything and nothing – it has no character – it enjoys light and shade – it lives in gusto,[3] be it foul or fair, high or low, rich or poor, mean or elevated. It has as much delight in conceiving an Iago as an Imogen.[4] What shocks the virtuous philosopher delights the chameleon poet. It does no harm from its relish of the dark side of things, any more than from its taste for the bright one – because they both end in speculation. A poet is the most unpoetical of any thing in existence, because he has no identity, he is continually in for – and filling – some other body. The sun, the moon, the sea, and men and women who are creatures of impulse, are poetical, and have about them an unchangeable attribute; the poet has none, no identity – he is certainly the most unpoetical of all God's creatures. If, then, he has no self, and if I am a poet, where is the wonder that I should say I would write no more? Might I not at that very instant have been cogitating on the characters of Saturn and Ops?[5] It is a wretched thing to confess, but is a very fact that not one word I ever utter can be taken for granted as an opinion growing out of my identical nature – how can it, when I have no nature? When I am in a room with people, if I ever am free from speculating on creations of my own brain, then not myself goes home to myself: but the identity of everyone in the room begins so to press upon me, that I am, in a very little time, annihilated – not only among men; it would be the same in a nursery of children. I know not whether I make myself wholly understood. I hope enough so to let you see that no dependence is to be placed on what I said that day.

In the second place I will speak of my views, and of the life I purpose to myself. I am ambitious of doing the world some good – if I should be spared, that may be the work of maturer years. In the interval I will assay to reach to as high a summit in poetry as the nerve bestowed upon me will suffer. The faint conceptions I have of poems to come brings the blood frequently into my forehead. All I hope is that I may not lose all interest in human affairs, that the solitary indifference I feel for

### Notes

Letter from John Keats to Richard Woodhouse

[1] *genus irritabile* from Horace, *Epistles* II ii 102.

[2] *Troilus and Cressida* I ii 15–16: 'he is a very man *per se*, / And stands alone.'

[3] *gusto* as an admirer of Hazlitt, Keats uses this word as meaning 'power or passion defining any object'; that is to say, it is one of the highest attributes of the creative imagination.

[4] Iago is the villain of *Othello*, Imogen the daughter to Cymbeline by a former Queen in *Cymbeline*.

[5] Saturn and Ops are characters in 'Hyperion'. Ops is usually identified with Cybele, wife of Saturn.

applause, even from the finest spirits, will not blunt any acuteness of vision I may have. I do not think it will – I feel assured I should write from the mere yearning and fondness I have for the beautiful, even if my night's labours should be burnt every morning and no eye ever shine upon them.

But even now I am perhaps not speaking from myself, but from some character in whose soul I now live. I am sure, however, that this next sentence is from myself. I feel your anxiety, good opinion, and friendliness, in the highest degree, and am

Yours most sincerely
John Keats

## *Hyperion: A Fragment* (composed late September–1 December 1818; abandoned April 1819)[1]

### *Book I*

Deep in the shady sadness of a vale
Far sunken from the healthy breath of morn,
Far from the fiery noon, and eve's one star,
Sat grey-haired Saturn,[2] quiet as a stone,
Still as the silence round about his lair;
Forest on forest hung about his head
Like cloud on cloud. No stir of air was there,
Not so much life as on a summer's day
Robs not one light seed from the feathered grass,
But where the dead leaf fell, there did it rest.
A stream went voiceless by, still deadened more
By reason of his fallen divinity
Spreading a shade; the naiad[3] mid her reeds
Pressed her cold finger closer to her lips.
   Along the margin-sand large footmarks went,
No further than to where his feet had strayed,
And slept there since. Upon the sodden ground
His old right hand lay nerveless,[4] listless, dead,
Unsceptred; and his realmless eyes were closed,
While his bowed head seemed list'ning to the earth,
His ancient mother, for some comfort yet.
   It seemed no force could wake him from his place;
But there came one who, with a kindred hand
Touched his wide shoulders, after bending low

## Notes

Hyperion: Book I

[1] 'I recollect at this moment the origin of the *Hyperion*', Severn wrote in 1845. 'Keats was abusing Milton to me, and a friend whose name I forget, but who was rather stern. I had expressed my great admiration and delight in Milton, when this friend, turning to Keats, said "Keats, I think it great reproach to you that Severn should admire and appreciate Milton, and you a poet should know nothing of him, for you confess never to have read him, therefore your dislike goes for nothing." After this, Keats took up Milton and became an ardent admirer and soon began the *Hyperion*. I mention this to show that his likings and dislikings were extraordinary'. When it first appeared, Leigh Hunt hailed it as 'a fragment – a gigantic one, like a ruin in the desert, or the bones of a mastodon. It is truly of a piece with its subject, which is the downfall of the elder gods' (*The Indicator*, 2 and 9 August 1820). Keats never finished this attempt to recast 'Paradise Lost' in pagan terms.

[2] *grey-haired Saturn* Hyperion's brother, leader of the Titans and father of the rebellious Jupiter. As the poem opens Saturn and the Titans are defeated. The Titans were a godlike race expelled from heaven by Jupiter in Greek myth.

[3] *naiad* water-nymph.

[4] *nerveless* weak.

With reverence, though to one who knew it not.
She was a goddess of the infant world;
By her in stature the tall Amazon
Had stood a pigmy's height – she would have ta'en
Achilles by the hair and bent his neck,
Or with a finger stayed Ixion's wheel.[5]
Her face was large as that of Memphian sphinx,[6]
Pedestalled haply in a palace court
When sages looked to Egypt for their lore.
But oh, how unlike marble was that face!
How beautiful, if sorrow had not made
Sorrow more beautiful than Beauty's self.
There was a listening fear in her regard,
As if calamity had but begun;
As if the vanward clouds of evil days
Had spent their malice, and the sullen rear
Was with its stored thunder labouring up.[7]
One hand she pressed upon that aching spot
Where beats the human heart, as if just there,
Though an immortal, she felt cruel pain;
The other upon Saturn's bended neck
She laid, and to the level of his ear
Leaning with parted lips, some words she spake
In solemn tenor and deep organ tone,
Some mourning words which in our feeble tongue
Would come in these like accents (oh how frail
To[8] that large utterance of the early gods!),
'Saturn, look up! – though wherefore, poor old King?
I have no comfort for thee, no, not one;
I cannot say, "Oh wherefore sleepest thou?"
For heaven is parted from thee, and the earth
Knows thee not, thus afflicted, for a god;
And ocean too, with all its solemn noise,
Has from thy sceptre passed, and all the air
Is emptied of thine hoary majesty.
Thy thunder, conscious of the new command,[9]
Rumbles reluctant o'er our fallen house,
And thy sharp lightning in unpractised hands
Scorches and burns our once serene domain.[10]
Oh aching time! Oh moments big as years!
All as ye pass swell out the monstrous truth,

## Notes

[5] *Ixion's wheel* Ixion was banished from heaven and sentenced to be tied to a burning and spinning wheel in Hades for eternity.

[6] *Memphian sphinx* Memphis was a city in Egypt. Keats saw a sphinx in the British Museum, early in 1819.

[7] *As if the vanward clouds…up* Calamity is compared to clouds building up before a storm, followed by the cloud mass; the storm itself is compared to the artillery moving in the wake of advancing troops.

[8] *To* i.e. compared with.

[9] *conscious of the new command* Jupiter is the new thunderer.

[10] *our once serene domain* the Saturnian golden age.

And press it so upon our weary griefs
That unbelief has not a space to breathe.
Saturn, sleep on! Oh thoughtless, why did I
Thus violate thy slumbrous solitude?
Why should I ope thy melancholy eyes?
Saturn, sleep on, while at thy feet I weep!'
　As when, upon a tranced summer night,
Those green-robed senators of mighty woods,
Tall oaks, branch-charmed by the earnest stars,
Dream, and so dream all night without a stir,
Save from one gradual solitary gust
Which comes upon the silence, and dies off
As if the ebbing air had but one wave;
So came these words and went, the while in tears
She touched her fair large forehead to the ground,
Just where her falling hair might be outspread,
A soft and silken mat for Saturn's feet.
One moon, with alteration slow, had shed
Her silver seasons four upon the night,
And still these two were postured motionless,
Like natural sculpture in cathedral cavern[11] –
The frozen god still couchant[12] on the earth,
And the sad goddess weeping at his feet.
Until at length old Saturn lifted up
His faded eyes, and saw his kingdom gone,
And all the gloom and sorrow of the place,
And that fair kneeling goddess, and then spake
As with a palsied[13] tongue, and while his beard
Shook horrid[14] with such aspen[15] malady:
'Oh tender spouse of gold Hyperion,[16]
Thea, I feel thee ere I see thy face;
Look up, and let me see our doom in it,
Look up, and tell me if this feeble shape
Is Saturn's; tell me if thou hear'st the voice
Of Saturn; tell me if this wrinkling brow,
Naked and bare of its great diadem,[17]
Peers like the front[18] of Saturn. Who had power
To make me desolate? Whence came the strength?
How was it nurtured to such bursting forth,
While Fate seemed strangled in my nervous[19] grasp?
But it is so, and I am smothered up
And buried from all godlike exercise
Of influence benign on planets pale,[20]

## Notes

[11] *Like natural sculpture in cathedral cavern* The motionless gods are compared to huge rock formations.

[12] *couchant* lying down.

[13] *palsied* trembling.

[14] *horrid* bristling.

[15] *aspen* the leaves of the aspen tremble in the slightest breeze.

[16] *tender spouse of gold Hyperion* Thea is the sister and third wife of Hyperion.

[17] *diadem* crown.

[18] *front* forehead.

[19] *nervous* muscular.

[20] *And buried…pale* Jupiter has taken control of the planets.

Of admonitions to the winds and seas,
Of peaceful sway above man's harvesting,
And all those acts which deity supreme
Doth ease its heart of love in. I am gone
Away from my own bosom; I have left
My strong identity, my real self,[21]
Somewhere between the throne and where I sit
Here on this spot of earth. Search, Thea, search!
Open thine eyes eterne,[22] and sphere them round
Upon all space – space starred, and lorn of light;
Space regioned with life-air, and barren void;
Spaces of fire, and all the yawn of hell.
Search, Thea, search! And tell me if thou seest
A certain shape or shadow, making way
With wings or chariot fierce to repossess
A heaven he lost erewhile: it must – it must
Be of ripe progress; Saturn must be King.
Yes, there must be a golden victory;
There must be gods thrown down, and trumpets blown
Of triumph calm, and hymns of festival
Upon the gold clouds metropolitan,[23]
Voices of soft proclaim, and silver stir
Of strings in hollow shells; and there shall be
Beautiful things made new, for the surprise
Of the sky-children. I will give command:
Thea! Thea! Thea! Where is Saturn?'
    This passion lifted him upon his feet,
And made his hands to struggle in the air,
His Druid locks[24] to shake and ooze with sweat,
His eyes to fever out, his voice to cease.
He stood, and heard not Thea's sobbing deep;
A little time, and then again he snatched
Utterance thus: 'But cannot I create?
Cannot I form? Cannot I fashion forth
Another world, another universe,
To overbear and crumble this to naught?
Where is another chaos? Where?' That word
Found way unto Olympus,[25] and made quake
The rebel three.[26] Thea was startled up,
And in her bearing was a sort of hope
As thus she quick-voiced spake, yet full of awe:
'This cheers our fallen house; come to our friends,[27]
Oh Saturn, come away and give them heart!

## Notes

[21] *My strong identity, my real self* Titans depend on their identity for their power.

[22] *eterne* eternal.

[23] *the gold clouds metropolitan* The clouds are the gods' metropolis.

[24] *Druid locks* i.e. long-haired.

[25] *Olympus* the mountain that provided Jupiter with his seat of power.

[26] *The rebel three* Saturn's sons – Jupiter, Neptune and Pluto.

[27] *our friends* the rest of the Titans.

I know the covert,[28] for thence came I hither.'
Thus brief, then with beseeching eyes she went
With backward footing through the shade a space;
He followed, and she turned to lead the way
Through aged boughs that yielded like the mist
Which eagles cleave upmounting from their nest.
   Meanwhile in other realms big tears were shed,
More sorrow like to this, and suchlike woe
Too huge for mortal tongue or pen of scribe.
The Titans fierce, self-hid, or prison-bound,
Groaned for the old allegiance once more,
And listened in sharp pain for Saturn's voice.
But one of the whole mammoth-brood still kept
His sov'reignty, and rule, and majesty:
Blazing Hyperion on his orbed fire[29]
Still sat, still snuffed the incense, teeming up
From man to the sun's god – yet unsecure.
For as among us mortals omens drear
Fright and perplex, so also shuddered he –
Not at dog's howl, or gloom-bird's[30] hated screech,
Or the familiar visiting of one
Upon the first toll of his passing-bell,[31]
Or prophesyings of the midnight lamp,
But horrors portioned[32] to a giant nerve
Oft made Hyperion ache. His palace bright,
Bastioned with pyramids of glowing gold,
And touched with shade of bronzed obelisks,
Glared a blood-red through all its thousand courts,
Arches, and domes, and fiery galleries;
And all its curtains of aurorean[33] clouds
Flushed angerly,[34] while sometimes eagle's wings
(Unseen before by gods or wondering men)
Darkened the place; and neighing steeds were heard,
Not heard before by gods or wondering men.
Also, when he would taste the spicy wreaths
Of incense, breathed aloft from sacred hills,
Instead of sweets, his ample palate took
Savour of poisonous brass and metal sick.
And so, when harboured in the sleepy west
After the full completion of fair day,
For rest divine upon exalted couch
And slumber in the arms of melody,
He paced away the pleasant hours of ease

## Notes

[28] *covert* hiding-place.

[29] *orbed fire* the sun, of which Hyperion is god.

[30] *gloom-bird* owl.

[31] *passing-bell* death-bell.

[32] *portioned* proportioned.

[33] *aurorean* roseate.

[34] *His palace…angerly* Hyperion's palace is part-Roman and part-Egyptian.

With stride colossal on from hall to hall;
While far within each aisle and deep recess
His winged minions in close clusters stood,
Amazed and full of fear, like anxious men
Who on wide plains gather in panting troops
When earthquakes jar their battlements and towers.
Even now, while Saturn, roused from icy trance,
Went step for step with Thea through the woods,
Hyperion, leaving twilight in the rear,
Came slope[35] upon the threshold of the west;
Then, as was wont, his palace-door flew ope
In smoothest silence, save what solemn tubes[36]
Blown by the serious zephyrs[37] gave of sweet
And wandering sounds, slow-breathed melodies;
And like a rose in vermeil[38] tint and shape,
In fragrance soft, and coolness to the eye,
That inlet to severe magnificence
Stood full-blown, for the god to enter in.
    He entered, but he entered full of wrath;
His flaming robes streamed out beyond his heels
And gave a roar as if of earthly fire,
That scared away the meek ethereal Hours[39]
And made their dove-wings tremble. On he flared,
From stately nave to nave, from vault to vault,
Through bowers of fragrant and enwreathed light
And diamond-paved lustrous long arcades,
Until he reached the great main cupola.[40]
There standing fierce beneath, he stamped his foot,
And from the basements deep to the high towers
Jarred his own golden region; and before
The quavering thunder thereupon had ceased,
His voice leaped out, despite of godlike curb,
To this result: 'Oh dreams of day and night!
Oh monstrous forms! Oh effigies of pain!
Oh spectres busy in a cold, cold gloom!
Oh lank-eared phantoms of black-weeded pools!
Why do I know ye? Why have I seen ye? Why
Is my eternal essence[41] thus distraught
To see and to behold these horrors new?
Saturn is fallen, am I too to fall?
Am I to leave this haven of my rest,
This cradle of my glory, this soft clime,
This calm luxuriance of blissful light,
These crystalline pavilions and pure fanes[42]

## Notes

[35] *slope* sloping downward.
[36] *solemn tubes* of a musical instrument, such as an organ.
[37] *zephyrs* breezes.
[38] *vermeil* scarlet.
[39] *Hours* 'Horae', attendant nymphs of the sun.
[40] *cupola* dome.
[41] *essence* being.
[42] *fanes* temples.

Of all my lucent[43] empire? It is left
Deserted, void, nor any haunt of mine.
The blaze, the splendour, and the symmetry,
I cannot see – but darkness, death and darkness.
Even here, into my centre of repose,
The shady visions come to domineer,
Insult, and blind, and stifle up my pomp.
Fall? No, by Tellus[44] and her briny robes!
Over the fiery frontier of my realms
I will advance a terrible right arm
Shall scare that infant thunderer, rebel Jove,
And bid old Saturn take his throne again.'
He spake, and ceased, the while a heavier threat
Held struggle with his throat but came not forth;
For as in theatres of crowded men
Hubbub increases more they call out 'Hush!'
So at Hyperion's words the phantoms pale
Bestirred themselves, thrice horrible and cold,
And from the mirrored level where he stood
A mist arose as from a scummy marsh.
At this, through all his bulk an agony
Crept gradual from the feet unto the crown,
Like a lithe serpent vast and muscular
Making slow way, with head and neck convulsed
From over-strained might. Released, he fled
To the eastern gates, and full six dewy hours
Before the dawn in season due should blush,
He breathed fierce breath against the sleepy portals,[45]
Cleared them of heavy vapours, burst them wide
Suddenly on the ocean's chilly streams.
The planet orb of fire whereon he rode
Each day from east to west the heavens through,
Spun round in sable curtaining of clouds;
Not therefore veiled quite, blindfold and hid,
But ever and anon the glancing spheres,
Circles, and arcs, and broad-belting colure,[46]
Glowed through, and wrought upon the muffling dark
Sweet-shaped lightnings from the nadir deep
Up to the zenith – hieroglyphics old[47]
Which sages and keen-eyed astrologers
Then living on the earth, with labouring thought
Won from the gaze of many centuries –
Now lost, save what we find on remnants huge
Of stone, or marble swart,[48] their import gone,

## Notes

[43] *lucent* shining.

[44] *Tellus* mother of the Titans, married to her brother Saturn.

[45] *portals* gateways.

[46] *colure* Technical term for 'each of two great circles which intersect each other at right angles at the poles, and divide the equinoctial and the ecliptic into four equal parts' (*Oxford English Dictionary*).

[47] *hieroglyphics old* signs of the zodiac.

[48] *swart* black.

Their wisdom long since fled. Two wings this orb
Possessed for glory, two fair argent[49] wings
Ever exalted at the god's approach;
And now from forth the gloom their plumes immense
Rose one by one, till all outspreaded were,
While still the dazzling globe maintained eclipse,
Awaiting for Hyperion's command.
Fain would he have commanded, fain took throne
And bid the day begin, if but for change.
He might not – no, though a primeval god;
The sacred seasons might not be disturbed.
Therefore the operations of the dawn
Stayed in their birth, even as here 'tis told.
Those silver wings expanded sisterly,
Eager to sail their orb; the porches wide
Opened upon the dusk demesnes[50] of night;
And the bright Titan, frenzied with new woes,
Unused to bend, by hard compulsion bent
His spirit to the sorrow of the time;
And all along a dismal rack of clouds,[51]
Upon the boundaries of day and night,
He stretched himself in grief and radiance faint.
There as he lay, the heaven with its stars
Looked down on him with pity, and the voice
Of Coelus,[52] from the universal space,
Thus whispered low and solemn in his ear:
'Oh brightest of my children dear, earth-born
And sky-engendered, son of mysteries
All unrevealed even to the powers[53]
Which met at thy creating; at whose joys
And palpitations sweet, and pleasures soft,
I, Coelus, wonder how they came and whence,
And at the fruits thereof what shapes they be,
Distinct and visible – symbols divine,
Manifestations of that beauteous life
Diffused unseen throughout eternal space.
Of these new-formed art thou, oh brightest child!
Of these, thy brethren and the goddesses!
There is sad feud among ye, and rebellion
Of son against his sire.[54] I saw him fall,
I saw my first-born[55] tumbled from his throne!
To me his arms were spread, to me his voice
Found way from forth the thunders round his head!
Pale wox[56] I, and in vapours hid my face.
Art thou, too, near such doom? Vague fear there is,

## Notes

[49] *argent* silver.
[50] *demesnes* domains, regions.
[51] *rack of clouds* cloud-mass.
[52] *Coelus* father of the Titans.
[53] *the powers* Coelus and Terra (parents of the Titans).
[54] *son against his sire* i.e. Jupiter's rebellion against Saturn.
[55] *my first-born* Saturn.
[56] *wox* became.

For I have seen my sons most unlike gods.
Divine ye were created, and divine
In sad demeanour, solemn, undisturbed,
Unruffled, like high gods, ye lived and ruled.
Now I behold in you fear, hope, and wrath,
Actions of rage and passion – even as
I see them on the mortal world beneath,
In men who die. This is the grief, oh son;
Sad sign of ruin, sudden dismay, and fall!
Yet do thou strive; as thou art capable,
As thou canst move about, an evident god,[57]
And canst oppose to each malignant hour
Ethereal presence. I am but a voice;
My life is but the life of winds and tides,
No more than winds and tides can I avail –
But thou canst. Be thou therefore in the van
Of circumstance;[58] yea, seize the arrow's barb
Before the tense string murmur.[59] To the earth!
For there thou wilt find Saturn and his woes.
Meantime I will keep watch on thy bright sun,
And of thy seasons be a careful nurse.'
Ere half this region-whisper had come down,
Hyperion arose, and on the stars
Lifted his curved lids, and kept them wide
Until it ceased, and still he kept them wide,
And still they were the same bright, patient stars.
Then with a slow incline of his broad breast,
Like to a diver in the pearly seas,
Forward he stooped over the airy shore
And plunged all noiseless into the deep night.

## *Book II*

Just at the self-same beat of Time's wide wings
Hyperion slid into the rustled air,
And Saturn gained with Thea that sad place
Where Cybele and the bruised Titans mourned.
It was a den where no insulting[1] light
Could glimmer on their tears; where their own groans
They felt, but heard not, for the solid roar
Of thunderous waterfalls and torrents hoarse,
Pouring a constant bulk, uncertain where.[2]
Crag jutting forth to crag, and rocks that seemed
Ever as if just rising from a sleep,

### Notes

[57] *an evident god* Saturn has being; Coelus is the sky, and is just a place – he cannot move around and has no 'essence'.

[58] *the van / Of circumstance* i.e. act, take the initiative.

[59] *seize…murmur* i.e. shoot your arrow before someone shoots at you.

Hyperion: Book II

[1] *insulting* The light would be an insulting reminder of their loss of power.

[2] *for the solid roar…where* Keats recollects the waterfalls he had seen on his walking tour of the Lake District and Scotland, summer 1818.

Forehead to forehead held their monstrous horns;
And thus in thousand hugest fantasies
Made a fit roofing to this nest of woe.
Instead of thrones, hard flint they sat upon,
Couches of rugged stone, and slaty ridge
Stubborned with iron. All were not assembled,
Some chained in torture and some wandering.
Coeus, and Gyges, and Briareus,
Typhon, and Dolor, and Porphyrion,
With many more, the brawniest in assault,
Were pent in regions of laborious breath,
Dungeoned in opaque element to keep
Their clenched teeth still clenched, and all their limbs
Locked up like veins of metal, cramped and screwed;
Without a motion, save of their big hearts
Heaving in pain, and horribly convulsed
With sanguine feverous boiling gurge[3] of pulse.[4]
Mnemosyne[5] was straying in the world;
Far from her moon had Phoebe[6] wandered;
And many else were free to roam abroad,
But for the main, here found they covert[7] drear.
Scarce images of life, one here, one there,
Lay vast and edgeways; like a dismal cirque
Of Druid stones upon a forlorn moor,[8]
When the chill rain begins at shut of eve
In dull November, and their chancel vault,[9]
The heaven itself, is blinded throughout night.
Each one kept shroud,[10] nor to his neighbour gave
Or word, or look, or action of despair.
Creus was one; his ponderous iron mace
Lay by him, and a shattered rib of rock
Told of his rage ere he thus sank and pined.
Iapetus another – in his grasp
A serpent's plashy[11] neck, its barbed tongue
Squeezed from the gorge,[12] and all its uncurled length
Dead, and because[13] the creature could not spit
Its poison in the eyes of conquering Jove.
Next Cottus; prone he lay, chin uppermost
As though in pain, for still upon the flint
He ground severe his skull, with open mouth
And eyes at horrid working.[14] Nearest him

## Notes

[3] *gurge* whirlpool.

[4] *pulse* i.e. that of blood in the heart.

[5] *Mnemosyne* mother of the Muses by Jupiter, included among the Titans. She is seeking Apollo.

[6] *Phoebe* goddess of the moon.

[7] *covert* shelter.

[8] *Druid stones upon a forlorn moor* Keats visited the Castlerigg stone circle near Keswick in June 1818.

[9] *their chancel vault* The stones and the darkness evoke the atmosphere of a church.

[10] *shroud* shrouded.

[11] *plashy* marked as if splashed with colour.

[12] *gorge* throat.

[13] *and because* i.e. and all this because.

[14] *at horrid working* looking round in a frightening manner.

Asia, born of most enormous Caf,
Who cost her mother Tellus keener pangs,
Though feminine, than any of her sons.
More thought than woe was in her dusky face,
For she was prophesying of her glory,
And in her wide imagination stood
Palm-shaded temples and high rival fanes
By Oxus or in Ganges' sacred isles.[15]
Even as Hope upon her anchor[16] leans,
So leant she, not so fair, upon a tusk
Shed from the broadest of her elephants.
Above her, on a crag's uneasy shelve,[17]
Upon his elbow raised, all prostrate else,
Shadowed Enceladus – once tame and mild
As grazing ox unworried in the meads,
Now tiger-passioned, lion-thoughted, wroth,
He meditated, plotted, and even now[18]
Was hurling mountains in that second war[19]
Not long delayed, that scared the younger gods
To hide themselves in forms of beast and bird.
Not far hence Atlas; and beside him prone
Phorcus, the sire of Gorgons. Neighboured close
Oceanus, and Tethys, in whose lap
Sobbed Clymene among her tangled hair.[20]
In midst of all lay Themis, at the feet
Of Ops the queen, all clouded round from sight;
No shape distinguishable, more than when
Thick night confounds the pine-tops with the clouds:
And many else whose names may not be told.
For when the muse's wings are air-ward spread
Who shall delay her flight? And she must chaunt
Of Saturn and his guide, who now had climbed
With damp and slippery footing from a depth
More horrid[21] still. Above a sombre cliff
Their heads appeared, and up their stature grew
Till on the level height their steps found ease;
Then Thea spread abroad her trembling arms
Upon the precincts of this nest of pain,
And sidelong fixed her eye on Saturn's face.
There saw she direst strife, the supreme god
At war with all the frailty of grief,
Of rage, of fear, anxiety, revenge,
Remorse, spleen, hope, but most of all despair.

## Notes

[15] *For she was…sacred isles* Asia will become the goddess of a future cult.

[16] *anchor* traditional emblem of hope; see Hebrews 6:19.

[17] *shelve* slope.

[18] *even now* i.e. in his imagination.

[19] *that second war* presumably to have been the subject of a further book of the poem, never written.

[20] *her tangled hair* a recollection of 'Lycidas' 69: 'the tangles of Neaera's hair.'

[21] *horrid* frightening.

Against these plagues he strove in vain, for Fate
Had poured a mortal oil upon his head,
A disanointing poison,[22] so that Thea,
Affrighted, kept her still, and let him pass
First onwards in, among the fallen tribe.
   As with us mortal men, the laden heart
Is persecuted more, and fevered more,
When it is nighing to the mournful house
Where other hearts are sick of the same bruise;
So Saturn, as he walked into the midst,
Felt faint, and would have sunk among the rest,
But that he met Enceladus' eye,
Whose mightiness and awe of him, at once
Came like an inspiration – and he shouted,
'Titans, behold your god!' At which some groaned,
Some started on their feet, some also shouted,
Some wept, some wailed, all bowed with reverence;
And Ops, uplifting her black folded veil,
Showed her pale cheeks and all her forehead wan,
Her eyebrows thin and jet, and hollow eyes.
There is a roaring in the bleak-grown pines
When winter lifts his voice; there is a noise
Among immortals when a god gives sign,
With hushing finger, how he means to load
His tongue with the full weight of utterless[23] thought,
With thunder, and with music, and with pomp:
Such noise is like the roar of bleak-grown pines,
Which, when it ceases in this mountained world,
No other sound succeeds; but ceasing here,
Among these fallen, Saturn's voice therefrom
Grew up like organ, that begins anew
Its strain, when other harmonies, stopped short,
Leave the dinned air vibrating silverly.[24]
Thus grew it up: 'Not in my own sad breast,
Which is its own great judge and searcher-out,
Can I find reason why ye should be thus;
Not in the legends of the first of days,
Studied from that old spirit-leaved book[25]
Which starry Uranus with finger bright
Saved from the shores of darkness, when the waves
Low-ebbed still hid it up in shallow gloom,
And the which book ye know I ever kept
For my firm-based footstool – ah, infirm!

## Notes

[22] *A disanointing poison* the ointment deprives Saturn of his godhead.
[23] *utterless* unutterable.
[24] *silverly* with a silvery sound.
[25] *that old spirit-leaved book* an imaginary book dating from the beginning of time, recording the first stages of the evolution of the world.

Not there, nor in sign, symbol, or portent
Of element, earth, water, air, and fire,
At war, at peace, or inter-quarrelling
One against one, or two, or three, or all
Each several one against the other three,
As fire with air loud warring when rainfloods
Drown both, and press them both against earth's face,
Where, finding sulphur, a quadruple wrath
Unhinges the poor world – not in that strife,
Wherefrom I take strange lore and read it deep,
Can I find reason why ye should be thus.
No, nowhere can unriddle, though I search
And pore on nature's universal scroll
Even to swooning, why ye divinities,
The first-born of all shaped and palpable gods,
Should cower beneath what, in comparison,
Is untremendous might. Yet ye are here,
O'erwhelmed, and spurned, and battered – ye are here!
Oh Titans, shall I say "Arise"? Ye groan;
Shall I say "Crouch"? Ye groan. What can I then?
Oh heaven wide! Oh unseen parent dear!
What can I? Tell me, all ye brethren gods,
How we can war, how engine our great wrath;[26]
Oh speak your counsel now, for Saturn's ear
Is all a-hungered. Thou, Oceanus,
Ponderest high and deep, and in thy face
I see, astonied,[27] that severe content
Which comes of thought and musing – give us help!'
   So ended Saturn, and the god of the sea,[28]
Sophist and sage from no Athenian grove,[29]
But cogitation in his watery shades,
Arose, with locks not oozy,[30] and began,
In murmurs, which his first-endeavouring tongue
Caught infant-like from the far-foamed sands:
'Oh ye, whom wrath consumes, who, passion-stung,
Writhe at defeat, and nurse your agonies!
Shut up your senses, stifle up your ears,
My voice is not a bellows unto ire.
Yet listen, ye who will, whilst I bring proof
How ye, perforce, must be content to stoop;
And in the proof much comfort will I give,
If ye will take that comfort in its truth.
We fall by course of nature's law, not force
Of thunder, or of Jove. Great Saturn, thou
Hast sifted well the atom-universe;[31]

## Notes

[26] *engine our great wrath* turn our wrath into an instrument of war.

[27] *astonied* astonished; an archaism used by Spenser and Milton.

[28] *the god of the sea* Oceanus, father of all the gods.

[29] *no Athenian grove* Oceanus did not gain his wisdom from an academy in Athens. Plato established his 'Academia' (academy) in Academus's grove.

[30] *locks not oozy* Oceanus is not in the sea; Keats is also alluding to 'Lycidas' 175: 'With nectar pure his oozy locks he laves.'

[31] *atom-universe* Although Keats may be echoing Milton ('Paradise Lost' ii 900), he was aware that John Dalton (1766–1844) had proposed in 1801 that all elements are composed of fundamental units, or 'atoms', that are specific to that element.

But for this reason, that thou art the King,
And only blind from sheer supremacy,
One avenue was shaded from thine eyes
Through which I wandered to eternal truth.
And first, as thou wast not the first of powers,
So art thou not the last; it cannot be.
Thou art not the beginning nor the end.[32]
From chaos and parental darkness came
Light, the first fruits of that intestine broil,[33]
That sullen ferment which for wondrous ends
Was ripening in itself. The ripe hour came,
And with it light, and light, engendering
Upon its own producer,[34] forthwith touched
The whole enormous matter into life.
Upon that very hour, our parentage,
The heavens and the earth, were manifest;
Then thou first-born, and we the giant-race,
Found ourselves ruling new and beauteous realms.
Now comes the pain of truth, to whom 'tis pain;[35]
Oh folly! for to bear all naked truths,
And to envisage circumstance, all calm,
That is the top of sovereignty. Mark well!
As heaven and earth are fairer, fairer far
Than chaos and blank darkness, though once chiefs;
And as we show beyond[36] that heaven and earth
In form and shape compact and beautiful,
In will, in action free, companionship,
And thousand other signs of purer life –
So on our heels a fresh perfection treads,
A power more strong in beauty, born of us
And fated to excel us, as we pass
In glory that old darkness. Nor are we
Thereby more conquered than by us the rule
Of shapeless chaos. Say, doth the dull soil
Quarrel with the proud forests it hath fed,
And feedeth still, more comely than itself ?
Can it deny the chiefdom of green groves?
Or shall the tree be envious of the dove
Because it cooeth, and hath snowy wings
To wander wherewithal and find its joys?
We are such forest trees, and our fair boughs
Have bred forth not pale solitary doves
But eagles golden-feathered, who do tower
Above us in their beauty, and must reign
In right thereof; for 'tis the eternal law

## Notes

[32] *Thou art not the beginning nor the end* Revelation 1:8: 'I am Alpha and Omega, the beginning and the ending, saith the Lord.'

[33] *intestine broil* civil war.

[34] *its own producer* the darkness of chaos.

[35] *to whom 'tis pain* for those to whom it is pain.

[36] *show beyond* are manifestly superior to.

That first in beauty should be first in might –
Yea, by that law another race may drive
Our conquerors to mourn as we do now.
Have ye beheld the young god of the seas,[37]
My dispossessor? Have ye seen his face?
Have ye beheld his chariot, foamed along
By noble winged creatures he hath made?
I saw him on the calmed waters scud,
With such a glow of beauty in his eyes
That it enforced me to bid sad farewell
To all my empire; farewell sad I took,
And hither came to see how dolorous fate
Had wrought upon ye, and how I might best
Give consolation in this woe extreme.
Receive the truth, and let it be your balm.'
   Whether through posed[38] conviction, or disdain,
They guarded silence when Oceanus
Left murmuring, what deepest thought can tell?
But so it was; none answered for a space,
Save one whom none regarded, Clymene.[39]
And yet she answered not, only complained
With hectic[40] lips, and eyes up-looking mild,
Thus wording timidly among the fierce:
'Oh father, I am here the simplest voice,
And all my knowledge is that joy is gone,
And this thing woe crept in among our hearts,
There to remain for ever, as I fear.
I would not bode of evil, if I thought
So weak a creature could turn off the help
Which by just right should come of mighty gods;
Yet let me tell my sorrow, let me tell
Of what I heard, and how it made we weep,
And know that we had parted from all hope.
I stood upon a shore, a pleasant shore
Where a sweet clime was breathed from a land
Of fragrance, quietness, and trees, and flowers.
Full of calm joy it was, as I of grief,
Too full of joy and soft delicious warmth –
So that I felt a movement in my heart
To chide, and to reproach that solitude
With songs of misery, music of our woes;
And sat me down, and took a mouthed shell
And murmured into it, and made melody.
Oh melody no more! For while I sang,
And with poor skill let pass into the breeze
The dull shell's echo, from a bowery strand[41]

## Notes

[37] *the young god of the seas* Neptune, traditionally depicted as riding a chariot over the sea.
[38] *posed* feigned.
[39] *Clymene* daughter of Oceanus and Tethys.
[40] *hectic* feverish.
[41] *bowery strand* sheltered seashore.

Just opposite, an island of the sea,
There came enchantment with the shifting wind,
That did both drown and keep alive my ears.
I threw my shell away upon the sand
And a wave filled it, as my sense was filled
With that new blissful golden melody.
A living death was in each gush of sounds,
Each family of rapturous hurried notes
That fell, one after one, yet all at once,
Like pearl beads dropping sudden from their string;
And then another, then another strain,
Each like a dove leaving its olive perch,
With music winged instead of silent plumes,
To hover round my head, and make me sick
Of joy and grief at once.[42] Grief overcame,
And I was stopping up my frantic ears,
When, past all hindrance of my trembling hands,
A voice came sweeter, sweeter than all tune,
And still it cried, "Apollo! Young Apollo!
The morning-bright Apollo! Young Apollo!"
I fled, it followed me, and cried "Apollo!"
Oh father and oh brethren, had ye felt
Those pains of mine – oh Saturn, hadst thou felt,
Ye would not call this too indulged tongue
Presumptous in thus venturing to be heard.'
  So far her voice flowed on, like timorous brook
That, lingering along[43] a pebbled coast,
Doth fear to meet the sea – but sea it met
And shuddered; for the overwhelming voice
Of huge Enceladus[44] swallowed it in wrath –
The ponderous syllables, like sullen waves
In the half-glutted[45] hollows of reef-rocks,
Came booming thus, while still upon his arm
He leaned (not rising, from supreme contempt):
'Or shall we listen to the over-wise,
Or to the over-foolish, giant gods?
Not thunderbolt on thunderbolt, till all
That rebel Jove's whole armoury were spent,
Not world on world upon these shoulders piled
Could agonize me more than baby-words
In midst of this dethronement horrible.
Speak! Roar! Shout! Yell, ye sleepy Titans all!
Do ye forget the blows, the buffets vile?
Are ye not smitten by a youngling arm?[46]

## Notes

[42] *Of joy and grief at once* joy at the music; grief that her music is surpassed.
[43] *lingering along* meandering towards.
[44] *Enceladus* one of the most powerful of the Titans.
[45] *half-glutted* half-filled.
[46] *youngling arm* inexperienced arm.

Dost thou forget, sham monarch of the waves,
Thy scalding in the seas? What, have I roused
Your spleens with so few simple words as these?
Oh joy, for now I see ye are not lost!
Oh joy, for now I see a thousand eyes
Wide glaring for revenge!' As this he said,
He lifted up his stature vast, and stood,
Still without intermission speaking thus:
'Now ye are flames, I'll tell you how to burn
And purge the ether of our enemies;[47]
How to feed fierce the crooked stings of fire[48]
And singe away the swollen clouds of Jove,
Stifling that puny essence in its tent.
Oh let him feel the evil he hath done –
For though I scorn Oceanus' lore,
Much pain have I for more than loss of realms.
The days of peace and slumberous calm are fled;
Those days, all innocent of scathing war,
When all the fair Existences of heaven
Came open-eyed to guess what we would speak –
That was before our brows were taught to frown,
Before our lips knew else but solemn sounds;
That was before we knew the winged thing,
Victory, might be lost, or might be won.
And be ye mindful that Hyperion,
Our brightest brother, still is undisgraced –
Hyperion, lo! His radiance is here!'
   All eyes were on Enceladus' face,
And they beheld, while still Hyperion's name
Flew from his lips up to the vaulted rocks,[49]
A pallid gleam across his features stern –
Not savage, for he saw full many a god
Wroth as himself. He looked upon them all,
And in each face he saw a gleam of light,
But splendider in Saturn's, whose hoar locks
Shone like the bubbling foam about a keel
When the prow sweeps into a midnight cove.
In pale and silver silence they remained,
Till suddenly a splendour, like the morn,
Pervaded all the beetling[50] gloomy steeps,
All the sad spaces of oblivion,
And every gulf, and every chasm old,
And every height, and every sullen depth,
Voiceless, or hoarse with loud tormented streams,
And all the everlasting cataracts,
And all the headlong torrents far and near,

## Notes

[47] *the ether of our enemies* the air our enemies breathe.

[48] *the crooked stings of fire* flashes of lightning.

[49] *the vaulted rocks* The rocks form a roof above them.

[50] *beetling* overhanging.

Mantled[51] before in darkness and huge shade,
Now saw the light and made it terrible.
It was Hyperion: a granite peak
His bright feet touched, and there he stayed to view
The misery his brillance had betrayed
To the most hateful seeing of itself.[52]
Golden his hair of short Numidian curl,
Regal his shape majestic, a vast shade
In midst of his own brightness, like the bulk
Of Memnon's image at the set of sun
To one who travels from the dusking east;[53]
Sighs, too, as mournful as that Memnon's harp
He uttered, while his hands contemplative
He pressed together, and in silence stood.
Despondence seized again the fallen gods
At sight of the dejected King of Day,
And many hid their faces from the light.
But fierce Enceladus sent forth his eyes
Among the brotherhood, and at their glare
Uprose Iapetus, and Creus too,
And Phorcus, sea-born, and together strode
To where he towered on his eminence.[54]
There those four shouted forth old Saturn's name;
Hyperion from the peak loud answered, 'Saturn!'
Saturn sat near the mother of the gods,
In whose face was no joy, though all the gods
Gave from their hollow throats the name of 'Saturn!'

## *Book III*

Thus in alternate uproar and sad peace,
Amazed were those Titans utterly.
Oh leave them, muse! Oh leave them to their woes,
For thou art weak to sing such tumults dire;
A solitary sorrow best befits
Thy lips, and antheming a lonely grief.
Leave them, oh muse! For thou anon wilt find
Many a fallen old divinity[1]
Wandering in vain about bewildered shores.
Meantime touch piously the Delphic harp,[2]

## Notes

[51] *Mantled* cloaked, obscured.

[52] *The misery…itself* Hyperion's radiance throws the misery of the Titans into sharper relief.

[53] *Memnon's image…east* The statue was in fact one of a pair representing the Egyptian King Amenhotep III, outside his funerary temple on the west bank at Thebes, mentioned by Juvenal in his fifteenth satire. The eighteenth- and early nineteenth-century English poets believed that the statue held a lyre which, when struck by the sun at dawn or sunset, sounded forth.

[54] *eminence* mountain.

HYPERION: BOOK III

[1] *divinity* god.

[2] *the Delphic harp* i.e. the divinely inspired harp.

And not a wind of heaven but will breathe
In aid soft warble from the Dorian flute;[3]
For lo! 'tis for the father of all verse.[4]
Flush everything that hath a vermeil[5] hue,
Let the rose glow intense and warm the air,
And let the clouds of even and of morn
Float in voluptuous fleeces o'er the hills;
Let the red wine within the goblet boil,
Cold as a bubbling well; let faint-lipped shells
On sands or in great deeps, vermilion turn
Through all their labyrinths; and let the maid
Blush keenly, as with some warm kiss surprised.
Chief isle of the embowered Cyclades,[6]
Rejoice, oh Delos,[7] with thine olives green,
And poplars, and lawn-shading palms, and beech
In which the zephyr breathes the loudest song,
And hazels thick, dark-stemmed beneath the shade.
Apollo is once more the golden theme!
Where was he when the giant of the sun[8]
Stood bright amid the sorrow of his peers?
Together had he left his mother fair
And his twin-sister[9] sleeping in their bower,
And in the morning twilight wandered forth
Beside the osiers of a rivulet,
Full ankle-deep in lilies of the vale.
The nightingale had ceased, and a few stars
Were lingering in the heavens, while the thrush
Began calm-throated. Throughout all the isle
There was no covert,[10] no retired cave
Unhaunted by the murmurous noise of waves,
Though scarcely heard in many a green recess.
He listened and he wept, and his bright tears
Went trickling down the golden bow he held.
Thus with half-shut suffused[11] eyes he stood,
While from beneath some cumbrous boughs hard by
With solemn step an awful goddess[12] came,
And there was purport in her looks for him,
Which he with eager guess began to read
Perplexed, the while melodiously he said:
'How cam'st thou over the unfooted sea?
Or hath that antique mien and robed form

## Notes

[3] *the Dorian flute* flute of classical Greece. Keats echoes 'Paradise Lost' i 550–1: 'the Dorian mood / Of flutes and soft recorders.' He marked the lines in his copy of Milton with the comment: 'The light and shade ... the sorrow, the pain, the sad-sweet melody.'

[4] *the father of all verse* Apollo, god of the sun and poetry.

[5] *vermeil* bright scarlet.

[6] *Cyclades* a cluster of islands in the Aegean.

[7] *Delos* island in the centre of the Cyclades, sacred to Apollo as it was his birthplace.

[8] *the giant of the sun* Hyperion.

[9] *mother...twin-sister* Latona and Diana.

[10] *covert* hiding-place.

[11] *suffused* tearful.

[12] *an awful goddess* The awe-inspiring goddess is Mnemosyne, mother of the Muses by Jupiter, and another Titan. She has abandoned the Titans and joined Apollo.

Moved in these vales invisible till now?
Sure I have heard those vestments[13] sweeping o'er
The fallen leaves, when I have sat alone
In cool mid-forest. Surely I have traced
The rustle of those ample skirts about
These grassy solitudes, and seen the flowers
Lift up their heads, as still the whisper passed.
Goddess! I have beheld those eyes before,
And their eternal calm, and all that face,
Or I have dreamed.' 'Yes', said the supreme shape,
'Thou hast dreamed of me; and awaking up
Didst find a lyre all golden by thy side,
Whose strings touched by thy fingers, all the vast
Unwearied ear of the whole universe
Listened in pain and pleasure at the birth
Of such new tuneful wonder. Is't not strange
That thou shouldst weep, so gifted? Tell me, youth,
What sorrow thou canst feel – for I am sad
When thou dost shed a tear. Explain thy griefs
To one who in this lonely isle hath been
The watcher of thy sleep and hours of life,
From the young day when first thy infant hand
Plucked witless the weak flowers, till thine arm
Could bend that bow heroic to all times.
Show thy heart's secret to an ancient power
Who hath forsaken old and sacred thrones
For prophecies of thee, and for the sake
Of loveliness new born.' Apollo then,
With sudden scrutiny and gloomless eyes,[14]
Thus answered, while his white melodious throat
Throbbed with the syllables: 'Mnemosyne!
Thy name is on my tongue I know not how;
Why should I tell thee what thou so well seest?
Why should I strive to show what from thy lips
Would come no mystery? For me, dark, dark
And painful, vile oblivion seals my eyes.
I strive to search wherefore I am so sad
Until a melancholy numbs my limbs;
And then upon the grass I sit and moan
Like one who once had wings. Oh why should I
Feel cursed and thwarted, when the liegeless air[15]
Yields to my step aspirant? Why should I
Spurn the green turf as hateful to my feet?
Goddess benign, point forth some unknown thing.
Are there not other regions than this isle?
What are the stars? There is the sun, the sun!

## Notes

[13] *vestments* clothes.

[14] *gloomless eyes* Apollo's gloom lifts at hearing Mnemosyne.

[15] *the liegeless air* the air has no master ('liege').

And the most patient brilliance of the moon!
And stars by thousands! Point me out the way
To any one particular beauteous star,
And I will flit into it with my lyre
And make its silvery splendour pant with bliss.
I have heard the cloudy thunder. Where is power?
Whose hand, whose essence, what divinity
Makes this alarum[16] in the elements
While I here idle listen on the shores
In fearless yet in aching[17] ignorance?
Oh tell me, lonely goddess, by thy harp
That waileth every morn and eventide,
Tell me why thus I rave about these groves!
Mute thou remainest, mute! Yet I can read
A wondrous lesson in thy silent face:
Knowledge enormous[18] makes a god of me.
Names, deeds, grey legends, dire events, rebellions,
Majesties, sovran[19] voices, agonies,
Creations and destroyings, all at once
Pour into the wide hollows of my brain
And deify me, as if some blithe wine
Or bright elixir peerless I had drunk,
And so become immortal.' Thus the god,
While his enkindled eyes, with level glance
Beneath his white soft temples, steadfast kept
Trembling with light upon Mnemosyne.
Soon wild commotions shook him, and made flush
All the immortal fairness of his limbs,
Most like the struggle at the gate of death;
Or liker still to one who should take leave
Of pale immortal death, and with a pang
As hot as death's is chill, with fierce convulse[20]
Die into life. So young Apollo anguished;
His very hair, his golden tresses famed
Kept undulation round his eager neck.
During the pain Mnemosyne upheld
Her arms as one who prophesied. At length
Apollo shrieked – and lo! from all his limbs
Celestial[21]...

## Notes

[16] *alarum* turmoil.

[17] *aching* longing.

[18] *Knowledge enormous* Knowledge of suffering has made a god of Apollo. See Keats's admiring comments on Wordsworth for his ability to portray a world 'full of misery and heartbreak, pain, sickness, and oppression'.

[19] *sovran* sovereign.

[20] *convulse* convulsion.

[21] In his annotated copy of 'Endymion' (1818), Reviewing the poem, Leigh Hunt remarked: 'If any living poet could finish this fragment, we believe it is the author himself. But perhaps he feels that he ought not' (*The Indicator*, 2 and 9 August 1820). By the time those comments were published Keats was suffering frequent episodes of blood-spitting, and was preparing his final departure for Italy.

## *The Eve of St Agnes* (composed 18 January–2 February 1819)[1]

I

St. Agnes' Eve – ah, bitter chill it was!
The owl, for all his feathers, was a-cold;
The hare limped trembling through the frozen grass,
And silent was the flock in woolly fold.
Numb were the beadsman's[2] fingers, while he told[3]
His rosary, and while his frosted breath,
Like pious incense from a censer old,
Seemed taking flight for heaven, without a death,
Past the sweet Virgin's picture, while his prayer he saith.

II

His prayer he saith, this patient, holy man;
Then takes his lamp and riseth from his knees,
And back returneth, meagre,[4] barefoot, wan,
Along the chapel aisle by slow degrees.
The sculptured dead on each side seem to freeze,
Imprisoned in black, purgatorial rails;
Knights, ladies, praying in dumb orat'ries,[5]
He passeth by; and his weak spirit fails
To think how they may ache in icy hoods and mails.

III

Northward he turneth through a little door,
And scarce three steps ere music's golden tongue
Flattered to tears this aged man and poor;
But no – already had his deathbell rung,
The joys of all his life were said and sung –
His was harsh penance on St Agnes' Eve:
Another way he went, and soon among
Rough ashes sat he for his soul's reprieve,[6]
And all night kept awake, for sinners' sake to grieve.

## Notes

The Eve of St Agnes

[1] The inspiration for this poem was the superstition that on St Agnes' Eve (20 January) virgins might use various means of divination to conjure up an image of their future husbands. Keats originally composed the poem between 18 January and 2 February 1819; he revised it in September, much to the dismay of Woodhouse, who communicated his feelings to Keats's publishers, Taylor and Hessey. Although Woodhouse later noted that 'Keats left it to his publishers to adopt which [alterations] they pleased', Keats went through the proofs of the poem as printed in 1820, and insisted that some of the revisions be allowed to stand. Some of the more controversial revisions, not included in 1820, are given in footnotes.

[2] *beadsman* one paid to pray for others.

[3] *told* counted.

[4] *meagre* thin.

[5] *Knights…orat'ries* Keats probably saw the sculptured effigies on the tombstones in Chichester Cathedral, January 1819. An oratory is a small chapel.

[6] *reprieve* redemption.

IV

That ancient beadsman heard the prelude[7] soft,
And so it chanced, for many a door was wide
From hurry to and fro. Soon, up aloft,
The silver, snarling trumpets 'gan to chide;
The level chambers, ready with their pride,
Were glowing to receive a thousand guests;
The carved angels, ever eager-eyed,
Stared, where upon their heads the cornice[8] rests,
With hair blown back, and wings put crosswise on their breasts.

V

At length burst in the argent[9] revelry,
With plume, tiara, and all rich array,
Numerous as shadows haunting fairily
The brain, new stuffed in youth, with triumphs gay
Of old romance. These let us wish away,
And turn, sole-thoughted, to one lady there,
Whose heart had brooded all that wintry day
On love, and winged St Agnes' saintly care,
As she had heard old dames full many times declare.

VI

They told her how, upon St Agnes' Eve,
Young virgins might have visions of delight,
And soft adorings from their loves receive
Upon the honeyed middle of the night,
If ceremonies due they did aright –
As, supperless to bed they must retire,
And couch supine their beauties, lily-white;
Nor look behind, nor sideways, but require
Of heaven with upward eyes for all that they desire.[10]

VII

Full of this whim was thoughtful Madeline.
The music, yearning like a god in pain,
She scarcely heard; her maiden eyes divine,
Fixed on the floor, saw many a sweeping train[11]
Pass by – she heeded not at all; in vain
Came many a tiptoe, amorous cavalier,
And back retired, not cooled by high disdain,
But she saw not; her heart was otherwhere.
She sighed for Agnes' dreams, the sweetest of the year.

## Notes

[7] *prelude* introductory music.

[8] *cornice* ornamental moulding between the wall and ceiling.

[9] *argent* silver.

[10] At this point in the manuscript version of the poem, Keats inserted an additional stanza, intended to clarify the narrative:

> 'Twas said her future lord would there appear
> Offering, as sacrifice (all in the dream),
> Delicious food, even to her lips brought near,
> Viands, and wine, and fruit, and sugared cream,
> To touch her palate with the fine extreme
> Of relish; then soft music heard, and then
> More pleasures followed in a dizzy stream,
> Palpable almost; then to wake again
> Warm in the virgin morn, no weeping Magdalen.

[11] *train* long skirts and robes sweeping along the floor.

VIII

She danced along with vague, regardless eyes;
Anxious her lips, her breathing quick and short.
The hallowed hour was near at hand: she sighs
Amid the timbrels[12] and the thronged resort
Of whisperers in anger, or in sport,
Mid looks of love, defiance, hate, and scorn,
Hoodwinked with fairy fancy – all amort,[13]
Save to St Agnes and her lambs unshorn,[14]
And all the bliss to be before tomorrow morn.

IX

So, purposing each moment to retire,
She lingered still. Meantime, across the moors
Had come young Porphyro, with heart on fire
For Madeline. Beside the portal doors,
Buttressed from moonlight,[15] stands he, and implores
All saints to give him sight of Madeline
But for one moment in the tedious hours,
That he might gaze and worship all unseen,
Perchance speak, kneel, touch, kiss – in sooth such things have been.

X

He ventures in – let no buzzed whisper tell;
All eyes be muffled, or a hundred swords
Will storm his heart, love's fev'rous citadel.
For him those chambers held barbarian hordes,[16]
Hyena foemen, and hot-blooded lords
Whose very dogs would execrations howl
Against his lineage;[17] not one breast affords
Him any mercy in that mansion foul,
Save one old beldame,[18] weak in body and in soul.

XI

Ah, happy chance! The aged creature came,
Shuffling along with ivory-headed wand
To where he stood, hid from the torch's flame
Behind a broad hall-pillar, far beyond
The sound of merriment and chorus bland.[19]
He startled her; but soon she knew his face,
And grasped his fingers in her palsied hand,
Saying, 'Mercy, Porphyro! Hie thee from this place;
They are all here tonight, the whole bloodthirsty race!

## Notes

[12] *timbrels* tambourines.

[13] *amort* listless, inanimate.

[14] *her lambs unshorn* The Feast of St Agnes is celebrated, 21 January, at Sant' Agnese fuori le Mura in Rome by the presentation and blessing of two unshorn lambs.

[15] *Buttressed from moonlight* Porphyro stands in the shade of a buttress.

[16] *barbarian hordes* the barbarians who attacked Rome.

[17] *Against his lineage* Madeline's and Porphyro's families are at war.

[18] *beldame* old lady.

[19] *bland* soothing.

XII

Get hence! Get hence! There's dwarfish Hildebrand –
He had a fever late, and in the fit
He cursed thee and thine, both house and land;
Then there's that old Lord Maurice, not a whit
More tame for his grey hairs. Alas me! Flit,
Flit like a ghost away!' 'Ah, gossip[20] dear,
We're safe enough; here in this armchair sit
And tell me how –' 'Good Saints! Not here, not here;
Follow me, child, or else these stones will be thy bier.'

XIII

He followed through a lowly arched way,
Brushing the cobwebs with his lofty plume,
And as she muttered, 'Wel-a – wel-a-day!'[21]
He found him in a little moonlight room,
Pale, latticed, chill, and silent as a tomb.
'Now tell me where is Madeline', said he,
'Oh tell me, Angela, by the holy loom
Which none but secret sisterhood may see,
When they St Agnes' wool are weaving piously.'[22]

XIV

'St Agnes! Ah! It is St Agnes' Eve –
Yet men will murder upon holy days!
Thou must hold water in a witch's sieve
And be liege-lord[23] of all the elves and fays
To venture so; it fills me with amaze
To see thee, Porphyro! St Agnes' Eve!
God's help! My lady fair the conjuror plays[24]
This very night. Good angels her deceive![25]
But let me laugh awhile, I've mickle[26] time to grieve.'

XV

Feebly she laugheth in the languid moon,
While Porphyro upon her face doth look
Like puzzled urchin on an aged crone
Who keepeth closed a wondrous riddle-book,
As spectacled she sits in chimney nook.
But soon his eyes grew brilliant, when she told
His lady's purpose; and he scarce could brook[27]
Tears, at the thought of those enchantments cold,[28]
And Madeline asleep in lap of legends old.

## Notes

[20] *gossip* talkative old lady.

[21] *Wel-a – wel-a-day* Keats is probably recalling Coleridge, 'Christabel' 252. It was a fairly recent publication, having been issued at Byron's request in 1816, eighteen years after Coleridge began to write it.

[22] *by the holy loom…piously* The wool from the sheep presented and blessed on The Feast of St Agnes is spun and woven by nuns.

[23] *liege-lord* master.

[24] *the conjuror plays* Madeline is attempting to conjure visions of her future husband.

[25] *Good angels her deceive* Let angels send her instead good dreams.

[26] *mickle* much.

[27] *brook* restrain.

[28] *enchantments cold* If Madeline is successful she will see only cold visions, not a living being.

XVI

Sudden a thought came like a full-blown rose,
Flushing his brow, and in his pained heart
Made purple riot;[29] then doth he propose
A stratagem that makes the beldame start:
'A cruel man and impious thou art –
Sweet lady, let her pray, and sleep, and dream
Alone with her good angels, far apart
From wicked men like thee. Go, go! I deem
Thou canst not surely be the same that thou didst seem.'

XVII

'I will not harm her, by all saints I swear',
Quoth Porphyro, 'Oh may I ne'er find grace
When my weak voice shall whisper its last prayer,
If one of her soft ringlets I displace,
Or look with ruffian passion in her face;
Good Angela, believe me by these tears,
Or I will, even in a moment's space,
Awake, with horrid shout, my foemen's ears,
And beard[30] them, though they be more fanged than wolves and bears.'

XVIII

'Ah, why wilt thou affright a feeble soul?
A poor, weak, palsy-stricken, churchyard thing,
Whose passing-bell[31] may ere the midnight toll;
Whose prayers for thee, each morn and evening,
Were never missed!' Thus plaining, doth she bring
A gentler speech from burning Porphyro;
So woeful, and of such deep sorrowing,
That Angela gives promise she will do
Whatever he shall wish, betide her weal or woe[32] –

XIX

Which was to lead him, in close secrecy,
Even to Madeline's chamber, and there hide
Him in a closet, of such privacy
That he might see her beauty unespied,
And win perhaps that night a peerless bride,
While legioned fairies paced the coverlet
And pale enchantment held her sleepy-eyed.
Never on such a night have lovers met,
Since Merlin paid his Demon all the monstrous debt.[33]

Notes

[29] *Made purple riot* i.e. made his heart beat excitedly.

[30] *beard* defy.

[31] *passing-bell* death-bell.

[32] *betide her weal or woe* whether good or ill befalls her.

[33] *Since Merlin paid his Demon all the monstrous debt* The precise reference of this line has puzzled commentators. Merlin was the son of a Welsh princess and a demon-father, from whom he inherited his magical powers.

XX

'It shall be as thou wishest', said the Dame,
'All cates[34] and dainties shall be stored there
Quickly on this feast-night; by the tambour frame[35]
Her own lute thou wilt see. No time to spare,
For I am slow and feeble, and scarce dare
On such a catering trust my dizzy head.
Wait here, my child, with patience; kneel in prayer
The while. Ah! Thou must needs the lady wed,
Or may I never leave my grave among the dead.'

XXI

So saying, she hobbled off with busy fear.
The lover's endless minutes slowly passed;
The dame returned, and whispered in his ear
To follow her, with aged eyes aghast
From fright of dim espial.[36] Safe at last,
Through many a dusky gallery, they gain
The maiden's chamber, silken, hushed, and chaste,
Where Porphyro took covert,[37] pleased amain.
His poor guide hurried back with agues in her brain.

XXII

Her falt'ring hand upon the balustrade,
Old Angela was feeling for the stair,
When Madeline, St Agnes' charmed maid,[38]
Rose, like a missioned spirit, unaware.
With silver taper's light, and pious care,
She turned, and down the aged gossip led
To a safe level matting. Now prepare,
Young Porphyro, for gazing on that bed:
She comes, she comes again, like ring-dove frayed[39] and fled.

XXIII

Out went the taper as she hurried in;
Its little smoke, in pallid moonshine, died.
She closed the door, she panted, all akin
To spirits of the air, and visions wide –
No uttered syllable, or woe betide![40]
But to her heart, her heart was voluble,[41]
Paining with eloquence her balmy[42] side,
As though a tongueless nightingale should swell
Her throat in vain, and die, heart-stifled, in her dell.

## Notes

[34] *cates* delicacies.

[35] *tambour frame* embroidery frame.

[36] *aghast…dim espial* terrified of not being able to see the dangers around them.

[37] *took covert* hid himself.

[38] *maid* maiden.

[39] *frayed* frightened.

[40] *No uttered syllable, or woe betide* If she speaks she will break the spell.

[41] *voluble* beating fast with excitement.

[42] *balmy* soft and fragrant.

XXIV

A casement high and triple-arched there was,
All garlanded with carven imag'ries[43]
Of fruits, and flowers, and bunches of knot-grass,
And diamonded with panes of quaint device,
Innumerable of stains and splendid dyes,
As are the tiger-moth's deep-damasked wings;
And in the midst, 'mong thousand heraldries,
And twilight saints, and dim emblazonings,
A shielded scutcheon[44] blushed with blood of queens and kings.

XXV

Full on this casement[45] shone the wintry moon,
And threw warm gules[46] on Madeline's fair breast,
As down she knelt for heaven's grace and boon;[47]
Rose-bloom fell on her hands, together pressed,
And on her silver cross soft amethyst,
And on her hair a glory,[48] like a saint:
She seemed a splendid angel, newly dressed,
Save wings, for heaven. Porphyro grew faint;
She knelt, so pure a thing, so free from mortal taint.

XXVI

Anon his heart revives; her vespers[49] done,
Of all its wreathed pearls her hair she frees,
Unclasps her warmed jewels one by one,
Loosens her fragrant bodice – by degrees
Her rich attire creeps rustling to her knees.
Half-hidden, like a mermaid in seaweed,
Pensive awhile she dreams awake, and sees
In fancy, fair St Agnes in her bed,
But dares not look behind, or all the charm is fled.

XXVII

Soon, trembling in her soft and chilly nest,
In sort of wakeful swoon, perplexed she lay,
Until the poppied warmth of sleep oppressed
Her soothed limbs, and soul fatigued away –
Flown like a thought, until the morrow-day,
Blissfully havened both from joy and pain,
Clasped like a missal where swart paynims pray;[50]
Blinded alike from sunshine and from rain,
As though a rose should shut, and be a bud again.

Notes

[43] *imag'ries* designs.
[44] *shielded scutcheon* coat-of-arms with royal quarterings on a field of gules.
[45] *casement* window.
[46] *gules* red light.
[47] *boon* blessing.
[48] *glory* halo.
[49] *vespers* evening prayers.
[50] *Clasped like a missal where swart paynims pray* clasped like a prayer-book carried by a believer through a pagan country.

XXVIII

Stol'n to this paradise, and so entranced,
Porphyro gazed upon her empty dress,
And listened to her breathing, if it chanced
To wake into a slumberous tenderness;
Which when he heard, that minute did he bless,
And breathed himself, then from the closet crept,
Noiseless as fear in a wide wilderness –
And over the hushed carpet, silent stepped
And 'tween the curtains peeped, where lo! – how fast she slept.

XXIX

Then by the bedside, where the faded moon
Made a dim, silver twilight, soft he set
A table, and, half anguished, threw thereon
A cloth of woven crimson, gold, and jet.
Oh for some drowsy Morphean amulet![51]
The boisterous, midnight, festive clarion,[52]
The kettle-drum, and far-heard clarionet,
Affray his ears, though but in dying tone;
The hall door shuts again, and all the noise is gone.

XXX

And still she slept an azure-lidded sleep
In blanched linen, smooth and lavendered,
While he from forth the closet brought a heap
Of candied apple, quince, and plum, and gourd;[53]
With jellies soother[54] than the creamy curd,
And lucent syrups tinct with cinnamon;[55]
Manna[56] and dates, in argosy[57] transferred
From Fez;[58] and spiced dainties, every one
From silken Samarcand to cedared Lebanon.

XXXI

These delicates he heaped with glowing hand
On golden dishes and in baskets bright
Of wreathed silver; sumptuous they stand
In the retired quiet of the night,
Filling the chilly room with perfume light.
'And now, my love, my seraph fair, awake!
Thou art my heaven, and I thine eremite.[59]
Open thine eyes, for meek St Agnes' sake,
Or I shall drowse beside thee, so my soul doth ache.'

## Notes

51 *Morphean amulet* sleeping pill.
52 *clarion* trumpet.
53 *gourd* melon.
54 *soother* more soothing.
55 *lucent syrups tinct with cinnamon* clear syrups tinged with cinnamon.
56 *Manna* probably an exotic fruit.
57 *argosy* large merchant ship.
58 *Fez* in northern Morocco.
59 *eremite* hermit.

XXXII

Thus whispering, his warm, unnerved[60] arm
Sank in her pillow. Shaded was her dream
By the dusk curtains; 'twas a midnight charm
Impossible to melt as iced stream.
The lustrous salvers in the moonlight gleam,
Broad golden fringe[61] upon the carpet lies;
It seemed he never, never could redeem
From such a steadfast spell his lady's eyes;
So mused awhile, entoiled in woofed[62] fantasies.

XXXIII

Awakening up, he took her hollow lute;
Tumultuous, and, in chords that tenderest be,
He played an ancient ditty, long since mute,
In Provence called, 'La belle dame sans mercy',[63]
Close to her ear touching the melody –
Wherewith disturbed, she uttered a soft moan.
He ceased – she panted quick – and suddenly
Her blue affrayed[64] eyes wide open shone;
Upon his knees he sank, pale as smooth-sculptured stone.

XXXIV

Her eyes were open, but she still beheld,
Now wide awake, the vision of her sleep –
There was a painful change, that nigh expelled
The blisses of her dream so pure and deep.
At which fair Madeline began to weep
And moan forth witless words with many a sigh,
While still her gaze on Porphyro would keep;
Who knelt, with joined hands and piteous eye,
Fearing to move or speak, she looked so dreamingly.

XXXV

'Ah, Porphyro!' said she, 'but even now
Thy voice was at sweet tremble in mine ear,
Made tuneable with every sweetest vow,
And those sad eyes were spiritual[65] and clear.
How changed thou art! How pallid, chill, and drear!
Give me that voice again, my Porphyro,
Those looks immortal, those complainings dear!
Oh leave me not in this eternal woe,
For if thou diest, my love, I know not where to go.'

## Notes

[60] *unnerved* weak.
[61] *golden fringe* of the tablecloth.
[62] *woofed* woven.
[63] *La belle dame sans mercy* title of a poem by Alain Chartier, 1424 – as well as one by Keats.
[64] *affrayed* startled.
[65] *spiritual* lacking bodily substance.

XXXVI

Beyond a mortal man impassioned far
At these voluptuous accents, he arose
Ethereal, flushed, and like a throbbing star
Seen mid the sapphire heaven's deep repose;
Into her dream he melted, as the rose
Blendeth its odour with the violet –
Solution sweet.[66] Meantime the frost-wind blows
Like love's alarum pattering the sharp sleet
Against the window-panes; St Agnes' moon hath set.

XXXVII

'Tis dark; quick pattereth the flaw-blown sleet.[67]
'This is no dream, my bride, my Madeline!'
'Tis dark; the iced gusts still rave and beat.
'No dream, alas! Alas, and woe is mine!
Porphyro will leave me here to fade and pine.
Cruel! What traitor could thee hither bring?
I curse not, for my heart is lost in thine,
Though thou forsakest a deceived thing,
A dove forlorn and lost with sick unpruned[68] wing.'

XXXVIII

'My Madeline! Sweet dreamer! Lovely bride!
Say, may I be for aye thy vassal blessed?
Thy beauty's shield, heart-shaped and vermeil dyed?
Ah, silver shrine, here will I take my rest
After so many hours of toil and quest,
A famished pilgrim, saved by miracle.
Though I have found, I will not rob thy nest,
Saving of thy sweet self – if thou think'st well
To trust, fair Madeline, to no rude infidel.

XXXIX

Hark! 'Tis an elfin-storm from fairy land,
Of haggard seeming,[69] but a boon[70] indeed.
Arise, arise! The morning is at hand;

## Notes

[66] The revised version of lines 314–22 reads:

See, while she speaks, his arms encroaching slow,
Have zoned her, heart to heart – loud, loud the dark
winds blow!
For on the midnight came a tempest fell;
More sooth, for that his quick rejoinder flows
Into her burning ear – and still the spell
Unbroken guards her in serene repose.
With her wild dream he mingled, as a rose
Marryeth its odour to a violet.
Still, still she dreams; louder the frost-wind blows ...

[67] *flaw-blown sleet* sleet blown by a sudden, tempestuous gust of wind.

[68] *unpruned* unpreened.

[69] *haggard seeming* wild appearance.

[70] *boon* blessing.

The bloated wassaillers will never heed.
Let us away, my love, with happy speed;
There are no ears to hear, or eyes to see,
Drowned all in Rhenish[71] and the sleepy mead.
Awake! Arise, my love, and fearless be,
For o'er the southern moors I have a home for thee.'

XL

She hurried at his words, beset with fears,
For there were sleeping dragons[72] all around,
At glaring watch, perhaps, with ready spears;
Down the wide stairs a darkling[73] way they found.
In all the house was heard no human sound;
A chain-drooped lamp was flickering by each door;
The arras,[74] rich with horseman, hawk, and hound
Fluttered in the besieging wind's uproar,
And the long carpets rose along the gusty floor.

XLI

They glide, like phantoms, into the wide hall;
Like phantoms to the iron porch they glide,
Where lay the porter, in uneasy sprawl,
With a huge empty flagon by his side;
The wakeful bloodhound rose and shook his hide,
But his sagacious eye an inmate owns.
By one, and one, the bolts full easy slide,
The chains lie silent on the footworn stones –
The key turns, and the door upon its hinges groans.

XLII

And they are gone – aye, ages long ago
These lovers fled away into the storm.
That night the Baron dreamt of many a woe,
And all his warrior-guests, with shade and form
Of witch and demon, and large coffin-worm,
Were long be-nightmared. Angela the old
Died palsy-twitched, with meagre face deform;
The beadsman, after thousand aves told,
For aye unsought for, slept among his ashes cold.

## Notes

[71] *Rhenish* wine from the Rhine valley.

[72] *dragons* dragoons.

[73] *darkling* dark.

[74] *arras* tapestry.

# *Journal-Letter from John Keats to George and Georgiana Keats, 14 February–3 May 1819* (extracts)[1]

[16 April 1819] Last Sunday I took a walk towards Highgate and, in the lane that winds by the side of Lord Mansfield's park, I met Mr Green, our demonstrator at Guy's, in conversation with Coleridge.[2] I joined them, after enquiring by a look whether it would be agreeable. I walked with him at his alderman[3]-after-dinner pace for near two miles, I suppose. In those two miles he broached a thousand things; let me see if I can give you a list. Nightingales, poetry – on poetical sensation – metaphysics – different genera and species of dreams – nightmare – a dream accompanied by a sense of touch – single and double touch – a dream related – first and second consciousness – the difference explained between will and volition – so many metaphysicians from a want of smoking – the second consciousness – monsters – the kraken[4] – mermaids – Southey believes in them – Southey's belief too much diluted – a ghost story – Good morning – I heard his voice as he came towards me – I heard it as he moved away – I had heard it all the interval (if it may be called so). He was civil enough to ask me to call on him at Highgate[5] goodnight! It looks so much like rain I shall not go to town to day, but put it off till tomorrow....

[21 April 1819] The common cognomen[6] of this world among the misguided and superstitious is 'a vale of tears', from which we are to be redeemed by a certain arbitrary interposition of God and taken to Heaven. What a little, circumscribed, straitened notion! Call the world, if you please, 'the Vale of Soul-Making'. Then you will find out the use of the world. (I am speaking now in the highest terms for human nature, admitting it to be immortal – which I will here take for granted for the purpose of showing a thought which has struck me concerning it.) I say 'Soul-Making' soul, as distinguished from an intelligence – there may be intelligences or sparks of the divinity in millions, but they are not souls till they acquire identities, till each one is personality itself.

Intelligences are atoms of perception. They know and they see and they are pure – in short, they are God. How then are souls to be made? How then are these sparks which are God to have identity[7] given them – so as ever to possess a bliss peculiar to each one's individual existence? How, but by the medium of a world like this? This point I sincerely wish to consider because I think it a grander system of salvation than the Christian religion – or rather it is a system of spirit-creation. This is effected by three grand materials acting the one upon the other for a series of years. These three materials are the intelligence; the human heart (as distinguished from intelligence or mind); and the world or elemental space suited for the proper action of mind and heart on each other for the purpose of forming the soul or intelligence destined to possess the sense of identity. I can scarcely express what I but dimly perceive, and yet I think I perceive it. That you may judge the more clearly I will put it in the most homely form possible: I will call the *world* a school instituted for the purpose of teaching little children to read; I will call the *human heart* the hornbook[8] used in that school; and I will call the *child able to read it* the soul made from that school and its hornbook.

## Notes

Journal-Letter from John Keats to George and Georgiana Keats

[1] The lengthy journal-letter from which these two extracts are taken is one of Keats's most entertaining and illuminating.

[2] This meeting took place in the grounds of Kenwood House, seat of William Murray, Lord Mansfield (1705–93). Joseph Henry Green (1791–1863) was Coleridge's literary executor, and had been Keats's demonstrator at Guy's Hospital, 1815–16.

[3] *alderman* '[portly, elderly] dignitary'.

[4] *kraken* mythical sea-monster of enormous size.

[5] Coleridge was at this time resident at Highgate in north London, at the home of Dr James Gillman.

[6] *cognomen* nickname.

[7] *identity* Rollins suggests that Keats must have been reading John Locke's *Essay Concerning Human Understanding* (1690), Book II, chapter 27, 'Of Identity or Diversity'.

[8] *hornbook* In Keats's day, children learned the alphabet from a leaf of paper mounted on a piece of wood with a handle. The paper was protected by a thin piece of horn.

Do you not see how necessary a world of pains and troubles is to school an intelligence and make it a soul, a place where the heart must feel and suffer in a thousand diverse ways? Not merely is the heart a hornbook, it is the mind's Bible, it is the mind's experience, it is the teat from which the mind or intelligence sucks its identity. As various as the lives of men are, so various become their souls, and thus does God make individual beings, souls, identical souls of the sparks of his own essence. This appears to me a faint sketch of a system of salvation which does not affront our reason and humanity; I am convinced that many difficulties which Christians labour under would vanish before it.

There is one which even now strikes me: the salvation of children. In them the spark or intelligence returns to God without any identity, it having had no time to learn of, and be altered by, the heart – or seat of the human passions. It is pretty generally suspected that the Christian scheme has been copied from the ancient Persian and Greek philosophers. Why may they not have made this simple thing even more simple for common apprehension, by introducing mediators and personages in the same manner as in the heathen mythology abstractions are personified? Seriously, I think it probable that this system of soul-making may have been the parent of all the more palpable and personal schemes of redemption, among the Zoroastrians,[9] the Christians, and the Hindus.[10] For as one part of the human species must have their carved Jupiter, so another part must have the palpable and named mediator and saviour – their Christ, their Oromanes,[11] and their Vishnu.[12]

If what I have said should not be plain enough, as I fear it may not be, I will put you in the place where I began in this series of thoughts. I mean, I began by seeing how man was formed by circumstances – and what are circumstances, but touchstones[13] of his heart? And what are touchstones, but provings of his heart? And what are provings of his heart, but fortifiers or alterers of his nature? And what is his altered nature, but his soul? And what was his soul before it came into the world and had these provings and alterations and perfectionings? An intelligence without identity – and how is this identity to be made? Through the medium of the heart? And how is the heart to become this medium, but in a world of circumstances?

## *La Belle Dame Sans Merci: A Ballad* (composed 21 April 1819)[1]

I

Oh what can ail thee, knight-at-arms,
Alone and palely loitering?
The sedge has withered from the lake,
And no birds sing.

## Notes

[9] *Zoroastrians* followers of the Zoroastrian religion, which originated in India and spread to Persia (modern-day Iran).

[10] For Keats, Christianity derives from ancient philosophies, offering a redemptive scheme which is as valid as Hinduism and Zoroastrianism.

[11] *Oromanes* Oromanes or Ahriman is the evil spirit in the dualistic doctrine of Zoroastrianism, who is opposed to Ormuzd, the deity of light. Keats is thus mistaken in thinking of him as a 'mediator and saviour'. Numerous sources for Keats's knowledge of Oromanes are suggested. Rollins suggests that he was probably an admirer of J.R. Planché's *Abudah, or the Talisman of Oromanes*, performed during Easter 1819 in London. Ronald Tetreault points out to me that in 1813–16 Thomas Love Peacock projected (and wrote part of ) a twelve-Book epic poem entitled *Ahrimanes*, about which Keats may have known.

[12] *Vishnu* preserver of the universe in Hindu mythology.

[13] *touchstones* anything that can be used to test the authenticity of something else.

La Belle Dame Sans Merci

[1] The poem's title derives from Alain Chartier's poem of 1424, which existed in a translation believed in Keats's day to be by Chaucer. Keats's poem, believed to be one of his finest, was published in a revised version in Hunt's magazine *The Indicator*, 10 May 1820, over the signature, 'Caviare'. It is widely agreed that the manuscript version, published here, is the better of the two.

2

Oh what can ail thee, knight-at-arms,
So haggard and so woe-begone?
The squirrel's granary is full,
And the harvest's done.

3

I see a lily on thy brow
With anguish moist and fever dew,
And on thy cheeks a fading rose
Fast withereth too.

4

I met a lady in the meads,
Full beautiful – a fairy's child;
Her hair was long, her foot was light,
And her eyes were wild.

5

I made a garland for her head,
And bracelets too, and fragrant zone;[2]
She looked at me as she did love,
And made sweet moan.

6

I set her on my pacing steed,
And nothing else saw all day long,
For sidelong would she bend, and sing
A fairy's song.

7

She found me roots of relish sweet,
And honey wild and manna dew,[3]
And sure in language strange she said,
'I love thee true'.

8

She took me to her elfin grot
And there she wept, and sighed full sore,
And there I shut her wild wild eyes
With kisses four.[4]

## Notes

[2] *fragrant zone* belt made out of flowers.

[3] *honey wild and manna dew* Keats is recalling the conclusion of Coleridge's 'Kubla Khan': 'For he on honey-dew hath fed / And drank the milk of paradise.'

[4] *kisses four* Sending this poem to his brother George, Keats wrote: 'Why four kisses? you will say. Why four? Because I wish to restrain the headlong impetuosity of my Muse. She would have fain said "score" without hurting the rhyme – but we temper the imagination (as the critics say) with judgment. I was obliged to choose an even number, that both eyes might have fair play: and to speak truly I think two a piece quite sufficient. Suppose I had said "seven"? There would have been three and a half apiece, a very awkward affair'.

9

And there she lullèd me asleep,
   And there I dreamed – ah, woe betide! –
The latest dream I ever dreamed
      On the cold hill's side.

10

I saw pale kings and princes too,
   Pale warriors, death-pale were they all;
They cried, 'La belle dame sans merci
      Hath thee in thrall!'

11

I saw their starved lips in the gloam[5]
   With horrid warning gapèd wide,
And I awoke and found me here
      On the cold hill's side.

12

And this is why I sojourn here,
   Alone and palely loitering,
Though the sedge is withered from the lake,
      And no birds sing.

## *Ode to Psyche* (composed 21–30 April 1819)[1]

Oh goddess! Hear these tuneless numbers,[2] wrung
   By sweet enforcement and remembrance dear,
And pardon that thy secrets should be sung
   Even into thine own soft-conchèd[3] ear.
Surely I dreamt today, or did I see
   The wingèd Psyche with awakened eyes?
I wandered in a forest thoughtlessly,[4]
   And, on the sudden, fainting with surprise,
Saw two fair creatures, couchèd side by side
   In deepest grass, beneath the whisp'ring roof
Of leaves and trembled blossoms, where there ran
      A brooklet, scarce espied.[5]

## Notes

[5] *gloam* twilight.

Ode to Psyche

[1] According to Keats's source, Lemprière's *Bibliotheca Classica* (1788), Psyche was 'a nymph whom Cupid [Eros] married and carried to a place of bliss, where he long enjoyed her company. Venus put her to death because she had robbed the world of her son; but Jupiter, at the request of Cupid, granted immortality to Psyche. The word signifies *the soul*, and this personification of Psyche is posterior to the Augustan age, though still it is connected with ancient mythology. Psyche is generally represented with the wings of a butterfly, to intimate the lightness of the soul, of which the butterfly is the symbol, and on that account, among the ancients, when a man has just expired, a butterfly appeared fluttering above, as if rising from the mouth of the deceased.'

[2] *tuneless numbers* his poetry.

[3] *soft-conchèd* her ear is shaped like a conch-shell.

[4] *thoughtlessly* without an anxious thought.

[5] *scarce espied* seen only with difficulty.

Mid hushed, cool-rooted flowers, fragrant-eyed,
Blue, silver-white, and budded Tyrian,[6]
They lay calm-breathing on the bedded grass;
Their arms embraced, and their pinions[7] too;
Their lips touched not, but had not bade adieu,
As if disjoined by soft-handed slumber,
And ready still past kisses to outnumber
At tender eye-dawn of aurorean[8] love.
The winged boy[9] I knew;
But who wast thou, oh happy, happy dove?
His Psyche true!

Oh latest born and loveliest vision far
Of all Olympus' faded hierarchy![10]
Fairer than Phoebe's sapphire-regioned star,[11]
Or Vesper,[12] amorous glow-worm of the sky;
Fairer than these, though temple thou hast none,
Nor altar heaped with flowers;
Nor virgin-choir to make delicious moan
Upon the midnight hours;
No voice, no lute, no pipe, no incense sweet
From chain-swung censer teeming;
No shrine, no grove, no oracle, no heat
Of pale-mouthed prophet dreaming.[13]

Oh brightest! though too late for antique vows,
Too, too late for the fond believing lyre,[14]
When holy were the haunted forest boughs,
Holy the air, the water and the fire;
Yet even in these days so far retired
From happy pieties, thy lucent fans,[15]
Fluttering among the faint Olympians,
I see, and sing, by my own eyes inspired.
So let me be thy choir, and make a moan
Upon the midnight hours;
Thy voice, thy lute, thy pipe, thy incense sweet
From swinged censer teeming;
Thy shrine, thy grove, thy oracle, thy heat
Of pale-mouthed prophet dreaming.

Yes, I will be thy priest, and build a fane[16]
In some untrodden region of my mind,
Where branched thoughts, new grown with pleasant pain,
Instead of pines shall murmur in the wind;
Far, far around shall those dark-clustered trees
Fledge the wild-ridged mountains steep by steep;

## Notes

[6] *Tyrian* purple, after the dye made at Tyre.

[7] *pinions* wings.

[8] *aurorean* roseate.

[9] *The winged boy* Cupid.

[10] *Olympus' faded hierarchy* The gods of Olympus are faded because they are no longer believed in.

[11] *Phoebe's sapphire-regioned star* the moon, of which Phoebe is goddess.

[12] *Vesper* evening star.

[13] *No heat…dreaming* There are no prophets inspired to speak on Psyche's behalf.

[14] *fond believing lyre* hymns sung by the unquestioningly devoted.

[15] *lucent fans* shining wings.

[16] *fane* temple.

And there by zephyrs, streams, and birds, and bees,
The moss-lain dryads[17] shall be lulled to sleep;
And in the midst of this wide quietness
A rosy sanctuary will I dress
With the wreathed trellis of a working brain,
With buds, and bells, and stars without a name,
With all the gardener Fancy e'er could feign,[18]
Who, breeding flowers, will never breed the same:
And there shall be for thee all soft delight
That shadowy thought can win –
A bright torch, and a casement[19] ope at night,
To let the warm Love in!

## *Ode to a Nightingale* (composed May 1819)[1]

1

My heart aches, and a drowsy numbness pains
My sense, as though of hemlock[2] I had drunk,
Or emptied some dull opiate to the drains[3]
One minute past,[4] and Lethe-wards[5] had sunk;
'Tis not through envy of thy happy lot,
But being too happy in thine happiness,
That thou, light-winged dryad[6] of the trees,
In some melodious plot
Of beechen green, and shadows numberless,
Singest of summer in full-throated ease.

2

Oh for a draught of vintage![7] that hath been
Cooled a long age in the deep-delved earth,
Tasting of flora and the country green,
Dance, and Provençal song, and sunburnt mirth!
Oh for a beaker full of the warm south,[8]
Full of the true, the blushful Hippocrene,[9]
With beaded bubbles winking at the brim,
And purple-stained mouth;
That I might drink, and leave the world unseen,
And with thee fade away into the forest dim –

## Notes

[17] *dryads* wood-nymphs.
[18] *feign* invent.
[19] *casement* window.

Ode to a Nightingale

[1] Twenty years after the event, Keats's friend Charles Brown recorded how this poem was composed: 'In the spring of 1819 a nightingale had built her nest near my house. Keats felt a tranquil and continual joy in her song; and one morning he took his chair from the breakfast-table to the grass-plot under a plumtree, where he sat for two or three hours. When he came into the house, I perceived he had some scraps of paper in his hand, and these he was quietly thrusting behind the books. On enquiry, I found those scraps, four or five in number, contained his poetic feeling on the song of our nightingale. The writing was not well legible; and it was difficult to arrange the stanzas on so many scraps. With his assistance I succeeded, and this was his "Ode to a Nightingale", a poem which has been the delight of everyone.'
[2] *hemlock* can be used as a sedative; it should be noted that Keats is not saying that he has actually taken hemlock.
[3] *drains* dregs.
[4] *past* ago.
[5] *Lethe-wards* towards Lethe, river of forgetfulness in Hades, from which souls drank to forget their past lives.
[6] *dryad* wood-nymph.
[7] *vintage* wine.
[8] *warm south* wine from the Mediterranean.
[9] *Hippocrene* spring sacred to the Muses on Mt Helicon. Keats means wine.

3

Fade far away, dissolve, and quite forget
What thou among the leaves hast never known,
The weariness,[10] the fever, and the fret
Here, where men sit and hear each other groan;
Where palsy shakes a few, sad, last grey hairs,
Where youth grows pale, and spectre-thin, and dies;[11]
Where but to think is to be full of sorrow
And leaden-eyed despairs;
Where Beauty cannot keep her lustrous eyes,
Or new Love pine at them beyond tomorrow.

4

Away! Away! For I will fly to thee,
Not charioted by Bacchus and his pards,[12]
But on the viewless[13] wings of Poesy,
Though the dull brain perplexes and retards;
Already with thee! Tender is the night,
And haply[14] the Queen Moon is on her throne,
Clustered around by all her starry fays;[15]
But here there is no light
Save what from heaven is with the breezes blown
Through verdurous glooms and winding mossy ways.

5

I cannot see what flowers are at my feet,
Nor what soft incense hangs upon the boughs,
But, in embalmed darkness,[16] guess each sweet
Wherewith the seasonable month[17] endows
The grass, the thicket, and the fruit-tree wild,
White hawthorn, and the pastoral eglantine,
Fast-fading violets covered up in leaves,
And mid-May's eldest child,
The coming musk-rose,[18] full of dewy wine,
The murmurous haunt of flies on summer eves.

6

Darkling[19] I listen; and for many a time
I have been half in love with easeful Death,
Called him soft names in many a mused rhyme,
To take into the air my quiet breath;

## Notes

[10] *weariness* Wordsworth had written of 'hours of weariness' amid the 'din / Of towns and cities' in 'Tintern Abbey' 26–8.

[11] *Where youth…dies* often taken to refer to the death of Tom Keats from consumption, 1 December 1818; cf. Wordsworth, 'Excursion' iv 760: 'While man grows old, and dwindles, and decays.'

[12] *Not charioted by Bacchus and his pards* Keats's source, Lemprière's *Bibliotheca Classica* (1788), recorded that when Bacchus (god of wine) travelled east, he 'was drawn in a chariot by a lion and a tyger and was accompanied by Pan and Silenus and all the satyrs'.

[13] *viewless* invisible.

[14] *haply* perhaps.

[15] *fays* fairies.

[16] *embalmed darkness* The night is full of the scent of plants.

[17] *the seasonable month* May.

[18] *The coming musk-rose* usually flowers in June.

[19] *Darkling* in darkness.

Now more than ever seems it rich to die,
To cease upon the midnight with no pain,
While thou art pouring forth thy soul abroad
In such an ecstasy!
Still wouldst thou sing, and I have ears in vain –
To thy high requiem become a sod.

7

Thou wast not born for death, immortal bird!
No hungry generations tread thee down;
The voice I hear this passing night was heard
In ancient days by emperor and clown:[20]
Perhaps the self-same song that found a path
Through the sad heart of Ruth, when, sick for home,
She stood in tears amid the alien corn;[21]
The same that oft-times hath
Charmed magic casements, opening on the foam
Of perilous seas, in fairy lands forlorn.

8

Forlorn! The very word is like a bell
To toll me back from thee to my sole self!
Adieu! The fancy cannot cheat so well
As she is famed to do, deceiving elf.
Adieu! Adieu! Thy plaintive anthem fades
Past the near meadows, over the still stream,
Up the hillside, and now 'tis buried deep
In the next valley-glades:
Was it a vision, or a waking dream?
Fled is that music – do I wake or sleep?

## *Ode on a Grecian Urn* (composed *c.*May 1819)[1]

1

Thou still unravished bride of quietness,
Thou foster-child of silence and slow time,[2]
Sylvan historian,[3] who canst thus express
A flowery tale more sweetly than our rhyme –

## Notes

[20] *clown* peasant.

[21] *Through the...corn* Ruth was forced, by famine, to leave home and labour in the fields of her kinsman, Boaz (Ruth 2:1–2).

Ode on a Grecian Urn

[1] The inspiration for this poem came from a variety of sources, including the Townley Vase and the Elgin Marbles, both at the British Museum.

[2] *foster-child of silence and slow time* The potter who made the vase is dead, leaving it to be fostered by time and silence.

[3] *Sylvan historian* The vase is a historian because it tells a story; 'sylvan' refers to the pastoral scenes it depicts.

What leaf-fringed legend haunts about thy shape
Of deities or mortals, or of both,
In Tempe or the dales of Arcady?[4]
What men or gods are these? What maidens loath?
What mad pursuit? What struggle to escape?
What pipes and timbrels?[5] What wild ecstasy?

2

Heard melodies are sweet, but those unheard
Are sweeter; therefore, ye soft pipes, play on –
Not to the sensual[6] ear, but, more endeared,
Pipe to the spirit ditties of no tone:
Fair youth, beneath the trees, thou canst not leave
Thy song, nor ever can those trees be bare;
Bold lover, never, never canst thou kiss,
Though winning near the goal – yet do not grieve;
She cannot fade, though thou hast not thy bliss,
For ever wilt thou love, and she be fair!

3

Ah, happy, happy boughs! that cannot shed
Your leaves, nor ever bid the spring adieu;
And, happy melodist, unwearied,
For ever piping songs for ever new;
More happy love, more happy, happy love!
For ever warm and still to be enjoyed,
For ever panting and for ever young;
All breathing human passion far above,
That leaves a heart high-sorrowful and cloyed,
A burning forehead, and a parching tongue.

4

Who are these coming to the sacrifice?
To what green altar, oh mysterious priest,
Lead'st thou that heifer lowing at the skies,
And all her silken flanks with garlands dressed?
What little town by river or seashore,
Or mountain-built with peaceful citadel,
Is emptied of this folk, this pious morn?
And, little town, thy streets for evermore
Will silent be, and not a soul to tell
Why thou art desolate, can e'er return.

## Notes

[4] Tempe and Arcadia, places known in classical times for their beauty and the happiness of their inhabitants.

[5] *timbrels* tambourines.

[6] *sensual* of sense.

5

Oh Attic[7] shape! Fair attitude! With brede[8]
Of marble men and maidens overwrought,[9]
With forest branches and the trodden weed;
Thou, silent form, dost tease us out of thought
As doth eternity. Cold Pastoral!
When old age shall this generation waste,
Thou shalt remain, in midst of other woe
Than ours, a friend to man, to whom thou say'st,
'Beauty is truth, truth beauty'; that is all
Ye know on earth, and all ye need to know.

## *Ode on Melancholy* (composed *c.* May 1819)[1]

1

No, no, go not to Lethe, neither twist
Wolfsbane,[2] tight-rooted, for its poisonous wine;
Nor suffer thy pale forehead to be kissed
By nightshade,[3] ruby grape of Proserpine;[4]
Make not your rosary of yew-berries,[5]
Nor let the beetle, nor the death-moth[6] be
Your mournful Psyche, nor the downy owl
A partner in your sorrow's mysteries;
For shade to shade will come too drowsily,
And drown the wakeful anguish of the soul.

2

But when the melancholy fit shall fall
Sudden from heaven like a weeping cloud,
That fosters the droop-headed flowers all,
And hides the green hill in an April shroud;
Then glut thy sorrow on[7] a morning rose,
Or on the rainbow of the salt sand-wave,
Or on the wealth of globed peonies;
Or if thy mistress some rich anger shows,
Imprison her soft hand, and let her rave,
And feed deep, deep upon her peerless eyes.

## Notes

[7] *Attic* Grecian.

[8] *brede* braid.

[9] *overwrought* fashioned over the surface of the urn.

Ode on Melancholy

[1] When first composed, the poem had the following opening stanza:

Though you should build a bark of dead men's bones,
And rear a phantom gibbet for a mast,
Stitch creeds together for a sail, with groans
To fill it out, bloodstained and aghast;
Although your rudder be a dragon's tail,
Long severed, yet still hard with agony,
Your cordage large uprootings from the skull
Of bald Medusa, certes you would fail
To find the Melancholy – whether she
Dreameth in any isle of Lethe dull.

[2] *Wolfsbane* aconite, a poisonous plant.

[3] *nightshade* a poisonous plant with bright red berries.

[4] *Proserpine* Queen of the Underworld.

[5] *yew-berries* Yew-trees have small red berries which are poisonous.

[6] *death-moth* The death's head moth has markings which resemble a human skull.

[7] *glut…on* enjoy to the full … by thinking of.

3

She dwells with Beauty – Beauty that must die;
And Joy, whose hand is ever at his lips
Bidding adieu; and aching Pleasure nigh,
Turning to poison while the bee-mouth sips.
Aye, in the very temple of Delight
Veiled Melancholy has her sovran shrine,
Though seen of none save him whose strenuous tongue
Can burst Joy's grape against his palate fine;
His soul shall taste the sadness of her might,
And be among her cloudy trophies hung.

## *Ode on Indolence* (composed between 19 March and 9 June 1819)[1]

*They toil not, neither do they spin.*[2]

I

One morn before me were three figures seen,
With bowed necks and joined hands, side-faced;
And one behind the other stepped serene,
In placid sandals and in white robes graced;
They passed, like figures on a marble urn,
When shifted round to see the other side;
They came again, as when the urn once more
Is shifted round, the first-seen shades return –
And they were strange to me, as may betide
With vases, to one deep in Phidian lore.[3]

2

How is it, shadows, that I knew ye not?
How came ye muffled in so hush[4] a masque?[5]
Was it a silent deep-disguised plot
To steal away, and leave without a task
My idle days? Ripe was the drowsy hour;
The blissful cloud of summer indolence
Benumbed my eyes; my pulse grew less and less;
Pain had no sting, and pleasure's wreath no flower –
Oh why did ye not melt, and leave my sense
Unhaunted quite of all but – nothingness?

Notes

ODE ON INDOLENCE

[1] This poem was not included in Keats's 1820 volume.

[2] Matthew 6:28: 'Consider the lilies of the field, how they grow; they toil not, neither do they spin.'

[3] *Phidian lore* sculpture; Phidias (born *c.*500 BCE) may have designed and probably supervised construction of the Elgin marbles.

[4] *hush* silent.

[5] *masque* procession.

3

A third time passed they by, and, passing, turned
 Each one the face a moment whiles to me;
Then faded, and to follow them I burned
 And ached for wings, because I knew the three:
The first was a fair maid, and Love her name;
 The second was Ambition, pale of cheek
  And ever watchful with fatigued eye;
   The last, whom I love more, the more of blame
Is heaped upon her, maiden most unmeek,
 I knew to be my demon Poesy.

4

They faded, and, forsooth, I wanted wings!
 Oh folly! What is love? And where is it?
And, for that poor ambition – it springs
 From a man's little heart's short fever-fit;[6]
For Poesy! No, she has not a joy –
 At least for me – so sweet as drowsy noons,
  And evenings steeped in honeyed indolence.
   Oh for an age so sheltered from annoy,[7]
That I may never know how change the moons,
 Or hear the voice of busy common sense!

5

A third time came they by – alas, wherefore?
 My sleep had been embroidered with dim dreams;
My soul had been a lawn besprinkled o'er
 With flowers, and stirring shades, and baffled beams;
The morn was clouded, but no shower fell,
 Though in her lids hung the sweet tears of May;
  The open casement pressed a new-leaved vine,
   Let in the budding warmth and throstle's lay –
Oh shadows, 'twas a time to bid farewell!
 Upon your skirts had fallen no tears of mine.

6

So ye three ghosts, adieu! Ye cannot raise
 My head cool-bedded in the flowery grass,
For I would not be dieted with praise –
 A pet-lamb in a sentimental farce![8]
Fade softly from my eyes, and be once more
 In masque-like figures on the dreamy urn;
  Farewell! I yet have visions for the night,
   And for the day faint visions there is store.
Vanish, ye phantoms, from my idle sprite,
 Into the clouds, and never more return!

## Notes

[6] *fever-fit* An echo of *Macbeth* III ii 23: 'After life's fitful fever he sleeps well.'

[7] *annoy* harm.

[8] *For I would not…farce* Keats is saying that praise from reviewers is worthless, as it is as patronizing as the stroking of a lamb.

# *Lamia* (Part I written *c.*28 June and 11 July 1819, Part II written 12 August and *c.*5 September 1819, revised March 1820)[1]

## *Part I*

Upon a time, before the fairy broods
Drove nymph and satyr from the prosperous woods,[2]
Before King Oberon's bright diadem,
Sceptre, and mantle, clasped with dewy gem,
Frighted away the dryads[3] and the fauns
From rushes green, and brakes, and cowslipped lawns,[4]
The ever-smitten Hermes[5] empty left
His golden throne, bent warm on amorous theft.
From high Olympus had he stolen light
On this side of Jove's clouds, to escape the sight
Of his great summoner, and made retreat
Into a forest on the shores of Crete,
For somewhere in that sacred island[6] dwelt
A nymph to whom all hoofed satyrs knelt,
At whose white feet the languid Tritons[7] poured
Pearls, while on land they withered and adored.
Fast by the springs where she to bathe was wont,
And in those meads where sometime she might haunt,
Were strewn rich gifts, unknown to any muse,[8]
Though fancy's casket were unlocked to choose.
'Ah, what a world of love was at her feet!'
So Hermes thought, and a celestial heat
Burnt from his winged heels to either ear,
That from a whiteness, as the lily clear,
Blushed into roses mid his golden hair,
Fallen in jealous curls about his shoulders bare.
   From vale to vale, from wood to wood, he flew,
Breathing upon the flowers his passion new,
And wound with many a river to its head

## Notes

Lamia: Part I

[1] When the poem was published in 1820, Keats added a note providing the source for this poem: '"Philostratus, in his fourth book *de Vita Apollonii*, hath a memorable instance in this kind, which I may not omit, of one Menippus Lycius, a young man twenty-five years of age, that going betwixt Cenchreas and Corinth, met such a phantasm in the habit of a fair gentlewoman, which taking him by the hand, carried him home to her house in the suburbs of Corinth, and told him she was a Phoenician by birth, and if he would tarry with her, he should hear her sing and play, and drink such wine as never any drank, and no man should molest him; but she, being fair and lovely, would live and die with him, that was fair and lovely to behold. The young man, a philosopher, otherwise staid and discreet, able to moderate his passions, though not this of love, tarried with her a while to his great content, and at last married her, to whose wedding, amongst other guests, came Apollonius; who, by some probable conjectures, found her out to be a serpent, a lamia; and that all her furniture was, like Tantalus's gold, described by Homer, no substance but mere illusions. When she saw herself descried, she wept, and desired Apollonius to be silent, but he would not be moved, and thereupon she, plate, house, and all that was in it, vanished in an instant: many thousands took notice of this fact, for it was done in the midst of Greece." Burton's *Anatomy of Melancholy* Part 3. Sect. 2. Memb. 1. Subs. 1.'

[2] *prosperous woods* the woods were more widespread than now.

[3] *dryads* wood-nymphs.

[4] *before the fairy broods…lawns* i.e. before medieval fairy-lore had superseded classical myth.

[5] *The ever-smitten Hermes* or Mercury, messenger of the gods, celebrated for his numerous love affairs.

[6] *sacred island* Crete was sacred as the birthplace of Zeus.

[7] *Tritons* sea-gods – half-man, half-fish.

[8] *unknown to any muse* beyond the imagination of any poet.

To find where this sweet nymph prepared her secret bed –
In vain; the sweet nymph might nowhere be found.
And so he rested on the lonely ground,
Pensive, and full of painful jealousies
Of the wood-gods, and even the very trees.
There as he stood, he heard a mournful voice,
Such as once heard, in gentle heart, destroys
All pain but pity. Thus the lone voice spake:
'When from this wreathed tomb shall I awake?
When move in a sweet body fit for life
And love and pleasure, and the ruddy strife
Of hearts and lips? Ah, miserable me!'
The god, dove-footed, glided silently
Round bush and tree, soft-brushing, in his speed,
The taller grasses and full-flowering weed,
Until he found a palpitating snake,
Bright, and cirque-couchant[9] in a dusky brake.
She was a gordian[10] shape of dazzling hue,
Vermilion-spotted, golden, green, and blue;
Striped like a zebra, freckled like a pard,[11]
Eyed like a peacock, and all crimson barred;
And full of silver moons that, as she breathed,
Dissolved, or brighter shone, or interwreathed
Their lustres with the gloomier tapestries –
So rainbow-sided, touched with miseries,
She seemed at once some penanced lady elf,
Some demon's mistress, or the demon's self.
Upon her crest she wore a wannish fire
Sprinkled with stars, like Ariadne's tiar;[12]
Her head was serpent but – ah, bitter-sweet! –
She had a woman's mouth with all its pearls complete.
And for her eyes: what could such eyes do there
But weep and weep, that they were born so fair? –
As Proserpine[13] still weeps for her Sicilian air.
Her throat was serpent, but the words she spake
Came, as through bubbling honey, for love's sake,
And thus; while Hermes on his pinions lay,
Like a stooped falcon ere he takes his prey.
'Fair Hermes, crowned with feathers, fluttering light,
I had a splendid dream of thee last night:
I saw thee sitting on a throne of gold
Among the gods upon Olympus old,
The only sad one – for thou didst not hear
The soft, lute-fingered Muses chaunting clear,
Nor even Apollo when he sang alone,

## Notes

[9] *cirque-couchant* lying in circular coils.

[10] *gordian* intricately knotted.

[11] *pard* leopard.

[12] *Ariadne's tiar* Ariadne was loved by Bacchus, god of wine. He gave her a crown of seven stars which, after her death, was made into a constellation. Keats probably has in mind Titian's painting, *Bacchus and Ariadne*, now in the National Gallery, London.

[13] Proserpine, gathering flowers in the Vale of Enna in Sicily, was carried off by Pluto, king of the underworld, to be his queen.

Deaf to his throbbing throat's long, long melodious moan.
I dreamt I saw thee, robed in purple flakes,[14]
Break amorous through the clouds, as morning breaks,
And, swiftly as a bright Phoebean dart,[15]
Strike for the Cretan isle – and here thou art!
Too gentle Hermes, hast thou found the maid?'
Whereat the star of Lethe[16] not delayed
His rosy eloquence, and thus enquired:
'Thou smooth-lipped serpent, surely high inspired!
Thou beauteous wreath, with melancholy eyes,
Possess whatever bliss thou canst devise,
Telling me only where my nymph is fled –
Where she doth breathe!' 'Bright planet, thou hast said',
Returned the snake, 'but seal with oaths, fair God!'
'I swear', said Hermes, 'by my serpent rod,
And by thine eyes, and by thy starry crown!'
Light flew his earnest words among the blossoms blown.
Then thus again the brilliance feminine:
'Too frail of heart! for this lost nymph of thine,
Free as the air, invisibly she strays
About these thornless wilds; her pleasant days
She tastes unseen; unseen her nimble feet
Leave traces in the grass and flowers sweet;
From weary tendrils and bowed branches green
She plucks the fruit unseen, she bathes unseen:
And by my power is her beauty veiled
To keep it unaffronted, unassailed
By the love-glances of unlovely eyes,
Of satyrs, fauns, and bleared Silenus'[17] sighs.
Pale grew her immortality, for woe
Of all these lovers, and she grieved so
I took compassion on her, bade her steep
Her hair in weird syrups that would keep
Her loveliness invisible, yet free
To wander as she loves, in liberty.
Thou shalt behold her, Hermes, thou alone,
If thou wilt, as thou swearest, grant my boon!'
    Then once again, the charmed god began
An oath, and through the serpent's ears it ran
Warm, tremulous, devout, psalterian.[18]
Ravished, she lifted her Circean[19] head,
Blushed a live damask, and swift-lisping said:
'I was a woman, let me have once more
A woman's shape, and charming as before.
I love a youth of Corinth – oh the bliss!

## Notes

[14] *purple flakes* fleecy clouds, coloured by the sun.

[15] *Phoebean dart* a ray of the sun, Phoebus being god of the sun.

[16] *the star of Lethe* Hermes, so-called because he led the souls of the dead to Hades over Lethe, the river of forgetfulness.

[17] Silenus, a demi-god of the woods, was foster-father of Bacchus.

[18] *psalterian* like the sound of a psaltery, an antique stringed instrument.

[19] *Circean* Circe was the enchantress who was capable of turning men into animals.

Give me my woman's form, and place me where he is.
Stoop, Hermes, let me breathe upon thy brow,
And thou shalt see thy sweet nymph even now.'
The god on half-shut feathers sank serene,
She breathed upon his eyes, and swift was seen
Of both the guarded nymph near-smiling[20] on the green.
It was no dream – or say a dream it was,
Real are the dreams of gods, and smoothly pass
Their pleasures in a long immortal dream.
One warm, flushed moment, hovering, it might seem
Dashed by the wood-nymph's beauty, so he burned;
Then, lighting on the printless verdure, turned
To the swooned[21] serpent, and with languid arm
Delicate, put to proof the lithe caducean charm.[22]
    So done, upon the nymph his eyes he bent
Full of adoring tears and blandishment,
And towards her stepped; she, like a moon in wane,
Faded before him, cowered, nor could restrain
Her fearful sobs, self-folding like a flower
That faints into itself at evening hour.
But the god fostering her chilled hand,
She felt the warmth, her eyelids opened bland,
And, like new flowers at morning song of bees,
Bloomed, and gave up her honey to the lees;[23]
Into the green-recessed woods they flew,
Nor grew they pale, as mortal lovers do.
    Left to herself, the serpent now began
To change; her elfin blood in madness ran,
Her mouth foamed, and the grass, therewith besprent,[24]
Withered at dew so sweet and virulent.
Her eyes in torture fixed, and anguish drear,
Hot, glazed, and wide, with lid-lashes all sear,[25]
Flashed phosphor and sharp sparks, without one cooling tear.
The colours all inflamed throughout her train,
She writhed about, convulsed with scarlet pain;
A deep volcanian yellow took the place
Of all her milder-mooned body's grace,
And, as the lava ravishes the mead,[26]
Spoilt all her silver mail, and golden brede,
Made gloom of all her frecklings, streaks and bars,
Eclipsed her crescents, and licked up her stars.
So that in moments few she was undressed
Of all her sapphires, greens, and amethyst,
And rubious-argent;[27] of all these bereft,
Nothing but pain and ugliness were left.

## Notes

[20] *near-smiling* smiling nearby.

[21] *swooned* with love.

[22] *lithe caducean charm* an olive staff wound about with two intertwined ('lithe') snakes at one end.

[23] *gave up her honey to the lees* surrendered totally.

[24] *besprent* sprinkled – an archaism even in Keats's day.

[25] *sear* scorched.

[26] *lava ravishes the mead* lava buries and burns the grass.

[27] *rubious-argent* silver embedded with rubies.

Still shone her crown – that vanished, also she
Melted and disappeared as suddenly,
And in the air, her new voice luting soft,
Cried, 'Lycius! Gentle Lycius!' Borne aloft
With the bright mists about the mountains hoar
These words dissolved – Crete's forests heard no more.
   Whither fled Lamia, now a lady bright,
A full-born beauty new and exquisite?
She fled into that valley they pass o'er
Who go to Corinth from Cenchreas' shore,
And rested at the foot of those wild hills,
The rugged founts of the Peraean rills,
And of that other ridge whose barren back
Stretches, with all its mist and cloudy rack,
South-westward to Cleone. There she stood
About a young bird's flutter from a wood,
Fair on a sloping green of mossy tread,
By a clear pool, wherein she passioned
To see herself escaped from so sore ills,
While her robes flaunted[28] with the daffodils.
   Ah, happy Lycius! For she was a maid
More beautiful than ever twisted braid,
Or sighed, or blushed, or on spring-flowered lea
Spread a green kirtle[29] to the minstrelsy –
A virgin purest lipped, yet in the lore
Of love deep learned to the red heart's core;
Not one hour old, yet of sciential[30] brain
To unperplex bliss from its neighbour pain;
Define their pettish limits, and estrange
Their points of contact, and swift counterchange;
Intrigue with the specious chaos, and dispart
Its most ambiguous atoms with sure art,
As though in Cupid's college she had spent
Sweet days a lovely graduate, still unshent,[31]
And kept his rosy terms in idle languishment.
   Why this fair creature chose so fairily
By the wayside to linger, we shall see;
But first 'tis fit to tell how she could muse
And dream, when in the serpent prison-house,
Of all she list, strange or magnificent;
How, ever, where she willed, her spirit went –
Whether to faint Elysium,[32] or where
Down through tress-lifting waves the nereids[33] fair
Wind into Thetis'[34] bower by many a pearly stair,
Or where god Bacchus drains his cups divine,

## Notes

[28] *flaunted* waved vigorously.
[29] *kirtle* woman's gown.
[30] *sciential* wise.
[31] *unshent* unspoilt.
[32] *Elysium* paradisal place of rest where Greek heroes were believed to spend an afterlife revelling and sporting in the sunshine.
[33] *nereids* water-nymphs.
[34] *Thetis* sea-deity, the daughter of Nereus and Doris.

Stretched out at ease beneath a glutinous[35] pine,
Or where in Pluto's[36] gardens palatine[37]
Mulciber's columns gleam in far piazzian line.[38]
And sometimes into cities she would send
Her dream, with feast and rioting to blend;
And once, while among mortals dreaming thus,
She saw the young Corinthian Lycius
Charioting foremost in the envious race
Like a young Jove with calm uneager face
And fell into a swooning love of him.
Now on the moth-time[39] of that evening dim
He would return that way, as well she knew,
To Corinth from the shore – for freshly blew
The eastern soft wind, and his galley now
Grated the quaystones with her brazen prow
In port Cenchreas, from Egina isle
Fresh anchored, whither he had been awhile
To sacrifice to Jove, whose temple there
Waits with high marble doors for blood and incense rare.
Jove heard his vows, and bettered his desire;
For by some freakful chance he made retire
From his companions, and set forth to walk,
Perhaps grown wearied of their Corinth talk.
Over the solitary hills he fared,
Thoughtless at first, but ere eve's star appeared
His fantasy was lost where reason fades,
In the calmed twilight of Platonic shades.[40]
　Lamia beheld him coming, near, more near –
Close to her passing, in indifference drear,
His silent sandals swept the mossy green;
So neighboured to him, and yet so unseen
She stood. He passed, shut up in mysteries,
His mind wrapped like his mantle, while her eyes
Followed his steps, and her neck regal white
Turned, syllabling thus: 'Ah, Lycius bright,
And will you leave me on the hills alone?
Lycius, look back, and be some pity shown!'
He did, not with cold wonder fearingly,
But Orpheus-like at an Eurydice[41] –
For so delicious were the words she sung,
It seemed he had loved them a whole summer long.
And soon his eyes had drunk her beauty up,

## Notes

[35] *glutinous* resinous.

[36] Pluto was king of the underworld.

[37] *palatine* palatial.

[38] *in far piazzian line* the construction resembles a piazza – a square or colonnaded walkway surrounded by buildings. Keats is recalling the construction of Pandemonium by Mulciber (Vulcan) in *Paradise Lost* i 713–15.

[39] *moth-time* early evening.

[40] *In the calm…shades* Lycius begins his walk unthinkingly, but starts to meditate on Plato's mystic philosophy.

[41] Orpheus nearly managed to reclaim his wife, Eurydice, from Hades, but lost her forever when he looked back at her out of curiosity.

Leaving no drop in the bewildering cup,
And still the cup was full – while he, afraid
Lest she should vanish ere his lip had paid
Due adoration, thus began to adore;
Her soft look growing coy, she saw his chain[42] so sure.
'Leave thee alone! Look back! Ah, goddess, see
Whether my eyes can ever turn from thee!
For pity do not this sad heart belie –
Even as thou vanishest so I shall die.
Stay, though a Naiad of the rivers, stay!
To thy far wishes will thy streams obey;
Stay, though the greenest woods be thy domain,
Alone they can drink up the morning rain!
Though a descended Pleiad,[43] will not one
Of thine harmonious sisters keep in tune
Thy spheres,[44] and as thy silver proxy shine?
So sweetly to these ravished ears of mine
Came thy sweet greeting, that if thou shouldst fade
Thy memory will waste me to a shade:
For pity do not melt!'
'If I should stay',
Said Lamia, 'here, upon this floor of clay,
And pain my steps upon these flowers too rough,
What canst thou say or do of charm enough
To dull the nice remembrance of my home?
Thou canst not ask me with thee here to roam
Over these hills and vales, where no joy is –
Empty of immortality and bliss!
Thou art a scholar, Lycius, and must know
That finer spirits cannot breathe below
In human climes, and live. Alas, poor youth,
What taste of purer air hast thou to soothe
My essence? What serener palaces,
Where I may all my many senses please,
And by mysterious sleights a hundred thirsts appease?
It cannot be. Adieu!'
So said, she rose
Tiptoe with white arms spread. He, sick to lose
The amorous promise of her lone complain,[45]
Swooned, murmuring of love, and pale with pain.
The cruel lady, without any show
Of sorrow for her tender favourite's woe –
But rather, if her eyes could brighter be,
With brighter eyes and slow amenity,
Put her new lips to his, and gave afresh

## Notes

[42] *chain* the metaphorical 'chain' of love.

[43] The Pleiades were the seven daughters of Atlas, who became a constellation after death.

[44] *Thy spheres* Reference to the music which the heavenly bodies were believed to make as they circled the earth.

[45] *complain* complaint.

The life she had so tangled in her mesh;
And as he from one trance was wakening
Into another, she began to sing,
Happy in beauty, life, and love, and everything,
A song of love, too sweet for earthly lyres,
While, like held breath, the stars drew in their panting fires.
  And then she whispered in such trembling tone,
As those who, safe together met alone
For the first time through many anguished days,
Use other speech than looks – bidding him raise
His drooping head, and clear his soul of doubt,
For that she was a woman, and without
Any more subtle[46] fluid in her veins
Than throbbing blood, and that the self-same pains
Inhabited her frail-strung heart as his.
And next she wondered how his eyes could miss
Her face so long in Corinth, where, she said,
She dwelt but half retired, and there had led
Days happy as the gold coin could invent
Without the aid of love – yet in content
Till she saw him, as once she passed him by,
Where 'gainst a column he leant thoughtfully
At Venus' temple porch, mid baskets heaped
Of amorous herbs and flowers, newly reaped
Late on that eve, as 'twas the night before
The Adonian feast;[47] whereof she saw no more,
But wept alone those days, for why should she adore?
  Lycius from death awoke into amaze
To see her still, and singing so sweet lays;
Then from amaze into delight he fell
To hear her whisper woman's lore so well;
And every word she spake enticed him on
To unperplexed delight and pleasure known.
Let the mad poets say whate'er they please
Of the sweets of fairies, peris,[48] goddesses;
There is not such a treat among them all,
Haunters of cavern, lake, and waterfall,
As a real woman, lineal indeed
From Pyrrha's pebbles[49] or old Adam's seed.
Thus gentle Lamia judged, and judged aright,
That Lycius could not love in half a fright,
So threw the goddess off, and won his heart
More pleasantly by playing woman's part
With no more awe than what her beauty gave,
That, while it smote, still guaranteed to save.

## Notes

[46] *subtle* rarefied.

[47] *The Adonian feast* A fertility ritual held annually in Venus's temple. Adonis was the beautiful young man in love with Venus, killed by a boar while hunting.

[48] *peris* superhuman beings or good genii from Persian myth.

[49] Exasperated by the crimes of humanity, Jupiter is said to have sent a flood that covered the world. The only ones to be saved, Deucalion and Pyrrha, repopulated the world by throwing stones behind them which turned into men and women.

Lycius to all made eloquent reply,
Marrying to every word a twinborn sigh;
And last, pointing to Corinth, asked her sweet,
If 'twas too far that night for her soft feet.
The way was short, for Lamia's eagerness
Made, by a spell, the triple league decrease
To a few paces – not at all surmised
By blinded Lycius, so in her comprised.[50]
They passed the city gates, he knew not how,
   So noiseless, and he never thought to know.
As men talk in a dream, so Corinth all,
Throughout her palaces imperial,
And all her populous streets and temples lewd[51]
Muttered like tempest in the distance brewed
To the wide-spreaded night above her towers.
Men, women, rich and poor, in the cool hours,
Shuffled their sandals o'er the pavement white,
Companioned or alone, while many a light
Flared here and there from wealthy festivals,
And threw their moving shadows on the walls,
Or found them clustered in the corniced shade
Of some arched temple door or dusky colonnade.
   Muffling his face, of greeting friends in fear,
Her fingers he pressed hard, as one came near
With curled gray beard, sharp eyes, and smooth bald crown,
Slow-stepped, and robed in philosophic gown.
Lycius shrank closer as they met and passed
Into his mantle, adding wings to haste,
While hurried Lamia trembled. 'Ah', said he,
'Why do you shudder, love, so ruefully?
Why does your tender palm dissolve in dew?'
'I'm wearied', said fair Lamia. 'Tell me who
Is that old man? I cannot bring to mind
His features. Lycius, wherefore did you blind
Yourself from his quick eyes?' Lycius replied,
'Tis Apollonius[52] sage, my trusty guide
And good instructor. But tonight he seems
The ghost of folly haunting my sweet dreams.'
   While yet he spake they had arrived before
A pillared porch with lofty portal door,
Where hung a silver lamp, whose phosphor[53] glow
Reflected in the slabbed steps below,
Mild as a star in water – for so new

## Notes

[50] *comprised* absorbed.

[51] *lewd* Keats is thinking of Robert Burton's description of Corinth: 'It was plenty of all things, which made Corinth so infamous of old, and the opportunity of the place to entertain those foreign comers, every day strangers came in, at each gate, from all quarters. In that one temple of Venus a thousand whores did prostitute themselves … all nations resorted thither as to a school of Venus' (*Anatomy of Melancholy* III 2 ii 1).

[52] Apollonius of Tyana, philosopher of the first century CE, whose life was recorded by Philostratus. He advocated strict moral and religious reform, and was credited with magic powers.

[53] *phosphor* phosphorescent.

And so unsullied was the marble hue,
So through the crystal polish, liquid fine,
Ran the dark veins, that none but feet divine
Could e'er have touched there. Sounds Aeolian[54]
Breathed from the hinges, as the ample span
Of the wide doors disclosed a place unknown
Some time to any, but those two alone,
And a few Persian mutes, who that same year
Were seen about the markets; none knew where
They could inhabit – the most curious
Were foiled, who watched to trace them to their house.
And but the flitter-winged verse must tell,
For truth's sake, what woe afterwards befell;
'Twould humour many a heart to leave them thus,
Shut from the busy world of more incredulous.

## *Part II*

Love in a hut,[1] with water and a crust,
Is (Love forgive us!) cinders, ashes, dust;
Love in a palace is perhaps at last
More grievous torment than a hermit's fast:
That is a doubtful tale from fairyland,
Hard for the non-elect to understand.
Had Lycius lived to hand his story down
He might have given the moral a fresh frown
Or clenched it quite[2] – but too short was their bliss
To breed distrust and hate, that make the soft voice hiss.
Besides, there, nightly, with terrific glare,
Love, jealous[3] grown of so complete a pair,
Hovered and buzzed his wings with fearful roar
Above the lintel of their chamber door,
And down the passage cast a glow upon the floor.[4]
  For all[5] this came a ruin: side by side
They were enthroned in the eventide,
Upon a couch, near to a curtaining
Whose airy texture, from a golden string,
Floated into the room, and let appear
Unveiled the summer heaven, blue and clear,
Betwixt two marble shafts.[6] There they reposed
Where use had made it sweet, with eyelids closed,
Saving a tithe[7] which love still open kept,
That they might see each other while they almost slept –
When, from the slope side of a suburb hill,

### Notes

[54] *Sounds Aeolian* i.e. like the sounds of an Aeolian harp.

LAMIA: PART II

[1] *hut* cottage.

[2] *clenched it quite* proved it conclusively.

[3] *jealous* protective.

[4] *Love...floor* Cupid guards perfect love from intrusion.

[5] *For all* in spite of.

[6] *marble shafts* two marble pillars supporting the lintel of the window.

[7] *tithe* a tenth.

Deafening the swallow's twitter, came a thrill
Of trumpets. Lycius started – the sounds fled,
But left a thought, a buzzing in his head.
For the first time, since first he harboured in
That purple-lined palace of sweet sin,
His spirit passed beyond its golden bourn[8]
Into the noisy world almost forsworn.
The lady, ever watchful, penetrant,[9]
Saw this with pain, so arguing a want
Of something more, more than her empery[10]
Of joys; and she began to moan and sigh
Because he mused beyond her, knowing well
That but a moment's thought is passion's passing-bell.
'Why do you sigh, fair creature?' whispered he.
'Why do you think?' returned she tenderly;
'You have deserted me; where am I now?
Not in your heart while care weighs on your brow.
No, no, you have dismissed me, and I go
From your breast houseless – aye, it must be so.'
He answered, bending to her open eyes,
Where he was mirrored small in paradise:
'My silver planet,[11] both of eve and morn!
Why will you plead yourself so sad forlorn
While I am striving how to fill my heart
With deeper crimson and a double smart?
How to entangle, trammel up[12] and snare
Your soul in mine, and labyrinth you there
Like the hid scent in an unbudded rose?
Aye, a sweet kiss – you see your mighty woes.
My thoughts! Shall I unveil them? Listen then!
What mortal hath a prize, that other men
May be confounded and abashed withal,
But lets it sometimes pace abroad majestical
And triumph, as in thee I should rejoice
Amid the hoarse alarm of Corinth's voice?
Let my foes choke, and my friends shout afar,
While through the thronged streets your bridal car
Wheels round its dazzling spokes!'
The lady's cheek
Trembled; she nothing said but, pale and meek,
Arose and knelt before him, wept a rain
Of sorrows at his words; at last with pain
Beseeching him, the while his hand she wrung
To change his purpose. He thereat was stung,
Perverse, with stronger fancy to reclaim

## Notes

[8] *bourn* realm, domain.

[9] *penetrant* perceptive, acute.

[10] *empery* empire.

[11] *silver planet* Venus, star of morning and evening.

[12] *trammel up* enmesh.

Her wild and timid nature to his aim –
Besides, for all his love, in self-despite,
Against his better self, he took delight
Luxurious in her sorrows, soft and new.
His passion, cruel grown, took on a hue
Fierce and sanguineous[13] as 'twas possible
In one whose brow had no dark veins to swell.
Fine was the mitigated[14] fury, like
Apollo's presence when in act to strike
The serpent[15] – ha, the serpent! Certes[16] she
Was none. She burnt, she loved the tyranny,
And, all subdued, consented to the hour
When to the bridal he should lead his paramour.
  Whispering in midnight silence, said the youth:
'Sure some sweet name thou hast, though, by my truth,
I have not asked it, ever thinking thee
Not mortal, but of heavenly progeny,
As still I do. Hast any mortal name,
Fit appellation for this dazzling frame?
Or friends or kinsfolk on the citied earth,
To share our marriage feast and nuptial mirth?'
'I have no friends', said Lamia, 'no, not one;
My presence in wide Corinth hardly known.
My parents' bones are in their dusty urns
Sepulchred, where no kindled incense burns,
Seeing all their luckless race are dead, save me –
And I neglect the holy rite for thee.
Even as you list invite your many guests;
But if, as now it seems, your vision rests
With any pleasure on me, do not bid
Old Apollonius – from him keep me hid.'
Lycius, perplexed at words so blind and blank,
Made close enquiry, from whose touch she shrank,
Feigning a sleep – and he to the dull shade
Of deep sleep in a moment was betrayed.[17]
  It was the custom then to bring away
The bride from home at blushing shut of day
Veiled in a chariot, heralded along
By strewn flowers, torches, and a marriage song,
With other pageants – but this fair unknown
Had not a friend. So being left alone
(Lycius was gone to summon all his kin)
And knowing surely she could never win
His foolish heart from its mad pompousness,[18]
She set herself, high-thoughted, how to dress

## Notes

[13] *sanguineous* red with anger.

[14] *mitigated* moderated.

[15] Apollo killed a huge dragon (called Python) at Delphi, where he established his shrine.

[16] *Certes* certainly.

[17] *to the dull shade...betrayed* Lycius is tricked into a deep sleep by Lamia's magic spell.

[18] *pompousness* love of display.

The misery in fit magnificence.
She did so, but 'tis doubtful how and whence
Came, and who were her subtle[19] servitors.
About the halls, and to and from the doors
There was a noise of wings, till in short space
The glowing banquet-room shone with wide-arched grace.
A haunting music, sole perhaps and lone
Supportress of the fairy-roof, made moan
Throughout, as fearful the whole charm might fade.
Fresh carved cedar, mimicking a glade
Of palm and plantain,[20] met from either side
High in the midst, in honour of the bride –
Two palms and then two plantains, and so on,
From either side their stems branched one to one
All down the aisled place; and beneath all
There ran a stream of lamps straight on from wall to wall.
   So canopied, lay an untasted feast
Teeming with odours. Lamia, regal dressed,
Silently paced about, and as she went,
In pale contented sort of discontent,
Missioned her viewless[21] servants to enrich
The fretted[22] splendour of each nook and niche.
Between the tree-stems, marbled plain at first,
Came jasper panels; then anon there burst
Forth creeping imagery of slighter trees,
And with the larger wove in small intricacies.
Approving all, she faded[23] at self-will,
And shut the chamber up, close, hushed and still,
Complete and ready for the revels rude,
When dreadful guests would come to spoil her solitude.
   The day appeared, and all the gossip rout.
Oh senseless Lycius! Madman! Wherefore flout
The silent-blessing fate, warm cloistered hours,
And show to common eyes these secret bowers?
The herd approached – each guest, with busy brain,
Arriving at the portal, gazed amain,
And entered marvelling, for they knew the street,
Remembered it from childhood all complete
Without a gap, yet ne'er before had seen
That royal porch, that high-built fair demesne.[24]
So in they hurried all, mazed, curious and keen,
Save one who looked thereon with eye severe,
And with calm-planted steps walked in austere;
'Twas Apollonius; something too he laughed,
As though some knotty problem, that had daffed[25]

## Notes

[19] *subtle* invisible.
[20] *plantain* a tropical tree-like plant.
[21] *viewless* invisible.
[22] *fretted* carved.
[23] *faded* disappeared, as if by magic.
[24] *demesne* palace.
[25] *daffed* toyed with, baffled.

His patient thought, had now begun to thaw
And solve and melt – 'twas just as he foresaw.
He met within the murmurous vestibule
His young disciple. ''Tis no common rule,
Lycius', said he, 'for uninvited guest
To force himself upon you, and infest
With an unbidden presence the bright throng
Of younger friends – yet must I do this wrong,
And you forgive me.' Lycius blushed, and led
The old man through the inner doors broad-spread;
With reconciling words and courteous mien
Turning into sweet milk the sophist's[26] spleen.
Of wealthy lustre was the banquet-room,
Filled with pervading brilliance and perfume;
Before each lucid[27] panel fuming stood
A censer fed with myrrh and spiced wood,
Each by a sacred tripod held aloft
Whose slender feet wide-swerved upon the soft
Wool-woofed carpets; fifty wreaths of smoke
From fifty censers their light voyage took
To the high roof, still mimicked as they rose
Along the mirrored walls by twin-clouds odorous.
Twelve sphered tables, by silk seats ensphered,
High as the level of a man's breast reared
On libbard's[28] paws, upheld the heavy gold
Of cups and goblets, and the store thrice told
Of Ceres' horn,[29] and, in huge vessels, wine
Come from the gloomy tun[30] with merry shine.
Thus loaded with a feast the tables stood,
Each shrining in the midst the image of a god.
When in an ante-chamber every guest
Had felt the cold full sponge to pleasure pressed
By minist'ring slaves upon his hands and feet,
And fragrant oils with ceremony meet
Poured on his hair, they all moved to the feast
In white robes, and themselves in order placed
Around the silken couches, wondering
Whence all this mighty cost and blaze of wealth could spring.
Soft went the music the soft air along,
While fluent Greek a vowelled undersong
Kept up among the guests, discoursing low
At first, for scarcely was the wine at flow;
But when the happy vintage touched their brains,
Louder they talk, and louder come the strains
Of powerful instruments. The gorgeous dyes,

## Notes

[26] *sophist* philosopher.
[27] *lucid* shining.
[28] *libbard's* leopard's.
[29] *Ceres' horn* the horn of plenty.
[30] *tun* cask.

The space, the splendour of the draperies,
The roof of awful richness, nectarous cheer,
Beautiful slaves and Lamia's self appear,
Now, when the wine has done its rosy deed,
And every soul from human trammels freed,
No more so strange – for merry wine, sweet wine,
Will make Elysian shades not too fair, too divine.[31]
   Soon was god Bacchus at meridian height;
Flushed were their cheeks, and bright eyes double bright.
Garlands of every green, and every scent
From vales deflowered, or forest-trees branch-rent,
In baskets of bright osiered[32] gold were brought
High as the handles heaped, to suit the thought
Of every guest – that each, as he did please,
Might fancy-fit his brows, silk-pillowed at his ease.
   What wreath for Lamia? What for Lycius?
What for the sage, old Apollonius?
Upon her aching forehead be there hung
The leaves of willow and of adder's tongue;[33]
And for the youth – quick, let us strip for him
The thyrsus,[34] that his watching eyes may swim
Into forgetfulness; and, for the sage,
Let spear-grass and the spiteful thistle wage
War on his temples. Do not all charms fly
At the mere touch of cold philosophy?
There was an awful[35] rainbow once in heaven:
We know her woof, her texture – she is given
In the dull catalogue of common things.
Philosophy will clip an angel's wings,
Conquer all mysteries by rule and line,
Empty the haunted air, and gnomed mine,
Unweave a rainbow, as it erewhile made
The tender-personed Lamia melt into a shade.
   By her glad Lycius sitting in chief place
Scarce saw in all the room another face
Till, checking his love trance, a cup he took
Full brimmed, and opposite sent forth a look
'Cross the broad table, to beseech a glance
From his old teacher's wrinkled countenance,
And pledge him. The bald-head philosopher
Had fixed his eye without a twinkle or stir
Full on the alarmed beauty of the bride,
Brow-beating her fair form, and troubling her sweet pride.
Lycius then pressed her hand, with devout touch,

## Notes

[31] Wine makes the idyllic world of the Elysian fields seem less remote.

[32] *osiered* woven.

[33] *The leaves of willow and of adder's tongue* emblems of grief; adder's tongue is a fern once used as a medicine for its soothing properties.

[34] Lycius's wreath is made from the ivy and vine-leaves wrapped round Bacchus's thyrsus (wand).

[35] *awful* awesome, awe-inspiring.

As pale it lay upon the rosy couch:
'Twas icy, and the cold ran through his veins –
Then sudden it grew hot, and all the pains
Of an unnatural heat shot to his heart.
'Lamia, what means this? Wherefore dost thou start?
Know'st thou that man?' Poor Lamia answered not.
He gazed into her eyes, and not a jot
Owned they the lovelorn piteous appeal;
More, more he gazed; his human senses reel;
Some hungry spell that loveliness absorbs –
There was no recognition in those orbs.
'Lamia!' he cried – and no soft-toned reply.
The many heard, and the loud revelry
Grew hush; the stately music no more breathes;
The myrtle sickened in a thousand wreaths.
By faint degrees, voice, lute, and pleasure ceased;
A deadly silence step by step increased
Until it seemed a horrid presence there,
And not a man but felt the terror in his hair.
'Lamia!' he shrieked – and nothing but the shriek
With its sad echo did the silence break.
'Begone, foul dream!' he cried, gazing again
In the bride's face, where now no azure vein
Wandered on fair-spaced temples; no soft bloom
Misted the cheek; no passion to illume
The deep-recessed vision – all was blight.
Lamia, no longer fair, there sat a deadly white.
  'Shut, shut those juggling[36] eyes, thou ruthless man!
Turn them aside, wretch, or the righteous ban
Of all the gods, whose dreadful images
Here represent their shadowy presences,
May pierce them on the sudden with the thorn
Of painful blindness – leaving thee forlorn,
In trembling dotage to the feeblest fright
Of conscience, for their long offended might,
For all thine impious proud-heart sophistries,
Unlawful magic, and enticing lies.
Corinthians, look upon that gray-beard wretch!
Mark how, possessed, his lashless eyelids stretch
Around his demon eyes! Corinthians, see!
My sweet bride withers at their potency.'
  'Fool!' said the sophist, in an undertone
Gruff with contempt; which a death-nighing moan
From Lycius answered, as heart-struck and lost,
He sank supine beside the aching ghost.
'Fool! Fool!' repeated he, while his eyes still

Notes

[36] *juggling* conjuring.

Relented not, nor moved. 'From every ill
Of life have I preserved thee to this day,
And shall I see thee made a serpent's prey?'
Then Lamia breathed death breath; the sophist's eye,
Like a sharp spear, went through her utterly,
Keen, cruel, perceant,[37] stinging; she, as well
As her weak hand could any meaning tell,
Motioned him to be silent – vainly so,
He looked and looked again a level 'No!'
  'A serpent!' echoed he – no sooner said,
Than with a frightful scream she vanished,
And Lycius' arms were empty of delight,
As were his limbs of life from that same night.[38]
On the high couch he lay – his friends came round,
Supported him; no pulse or breath they found,
And, in its marriage robe, the heavy body wound.

## *To Autumn* (composed *c.*19 September 1819)[1]

I

Season of mists and mellow fruitfulness,
  Close bosom-friend of the maturing sun,
Conspiring with him how to load and bless
  With fruit the vines that round the thatch-eaves run;
To bend with apples the mossed cottage-trees,
  And fill all fruit with ripeness to the core;
    To swell the gourd,[2] and plump the hazel shells
With a sweet kernel; to set budding more,
  And still more, later flowers for the bees,
  Until they think warm days will never cease,
    For summer has o'er-brimmed their clammy cells.

2

Who hath not seen thee oft amid thy store?
  Sometimes whoever seeks abroad may find
Thee sitting careless[3] on a granary floor,
  Thy hair soft-lifted by the winnowing wind;
Or on a half-reaped furrow sound asleep,
  Drowsed with the fume of poppies,[4] while thy hook[5]
    Spares the next swath[6] and all its twined flowers;
And sometimes like a gleaner[7] thou dost keep

### Notes

[37] *perceant* piercing.

[38] Apollonius saves Lycius from Lamia, killing him in the process.

To Autumn

[1] For commentary on the poem see headnote.

[2] *gourd* melon.

[3] *careless* without care.

[4] *Drowsed…poppies* poppies are associated with sleep.

[5] *hook* blade for reaping corn.

[6] *swath* width of corn cut by a scythe.

[7] *gleaner* one who gathers stray ears of corn missed by the reapers.

Steady thy laden head across a brook;
Or by a cider-press, with patient look,
Thou watchest the last oozings hours by hours.

3

Where are the songs of spring? Aye, where are they?
Think not of them, thou hast thy music too –
While barred clouds bloom the soft-dying day,
And touch the stubble-plains with rosy hue;
Then in a wailful choir the small gnats mourn
Among the river sallows,[8] borne aloft
Or sinking as the light wind lives or dies;
And full-grown lambs loud bleat from hilly bourn,
Hedge-crickets sing, and now with treble soft
The redbreast whistles from a garden-croft,
And gathering swallows twitter in the skies.

## *The Fall of Hyperion: A Dream* (composed between late July and 21 September 1819)[1]

### *Canto I*

Fanatics[2] have their dreams, wherewith they weave
A paradise for a sect; the savage too
From forth the loftiest fashion of his sleep[3]
Guesses at heaven; pity these have not
Traced upon vellum or wild Indian leaf
The shadows of melodious utterance.
But bare of laurel they live, dream and die;
For Poesy alone can tell her dreams,
With the fine spell of words alone can save
Imagination from the sable charm
And dumb enchantment. Who alive can say
'Thou art no poet; may'st not tell thy dreams'?
Since every man whose soul is not a clod
Hath visions, and would speak, if he had loved
And been well nurtured in his mother tongue.
Whether the dream now purposed to rehearse
Be poet's or fanatic's will be known
When this warm scribe my hand is in the grave.
Methought I stood where trees of every clime,

Notes

[8] *sallows* willows.

The Fall of Hyperion: Canto I

[1] This reconceived version of 'Hyperion' was first published in 1857. Keats gave it up because 'there were too many Miltonic inversions in it. Miltonic verse cannot be written but in an artful or rather artist's humour. I wish to give myself up to other sensations. English ought to be kept up. It may be interesting to you to pick out some lines from Hyperion and put a mark X to the false beauty proceeding from art, and one | | to the true voice of feeling. Upon my soul 'twas imagination; I cannot make the distinction. Every now and then there is a Miltonic intonation – but I cannot make the division properly'.

[2] *Fanatics* religious fanatics.

[3] *the loftiest fashion of his sleep* the depths of his dreams.

Palm, myrtle, oak, and sycamore, and beech,
With plantain,[4] and spice-blossoms, made a screen;
In neighbourhood of fountains, by the noise
Soft-showering in mine ears, and, by the touch
Of scent, not far from roses. Turning round,
I saw an arbour with a drooping roof
Of trellis vines, and bells, and larger blooms,
Like floral censers swinging light in air;
Before its wreathed doorway, on a mound
Of moss, was spread a feast of summer fruits,
Which nearer seen, seemed refuse of a meal
By angel tasted, or our mother Eve;
For empty shells were scattered on the grass,
And grape-stalks but half bare, and remnants more,
Sweet smelling, whose pure kinds I could not know.
Still was more plenty than the fabled horn[5]
Thrice emptied could pour forth, at banqueting
For Proserpine[6] returned to her own fields,
Where the white heifers low. And appetite
More yearning than on earth I ever felt
Growing within, I ate deliciously;
And, after not long, thirsted, for thereby
Stood a cool vessel of transparent juice
Sipped by the wandered bee, the which I took,
And, pledging all the mortals of the world,
And all the dead whose names are in our lips,
Drank. That full draught is parent of my theme.
No Asian poppy nor elixir fine
Of the soon-fading jealous Caliphat,[7]
No poison gendered in close monkish cell
To thin the scarlet conclave of old men,[8]
Could so have rapt[9] unwilling life away.
Among the fragrant husks and berries crushed,
Upon the grass I struggled hard against
The domineering potion, but in vain –
The cloudy swoon came on, and down I sunk
Like a Silenus[10] on an antique vase.
How long I slumbered 'tis a chance to guess.
When sense of life returned, I started up
As if with wings; but the fair trees were gone,
The mossy mound and arbour were no more.

## Notes

[4] *plantain* tropical tree-like plant.

[5] *the fabled horn* the cornucopia of plenty.

[6] Proserpine was Ceres's daughter; she was carried off to hell by Pluto. To soothe Ceres's grief, Jupiter decided that Proserpine should spend half the year in hell, and the other half on earth.

[7] *No Asian poppy...Caliphat* the Caliphs ruled the Muslim world after the death of Mohammed. They were believed to use poison as a means of political intrigue.

[8] *the scarlet conclave of old men* Cardinals elect a Pope in 'scarlet conclave'.

[9] *rapt* taken.

[10] *Silenus* attendant of Bacchus, who would sink down in a drunken stupor.

I looked around upon the carved sides
Of an old sanctuary with roof august,
Builded so high, it seemed that filmed clouds
Might spread beneath, as o'er the stars of heaven.
So old the place was, I remembered none
The like upon the earth – what I had seen
Of grey cathedrals, buttressed walls, rent towers,
The superannuations[11] of sunk realms,
Or nature's rocks toiled hard in waves and winds,
Seemed but the faulture[12] of decrepit things
To that eternal domed monument.
Upon the marble at my feet there lay
Store of strange vessels, and large draperies
Which needs had been of dyed asbestos wove,
Or in that place the moth could not corrupt,[13]
So white the linen; so, in some, distinct
Ran imageries[14] from a sombre loom.
All in a mingled heap confused there lay
Robes, golden tongs, censer and chafing-dish,[15]
Girdles, and chains, and holy jewelleries.
  Turning from these with awe, once more I raised
My eyes to fathom the space every way;
The embossed roof, the silent massy range
Of columns north and south, ending in mist
Of nothing; then to eastward, where black gates
Were shut against the sunrise evermore.
Then to the west I looked, and saw far off
An image,[16] huge of feature as a cloud,
At level of whose feet an altar slept,
To be approached on either side by steps,
And marble balustrade, and patient travail
To count with toil the innumerable degrees.
Towards the altar sober-paced I went,
Repressing haste as too unholy there;
And, coming nearer, saw beside the shrine
One minist'ring;[17] and there arose a flame.
When in mid-May the sickening east wind
Shifts sudden to the south, the small warm rain
Melts out the frozen incense from all flowers,
And fills the air with so much pleasant health
That even the dying man forgets his shroud;
Even so that lofty sacrificial fire,
Sending forth Maian incense,[18] spread around

## Notes

[11] *superannuations* ruins, obsolete remains.

[12] *faulture* weakness.

[13] *Or in…corrupt* heaven; Matthew 6:19–20: 'Lay not up for yourselves treasures upon earth, where moth and rust doth corrupt and where thieves break through and steal.'

[14] *imageries* patterns in the cloth, embroidered designs.

[15] *chafing-dish* censer. This is a list of items used in religious rites.

[16] *An image* of Saturn.

[17] *One minist'ring* Moneta, the priestess of the temple.

[18] *Maian incense* flowery scent.

Forgetfulness of everything but bliss,
And clouded all the altar with soft smoke,
From whose white fragrant curtains thus I heard
Language pronounced: 'If thou canst not ascend
These steps, die on that marble where thou art.
Thy flesh, near cousin to the common dust,
Will parch for lack of nutriment; thy bones
Will wither in few years, and vanish so
That not the quickest eye could find a grain
Of what thou now art on that pavement cold.
The sands of thy short life are spent this hour,
And no hand in the universe can turn
Thy hourglass, if these gummed leaves[19] be burnt
Ere thou canst mount up these immortal steps.'
　I heard, I looked – two senses both at once,
So fine, so subtle, felt the tyranny
Of that fierce threat and the hard task proposed.
Prodigious seemed the toil; the leaves were yet
Burning, when suddenly a palsied chill
Struck from the paved level up my limbs,
And was ascending quick to put cold grasp
Upon those streams that pulse beside the throat.[20]
I shrieked, and the sharp anguish of my shriek
Stung my own ears – I strove hard to escape
The numbness, strove to gain the lowest step.
Slow, heavy, deadly was my pace; the cold
Grew stifling, suffocating, at the heart;
And when I clasped my hands I felt them not.
One minute before death, my iced foot touched
The lowest stair; and as it touched, life seemed
To pour in at the toes. I mounted up,
As once fair angels on a ladder flew
From the green turf to heaven. 'Holy Power',
Cried I, approaching near the hornèd shrine,[21]
'What am I that should so be saved from death?
What am I, that another death come not
To choke my utterance sacrilegious here?'
Then said the veiled shadow:[22] 'Thou hast felt
What 'tis to die and live again before
Thy fated hour. That thou hadst power to do so
Is thy own safety; thou hast dated on
Thy doom.'[23] 'High Prophetess', said I, 'purge off

## Notes

[19] *gummed leaves* leaves of aromatic trees.

[20] *those streams…throat* Having had a medical training, Keats would have known that he was referring to the carotid arteries which carry blood to the neck.

[21] *the hornèd shrine* It was believed that altars in ancient times were adorned with animal horns.

[22] *veiled shadow* Moneta, as at l. 211 below.

[23] *dated on / Thy doom* postponed your death.

Benign, if so it please thee, my mind's film.'[24]
'None can usurp this height', returned that shade,
'But those to whom the miseries of the world
Are misery, and will not let them rest.
All else who find a haven in the world,
Where they may thoughtless sleep away their days,
If by a chance into this fane[25] they come,
Rot on the pavement where thou rotted'st half.'
'Are there not thousands in the world', said I,
Encouraged by the sooth[26] voice of the shade,
'Who love their fellows even to the death;
Who feel the giant agony of the world;
And more, like slaves to poor humanity,
Labour for mortal good? I sure should see
Other men here – but I am here alone.'
'They whom thou spak'st of are no vision'ries,'
Rejoined that voice, 'They are no dreamers weak,
They seek no wonder but the human face,[27]
No music but a happy-noted voice,
They come not here, they have no thought to come –
And thou art here, for thou art less than they.
What benefit canst thou do, or all thy tribe,
To the great world? Thou art a dreaming thing,
A fever of thyself.[28] Think of the earth;
What bliss even in hope is there for thee?
What haven? Every creature hath its home;
Every sole[29] man hath days of joy and pain,
Whether his labours be sublime or low –
The pain alone; the joy alone; distinct.
Only the dreamer venoms all his days,[30]
Bearing more woe than all his sins deserve.
Therefore, that happiness be somewhat shared,
Such things as thou art are admitted oft
Into like gardens thou didst pass erewhile,
And suffered in[31] these temples; for that cause
Thou standest safe beneath this statue's knees.'
'That I am favoured for unworthiness,
By such propitious parley medicined
In sickness not ignoble, I rejoice –
Aye, and could weep for love of such award.'
So answered I, continuing, 'If it please,

## Notes

[24] *purge off...film* help me to understand clearly.
[25] *fane* temple.
[26] *sooth* smooth.
[27] *They seek no wonder but the human face* Miriam Allott suggests comparison with Keats's letter to John Taylor, 17 November 1819: 'Wonders are no wonders to me. I am more at home amongst men and women. I would rather read Chaucer than Ariosto.'
[28] *A fever of thyself* i.e. he is prone to feverish fits of poetic inspiration. This kind of fever is healthy.
[29] *sole* single.
[30] *Only the dreamer venoms all his days* with the awareness of human misery.
[31] *suffered in* allowed to enter.

Majestic shadow, tell me – sure not all
Those melodies sung into the world's ear
Are useless? Sure a poet is a sage,
A humanist,[32] physician to all men.
That I am none I feel, as vultures feel
They are no birds when eagles are abroad.
What am I then? Thou spakest of my tribe –
What tribe?' The tall shade veiled in drooping white
Then spake, so much more earnest, that the breath
Moved the thin linen folds that drooping hung
About a golden censer from the hand
Pendent: 'Art thou not of the dreamer tribe?
The poet and the dreamer are distinct,
Diverse, sheer opposite, antipodes.
The one pours out a balm upon the world,
The other vexes it.' Then shouted I
Spite of myself, and with a Pythia's spleen:[33]
'Apollo![34] Faded, far-flown Apollo!
Where is thy misty pestilence[35] to creep
Into the dwellings, through the door crannies,
Of all mock lyrists, large self-worshippers,
And careless hectorers in proud bad verse?[36]
Though I breathe death with them it will be life
To see them sprawl before me into graves.
Majestic shadow, tell me where I am;
Whose altar this; for whom this incense curls;
What image this, whose face I cannot see,
For the broad marble knees; and who thou art,
Of accent feminine, so courteous.'
   Then the tall shade, in drooping linens veiled,
Spake out, so much more earnest, that her breath
Stirred the thin folds of gauze that drooping hung
About a golden censer from her hand
Pendent – and by her voice I knew she shed
Long-treasured tears: 'This temple sad and lone
Is all spared[37] from the thunder of a war[38]
Foughten long since by giant hierarchy
Against rebellion. This old image here,
Whose carved features wrinkled as he fell,
Is Saturn's; I, Moneta,[39] left supreme,
Sole priestess of his desolation.'
I had no words to answer, for my tongue,

## Notes

[32] *humanist* humanitarian.

[33] *a Pythia's spleen* Oracles in the temple of Apollo, god of poetry and prophecy, at Delphi were delivered by a priestess called 'the Pythia', whose wild and incoherent speeches were transcribed.

[34] *Apollo!* Son of Jupiter.

[35] *thy misty pestilence* Apollo was associated with plagues and diseases.

[36] *careless hectorers in proud bad verse* Suggested candidates include Byron, Wordsworth and Moore. In September 1819 Keats referred to *Don Juan* as 'Lord Byron's last flash poem'.

[37] *Is all spared* is all that is spared.

[38] *war* that of the Titans against the Olympians.

[39] *Moneta* Mnemosyne, mother of the Muses.

Useless, could find about its roofed home
No syllable of a fit majesty
To make rejoinder to Moneta's mourn.
There was a silence while the altar's blaze
Was fainting for sweet food. I looked thereon,
And on the paved floor, where nigh were piled
Faggots of cinnamon, and many heaps
Of other crisped spice-wood – then again
I looked upon the altar, and its horns
Whitened with ashes, and its lang'rous flame,
And then upon the offerings again;
And so by turns, till sad Moneta cried,
'The sacrifice is done, but not the less
Will I be kind to thee for thy goodwill.
My power, which to me is still a curse,
Shall be to thee a wonder; for the scenes
Still swooning vivid through my globed brain[40]
With an electral[41] changing misery,
Thou shalt with those dull mortal eyes behold,
Free from all pain, if wonder pain thee not.'
As near as an immortal's sphered words
Could to a mother's soften, were these last.
But yet I had a terror of her robes,
And chiefly of the veils, that from her brow
Hung pale, and curtained her in mysteries,
That made my heart too small to hold its blood.
This saw that goddess, and with sacred hand
Parted the veils. Then saw I a wan face,
Not pined[42] by human sorrows, but bright-blanched
By an immortal sickness which kills not;
It works a constant change, which happy death
Can put no end to; deathwards progressing
To no death was that visage; it had passed
The lily and the snow; and beyond these
I must not think now, though I saw that face –
But for her eyes I should have fled away.
They held me back with a benignant light,
Soft-mitigated by divinest lids
Half-closed, and visionless[43] entire they seemed
Of all external things – they saw me not,
But in blank splendour beamed like the mild moon,
Who comforts those she sees not, who knows not
What eyes are upward cast. As I had found
A grain of gold upon a mountain's side,
And twinged with avarice strained out my eyes

## Notes

[40] *the scenes…brain* The scenes are vivid enough in her memory to make her swoon.

[41] *electral* charged as if by electricity.

[42] *pined* wasted.

[43] *visionless* The eyes do not see the outside world, but are directed on inner visions.

To search its sullen[44] entrails rich with ore,
So at the view of sad Moneta's brow
I ached to see what things the hollow brain
Behind enwombed, what high tragedy
In the dark secret chambers of her skull
Was acting, that could give so dread a stress
To her cold lips, and fill with such a light
Her planetary eyes, and touch her voice
With such a sorrow. 'Shade of Memory!'[45]
Cried I, with act adorant at her feet,
'By all the gloom hung round thy fallen house,
By this last temple, by the golden age,[46]
By great Apollo, thy dear foster child,[47]
And by thyself, forlorn divinity,
The pale omega[48] of a withered race,
Let me behold, according as thou said'st,
What in thy brain so ferments to and fro.'
No sooner had this conjuration passed
My devout lips, than side by side we stood,
Like a stunt bramble by a solemn pine,
Deep in the shady sadness of a vale,
Far sunken from the healthy breath of morn,
Far from the fiery noon and eve's one star.
Onward I looked beneath the gloomy boughs,
And saw what first I thought an image huge,
Like to the image pedestalled so high
In Saturn's temple. Then Moneta's voice
Came brief upon mine ear: 'So Saturn sat
When he had lost his realms.' Whereon there grew
A power within me of enormous ken[49]
To see as a god sees, and take the depth
Of things as nimbly as the outward eye
Can size and shape pervade. The lofty theme
At those few words hung vast before my mind,
With half-unravelled web. I set myself
Upon an eagle's watch, that I might see,
And seeing ne'er forget. No stir of life
Was in this shrouded vale, not so much air
As in the zoning[50] of a summer's day
Robs not one light seed from the feathered grass,
But where the dead leaf fell there did it rest.
A stream went voiceless by, still deadened more

## Notes

[44] *sullen* gloomy.

[45] *Shade of Memory* Moneta, whose other name, Mnemosyne, means 'memory'.

[46] *the golden age* of Saturn's rule.

[47] *Apollo, thy dear foster child* Apollo was the son of Jupiter by Latona. Moneta was Jupiter's wife at the time.

[48] *omega* survivor (omega is the final letter of the Greek alphabet).

[49] *ken* sight.

[50] *zoning* duration.

By reason of the fallen divinity
Spreading more shade; the naiad[51] mid her reeds
Pressed her cold finger closer to her lips.
Along the margin sand large footmarks went
No farther than to where old Saturn's feet
Had rested, and there slept – how long a sleep!
Degraded, cold, upon the sodden ground
His old right hand lay nerveless,[52] listless, dead,
Unsceptred; and his realmless eyes were closed,
While his bowed head seemed listening to the earth,
His ancient mother,[53] for some comfort yet.
  It seemed no force could wake him from his place;
But there came one who, with a kindred hand
Touched his wide shoulders, after bending low
With reverence, though to one who knew it not.
Then came the grieved voice of Mnemosyne,
And grieved I hearkened: 'That divinity
Whom thou saw'st step from yon forlornest wood,
And with slow pace approach our fallen King,
Is Thea,[54] softest-natured of our brood.'
I marked the goddess in fair statuary[55]
Surpassing wan Moneta by the head,
And in her sorrow nearer woman's tears.
There was a listening fear in her regard,
As if calamity had but begun;
As if the vanward clouds of evil days
Had spent their malice, and the sullen rear
Was with its stored thunder labouring up.[56]
One hand she pressed upon that aching spot
Where beats the human heart, as if just there,
Though an immortal, she felt cruel pain;
The other upon Saturn's bended neck
She laid, and to the level of his hollow ear,
Leaning with parted lips, some words she spake
In solemn tenor and deep organ tune –
Some mourning words, which in our feeble tongue
Would come in this-like accenting (how frail
To that large utterance of the early gods!):
'Saturn, look up! And for what, poor lost King?
I have no comfort for thee – no, not one;
I cannot cry, "Wherefore thus sleepest thou?"
For heaven is parted from thee, and the earth
Knows thee not, so afflicted, for a god;
And ocean too, with all its solemn noise,
Has from thy sceptre passed, and all the air

## Notes

[51] *naiad* water-nymph.

[52] *nerveless* weak.

[53] *His ancient mother* Tellus (earth).

[54] *Thea* daughter of Uranus and Terra.

[55] *statuary* stature.

[56] *As if the vanward clouds…up* Calamity is compared with clouds building up before a storm, followed by the cloud mass; the storm itself is compared with artillery moving in the wake of advancing troops.

Is emptied of thine hoary majesty.
Thy thunder, captious[57] at the new command,
Rumbles reluctant o'er our fallen house;
And thy sharp lightning in unpractised hands
Scorches and burns our once serene domain.[58]
With such remorseless speed still come new woes
That unbelief has not a space to breathe.
Saturn, sleep on. Me thoughtless, why should I
Thus violate thy slumbrous solitude?
Why should I ope thy melancholy eyes?
Saturn, sleep on, while at thy feet I weep.'
    As when, upon a tranced summer night,
Forests, branch-charmed by the earnest stars,
Dream, and so dream all night, without a noise,
Save from one gradual solitary gust
Swelling upon the silence, dying off,
As if the ebbing air had but one wave;
So came these words, and went, the while in tears
She pressed her fair large forehead to the earth,
Just where her fallen hair might spread in curls,
A soft and silken mat for Saturn's feet.
Long, long those two were postured motionless,
Like sculpture builded up upon the grave
Of their own power. A long awful time
I looked upon them; still they were the same,
The frozen god still bending to the earth,
And the sad goddess weeping at his feet;
Moneta silent. Without stay or prop
But my own weak mortality, I bore
The load of this eternal quietude,
The unchanging gloom, and the three fixed shapes
Ponderous upon my senses a whole moon.
For by my burning brain I measured sure
Her silver seasons shedded on the night,
And every day by day methought I grew
More gaunt and ghostly; oftentimes I prayed
Intense, that death would take me from the vale
And all its burdens; gasping with despair
Of change, hour after hour I cursed myself –
Until old Saturn raised his faded eyes,
And looked around and saw his kingdom gone,
And all the gloom and sorrow of the place,
And that fair kneeling goddess at his feet.
As the moist scent of flowers, and grass, and leaves
Fills forest dells with a pervading air

## Notes

[57] *captious* objecting querulously.

[58] *our once serene domain* the Saturnian golden age.

Known to the woodland nostril, so the words
Of Saturn filled the mossy glooms around,
Even to the hollows of time-eaten oaks,
And to the windings in the foxes' hole,
With sad low tones, while thus he spake, and sent
Strange musings to the solitary Pan:[59]
'Moan, brethren, moan, for we are swallowed up
And buried from all godlike exercise
Of influence benign on planets pale,
And peaceful sway above man's harvesting,
And all those acts which deity supreme
Doth ease its heart of love in. Moan and wail.
Moan, brethren, moan, for lo! the rebel spheres
Spin round, the stars their ancient courses keep,
Clouds still with shadowy moisture haunt the earth,
Still suck their fill of light from sun and moon,
Still buds the tree, and still the seashores murmur.
There is no death in all the universe,
No smell of death – there shall be death. Moan, moan,
Moan, Cybele,[60] moan, for thy pernicious babes
Have changed a god into a shaking palsy.
Moan, brethren, moan, for I have no strength left,
Weak as the reed – weak – feeble as my voice –
Oh, oh, the pain, the pain of feebleness.
Moan, moan, for still I thaw – or give me help:
Throw down those imps,[61] and give me victory.
Let me hear other groans, and trumpets blown
Of triumph calm, and hymns of festival
From the gold peaks of heaven's high-piled clouds;
Voices of soft proclaim, and silver stir
Of strings in hollow shells; and let there be
Beautiful things made new, for the surprise
Of the sky-children.' So he feebly ceased,
With such a poor and sickly sounding pause,
Methought I heard some old man of the earth
Bewailing earthly loss; nor could my eyes
And ears act with that pleasant unison of sense
Which marries sweet sound with the grace of form,
And dolorous accent from a tragic harp
With large-limbed visions. More I scrutinized:
Still fixed he sat beneath the sable trees,
Whose arms spread straggling in wild serpent forms,
With leaves all hushed; his awful presence there
Now all was silent, gave a deadly lie
To what I erewhile heard – only his lips

## Notes

[59] Pan is the natural world, solitary after the passing of the golden age.

[60] *Cybele* mother of all the gods.

[61] *those imps* his own children, the Olympians, by whom he has been usurped.

Trembled amid the white curls of his beard.
They told the truth, though, round the snowy locks
Hung nobly, as upon the face of heaven
A midday fleece of clouds. Thea arose
And stretched her white arm through the hollow dark,
Pointing some whither, whereat he too rose
Like a vast giant seen by men at sea
To grow pale from the waves at dull midnight.
They melted from my sight into the woods;
Ere I could turn, Moneta cried, 'These twain
Are speeding to the families of grief,
Where roofed in by black rocks they waste in pain
And darkness for no hope.' And she spake on,
As ye may read who can unwearied pass
Onward from the antechamber of this dream,
Where even at the open doors awhile
I must delay, and glean my memory
Of her high phrase – perhaps no further dare.

## *Canto II*

'Mortal, that thou may'st understand aright,
I humanize my sayings to thine ear,
Making comparisons of earthly things;
Or thou might'st better listen to the wind,
Whose language is to thee a barren noise,
Though it blows legend-laden through the trees.
In melancholy realms big tears are shed,
More sorrow like to this, and suchlike woe
Too huge for mortal tongue, or pen of scribe.
The Titans[1] fierce, self-hid or prison-bound,
Groan for the old allegiance once more,
Listening in their doom for Saturn's voice.
But one of our whole eagle-brood still keeps
His sov'reignty, and rule, and majesty;
Blazing Hyperion on his orbed fire[2]
Still sits, still snuffs the incense teeming up
From man to the sun's god – yet unsecure.
For as upon the earth dire prodigies[3]
Fright and perplex, so also shudders he;
Nor at dog's howl, or gloom-bird's even screech,[4]
Or the familiar visitings of one

## Notes

THE FALL OF HYPERION: CANTO II

[1] *The Titans* a god-like race expelled from heaven by Jupiter in Greek myth.

[2] *orbed fire* the sun; Hyperion is god of the sun.

[3] *prodigies* unnatural events.

[4] *gloom-bird's even screech* owl's hooting in the evening.

Upon the first toll of his passing-bell,[5]
But horrors, portioned[6] to a giant nerve,
Make great Hyperion ache. His palace bright,
Bastioned with pyramids of glowing gold,
And touched with shade of bronzed obelisks,
Glares a blood-red through all the thousand courts,
Arches, and domes, and fiery galleries;
And all its curtains of aurorean[7] clouds
Flush angerly[8] – when he would taste the wreaths
Of incense breathed aloft from sacred hills,
Instead of sweets, his ample palate takes
Savour of poisonous brass and metals sick.
Wherefore, when harboured in the sleepy west,
After the full completion of fair day,
For rest divine upon exalted couch
And slumber in the arms of melody,
He paces through the pleasant hours of ease
With strides colossal, on from hall to hall,
While far within each aisle and deep recess
His winged minions in close clusters stand
Amazed, and full of fear; like anxious men
Who on a wide plain gather in sad troops
When earthquakes jar their battlements and towers.
Even now, while Saturn, roused from icy trance,
Goes step for step with Thea from yon woods,
Hyperion, leaving twilight in the rear,
Is sloping to the threshold of the west.
Thither we tend.' Now in clear light I stood,
Relieved from the dusk vale. Mnemosyne
Was sitting on a square-edged polished stone,
That in its lucid depth reflected pure
Her priestess-garments. My quick eyes ran on
From stately nave to nave, from vault to vault,
Through bowers of fragrant and enwreathed light
And diamond-paved lustrous long arcades.
Anon rushed by the bright Hyperion;
His flaming robes streamed out beyond his heels,
And gave a roar, as if of earthly fire,
That scared away the meek ethereal hours[9]
And made their dove-wings tremble. On he flared...

## Notes

[5] *passing-bell* death-bell.

[6] *portioned* proportioned.

[7] *aurorean* roseate.

[8] *His palace...angerly* Hyperion's palace is part Greek, part Byzantine and part Egyptian.

[9] *hours* Latin 'Horae', attendant nymphs of the sun.

## *Bright Star, Would I Were Steadfast as Thou Art* (composed October–December 1819)[1]

Bright star, would I were steadfast as thou art –
Not in lone splendour hung aloft the night
And watching, with eternal lids apart,
Like nature's patient, sleepless eremite,[2]
The moving waters[3] at their priestlike task
Of pure ablution[4] round earth's human shores,
Or gazing on the new soft-fallen mask
Of snow upon the mountains and the moors;
No – yet still steadfast, still unchangeable,
Pillowed upon my fair love's ripening breast,
To feel for ever its soft swell and fall,
Awake for ever in a sweet unrest,
Still, still to hear her tender-taken breath,
And so live ever – or else swoon to death.

## *This Living Hand, Now Warm and Capable* (composed towards the end of 1819)[1]

This living hand, now warm and capable
Of earnest grasping, would, if it were cold
And in the icy silence of the tomb,
So haunt thy days and chill thy dreaming nights
That thou would wish thine own heart dry of blood,
So in my veins red life might stream again,
And thou be conscience-calmed. See, here it is –
I hold it towards you.

### Notes

Bright Star, Would I Were Steadfast as Thou Art

[1] This sonnet was published first in 1838. It has traditionally been thought of as Keats's last poem, but editors now place it in late 1819.

[2] *eremite* anchorite, hermit.

[3] *The moving waters* cf. Wordsworth, 'The Excursion' ix 9: 'The moving waters and the invisible air.'

[4] *ablution* cleansing. The ebb and flow of the waters are like a religious ritual.

This Living Hand, Now Warm and Capable

[1] First published 1898. This is probably a jotting for use in a play or poem.

# Index of First Lines



*Romanticism: An Anthology*, Fifth Edition. Edited by Duncan Wu.

Companion website: www.wiley.com/go/Wu/Romanticism5e

# Index to Headnotes and Notes

Page numbers followed by 'n' or 'nn' refer to notes; page numbers followed by '(nn)' refer to page ranges containing notes; all other page numbers refer to headnotes.




*Romanticism: An Anthology*, Fifth Edition. Edited by Duncan Wu.



Companion website: www.wiley.com/go/Wu/Romanticism5e